ENCYCLOPEDIA OF MAJOR LEAGUE BASEBALL

AMERICAN LEAGUE

Other Books by Peter C. Bjarkman ("Dr. Baseball")

The Baseball Scrapbook
Encyclopedia of Major League Baseball Team Histories: American League **(Editor)**
Encyclopedia of Major League Baseball Team Histories: National League **(Editor)**
Baseball & the Game of Life: Stories for the Thinking Fan **(Editor)**
Baseball & the Game of Ideas: Essays for the Serious Fan **(Editor)**
The History of the NBA
The Brooklyn Dodgers
Baseball's Great Dynasties: The Dodgers
Baseball's Great Dynasties: The Reds
The Toronto Blue Jays
Roberto Clemente (juvenile)
Duke Snider (juvenile)
Ernie Banks (juvenile)
Warren Spahn (juvenile)

ENCYCLOPEDIA OF MAJOR LEAGUE BASEBALL

AMERICAN LEAGUE

TEAM HISTORIES

Edited by
Peter C. Bjarkman, Dr. Baseball

Updated and Revised Edition

Carroll & Graf Publishers/Richard Gallen
New York

Published by arrangement with Meckler Publishing, a division of Meckler
Corporation.

First Carroll & Graf/Richard Gallen edition 1993

Carroll & Graf Publishers, Inc.
260 Fifth Avenue
New York, NY 10001

Library of Congress Cataloging-in-Publication Data

Encyclopedia of major league baseball : American League team histories
  / edited by Peter C. Bjarkman.
     p.   cm.
  Rev. ed. of: Encyclopedia of major league baseball team histories.
©1991.
  Includes bibliographical references.
  ISBN 0-88184-974-X : $14.95
  1. American League of Professional Baseball Clubs—History.
2. American League of Professional Baseball Clubs—Records.
I. Bjarkman, Peter C.   II. Encyclopedia of major league baseball
team histories.
GV875.A15E53   1993
796.357'64'0973—dc20   93-20025
                                                         CIP

Manufactured in the United States of America

For Ronnie Wilbur

A true American League fan, and the better
half of the best double play combination going!

Contents

Acknowledgments

This book (like most such group projects) would never have become a reality without the assistance and support of numerous people, all of whom gave selflessly of their time and talents. Most especially, this American League volume represents a labor of love by the 10 contributing authors whose individual chapters bear their personal bylines. If each had not been quite so knowledgeable in the field of baseball history, quite so receptive to editorial suggestion, and quite so dedicated to meeting strict deadlines, this volume would never have taken its present shape or achieved its planned dimensions.

But the book represented here is also equally indebted to baseball fan and publisher Alan Meckler, who is most responsible for its original conception, and to Meckler Corporation Vice President Anthony Abbott, whose continued editorial support and wisdom kept the work properly on target and firmly on schedule. There are others who made significant contributions along the way and who thus merit acknowledgment by name, even if their specific contributions cannot be fully detailed here. This list includes: Ronnie Wilbur, William Friday, Lonnie Wheeler, John S. Bowman, Lloyd Johnson, Tony Formo, Gerald Vaughn, Allen Hye, Pete Cava, Rob Plapinger, Bernard Titowsky, Jim Martin, William Humber, and Rich Westcott. A very special debt of gratitude is also owed by the project editor to Bruce L. Prentice of the Canadian Baseball Hall of Fame, as well as to Howard Starkman of the Toronto Blue Jays, Dan Evans of the Chicago White Sox, and John Blake of the Texas Rangers. To you all, then, may all your summer days be glorious doubleheaders!

Peter C. Bjarkman
West Lafayette, Indiana

Introduction
Historical Perspectives
on the Junior Circuit
PETER C. BJARKMAN

*Belonging and caring is what our games are all about . . .
which is a capacity or an emotion that has almost gone out
of our lives. And so it seems possible that we have come to a
time when it no longer matters so much what the caring is
about, how frail or foolish is the object of that concern, as
long as the feeling itself can be saved. Naivete—the infantile
and ignoble joy that sends a grown man or woman to dancing
and shouting with joy in the middle of the night over the
haphazardous flight of a distant ball—seems a small price to
pay for such a gift.*

Roger Angell, *Five Seasons*

The gift of which Roger Angell writes in this passage (lines inspired by Carlton Fisk's memorable home run which captured a crucial 1975 World Series contest for his beloved Boston Red Sox) is that marvelous national passion we all know as American baseball. Mr. Angell is only one, of course—albeit perhaps the most poetic and insightful—among contemporary literary voices who extol the love and passion Americans expend upon this most perfect, symbolic, and profound of man's sporting spectacles. An estimated 50 million paying fans will pass through the turnstiles of major league ballparks during the 1992 summer season; in this very same summer one ballclub (Canada's Toronto Blue Jays) will again become the only pro franchise ever to attract an annual attendance in excess of four million to the home ballpark. Millions more will watch the national game from the comfort of their living rooms or dens, beneficiaries of a bonanza $375 million yearly deal between big league baseball, ESPN, and the Columbia Broadcasting System. What was already being touted as the American national pastime as early as the 1890s has clearly enough become the North American obsession at the turn of the 1990s.

And baseball's appeal extends (like that of no other sport) far beyond the actions of the playing field itself. Poets from Walt Whitman to Robert Frost and novelists from Mark Twain to Phillip Roth have invented huge life-mirroring metaphors from the nation's big-league diamonds. Adults as well as children today support a billion-dollar industry in bubble gum trading cards and other nostalgic baseball memorabilia. Millionaire superstars of the game provide not only the nation's highest paid media celebrities, but also its longstanding national folk heroes—from the arch-villain Ty Cobb to the Bunyanesque Babe Ruth to the Achilles Heel of Pete Rose. Such is the blissful marriage today enjoyed by baseball and popular culture that historians Joel Zoss and John S. Bowman (*Diamonds in the Rough—The Untold History of Baseball*, Macmillan, 1990) are able to provide the literary gem of the current sporting season by writing a book devoted entirely to exploring baseball's connections to stage and screen, to verse and fiction, to music, to visual arts, to the nation's ethnic diversity and racial integration, even to substance abuse and to wartime and peacetime culture. Clearly no other sporting spectacle—perhaps no other facet of our national culture—reflects as thoroughly everything that is so indelibly American.

Baseball's unique attraction stems largely from two defining images (visages, if you will) of this distinctly nineteenth-century ceremonial bat and ball game. The first of these is professional baseball's rich historical tradition and thus its consequent roots in memory and nostalgia. Baseball is first and foremost a game of the mind—a spectacle befitting lazy summer hours, an endless source for reflection and discussion during the lengthy pause between thrown pitch and batted ball, a drama best attuned to radio and thus to the imagination—the imagination which alone adequately captures and recreates the stately flow of the game's timeless progress. It is in this sense that the national pastime is, in Jim O'Donnell's apt phrase, a game of both recreation and re-creation. Baseball always plays best in the "interior stadium of the mind" as Angell has best dubbed it. And as a strict game of the mind it is most clearly a game of memory, of passion for earlier times, and especially for days of childhood. Millions of Americans, for generations, have marked and measured the events of their humdrum daily lives through their baseball memories. "Each man's 'Golden Age' is the era his nostalgia is most loyal to," observes baseball poet Marvin Cohen, and thus each American male (and many a female to boot) is fiercely loyal to the cherished baseball heroes and baseball scenes of his or her own childhood years.

Baseball's second appeal lies in its humanness, in its appeal to altogether human and thus inevitably flawed and failed heroes, and in its bittersweet mixture of the tragic and comic elements always prevalent in our shared human experience. Baseball's most memorable moments are its indelible images of heroic defeat: Carl Yastrzemski failing for all New England in the final desperate moments of the 1978 league playoff series with the hated rival Yankees; the archetypal fictional slugger "Casey of Mudville" brought directly to flesh time and again through so many dramatic scenes played out on big-league diamonds across the nation. And to balance such tragic tales of pennants lost and noble heroes struck out is the omnipresent element of pure zaniness: perhaps the comic pathos of three Daffy Dodgers simultaneously hugging third, or the spindly legged and barrel-bellied Babe Ruth rudely disappointing the New York faithful with his gigantic bellyache which cost another certain Yankee pennant parade, or the arch prankster Casey Stengel astounding teammates, home plate arbiter, and fans alike by releasing a captured sparrow from beneath his cap in a heated moment of big-league play.

Baseball is the most democratic of all man's theatric games: each action-packed play on the field is spread openly before the spectator to be minutely judged by its merit alone; the game's meticulous statistics hold each player fully accountable for his own deeds and misdeeds over the long summer's play; all numbers must be tallied and balanced (for each run earned there is a debit in the pitcher's column); and each man is ultimately accountable in the game's final ledger or box score. No single play escapes our sight and our immediate judgment: base hit, missed signal, dropped or caught ball, errant throw—each unfolds in full view and is understood by even the casual informed fan for its full significance in the unfolding drama of play. No shortstop or outfielder shares responsibility for his misplayed ball with any teammate. It is also by turn the most starkly human of all our games: the players are of human proportion and visage—they are neither freakish padded and helmeted warriors nor seven-foot behemoths performing superhuman acrobatic feats beyond the grasp of mere mortal contestants. Each American boy and girl thus grows up believing in his heart of hearts that—for the briefest of moments—he or she too could step onto the lush field with childhood heroes and play the game. And of course millions do each summer as children in little league or school play, or as adults in co-ed softball leagues around the land.

Roger Angell again provides perhaps the best assessment of what constitutes the human appeal of the lionized baseball hero in American life. Here Angell adroitly summarizes the remarkable performance of Red Sox slugger Yastrzemski in the final days of the thrilling 1967 pennant race. Yaz had produced in that glorious final month of 1967 perhaps the most stirring extended performance by a single player under pressure in all baseball history. And for the attuned baseball observer Yastrzemski's heroic efforts and ultimate inevitable failure during the World Series play which followed was truly mythic in proportion: "There is something sad here—perhaps the thought that for Yastrzemski, more than for anyone else, this summer could never come again. He had become a famous star with all the prizes and ugly burdens we place on the victims of such celebrity. From now on he would be set apart from us and his teammates and the easy time of his youth" (Angell, 1972, 187).

Baseball's individual and collective memories exploit and amplify at least three byproducts of the American national game—both the game as it is played on the professional field and the personal baseball fantasies of remembered big-league games which live on in our own private memories. One crucial element is the memory of distinct baseball places. First there are those private spots (locales) in which we first enjoyed baseball play over the radio. These are the places (the darkness of a childhood bedroom or aromatic front seat of a family sedan) where we once heard news of the important games by which we measured our childhood and the daily passage of our lives. But most important are the public locales of the ball games themselves, the nation's baseball stadiums. Big-league ballparks acquire their own spiraling careers and colorful personalities (what William Humber recalls as the soggy-blanket atmosphere of the Polo Grounds or the crackling autumn sunshine of Fenway Park) and have a thriving immortal life of their own. Time moves differently within a ballpark, marked and measured only by the events of the game itself; each stadium has a unique face and each houses ghosts of countless heroes who have swung from the same batter's box and hurled from the same pitcher's mound. Memories of baseball experience are always memories of our earliest visits to the nation's sacred ballparks.

Angell knowingly boasts that the history and tradition of any professional baseball team is often indistinguishable from the history and tradition of the ballpark in which it plays. By turn, those franchises with the richest historical traditions are those legendary teams with historic, decaying, and unaltered ballparks. These are also the teams which capture the loyal fandom of Angell and of most true baseball fans as well. Foremost here are the Boston Red Sox with their intimate and pastoral Fenway Park; the Detroit Tigers housed in creaky Tiger Stadium; and the New York Yankees sporting that gigantic "House that Ruth Built" in the heart of massive Gotham. And to a somewhat lesser extent (perhaps only because apparently cheapened by the relentless hype of modern-day TV hucksters like baseball pitchmen Harry Caray and Dwayne Staats, and thus not so natural and unprompted an outpouring of pure fan nostalgia) stand the long-suffering Chicago Cubs with their hallowed Wrigley Field, ennobled by its ivy-clad walls and venerable tradition as the last remaining holdout against the encroachments of prime-time arc-light baseball.

We must note by contrast that those professional ballclubs most divorced from baseball's rich historical traditions are those that have abandoned their most binding link with the nation's past—scrapping their unique old-style urban parks and replacing them with colorless, sterile, and tradition-poor multipurpose suburban arenas, built adjacent to sprawling full-access freeways (sometimes even domed) and largely indistinguishable from each other. These stadia are built by the city's fathers for cohabitation with the local professional football franchise (usually the prime occupant) and thus are uniform circular monoliths offering little recognizable baseball ambience and nothing of distinctive ballpark character. (The very preference for calling such present-day arenas "stadiums" rather than "parks" or "fields" is reflective of this loss of baseball's nineteenth-century pastoral roots.) Such is the distasteful saga surrounding the Los Angeles Dodgers and their multitiered suburban Taj Mahal of ballparks, dubbed unaffectionately yet appropriately by Roger Angell as O'Malley Safeway. It is the equally distressing story of the 1970s-vintage Cincinnati Reds (baseball's oldest franchise and once proud occupants of unique Crosley Field) and the 1960s-era St. Louis Cardinals (late of Sportsman's Park), two of the National League's most ancient ballclubs which in recent decades replaced decaying downtown ballparks with circular football structures distasteful to all that is baseball ambience. In the cases of Cincinnati and St. Louis (as Angell himself observes) such ballpark renovation was the natural fallout of a city's desperate efforts to combat rampantly encroaching urban decay. Franchises such as the Reds and Cardinals (along with the cities which house them) thus sacrifice the appeal of tradition and history for a newer American myth touting rebirth, regeneration, and that obsession with change which is called progress. Yet in purely baseball terms, something always seems lost in the bargain.

Baseball memory (unlike all other sports in degree) is also the lasting memory of human heroes, of chosen personal favorites among the several hundred exceptionally talented men who emerge larger than life each summer by playing the game of baseball to perfection. Or of those lesser ballplayers on whom a fortuitous moment of fate has ironically smiled—perhaps a Bobby Thomson, Bill Mazeroski, Don Larsen, or Dave Henderson. Above all else baseball is mythic in its dimensions, and myth does not survive or prosper without the cult of the mythic hero. It is this cult of baseball personalities and the inherent mythic structure of the game which explains its irrepressible literary quality as well. But it is also the starkly human element surrounding baseball heroes that makes baseball memories so enduring. We identify intimately with our baseball heroes as with no other American public figures, in contrast to football and basketball players who are far too big in physical stature; their action is far too violent and frenetic; and each accomplishment is far too predictable and therefore not nearly heroic enough to feed our memory.

Cultural historian Murray Ross (1971, 33-34) captures this point for us by contrasting the lovably human baseball hero Babe Ruth with the forbidding (even terrifying) and godlike football hero Jim Brown. The latter was excessively muscular and of near-perfect physique, a heroic figure with expressionless face hidden within a warrior's helmet and suit of armor—an invincible embodiment of speed and power within an over-inflated human shape. The former remains for all time an absurd caricature on spindly legs supporting a Santa-sized torso, an impressive yet awkward specimen whose delicate short stride mitigated his awesome athletic skill and rendered him somehow poignant and vulnerable, a comic figure dressed up in baggy suit and schoolboy cap—ultimately an embodiment of boyish innocence.

Finally, there is yet another aspect to baseball identification. If we identify with individual players and their legendary diamond feats, we identify equally with hometown teams—usually with that favorite big-league ballclub whose appeal was passed on to us from our fathers and grandfathers—who in turn had received such blood-deep loyalties from their own fathers, as they were passed down from generation to generation as a family legacy alongside religion, ethnic heritage, and national identity itself. Each fan suffers religiously for years with the annual fate of a hometown favorite team, a team doomed to lose as often as it wins in even the best of seasons. (For the beauty of baseball is that the best team and the worst team usually finish the season within reasonable striking distance of a .500 record.) Again as with no other sport, baseball fans develop lifelong and passionate affinities for the home team. We live and die with that team, and its fortunes seemingly are those of our own lives. And usually that favorite ballclub also exposes the geographical roots from which each of us springs; the hometown ballpark and the local (or at least regional) big-league team provides a vital sense of urban or regional identity and solidarity—the kind of belonging to which Roger Angell alludes and which sport alone now seems to provide in a world of such diverse and alienating transient environments. It is one of baseball's purest joys and one of America's most honored rituals—and also the clearest barometer of civic pride—to rise each summer morning and scan the local newspaper sports section, checking box scores and league standings in order to find out where one's city now stands in relation to another by noting the successes of the local ball team.

The chapters which follow here capture for us all three types of baseball's richest memories. In the histories of each American League club are found the fortunes and failures of our long-suffering favorite hometown teams, carefully traced here by talented baseball historians who have crystallized those moments and developments which best illustrate the ebb and fortune of each individual team. There are also the personalities of team owners, managers, and star players which parallel and often shape the evolving histories of each team. Down through the years the American League has featured baseball's greatest individual heroes as well as its most fabled personalities—Ty Cobb, Cy Young, Charles Comiskey, Nap Lajoie, Connie Mack, Clark Griffith, Lefty Grove, Grover Cleveland Alexander, Ted Williams—and the noblest of all classic American baseball heroes, the enigmatic and graceful Joltin' Joe DiMaggio. Resurrected in these pages are the legions of legendary Bronx Bombers stretching from Ruth and Gehrig, to Bill Dickey and Joe McCarthy, to Mantle and Berra and Whitey Ford, to Billy Martin and Reggie Jackson and Don Mattingly. The legendary Walter Johnson lives here again in the memory of Washington Senators fans, as does Yaz, Jimmie Foxx, Johnny Pesky, and Bobby Doerr for Beantowners, or Greenberg, Kaline, and Mickey Lolich for hometown Detroiters. And finally there is the story of the sacred ballparks—Fenway Park, Yankee Stadium, and Tiger Stadium among those that live on; Griffith Stadium, Comiskey Park, and Sportsman's Park among those which have now passed from the nation's landscape, yet will never fade from the collective memories of all true American League fans. From hometown teams to legendary heroes to ancient ballparks, professional baseball as we know it today has evolved and flourished throughout the nearly century-long history of the American League.

Dubbed by writers and fans as the Junior Circuit and founded only at the turn of the century some 25 years after its National League forerunner, the American League would seem to many to be the league of modernity and novelty, an upstart creation which repeatedly loses sight of fabled baseball tradition. Many baseball chronicles have suggested as much. From this vantage point, the American League is that less-respected "new kid on the block"—likely to flout all that the tradition-minded baseball fan holds sacred. Those arguing in this vein repeatedly point myopically to the hotly debated issue of the designated hitter and its supposed encroachment on the game's intricate managerial strategies. But this argument is the sporting world's biggest red herring. One can only ask if a pitcher permitted to bat in Houston's Astrodome or on the circular carpeted venues which imitate baseball fields in Cincinnati or St. Louis is truly more in synch with pre-World-War-II baseball than an American League designated hitter taking his cuts in such venerable grass-filled parks as Fenway or Tiger Stadium? There is, after all, something to be said here for the physical appearance of the game—its fresh meadow smells, its natural wood sounds, its outdoor spectacle, and traditional outfield dimensions.

The argument can be made just as convincingly that the younger American League is in fact the proper home of unrivalled respect for baseball's most sacred traditions, while the so-called Senior Circuit is in reality the repeated source of unrivalled innovation and of monumental baseball change. The game's few bold engineers of progress have most certainly been Branch Rickey, Walter O'Malley, and Larry MacPhail—National Leaguers all. It was the Nationals, recall, that first broke the odious color barrier in the modern era of the previously segregated national sport. It was also the New York National League franchises of O'Malley and Horace Stoneham that first boldly transported the game to the West Coast. Walter O'Malley and his vision of West Coast play pioneered an age of intercontinental baseball we now take for granted. And while O'Malley and his National League cronies were changing the face of the baseball map to correspond to a new nation of jet travel and intercontinental communication, backward-looking American League owners still balked at Clark Griffith's repeated pleas for permission to carry out his own devoutly-wished-for franchise move to the baseball frontier in Minnesota. It was also the National League (this time under Larry MacPhail) which first dared nighttime baseball (a fact often lost in the hoopla of current media-hype surrounding the traditionalist stance of the Chicago Cubs). And finally it was the National League's Atlanta-based franchise (under entrepreneurial Ted Turner) and the Chicago Cubs (for all their pseudo-traditionalism regarding quaint Wrigley Field) which together launched the modern age of satellite nationwide cable television baseball. A third National League ballclub, the New York Mets, has now also joined the Senior Circuit's revolutionary and highly profitable superstation triumvirate.

The American League, on the other hand, maintains almost exclusively those few remaining old-style and tradition-etched ballparks which create the true essence and ambience of the old-time game. Such anachronistic concrete and steel urban parks remain in New York, Boston, Cleveland, Detroit, Baltimore (until 1991), and Chicago (through 1990) among American League cities; but only Chicago's Wrigley Field survives among National League exemplars of such early-day architectural wonders. It is the American League, then, that seemingly maintains the greatest living storehouses of baseball tradition and baseball memory. On the same mound where Roger Clemens now hurls once stood the immortal Cy Young. Ruth, DiMaggio, Mantle, and now Mattingly, have stood in the same batter's box. Ozzie Gullien patrols the same Comiskey Park infield as did Eddie Collins and Buck Weaver in a dimmer age. Baseball history in Riverfront Stadium (Cincinnati), Three Rivers Stadium (Pittsburgh), Veterans Stadium (Philadelphia), or Busch Stadium (St. Louis) fails to reach even the dawn of divisional play barely two decades ago.

It is not surprising (or overly ironic) that the newer American League (the "Junior" Circuit) would approximate what Angell sees as the Jamesian European historical posture: European culture with its crumbling urban and family facades (rather like the decay of old yet still charming ballparks) is ultimately "redeemed by its weighty regard for the past and its sense of tradition" (Palmer, 1986, 24). This image of outward decay and ennobling age bolstered by cultured tradition and a sense of history (viz. the Tigers of Detroit or Pale Hose of Chicago) is at the very heart of our conception of American League baseball as well. Nor is it surprising that the considerably older National League (with its roots firmly planted in the last quarter of the nineteenth century) would seem more representative of what D.H. Lawrence portrayed as the New American myth: the sloughing off of old forms and the shedding of old skin, the emancipation from the bonds of history, and the birth of new forms and radically new traditions. The innovations of National League moguls MacPhail, Rickey, O'Malley, and Horace Stoneham (racial integration, nighttime games, West Coast baseball) establish the very image in baseball of a New World pioneering spirit based in progress and change.

Unconsciously no doubt, such fathers of American League baseball as Ban Johnson, Charles Comiskey, Connie Mack, Clark and Calvin Griffith, and dozens more in recent decades—perhaps overly sensitized to their youthful "Johnny-Come-Lately" legacy—have seemingly struggled (albeit often quite haphazardly) to maintain that visible display of tradition and historical perspective deemed by commentators and fans alike as essential to our nineteenth-century pastoral game. This sense of tradition surfaces in the modern baseball period most visibly with the strict maintenance of old neighborhood ballparks.[1] A full half of American League parks date back to baseball's Golden Age in the 1950s and four even stretch past the period between the two Great Wars, while Wrigley Field remains the single National League landmark predating the Kennedy assassination and the Eisenhower Cold War years. Yet baseball's hoary tradition has other less noticeable manifestations as well: a dogged long-time resistance to westward expansion in the Junior Circuit (which the older league launched with the Braves' flight into Milwaukee in 1953), a favoring in the nation's older American League parks for the aesthetic joys of natural grass, and the preference for old appearances. American League umpires were the last to give up the old-style chest protectors worn outside the uniform jacket. Little-League-style protective headgear was introduced several times in the Senior Circuit (first by the Dodgers, as another of Branch Rickey's surprising innovations, and then by the Rickey-owned Pirates) before being adopted by any American League clubs. Natural grass fields still grace all but two (Kansas City and Toronto) of the American League's 12 open-air ballparks. By contrast, odious plastic carpets (usually installed for the primary benefit of a city's NFL franchise) now blight exactly half (six) of the Senior Circuit's newer and less fan-friendly parks.

Thus the popular conception of the National League as the protector of tradition and the American League as the arena for baseball change is simply not borne out by the historical facts surrounding the past century of major league play. The National League has in fact been the sole catalyst for true innovation and radical baseball experimentation (see the National League volume of this present two-volume set, especially the introduction). It was Senior Circuit teams that broke baseball's noxious color barrier, then expanded boldly to the West Coast, then first played indoor baseball in Houston's wondrous Astrodome (the American League did not go indoors until 1977), later flooding the national pastime with artificial turf fields, and finally tearing down the bulk of America's landmark ballparks (Sportsman's Park, Crosley and Forbes Fields, the Polo Grounds, Ebbets Field, Shibe Park) with pure abandon. Alongside such radical reshaping of the appearance and format of the game, the much-debated Designated Hitter Rule is merely a minor tinkering with one of the game's less visible and less baseball-pure details.

It is important that the much-discussed Designated Hitter Rule be put in its proper place. This subtle variation in the game's format (removing the pitcher from the batting order and replacing him with a designated batter in a calculated effort to increase the game's offensive display) was a response to what had become baseball's dull predictability in the late sixties and early seventies. This rule change was at the time a successful boon to reversing falling attendance in American League parks (though certainly not the only innovation to reverse the game's slide; renewed competitive balance achieved through free agency and divisional play were even more salubrious factors). In this sense the DH Rule was no different in intent or kind than the introduction of a more lively ball during the twenties and again in the late thirties—a ploy to increase offensive fireworks. But the impact on managerial strategy which the rule entailed (removing the decision to pinch hit for a pitcher in crucial situations and thus also removing the manager's quandary about keeping an effective pitcher on the mound) is altogether minimal when compared with the strategic impact in the National League of a whole fleet of new symmetrical ballparks featuring artificial turf. Old-style odd-shaped ballparks like Forbes Field or the Polo Grounds mandated crucial managerial strategy decisions regarding an entire lineup and not just a single pitcher's spot in the batting order. Different parks required different designs of the lineup—some required righthanded batting power, some mandated fleet fielders and baserunners, some rewarded sluggers, while others clearly favored contact hitters. And any manager who deftly designed his lineup for unfair advantage on the home field had to adjust equally for each road stop around the circuit. Lineups had to be constantly juggled and strategy was challenged by the eccentricity of each new park. While the preponderance of plastic fields in present National League play dictates strategy as well, they do so with an evenness which narrows rather than expands the manager's play-by-play responsibility. Removal of the smaller grass-covered older parks and their replacement with cavernous carpeted multipurpose arenas cuts severely into home-run production, returns the stolen base to prominence, demands a new breed of fleet-footed (but not necessarily strong-armed) outfielders, and reduces the joys of the unpredictable strange bounce to the list of an endangered species. Outfielders no longer dive for pop flies, the bunt (one of the venerable standbys of managerial strategy) is a lost art without grass, infielders are no longer compelled to play the sharply hit bouncer against the infield dirt, but wait back for a true bounce on the pool-table-like artificial surface, and the look and smell of the summer game have disappeared along with baseball's familiar strategies and styles of play. It was ultimately the arrival of Monsanto (the industry leader in plastic athletic turf) and not Ron Blomberg (the American League's first DH) which shifted forever the cherished traditional strategies of big-league offensive and defensive play.

The American League from the first has resisted change in matters far more crucial to the game's historical evolution than the overblown case of a Designated Hitter Rule; the result has admittedly been sometimes nothing short of reactionary and threatening to the game's best interests. While the first black players in the Junior Circuit (Larry Doby and Satchel Paige with Cleveland and Hank Thompson and Willard Brown in St. Louis) were quick to appear behind Jackie Robinson, the American League was indeed slow with widespread integration across all of its eight ballclubs. The circuit's three most traditional franchises were, as expected, the league's worst foot-draggers. The Detroit Tigers did not integrate until 1958 when the threat of boycott by civil rights groups prompted the promotion of minor-league third baseman Ossie Virgil; the Yankees (burying Vic Power in their minor league system as unfitting of the proper Yankee mold) were glacial to react and did not bring a first black on board until Elston Howard in 1955; and the Red Sox (passing up both Jackie Robinson and Willie Mays along the way) did not promote a black until journeyman Pumpsie Green a full 12 seasons after Robinson in Brooklyn (Tygiel, 1983, Chapter 11). Westward expansion (to Los Angeles and Minnesota in 1961) was also slow in coming and long resisted throughout the league, as Calvin Griffith's repeated efforts to move his nearly moribund Senators met stonefaced rejection by Junior Circuit owners.

Nighttime baseball in the American League also followed a full laggard's step behind the innovations of Larry MacPhail of the National League's Cincinnati Reds (where big-league night baseball made its debut on May 24, 1935); while the National League's Wrigley Field remained an anomaly in this regard until the present decade, night ball was still not played in Detroit's Briggs Stadium until well after the Second World War (June 15, 1948) and one other American League park (Fenway) lingered until war's end (June 16, 1947) as well. (It should be noted here that the persistence of Wrigley Field in maintaining the tradition of daytime baseball owes as much to accident as it does to any dedication in the Wrigley family toward baseball's daylight tradition; William Wrigley had intended lights for the old park way back in 1941 but donated them to the war effort in a fit of patriotism, and the project never got off the ground again until it suddenly became a point of city pride in later decades to resist such modernization.) In this most visible sense of night baseball, as in the case of racial integration and continental expansion, the Junior Circuit sadly lagged in the very innovations which kept full pace with a changing American society and ultimately saved the game from fatal stagnation.

But while the negative side may well be that important and necessary game-saving innovation lagged in American League cities, the positive side here is that in at least two of the most visible aspects of the game, the American League indeed remains the truest symbol of baseball's all-pervasive respect for tradition and changelessness. Historic ballparks are the existing legacy of American League bonding with baseball's glorious past. But also not to be ignored is the monopoly within the Junior Circuit of the game's greatest and most colorful players. Baseball's appeal is ultimately through the figure of the baseball folk hero, with all his most human and thus starkly flawed elements. And again it has been the American League which has offered the greatest names among baseball's wealth of heroes. Almost any all-time major league all-star roster would conservatively feature at least six positions staffed by Junior Circuit greats: Ruth, Cobb, and DiMaggio in the outfield; Gehrig and Cal Ripken, Jr. (name a better shortstop) in the infield; and Walter Johnson as the game's greatest righthanded hurler. While Hank Aaron bested Ruth's long-unchallenged standard for roundtrippers, he offers no match for the Babe as the nation's most legendary of sporting heroes. Similarly, Pete Rose finally chased down Ty Cobb through stubbornness and shear longevity, yet the scandal-plagued Rose will never hold the same regard in the annals of the game's greatest natural batsmen (American Leaguer Ted Williams seems the more likely candidate here). "Teddy Ballgame" Williams is a culture hero far beyond the proportions of National Leaguer Stan Musial, despite the latter's awe-inspiring string of hitting records. While most dedicated and impartial fans would today judge Willie Mays the game's greatest outfielder and perhaps even its greatest all-around player, the lack of a career-long New York venue and the issue of race has kept Mays deep in the shadow of an unfulfilled Mickey Mantle as the darling of the nation's fans. And no player—perhaps not even Ruth—maintains the unshakeable grip on the American imagination which remains the proud badge of the incomparable Yankee Clipper, Joe DiMaggio. Ruth and DiMaggio—American Leaguers both—stand apart from all the nation's other sporting heroes as the very images and essence of baseball's comic and tragic dimensions.

But above all else, American League tradition sustains baseball's most venerable franchises. Marty Appel recounts in pages to follow the inauspicious beginnings, unmatched glory years, and recent thin summers of a proud New York Yankees organization which boasts the most glorious and celebrated winning record in all American sport. Morris Eckhouse touts the conservatism, stability and consistency which has been the legacy of the Detroit Tigers and their glorious past from Cobb through Greenberg, on to Al Kaline, Norm Cash, and Harvey Kuenn, and down to the successful teams of the 1980s under personable manager Sparky Anderson. Fred Ivor-Campbell lovingly recounts the fateful saga of the Boston Red Sox and their "unceasing ribbon of bad news" which has flowed so endless across the decades from the stately island of Fenway Park. If ever there has been a ball team plagued by last-minute defeat and enriched with ennobled fallen heroes it has been the Red Sox—from Williams to Fisk and from Mel Parnell to Roger Clemens. Rocked by the outrageous trade of Babe Ruth and stunned by Johnny Pesky's fateful moment of hesitation and by the incredible seeing-eye ground ball which alluded Bill Buckner's outstretched glove, Red Sox partisans still pine away for that one perfect season when the ultimate trophy will finally be theirs.

Bill Felber, in turn, explores with humor and insight the most unlikely success story in all professional baseball history, as he recounts fondly how the nation's most consistent losers, the old St. Louis Browns, became by a most fortuitous change of venue one of its most consistent winners, the new Baltimore Orioles of the past three decades. And in one of the most stirring chapters of American League history, Norman Macht recounts the 50 years in which ageless Connie Mack, baseball's grandest old man, lovingly built the pioneering American League ballclub known as the Athletics; an account supplemented and nearly negated by the few short seasons in which first Arnold Johnson and then Charlie Finley carted the same franchise greedily across the countryside, haphazardly trying to dismantle what Mack had so painstakingly constructed.

The stories of all other American League franchises are told here as well. These include some of the game's oldest and most storied ballclubs—the Cleveland Indians (Morris Eckhouse) who have won but two pennants since the fateful season of 1920, when star shortstop Ray Chapman became baseball's lone on-field fatality and unheralded second sacker Bill Wambsganss turned the first and last World Series unassisted triple play; the ill-starred Chicago White Sox (Rich Lindberg) whose last powerhouse team seven full decades ago earned lasting infamy by conspiring to throw the sport's only illegitimate World Series Classic; the woeful Washington Senators under "Old Fox" Clark Griffith, whose decades of inept play inevitably inspired baseball's most famous epithetic barb—"first in war, first in peace, but last in the American League!" Also featured are baseball's newest teams: the Toronto Blue Jays, who have enjoyed expansion success and box office bonanza rivaling even the miracle New York Mets of the 1960s; and the Seattle Mariners (James O'Donnell), who have already authored an unparalleled saga of futility which leaves them as baseball's only twentieth-century franchise never to enjoy a single winning season; the Texas Rangers, Kansas City Royals (Bill Carle), and Milwaukee Brewers (Paul Adomites), representing opposite poles of baseball's expansion fortunes and misfortunes, one a fan-poor perennial loser and the other two providing unparalleled sagas of loyal hometown fan enthusiasm; California's Angels (Richard E. Beverage), a team tragically shadowed by uncanny ill-fortune ever since their 1961 inception as the Junior Circuit's first West Coast resident; and finally the Twins of Minnesota and of ambitious Calvin Griffith, a ballclub which finally escaped the baseball doldrums of the nation's capital in the early 1960s, yet did altogether little to escape the cellar of the American League over the next three frustrating decades.

This volume has set out to capture, then, something of the inspired diamond traditions and the numerous on-field and off-field legends that sustain American League history. Each chapter inevitably reflects the unique writing style and scholarly approach of the individual author, as well as differing approaches to historical review dictated by the unparalleled franchise history of each individual ballclub. If the story of the Toronto Blue Jays inescapably reflects the joyous optimism of expansion-era baseball, those of the Seattle Mariners and Texas Rangers will undoubtedly provide painful lessons in the pitfalls of franchise mismanagement during this age of coast-to-coast and border-to-border big-league venues. And if the Detroit Tigers and Boston Red Sox offer the true zenith in baseball's rich tradition of immortal heroes and enshrined baseball legends, so too do the New York Yankees boast the noblest and proudest winning tradition in all of American sport. If the Chicago White Sox (as Rich Lindberg contends) seem doomed to remain a second-class organization within the nation's second grand city, so too do the Detroit Tigers remain (in Morris Eckhouse's phrase) the only major league ballclub which has enjoyed so extended and exclusive a monopoly on an entire populous state. Taken together, these team histories reflect the most spectacular moments, bizarre events, and storied traditions of American League baseball, alongside the fabled past of each and every club. What follows is a rare team-by-team history of baseball written by some of the game's foremost current scholars. This is a history which focuses on the story of each team—its indelibly remembered and inevitably forgotten heroes and goats, late-season pennants unpredictably won and predictably lost, colorful and often tyrannical franchise owners, nostalgic and historic ballpark landmarks, and much, much more. In these pages the fan can relive the exciting saga of a favorite local or childhood home team, and at the same time survey as well the entire history of baseball's youngest yet most tradition-bound league.

Note

1. For fans wishing to pursue this enthralling and controversial story of evolution in North America's ballparks, nowhere is this history better capsulized than in William Humber's delightful chapter on the subject in *Let's Play Ball*, 1989. Humber provides a delicately balanced picture of the role of ballparks in modern baseball lore, suggesting both pros and cons of the inevitable evolution of past decades, from steel-and-concrete neighborhood parks in the pre-World-War-II era (Shibe Park, Ebbets Field, Polo Grounds, and the like) which intimately reflected idiosyncracies of their colorful neighborhood settings, to the circular, carpeted, and generic multi-purpose stadia of the 1970s and 1980s (Riverfront Stadium in Cincinnati being the ideal archetype). While the astroturf stadium was designed to perfect baseball play by removing the role of nature's elements and the quaint peculiarities of odd outfield dimensions and imperfect infield gravel, it has only in the end robbed the game of its traditional sights and smells and extenuated discrepancies between home fields (those that are grass and those that are not). Yet the modern stadium has also been a boon to baseball's greatest-ever attendance bonanza. No one codifies these issues more insightfully than Humber.

References

Angell, Roger. 1972. *The Summer Game.* New York: The Viking Press (New York: Ballantine Books, 1984).

———. 1977. *Five Seasons: A Baseball Companion.* New York: Simon and Schuster (New York: Popular Library, 1978).

Humber, William. 1989. *Let's Play Ball! Inside the Perfect Game.* Toronto, Ontario: Lester and Orpen Dennys Publishers.

Palmer, William. 1986. "History, Tradition, and Hubris: The Baseball Universe of Roger Angell." *Journal of Popular Culture* 20:2 (Fall):17-28.

Ross, Murray. 1971. "Football Red and Baseball Green: The Heroics and Bucolics of American Sport." *Chicago Review* 22(2): 30-40.

Tygiel, Jules. 1983. *Baseball's Great Experiment: Jackie Robinson and His Legacy.* New York: Oxford University Press.

Zoss, Joel, and John S. Bowman. 1989. *Diamonds in the Rough: The Untold History of Baseball.* New York: Macmillan Publishing Company (London: Collier Macmillan Publishers, 1989).

1

Boston Red Sox
Their Foot Shall Slide . . . Baseball's Most Potent Myth

FREDERICK IVOR-CAMPBELL

Through the end of World War I the Boston Red Sox were one of baseball's most powerful teams, winners of six American League pennants and all five World Series they entered. But in 1919 they began a long decline, which ended only after the wealthy Tom Yawkey bought the club in 1933. In 1946 the team Yawkey built won a seventh Red Sox pennant, and the Sox have since increased their pennant total to 10. But not since 1918 have the Red Sox won a World Series. Their four narrow Series losses, and their near misses in several pennant chases since 1946, have given rise to what might be called The Myth, the conviction that the Sox are fated to come close to ultimate victory, only to lose. The Myth has so strengthened its grip through frequent renewal that some Sox devotees have come to honor Red Sox failure—cautionary like a fiery sermon, cathartic like classical tragedy—as a finer thing than airy, unsubstantial victory.

Boston was not on the original list of eastern cities into which Ban Johnson planned to move his fledgling American League in 1901 as part of his scheme to raise the league to major league status. But when he learned that another league with major league aspirations planned a Boston franchise, he dropped Buffalo from his league to make room for a new Boston club. Johnson persuaded American League Vice President Charles W. Somers to bankroll the new club, vacant land was found for a ballpark along the Huntington Avenue trolley line, star third baseman Jimmy Collins was lured away from Boston's National League Beaneaters in mid-March to manage and play third for the new club, and the Boston Americans were in business.

The American League invasion of Boston helped expand its skirmish with the National League into a full-scale baseball war. Collins persuaded three more Beaneaters to desert to the American League club, but his biggest catch was pitcher Cy Young, hired away from the St. Louis Cardinals along with his favorite catcher Lou Criger.

Boston's Americans were immediately competitive in the new major league; they drew nearly twice as many fans in 1901 as their local rivals, and continued to outdraw the Beaneaters (who soon became known as the Braves) every season for two decades, sometimes by margins greater than four to one.

The Americans began slowly, losing seven of their first nine games on the road while their park was hurried to completion. But they recovered to grab a share of the league lead in August before slipping to second behind the Chicago White Sox, four games back. The team superstar was Cy Young, whose 33 wins led other league hurlers by a wide margin, and whose 1.62 earned run average was a full 80 points lower than that of his closest rival.

The next year Boston's Americans lured pitcher Bill Dinneen from the Beaneaters. Young's league-leading 32 wins and Dinneen's 21 provided nearly 70 percent of the team's 77 victories—only two fewer than the year before. But with stiff competition from several clubs this year, Boston did well to finish third.

Long Tom Hughes joined Young and Dinneen among Boston's 20-game winners in 1903, providing the margin of superiority that thrust the team into the league lead in mid-June and carried them steadily upward to a 14½-game pennant-winning margin over runner-up Philadelphia.

The American and National Leagues had ended their war in January 1903, with a "National Agreement" that would govern Organized Baseball. The agreement said nothing about a post-season World Series, but in mid-September, after it had become clear who the pennant winners would be, Pittsburgh owner Barney Dreyfuss and the new Boston president, Henry J. Killilea (a Milwaukee lawyer who, after helping negotiate the National Agreement, had purchased from Somers a controlling interest in the Boston Americans) signed an agreement for a best-of-nine Series at season's end.

For a time, though, it seemed that the Series might not come off. Boston's player contracts expired at the end of September, and the players demanded the club's entire share of ticket proceeds as payment for extending their season into October. They balked at Killilea's offer of two weeks' extra salary, but gave in when he sweetened the pot a bit.

The Pirates—easy winners of their third straight National League pennant, champions of the senior (and presumed stronger) league— were Series favorites, even though only one of their top three pitchers was at full strength. But after winning three of the Series' first four games behind the healthy arm of Deacon Phillippe, the Pirates lost the next four—and the Series—to the upstart American Leaguers. In

November, Boston manager Collins was signed to a new three-year contract.

But owner Killilea bailed out. Criticized by the press for keeping his owner's share of the World Series take (Pirate owner Dreyfuss had given his share to his players) and for other "skinflint" business practices (like charging visiting baseball writers for their Series seats), Killilea first replaced his unpopular business manager, then decided to sell the club to local ownership. General Charles H. Taylor, owner and publisher of the Boston *Globe*, purchased the club and turned over the reins to his son John I., a sports enthusiast in need of something to occupy his time (Lieb, 1947, 47–50).

John I.'s first season as club president was rewarded by Boston's tightest pennant race in its first 47 years—and a 64 percent increase in attendance that put the club at the head of the American League. Best of all for Boston fans, the race ended in a second straight Boston pennant.

The Pilgrims (as the newspapers sometimes called the team) leaped quickly into the league lead and held it through midseason behind the strong pitching of Young and Dinneen, and of veteran Jesse Tannehill, who had been acquired from New York's American League Highlanders in a trade for Long Tom Hughes (engineered by league president Ban Johnson as an effort to strengthen the weaker New York club) (Lieb, 1947, 52). In April Young began a streak of 25½ consecutive hitless innings, the climax of which was a perfect game on May 5 against the Philadelphia Athletics. By early August both New York and Chicago were closing in on Boston; by mid-month they had dropped the Pilgrims to third. But on August 17 Tannehill stopped the White Sox with the second Boston no-hitter of the season, and through the rest of the season—as Chicago dropped out of the race—Boston and New York traded the lead back and forth.

The battle continued to the final day, when the contenders met for a doubleheader in New York. Boston, 1½ games ahead, could clinch the flag with one win; the Highlanders needed a sweep. The first game began well for New York, as Highlander ace Jack Chesbro blanked Boston through six innings while his teammates scored twice off Bill Dinneen. But a Highlander error in the seventh let in the tying runs, and in the top of the ninth Chesbro's wild pitch high over his catcher's head let in the tie-breaker. Dinneen held New York in the last of the ninth and the Pilgrims were repeat champions. (New York won the nightcap in 10 innings, 1–0.) There was no World Series for Boston, however, as John McGraw, manager of the National League champion New York Giants, refused to play the American Leaguers.[1]

The Pilgrims plunged in 1905, and only a late-season spurt carried them above .500 into fourth place. In 1906 the pitching—Boston's chief strength to this point—fell apart and the club dropped to the bottom of the league with 105 losses, 45½ games out of first. Manager Collins, fading as a player and cracking under the strain of the team's decline, was fired; his replacement as manager, center fielder Chick Stahl, committed suicide the following spring.

As President Taylor began trading away Boston's aging heroes, the team rose to seventh in 1907 and to fifth in 1908. When Taylor traded Cy Young to Cleveland in February 1909, just before Young's 42d birthday, Boston's press and fans were outraged, for he had been since 1901 the team's one superstar and was still pitching effectively. But a new superstar emerged to capture the fans' attention, and the club in 1909 set a Boston attendance record that would stand until the Ted Williams era 31 years later. Nearly 669,000 fans turned out to watch 21-year-old center fielder Tris Speaker spark a revival with his bat and glove that lifted the team to third place.

Meanwhile, when Boston's National League club abandoned the last traces of red in their stockings after the 1907 season, Taylor quickly appropriated the color for his Americans and proclaimed them the Red Sox (Lieb, 1947, 6).

Although the Red Sox slipped in the standings the next two years, a team was emerging that would carry them back to the top in 1912. Harry Hooper and Duffy Lewis joined Speaker in the outfield, and the young fastballer Joe Wood was beginning to develop his reputation as "Smokey Joe." Equally exciting, the Taylors built a concrete and steel ballpark after the 1911 season near the Fenway, a section of Boston's famed chain of parks. The Taylors owned the ballpark, but shortly after starting construction they sold half the club to a group headed by Jim McAleer, retiring manager of the Washington Senators, who became the new Red Sox president. Garland "Jake" Stahl (Chick's brother) was lured back to the game after a year as a Chicago banker to play first base and manage the Sox.

The Red Sox celebrated their new park with one of their greatest seasons ever. In early June they passed the slumping White Sox to take first place, and never looked back. By season's end they had recorded what is still a team-high 105 victories for a pennant-winning margin of 14 games. Tris Speaker, with a combination of heavy hitting and sparkling fielding, was the most productive position player in the majors, while his roommate Joe Wood—with a Red Sox record 34 wins—ranked only behind Washington's Walter Johnson among major league pitchers.[2] In one of baseball's great pitching duels, Wood beat Johnson, 1–0, before a huge crowd at Fenway Park on September 6, keeping his winning streak alive at 14 games. (Wood would win two more games before losing.)

The World Series, against McGraw's Giants, turned out to be one of the most memorable Series ever. The teams stood even after three games, each with a one-run win and a share in an 11-inning tie. But

Wood held New York to one run in winning Game Four, and Boston rookie Hugh Bedient overwhelmed the Giants with a three-hitter in Game Five. After a Sunday off, with Smokey Joe ready to go again in Game Six, even Giant fans could sense an early end to the Series. But Sox president McAleer insisted that manager Stahl pitch rookie Buck O'Brien and rest Wood for the seventh game, should it be needed. Not only did the Giants defeat O'Brien with five first-inning runs, but the next day in Boston they chased Wood with *six* runs in the first, evening the Series with an 11–4 victory.

Because an eighth game had not been expected, and because the clubs hadn't decided until after the seventh game where to hold the finale (a coin toss gave it to Boston), Fenway Park was only half filled for what is still on the short list of greatest World Series games. Wood (who had hurled only the first inning the day before) relieved Bedient with the score tied 1–1 in the eighth, and preserved the tie into the tenth, when a double and single gave the Giants the go-ahead run. If Giant hurler Christy Mathewson could hold the Sox in the last of the tenth the New Yorkers would be champions. But center fielder Fred Snodgrass opened the inning with his historic muff of an easy fly, and although he made a fine catch on the next play, the tide had turned in Boston's favor. Matty walked a batter, then watched as his first baseman and catcher let Tris Speaker's pop foul drop between them. Speaker, given new life, singled home the tying run and, after an intentional walk filled the bases, Sox third baseman Larry Gardner sent a long fly out to right that drove home the winning run with the world title attached.

From 1912 through 1914 Speaker enjoyed the three finest seasons of his career, but injuries to other key players in 1913—especially Joe Wood, who lost two months to a broken hand—contributed to a disappointing season that saw the Sox struggle to finish fourth. The team improved its record after president McAleer replaced manager Stahl in midseason with catcher Bill Carrigan, but the "public humiliation" of Stahl's firing angered league president Johnson. That winter Johnson engineered the sale of the half interest in the club owned by the McAleer group to Joe Lannin, a Canadian-born Boston entrepreneur and baseball fan (Lieb, 1947, 116–17). Carrigan remained manager, though, and in 1914 led the Sox, after a rocky start, to second place, with a pitching staff that outdistanced the league in ERA, paced by sophomore Hubert "Dutch" Leonard's remarkable 1.01, the best performance by a major league starter in the past century.

Tris Speaker, with what was for him an off year, headed a Red Sox offense in 1915 that was hardly overwhelming. But the Sox had by then put together a pitching staff of remarkable strength and

balance. Its ace was sophomore Ernie Shore (19–8, 1.64 ERA), followed by Joe Wood (15–5, and a league best 1.49 ERA) and Rube
Foster (19–8, 2.11 ERA). Twenty-year-old Babe Ruth, who had spent
much of 1914 in minor league Providence, shone in his rookie big-
league season with 18 wins (helped along by his .315 batting). Dutch
Leonard rounded out the top five with 15 victories, and rookie Carl
Mays provided league-leading relief. The Sox began slowly and en-
tered June at .500, in fourth place. But by late July they had overtaken
Chicago for the lead, and by taking two crucial late-season series from
Detroit, held off the surging Tigers to capture the flag by 2½ games.

Joe Wood's continuing arm troubles brought his pitching career
to a virtual end before the season was over, and he saw no action in
the World Series. Neither did Ruth, as a pitcher, though he went to
bat once as a pinch hitter. But after Shore lost the opener to Grover
Cleveland Alexander, Foster (who singled home his own winning run
in the ninth) and Leonard stifled Philadelphia's Phillies with matching
three-hit, 2–1 victories. Shore yielded seven Phillie hits in Game Four,
but emerged the Sox' third straight 2–1 winner. And although Foster
gave the Phillies four early runs in Game Five, he held them scoreless
over the final five innings as Duffy Lewis homered to tie the game in
the eighth, and Harry Hooper (who had homered in the third inning)
homered a second time in the top of the ninth for the Series-winning
run. Games Three and Four drew Series-record crowds of more than
40,000 to Boston's new Braves Field, lent to the Sox by the Braves
(who had borrowed Fenway Park for their own World Series play the
year before).

Joe Lannin, who in one of his first decisions as Red Sox president
had doubled Tris Speaker's salary rather than lose him to the upstart
Federal League, cut back his star's pay to its original $9,000 for 1916,
now that the Federal League had folded. Speaker held out, refusing
to report for spring training, and on the eve of opening day Lannin
traded him to Cleveland. The Speaker-less Sox hit 10 points lower
than the year before, and although they began to win consistently in
June, they struggled in a tight six-way race before surging to the front
for a few weeks in August and September. Along the way Babe Ruth
emerged as the staff ace with three straight shutouts; shortstop Everett
Scott began what would become a record string (until Lou Gehrig and
Cal Riphen surpassed it) of 1,307 consecutive games played; and Rube
Foster and Dutch Leonard twirled no-hitters. Mid-September found
Boston in a virtual tie with the red-hot Tigers and surging White Sox,
and in third place a day later as they dropped the opener of a crucial
series in Chicago. But the Red Sox rallied to win the final two from
the Pale Sox, then disposed of the Tigers with a three-game sweep in

Detroit. Ruth led the club with 23 wins (and the league with his 1.75 ERA), and Carl Mays replaced Wood in Boston's balanced rotation, gaining 18 victories, 12 of them as a starter.

Once again the Sox played their Series home games at Braves Field, and once again disposed of their National League rivals—this time the Brooklyn Robins—in five games. In Game One Mays relieved Ernie Shore with the bases loaded and two out in the ninth. One run scored on an infield single, but Mays retired the next batter to preserve a 6–5 win. Ruth at last got his chance to pitch a World Series game, and made the most of his opportunity. He gave up a solo homer in the first inning of Game Two, but drove in the tying run himself in the third while holding Brooklyn scoreless for 13 innings, until the Sox scored in the last of the 14th to increase Boston's Series advantage to two games. Brooklyn held on to an early lead for a 4–3 win as the Series moved to Brooklyn. But in Game Four Dutch Leonard, after yielding two runs (only one earned) to the Robins in the first inning, blanked them the rest of the way as he watched his teammates score six times. Back in Boston—where the Columbus Day crowd of over 42,000 set a Series attendance mark that stood until Yankee Stadium was completed in 1923—Shore held Brooklyn to three singles and one run as the Sox scored four to put away their fourth world title.

Catcher-manager Carrigan left baseball after the season for a banking career in his native Maine, but his departure turned out not to be the club's greatest loss of the post-season. Although president Lannin had gradually acquired a controlling share of the club from the Taylors, he had found running a major league franchise a strain on his somewhat fragile health. In December he sold the Sox to Harry Frazee, a New York theater owner and producer, and his associate Hugh J. Ward. Ward stayed around long enough to see Sox second baseman Jack Barry named manager, then left for Australia, leaving the running of the club to Frazee (Lieb, 1947, 153–56).

Mays and Ruth, combining strong bats and solid fielding with their effective pitching, were the league's most productive moundsmen in 1917. But the season's pitching highlight was Ernie Shore's perfect game in June. Shore, replacing Ruth, who had been ejected for hitting an umpire after walking the leadoff batter, promptly picked off the baserunner and retired the next 26 men to face him. Through August, Boston hung close to the front-running White Sox, but leveled off in September as Chicago spurted ahead, and finished second, nine games back.

The Red Sox lost several top players—including manager Barry— to military service in World War I before and during the 1918 season. But Frazee had prepared for the roster turmoil by trading with Connie Mack's Athletics for some of his top players. In February he signed

Ed Barrow, who had just quit as International League president, to manage the club (Barrow, 1951, 86–89).

In 1918 Barrow, recognizing Babe Ruth's hitting ability, frequently played his star in left field on days he was not pitching. Ruth blossomed as a slugger, and although he played in only 95 of the team's 126 games, he tied for the major league lead in home runs (with 11), while leading the majors in slugging as well. Boston started strong, and although New York challenged for the lead throughout June, the Sox pulled away in July, and held on to reach Labor Day 2½ games ahead of Cleveland. That made them league champions, as the government had demanded that the season end a month early to save on wartime travel and encourage ballplayers to enter war service. The government permitted the playing of the World Series, however.

Fielding superiority gave the Red Sox the victory over Chicago's Cubs in six games. The Cubs outhit and outpitched the Sox, but Boston committed only one error, and made a number of spectacular plays in the field. Left fielder George Whiteman made a homer-saving catch in Game Three that meant the difference between loss and victory, and Chicago errors gave Boston the winning runs in Games Four and Six. Babe Ruth pitched a shutout in the opener and 7⅓ more scoreless innings in Game Four to extend to 29⅔ a World Series record for consecutive scoreless innings (begun in 1916) that Ruth proclaimed his "proudest achievement" in baseball (Ruth, 1948, 65).[3]

Boston fans deplored the delay of Game Five by nearly an hour while the players argued (unsuccessfully) for a larger share of the Series take, and only 15,238 showed up at Fenway the next day (the smallest World Series crowd in nearly a decade) to watch Carl Mays hurl the Sox to their fifth world championship with a three-hit, 2–1 victory. How could they know that 72 years later Red Sox fans would still be watching for world championship number six?

Harry Frazee had bought the Red Sox mostly with IOUs, planning to pay them off from club profits. But as the nation went to war in 1917, attendance at Fenway dropped 22 percent from the year before. And in war-shortened 1918, Sox attendance hit a new low. With the war's end in the fall of 1918, and the restoration of a longer season, Frazee could expect increased attendance in 1919. But he also found himself with a surplus of talent as players returned from the service. Thus, innocently, began what came to be known as "the rape of the Red Sox" (Lieb, 1947, 178), with the trade to the Yankees of Dutch Leonard, Ernie Shore, and Duffy Lewis for four lesser lights and $15,000 in mid-December 1918. In July the moody Carl Mays deserted the team; Frazee sent him to the Yankees (in a deal that league president Johnson tried but failed to block) for two players and $40,000.

The Red Sox finished sixth in 1919, but Babe Ruth, now playing mostly in the outfield, brought crowds to the park by hitting 29 home runs, a new season record. Attendance climbed toward prewar levels, but Frazee was still in deep trouble—in addition to his Red Sox debts, he was losing money on his theatrical productions—and in December he arranged to sell Babe Ruth to the Yankees for $100,000 and a secret $300,000 mortgage on Fenway Park. Boston fans were devastated by the sale, and deserted the Sox in 1920 to follow the Braves, who for the first time ever outdrew the Red Sox in Boston. The Sox finished fifth, and that October manager Barrow jumped ship for the Yankees, where as business manager he helped complete the Red Sox's destruction.

The Sox finished fifth again in 1921, although new manager Hugh Duffy brought them a few wins closer to .500. Pitcher Sad Sam Jones enjoyed one of the best seasons of his career, as did Bullet Joe Bush. Shortstop Everett Scott continued to set a new record with every consecutive game he played. In December all three were sent to the Yankees. In July 1922, while the Red Sox spiraled downward to their first last-place finish in 16 years, third baseman Joe Dugan and outfielder Elmer Smith, who had come to Boston in off-season trades and were hitting well, were sent to the Yankees for four players and $50,000, a trade that so enraged the St. Louis Browns (who were battling New York for the pennant) that a rule was subsequently adopted forbidding player sales for more than the waiver price after June 15th each season.

The Yankees recognized a potential for greatness in Red Sox pitcher Herb Pennock, and gave Frazee $50,000 and three players for him in January 1923. But Frazee's financial worries wouldn't go away, and as the Sox plummeted toward the cellar again—and attendance sank even below that of the short 1918 season—Frazee at last yielded to Ban Johnson's wishes and sold the club (Lieb, 1947, 193). The buyers were a group of Ohioans headed by J. A. Robert Quinn (who resigned as business manager of the Browns), and backed principally by millionaire Palmer Winslow.

One bright spot in the 1923 season was the pitching of veteran Howard Ehmke, acquired from Detroit the previous fall, who en route to his 20 wins for the Sox (nearly a third of their season total) hurled a no-hitter against Philadelphia on September 7, and followed it up in his next outing with a near-perfect game against the pennant-bound Yankees that was spoiled only by a leadoff single on a bobbled ball that might just as easily have been ruled an error (Lieb, 1947, 189–90).

Fenway attendance nearly doubled in 1924, Quinn's first season as Red Sox president, and the team battled among the league leaders into June before tailing off to seventh. But then followed six straight seasons in which the club didn't even offer a serious challenge for *seventh* place. Pitcher Red Ruffing could compile a record of just 39–96 with the Red Sox; traded (for a player and $50,000) to the Yankees in 1930, he went 231–124 and wound up in the Hall of Fame.

Millionaire Winslow died in 1926, and with him Quinn's one source of ready cash to plug the club's deepening financial hole (Lieb, 1947, 194). The Sox rallied late in 1931 to rise from last place in mid-September to sixth (just one percentage point out of fifth) by season's end. (This was the year Earl Webb spanked what is still a major-league record 67 doubles.) But they couldn't abide the rarified atmosphere, and ended the next season with the worst record in the team's history: last place with 111 losses, 64 games out of first. Home attendance fell below 200,000 for the first (and only) time. The club, like the nation, was mired in the Great Depression. Just in time, Tom Yawkey turned 30.

Thomas A. Yawkey, the adopted son of his uncle William Yawkey, onetime part owner of the Detroit Tigers, was a wealthy sportsman and baseball fan who wanted a team of his own. When he learned the Red Sox could be purchased, he sought out his boyhood idol, Eddie Collins (then coaching for the Athletics), and secured his agreement to join the Sox as their first general manager. Then, on February 25, 1933, four days after his 30th birthday had brought him a major portion of his inheritance, he bought the club.

Three weeks after the sale was completed in April, Yawkey acquired catcher Rick Ferrell and pitcher Lloyd Brown from the Browns for a player and an undisclosed sum of money, and a few days later sent $100,000 to the Yankees for veteran pitcher George Pipgras and rookie infielder Bill Werber. The years of selling Sox stars were over; the years of buying stars had begun. Yawkey's quick fix spurred the Red Sox out of the cellar in 1933—up only one place, to seventh, but with 20 more wins than the previous year. Attendance rose 47 percent over 1932.

That winter Yawkey rebuilt Fenway Park from the ground up, retaining the unique configuration of the playing field but thoroughly modernizing the stands. He continued to rebuild the team as well through purchases from other major league clubs. Some veterans, like Rube Walberg and Max Bishop, were nearing the end of their careers but others, like pitchers Lefty Grove and Wes Ferrell (Rick's brother), shortstop-manager Joe Cronin (whose purchase from Washington in the fall of 1934 cost Yawkey a quarter million dollars), and slugging first baseman Jimmie Foxx (acquired in December 1935), more than repaid the fortune spent for them.

With the attraction of a renewed team in a renewed ballpark, home attendance in 1934 more than doubled over the previous year, rising above 600,000 for the first time in a quarter century. As the team rose to fourth place, their best finish since 1918, they outdrew the Braves for the first time in five years.

The Red Sox finished fourth again in 1935, then fell to sixth the next year. In 1937, while they rose only one place, to fifth, a 12-game win streak lifted them into second place briefly in August, and they compiled their best won-lost record in 19 years.

Lefty Grove had won 14 games in 1938 when he injured his arm fielding a bunt in mid-July, and won no more games that year. The Sox, who were in third place and playing well, leveled off for a month, but recovered in August to move into second, and with a September spurt hung on to second place, finishing just 9½ games behind the Yankees. Boston's .299 team batting average led the league, and Jimmie Foxx earned league titles in batting, slugging, walks, RBIs, and total bases. His 50 home runs trailed Tiger Hank Greenberg's 58, but established a Red Sox record that still stands. In the shadow of the Sox' imported stars, a young second baseman played his first full major league season: Bobby Doerr, a harbinger of GM Collins's program to continue the team buildup with prospects seasoned in the minors.

As the veteran stars gradually gave way to younger players over the next four years, the team remained among the league's strongest. Three times—in 1939, 1941, and 1942—the Sox finished second, although in none of these years did they seriously challenge the powerful Yankees for the pennant. In 1940 they rose to first place in May, but played .500 ball the rest of the season, finishing fourth. Ted Williams, a brash, skinny outfielder the Sox had purchased from minor league San Diego in December 1937, was brought up to the big club in 1939 after a year of seasoning in Minneapolis, and quickly captured the attention of the baseball world with his consistency and power at the plate—and with his prickly temperament. In his second season he moved past Foxx as the team's top slugger.

The Red Sox were lucky to acquire Williams. Yawkey was not an innovator, and was slow even to adopt the successful innovations of others. He never matched Branch Rickey, for example, in the development of young talent. Rickey's Cardinals, and the Detroit Tigers, had scouted Williams in high school, and the Cardinals brought him to a tryout camp and offered him a contract. The Yankees also wanted to sign him, but perhaps balked at his mother's insistence on a $1,000 signing bonus (Williams, 1969, 35–37). The Red Sox didn't discover Williams until he was already playing for San Diego, with whom the Sox had a working agreement. Even Yawkey hesitated to pay the bonus the Williamses demanded, but Eddie Collins apparently convinced his boss of Williams's potential, and the Kid was signed (Williams, 1969, 43).

By 1941 Williams was baseball's dominant player. His on-base percentage of .551 that year set a standard that may endure forever; only Williams himself has since come within 35 points of it. And only two players besides Williams have since come within 20 points of his .406 batting average that year. The next season, rookie Johnny Pesky (who replaced manager Cronin at shortstop and whacked a league-leading 205 hits) and sophomore hurler Tex Hughson (22–6, 2.59 ERA) joined the growing number of farm-grown Red Sox standouts.

World War II had by 1943 drawn off many of baseball's best. From the Red Sox, Pesky, Williams, and Dom DiMaggio (Joe's little brother, since 1940 a fixture in the Red Sox outfield) headed the list of players to enter military service. Not even Tex Hughson's second strong season on the mound could bring him or the club a winning year in 1943; Boston finished seventh.

Although he played only 125 games in 1944, Bobby Doerr enjoyed his most productive season at the bat, leading the league in slugging. Tex Hughson dropped his ERA to a career-best 2.26, winning 18 games by early August. And catcher Hal Wagner, acquired in a June trade, hit a team-high .332 in 66 games. The Sox battled in the midst of a tight field through June, and by mid-August had established themselves in second place with hopes of catching the slumping St. Louis Browns. But just then Doerr, Hughson, and Wagner were called to war. The Sox dropped quickly to fourth, where they finished at exactly .500, 12 games out. They fell farther, to seventh, in 1945, the final war year, but there was a bright spot in the performance of pitcher Dave Ferriss (released from the Army in February because of asthma), who made his major league debut with back-to-back shutouts, and 21 season victories.

Ferriss proved that he was no wartime fluke the next season when he won 25 games for Yawkey's first pennant winner. With the war over, the Red Sox were back at full strength in 1946, and with a host of young players at the height of their careers, they made a shambles of the pennant race. Williams with his smoking bat and Doerr with solid hitting and his best year defensively ranked one-two among American League position players, and the pitching of Ferriss and Hughson placed them among the league's top winners. By mid-May the Sox were nearly 20 games above .500 with a solid lead that proved unchallengeable. Detroit surged in September to pass New York for second place, but still finished 12 games behind Boston. The Sox in 1946 attracted more than 1.4 million fans to Fenway, breaking their old attendance mark by nearly 700,000. The record was set without night baseball, but owner Yawkey would capitulate to the changing times and install lights at the park for the 1947 season, 12 years after Cincinnati had pioneered the way.

Well rested after their easy pennant victory, the Red Sox were favored to take the World Series from the St. Louis Cardinals (who had been caught by the Dodgers in regulation play, but triumphed in the first major league tiebreaker playoff series). The Sox won the opener on veteran Rudy York's home run in the 10th inning, but the next day the Cards' Harry Brecheen shut them out 3–0. The Sox responded in kind as the Series moved to Boston for Game Three: York walloped a three-run homer in the first inning and Dave Ferriss spaced six hits for a 4–0 win.

In this seesaw Series, the Cardinals evened things up with an embarrassing 20-hit 12–3 win in Game Four, but the Sox' Joe Dobson held them to just four hits (and three unearned runs) the next day as his teammates scored six runs to take the Series advantage for the third time.

Back in St. Louis, the Cards for the third time tied the Series, as Brecheen won his second game, 4–1. The way the Series was going, it was Boston's turn to win Game Seven. The Sox rallied to tie the game at 3–3 in the eighth, but in the bottom of the inning Cardinal baserunner Enos Slaughter scored from first on Harry Walker's two-out hit to left center, which was hesitantly relayed to the plate by Sox shortstop Johnny Pesky. Reliever Brecheen stifled another Boston scoring threat in the ninth to take his third win of the Series and hand the Red Sox their first World Series defeat.

It would be 21 years until the next Red Sox pennant. With Pesky's hesitation, the Red Sox had begun to construct The Myth. Since 1946 Sox near-misses have gradually supplanted the spider Jonathan Edwards held over the fiery pit as New England's signal object lesson; since 1946 the Red Sox have repeatedly performed on their green stage New England's answer to Greek tragedy.

The Sox were pre-season favorites to repeat as American League champions in 1947. Offensively they proved still formidable. But three of the team's top four pitchers of 1946 slipped badly in 1947; only the improvement of Joe Dobson and Earl Johnson's career season in both relief and starting assignments kept the Sox from sliding lower than third. At the end of the season, manager Cronin took over from the aging Eddie Collins as general manager. Replacing Cronin was Joe McCarthy, manager of nine winners (and seven World Series victors) with the Cubs and Yankees.

In November Boston turned to the St. Louis Browns for pitching—and more, sending 10 players and $375,000 to St. Louis for pitchers Jack Kramer and Ellis Kinder, slugging shortstop Vern Stephens, and utility infielder Billy Hitchcock. Stephens helped Williams and Doerr rebuild the Sox offense into a league powerhouse, but just as important to Boston's recovery in 1948 was the pitching of

Mel Parnell, who in his first full big-league season won 15 games and led the club in earned run average. The Sox began slowly, and found themselves on Memorial Day nine games below .500, in seventh place. But then they caught fire, shooting up to fourth place by late June, and into a virtual four-way tie for first on August 3. As August passed into September, Philadelphia dropped out of the race and the Sox took a narrow lead which they held for nearly a month. A pair of late-September losses, though, dropped them into a three-way tie, then Cleveland moved into the lead, leaving the Yankees and Red Sox tied in second place for five days. But in the final two games of the regular season, Cleveland split with Detroit, and the Sox defeated the Yankees twice to finish even with the Indians.

Joe McCarthy chose the veteran Denny Galehouse to face Cleveland in the one-game tiebreaker at Fenway Park the next day, although Parnell and Kinder—both with better season records—were also rested. The result was an 8–3 rout, as Indian manager-shortstop Lou Boudreau homered twice to lead his club into the World Series. The only consolation for Boston was that the tight race had boosted their home attendance over 1.5 million for the first time.

Again in 1949 the Red Sox started slowly. Winning at home, but losing on the road, they hovered around .500 into July. But on July 24 the Sox began one of their most impressive surges ever, winning 28 of their next 35 games to pull themselves by late August to within 1½ games of New York. Three straight losses dropped them back a bit, but they recovered to pull within half a game of the front-runner on Labor Day. After splitting a two-game series in New York, the Sox lost two of their next three and trailed the Yankees by two games when they next met at Fenway on September 24. Ellis Kinder, after a night of heavy drinking (Halberstam, 1989, 224–25), stopped New York 3–0 for his 13th win in a row (his 18th straight win as a starter). The next day Mel Parnell topped the Yankees 4–1 for his 25th win. For the first time all season the Sox held a share of first place. The next day the teams moved to New York for a third game, and the Sox edged the Yankees 7–6, to take the lead by themselves.

The Red Sox won another game to run their win streak to 11, but then split their next two before returning to Yankee Stadium for the final two games of the season. The Bosox led New York by a game: one win would give them the cherished pennant. Parnell started the first game, aiming for a 26th victory, but the Yankees won 5–4 and the two teams were again tied as they entered the final game.

The Yankees scored a run in the first inning off Kinder, but entered the last of the eighth still ahead only 1–0. In a managerial move that in retrospect seemed ill conceived, McCarthy lifted Kinder for a pinch hitter earlier in the inning, and the Yankees faced a tired

Parnell. By the time the Yankees had finished scoring off Parnell and Tex Hughson, his successor, they led 5–0. The Sox scored three runs in the ninth and put an additional runner on first before a foul out ended their season. Ted Williams and Vern Stephens had captured the league's two top spots in home runs, slugging, total bases, and RBIs. Dom DiMaggio had hit safely in what is still a Red Sox record 34 consecutive games. Mel Parnell had turned in the league's best season on the mound, and Kinder had put together his finest season as a starter. The Red Sox had compiled an astonishing 61–16 won-lost mark at home that duplicated their 1946 record, and had drawn, for the fourth year in a row, a record number of fans to Fenway. But their road ledger was just 35–42, and for the second year in a row they wound up one game back in second place.

In 1949 the Red Sox had turned down an opportunity to purchase young Willie Mays—who was enthusiastically recommended by Boston scout George Digby—for $5,000 from the Birmingham Black Barons (Halberstam, 1989, 184–87). On May 13, 1950, the Sox released their first black minor league player, Negro League veteran Piper Davis, who was leading the Scranton club at the bat and on the basepaths, thereby saving themselves the $7,500 they would have had to pay the Black Barons had they retained Davis until May 15 (Tygiel, 1983, 261–63).

Tom Yawkey may not have been more racist than other club owners of his time, but many player decisions were made by racist subordinates. And Yawkey was no pioneer. Handed a golden opportunity to integrate Organized Baseball in April 1945, when (under pressure from the Boston city council) the Red Sox gave a tryout at Fenway Park to three Negro leaguers—one of them Kansas City Monarch rookie Jackie Robinson—Sox officials found excuses not to consider hiring any of the three (Hirshberg, 1973, 144–45). The Red Sox would not field a black player until 14 years after this Fenway tryout, only three years before Robinson's induction into the Hall of Fame. By then, every other major league club had been integrated.

But in 1950 the Sox management saw little need to expand their search for players into new and possibly disrupting areas. They already had the strongest team in the game—at the plate, anyway. The team hit .302 that year—the last major league club to surpass .300—and was one of few teams ever to score more than 1,000 runs in a season.

After a strong start the 1950 Sox stalled in midsummer. Ted Williams broke his elbow in the All-Star Game, and manager Joe McCarthy retired. Under former coach Steve O'Neill, the club surged in September to within a game of the front-running Yankees before dropping back to third, four games out. All the Red Sox power couldn't overcome the weakness of a pitching staff on which only Mel Parnell could hold the opposition to fewer than four earned runs per game.

Sox pitching improved in 1951, but their hitting fell off 36 points and, while their 804 runs scored again led the league, they averaged nearly 1½ fewer runs per game than the year before. From July to mid-September the Sox played at or near the top, but a late-season plunge left them 11 games back in third place. Still, this was closer than they would finish for 16 future years.

Over the next nine seasons, as the Williams era slowly wound down, the Red Sox went nowhere. Long before Williams himself retired, the others who had formed Yawkey's first youth movement were gone: pitchers Tex Hughson and Dave Ferriss had worn out their arms before 1950; Bobby Doerr retired with a bad back before the close of the 1951 season; Johnny Pesky was traded to Detroit; and Dom DiMaggio retired one month into the 1953 season.

Sox nemesis Lou Boudreau was hired from Cleveland to manage Boston in October 1951. A month after his appointment he announced that Williams could be traded. A month after that, he decided to keep him. The Marines had other plans, however, and recalled Williams to active duty: he spent most of the 1952 and 1953 seasons as a combat pilot in Korea.

The Sox remained in contention until September 1952, when they slumped from third to sixth, with their first sub-.500 finish in seven years. (Rookie outfielder Jim Piersall dropped out the last half of the season to seek treatment of the mental illness he describes in his book *Fear Strikes Out*.) Mel Parnell and Ellis Kinder came back strongly the next year, Maurey McDermott enjoyed his finest season on the mound, and the Sox rebounded to fourth place. Kinder's effectiveness diminished in 1954, though, and Parnell broke his pitching arm. McDermott was traded to Washington for outfielder Jackie Jensen. Jensen complemented Ted Williams's league-leading offense, and the team again finished fourth. The high finish is deceptive, however, for the club wound up well below .500, a full 25 games out of third place, and 42 games out of first—their most distant finish since the disaster of 1932. In October manager Boudreau was fired, and replaced by one-time Sox third baseman Mike "Pinky" Higgins.

Ted Williams missed a third of 1955 with back trouble, and promising sophomore first baseman Harry Agganis died of a pulmonary embolism in late June after developing pneumonia in May. But Jensen and first baseman Norm Zauchin added their power to that of Williams, and sophomore Frank Sullivan proved the league's most effective pitcher. The club reversed a poor start with a rush in June and July that brought them into the thick of a tight four-team race in

August before they leveled off to yet another fourth-place finish—though this time just 12 games out. No one challenged the Yankees in 1956, but Boston battled into September for second place before falling off to their fourth straight fourth-place conclusion. The sentimental highlight of the year was the midsummer no-hitter Mel Parnell hurled against Chicago in what was to be his final big-league season.

Boston rose a notch to third place in 1957. Although the team never contended for first, Ted Williams (who turned 39 in August) made it exciting for Sox fans with one of his most splendid seasons, homering 38 times (his highest total in eight years) while batting .388, tops in the majors since his .406 in 1941.

Nineteen fifty-eight was another runaway Yankee year, and the Sox stirred little excitement in finishing another distant third. In January 1959 Joe Cronin was elected president of the American League, and was replaced as Sox general manager by Bucky Harris, who had been Yawkey's first managerial appointee in 1934. The Sox spent most of the 1959 season below .500, and only a September push lifted them as high as fifth. Manager Higgins was fired July 3 (he would be called back in 1960), and Pumpsie Green arrived a couple of weeks later to complete the racial integration of the major leagues. For the only time in his career Ted Williams—plagued by a pinched nerve in his neck—hit below .300 (Williams, 1969, 230–31).

Williams, now 41, recovered enough to return in 1960 for one final season. He played in only 10 more games than he had in 1959, but hit 19 more home runs; his season total of 29 (the last of them hit in his final at bat) brought his career total to 521, at the time third best ever behind only Babe Ruth and Jimmie Foxx. Jackie Jensen, who quit baseball in January because of his fear of flying, sat out the season, although he would try one final time to overcome his fear in 1961.

As a team, the Sox had a terrible season, finishing seventh and introducing a seven-year slump in Sox fortunes, the most sustained depression of Tom Yawkey's ownership. The Sox finished as high as sixth only once (in 1961), and twice finished seventh (1960, 1963), twice eighth (1962, 1964), and twice ninth (1965, 1966). Because the American League added two teams in 1961, the Sox' eighth- and ninth-place finishes were not the league's lowest, but their closest finish in these years was 19 games from the top in 1962. In the worst of these seasons—1965—they lost 100 games and finished 40 games back.

During this depression only 1963 saw the Sox contend at all seriously; they remained close to the top into July before falling out of the race. Newly acquired first baseman Dick Stuart brought power to the club in his two years with the Sox. But his awkward fielding (which earned him the nickname "Dr. Strangeglove"), and his concern only for his own hitting rather than team success (Hirshberg, 1973,

79), brought his Boston career to an early end. In 1963 left fielder Carl Yastrzemski, in his third big-league season, won the first of his three batting crowns. Pitcher Bill Monbouquette crafted his only 20–win season, and sophomore reliever Dick Radatz enjoyed the finest year of his career, the second of three straight seasons as the league's top reliever.

There were few other highlights during these years, but among them were three no-hit performances: by Earl Wilson (who won his own game with a home run) and Monbouquette in 1962, and by Dave Morehead in 1965 (the last no-hitter to date by a Sox pitcher). Also in 1965, 20-year-old outfielder Tony Conigliaro ("Tony C"), in his second Sox season, became the youngest player ever to lead the league in home runs.

Mike Higgins, elevated from manager to general manager after the 1962 season, proved no more adept at building a winning team than Joe Cronin or Bucky Harris had. But near the end of the 1965 season, Yawkey replaced Higgins with the club's business manager, Dick O'Connell. A year later, O'Connell named Dick Williams to manage the Sox for 1967.

Williams, a former utility player, had found success managing minor league Toronto. In contrast to his predecessors, Williams was a strict taskmaster who (for one season, at least) brought the Red Sox together as a team to a degree previous managers had been unable to do. Some players viewed him as cold and uncaring, but they respected his managerial ability and responded to his determination to succeed.

Rookie pitcher Billy Rohr's first big-league win, an April one-hitter (a no-hitter for 8⅔ innings) against the Yankees, was the high point of the first half of the Red Sox' 1967 season. The team was playing better than usual, but at the All-Star break (by which time Rohr was back in the minors) they stood just two games above .500, in fifth place, six games out of first. But on July 14 the Sox exploded for an 11–5 win over Baltimore and the season that became known as "The Impossible Dream" shifted into high gear.

The Sox won 10 games before their next loss, to pull themselves within half a game of first place. They played below .500 for the next month, dropping back to fourth, but then won seven straight to gain a virtual tie for first. Even the tragic beaning of Tony C. in mid-August failed to stop Boston's momentum, although it knocked Conigliaro out of the game for the rest of 1967 and all of 1968. Through the final two months of the season, in a four-way struggle that John Davenport has called "the ultimate mind-boggler of pennant races" (Davenport, 1981, 119), the Red Sox battled Minnesota, Detroit, and Chicago. At no time after August 6 were the four clubs more than 3½ games apart. Three times they were separated by one game or less, including a virtual four-way tie on September 6. The White Sox ended their season with five straight losses, but Boston and Minnesota came to the final day tied, with one more game at Fenway, while Detroit, a half game back, faced California in a doubleheader. The Sox beat the Twins, 5–3, while the Tigers were winning their first game in Detroit. If the Tigers could defeat the Angels in the nightcap they would tie the Sox, forcing a playoff. But they lost, and Tom Yawkey had his second pennant. There were Red Sox heroes aplenty during the stretch run, but Carl Yastrzemski's six RBIs (including a three-run homer) in the final two must-win games stand out. In both games Yaz's hitting meant the difference between loss and victory—and assured him the triple crown, a height no major leaguer has scaled since.

In the World Series opener the St. Louis Cardinals, behind Bob Gibson's 10-strikeout pitching, edged the Red Sox 2–1, but the Sox' Jim Lonborg shut out the Cards on one hit the next day (as Yaz homered twice). In St. Louis the Cardinals took the next two games (Game Four was a Gibson shutout), but Lonborg stopped the Sox slide with a three-hit, 3–1 win in Game Five. Back in Boston the Sox evened the Series with an 8–4 victory that featured four Red Sox homers. But in the finale Gibson homered in his own behalf against an overmatched Lonborg, yielding just three hits while fanning 10 in the 7–2 game. As in 1946, Yawkey's hopes for a world title were frustrated by the Cardinals in the seventh game. But in the euphoria of the Sox' "impossible" recovery from years near the bottom, the team's World Series defeat barely roused The Myth.

With an increase of nearly a million fans over 1966, the 1967 Red Sox led the American League in home attendance for the first time in 52 years, and set a new club record of more than 1.7 million. Baseball was once again big in Boston, and nearly two million fans turned out to see the Sox in 1968 (setting a Fenway record that would stand for nine years), even though the team managed to finish no better than a distant fourth. Slugger Ken Harrelson, who had signed on with the dream team the previous August, helped ease the loss of Tony C. with his finest season, and pitcher Ray Culp, acquired the previous November, hurled four straight shutouts in a 16–6 season that partially redeemed the ineffectiveness of Jim Lonborg, who had wrenched his knee in a Christmas Eve skiing accident. Yaz again led the league in batting, although in this "year of the pitcher" he averaged only .301, a record low for a major league batting champion.

Harrelson was traded away early in the 1969 season, but Yastrzemski, shortstop Rico Petrocelli, center fielder Reggie Smith, and Tony Conigliaro (with an impressive comeback) powered Boston to home run and slugging league titles in 1969 and 1970. When Yaz's production fell off in 1971, first baseman George Scott recovered much of his 1967 form to take up the slack. But no one challenged Baltimore in the American League East those years, and Boston finished each season well back in third place.

The ballplayers wiped out the first 13 days of the 1972 season with a strike, which left the clubs with an unequal number of games to play, depriving the Red Sox (as it turned out) of a chance to win the division championship. Manager Williams had been fired late in the 1969 season, and the Sox were now led by Eddie Kasko, promoted from the triple-A Louisville club. Tony C. had been traded in October 1970, and just before the 1972 season, in one of Boston's worst trades ever, the emerging relief ace Sparky Lyle was sent to the Yankees for infielder Danny Cater, whose best years were behind him. But the Sox had acquired pitcher Luis Tiant (whom no one else wanted) in May 1971, and speedster Tommy Harper and pitcher Marty Pattin that October. All three contributed much to Boston's pennant run, as did rookie catcher Carlton Fisk, who burst on the scene with the best season of his long career.

In late summer, after a dreadful start and a long climb to rise above .500, the Sox leaped from fourth to first and held Detroit at bay until the season's final series, when they lost the first two of three games to the Tigers to hand them the division crown. Boston beat Detroit in the final game, but since (because of the strike) they had played one game fewer than the Tigers, they remained half a game back, their closest finish ever.[4]

Pitcher Bill Lee—one of the Sox' more memorable free spirits— was moved from the bullpen into the starting rotation in 1973, and with Luis Tiant anchored a transitional squad that in 1973 and 1974 offered strong challenges for the division title until late summer. In 1974, under new manager Darrell Johnson (the third manager in a row to be elevated from the club's top farm—by this time located in Pawtucket, Rhode Island), Boston occupied first place through much of the summer before sliding to third with a three-week slump in September.

Offense was the story of Boston's division crown in 1975. Led by a pair of rookie outfielders up from Pawtucket, Fred Lynn and Jim Rice, who between them drove in 207 runs, and bolstered by the heavy hitting of Cecil Cooper (in limited service as first baseman and designated hitter) and Carlton Fisk (who returned in late June after losing nearly a year to injuries), the Sox took league titles in batting and slugging, and scored 108 more runs than their closest divisional rival to make even their below-average pitching staff look good.[5]

Boston broke out of its May doldrums to take first place late in the month; by June 29, the Sox were in front to stay. A 10-game win streak in July put them well ahead of Baltimore, their only late-season challenger, and they clinched their first division championship when the Orioles lost a doubleheader on September 27. Jim Rice had broken his arm in a game six days earlier and would miss post-season play; Fred Lynn would become the first rookie ever named American League most valuable player.

The Red Sox defeated reigning world champion Oakland in the League Championship Series with surprising ease. Luis Tiant's three-hitter in the opening game set the tone, and the Sox swept the A's in three games. The World Series against Cincinnati's "Big Red Machine," though, was another story.

Tiant shut out the Reds 6–0 in the Boston opener, but the Sox lost a pair of heartbreakers, 3–2 in Game Two as Cincinnati came back with a pair of ninth-inning runs, and 6–5 in Game Three at Cincinnati, when (after Sox right fielder Dwight Evans had tied the score with a two-run homer in the ninth) the Reds' Joe Morgan rapped a long bases-loaded hit in the last of the 10th. The Sox bounced back with a five-run fourth inning in Game Four to take a close win (5–4) of their own (Tiant's second complete-game victory), but the Reds regained their Series advantage with a 6–2 victory the next day.

A travel day and three rainouts brought Tiant back to the mound at Fenway for Game Six. Fred Lynn gave the Sox a quick boost with his three-run homer in the first inning. But the Reds tied the score in the fifth, took a two-run lead in the seventh, and finally drove out Tiant with a leadoff homer in the eighth. Boston pinch hitter Bernie Carbo evened the score again with a three-run blast in the bottom of the eighth, but there the score stood through 3½ scoreless innings (which included a leaping catch in the 11th by Dwight Evans in deep right that prevented one—and probably two—Cincinnati runs), until Carlton Fisk led off the Boston 12th with a home run memorably captured on TV by a low-level camera angle that has ever after been known as "the Fisk." The game itself was immediately labeled the greatest in World Series history—and so it remains. But the Red Sox needed one more win to break the grip of The Myth.

They didn't get it. Boston scored first in Game Seven with three runs in the third inning, but the Reds tied the score in the seventh, and in the ninth pushed across what proved to be the deciding run as the Sox went down in order in their final turn at bat.

The Red Sox, who had now gone 57 years without a world championship, were still counting. But Tom Yawkey's years had run out. On July 9, 1976, in his 44th year of club ownership, he died of leukemia.

Ten days after Yawkey's death, manager Darrell Johnson was fired as the Sox plummeted toward the bottom of the division, and was replaced by coach Don Zimmer. Under Zimmer, a no-nonsense man of the old school who had little rapport with counterculture types like Bill Lee, and little use for suspected malingerers, the Sox reversed course, working their way back above the .500 mark, and capturing third place by half a game at the very end of the season.

In 1977 and 1978, Zimmer's first two full years at the helm, the Red Sox enjoyed their most successful seasons since 1950, and even his less imposing 1979 squad won more than 90 games. His teams drew record numbers to Fenway three years running—more than two million fans a year—but they couldn't win the division championship.

They came close in 1977, with a blend of power (eight players numbered their home runs in double figures) and the league's best relief pitching from Bill Campbell, who had signed as a free agent the previous November. The Sox battled Baltimore and New York for the lead from May into September, when the Yankees burst ahead, leaving the Sox and Orioles tied 2½ games back at the finish.

The years 1977–1978 saw major changes in ownership and front office personnel. Tom Yawkey's widow Jean, on behalf of the Yawkey estate, had put the club and Fenway Park up for sale in April 1977, and late in September announced a purchase agreement with Haywood Sullivan, the club's director of player personnel, and former Sox trainer Edward "Buddy" LeRoux, with Mrs. Yawkey and others listed as limited partners. The league withheld its approval of the sale, however, until the following May, after its financing had been strengthened by the addition of Mrs. Yawkey and the Yawkey estate as a third general partner. Meanwhile, Mrs. Yawkey fired general manager Dick O'Connell, who had tightened a ragged administration and built the contending Sox teams of the 1970s.[6]

Manager Zimmer found his club even stronger in 1978 than 1977. Chief among the off-season acquisitions were pitchers Mike Torrez and Dennis Eckersley, and second-baseman Jerry Remy. The Sox jumped out to their best start since 1946, and by mid-July stood more than 30 games above .500, 8½ games ahead of second-place Milwaukee and 13 ahead of the drooping Yankees. From July 17–19 the Sox margin over New York peaked at 14 games. Jim Rice was on his way to the best season of his career, but injuries to several key players began to take their toll, and the Sox saw the Brewers close to within 4½ games and the Yankees to 6½ in less than two weeks. Milwaukee faded away and the Sox recovered, but as August turned into September the Sox began another slump while New York continued its surge; in four games at Fenway the Yankees overwhelmed the Red Sox (42 runs to nine, dubbed the "Boston Massacre") as they swept to a tie for the lead. With two more wins over the Sox in New York a few days later the Yankees moved 3½ games in front. But Boston won the third game of the series, and in the final week of the season closed the gap to one game while winning their final eight. New York held their lead until a final-game loss dropped them into a tie with Boston.

The outcome of the tiebreaker playoff game at Fenway the next day moved Harvard classics professor Emily Vermeule to equate the Red Sox with heroes of Greek tragedy (Vermeule, 1987, 222–23). Carl Yastrzemski opened the scoring with a home run off Yankee ace Ron Guidry in the second inning, and the Sox scored a second run in the sixth. But in the top of the seventh, with two men on base and two out, Yankee Bucky Dent lofted a ball to left that earlier in the game would have drifted down into the outfield. But the wind had shifted and now carried the fly over Fenway's high but close-in "green monster" for a three-run lead-changing home run. One batter (and walk) later, Sox starter Mike Torrez was pulled for Bob Stanley, who in his second big-league season had shown himself one of the league's best relievers. But this time, the first man he faced doubled to make the Yankee lead 4–2, and one inning later Reggie Jackson homered to increase it to 5–2.

Yankee reliever Goose Gossage was pitching in the eighth when the Sox followed Jerry Remy's double with three singles to narrow the Yankee lead to 5–4. In the last of the ninth the Sox put men on third and first, but with two away, Yaz popped up to the third baseman, and the Red Sox season was over.

The next three years were anticlimatic. Expectations were high for 1979, and the team remained a league powerhouse. Fred Lynn rebounded from a couple of sub-par seasons with his best year ever, and Yaz reached a pair of milestones, becoming the first American Leaguer to acquire both 400 home runs and 3,000 hits. But although the Sox chased Baltimore for the division lead into August, a late-season slump dropped them deep into third place, where they remained.

Veteran first baseman Tony Perez, signed as a free agent in November, helped supply power to a 1980 Red Sox lineup disrupted by injuries to Rice (in June) and Lynn (in August). But despite an August revival the team offered no challenge to the leaders. Manager Zimmer was fired during a Sox slump just four games from the end of the season, and club finished a distant fourth.

That winter, through front office bungling, Boston lost catcher Carlton Fisk to free agency (he joined the White Sox) and Fred Lynn to California in a trade that gained the Sox less than Lynn's value in the player market.[7] Nevertheless, in strike-divided 1981, the Sox' first season under former Yankee manager Ralph Houk, veteran outfielder Dwight Evans led the league in total bases and runs created to pace an otherwise ordinary team to a run for the second-half division title before they settled back into a second-place tie, 1½ games out.

Evans continued to wield one of the league's most authoritative bats in 1982, but the Sox, after leading their division much of the first half, leveled off and were overtaken by Milwaukee and Baltimore. Injuries took a toll, but third baseman Carney Lansford's sprained ankle opened a place in the lineup for rookie Wade Boggs, who although he came to the plate too little to qualify for a batting title, hit for an average (.349) 17 points higher than that of any major league regular that season.

Slugger Tony Armas (acquired from Oakland) joined Rice and Evans in 1983 to form for two years one of the game's most potent outfields. Wade Boggs won his first batting crown, and Carl Yastrzemski wound up his 23-year career on the season's last day with his 3,419th hit. But the season in the front office was in many ways more interesting than the one on the field.

On June 5 part-owner Buddy LeRoux called a news conference to announce that he and two limited partners were taking control of the Red Sox. Shortly afterward co-owner Haywood Sullivan called a news conference to say that LeRoux would do no such thing (Gammons, 1985, 254–57). That day the Sox were in first place; at season's end they were in sixth place, with their first sub-.500 finish in 17 years. The LeRoux group failed in their takeover attempt and, after a year-long battle in the courts, were forced to relinquish their shares in the club to Sullivan and Jean Yawkey.[8] In the spring of 1984, Sullivan relinquished his function as general manager to James "Lou" Gorman, who arrived fresh from rebuilding the New York Mets.

The Armas-Evans-Rice outfield combined to drive in 349 runs and power the Sox back above .500 and into fourth place in 1984. In October John McNamara, who had resigned as manager at California, was named to replace Ralph Houk, who retired.

The 1985 Red Sox remained an offensive power despite the loss of Armas to injury much of the season. Wade Boggs hit safely 240 times (the most hits by a major leaguer since 1930) in fashioning his second batting crown. But the team slipped back to fifth, with an 81–81 record.

There were many reasons for the Red Sox turnaround in 1986, but the contributions of two players—pitcher Roger Clemens and designated hitter Don Baylor—stand out. Clemens, fully recovered from two seasons of arm problems, won his first 14 decisions before suffering a loss, completing the season at 24–4, with the league's best ERA. Baylor, acquired from the Yankees just before the start of the season, hit a team-high 31 home runs and drove in 94, but more crucial to the Sox' success, provided leadership that spurred the players by the force of his personality and example (and by such devices as a "kangaroo court" in which he assessed small fines for sloppy or careless play) to a level of team effort rare for the notoriously individualistic Sox.

On April 29 Clemens struck out 20 Seattle Mariners to erase a record for a nine-inning game that had stood nearly 102 years. In one July stretch in which Boston won only three of 13 games, Clemens won three, losing none. Clemens and late-season standout Bruce Hurst together went 9–0 in September to carry Boston to an unbeatable division lead.

Boston would have been eliminated by California in the League Championship Series had the LCS not been expanded from five to seven games a year earlier. The teams split the first two games in Boston, but when the series moved to California, the Angels took the lead with a 5–3 win in Game Three, and increased it the next day with a come-from-behind 4–3 triumph in 11 innings. A day later the Red Sox found themselves one strike away from elimination. But Sox batter Dave Henderson (who had come to the club from Seattle in August) fouled off one pitch, then homered to put the Sox ahead. California evened the score in the last of the ninth, but Henderson drove in the tiebreaker in the 11th, and reliever Calvin Schiraldi (the goat of the previous day's loss) held the Angels in the last of the 11th to preserve the Sox' win. Boston handily defeated the demoralized Angels in the final two games in Boston, 10–4 and 8–1. It was as though Henderson had ripped loose The Myth and left it behind in California.

Although New York's mighty Mets were favored over Boston in the World Series, the Sox took the first two games in New York. The Mets bounced back with a pair of wins in Boston, but Bruce Hurst restored the advantage to the Sox in Game Five with his second Series win.

Back in New York for Game Six the Sox scored first, but at the end of nine the score stood tied at 3–3. Henderson put Boston ahead with a leadoff homer in the 10th inning, and the Sox scored a fifth run with a pair of hits to give them a two-run lead. In the bottom of the tenth, the first two Met batters flied out, but the next two singled. Pitcher Schiraldi got two strikes on Ray Knight, and the Sox prepared to rush onto the field to celebrate their first world championship in 68 years. But Knight singled home a fourth Met run, and Bob Stanley replaced Schiraldi on the mound. Once more the Sox came within a strike of victory. Then The Myth—out of its element in the gaudy California sunlight—returned East to reclaim its hold over the millions watching in households throughout New England. Stanley hurled a wild pitch and the tying run came home.[9] Then, in the most famous

Series bungle since Snodgrass's muff, Mookie Wilson's grounder went through the legs of first baseman Bill Buckner and the Series was even at three games apiece.

The rain that postponed Game Seven for a day made possible Bruce Hurst's return to the mound for a third time. But the Sox were no longer confident. "After Game Six," Don Baylor wrote later, "we felt outnumbered and overwhelmed" (Baylor 1989, 267).

Hurst held the Mets scoreless through five innings of the finale as Boston took a lead with three runs in the second. But when Hurst weakened in the sixth the Mets evened the score, and two innings of ineffective Sox relief gave the Mets five more runs, and the Series. The one or two columnists who attempted to discount The Myth sounded as though they were whistling in the dark.

Wade Boggs hit for power as well as average in 1987, Dwight Evans (at age 35) wielded the most potent bat of his career, and Roger Clemens, after a holdout and slow start, recovered to pitch better than anyone else in the league. But salary squabbles, injuries, and age weakened the American League champions; they never rose above .500, and finished in fifth place. Before the season was over, Buckner, Baylor, and Henderson all had been released or traded.

Several rookies up from Pawtucket—most notably outfielders Mike Greenwell and Ellis Burks—showed enough promise to give Red Sox fans new hope for 1988, and the club's December acquisition from the Chicago Cubs of star reliever Lee Smith, which strengthened the team at its weakest point, elevated that hope. But it was not until the club replaced manager McNamara with coach Joe Morgan at midseason that the Sox began to stir. Morgan inserted rookie Jody Reed at shortstop as a regular, and piloted the club to 19 wins in his first 20 games to move the Sox into a tie for first place. A month later the Sox moved into first to stay. Although "Morgan's miracle" faded as the Sox lost seven of their final eight games, the team had built enough of a lead early in September to secure the division crown by one game. For the fifth year in a row the Sox drew more fans to Fenway than the year before—nearly 2.5 million, which broke the club record set nine years earlier.

Oakland's favored Athletics swept Boston in the League Championship Series, although the first two games, in Boston, were closely contested. Hurst pitched well, and Boston tied Oakland in the seventh inning of Game One before losing 2–1; Clemens held the A's scoreless for six innings the next day before weakening. In Oakland for Game Three, the Sox even took an early 5–0 lead before being battered 10–6. Only in the fourth game, a 4–1 loss, did Boston never lead or tie.

At the dawn of the 1990s it truly looked like New England's favorite team might be back in business for another serious run at that always-elusive world championship banner. Over the course of the 1990 season Joe Morgan's men were able to survive a tight pennant chase with the talented Toronto Blue Jays before once again stumbling at the hands of Tony LaRussa's powerhouse Oakland team in an abbreviated four-game ALCS showdown. By the third season of the new decade, however, things seemed to come apart faster in Beantown than an unravelling ball of yarn. Boggs appeared to have lost his magic hitting wand almost overnight, slumping to an unheard of .259 mark, eighty-plus points below his career standard. Clemens did win a third-straight ERA title in 1992, but a late season slide prevented another 20-win campaign and possible fourth Cy Young trophy. The result was an altogether embarrassing basement finish. Once again rebuilding was the order of the day in Boston, a city where pennants were scarce and a fatalistic optimism was always the baseball hallmark.

Notes

1. New York as well as Boston fans were disappointed not to see the champions face off, and before another season had ended the World Series was established officially and permanently.

2. My comments on player rankings and my evaluation of players' seasons are based in large part on the new statistics found in John Thorn and Peter Palmer, eds., *Total Baseball* (New York: Warner Books, 1989). For traditional statistics I have used as my ultimate authority Joseph L. Reichler, ed., *The Baseball Encyclopedia*, Seventh Edition (New York: Macmillan, 1988); this is also my source for most player trade information. For attendance figures I have used the *Boston Red Sox Media Guide 1989*, p. 111, and (for the Braves) the *Official Baseball Dope Book*, 1984 Edition (St. Louis: The Sporting News, 1984), pp. 56–57. In tracing the major league pennant races since 1901, nothing beats John Warner Davenport, *Baseball's Pennant Races: A Graphic View* (Madison, Wis.: First Impressions, 1981).

3. Ruth's record stood until 1961, when Whitey Ford pushed it to 32 innings; Ford added a 33rd inning to his record the following year.

4. The playoffs of the Red Sox' 1948 and 1978 ties are considered part of the regular season for statistical purposes. Boston's playoff losses thus left them in these years a full game behind the pennant winner.

5. Of the regular pitchers, only Rogelio Moret (in his first full major league season) finished with an ERA better than the league average.

6. See Peter Gammons, *Beyond the Sixth Game* (1985), pp. 193–97, for details of the infighting during the change of ownership.

7. Gammons, pp. 198–207, provides a detailed examination of Boston's dealings with Fisk, Lynn, and Rick Burleson in the winter of 1980–81.

8. Jean Yawkey (as majority owner of the JRY Corporation, a general partner) and Sullivan (the other general partner) now control the Red Sox. Yawkey, club president since August 1976, retains that title; Sullivan is CEO/COO. In the resolution of differences, Yawkey has two votes to Sullivan's one.

9. Or catcher Gedman let by a passed ball, as many feel the play should have been scored. Disputes over the official scoring of the play not only occupied fans and writers, but even caused rifts between Red Sox players.

References

Angell, Roger. 1988. "The Sporting Scene: Celebration." *The New Yorker* 64 (22 August): 59.

Barrow, Edward Grant, with James M. Kahn. 1951. *My Fifty Years in Baseball.* New York: Coward-McCann.

Baylor, Don, with Claire Smith. 1989. *Don Baylor—Nothing But the Truth: A Baseball Life.* New York: St. Martin's.

Davenport, John Warner. 1981. *Baseball's Pennant Races: A Graphic View.* Madison, Wis.: First Impressions.

Gammons, Peter. 1985. *Beyond the Sixth Game.* Boston: Houghton Mifflin.

Halberstam, David. 1989. *Summer of '49.* New York: Morrow.

Hirshberg, Al. 1973. *What's the Matter with the Red Sox?* New York: Dodd, Mead.

Lieb, Frederick G. 1947. *The Boston Red Sox.* New York: Putnam's.

Ruth, Babe, as told to Bob Considine. 1948. *The Babe Ruth Story.* New York: Dutton.

Tygiel, Jules. 1983. *Baseball's Great Experiment: Jackie Robinson and His Legacy.* New York: Oxford Univ. Press.

Vermeule, Emily. 1987. "It's Not a Myth—They're Immortal." In *The Red Sox Reader,* edited by Dan Riley. Thousand Oaks, Calif.: Ventura Arts.

Williams, Ted, with John Underwood. 1969. *My Turn at Bat: The Story of My Life.* New York: Simon and Schuster.

Annotated Bibliography

Barrow, Edward Grant, with James M. Kahn. *My Fifty Years in Baseball.* New York: Coward-McCann, 1951.

As Red Sox manager in 1918–1920, Barrow led the club to a world championship, converted Babe Ruth from pitcher to outfielder, and saw owner Harry Frazee begin to sell off the Sox' best players to the Yankees before he himself left Boston to join the Yankee front office.

Boston Red Sox: The Complete Record of Red Sox Baseball. New York: Macmillan, 1984.

Here are complete stats from the Macmillan *Baseball Encyclopedia* computer bank, plus year-by-year historical summaries by Henry and Harold Berry, a section of photos, Pete Palmer's statistical study of Fenway Park's effect on hitters and pitchers, and John Warner Davenport's priceless charts and graphs of Sox performance through each season.

Clark, Ellery H., Jr. *Boston Red Sox: 75th Anniversary History 1901–1975.* Hicksville, N.Y.: Exposition Press, 1975.

———. *Red Sox Forever.* Hicksville, N.Y.: Exposition Press, 1977.

———. *Red Sox Fever.* Hicksville, N.Y.: Exposition Press, 1979.

This trilogy, a quirky tribute to the Sox by one of its oldest and most knowledgeable fans, features such things as vintage photos and cartoons, and excerpts of letters to Clark from Red Sox players from Jesse Tannehill to Rick Burleson.

Clemens, Roger, with Peter Gammons. *Rocket Man: The Roger Clemens Story.* Lexington, Mass.: Stephen Greene, 1987.

One hundred pages of this 161-page autobiography are devoted to a detailed look at the Red Sox' pennant winning 1986 season from the perspective of its ace hurler.

Coleman, Ken, and Dan Valenti. *The Impossible Dream Remembered: The 1967 Red Sox.* Lexington, Mass.: Stephen Greene, 1987.

This day-by-day chronicle of the Sox' 1967 pennant season by a broadcaster who covered every game also includes player interviews, commen-
tary, anecdotes, photos, and stats. This is one of the very best baseball
books of its kind: informative, entertaining, nicely organized, and well
written.

Conigliaro, Tony, with Jack Zanger. *Seeing It Through*. New York: Macmillan,
1970.

Conigliaro's vivid account of his recovery and comeback from a near-fatal
beaning during the 1967 season was written just before what turned out
to be in some ways the best year of his playing career.

Cunningham, Bill. "The Boston Red Sox." In *The American League*, edited by
Ed Fitzgerald, 122–63. New York: Grosset & Dunlap, rev. ed., 1966.

A short history of the Red Sox through 1965, this is one in a collection of
team histories published originally in *Sport* magazine.

Frommer, Harvey. *Baseball's Greatest Rivalry: The New York Yankees and Boston
Red Sox*. Rev. ed. New York: Atheneum, 1984.

This lively review of highlights in a long and deeply felt rivalry concludes
with a 34-page section of player and team statistics.

Gammons, Peter. *Beyond the Sixth Game*. Boston: Houghton Mifflin, 1985.

Gammons, a close follower of Red Sox baseball, traces the effects on
baseball of the 1975 Messersmith-McNally free-agency decision through
its effect on the Red Sox. This is a trenchant (though sometimes repetitive)
study of nine years (1976–1985) in the life of the Red Sox, and of baseball
itself.

Halberstam, David. *Summer of '49*. New York: Morrow, 1989.

This absorbing look at the 1949 Red Sox-Yankees pennant race includes
memorable portraits of Red Sox players and Boston columnist Dave Egan.
But except for full accounts of the season's final two games, the book is
skimpy on details of the race itself.

Hirshberg, Al. *What's the Matter with the Red Sox?* New York: Dodd, Mead,
1973.

Hirshberg, writing near the end of Tom Yawkey's life, examines Yawkey's
four decades of Red Sox ownership in an attempt to answer the question
why Yawkey, with all his money and desire, had been unable to build a
world championship team. Among the topics explored in his thought-
provoking study are Yawkey's sometimes questionable choice of subordinates, and the club's foot-dragging in the matter of racial integration.

Honig, Donald. *The Boston Red Sox: An Illustrated Tribute*. New York: St. Martin's, 1984.

Black and white photos—mostly portraits and posed action shots—with
brief historical text picture the Sox from the club's beginnings through
Yaz's retirement in 1983. Bland, but nice.

Hough, John, Jr. *A Player for a Moment: Notes from Fenway Park*. San Diego:
Harcourt Brace Jovanovich, 1988.

Novelist Hough blends personal reminiscence as a lifelong Red Sox fan
with close—and sometimes insightful—observation of the 1987 Sox and
their disappointing season.

Lieb, Frederick G. *The Boston Red Sox*. New York: Putnam's, 1947.

One of the best volumes in the classic Putnam's series, Lieb's work is still
the definitive history of the Red Sox' first 45 years.

Liss, Howard. *The Boston Red Sox*. New York: Simon and Schuster, 1982.

This brisk romp (158 pages) is not "the complete history" the dust jacket
claims it to be, but it is a useful and competent survey—even though Liss

confuses the reader by implying that Red Sox history begins with the Boston Red Stockings of 1871.

McSweeney, Bill. *The Impossible Dream: The Story of the Miracle Boston Red Sox.* New York: Coward-McCann, 1968.

After a brief survey of early Sox history, McSweeney offers chapters on Tom Yawkey, Joe Cronin, Ted Williams, and a long chapter on the Sox' two-decade decline after 1946. The second half of the book is a breezy narrative account of the Sox' 1967 pennant year.

Mercurio, John A. *Chronology of Red Sox Records.* New York: Perennial-Harper & Row, 1989.

More than 200 different Red Sox players and managers have held the team record in one category or another; they and their records are all here in this handy compilation.

Piersall, Jim, and Al Hirshberg. *Fear Strikes Out: The Jim Piersall Story.* Boston: Atlantic-Little, Brown, 1955.

Piersall's story of recovery from his mental illness that disrupted the 1952 Red Sox was made into a movie. The book and film did much to convince the public that mental illness is treatable, and not a cause for shame, not something that should be hidden and denied.

Red Sox Reader, The. Edited by Dan Riley. Thousand Oaks, Calif.: Ventura Arts, 1987.

This anthology of writing about the Red Sox includes several classics, like John Updike's "Hub Fans Bid Kid Adieu" and Thomas Boswell's "The Greatest Game Ever Played" (the 1978 Sox-Yankee tiebreaker playoff game).

Shaughnessy, Dan. *One Strike Away: The Story of the 1986 Red Sox.* New York: Peter Weed-Beaufort, 1987.

Shaughnessy, who followed the Sox' pennant-winning season of 1986 for the Boston *Globe*, provides a thorough and entertaining account of the year that culminated in the nearest miss of all.

Walton, Edward H. *This Date in Boston Red Sox History.* New York: Scarborough-Stein and Day, 1978.

A 285-page compendium of Red Sox facts and figures, from the birth date of Frank Fuller (who played for the Sox in 1923) to box scores of all Sox World Series games.

———. *Red Sox Triumphs and Tragedies.* New York: Scarborough-Stein and Day, 1980.

This sequal to Walton's earlier book is nearly 100 pages longer, and supplements its facts and figures with a number of anecdotes and essays.

Williams, Ted, with John Underwood. *My Turn at Bat: The Story of My Life.* New York: Simon and Schuster, 1969.

This frank and thoughtful autobiography of the Red Sox' greatest hitter has come to be recognized as a baseball classic. The fact that it was not written until several years after Williams's retirement as a player gave Williams time for reflection, time to develop a perspective on his life and career that quickie autobiographies almost always lack.

Yastrzemski, Carl, with Al Hirshberg. *Yaz.* New York: Viking, 1968.

In 1967 Yaz fashioned what turned out to be the greatest season of his career. Al Hirshberg was there to help him capture it in print before the memories could grow cold.

Year-by-Year Standings and Season Summaries

Year	Pos.	Record	Pct.	GB	Manager	Player	BA	Player	HR	Player	W-L	ERA
1901	2nd	79–57	.581	4.0	J.J. Collins	Freeman	.345	Freeman	12	Young	33–10	1.62
1902	3rd	77–60	.562	6.5	J.J. Collins	Dougherty	.342	Freeman	11	Young	32–11	2.15
1903	1st	91–47	.659	+14.5	J.J. Collins	Dougherty	.331	Freeman	13	Young	28–9	2.08
1904	1st	95–59	.617	+1.5	J.J. Collins	C. Stahl	.295	Freeman	7	Young	26–16	1.97
1905	4th	78–74	.513	16	J.J. Collins	J.J. Collins	.276	Ferris	6	Young	18–19	1.82
1906	8th	49–105	.318	45.5	J.J. Collins C. Stahl	Grimshaw	.290	C. Stahl	4	Tannehill	13–11	3.16
1907	7th	59–90	.396	32.5	Huff Unglaub Young McGuire	Congalton	.286	Ferris	4	Young	21–15	1.99
1908	5th	75–79	.487	15.5	McGuire Lake	Gessler	.308	Gessler	3	Young	21–11	1.26
1909	3rd	88–63	.583	9.5	Lake	Lord	.311	Speaker	7	Arellanes	16–12	2.18
										Cicotte	13–5	1.97
1910	4th	81–72	.529	22.5	Donovan	Speaker	.340	G. Stahl	10	R. Collins	13–11	1.62
1911	5th	78–75	.510	24	Donovan	Speaker	.327	Speaker	8	Wood	23–17	2.02
1912	1st	105–47	.691	+14	G. Stahl	Speaker	.383	Speaker	10	Wood	34–5	1.91
1913	4th	79–71	.527	15.5	G. Stahl Carrigan	Speaker	.363	Hooper	4	Leonard	14–16	2.39
1914	2nd	91–62	.595	8.5	Carrigan	Speaker	.338	Speaker	4	Leonard	19–5	1.01
1915	1st	101–50	.669	+2.5	Carrigan	Speaker	.322	Ruth	4	Shore	19–8	1.64
1916	1st	91–63	.591	+2	Carrigan	Gardner	.308	Gainer	3	Ruth	23–12	1.75
								Ruth	3			
								Walker	3			
1917	2nd	90–62	.592	9	Barry	Lewis	.302	Hooper	3	Mays	22–9	1.74

Year	Pos.	Record	Pct.	GB	Manager	Player	BA	Player	HR	Player	W-L	ERA
1918	1st	75–51	.595	+2.5	Barrow	Hooper	.289	Ruth	11	Mays	21–13	2.21
1919	6th	66–71	.482	20.5	Barrow	Ruth	.322	Ruth	29	Pennock	16–8	2.71
1920	5th	72–81	.471	25.5	Barrow	Hooper	.312	Hooper	7	Pennock	16–13	3.68
1921	5th	75–79	.487	23.5	Duffy	Pratt	.324	Pratt	5	Jones	23–16	3.22
1922	8th	61–93	.396	33	Duffy	Harris	.316	Burns	12	Quinn	13–15	3.48
1923	8th	61–91	.401	37	Chance	Harris	.335	Harris	13	Ehmke	20–17	3.78
1924	7th	67–87	.435	25	Fohl	Boone	.333	Boone	13	Ehmke	19–17	3.46
1925	8th	47–105	.309	49.5	Fohl	Boone	.330	Todt	11	Ehmke	9–20	3.73
1926	8th	46–107	.301	44.5	Fohl	Flagstead	.299	Todt	7	Wiltse	8–15	4.22
1927	8th	51–103	.331	59	Carrigan	Myer	.288	Todt	6	Harriss	14–21	4.18
1928	8th	57–96	.373	43.5	Carrigan	Myer	.313	Todt	12	Morris	19–15	3.53
1929	8th	58–96	.377	48	Carrigan	Rothrock	.300	Rothrock	6	Gaston	12–19	3.73
										MacFayden	10–18	3.62
1930	8th	52–102	.338	50	Wagner	Webb	.323	Webb	16	Gaston	13–20	3.92
1931	6th	62–90	.408	45	J.F. Collins	Webb	.333	Webb	14	Moore	11–13	3.88
1932	8th	43–111	.279	64	J.F. Collins McManus	Alexander	.372	Jolley	18	Durham	6–13	3.80
1933	7th	63–86	.423	34.5	McManus	R.C. Johnson	.313	R.C. Johnson	10	Rhodes	12–15	4.03
1934	4th	76–76	.500	24	Harris	Werber	.321	Werber	11	Ostermueller	10–13	3.49
1935	4th	78–75	.510	16	Cronin	R.C. Johnson	.315	Werber	14	Grove	20–12	2.70
1936	6th	74–80	.481	28.5	Cronin	Foxx	.338	Foxx	41	Grove	17–12	2.81
1937	5th	80–72	.526	21	Cronin	Cronin	.307	Foxx	36	Grove	17–9	3.02
1938	2nd	88–61	.591	9.5	Cronin	Foxx	.349	Foxx	50	Grove	14–4	3.08
1939	2nd	89–62	.589	17	Cronin	Foxx	.360	Foxx	35	Grove	15–4	2.54
1940	T4th	82–72	.532	8	Cronin	T. Williams	.344	Foxx	36	Grove	7–6	3.99
										Heving	12–7	4.01
1941	2nd	84–70	.545	17	Cronin	T. Williams	.406	T. Williams	37	Wagner	12–8	3.07
1942	2nd	93–59	.612	9	Cronin	T. Williams	.356	T. Williams	36	Hughson	22–6	2.59

Year	Pos.	Record	Pct.	GB	Manager	Player	BA	Player	HR	Player	W-L	ERA
1943	7th	68–84	.447	29	Cronin	Fox	.288	Doerr	16	Hughson	12–15	2.64
1944	4th	77–77	.500	12	Cronin	Doerr	.325	R.L. Johnson	17	Hughson	18–5	2.26
1945	7th	71–83	.461	17.5	Cronin	Newsome	.290	R.L. Johnson	12	Ferriss	21–10	2.96
1946	1st	104–50	.675	+12	Cronin	T. Williams	.342	T. Williams	38	Hughson	20–11	2.75
1947	3rd	83–71	.539	14	Cronin	T. Williams	.343	T. Williams	32	Dobson	18–8	2.95
1948	2nd	96–59	.619	1	McCarthy	T. Williams	.369	Stephens	29	Parnell	15–8	3.14
1949	2nd	96–58	.623	1	McCarthy	T. Williams	.343	T. Williams	43	Parnell	25–7	2.77
1950	3rd	94–60	.610	4	McCarthy O'Neill	Goodman	.354	Dropo	34	Parnell	18–10	3.61
1951	3rd	87–67	.565	11	O'Neill	T. Williams	.318	T. Williams	30	Parnell	18–11	3.26
1952	6th	76–78	.494	19	Boudreau	Goodman	.306	Gernert	19	Kinder	5–6	2.58
1953	4th	84–69	.549	16	Boudreau	Goodman	.313	Gernert	21	Kinder	10–6	1.85
										McDermott	18–10	3.01
										Parnell	21–8	3.06
1954	4th	69–85	.448	42	Boudreau	T. Williams	.345	T. Williams	29	Sullivan	15–12	3.14
1955	4th	84–70	.545	12	Higgins	Goodman	.294	T. Williams	28	Sullivan	18–13	2.91
1956	4th	84–70	.545	13	Higgins	T. Williams	.345	T. Williams	24	Brewer	19–9	3.50
										Sullivan	14–7	3.42
1957	3rd	82–72	.532	16	Higgins	T. Williams	.388	T. Williams	38	Sullivan	14–11	2.73
1958	3rd	79–75	.513	13	Higgins	T. Williams	.328	Jensen	35	Delock	14–8	3.38
1959	5th	75–79	.487	19	Higgins York Jurges	Runnels	.314	Jensen	28	Delock	11–6	2.95
1960	7th	65–89	.422	32	Jurges Higgins	Runnels	.320	T. Williams	29	Fornieles	10–5	2.64
1961	6th	76–86	.469	33	Higgins	Malzone	.266	Geiger	18	Monbouquette	14–14	3.39
										Schwall	15–7	3.22
1962	8th	76–84	.475	19	Higgins	Runnels	.326	Malzone	21	Radatz	9–6	2.24

Year	Pos.	Record	Pct.	GB	Manager	Player	BA	Player	HR	Player	W-L	ERA
1963	7th	76–85	.472	28	Pesky	Yastrzemski	.321	Stuart	42	Radatz	15–6	1.97
1964	8th	72–90	.444	27	Pesky	Bressoud	.293	Stuart	33	Radatz	16–9	2.29
					Herman							
1965	9th	62–100	.383	40	Herman	Yastrzemski	.312	A. Conigliaro	32	Monbouquette	10–18	3.70
1966	9th	72–90	.444	26	Herman	Yastrzemski	.278	A. Conigliaro	28	McMahon	8–7	2.65
					Runnels							
1967	1st	92–70	.568	+1	R. Williams	Yastrzemski	.326	Yastrzemski	44	Lonborg	22–9	3.16
										Stange	8–10	2.77
1968	4th	86–76	.531	17	R. Williams	Yastrzemski	.301	K. Harrelson	35	Santiago	9–4	2.25
American League East												
1969	3rd	87–75	.537	22	R. Williams	R. Smith	.309	Petrocelli	40	Lyle	8–3	2.54
					Popowski			Yastrzemski	40	Nagy	12–2	3.11
1970	3rd	87–75	.537	21	Kasko	Yastrzemski	.329	Yastrzemski	40	Culp	17–14	3.05
1971	3rd	85–77	.525	18	Kasko	R. Smith	.283	R. Smith	30	Siebert	16–10	2.91
1972	2nd	85–70	.548	0.5	Kasko	Fisk	.293	Fisk	22	Tiant	15–6	1.91
1973	2nd	89–73	.549	8	Kasko	R. Smith	.303	Fisk	26	Lee	17–11	2.75
1974	3rd	84–78	.519	7	D. Johnson	Yastrzemski	.301	Petrocelli	15	Tiant	22–13	2.92
								Yastrzemski	15			
1975	1st	95–65	.594	+4.5	D. Johnson	Lynn	.331	Rice	22	Moret	14–3	3.60
1976	3rd	83–79	.512	15.5	D. Johnson	Lynn	.314	Rice	25	Tiant	21–12	3.06
					Zimmer							
1977	T2nd	97–64	.602	2.5	Zimmer	Rice	.320	Rice	39	Campbell	13–9	2.96
1978	2nd	99–64	.607	1	Zimmer	Rice	.315	Rice	46	Eckersley	20–8	2.99
1979	3rd	91–69	.569	11.5	Zimmer	Lynn	.333	Lynn	39	Eckersley	17–10	2.99
								Rice	39			
1980	4th	83–77	.519	19	Zimmer	Stapleton	.321	Perez	25	Burgmeier	5–4	2.00
					Pesky							

Year	Pos.	Record	Pct.	GB	Manager	Player	BA	Player	HR	Player	W-L	ERA
1981	5th	30–26	.536	4	Houk	Lansford	.336	Evans	22	Burgmeier	4–5	2.85
	T2nd	29–23	.558	1.5								
1981*	5th	59–49	.546	2.5								
1982	3rd	89–73	.549	6	Houk	Rice	.309	Evans	32	Burgmeier	7–0	2.29
										Stanley	12–7	3.10
1983	6th	78–84	.481	20	Houk	Boggs	.361	Rice	29	Stanley	8–10	2.85
1984	4th	86–76	.531	18	Houk	Boggs	.325	Armas	43	Hurst	12–12	3.92
										Nipper	11–6	3.89
										Ojeda	12–12	3.99
										Stanley	9–10	3.54
1985	5th	81–81	.500	18.5	McNamara	Boggs	.368	Evans	29	Boyd	15–13	3.70
1986	1st	95–66	.590	+5.5	McNamara	Boggs	.357	Baylor	31	Clemens	24–4	2.48
1987	5th	78–84	.481	20	McNamara	Boggs	.363	Evans	34	Clemens	20–9	2.97
1988	1st	89–73	.549	+1	McNamara/Morgan	Boggs	.366	Greenwell	22	Clemens	18–12	2.93
1989	3rd	83–79	.512	6	Morgan	Boggs	.330	Esasky	30	Clemens	17–11	3.13
1990	1st	88–74	.543	+2	Morgan	Boggs	.302	Burks	21	Clemens	21–6	1.93
1991	2nd(T)	84–78	.519	7	Morgan	Boggs	.332	Clark	28	Clemens	18–8	2.62
1992	7th	73–89	.451	23	Hobson	Brunansky	.266	Brunansky	15	Clemens	18–11	2.41

*Split Season Totals (Players' Union Strike).

All-Time Red Sox Career and Season Records

Career Batting Leaders (1901–1992)

Games Played	Carl Yastrzemski	3,308
At Bats	Carl Yastrzemski	11,988
Runs Scored	Carl Yastrzemski	1,816
Hits	Carl Yastrzemski	3,419
Batting Average	Wade Boggs	.338
Home Runs	Ted Williams	521
Runs Batted In	Carl Yastrzemski	1,844
Stolen Bases	Harry Hooper	300
Strikeouts	Carl Yastrzemski	1,393

Career Pitching Leaders (1901–1992)

Innings Pitched	Cy Young	2,728.1
Earned Run Average	Joe Wood	1.99
Wins	Cy Young	193
Losses	Cy Young	112
Winning Percentage	Dave Ferriss	.684
Strikeouts	Roger Clemens	1,873
Walks	Mel Parnell	758
Games	Bob Stanley	637
Shutouts	Cy Young	38
Saves	Bob Stanley	132
Games Started	Cy Young	297
Complete Games	Cy Young	275

Single-Season Batting Records (1901–1992)

Batting Average	Ted Williams	.406	1941
Home Runs	Jimmie Foxx	50	1938
Home Runs (lefthanded)	Carl Yastrzemski	44	1967
Runs Batted In	Jimmie Foxx	175	1938
Runs Scored	Ted Williams	150	1949
Hits	Wade Boggs	240	1985
Singles	Wade Boggs	187	1985
Doubles	Earl Webb	67	1931
Triples	Chick Stahl	22	1904
	Tris Speaker	22	1913
Slugging Percentage	Ted Williams	.735	1941
Extra Base Hits	Jimmie Foxx	92	1938
Game-Winning RBIs	Mike Greenwell	23	1988
Sacrifices	Jack Barry	54	1917
Stolen Bases	Tommy Harper	54	1973
Pinch Hits	Joe Cronin	18	1943
Strikeouts	Butch Hobson	162	1977
Total Bases	Jim Rice	406	1978
Hitting Streak	Dom DiMaggio	34	1949
Grand Slam Home Runs	Babe Ruth	4	1919
On-Base Percentage	Ted Williams	.551	1941
Hit by Pitch	Don Baylor	35	1986

All-Time Red Sox Career and Season Records *(continued)*

Single-Season Pitching Records (1901–1992)

ERA (150+ innings)	Dutch Leonard	1.01	1914
ERA (100–149 innings)	Elmer Steele	1.83	1908
Wins	Joe Wood	34	1912
Losses	Red Ruffing	25	1928
Winning Pct. (10 decisions)	Elmer Myers	.900	1920
Strikeouts	Roger Clemens	291	1988
Walks	Mel Parnell	134	1949
Saves	Jeff Reardon	40	1991
Games	Dick Radatz	79	1964
Complete Games	Cy Young	41	1902
Games Started	Cy Young	43	1902
Shutouts	Cy Young	10	1904
	Joe Wood	10	1912
Innings Pitched	Cy Young	384.2	1902
Home Runs Allowed	Earl Wilson	37	1964
Consecutive Games Won (season)	Joe Wood	16	1912
Consecutive Games Lost (season)	Joe Harris	14	1906
Wild Pitches	Earl Wilson	21	1963

2

Chicago White Sox
Second Class in the Second City

RICHARD C. LINDBERG

When the city fathers of St. Petersburg, Florida, threatened to steal that cherished south side civic institution, the White Sox, columnist Mike Royko of the *Chicago Tribune* raised the hue and cry. Send them your socks, he said, your dirty, tired, torn socks. Within a week thousands of pairs of tattered hosiery arrived in the sunshine state—the windy city's flippant response to Florida's relentless crusade to land a permanent tenant for its Suncoast Dome.

Was this the best Chicago could do to stave off the exodus of this proud old franchise, its nineteenth-century roots preserved in the fabric of the Irish Bridgeport neighborhood?

Springtime 1988. Even the most optimistic Sox fan—and it takes a certain amount of fortitude to love this team, as we shall soon see—was ready to pronounce the last rights. Bill Veeck was dead. Charles Comiskey was a name from the dim and distant past. The fans were strangely silent and the press apathetic, as usual, to the White Sox plight. Meanwhile St. Petersburg offered the Sox owners lucrative financial inducements to move the team to Florida in a spacious new ballpark with a probable first-year attendance of two million, numbers not seen on the south side since 1984.

Comiskey Park was crumbling. Baseball's oldest stadium had long since outlived its usefulness according to structural engineers. The sightlines were poor, and the number of decent box seats were at a premium. Before the entire park came crashing down around them, Jerry Reinsdorf and Eddie Einhorn—the embattled owners who were under continuous heat from the fans—announced their intention to build a new stadium in the western suburbs of Chicago with the assistance of the state of Illinois. That was in July of 1986, the opening shot of a three-year melodrama that nearly culminated in the team's defection. The announcement was greeted with the usual skepticism. If Comiskey Park was so bad, why not just fix it up, grumbled long-time sportswriter Bill Gleason who likened the stadium to a rusty old battleship that could be repaired in dry-dock. Of course no one really knew where the team would play during a two-year renovation, or the dynamics of a temporary move. These owners were two guys from New York trying to hustle the good people of Chicago. That was the prevailing wisdom of most Sox fans longing for the days of "sport shirt" Bill Veeck. Forgotten during this latest Chisox imbroglio was the fact that Veeck himself seriously considered moving the team to Denver in 1980.

On November 4, 1986 the residents of Addison, Illinois, voted down an advisory referendum which would have paved the way for the White Sox suburban move. Residents of this white bedroom suburb wanted no part of the Sox, the traffic congestion, and—though no-one was willing to say it at the time—the fear of integration. Then in a surprise move the Illinois General Assembly passed funding legislation for a new stadium on December 5—directly across the street from old Comiskey Park. Mayor Harold Washington applauded the move. The Sox are Chicago's south side team, and here they shall remain, he said. The irretrievable link to the Comiskey past would be maintained, and a legacy that began in a Chicago hotel room on a cool autumn day in 1899 would be preserved. Sox fans breathed a premature sight of relief.

Playing the Game by Their Rules (1900–1903)

The team that was to become the White Sox arrived in Chicago via Sioux City, Iowa. The franchise was christened on November 20, 1893, when the Western League was incorporated at the Grand Hotel in Indianapolis. The fortunes of baseball were at a low ebb. The National League was weak and corrupt, and the Brotherhood War of 1890–91 seriously undermined the credibility of the owners—men who lacked vision and perception. There was plenty of room for growth and expansion on the minor league level.

Charles Comiskey was managing the Cincinnati Redlegs at the time. The 34-year-old journeyman was resting on past laurels. His St. Louis Browns were an American Association phenomenon in the 1880s, but the league withered and died on the vine in 1891. Comiskey was the son of a prominent Irish political boss who served his west side constituents faithfully for nearly 20 years. Son Charles was born on Lytle Street between 12th and Taylor in a teeming Irish ghetto, August 15, 1859. As a young man he played semi-pro baseball against the wishes of his father who believed that he could make more money apprenticed to a plumber. Comiskey had other ideas.[1]

Against his father's wishes Comiskey began his professional career in 1879, playing for the Dubuque Rabbits of the Northwestern League. In 1882 he joined Chris von der Ahe's Browns as a pitcher-first-baseman. The flamboyant St. Louis owner popularized Sunday base-ball and undercut his competitors with 25-cent admissions. In 1885, with Comiskey at the helm, the Browns played the powerful Chicago White Stockings to a draw in the forerunner of the modern World Series. A year later he knocked off Anson's boys four games to two.

Charles Comiskey remained with the Browns until 1890 when he bolted the league in order to head up the Chicago entry of the Player's Association. The so-called Brotherhood was the first "revolt" against the existing salary structure and trade restrictions imposed by organized baseball. The Chicago Pirates played in a makeshift wooden park directly east of the future Comiskey Park. The team played respectably and finished fourth, but the league itself was a financial loser. When it was disbanded, Charles Comiskey returned to the Browns for one year before signing on with the Reds. Unhappy in his new surroundings, the "Old Roman," as he was later known to his intimates, struck up a friendship with Ban Johnson, a sportswriter for the Cincinnati *Commercial Gazette*. The dynamic future president of the American League abandoned his law studies to become a police reporter in 1886. When they advanced him to the sports desk several years later, Johnson believed he had settled into a lifetime career.[2]

In the fall of 1893 Comiskey whispered to Johnson that there were rumblings afoot to revive the old Northwestern League. At first Johnson was reticent, but he attended the Indianapolis meeting as a disinterested observer who might give the story a needed plug in his newspaper. The dour-looking Johnson emerged from the meeting as president, secretary, and treasurer of the new eight-team circuit which included Milwaukee, Kansas City, Minneapolis, Toledo, Detroit, Sioux City, Grand Rapids, and Indianapolis. Each owner posted a $1,000 bond to prevent desertion and a schedule was drawn up for the 1894 season.[3]

Under the direction of W.H. Watkins, the Sioux City entry won the pennant in its maiden season, but attendance was dismal. At its second annual meeting in Chicago, the decision was made to transfer the ailing franchise to St. Paul where it might profit from a spirited civic rivalry with the Minneapolis club across the river. The first year had been a struggle and Johnson considered resigning his post in order to return to the newspaper business—unless his old friend Comiskey came on board in an executive capacity.[4] The Old Roman's contract with the Reds had expired, but owner John Brush, sensing that his manager was giving serious consideration to Johnson's proposal, attempted to block his path. Brush hated Ban Johnson for his many published attacks against the Redlegs. To lose Comiskey to this upstart league would be the greatest indignity.

A contract extension was proposed, but Charles Comiskey decided to cast his lot in St. Paul with the Western League. In 1895 the "Saints," or "Apostles," as they were called, finished second. The team remained competitive for the next four years, but was unable to sustain a contin-ued profit.

In 1899 Johnson addressed this situation by pressing the National League for permission to relocate the Saints to Chicago under the aegis of Comiskey. The city was a large enough market to support two teams, Johnson argued. With the exception of James T. Hart, owner of the National League White Stockings (Cubs), the magnates were agreeable to the plan with certain conditions. The Nationals feared that another group headed by Adolph Busch and Cap Anson were going to attempt to re-form the long dormant American Association. They were willing to grant concessions to this rather inconsequential minor league.

That is, everyone except Hart who correctly maintained that his base of support would erode. To assuage his fears and concerns Com-iskey and Johnson were forced to abide by several restrictions. The Chicago team could not build a park north of 35th Street, and Hart was permitted to draft two players off of Comiskey's team each year, subject to the terms of the National Agreement. On March 21, 1900, the agreement was signed and the nameless aggregate was permitted to move to Chicago in the new American League. At the suggestion of W.F. Golt of Indianapolis the name of the league was changed. This was all well and good for Johnson and the other team owners, but Comiskey needed a readily identifiable name. Under the terms of the 1900 agreement the Old Roman was not permitted to use the name Chicago in his business dealings. So he borrowed the nickname "White Stockings" from Hart's team. Since 1898, the year that Cap Anson was fired, the moniker had lost favor among National League fans. The White Stockings they became, until a headline writer allegedly short-ened the name for the sake of brevity.

With a borrowed name, no place to play, and second-class status in the Windy City, the leaky ship of state was finally launched. The scheduled opener against Milwaukee was less than a month away but Comiskey had no clue as to where his team was going to play. The old Brotherhood League park had stood on the boundary line established by James Hart. But after the league collapsed in financial ruin, the small wooden grandstand was torn down.

After careful consideration Charles Comiskey decided on a vacant lot four blocks south of the Brotherhood grounds at 39th and Went-worth. At the time of the 1893 Worlds Fair a cricket team known as the Chicago Wanderers played on the site, but had abandoned it in 1897. Small boys played rounders and kick-the-can amidst the weeds and garbage, as Comiskey stared unhappily at his new property. It took several thousand dollars of capital the Old Roman did not have to renovate the site in time for opening day. At length, he persuaded the First National Bank of Chicago to advance him a sum of money to build a grandstand. For nearly a month construction men labored furiously around the clock to build wooden seating. The work continued right up to game time, April 21, when American League baseball came to Chicago after a long winter of discontent and uncertainty.

The team that took the field (and lost 5–4) with the Milwaukee Brewers in that 1900 inaugural was a veteran club. All except Roy Patterson, the "St. Croix Boy Wonder," had seen major league action at one time or another. Frank Isbell, "Dummy" Hoy, and Dick Padden were Comiskey's offensive stars, if offense is the applicable word here. The 1900 White Sox finished last in hitting but won the pennant by a comfortable five-game margin.

In honor of their achievement a sporting goods firm presented the Old Roman and "slugger" Dick Padden (.284, one home run) with a five-foot bat, three days after the September 12 clincher. It was the city's first baseball championship since 1886, and Comiskey's last as a field manager.

His team of misfits were magic that year. In the counting house the results were equally encouraging. Comiskey had brought an exciting brand of baseball to the south side at popular prices. He undercut the Cubs by charging 25-cent admissions—half of what National League patrons paid to watch a fifth place ballclub.

When the season ended Johnson and Comiskey pressed ahead with an ambitious plan to expand to Philadelphia, Baltimore, and Washington. At the league meetings Johnson sought concessions from the National League. He purposely neglected to renew the National Agreement, with the hope that it might serve as leverage in getting John Brush and his cohorts to sanction a move into new markets. The National League seriously underestimated the tenacity of Charles Comiskey who wanted to bury them at all costs. Ban Johnson merely wanted coexistence and a balanced two-league system. These two dynamic baseball men had reached a fork in the road. Their 10-year friendship was coming apart at the seams just as the fledgling American League was beginning to flex some muscle. In 1901 "war" was declared as Comiskey and the other owners declared "open season" on National League stars. Not until the top stars were plucked off the N.L. rosters did the senior circuit awake to the gravity of the situation. Comiskey and his fellow magnates lured the top players with higher salaries and other financial inducements. It was strongly rumored that Clark Griffith was awarded shares of White Sox stock for joining up with Comiskey. This was not the case, however. Griffith was dissatisfied with the Cubs, and he encouraged Jimmy Callahan and Sandow Mertes to join him on the south side. A star pitcher for the Cubs during the 1890s, Griffith traveled to Pittsburgh in an unsuccessful attempt to lure away Honus Wagner. Though Comiskey would never allow an outsider to own a portion of the family business, he rewarded the Old Fox with the manager's chair for the 1901 season—the American League's second "inaugural."

Stocked with first-year "free agents" Callahan, Mertes, Griffith, Billy Sullivan, and Fielder Jones, the White Sox coasted to their second consecutive pennant. They claimed first place on July 18 and never looked back in a wild and woolly season characterized by violent confrontations with umpires. On August 21 Frank Shugarts and Jack Katoll were suspended by Ban Johnson for assaulting umpire Jack Haskell with a baseball. "He is incompetent to manage in *any* league,"[5] snapped Griffith. Johnson, who refused to allow National League players to intimidate his officials, stood by his decision. "Let them jump back to the National League if they want. Inexperienced playing managers have made all the trouble this year,"[6] Johnson said, in an obvious reference to Griffith. Charles Comiskey supported the league president's decision, but privately fumed against Johnson for singling out his players in the middle of a pennant race. Ban Johnson was stung by the insinuations of other A.L. owners that he had showed partiality in his dealings with Comiskey. Johnson was vain, impatient, and very sensitive to this kind of criticism. In the coming years he therefore went out of his way to *thwart* Comiskey whenever possible.

The White Sox wrapped up their second consecutive pennant on September 21, and met a team of American League All-Stars captained by Nap Lajoie in the post-season. Chicago played Lajoie's team to a four-game draw, capping off a financial *and* artistic success. Comiskey's team outdrew the Cubs by nearly 150,000 and had won the opening shot of the newest baseball "war."

Encouraged by his 1901 success, Charles Comiskey continued his marauding tactics against the Nationals. He signed George Davis, Danny Green, and Ed McFarland to 1902 contracts, but the team slipped to fourth place in the standings. With the exception of the dependable Roy Patterson, the pitching staff was composed of a collection of fading veterans. Jimmy Callahan fired the first club no-hitter on September 20, after being released from jail on an assault charge. He had slugged a Cleveland bellhop for poor room service.

Peace was finally reached with the Nationals in 1903, but Comiskey could only ask, at what price? Clark Griffith left the Sox to take over the managerial reins of the New York Yankees, transplanted from Baltimore. Griffith's defection was a foregone conclusion as early as August 29, 1902. He had actually left Chicago at the league president's urging in order to provide stability to the critical New York market— another controversial Johnson decision which Comiskey was forced to abide by.

The Sox were a team in transition. The 1903 edition finished next to last under the direction of hard-drinking, brawling Jimmy Callahan—one of Comiskey's prodigal sons who refused to accept discipline or observe simple training rules. He was too brash, and too inexperienced to make much of a difference at this juncture of his career. On June 5, 1904 Callahan gladly surrendered the job to someone who *was* ready to assume a leadership role for this rudderless team—Fielder Allison Jones. The little firebrand instilled discipline and made good use of the available talent.

Blue Skies, the Wind at the Backs (1906–1910)

Jones taught them to hit and run; exploit the opponent's every weakness and give them no quarter. He introduced the "motion" infield and the famous "body twist" slide. But the real tangible results were reflected in the pitching. Jones inherited a quartet of starting pitchers who had struggled in other organizations: Frank Owen, Doc White, Frank Smith, and Nick Altrock. Under his patient tutelage all four became big winners in 1904, and would anchor the team during most of the "Hitless Wonder" era. When Fielder Jones stepped in, there was a young, strapping rookie pitcher riding the pines. Callahan used the boy sparingly. He threw a trick pitch picked up from Elmer Stricklett, a luckless righthander who was cut in the spring. The boy's name was Edward Augustine Walsh, another "Son of Erin" whose cock-sure attitude appealed to Comiskey.

Ed Walsh emerged as a star in 1906 on the strength of a deadly spitter known as the "eel ball." That was the year that became etched in memory, when David slew Goliath and the White Sox proved once and for all that betting odds are for suckers. In 1905 Chicago narrowly missed winning the pennant. Over the winter Jones lost two thirds of his starting outfield and his old pal Jimmy Callahan who went off to play semi-pro baseball on the city's north side. Complicating matters were a long string of injuries and the strained relationship between Jones and several of his key pitchers. When the White Sox dropped to fourth place, 10 games out of first on July 29, even Comiskey was ready to write them off. He fled to his Wisconsin hunting lodge, refusing to come back until the team began posting some wins. The Old Roman did not have to wait long.

On August 1 the Sox trailed Connie Mack's A's and Griffith's Highlanders by nine full games. The next day Doc White blanked the Red Sox and Cy Young 3–0. Ed Walsh followed this up with a 4–0, one-hit whitewash on August 3. Chicago was on its way as winning became a state of mind on the south side. By the time their 19-game winning streak was finally stopped on August 25, the White Sox were sitting pretty with a 5½-game lead. They clawed and scratched the rest of the way, but held on to capture their third league championship, a remarkable achievement given the feeble hitting attack. For the second time in their history the Sox had won a pennant despite having the worst offense in the league. With a collective team batting average of .230, and just seven home runs, they truly were the "Hitless Wonders," a nickname believed to have been coined by Charles Dryden of the *Chicago Tribune*. On July 14 the headline on page one carried the good news: "Hitless Wonders Rally and Turn An Apparent New York Victory Into Defeat."[7]

This was a scrapping, hungry team. With any other manager perhaps the results would not have been quite as gratifying. In only one game during the record-setting streak were the White Sox able to field their starting lineup. The injuries took their toll, but not enough to deny them their first World Series appearance. In the Fall Classic the Sox squared off against the Cubs, a fitting showdown between the establishment and the upstarts. The Cubs of 1906 made a shambles of the National League pennant race, winning a record 116 games. Few people gave the White Sox "Davids" much of a chance to derail this Cubs' juggernaut. *Chicago Tribune* sportswriter Hugh Fullerton was said to have "doped" the precise outcome of each of the six games but that was easy to say after the fact.

This was more than a baseball championship series. It was *war*. Fans on both sides of town loaded their soggy tomatoes into paper sacks and brought them to the ballpark in anticipation of a friendly "debate" with the other team's fans. The first "subway" series began on October 8—except there was no subway in Chicago yet. From all corners of the city they came, by auto, omnibus, and on foot. Game One featured a pitcher's duel—no surprise there. It was the outcome that astonished everyone. The White Sox prevailed by a 2–1 score, thanks to the unheralded substitute George Rohe who banged home the first run of the game with a long triple into the carpenter's wood pile down the left-field line. When it was over Charles Murphy, owner of the Cubs, dismissed it as a fluke of nature—akin to snow in August. "One swallow does not make a summer!" he said. The next day Ed Reulbach fired a face-saving one hitter as the Cubs carried the day 7–1. "Watch our smoke!" Murphy promised.[8]

But there was to be no fire. At the Cubs West Side Park on October 11, Ed Walsh, not be outdone by Reulbach, tossed a two-hit 3–0 shutout. Again it was Rohe who provided the heroics. His bases-clearing triple drove home all the runs Walsh needed. "Whatever George Rohe may do from now on, he's signed for life with me," beamed the Old Roman, who released him just a year later.[9]

After being white-washed by Three Finger Brown in Game Four, the White Sox rallied behind Fielder Jones. Typifying the spirit of this club, Eddie Hahn was suited up and ready to play. The little fireplug, released by Clark Griffith and picked up by the Sox in mid-year, had his nose broken in Game Three by Cub pitcher Jack Pfiester. Hahn had the nose mended with strips of plaster. A small red rubber hose was inserted in the cast to help him breathe. In Game Six the bruised and bandaged house painter from Mississippi banged out four hits to lead the Sox to an 8–3 rout and the Series championship. While his players popped the champagne corks in the dressing room, Fielder Jones sat down with Comiskey in his private office. Flushed with success and caught in the reverie of the moment, the Old Roman wrote a check for $15,000 to be split "among the boys." Jones burst out of the office waving the check before a gaggle of reporters. "Look," he rasped. "Look what Commy has done! He has given me this check for $15,000 to be divided among the players. No man ever had the honor of working for a better hearted or more appreciated man than old Commy!" When the 1907 contracts arrived in the mail several months later the Hitless Wonders were disappointed to discover that the raises had been withheld. When asked if this could be an oversight on Comiskey's part, secretary Charles Fredericks reminded the "boys" of their World Series bonuses—which were factored into their new contracts. This was the essence of Comiskey, gifted with rare genius, yet impaired by a smallness, and a financial cunning that ultimately spelled doom for his franchise, which had emerged as Chicago's best-loved team during those halcyon days before the onset of the Black Sox Scandal.

> What city's in the baseball eye?
>   Chicago
> Who'll win the pennant by and by?
>   Chicago
> What team threw down the clan of Mack?
>   Chicago
> Who soon will hurl Clark Griffith back?
>   Chicago
> Who's Got 'em all upon the rack?
>   Chicago
>
> Grantland Rice (1906)[10]

The sweat and blood of his players had helped establish Comiskey as one of the most revered public figures in Chicago. This is not to say that his fellow owners treated their players any better. After the 1903 peace agreement the American League magnates proved to be as restrictive and greedy as John Brush, Andrew Freedman, and Frank Robison had been during the not-so-gay nineties. The Old Roman was a shrewd business man with a good marketing sense. He wined and dined the Chicago press corps lavishly and in return they bestowed precious column inches to the south side ballclub. He earned the loyalty of the sports writers by admitting them into the realm of the Woodland Bards, an exclusive club of show people, politicians, and civic leaders who accompanied Comiskey on his annual forays to the Jerome Hunting and Fishing Club, 12 miles north of Mercer, Wisconsin. Comiskey purchased this 800-acre resort in 1903. The Bards were indeed a celebrated group, whose membership included, at various times, Ring Lardner, George M. Cohan (honorary), Ban Johnson, August Herrmann of the National Commission, and Joe Farrell, long-time Chicago Blackhawks press agent. These worthy sports, and a flock of invited beat reporters as well, drank Comiskey's wine and consumed fresh venison—shot on the premises. The Bards cavorted about the grounds like small boys on a holiday, composing silly lyric verse which appealed to their host's vanity and ensured them a second invitation.

> For all his friends are welcome if they wish to make a call—
> There's always room for one more hat on the cabin wall—
> And there's always a drop for to warm your heart—
> And the eating is there for to name—
> If you call on him once, I'll lay odds that you'll call again.[11]

Yet Comiskey would at the same time require his players to launder their own uniforms. Decline set in after the championship season, hastened by the players dissatisfaction with Comiskey, and the usual rash of injuries that continued to plague this team. As hitless as ever, the Jones men battled right down to the last week of the 1907 and 1908 seasons before succumbing to the improved Tigers. In 1908 Ed Walsh, the "Big Reel" as he was called, won 40 games and saved seven. The over-reliance on Walsh no doubt contributed to the nagging arm problems he had to deal with in the coming years, but this didn't seem to matter to Comiskey who refused to pay him the $7,500 he held out for in 1909.

Following the heartbreak of 1908, Fielder Jones called it quits. Comiskey begged him to reconsider, but the fiery Sox manager owned some valuable acreage in Portland, Oregon, and didn't need baseball to sustain him. He told Comiskey in no uncertain terms that the only way he would return would be as part-owner. Commy quickly appointed his catcher Billy Sullivan to guide the 1909 edition but the results were not the same.

Twilight Years (1910–1920)

As early as 1903 Comiskey scouted the city for a new location for his White Sox to play. But he neither had the money nor the resources to finance a costly construction project. In 1909 he bought the property at 35th and Shields from the heirs of former Mayor John Wentworth for $100,000. A year later the second all-concrete-and-steel stadium in America—Comiskey Park—opened its doors at a location directly west of where the old Brotherhood grandstand once stood. Even though he was no longer restrained by James Hart's restrictions Comiskey elected to build on the 35th Street boundary line. The south side was beginning its racial transition from white ethnic Irish to black. The constituency the Sox owner marketed his product to was beginning to flee the neighborhood making the park an anachronism before it was a quarter-century old. Perhaps it was just a case of stubborn pride on Comiskey's part. He had to *prove* to the Cubs that the Sox could thrive in Bridgeport even after he was free to move to the north or west sides of the city.

Compounding the problem of logistics were the cost-cutting measures Charles Comiskey imposed on the architects. There would be no cantilevered grandstand which would have provided spectators with an unimpaired view of the field. Comiskey rejected a Beaux-art style similar to that of Shibe Park, and the sight lines in the corners made it difficult to see the infield. The new White Sox Park was notable only for its sheer massive size, which ultimately deprived its patrons of sorely needed intimacy. The "Baseball Palace of the World" opened on July 1, 1910 to favorable reviews from a generation obsessed by boldness and size. The deep-seeded problems of the stadium and its surrounding environs were years in the making, but were planted by Comiskey at a time when he thought the world was his oyster.

In their spacious new quarters the White Sox stumbled through the next five seasons. The team played .500 baseball under the direction of Hugh Duffy and Jimmy Callahan. Without Ed Walsh the White Sox might have tumbled into the nether regions of the American League, but the "Big Reel" from the Pennsylvania coal fields won 72 games from 1910–1912 before his arm finally gave out from overwork. The "Hitless Wonder" era was over as Charles Comiskey laid plans to dig his dusty old spikes in three continents.

Since the 1880s the Old Roman dreamed about a baseball world tour. Albert Spalding first blazed the trail in 1888, bringing the American game from the Orient to Europe. It was a coup de grace for the venerable old Spalding which must have made Commy envious. The idea burned in his mind for years. In 1910 Comiskey laid the groundwork by traveling to England with his wife and personal secretary. Beyond the hoopla of a European barnstorming tour, the Old Roman envisioned an expansion of baseball to the English-speaking lands with a large share of the credit going to him. The team was largely ignored while Comiskey, Ted Sullivan, and John McGraw mapped out plans for a tour to commence at the conclusion of the 1913 season. Comiskey disliked the Giants manager. Their differences extended back to 1902 when McGraw bolted the American League in mid-season to accept a job in New York. "He doesn't know the first thing about managing a baseball team," Comiskey said of McGraw when he forsaked the Baltimore team in 1902.[12]

Neither did McGraw know the first thing about high finance. Comiskey guaranteed the entire trip, underwriting all expenses. McGraw was oblivious to this fact and put up his entire fortune to cover "obligations." Comiskey, of course, remained silent about this matter as the good ship White Sox set sail for Japan and the Philippines on November 18, 1913. The entourage travelled to Japan, Ceylon, Australia, Egypt, Italy, France, and England, where they played a command performance before the King. On the mound for the Giants that day was a young pitcher on "loan" from Comiskey—Urban "Red" Faber, about to embark upon a 20-year odyssey with the Pale Hose. The Sox and the Giants played a total of 44 games in Europe and Asia, but at best the national game was viewed as a curiosity by the people Comiskey hoped to impress. The only bouquets awaiting the tourists were from the sportswriters and civic leaders who feted Comiskey at a gaudy banquet in Chicago's Congress Hotel in March 1914. More than 1,000 admirers hailed the Old Roman, chanting in unison: "the White Sox! May they always win; but win or lose, the White Sox!"[13]

Yet at the moment when Charles Comiskey's stars seemed to be in ascent, the storm clouds were already beginning to form. Ahead, triumphs untold, and then years of ashes and despair. The second great epoch of Chicago White Sox history began in 1915. With the distractions of the world tour out of the way, and Comiskey awakened to the threat posed by Charles Weeghman, owner of the local Federal League team, the Old Roman invested a portion of his capital in the procurement of star-caliber players who would return the Sox to preeminence in the junior circuit. On December 8, 1914 the contract of Eddie Collins was purchased from Connie Mack for $50,000. Collins, a Princeton-educated scholar, was not about to be led through the woods by the Old Roman. He insisted on a five-year guaranteed contract estimated to be worth $90,000 with bonuses.

On August 20, 1915, "Shoeless" Joe Jackson arrived from Cleveland for three disappointments: Ed Klepfer, Braggo Roth, and Larry Chappell. The financially strapped Indians were more interested in the $31,000 check Comiskey sent along than any of these three players. Jackson, the only player to hit .390 two years in a row, moved into left field where he once again demonstrated why he was second only to Cobb as the A.L.'s most feared batsman. In 1915 the Sox won 93 games with five new position players. There were few now who doubted Comiskey's ability to build winning ballclubs. Each time a veteran club began to slip, Comiskey would purchase quality players from the other

American League moguls, or reach down into the minors where his three trusted old friends Ted Sullivan, Joe Cantillon, and Frank Isbell might tip him off to a worthwhile prospect. This was the formula for success which worked like a charm for nearly 20 years.

The team that graced the Comiskey diamond from 1915 until its demise in 1920 is considered by old-timers to be one of the most "perfect" clubs in baseball history. Red Faber, the veteran Ed Cicotte acquired for a song in 1912, and the kid Lefty Williams were backed up by a supporting cast that included the no-hit pitcher Joe Benz, and "Reb" Russell of Bonham Texas, who just wanted a chance to play for the Sox and see the big cities. The hitting and inner defense was solid. Ray Schalk was one of the most capable catchers in the game, redefining the role of a backstop in an era when few members of his profession were able to play 100 games in a season. The pint-sized "Cracker" arrived in 1912. When Walsh first caught sight of him he laughed aloud at the idea of a schoolboy handling the deadly spitter. But Ray would handle the best of them in a distinguished 16-year career. His strong accurate throws to Collins were unerring; Schalk was the mortar between the bricks.

George "Buck" Weaver arrived at the White Sox training camp in Waco, Texas, a few months ahead of Schalk. In the winter of 1911 he worked long hours at a California stock ranch to get in shape for the tryout. In Pennsylvania his mother took sick, and grew progressively worse by the day. He wanted to go back, but he had barely enough money to afford a good dinner let alone a train trip back east. On the day when Weaver met up with Ping Bodie to begin the journey to the Sox spring camp he received the news that his mother had passed away. It would have been impossible to go to the funeral and still report to Jimmy Callahan in Texas at the same time. His father advised Buck not to attempt it, but to join the team and make the best of a tough situation. Weaver did not mention a word of this to his teammates. No one showed more enthusiasm in camp than this sprite 20-year-old infielder, who cried his eyes out in his hotel room many nights afterward. Years later when Buck Weaver was forced to eke out a living as a race track tout, a friend from the old days recalled with sadness his life and times. "Whether he was a Black Sox, White Sox, or Green Sox, I still say that Buck Weaver was the best third baseman I ever saw. In any event," the man said, his voice lowering, "even though he's dead Buck Weaver could play third base out of the dream book. And he could have been the best of them all."[14]

The Black Sox. Chicago's shame, America's tragedy. Perhaps their sellout was indicative of the deeper problems confronting America in the post-war era. The period of American innocence was over. Creeping bolshevism, racial tensions in the large urban areas, the Boston police strike, and growing lawlessness—all were changing Americans' view of their society. The Black Sox scandal reflected a growing cynicism and deeper despair permeating the nation. How could such a thing have happened, and what were the consequences for Charles Comiskey and his White Sox?

In 1917 Clarence Rowland's White Sox coasted to their third pennant and second World Series appearance. Their six-game victory over the New York Giants in the Championship Series was academic. They were simply the best team in baseball seemingly headed for a dynasty. The next year the roster was decimated by the war. Jackson and Williams went off to work in the shipyards while Faber and the eventual "clean Sox" served their time in the armed forces. This led to dissension in the ranks and great bitterness between two cliques on the ballclub.

The Black Sox—Jackson, Weaver, Oscar Felsch, "Chick" Gandil, "Swede" Risberg, Lefty Williams, and Ed Cicotte—were united in their mutual hatred of Comiskey and envious of the fat salary commanded by Eddie Collins. The owner's niggardly policy of making the players pay for the upkeep of their uniforms was later cited as an example of the kind of behavior that drove them into the arms of the gamblers. Comiskey's plantation style of management was certainly no different now than it had been in 1906 or 1910. Yet this particular team decided to cross the line. Perhaps it was symptomatic of the times in which they lived. More likely it was the culmination of a festering problem that Ban Johnson and his counterparts had shoved under the rug far too long. There was a tolerance of gambling. Big-city gangsters like Mont Tennes in Chicago and Arnold Rothstein were interested in the sport for years. The newspapers encouraged fans to place wagers by listing the "odds" on a daily basis. Society at large frowned on the "sporting fraternity" yet tacitly encouraged them.

Against this backdrop the bitterly divided White Sox captured first place on July 9, 1919, and held on the rest of the way. The first contact with the gamblers occurred at the Ansonia Hotel in New York City, September 17–18, during the team's last eastern swing. Ed Cicotte, who had no doubt discussed the "fix" with his seven disgruntled teammates on several prior occasions, told the gamblers that $10,000 would be his price. Jackson was offered $5,000 but he turned this down. It wasn't enough to do a "dirty deal" according to Cicotte's grand jury confession. Joe finally agreed to accept $5,000 after each game. The next clandestine meeting between Sport Sullivan, Abe Attell, and the players took place at the Warner Hotel in Chicago several days before the Series began on October 1. Cicotte demanded $10,000. When he returned home that night the money was tucked under his pillow. The fix was on.[15]

While Cicotte and company wrestled with their conscience, manager Kid Gleason was all smiles on the eve of the World Series. "Take those four fellows (Williams, Cicotte, Kerr, Faber) with Schalk behind the plate and I don't know where they can be beaten," Gleason beamed. "It won't make any difference to them whether they're playing the Reds for the world's championship or playing an exhibition game in a hick town."[16]

Cincinnati was no hick town. The Sinton Hotel was ablaze with excitement and anticipation as the upstart Reds prepared to clash with the seemingly invincible White Sox. On the morning of the game Kid Gleason called for a workout at Redland Field as a final tuneup. The entire team, including Gandil, Jackson, and their fellow conspirators, took infield and hitting practice. Sleepy Bill Burns, former Sox player turned gambler and the state's star witness, later testified that he had met the players in their hotel room that same morning. This was later contradicted by Kid Gleason under cross-examination, one of many puzzling inconsistencies in the state's case against the eight Black Sox.

Cicotte testified that he planned to walk the first batter of the game by prior agreement with the gamblers. Instead he beaned Morrie Rath. After that, he said, his conscience hurt him and he realized that he was doing wrong. He regretted his actions, yet inexplicably kept the gambler's advance money. The Sox were blown out of the box by a 9–1 score in Game One. They dropped Game Two by a 4–2 count but came back to win 3–0 behind the "busher" Dickie Kerr in Game Three. Comiskey heard all the ugly rumors during the Series, and was caught in a real quandary. If he failed to report his suspicions to a higher authority he risked forfeiture of his team according to league rules. By bringing this to light, he would still lose out, in a scandal of the greatest magnitude. Deciding that a coverup was not in his best interests he convened a late-night meeting with the two league presidents, Ban Johnson and John Heydler. "That's the whelp of a beaten cur!" snapped the American League president, whose petty squabbles with Comiskey over the years had become virulent hatred.[17]

The White Sox dropped five of the eight games played. Most observers preferred to believe that the White Sox were victimized by an inspired heady ballclub that was "up" for this Series. Hugh Fullerton of the *Chicago Tribune* took a different view, ominously noting that "yesterday's game also means the disruption of the Chicago White Sox ballclub. There are seven men on the team who will not be there when the gong sounds next spring."

Chick Gandil, the acknowledged ringleader, was the only member of the Black Sox absent in 1920. The rough-housing Chickie decided to sit it out when he was unable to land the kind of contract he felt he deserved. Comiskey knew Gandil was guilty, but spent two months trying to coax him to come back. When the news of the scandal failed to "break," Comiskey decided to keep the team together hoping that it would all blow over. In this sense the Old Roman was himself guilty of a coverup. Then after it came to light Commy was suddenly on the side of law and order, demanding that the rascals be thrown out for the good of the game. Comiskey's every move was coached by Alfred Austrian, senior partner of Mayer, Myer, Austrian, and Platt, one of Chicago's most prestigious law firms.

In 1920 the White Sox battled down to the wire with the Cleveland Indians. In some ways this club was even better than the 1919 edition. Faber, Cicotte, Kerr, and Williams won 20 apiece—a feat unmatched until the Baltimore Orioles' staff of Cuellar, Dopson, Palmer, and McNally equalled the mark in 1971. The real evidence of a fix began to manifest itself late in the 1920 season. The ugly rumors and innuendo boiled over into September as the White Sox and Indians battled right down to the closing days for the pennant. On August 18 the Sox began a crucial eastern road swing. When they arrived in New York on the 26th they enjoyed a comfortable 3½-game lead. Seven days and seven losses later Gleason's boys found themselves in third place. "As soft as two minute eggs most of the time!" commented one scribe. It is easy to see where Arnold Rothstein and his friends used their "persuasive" powers to inveigle the eight players to throw crucial league games. In the last week of the season with the pennant hanging in the balance a petty gambler named Billy Maharg spilled his gut to a sportswriter from the Philadelphia *North American* about the alleged World Series fix.

With the cards finally on the table Ban Johnson prevailed upon Charles MacDonald, presiding judge of the Cook County Court, to initiate a grand jury investigation. The carrot that the wily American League president dangled in front of the politically ambitious jurist was a possible appointment as high commissioner of baseball. Johnson would leave no stone unturned in his desire to ruin Comiskey.

On September 28 Cicotte and Jackson waived immunity and confessed to the hastily assembled grand jury. "Now Risberg threatens to bump me off if I squawk," the veteran Cicotte said. "That's why I had all the bailiffs with me when I left the grand jury room this afternoon. I'm not under arrest yet and I've got the idea that after what I told them old Joe Jackson isn't going to fall. But I'm not going to get far from my protectors until this blows over. Swede is a hard guy."[18]

Protectors indeed. "Mr. Comiskey and myself as counsel have been working on this for a year," Austrian said in a brave attempt to distance the Old Roman from the residue of scandal. There were more ulterior motives and snaking twists to this unfolding drama than kinks in the queen's necklace. Johnson wanted to harpoon Comiskey. The

Old Roman did not relish the though of losing his bankable cash commodity—the players. But neither could he risk his good name in a shady coverup, or by being too closely identified with the indicted players. Looking down the road Charles Comiskey perhaps saw this as a golden opportunity to replace Johnson, or at the very least diminish his power. By vigorously prosecuting the White Sox, Comiskey's arch-enemy was inadvertently writing his own baseball epitaph.

The jury trial of the torn and soiled Black Sox began on July 18, 1921. Since Illinois had no bribery statute on the books, a trumped-up conspiracy charge to defraud the business of Charles Comiskey, the people of Chicago, and the "honest" White Sox players was presented to the judge and jury. The chief conspirator of the "fix"— Arnold Rothstein—was notable only by his absence. Two lesser gamblers, Carl Zork and David Zelser, went on trial with the eight players who were represented by Michael Ahearn and Thomas Nash, the favored mouthpieces of Chicago gangland. Not so surprisingly, their services were being privately paid for by Comiskey.

During the trial figures were introduced by the defense lawyers which proved that the conspiracy had not, in fact, injured the business of Comiskey. During 1919 the team's gate receipts totaled $521,175.76. For the 1920 season this figure jumped to $910,206.59. No one, especially Charles Comiskey, was going to the poorhouse because of Gandil, Jackson, and company. For the disillusioned and broken-hearted White Sox fans who were the ultimate losers in all this, their consolation was in the World Series averages: Jackson, .375; Weaver, .324; McMullin, .500; Cicotte, 2.91 ERA. Felsch, Gandil, and Risberg, considered to be the real ringleaders of the fix, played poorly, however, suggesting that the conspiracy was an extremely half-hearted one.

The trial of the Black Sox closed on August 2, 1921. The prosecution's inability to establish a conspiracy within the narrow context of the indictments made acquittal inevitable. When the foreman announced the verdict everyone seemed pleased. Comiskey got his ballclub back. Baseball, as the last "clean" sport in America, was vindicated and the shattered faith of the fans was seemingly restored. However, Judge Kenesaw Mountain Landis decreed the next day that "no player who throws a ballgame, no player that undertakes or promises to throw a ballgame, no player that sits in conference with a bunch of crooked players and gamblers where the ways and means of throwing a game are discussed and does not promptly tell his club about it will ever play baseball." It was a long-winded denunciation from a man whose own courtroom was not unlike that of Judge Roy Bean. Landis—hired to save baseball from itself—had to do something to justify his salary. The harshness of the decision that effectively sentenced the

White Sox franchise to hell belied his later rulings. Landis seemed to operate under the belief that he had the right to pick and choose his victims. In the Ty Cobb-Tris Speaker affair of 1926 the judge absolved them of wrongdoing in the face of hard evidence that the two venerable old stars had wagered on the outcome of *their own* game back in 1919. Even Ban Johnson was not convinced of their innocence, and he urged Landis to banish them for the good of the game. His pleas fell on deaf ears.[19]

Once again Comiskey positioned himself in the glow of favorable publicity by standing behind the man who represented "integrity." "Those indicted players are on *my* ineligible list," he said. "It was not necessary for Judge Landis to put them on his, but I am glad he did as it justifies my position. There is absolutely no chance for any of them to play on *my* team again."[20]

One can only wonder what Comiskey might have said if the players were allowed to return to the club. A great but tragic team was decimated—ruined. And who was at fault? Comiskey for being a tightwad? The players for their stupidity and avarice? The corrupt baseball oligarchy for allowing events to get out of hand? There was enough collective guilt here so no one would be cheated. The White Sox were a dominant franchise before 1920, arguably the cornerstone team of the circuit. Afterward they were nothing. Perpetual underdogs. Losers. How could Comiskey have allowed this to happen?

> Do not be remembering the most natural man ever to wear spiked shoes—
> The canniest fielder and the longest hitter,
> Who squatted on his heels
> In a uniform muddied at the knees,
> Till the bleacher shadows grew long behind him.
> Who went along with Chick and Buck and Happy
> Because they treated him so friendly like—
> Hardly like Yankees at all.
> With Williams because Lefty was from the south too
> And with Risberg because the Swede was such a hard guy—
> Who made an X for his name and couldn't argue with Comiskey's
>   sleepers.
> But who could pick a line drive out of the air ten feet outside the foul
>   line.
> And rifle anything home from anywhere in the park.
> For Shoeless Joe is gone, long gone
> A long-yellow grass-blade between his teeth
> And the bleacher shadows behind him . . .
>
> Nelson Algren

The Depression Began Early (1921–1950)

The game had passed Charles Comiskey by. No longer would he be able to assemble a winning ballclub overnight. He tried hard but the results would never be the same. From Salt Lake City Comiskey purchased an infield—Earl Sheely, Ernie Johnson, and Eddie Mulligan. He traded Shano Collins and Nemo Liebold to acquire "grade-A" Harry Hooper, for name recognition, while the minor leagues were scoured for top talent. Comiskey truly believed that his wheeling and dealing would eventually restore winning baseball to the south side. Between 1920 and his death in 1931 he spent a million dollars in player procurement. The names of the supporting cast changed, but the results were always the same. Between 1921 and 1936 the Sox finished above .500 only twice. Ted Lyons arrived off the Baylor campus in 1923. But he and Faber could not carry the team on their backs. For every blue chip prospect with the grit and determination of Lyons there was a Maurice Archdeacon or Randy Moore to disappoint. Typical of the problems confronting Comiskey and his lieutenant Harry Grabiner were the yearly holdouts and widespread grumbling among the few star-caliber players on this team. After losing 93 games and finishing in seventh place in 1929, Peck's original bad boy, Art Shires, demanded $22,000 in salary. Willie Kamm, purchased for $100,000 in 1923, was a lengthy holdout when manager Donie Bush stripped him of his title of captain. Smead Jolley got lost en route to spring training, and in the midst of an early season losing streak that carried over to October, old Red Faber complained about his fielders' inability to catch the ball. "It's the ego racket," said Art "the Great" Shires, who had a way of putting matters into their proper perspective.[21]

In 1924 Comiskey embarked on a second world tour with McGraw, but no one outside of Chicago and New York noticed . . . or cared. Three years later the Old Roman decided to take advantage of the Babe Ruth gold rush by upperdecking the outfield grandstand for a cool $100,000. This costly renovation was not only unnecessary—the Sox filled these seats to capacity only seven times before 1941—but unwise. The cavernous dimensions already had made this park one of the most imposing structures in the majors. A second tier of seats in the outfield further deprived the stadium of sorely needed intimacy, and hastened the structural problems of the late 1980s. By contrast Wrigley Field, on the emerging "Gold Coast," was perceived as a cozy charming ballpark with inherent natural beauty. Only the most ardent Sox enthusiast could say the same about palatial Comiskey Park.

Comiskey operated up a blind alley for the remaining years of his life. He changed managers at will, replacing good men for the most arbitrary reasons. Eddie Collins—the only one who had been around during the glory years—was fired after the 1926 season, despite leading the team to its only winning seasons during this whole miserable period. Ray Schalk took over, but he lacked the necessary leadership skills and was unable to cope with the modern 1920s ballplayer, a breed apart from the Hitless Wonders. Just before the Sox broke winter camp in 1927 Johnny Mostil tried to kill himself with a straight razor. The fleet center fielder suffered from neuritis. That was the official reason offered by the Comiskeys for this inexplicable tragedy. What Schalk was apparently unaware of was the rumored infidelity between Mostil and Red Faber's wife. As it turned out Mostil recovered, but the vicious innuendo and internal dissension continued.

Charles Comiskey died at his Eagle River, Wisconsin, resort on October 26, 1931, a broken, embittered old man obsessed in the last few remaining years with his declining health. The strain of running the team had taken its toll, and in the last two years he had distanced himself from its day-to-day operation. Comiskey's only consolation was knowing that he had followed Ban Johnson to death's door by four months.

If this was baseball's golden age, Sox fans wanted no part of it. With each pennant the Cubs were winning (1929, 1932, 1935, 1938) new generations of Wrigley fans were being cultivated at the expense of the dreary White Sox, harbingers of the last-place finish. Ring Lardner was long gone. The Woodland Bards, what was left of them, were walking around with canes. In 1932 the Old Roman's son, J. Louis, took a hard look at this situation. A corpulent, but frail man, J. Lou outlined an ambitious plan of action.

The baseball organization needed an overhaul. Necessity dictated that the Sox emerge from the dark ages and start to build their own minor league system. For years the Old Roman purchased the contracts of top amateur players only to see them go belly up on the major league level. After nine years of careful preparation, the fledgling minor league operation was finally launched in 1939 under the direction of Billy Webb and Bob Tarleton. A working agreement was signed with the Dallas team of the Southwest League. Two new scouts were hired to supplement the work being done in Texas.

The Sox needed some stars for the fans to identify with. The best thing going in 1932 were "Fats" Fothergill and Carey "Him" Selph. During the World Series that year J. Lou completed the long-rumored purchase of three of Connie Mack's prized stallions—Jimmy Dykes, Al Simmons, and Mule Haas. Simmons turned out to be a bust, but the acquisition turned out to be a good one for the Sox down the road. Dykes took over as manager on May 15, 1934, and immediately instilled some fire and vinegar into the team.

By 1936 the White Sox were back in business and seemingly on the road to recovery. Luke Appling, the only Sox player to win a batting title (1936, 1943), was complemented by a quartet of promising young stars: Mike Kreevich, "Rip" Radcliff, Zeke Bonura, and Jackie Hayes. Their development was patiently nurtured by Dykes, and his two close advisors Mule Haas and "Muddy" Ruel. Comiskey Park had temporarily become "Philadelphia on the lake" and slowly the attendance barometer began to reflect the new mood in town.

The ebb and flow of White Sox history being what it is dictated that at the precise moment of triumph a new calamity would shortly follow. Tragedies invariably come in threes, and it was no different in 1939. First they would lose the services of Monty Stratton, a late-blooming pitcher who posted a 15–5 record in 1937. Stratton lost his leg as a result of a freakish hunting accident in 1938. Just before the lights were turned on for the first time in Comiskey Park, J. Lou passed away on July 18, 1939. His death was not unexpected, but with him went the drive, the energy, and the imagination that had brought the team back from among the missing.

The rebuilding process finally came to a grinding halt with the onset of World War II and the death of Billy Webb, who conceived the farm system. The trend of the 1940s was established on the very first opening day when Bob Feller fired a no-hitter against the ever-pale hose. The ace in the hole for Chicago during the lean war years was the ever-quotable Jimmy Dykes. The cigar-smoking Sox manager was a magician in making good use of the available talent. Gimpy veterans plucked off of other teams' rosters produced for Dykes in ways that were unimagined by his fellow managers. The times, they were 'a hard, and the attendance was lackluster, but the Sox endured. Grabiner and his new boss Grace Reidy Comiskey kept a close watch on the purse strings, while the stands echoed with the plaintive cry of "C'mon Luke!" And that too was stilled when Appling went off to fight the war in 1944.

After 12 years at the helm, Jimmy Dykes called it quits on May 24, 1946. The longest reigning Sox manager left his mark on the franchise. He won 899 games and lost a lot more, but the record does not accurately reflect his contribution. Dykes was an anchor in the storm. He was popular. He was *colorful*. For what is baseball, if not good marketing. If you own a team that is a perennial loser, you better stock it with some colorful personalities. Jimmy Dykes was a salty-tongued, umpire-baiting curmudgeon—ideal for the times he lived in. His replacement Ted Lyons steered the club through two bleak seasons. The old Baylor Bearcat wasn't the answer obviously, but he was a sentimental favorite of the fans—the winningest pitcher in team history with 260 big ones in the "W" column. The older he became the more effective he was, pitching exclusively on Sundays. With any other team this crafty knuckleballer might have won 500 games. That much was conceded by the members of the fourth estate who watched Lyons develop over the course of two decades.

After dropping 101 games in 1948 the great house cleaning began. Les O'Connor, a dismal failure as general manager, was given his walking papers. From the Big Ten and more recently the American Association came Frank "Trader" Lane, a physical fitness buff whose first move was to put the entire team on waivers. "There are no sacred cows on this club," he explained.

Out of the Ashes (1949–1962)

Young Chuck Comiskey had just completed his baseball apprenticeship with the Sox farm club affiliate at Waterloo, Iowa. The symbolic ties to the farms and fields of Iowa were cultivated years earlier by the Old Roman, when as a young stripling he began his playing career in Dubuque. The torch had been passed to a third generation of Comiskey, who promised Sox fans a new deal in his first Christmas message. "Up Donner!" "Up Blitzen!"

> For the best and most loyal fans in baseball, I wish the happiest and brightest of all Christmastides. Let us all join together in the wish for the New Year that the White Sox begin a surge upward in the American League standings that in years to come will ultimately bring another pennant to Comiskey Park. I assure you each member of the White Sox organization will do his best to make that dream come true.
>
> Chuck Comiskey[22]

The rebirth, foretold by Chuck in 1948, finally came to be in 1951 when Paul Richards was hired to pilot the young White Sox who had been given the complete makeover by Lane. Nellie Fox and Billy Pierce were acquired from Philadelphia and Detroit respectively. And on April 30, 1951, the final piece in the puzzle was in place when Orestes "Minnie" Minoso arrived in a tricky three-cornered deal with the A's and Indians. The next day he cracked the lineup—and the White Sox color barrier—with a flourish. Yankee hurler Vic Raschi's second offering was launched into the center-field bullpen. Minnie the Moocher and company were off and running in what was to become the most exciting decade in White Sox history. There would be only one pennant, but the memory of the Black Sox, and all the long dry years that followed were forgotten in the shout and tumult of the magnificent fifties.

A 14-game winning streak in mid-May propelled the "Go-Go" White Sox (the famous sobriquet, coined in 1951, encouraged such base thieves as Jim Busby, Minnie Minoso, and "Chico" Carrasquel) into a temporary lead in the American League pennant race. Their first place standing on June 10 marked the first time since 1920 that any Sox club led the pack this late in a season. Though they eventually wilted to a superior Yankee team, interest in the White Sox was finally rekindled. They passed the million mark in attendance for the first time, and an appreciative Mayor Martin Kennelly handed Chuck Comiskey the key to the city in a special ceremony. It unlocked the hearts and minds of Chicago fandom—which for too long had been infatuated with the downward-spiralling Cubs. Minnie, Nellie, Chico, and company won the close ones with the proven Comiskey formula: speed, defense, and pitching. By contrast the best thing going at the friendly confines was Harry Chiti and Moose Moryn. The shoe was at last on the other foot, and brother it felt good!

Paul Rapier Richards' greatest talent was with the pitchers. Billy Pierce, Virgil Trucks, and Bob Keegan became big winners under the guidance of the "Wizard of Waxahachie." Richards and Lane didn't always see eye to eye. The Sox manager always said that if left alone in a corner, "Trader" Lane would peddle away a pennant winner just because he needed something to do. His seven-year reign as Sox G.M. witnessed 241 player transactions involving 353 players. The alchemy worked best in the early years, when there were few bargaining chips and nothing to lose. After the Sox began their winning ways, and the fans whispered that forbidden word—pennant—relations between Lane and Richards, and Lane and Comiskey, and Lane and the world at large, became strained. Paul Richards was the first to go, when Grace Comiskey refused to grant him a three-year contract. He fled the south side on September 13, 1954, to head up baseball operations for the new Baltimore Orioles. After a heated showdown with Chuck Comiskey—a man he considered a novice—Frank Lane cashed in the chips on September 21, 1955.

A series of third-place finishes which would have been wonderful news back in 1932 was not enough to satisfy the Comiskeys or their fans in 1955. Marty Marion was brought in to manage the club in Louie Aparicio's rookie year. But the old Cardinal shortstop got under the skin of Chuck, and his new partner in the front office, John Rigney. With a club they believed strong enough to win it all in 1955, Marion came in third. Dick Donovan's appendectomy was the best excuse offered for his latest failure, and it earned the manager a temporary reprieve. A disastrous losing streak which accompanied a four-game sweep of the Yanks in June 1956 doomed the Sox to another treadmill third-place finish. Marty Marion was not long for the south side when news leaked out that Al Lopez, the genial "Señor" from Tampa, was about to be let go in Cleveland.

Lopez puffed a fat cigar to celebrate his new contract with the White Sox, signed on October 29, 1956. Jungle Jim Rivera, who helped put the go in go-go, offered the new Sox manager some timely advice. "It isn't everybody who can inherit a player like me when they get the job," he said.[23]

Al Lopez was the seventh son of a seventh son—and the only other manager to win pennants in the American League during the height of the Yankee decade (1949–1959) when the Bronx Bombers were compared to U.S. Steel for their methodical success. But even the astute Lopez was not given much of a chance by the sportswriters assembling in Tampa, Florida for the annual rites of spring in 1959. Two consecutive second-place finishes left the veteran scribes unconvinced. The 1958 edition lagged 10 games behind Casey Stengel's club in a generally weak field. The Sox were getting on in years. And still there was no longball threat, though Washington strong boy Roy Sievers was reportedly available for the right price.

Events off the field captured all the ink in the early months of 1959. A front office upheaval brought Bill Veeck and his bag of magic tricks to Chicago over the winter. The "battling Comiskeys" fought for control of the team in probate court which permitted Barnum Bill to sneak in through the front door. Young Chuck believed that the team was his by birthright. He had no reason to believe otherwise. Since Chuck was a boy in knee britches, his family prepared him for the day he would take over active management of the club, and now it was time to collect on some old promises. Unfortunately sister Dorothy owned 54 percent of the stock, and the years of internecine feuding with her brother and his side of the family discouraged her from selling her share of the team for a price Chuck was willing to pay. This courtroom drama dragged into March before a judge paved the way for Veeck and his partners.

Down in Florida Lopez told his new boss to relax and enjoy the ride. The Sox could do just fine without Sievers. Al Lopez said he had reason to believe that the Chicago pennant drought was about to end. As it turned out, the señor was the only one who truly believed this team had the firepower to go all the way. Writer William Barry Furlong wagered that the White Sox would not be in the money at season's end. If wrong, he promised to roll a peanut down State Street—with his nose.

Crippled with injuries and beset with salary holdouts, the New York Yankees were never a factor in 1959. The talented Cleveland club led the way during the early going, but the Go-Go Sox remained within striking distance until they captured the lead for good on July 22. Last in the league in home runs, the Sox paced the A.L. in fielding at .979 and pitching with a 3.29 ERA. Grizzled old Early Wynn proved that life begins at 39, when he bagged 22 victories to claim Cy Young honors. In his 10th season with the White Sox diminutive, tobacco-chewing Nellie Fox became the first Chisox player to win the coveted Most Valuable Player award. Fox at second, Jim Landis in center, and Sherm Lollar behind the plate. This was magic up the middle and the reason why the Sox were so devastating in one-run games. Their 35–15 record in this category was the best in baseball.

Bill Veeck left them laughing in the aisle with cow milking contests, a martian invasion (led by midget Eddie Gaedel), and Al Smith

Night, in which every Schmidt, Smith, Smithe, and Smythe was admitted for free in order to encourage the slumping White Sox left fielder. However, Al Smith dropped a fly ball which gave the Red Sox a 7–6 victory in front of all his namesakes. These diversions were but window dressing as the Sox went about their business in a workmanlike manner. The pennant was really won during a four-game set in Cleveland August 28–30. Trailing the Sox by only a game and a half, the pesky Indians needed to take three of four to get back into the race. Playing before the largest crowds of the year the Sox went into cavernous Municipal Stadium and took four straight. The next day the Cleveland *Plain Dealer* captured the gloom and remorse of their fans when they said "Go-Go Home White Sox!"[24]

The pennant was clinched during a return engagement on September 22. With two outs in the ninth inning and the Sox ahead 4–2, dangerous Vic Power stepped up to the plate with the bases full and one out. He faced relief specialist Gerry Staley, brought in from the bullpen to put out the fire. On the first pitch Power drove one up the middle, but Aparicio grabbed it and turned the double play. The pennant belonged to Chicago, and in the Windy City the sirens wailed. Those who were unfamiliar with baseball believed that the Russians were at the back door, forcing Mayor Richard Daley, and fire commissioner Robert Quinn—both Sox fans—to issue an apology. It was a night of celebration and revelry on the south side, but in retrospect it was the first death knell of the Go-Go era. Talk of an emerging White Sox dynasty was stilled when the Los Angeles Dodgers proved in the World Series that they were going to do more than just show up. The running game was stymied by Dodger catcher John Roseboro, and the lack of a long ball to complement the White Sox pop-gun attack convinced Veeck that he needed to wheel and deal over the winter. In hindsight this proved to be a tragic mistake, and the undoing of the White Sox in the next two decades.

Roy Sievers, Gene Freese, and Minnie Minoso arrived in time for opening day, 1960. The cost of these fading veterans was prohibitive. Bill Veeck, whose promotional genius was unquestioned, gutted the entire White Sox farm system, which had been carefully assembled by Chuck Comiskey and his lieutenants in the 1950s. The future stars of the sixties, a veritable all-star team, were sacrificed by Veeck who wanted to make his hay in 1960 while the frying pan was still hot. Departing the White Sox were Earl Battey, Johnny Callison, John Romano, Norman Cash, Don Mincher, and in later Veeck deals, Wes Covington and Al Worthington. It would take years to recover from these ill-advised moves. Always sensitive to criticism, Bill Veeck would defend his trades within the context of the times. But the facts are inescapable. The seeds of the White Sox undoing in 1968 and beyond were sewn up at the precise moment of their greatest triumph.

Go-Go, and Nearly Gone (1963–1970)

The erosion continued into 1962, when the White Sox dropped to fifth place. They were still a first-division team in the newly realigned American League, but the infusion of new talent to replace fading veterans was slow in coming. Top names on the Triple-A level included Tommy McCraw, Brian McCall, Joe Hicks, and J.C. Martin, remnants of what was once a good farm system. Bill Veeck bailed out of the picture on June 5, 1961 when he sold the team to Arthur C. Allyn, a Chicago businessman who did not have a clue as to what should be done.

Allyn elevated Edwin Short to the position of general manager. Short was a former radio disc jockey who had worked for years in the White Sox publicity and media relations department. His promotion came as a total surprise, and the members of the press corps wondered if there were any rabbits left inside the hat. That's what it would take because few people believed that Short had the know-how to rebuild the organization top to bottom.

He did better than expected, at least in the early years. Luis Aparicio, Nellie Fox, Billy Pierce, and Al Smith were all traded. Early Wynn was released after failing to register his 300th victory and Sievers disappeared as fast as he came. A blockbuster trade with the Orioles brought Pete Ward, Hoyt Wilhelm, and Dave Nicholson to town, and the arrival of Gary Peters and Joel Horlen after several earlier failures buoyed the White Sox to three consecutive second-place finishes, 1963–65. In 1964, one of the most thrilling pennant races in club history, the White Sox won their last nine games of the year only to finish one game behind the Yankees. The pitching was superb. Led by 20-game winner Gary Peters, and relief ace Hoyt Wilhelm, the staff posted a league-leading 2.72 ERA. Longtime Sox fans remember the 1950s as a good pitcher's decade on the south side. Unquestionably though, the Peters-Horlen-Tommy John tandem was the best since the Black Sox era. The big three were complemented by an outstanding bullpen that included, at various times, Eddie Fisher, Bob Locker, Don McMahon, and Wilbur Wood. With such second-line starters as Juan Pizarro, John Buzhardt, and Jim O'Toole, the Sox were capable of throwing a shutout on any given day. Of course there were the usual share of clunkers. Short elected to keep pitcher Bruce Howard over Dennis McLain based on one spring training game in 1963. But for the most part Short kept the Sox in the thick of things until the inevitable collapse finally occurred in 1968.

An era ended on November 4, 1965, when Al Lopez stepped down after eight seasons at the helm. The genial señor had his detractors in the Chicago press corps—columnist Bill Gleason never forgave Lopez for not starting Billy Pierce in the World Series—but his calm, assured manner translated into winning baseball. Eddie Stanky piloted the club through 1966–1968. The "Brat" was a firebrand, loved by the fans and universally hated by the players for his strict regimens and unforgiving attitudes. During the two and a half years Stanky managed the White Sox, he insulted rival managers, opposing players, and anybody who crossed his path. Stanky called Carl Yastrzemski an all-star from the neck down, Bill Rigney of the Angels a "television manager," and Charlie Dressen "bush." Stanky rewarded Tommy John with a new suit of clothes every time he tossed a complete game, and in the bowels of Comiskey Park he froze baseballs with head groundskeeper Gene Bossard to ensure that his pitchers had a competitive edge when they took the mound. Vintage Stanky.[25]

In 1967 the weak-hitting White Sox nearly stole a pennant. Ken Berry paced the hitters with a .241 average. And yet they remained right up there until the last week of the season, until dropping a twi-night doubleheader to the last-place Kansas City A's on September 27—Black Wednesday—the day the music died. Boston and Minnesota had both lost their games that day, and the Sox were primed to take over first place by virtue of beating a doormat. Only this doormat introduced a host of exciting rookies that night—Sal Bando, Reggie Jackson, and Joe Rudi. To add final insult to an injury that was slow to heal, Luke Appling managed the A's that night. The 1967 pennant race was over, and with it the White Sox 17-year reign in the first division of the American League.

With all that pitching, and the addition of Tommy Davis and Louie Aparicio for 1968 the Sox were an early season favorite to win the crown. They finished miserably, in eighth. The reasons were hard to pinpoint, since this was the same cast of characters that nearly won a pennant a year earlier. Was 1967 a fluke? No, that memorable summer was not just a flash in the pan. The Stanky Sox played as a cohesive unit, bound together in their mutual dislike of the manager. It was a mistake to trade Don Buford to Baltimore for Aparicio. The presence of Davis, and two late-season acquisitions, Ken Boyer, and Rocky Colavito, upset the delicate chemistry that catapulted the Sox to an early lead in 1967.[26] A year later the balance was gone. Not even the pitching could sustain them. Joel Horlen's best years were behind him, and Gary Peters could no longer carry the team or dominate the staff as he had done in 1963–64.

A ballclub that had won 89 games in 1967 lost 106 just three years later. The farm system was bereft of talent and the pitching that had sustained the franchise for so many years went south. And so did the attendance. Art Allyn called for the construction of a new downtown stadium but the city fathers took no action. The south side had been plagued by racial tensions since 1966. Nervous suburbanites stayed away because of a fear of black crime, unjustified as it was. Police statistics showed that the Bridgeport community was safer than the neighborhood the Cubs played in, but the reputation was firmly planted, and only a winning ballclub could reverse this ominous pattern. The resurgence of the Cubs in 1967 hurt the White Sox the most. Ernie Banks, Ron Santo, and company were colorful personalities. The Sox really had no one to excite the fans or provide the longball stimulus to make this team attractive to peripheral baseball fans.

Barely afloat in a sea of red ink, Art Allyn tinkered with the notion of selling the team to Milwaukee investors. This was avoided when brother John purchased the club at the conclusion of the moribund 1969 season. A Christmas card sent out by the front office summarized the prevailing mood on the south side, by pleading: "Oh come all ye faithful!"

The Team that Could Not Afford to be Poor (1971–1980)

It took another reshuffling and the infusion of new talent in the baseball organization to turn this floundering ballclub around. Ed Short, who had become increasingly monolithic and testy in his dealings with the media, was fired on September 2, 1970. The embattled Sox G.M. traded away productive veterans like Gary Peters without receiving commensurate value in return. A sorry collection of has-beens and never-weres populated the roster at the tail end of the Short (sided) era. Gary Bell, Lee Stange, Woodie Held, Barry Moore, and the lamentable Gerry "Wheat Germ Kid" Janeski were a few of the names passing in review before disbelieving eyes during those awful years.

In 1971 the Sox emerged from their three-year slide under a new manager, Chuck Tanner, and a dynamic, imaginative front office team headed by Roland Hemond and Stu Holcomb. The Sox trotted out in red pin-striped uniforms with a cast of characters that had arrived overnight. Rick Reichardt, Pat Kelly, Mike Andrews, and Tom Bradley were among the key Roland Hemond acquisitions that paced the 1971 comeback. Tanner converted Wilbur Wood to a starting role, and the portly knuckleballer responded with 22 wins and a nifty 1.91 ERA. What was still missing in the middle of the lineup was a bona fide power hitter—to sandwich around Melton, Reichardt, and Carlos May. That winter Richard Anthony Allen arrived from Los Angeles for Tommy John. The controversial mysterious Allen was called the "Savior" by Hemond for his 1972 heroics: 37 homers, 113 RBIs, and a .308 average. Certainly no clear thinking fan can look past Dick Allen and what he meant to the Sox for three years. But the team was improving without him. In the broadcast booth announcer Harry

Caray proved he was perfectly attuned to the White Sox market, a blue-collar beer drinking constituency largely ignored since Bill Veeck had left town.

Fearful that Allen might bolt if he suddenly became unhappy, Chuck Tanner devised two sets of rules, one for his temperamental star and another for everyone else. To placate Richie, his brother Hank occupied a spot on the roster in 1973 in order to help him qualify for the baseball pension. In 1974, a year in which Dick Allen led the league in home runs, and the team could manage only a modest .500 finish, the great enigma walked out. He was through with baseball, as he explained in his memoirs, because Ron Santo had a few ideas of his own about team leadership, and his old pal Chuck Tanner had suddenly decided to assert himself as manager. "Then one day Chuck came up to me and told me the dissension was ruining the team. He said, 'there's only room for one guy to run this team—and that's me.' That's when I knew things would never be the same. I decided it was time to go."[27] A talented athlete? There is no doubt. A pampered prima donna in Chicago? That much is also true. Allen was shown nothing but the warmest affection by the fans and media. He repaid it in kind, by walking out on John Allyn at a time when the harried Sox owner needed box office presence to sustain a meager profit.

In 1975 the Sox tumbled to fifth and attendance fell through the floor again. At season's end John Allyn was in a precarious fix. Unable to meet his payroll and facing a lawsuit from his brother Art, John listened to offers from a Seattle group headed by entertainer Danny Kaye. At the edge of the precipice he resisted the impulse to move the team at a fat profit in order to deal with Bill Veeck who had emerged from quiet retirement on the Maryland shores to submit a bid. It almost ended in disaster. At a league meeting on December 3, 1975, the owners voted the sale down 8–3 with one abstention. The other owners did not approve of Veeck's method of capitalization—or his way of doing business if the truth be known. They gave him 10 days to come up with an additional $1.2 million. It seemed like an impossible task, but Veeck was up to it. He found his million under the bushes and the smoky backrooms of Chicago. When things need to get done fast in clout city . . . you find the way.

At the critical hour dame fortune seems to always smile on this franchise. Veeck was given private assurances by baseball insiders that the controversial reserve clause would never be struck down. Had the Peter Seitz decision been handed down *before* the sale to Veeck had been finalized, it is likely that the team would have wound up in Seattle after all. Though he was no fan of the ancient and patently unfair reserve clause, it was the only weapon left in his cash-poor arsenal to build and maintain a competitive club. Free agency hamstrung Bill

Veeck and his limited partners, who by choice or design refused to participate in the money grubbing sweepstakes. As a result the Sox lost Richie Zisk and Oscar Gamble to Texas and San Diego following the unforgettable 1977 season.

That was the year that Bill Veeck inaugurated his "rent a player" scheme. Zisk and Gamble were picked up in trades during the off-season. Both players were at the end of their contracts and eligible for free agency. The Sox owner decided to take his chances and rent them, naively hoping that they would become so enchanted with the city and the team that perhaps they might come back in 1978. It was another Veeck fairy tale, but it made for lively discussion at any rate.

Stocked with his one-year sluggers, the "South Side Hitmen" pounded out a club-record 192 home runs and finished a surprising third. All previous attendance records were shattered with a winning ballclub and the usual grab bag of zany promotions.

Belly dancers frolicked in the outfield. On "Anti-Superstition Night" a coven of witches pronounced a hex on the opposing teams. A shower was installed in the center-field bleachers for the comfort of the fans, and a variety of ethnic festivals were staged for the benefit of Chicago's large immigrant population. It seemed so silly at the time. Would it not make more sense to divert the money paid to the owners of frisbee-catching dogs to Zisk and Gamble? But with each passing year the lunacy and free-wheeling antics of that era seem strangely missing. After the "Hit Men" summer, Richie Zisk and Oscar Gamble were never able to recapture the old magic with their new teams. What happened to them is a fable of free agency. Sometimes the million-dollar contract carries with it unintended pitfalls. They were the ultimate losers, not the Sox, in this strange new order.

Veeck lost other players to free agency, among them Jorge Orta and Steve Stone. So by 1980 the gags, the gimmicks, and the comical softball style uniforms ceased to be funny as writers and fans alike began to realize that the cupboard was permanently bare. Good players like Jim Spencer and Eric Soderholm were traded because Veeck could no longer pay their salaries. From 1976 to 1979 top draft picks in the January draft went unsigned, and the annual renovation program on deteriorating Comiskey Park was becoming more than Veeck could handle. Of course there were rumors—persistent allegations—that Bill Veeck sat on a pile of his investors' money which was available for the asking. But in every business endeavor going back to the time he owned the Indians, Veeck prided himself on returning a profit to his backers. In all likelihood he would not have tapped this resource even if he could.[28]

In July 1980, the Sox board of directors decided to accept bids from interested parties. For several years Bill Veeck had entertained notions about moving the team out of Chicago, and had spoken with

Denver investors about the possibility. Savior II would have sold out the fans if the conditions were right. Instead, he chose to deal with the DeBartolos of Youngstown, Ohio. The senior Ed DeBartolo soon agreed to purchase the club for $20 million on August 22, 1980. The real estate mogul who owned a string of race tracks remained non-committal about his plans for the White Sox. Many people believed the team was headed to New Orleans despite private assurances that the DeBartolo group would keep the Sox in Chicago.

Commissioner Bowie Kuhn, a man of enduring controversy, nixed the deal, and used his persuasive powers to "convince" the other owners to vote against DeBartolo. No doubt the commissioner was opposed to race track interests besmirching the fair name of baseball. But there were deeper, more pervasive reasons for Kuhn's steadfast opposition to DeBartolo. It has never been adequately explained, though an aid to Edward DeBartolo suggested that Kuhn was afflicted with anti-Italian biases. A second group headed up by Jerry Reinsdorf and Edward M. Einhorn of New York were given the thumbs up by Kuhn and the inner circle on January 29, 1981. Reinsdorf was a real estate mogul who built the Balcor Corporation into one of the nation's leading investment firms. Eddie Einhorn, who once worked as a hot dog vendor at Comiskey Park during the pennant year, had served as an executive producer for CBS sports.

Eddie and Jerry were not Veeck's first choice, and he made this abundantly clear in the next few years by boycotting the park and the team. Despite conciliatory attempts on the part of the new owners, Veeck harbored a deep mistrust and suspicion which the fans were quick to pick up on. Businesslike principles were introduced into an organization accustomed to shirt-sleeve staff meetings. Sales of hard liquor in the ballpark were halted when unbridled rowdy fans threatened to turn the stadium into the world's largest outdoor saloon. The embarrassing softball uniforms were mercifully discarded, and the new owners delved into the free agent market to come up with a trio of blue chips to complement youngsters Harold Baines and Richard Dotson: Carlton Fisk, Greg Luzinski, and Tom Paciorek. Overnight the pattern of losing was reversed. In the 1981 strike year the Sox posted their first winning campaign since the "Hit Men" year. Then just before the 1983 division title something happened which put Reinsdorf and company on the defensive.

It's Not How You Play the Game, It's the Superstation That Counts (1981–1992)

The Cubs were sold to the Tribune Company, a communications conglomerate that also owned WGN Radio and TV ("the World's Greatest Newspaper!", get it?). The benign Wrigleys always viewed the White Sox as their friendly competitors. Their casual, laid-back style permitted the Sox to occasionally gain the upper hand in a town that is admittedly pro-Cub. The truth is, the Chicago National League ballclub had been a slumbering giant for most of the 1970s. All this changed when the *Tribune* bought the Cubbies and began to aggressively market vines and ivy through its twin resources. Seen in 49 states on the cable, the north siders became a national entity while the Sox were relegated to a small UHF outlet seen only in Chicago, and the collar counties.[29]

Had Reinsdorf and Einhorn known of this impending transaction in January 1981, or been able to foresee the cable explosion, perhaps they might have backed away. Again fortune smiled on the White Sox at an opportune moment, forestalling another potential demise, as Eddie Einhorn outlined his marketing strategy. The Sox will be *Chicago's* team, not just a south side curiosity. In the winning seasons it is certainly possible. However the bloom was quickly off the rose when the Sox went into a dizzying tailspin after claiming the A.L. West crown in 1983 by a whopping 20 games. In those important rebuilding years it has been proven time and again that the White Sox cannot compete with the Cubs for the fan's dollar. This was especially true after 1984 when the Cubs won their own division title with colorful Harry Caray acting as the pied piper of the air waves.

An early casualty of the marketing war was Tony LaRussa, one of the finest young managers to emerge from the 1970s. Named by Bill Veeck to replace Don Kessinger in 1979, LaRussa quickly matured into the job. Young enough to understand the contemporary ballplayer, yet far enough removed so that his judgments were not tempered by personal prejudices, Tony LaRussa is a thinking man's manager. But he was sacrificed along with Roland Hemond and Dave Dombrowski, considered to be the architects of the team's success in the early 1980s. Their dismissal was a direct consequence of a reactive policy to what the "world's greatest newspaper" was doing across town.

After drawing two million fans in 1983–84, Einhorn and Reinsdorf noted with growing alarm a steady erosion of gate receipts and precious media support. Coverage of the White Sox began to diminish after 1983 despite heavy-handed denials by WGN and the *Tribune*. Nevertheless it was fact, not myth to most Sox fans. In the late 1970s Bill Veeck protested the injustice by counting column inches in the morning papers to see if his boys were getting a fair shake. Jerry and Eddie never went to these extremes to prove a point. They didn't *have* to. It was as plain to Sox fans as Harry Caray's billboard ads for Budweiser beer and the Cubs. ("Bud Man! Cub Fan!") It was painful.

Rarely after 1984 were the Sox mentioned in the same breath as the Cubs, especially on WGN whose unabashed grandstanding ran against the grain of journalistic objectivity. Their sports talk-show host Chuck Swirsky boasted of being a Cub fan (no word about the

Budweiser, however). "Hey, nobody's talking about the Sox these days!" he reminded one listener with an unmistakable touch of glee. A Sunday afternoon WGN gabfest known as "The Sportswriters" would devote, on the average, an hour to Cub news and a few minutes before the station break to the Sox. Disgruntled listeners would voice an objection from time to time, and referee Ben Bentley would half-heartedly attempt to steer the conversation back to the sorry Sox, usually with no success. "Okay, now we've talked about them," quipped one of Bentley's laconic panelists after a Sox fan's letter was read aloud over the air.

"I don't think what WGN is doing is right," observed a long-time sports reporter affiliated with the Sox flagship station WMAQ. "But they are who they are and they do what they want." In 1988 the Sox radio affiliate converted to an all-news format and scrapped many of their promotional tie-ins and call-in shows with the ballclub. At decade's end the team was nearly as invisible as it had been in 1969–70, regarded as the absolute nadir of Sox history. Even Carlton Fisk had difficulty landing celebrity endorsements. In 1989 the team crashed into the cellar for only the sixth time in their history. The marketing department and the baseball organization were at odds about the proper way to market this team. There was only one thing that was certain. If you can't beat 'em *join* 'em. The White Sox front office bit the bullet and signed a TV deal with WGN, whereby 45 games would be broadcast each year, beginning in 1990. It made a great deal of sense for the White Sox who were desperate to cultivate a younger generation of fans, not only in Chicago but outside the region. For WGN, always eager to corner the volatile local sports market, the White Sox were an important addition, albeit a losing one.

The elephant and mouse syndrome had preyed on the minds of nervous Sox executives saddled with a deteriorating ballclub playing in an archaic stadium. To stimulate the media and refocus attention back to the south side, broadcaster Ken "Hawk" Harrelson was promoted to vice president and general manager, replacing the low-key but quietly effective Roland Hemond for the 1986 season. This occurred at a time when the marketing department believed that citywide supremacy was an attainable dream. The eccentric Hawk was great in the booth but his ideas about running a ballclub bordered on the bizarre—like doing away with the farm system.

Then there was the problem of Tony LaRussa, who was a Hemond man. The Sox manager was understandably miffed by the strange new paths his team was heading in following a convincing division championship when the Sox ran away with everything except the kitchen sink. Tensions between Harrelson and LaRussa exploded in June 1986. Caught in the middle of a misguided marketing plan ("The

Hawk Wants *You!*"), Jerry Reinsdorf was forced to sink or swim with his new general manager. Tony was fired after logging seven years at the helm, and the ball of yarn quickly unraveled after that. Most Chicago fans were happy to see LaRussa go, as they bitterly recalled his many feuds with departed announcers Harry Caray and Jimmy Piersall years earlier. These same fans who still harbor a smoldering grudge against the closed-mouthed, misunderstood LaRussa have chosen to look past his undeniable accomplishments on the field. Given a new lease on life with the Oakland A's, LaRussa has emerged as a Cadillac manager.

Harrelson lasted less than a year. After the team stumbled out of the gate in 1986 the "Hawk" was seen less and less at the park. Promoting a flamboyant general manager instead of the team was an ill-conceived stratagem. Attendance continued to plummet downward. The losses mounted, and the farm system which Harrelson had disdained was stocked with journeymen minor leaguers. Soon the Hawk became as extinct as the Dodo Bird.

This was the worst of all times to announce to a skeptical city that Comiskey Park was about to fall down, but Reinsdorf and Einhorn set the ball in motion just when their credibility had sunk to an all-time low. For the next three seasons the game on the field took a backseat to the one question on everyone's lips: to build or not to build.

The End Is Only the Beginning, Comiskey Park Old and New

After Addison was ruled out as the future home of the Sox, and the mayor and the governor decreed that the new facility shall be built across the street, a period of inactivity followed. Nearly a year passed, and all the politicians could do was disagree on the appointees to the Illinois Sports Facilities Authority, given the task of land acquisition and sub-contracting. In St. Petersburg city officials began courting the White Sox, and there were more than a few members of the front office who would have welcomed a move to a sun-belt city where the team would enjoy a virtual monopoly over broadcasting, souvenir licensing, and the undivided attention of the press.

During their flirtation with St. Pete, Sox officials failed to consider one likely scenario. What would have happened if after two or three years in Florida the attendance fell off, and the large population of senior citizens became apathetic to baseball in a sterile indoor stadium with all the charm of the Seattle Kingdome? Florida, with its many outdoor diversions, is still an unproven commodity. Who is to say that a team is guaranteed immediate success by virtue of being the first to inhabit a geographic area?

When the 1988 season began, a move to Florida seemed to be in the cards. The original funding package was sent back to the Illinois

Legislature. In essence the stakes had been raised. It was now necessary to pass a two-per-cent hotel-motel tax to help fund construction costs, estimated to be in the neighborhood of $100 million. Legislators, especially those outside the Chicago metro area, were opposed to any bill that would divert money away from education and public works. "As long as Illinois is balancing its budget by not paying the bills of Public Aid patients in nursing homes and hospitals, and not supporting community mental health facilities, and not funding public education at every level to the extent of its commitment—I cannot see spending large sums of money even to keep the White Sox," said State Representative Mary Grace Stern.[30] The intangibles—what a team brings to a city in terms of prestige and seasonal tourist income—were largely ignored by these same fine representatives who needed to be "coaxed" by governor James Thompson.

In the capitol building in Springfield the governor faced an uphill battle. The vote was scheduled for June 30, 1988—the last day of the legislative session. Jerry and Eddie decided to maintain an uncharacteristic low profile during the deliberations. Their decision not to lobby for the passage of their stadium bill was a cause of concern to many legislators who concluded that the Sox owners wanted to move to Florida all along. Sox management was undoubtedly convinced that a move was inevitable.

Editorials in the two Chicago dailies generally supported the stadium bill, but there was no great civic outcry, no outraged indignation from Sox fans. Where was the groundswell? The loudest protests came from a handful of displaced residents whose homes were scheduled to be razed. The South Armour Square Coalition, as they called themselves, would be richly compensated and relocated to better housing in the same neighborhood. These assurances from the Stadium Authority did not placate the leaders of this group—some of whom came from the far north side to stir up long dormant racial hatred and trade on the collective prejudices of both black and white. It was an ugly, depressing situation that appeared to be hopeless.

The clock ticked down. Finally at the eleventh hour two grass-roots fan organizations emerged to take matters in hand. A small north side contingency known as "Sox Fans on Deck" began a petition drive. Operating out of a small, cramped law office in the heart of Cub territory, S.F.O.D. placed ads in downstate newspapers and solicited funds from well-known Sox fans across the city to pay for these costly placements. Within two weeks 30,000 signatures were gathered and presented to State Senator William Marovitz at a massive downtown rally held on June 17, 1988. The petitions were delivered to Springfield the next week. On June 27, just three days before the fateful vote, James T. Richards of suburban Oak Lawn chartered five busses to ferry as many Sox fans as he could find for a day-long excursion to the capitol for a little old-fashioned lobbying. Richards' group was called "Save Our Sox" (S.O.S), the name borrowed from an earlier, ill-advised attempt to save the park. Several hundred enthusiasts carrying placards and handbills camped on the front lawn, singing, cooking hotdogs, and arguing with the legislature—with one common purpose. Governor Thompson spoke with the group at length, urging them to summon their representatives from the chambers. The feeling was echoed across party lines, by Democratic Speaker of the House Michael Madigan, an arch foe of Thompson.

The matter was considered by the Illinois Senate and the House as its last item of business for the calendar year, shortly before midnight on June 30. In the waning moments the outcome hung in the balance. Looking tired and spent, the governor paced the aisles of both legislative branches collecting on every favor accumulated in his 12 years in office. Never has the state witnessed a more stirring drama in the corridors of power. Then as the last seconds were counted off the roll call was taken. The bill passed . . . by the skin of its teeth. The final count was 90–81.

Much hoopla surrounded the final historic season at the venerable Comiskey Park on Chicago's south side. Perhaps the single season's highlight, however, came on the very date of the doomed park's 80th anniversary celebration—July 1, 1990. On that historic afternoon New York Yankees journeyman righthander Andy Hawkins would hurl one of baseball's most bizarre yet memorable games. Hawkins would no-hit the punchless Chisox yet somehow manage to lose in the process when two dropped fly balls in the eighth frame handed the locals a cheap 4–0 victory. Yet the season-long sideshow promoting the old park's final curtain call was almost outstripped in the end by the on-field excitement, a healthy dose of pennant fever generated by a competitive young Chicago team which finished second to the veteran Oakland Athletics in the summer's thrilling title chase.

Bedecked in snappy black and silver pinstripes, the 1991 edition of these rennovated Chisox inaugurated a state-of-the-art replacement Comiskey Park with a second consecutive runner-up AL Western Division finish. The new park itself proved a major disappointment for baseball's tradition-minded fans, featuring distant vantage-points from upperdeck seating and a blaring scoreboard designed to blast commerical messages during every imaginable dead-space in the diamond action. If the atmosphere of the park was sterile and often jarring to the senses, however, the baseball itself was now decidedly better on Chicago's south side. A phenomenal new hitting star had been born in first sacker Frank Thomas, who slugged at a .318 pace in 1991 and at .323 in 1992.

And Jack McDowell finally justified management's patience with a 20–10 (3.18 ERA) 1992 ledger. Despite a somewhat disappointing third-place finish in 1992, under new skipper Gene Lamont the long-suffering Pale Hose seemed finally poised for a serious pennant challenge as diamond action headed into the mid-1990s.

Notes

1. Gus Axelson, *Commy: The Life Story of Charles Comiskey* (Chicago: Reilly & Lee, 1919), pp. 38–43. Comiskey was singled out by Ted Sullivan, an upperclassman at St. Mary's College in Kansas. Sullivan went on to organize the Dubuque Rabbits of the Northwestern League. He signed Comiskey to his first professional contract in 1879. See also Harold Dellinger's "Theodore Sullivan," in *Nineteenth Century Baseball Stars* (Cooperstown, N.Y.: Society for American Baseball Research, 1989), p. 120.

2. *Chicago Tribune*, April 23, 1924. In a revealing two-part series, Ban Johnson recounts his career: failures, triumphs, and the founding of the American League. The machinations employed by the wily National League owners to thwart his expansion plans into Chicago, Cleveland, and Philadelphia are discussed at length.

3. *Ibid.*, November 21, 1893. The Western League was formed in 1879, and revived by the magnates at this crucial Indianapolis meeting. For a good discussion of the American League's early development see: Harold Seymour's "The National League Meets Its Match," in *Baseball: The Early Years* (New York: Oxford University Press, 1960), pp. 307–342.

4. *Ibid.* At the second league meeting held a year later in Chicago's Wellington Hotel, Johnson intended to resign in order to return to his newspaper job. "One year in baseball convinced me it was mainly a matter of grief," he said. Jimmy Manning of the Kansas City team persuaded Johnson to hang on another year. One year turned into 33.

5. *Ibid.*, August 21, 1901. Clark Griffith threatened a walkout over this. Shugarts was blacklisted after trading blows with Haskell. The umpire instigated the brawl by pounding the Sox shortstop over the head with his face mask.

6. *Ibid.*

7. *Ibid.*, July 14, 1906. It is probable that the famous nickname was bandied about much earlier in the season. However this is the earliest published account of the "Hitless Wonders" that I have been able to locate.

8. *Ibid.*, October 10, 1906.

9. Dennis Bingham, "A Fan's Eye View of the World Series," *Baseball in Chicago* (Chicago: Society for American Baseball Research, 1986), p. 48. Quoted from contemporary newspaper copy.

10. *Chicago Inter Ocean*, October 15, 1906. Quote.

11. "The Home Plate," souvenir of the Woodland Bards. Chicago White Sox archives. Verse by Joseph Farrell. The annual forays to the Wisconsin north woods occurred at the end of each baseball season. Camp Jerome was an enclosed hunting resort and lodge. The grounds were stocked with fresh game in anticipation of the arrival of the Chicago "dudes." Comiskey entertained in grand style. One year he purchased a house boat in order to run excursions down the lower Mississippi River. The good ship "White Sox" ran aground about the same time as the ballclub.

12. *Chicago Tribune*, July 17, 1902. Quote. McGraw incurred Comiskey's wrath for what the Old Roman believed to be deliberate sabotage of the American League.

13. Banquet program, Congress Hotel testimonial, March 10, 1914, Chicago White Sox archives. The best account of the world tour can be found in the Axelson book, pp. 219–262.

14. *Chicago American*, February 1, 1956. Quoted from Leo Fischer's column eulogizing the memory of this unfairly maligned athlete. For years Weaver wrote letters to Judge Landis—no doubt unanswered—begging for redemption, and a small share of his baseball pension. One of these heart-rending letters was displayed by the Chicago Historical Society during its 1989 exhibit "the Black Sox." Weaver was working as a race track tout at the time of his death.

15. See: Harold Seymour, *Baseball: The Golden Age* (New York: Oxford University Press, 1971), pp. 274–399, for the most lucid account of the Black Sox scandal published to date. Also: the *Chicago Tribune*, July 26, 1921. According to Ed Cicotte the first contact with the gamblers occurred in New York, at the Hotel Ansonia, not in Boston which Eliot Asinof suggests in *Eight Men Out*.

16. *Chicago Tribune*, September 24, 1919. Kid Gleason to James Cruisinberry, quoted. In this same published account the paper noted with wonderment that "with the announcement of dates for the staging of the world's series betting on the great baseball classic picked up in Indianapolis today and quite a few freak wagers were offered and taken at the local betting boards."

17. Eliot Asinof, *Eight Men Out* (New York: Holt, Rinehart & Winston, 1963), p. 86, quoted. This animosity between Comiskey and Johnson was years in the making. The first strain in their relationship was a philosophical one. Comiskey was desirous of having the one team in Chicago, playing in one league—his own. Ban Johnson favored peaceful coexistence and a balanced two-league system. Minor resentments, professional jealousy, and various disagreements exploded into an all-out feud in 1918 when Johnson awarded John Picus Quinn, a highly regarded pitcher, to the Yankees on a technicality. After that, the two founders of the league were barely civil to each other.

18. *Chicago Tribune*, September 30, 1920. Quoted in the morning editions. Whether the kid in the streets actually walked up to Jackson and begged him to "say it ain't so" is a matter of speculation. The great slugger said many things without benefit of counsel, but in his slow southern backwoods way, Jackson was smart enough to realize that he had been hustled by the sharpers—Rothstein, Comiskey, Austrian, Gandil . . . "they've hung it on me," he sighed. "They ruined me when I went to the shipyards but I don't care what happens now. I guess I'm through with baseball. I wasn't wise enough like Chick was to beat them to it, but some of them will sweat it out before the show is over."

19. Seymour, *The Golden Age*, pp. 382–388. Landis offered the lame excuse that he could not concern himself with events that occurred prior to his appointment as commissioner. This seemed to contradict his pledge to root out all players implicated in gambling regardless of the circumstances.

20. *Chicago Tribune*, March 21, 1921. Quoted. The Black Sox had been placed on Landis's ineligible list long before the outcome of the trial was decided. Comiskey's comments were made in Paso Robles, Texas, while he was en route to the team's spring training headquarters in Waxahachie.

21. *Ibid.*, June 16, 1930. Art Shires and his teammate Bill Cissell were a hard-drinking, fast living duo. In the spring of 1929 the two Sox players were suspended for breaking curfew rules. These two gifted athletes might have enjoyed long rewarding careers, but this was not to be the case. Shires was traded to Washington when he refused to give up his rowdy habits, and Cissell buried himself in a bottle. The former bonus baby, purchased for $123,000 in 1927, lasted five seasons with the Sox before fading out. Years later he was

found dead in a tenement house not far from Comiskey Park. Chuck Comiskey paid his funeral expenses when no one else came forward. There is an uncom-firmed story—legend if you will—that the ghost of Cissell haunts Comiskey Park.

22. *White Sox Yarns*, December 1948. Chicago White Sox publication.

23. *Chicago Tribune*, October 30, 1956.

24. *Cleveland Plain Dealer*, August 31, 1959.

25. Rich Lindberg, *Who's on Third? The Chicago White Sox Story* (South Bend: Icarus Press, 1983), p. 120. The accusations of baseball freezing first surfaced in 1965 when Detroit pitcher Hank Aguirre accused Lopez of the treachery. The mystery deepened two years later when Eddie Stanky decided to make good use of a humidifier below the stands. According to Roger Bossard, second-generation Comiskey Park groundskeeper who was a mere apprentice at the time, the game balls were placed in a humidifier 12 days before a homestand. When they were removed a few hours before game time, the outer surfaces were dry but the centers gained over two ounces in moisture. The effect of course, deadened the flight of the ball. The reasoning being, of course, that if the Sox couldn't hit, neither shall the opponents.

26. Bob Vanderberg, *From Lane and Fain to Zisk and Fisk* (Chicago: Chicago Review Press, 1982), pp. 280–281. Tommy McCraw, a speedy first baseman who failed to live up to his press clippings, puts forth the theory that the "togetherness" of the 1967 team was disrupted by the presence of fading veterans in 1968.

27. Dick Allen and Tim Whitaker, *Crash: The Life and Times of Dick Allen* (New York: Ticknor & Fields, 1989), pp. 151–152. Richie "call me Dick" Allen was shown every consideration, and extended the greatest latitude by Chuck Tanner who patiently answered his critics by saying that his star player "leads by example." Allen commanded the largest salary of anyone on that ballclub and was honored by Chicago fans in ways unheard of during his Philadelphia years. Allen's decision to jump the Sox at the end of the 1974 season is simply inexcusable; a betrayal and sellout of the fans, his teammates, and the benevolent Mr. John Allyn who is the forgotten hero of that decade.

28. Phil Hersh, "Is Money Preventing the Sox From Cashing In?" *Chicago Sun-Times*, July 23, 1979. The White Sox were an impoverished franchise from the late 1960s on. The lack of cash in the till prevented them from maintaining Comiskey Park, participating in free agency, and holding on to the players developed in their own minor league system. Veeck was hardest hit by this changed economic picture. Had he kept the club a few more years, he would have received additional TV revenue in the new contract which would have ended his total dependence on gate receipts to sustain a profit. Nowadays it is possible to make money without drawing so much as a solitary fan.

29. The White Sox TV troubles began in 1948 when the FCC granted Chicago just one independent station frequency, WGN. By contrast New York City had two, WPIX, and WWOR. In the very beginning a number of Sox night home games were televised by WGN, but this quickly changed in the 1950s when the station developed a nighttime lineup of programs. Because WGN was unwilling to alter its programming to accommodate the Sox, the southsiders were seen less and less in the Chicago area. The White Sox games were aired on the weekends at home, provided they were played during the day. In 1968 Art Allyn chose to end the 20-year association with WGN in order to sign an agreement with an emerging UHF outlet, WFLD, channel 32. At the time the deal seemed like a good one for both parties. Allyn got the station to broadcast 144 games home and away, while channel 32 gained some exposure in the Chicago market. There were immediate problems. The

announcers Jack Drees and Dave Martin were boring, and anyone who wanted to see the Sox had to purchase a de-coder box in order to pick up the UHF signal. By the time the era of the "superstation" rolled around in the 1980s the White Sox were left out in the cold. While the Cubs were cultivating a nationwide audience, Einhorn and Reinsdorf contemplated the failures of their own pet project: Sportsvision, the pay-TV flop that was once regarded to be a pot of gold at the end of the rainbow. Sportsvision was sold, and was eventually absorbed into Sportschannel of New York.

30. Letter to the author, June 2, 1988. Ms. Stern was never swayed to vote for the stadium bill, though many legislative opponents changed their minds at the critical hour.

Annotated Bibliography

There is a scarcity of good secondary material about the American League's oldest franchise. Despite a long and colorful history, publishers have been reluctant in recent years to issue books about the team. The few that have appeared in bookstores have typically followed pennant-winning seasons or exciting years that have generally come after long dry spells. This pattern began all the way back in 1919 when Gus Axelson's biography of Charles Comiskey appeared—during the ill-fated 1919 World Series. Second class in the second city has often extended from the playing fields of Comiskey to the marketing departments of U.S. publishing houses.

Asinof, Eliot. *Eight Men Out: The Black Sox and the 1919 World Series*. New York: Holt, Rinehart and Winston, 1963. 302 pp.
   The story of the Black Sox is told in quasi-novel style. Asinof invented dialog between the players and the owner that should not be taken literally. Nevertheless the book remains a classic of baseball publishing, despite several glaring factual errors. For a deeper understanding of the events leading up to the Black Sox Scandal, and its tragic aftermath Harold Seymour's *Baseball: The Golden Age*, New York: Oxford University Press, 1971, pp. 274–399, is highly recommended.

Axelson, Gustav. *Commy: The Life Story of Charles A. Comiskey, The Grand Old Roman of Baseball and for Nineteen Years the President and Owner of the Chicago White Sox*. Chicago: Reilly & Lee, 1919. 320 pp.
   Until the long awaited biography of the "Old Roman" is finally released, Axelson's sympathetic treatment of Comiskey remains the only published biography in book-length form to date. The book appeared during the 1919 World Series to capitalize on the public's interest in the White Sox. The closing chapter contains a statement from Comiskey which has emerged as one of the great comic ironies of baseball history. "Crookedness and baseball do not mix. It [baseball] has become immeasurably more popular as the years have gone by. It will be greater yet. This year, 1919, is the greatest season of them all."

Berke, Art, and Paul Schmitt. *This Date In Chicago White Sox History*. New York: Stein & Day, 1982.
   The "day by day" concept of sports publishing has resulted in several fine editions of team history. This however, is not one of them. The research was slipshod and the book is unusually thin for the available subject matter. It appears that the authors did not spend enough time in front of the newspaper micro-film machines tracking down game results, trades, and the front office imbroglios that might have lent color and drama to the otherwise bland text. Instead, readers are subjected to a litany of player birthdates and events from the all-too-recent past.

Brown, Warren. *The Chicago White Sox*. New York: G.P. Putnam's Sons, 1952. 248 pp.

The story goes that Warren Brown, an esteemed newspaper columnist for the Hearst newspapers in Chicago, made a bet one day. He wagered that he could write the history of the White Sox and submit it to his publisher in the course of a weekend. When *The Chicago White Sox* appeared in 1952, the reporters on the sports desk of the *American* chuckled at the thought, and paid up. Brown covered the team for nearly 30 years prior to the publication of this team history—the first since the franchise was founded in 1900—and it sadly lacks the depth of the author's rich experience. The first 50 pages are a rehash of material that appeared in Axelson's earlier biography, and the wit and perception of Brown's "So They Tell Me" column is absent from the pages of this book.

Carmichael, John. "The Chicago White Sox." In *The American League*, 53–82. New York: Grosset & Dunlap, 1966.

Veteran baseball writer John Carmichael opened his "Barber Shop" column in the pages of the *Daily News* in the 1930s. For years the liveliest baseball discussion in town could be found here in the *News*. When he retired from the daily grind, Carmichael went to work for the White Sox in a public relations capacity. The genuine affection he felt for the embattled Comiskeys is reflected in this survey of major events of Chisox history. The team chapter was reprinted from the pages of *Sport Magazine* (June 1951), and updated in 1966.

Condon, David. *The Go-Go Chicago White Sox*. New York: Coward-McCann, 1960. 220 pp.

When the Sox captured their first pennant in 40 years the rush was on to celebrate the achievement in print form and souvenir paraphernalia. There were ashtrays, drinking glasses, pennants and this hastily assembled sketchbook which appeared in hard cover prior to the opening of the 1960 season. Condon inherited the fabled "Wake of the News Column" in the Chicago *Tribune*. The wake was lovingly handed down through generations from Ring Lardner to Charles Lait, to Arch Ward and finally to Condon—all great journalists in their own right. Yet I am sure that Dave Condon would be the first to admit that this book is not counted among his finer literary efforts. He races through the 1906 World Series, the Black Sox, and all the years in between before getting to the meat of the book: the 1959 player profiles. A year later the book was as obsolete as yesterday's newspaper.

Eskenazi, Gerald. *Bill Veeck: A Baseball Legend*. New York: McGraw-Hill, 1988. 182 pp.

Some people have a moment or a year. Bill Veeck had a midget. The Eddie Gaedel story is given wide play in this treatment of the major events of Bill Veeck's life, but little attention is paid to the Sox owner's private life. It is a shame, because the public and private Bill Veeck were often at odds. The temptation on the part of many baseball free thinkers who write for a living is to swallow the Veeck myth, hook, line, and sinker. Barnum Bill spent a lifetime ruffling the feathers of the baseball aristocracy; Spike Briggs, George Weiss, Ford Frick, et al. They were wealthy, arrogant men and therefore unworthy of respect, in Veeck's way of thinking. Yet the man who enjoyed tweeking the nose of the establishment was himself the son of a millionaire who sent him to the best private schools. His imperfections of character are revealed in the interviews conducted with persons better acquainted with Veeck than the New York-based author. Alfred Wright who reviewed Veeck's first book decided that his ramblings against the monied class were a pet obsession. Yet this south side folk hero flew to Denver hat in hand, to offer the White Sox on a platter to oil-man Marvin Davis. Why he desired to sell out the Chicago fans in this way remains a mystery, and one that is not adequately explained here. A quote from former announcer Jimmy Piersall captures the essence of Veeck best, I think, when he said: "In Cleveland he took over players already good. In Chicago, actually, he took that club down. His forte was communication with the press, communication with the public, and his promotions."

Gold, Eddie. *Eddie Gold's White Sox and Cubs Trivia Book.* Chicago: Follett Publishing Co., 1981. 142 pp.

Includes miscellaneous records, a listing of no-hitters, Sox players who played for the Cubs, and a thumbnail sketch of team history. The author writes a trivia column for the Chicago *Sun-Times*, and is an acknowledged expert on movies, the Cubs, and baseball minutiae. In the photograph accompanying his column, Mr. Gold wears a Cub baseball hat—which raised the hackles of the White Sox publicity department and fueled the old complaints about journalistic objectivity in the Windy City.

Lindberg, Richard. *Sox: The Complete Record of Chicago White Sox Baseball.* New York: Macmillan, 1984. 432 pp.

Graphics by John Warner Davenport. An off-shoot of the very successful *Macmillan Baseball Encyclopedia*, this volume is part of an ongoing series that blends statistics, graphic analysis, and narrative history into a pleasing package. Proper attention is devoted to the pre-1950 seasons, an element lacking from the earlier *Who's on Third?*

————. *Stuck on the Sox.* Evanston: Sassafrass Press, 1978. 191 pp.

A memoir of growing up on Chicago's northwest side during the Cub years of the mid to late 1960s. This small-sized paperback was the first book about the White Sox to appear on the newsstands since Condon's 1960 effort. *Stuck on the Sox* was a companion volume to Rick Schwab's *Stuck on the Cubs*, a local bestseller in 1977. Both books sold well and were to form the basis of a team series cutting across all professional sports. The plan was cancelled in consideration of the publisher's decision to market a line of pizza cookware.

————. *Who's On Third? The Chicago White Sox Story.* South Bend: Icarus Press, 1983. 287 pp.

The timing was right for a serious look at the White Sox, and the publication of this team history coincided with the club's 1983 division title. The publisher required that the format parallel Jim Langford's *The Game Is Never Over*. As a result, discussion of the pre-1950 period is limited. The focus is on the seasons, the personalities, and the off-field turmoil characterizing White Sox history since 1950. An all-time roster, off-beat records, and box scores from memorable games are included in a lavish index.

Logan, Bob. *Miracle on 35th Street: Winnin' Ugly With the 1983 White Sox.* South Bend: Icarus Press, 1983. 175 pp.

In an attempt to wring a last, fast buck out of the euphoria of the 1983 division title, the publisher recruited *Tribune* sportswriter Bob Logan to recount the highlights of the Sox late season dash to the playoffs. The story is told through player profiles and interviews, with a statistics section following the text. The 1984 swan-dive coupled with various production issues doomed the book to a quick death on the stands.

Luhrs, Victor. *The Great Baseball Mystery: the 1919 World Series.* Cranbury, N.J.: A.S. Barnes & Co., 1966. 318 pp.

The author offers a provocative hypothesis that the Redlegs would have won the World Series even if the Black Sox played it squarely. His contention is that the clean Sox played worse than Jackson and company.

Vanderberg, Bob. *From Lane and Fain to Zisk and Fisk*. Chicago: Chicago Review Press, 1982. 376 pp.

The emphasis here is on the players, managers, and front-office personnel since the mid-1950s. Vanderberg interviewed the men who put the go in go-go, including Jim Rivera, Minnie Minoso, and Luis Aparicio. The Frank Lane-Chuck Comiskey story is discussed. However Vanderberg neglected to get Chuck Comiskey's side of the story making this an uneven, judgmental account that ignores the contributions the young magnate made to rebuild the torn Sox in the early fifties. Taken as a whole, *Lane and Fain* is a good personal memoir; not up to *The Boys of Summer*, but interesting and nostalgic to Sox fans born in the "baby boom."

Veeck, Bill and Ed Linn. *The Hustler's Handbook*. New York: G.P. Putnam's Sons, 1965. 344 pp.

"You don't have to be a hustler to be a promoter," says Bill Veeck in his opening remarks, but it certainly helps. There is no doubt that in his lifetime Bill Veeck was both, though he would probably say he was more of the promoter. For White Sox fans interested in a new slant on the 1919 Black Sox see pp. 252–299, detailing Harry Grabiner's 1919 diary. The tell-all diary of Charles Comiskey's right-hand man was allegedly found in a crack in the wall under the stands of the ballpark by one Fred Krehbiel. The account is a fascinating one, but the diary is not in public domain. It would be good to take a second look.

———. *Veeck As In Wreck*. New York: G.P. Putnam's Sons, 1962. 380 pp.

Barnum Bill's autobiography enhanced his reputation as a baseball maverick, but the criticism of Chuck Comiskey is patently unfair. Young Chuck was capricious in his ways, and not without fault. Veeck acknowledges, but fails to pay a debt to the ancien Comiskey regime which *built* the team that won the 1959 pennant. His promotions and enthusiasm translated into record attendance, but the mechanisms were already in place by 1959. As a consequence the Sox were big winners, but the role of Chuck, Frank Lane, and John Rigney is diminished in this account.

Wittingham, Richard. *The Chicago White Sox: A Pictorial History*. Chicago: Contemporary Books, 1982. 153 pp.

Another fast start, renewed interest in the White Sox, and the promise of a championship that never materialized resulted in the publication of this thin volume of photographs punctuated by occasional narrative text and statistics. Too many of the photos have been previously published by the team in its yearbooks and game programs, which is regrettable since a good coffee-table-sized pictorial would be a welcome addition to the historiography.

Year-by-Year Standings and Season Summaries

Year	Pos.	Record	Pct.	GB	Manager	Player	BA	Player	HR	Player	W-L	ERA
1900*	1st	82–53	.608	+4	Comiskey	Padden	.284	Shugarts	5	Denzer	20–10	...
1901	1st	83–53	.610	+4	Griffith	Jones	.340	Mertes	5	Griffith	24–7	2.67
1902	4th	74–60	.552	8	Griffith	Jones	.321	Isbell	4	Patterson	20–12	3.06
1903	7th	60–77	.438	30.5	Callahan	Green	.309	Green	6	White	17–16	2.13
1904	3rd	89–65	.578	6	Callahan / Jones	Green	.265	Jones	3	Owen	21–15	1.94
1905	2nd	92–60	.605	2	Jones	Donahue	.287	Jones, Sullivan, Isbell	2	Altrock	22–12	1.88
1906	1st	93–58	.616	+3	Jones	Isbell	.279	Jones, Sullivan	2	Owen	22–13	2.33
1907	3rd	87–64	.576	5.5	Jones	Dougherty	.270	Rohe, Dougherty	2	Walsh	24–18	1.60
1908	3rd	88–64	.579	1.5	Jones	Dougherty	.278	Walsh, Jones, Isbell	1	Walsh	40–15	1.42
1909	4th	78–74	.513	20	Sullivan	Dougherty	.285	Hahn, Altizer, Dougherty, Cravath	1	Smith	25–17	1.80
1910	6th	68–85	.444	35.5	Duffy	Dougherty	.248	Gandil	2	Walsh	18–20	1.27
1911	4th	77–74	.510	24	Duffy	McIntyre	.323	Bodie	4	Walsh	27–18	2.22
1912	4th	78–76	.506	28	Callahan	Bodie	.294	Bodie, Lord	5	Walsh	27–17	2.15
1913	5th	78–74	.513	17.5	Callahan	Chase	.286	Bodie	8	Russell	22–16	1.91
1914	6thT	70–84	.455	30	Callahan	Fournier	.311	Benz	6	Benz	14–19	2.26
1915	3rd	93–61	.604	9.5	Rowland	E. Collins	.332	Scott	5	Scott	24–11	2.03
1916	2nd	89–65	.578	2	Rowland	Jackson	.341	Felsch	7	Russell	17–11	2.42
1917	1st	100–54	.649	+9	Rowland	Felsch	.308	Felsch	6	Cicotte	28–12	1.53
1918	6th	57–67	.460	17	Rowland	Weaver	.300	E. Collins	2	Cicotte	12–19	2.64

*American League designated as Minor League.

Year	Pos.	Record	Pct.	GB	Manager	Player	BA	Player	HR	Player	W-L	ERA
1919	1st	88–52	.629	+3.5	Gleason	Jackson	.351	Jackson	7	Cicotte	29–7	1.82
								Felsch	7			
1920	2nd	96–58	.623	2	Gleason	Jackson	.382	Felsch	14	Faber	23–13	2.99
1921	7th	62–92	.403	36.5	Gleason	E. Collins	.337	Sheely	11	Faber	25–15	2.48
1922	5th	77–77	.500	17	Gleason	E. Collins	.324	Falk	12	Faber	21–17	2.80
1923	7th	69–85	.448	30	Gleason	E. Collins	.360	Hooper	10	Faber	14–11	3.41
1924	8th	66–87	.431	25.5	Evers	Falk	.352	Hooper	10	Thurston	20–14	3.80
					Walsh							
					Collins							
1925	5th	79–75	.513	18.5	Collins	E. Collins	.346	Sheely	9	Lyons	21–11	3.26
1926	5th	81–72	.529	9.5	Collins	Falk	.345	Falk	8	Lyons	18–16	3.01
1927	5th	70–83	.458	39.5	Schalk	Falk	.327	Falk	9	Lyons	22–14	2.84
1928	5th	72–82	.468	29	Schalk	Kamm	.308	Metzler	3	Thomas	17–16	3.08
					Blackburne			Barrett	3			
1929	7th	59–93	.388	46	Blackburne	Reynolds	.317	Reynolds	11	Thomas	14–18	3.19
1930	7th	62–92	.403	40	Bush	Reynolds	.359	Reynolds	22	Lyons	22–15	3.78
1931	8th	56–97	.366	51.5	Bush	Blue	.304	Reynolds	6	Frazier	13–15	4.46
1932	7th	49–102	.325	56.5	Fonseca	Fothergill	.295	Kress	9	Lyons	10–15	3.28
1933	6th	67–83	.447	31	Fonseca	Simmons	.331	Simmons	14	Durham	10–6	4.48
1934	8th	53–99	.349	47	Fonseca	Simmons	.344	Bonura	27	Earnshaw	14–11	4.52
					Dykes							
1935	5th	74–78	.487	19.5	Dykes	Appling	.307	Bonura	21	Lyons	15–8	3.02
1936	3rd	81–70	.536	20	Dykes	Appling	.388	Bonura	12	Kennedy	21–9	4.63
1937	3rd	86–68	.558	16	Dykes	Bonura	.345	Bonura	19	Stratton	15–5	2.40
1938	6th	65–83	.439	32	Dykes	Steinbacher	.331	Walker	16	Stratton	15–9	4.01
1939	4th	85–69	.552	22.5	Dykes	McNair	.342	Kuhel	15	Rigney	15–8	3.70
1940	T5th	82–72	.532	8	Dykes	Appling	.348	Kuhel	27	Smith	14–9	3.21
1941	3rd	77–77	.500	24	Dykes	Wright	.322	Kuhel	12	Lee	22–11	2.37
1942	6th	66–82	.446	34	Dykes	Kolloway	.273	Moses	7	Lyons	14–6	2.10
1943	4th	82–72	.532	16	Dykes	Appling	.328	Kuhel	5	Grove	15–9	2.75
1944	7th	71–83	.461	18	Dykes	Hodgin	.295	Trosky	10	Dietrich	16–17	3.62
1945	6th	71–78	.477	15	Dykes	Cuccinello	.308	Dickshot	4	Lee	15–12	2.44
								Curtright	4			

Year	Pos.	Record	Pct.	GB	Manager	Player	BA	Player	HR	Player	W-L	ERA
1946	5th	74–80	.481	30	Dykes	Appling	.309	Wright	7	Caldwell	13–4	2.08
1947	6th	70–84	.455	27	Lyons	Wright	.324	York	15	Lopat	16–13	2.81
1948	8th	51–101	.336	44.5	Lyons	Appling	.314	Seerey	18	Haynes	9–10	3.97
1949	6th	63–91	.409	34	Lyons	Michaels	.308	Souchock	7	Wight	15–13	3.31
1950	6th	60–94	.390	38	Onslow Corriden	Robinson	.311	Zernial	29	Pierce	12–16	3.98
1951	4th	81–73	.526	17	Richards	Minoso	.324	Robinson	29	Pierce	15–14	3.03
1952	3rd	81–73	.526	14	Richards	Fox Robinson	.296	Robinson	22	Pierce	15–12	2.57
1953	3rd	89–65	.578	11.5	Richards	Minoso	.313	Minoso	15	Pierce	18–12	2.72
1954	3rd	94–60	.610	17	Richards Marion	Minoso	.320	Minoso	19	Trucks	19–12	2.79
1955	3rd	91–63	.591	5	Marion	Kell	.312	Dropo	19	Pierce	15–10	1.97
1956	3rd	85–69	.552	12	Marion	Minoso	.316	Doby	24	Pierce	20–9	3.32
1957	2nd	90–64	.584	8	Lopez	Fox	.317	Doby Rivera	14	Pierce	20–12	3.26
1958	2nd	82–72	.532	10	Lopez	Fox	.300	Lollar	20	Pierce	17–11	2.68
1959	1st	94–60	.610	+5	Lopez	Fox	.306	Lollar	22	Wynn	22–10	3.17
1960	3rd	87–67	.565	10	Lopez	Smith	.315	Sievers	28	Pierce	14–7	3.62
1961	4th	86–76	.531	23	Lopez	Robinson	.310	Smith	28	Pizarro	14–7	3.05
1962	5th	85–77	.525	11	Lopez	Robinson	.312	Smith	16	Herbert	20–9	3.27
1963	2nd	94–68	.580	10.5	Lopez	Ward	.295	Ward Nicholson	22	Peters	19–8	2.33
1964	2nd	98–64	.605	1	Lopez	Robinson	.301	Ward	23	Peters	20–8	2.50
1965	2nd	95–67	.586	7	Lopez	Buford, Berry	.283	Skowron Romano	18	Fisher	15–7	2.40
1966	4th	83–79	.512	15	Stanky	Agee	.273	Agee	22	John	14–11	2.62
1967	4th	89–73	.549	3	Stanky	Buford	.241	Ward	18	Horlen	19–7	2.06
1968	T7th	67–95	.414	36	Stanky Moss Lopez	Davis	.268	Ward	15	Wood	13–12	1.87
1969	5th	68–94	.420	29	Lopez Gutteridge	Williams	.304	Melton	23	Horlen	13–16	3.78

Year	Pos.	Record	Pct.	GB	Manager	Player	BA	Player	HR	Player	W-L	ERA
1970	6th	56–106	.346	42	Gutteridge / Adair / Tanner	Aparicio	.313	Melton	33	John	12–17	3.28
1971	3rd	79–83	.488	22.5	Tanner	May	.294	Melton	33	Wood	22–13	1.91
1972	2nd	87–67	.565	5.5	Tanner	Allen	.308	Allen	37	Wood	24–17	2.51
						May	.308					
1973	5th	77–85	.475	17	Tanner	Kelly	.280	Melton	20	Wood	24–20	3.46
								May				
1974	4th	80–80	.500	14	Tanner	Orta	.216	Allen	32	Kaat	21–13	2.92
1975	5th	75–86	.466	22.5	Tanner	Orta	.304	Johnson	18	Kaat	20–14	3.11
1976	6th	64–97	.398	25.5	Richards	Garr	.300	Spencer	14	Brett	10–12	3.32
								Orta	14			
1977	3rd	90–72	.556	12	Lemon	Garr	.300	gamble	31	Stone	15–12	4.52
1978	5th	71–90	.441	20.5	Lemon / Doby	Lemon	.300	Soderholm	20	Stone	12–12	4.37
1979	5th	73–87	.456	14	Kressinger / LaRussa	Lemon	.318	Lemon	17	Kravec	15–13	3.74
1980	5th	70–90	.438	26	LaRussa	Lemon	.292	Morrison	15	Burns	15–13	2.84
								Nordhagen				
1981	3rd	54–52	.509	8.5	LaRussa	Nordhagen	.308	Luzinski	21	Burns	10–6	2.64
1982	3rd	87–75	.537	6	LaRussa	Luzinski	.292	Baines	25	Hoyt	19–15	3.53
1983	1st	99–63	.611	+20	LaRussa	Paciorek	.307	Kittle	35	Hoyt	24–10	3.66
1984	T5th	74–88	.457	10	LaRussa	Baines	.304	Kittle	32	Seaver	15–11	3.95
1985	3rd	85–77	.525	6	LaRussa	Baines	.309	Fisk	37	Burns	18–11	3.96
1986	5th	72–90	.444	20	LaRussa / Rader/Fregosi	Baines	.296	Baines	21	Cowley	11–11	3.88
1987	5th	77–85	.475	8	Fregosi	Baines	.293	Calderon	28	Bannister	16–11	3.58
						Calderon						
1988	5th	71–90	.441	32.5	Fregosi	Gallagher	.303	Pasqua	20	Reuss	13–9	3.44
1989	7th	69–92	.429	29.5	Torborg	Martinez	.300	Calderon	14	Perez	11–14	5.01
1990	2nd	94–68	.580	9	Torborg	Johnson	.285	Fisk	18	Hibbard	14–9	3.16
1991	2nd	87–75	.537	8	Torborg	Thomas	.318	Thomas	32	McDowell	17–10	3.41
1992	3rd	86–76	.531	10	Lamont	Thomas	.323	Bell	25	McDowell	20–10	3.18

99

All-Time White Sox Career and Season Records

Career Batting Leaders (1901–1992)

Games Played	Luke Appling	2,422
At Bats	Luke Appling	8,857
Runs Scored	Luke Appling	1,319
Hits	Luke Appling	2,749
Batting Average	Joe Jackson	.339
Home Runs	Harold Baines	186
Runs Batted In	Luke Appling	1,116
Stolen Bases	Eddie Collins	366
Strikeouts	Harold Baines	782

Career Pitching Leaders (1901–1992)

Innings Pitched	Ted Lyons	4,161
Earned Run Average	Ed Walsh	1.81
Wins	Ted Lyons	260
Losses	Ted Lyons	230
Winning Percentage	Claude Williams	.648
Strikeouts	Billy Pierce	1,796
Walks	Urban Faber	1,213
Games	Urban Faber	669
Shutouts	Ed Walsh	58
Saves	Bobby Thigpen	200
Games Started	Ted Lyons	484
	Red Faber	484
Complete Games	Ted Lyons	356

Single-Season Batting Records (1901–1992)

Batting Average (502 ABs)	Luke Appling	.388	1936
Batting Average (100 games)	Joe Jackson	.382	1920
Home Runs	Dick Allen	37	1972
	Carlton Fisk	37	1985
Home Runs (lefthanded)	Oscar Gamble	31	1977
Runs Batted In	Henry Bonura	138	1936
Hits	Eddie Collins	222	1920
Singles	Eddie Collins	169	1920
Doubles	Frank Thomas	46	1992
Triples	Joe Jackson	21	1916
Slugging Percentage	Dick Allen	.603	1972
Extra Base Hits	Joe Jackson	74	1920
Game Winning RBIs	Harold Baines	22	1983
Sacrifices	George Davis	40	1905
Stolen Bases	Rudy Law	77	1983
Pinch Hits	Smoky Burgess	21	1966
Strikeouts	Dave Nicholson	175	1963
Total Bases	Joe Jackson	336	1920
Hitting Streak	Luke Appling	27	1936
Grand Slam Home Runs	Pete Ward	3	1964
Hit by Pitch	Minnie Minoso	23	1956

All-Time White Sox Career and Season Records *(continued)*

Single-Season Pitching Records (1901–1992)

ERA (150 innings)	Ed Walsh	1.27	1910
ERA (100 innings)	Ed Walsh	1.41	1909
Wins	Ed Walsh	40	1908
Losses	Pat Flaherty	25	1903
Winning Pct. (10 decisions)	Sandy Consuegra	.842	1954
Strikeouts	Ed Walsh	269	1908
Walks	Vern Kennedy	147	1936
Saves	Bobby Thigpen	57	1990
Games	Wilbur Wood	88	1968
Complete Games	Ed Walsh	42	1908
Games Started	Ed Walsh	49	1908
	Wilbur Wood	49	1972
Shutouts	Ed Walsh	12	1908
Innings Pitched	Ed Walsh	464	1908
Home Runs Allowed	Billly Pierce	33	1958
Consecutive Games Won (season)	LaMarr Hoyt	13	1983
Consecutive Games Lost (season)	Howard Judson	14	1949
Wild Pitches	Tommy John	17	1970

3
Cleveland Indians
Recent Wahoo Woes Overshadow Cleveland's Baseball Tradition

Morris A. Eckhouse

Triumphs have been few and far between for the Cleveland Indians, one of just four of the original eight American League franchises to remain in one city continuously since 1901. No non-expansion club has appeared in fewer World Series than the Tribe. Memories of great victories in 1920 and 1948 have sustained many Cleveland baseball fans, while a new generation hopes to someday experience the thrill of post-season play in the Forest City. The third World Series appearance, in 1954, was a harbinger of disappointment that would stretch through three major league expansions and three decades.

With the exception of 1908, Cleveland did not build a true pennant contender in the new American League until the late teens, after original club owner Charles Somers sold the team to Jim Dunn. Led by player-manager Tris Speaker, shortstop Ray Chapman, second baseman Bill Wambsganss, catcher Steve O'Neill, and pitchers Jim Bagby and Stan Coveleski, the Indians finished a close second to the Red Sox in 1918 and then to the White Sox in 1919. The addition of former Yankees ace pitcher Ray Caldwell in 1919 gave the Tribe a dominant pitching staff in 1920. With Bagby's club-record 31 wins, 24 from Coveleski, and 20 from Caldwell, Cleveland's big three matched the top trios of the 1908 White Sox and 1904 Yankees as the winningest threesomes in American League history. Babe Ruth was hitting homers like nobody's business and the White Sox were better than ever, despite rumors of wrongdoing in the 1919 World Series, but the lesser known Indians were right in the pennant chase in 1920.

On August 16th, leading the Yanks and White Sox by percentage points, the Indians began a road trip at the Polo Grounds in New York. The overcast day, Ray Chapman's plate-crowding batting stance, and Carl Mays' hard-to-follow submarine delivery combined to produce one of baseball's great tragedies. Leading off the fifth inning, Chapman hung his head over the plate, as usual, to face Mays. A fastball from the righthanded hurler came at Chapman's head. Unable to avoid the pitch, Chapman was struck in the left temple with such force that the ball ricocheted back at Mays as though it had hit the bat. Chapman collapsed with a fractured skull. He died early the following morning, becoming the only on-field fatality in major league history. The game of August 17th was postponed. After splitting the final two games at New York, postponement of the game at Boston on August 20 allowed team members to attend Chapman's funeral in Cleveland, still remembered as one of the grandest and saddest in the history of the city.

Returning to Boston, the Indians were shut out on both ends of a doubleheader. Harry Lunte briefly replaced Chapman, but he went down with an injured leg on Labor Day. The Indians acquired Joe Sewell for $6,000, from their New Orleans farm club to fill the void at short. Sewell's arrival coincided with a brief slump that dropped the Indians to second place behind the Yankees. Soon afterward Cleveland acquired pitcher Walter "Duster" Mails from Sacramento of the Pacific Coast League. Known as "The Great Mails," Duster was unbeatable, with seven wins and no defeats in September. By mid-September, New York's injury-riddled team was suffering a devastating four-game losing streak of its own, while both the Indians and White Sox were on winning tears. On September 23 Chicago invaded Cleveland to do battle for first place. Dickie Kerr beat Bagby in the first game, Mails won the second, but Chicago took the third and left town a half-game behind the leaders. On September 28, with the A.L. pennant in the balance, the Cook County grand jury returned indictments against eight members of the White Sox. Chicago owner Charles Comiskey immediately suspended the eight players, including former Cleveland star Joe Jackson. A makeshift White Sox squad lost two of its final three games. Caldwell's 20th win on October 1 and Bagby's 31st on October 2 clinched a first-ever pennant for the Cleveland Indians.[1]

The 1920 World Series, the second of three consecutive best-of-nine affairs, remains one of the most exciting in baseball history. Opening at Brooklyn, Coveleski, still considered the ace of the Cleveland staff despite Bagby's great season, earned a 3–1 win as O'Neill drove home two runs with a pair of doubles. Another spitballer, Burleigh Grimes, blanked Cleveland and Bagby, 3–0, in the second game. Sherry Smith gave Brooklyn the edge with a 2–1 win in Game Three. Moving to Dunn Field (a.k.a. League Park) in Cleveland, Coveleski took the fourth game, 5–1. The fifth game, October 10, is strikingly unique in World Series annals. Cleveland's Elmer Smith provided the first memorable moment in the first inning. With the bases loaded, Smith belted a home run off Grimes, the first grand slam in World Series history. In the fourth, Bagby became the first pitcher to hit a World Series homer with a three-run blast giving the Indians a 7–0 edge. In the fifth, Wambsganss executed the first and only unassisted triple play ever seen in the Fall Classic. With runners at first and second, pitcher Clarence Mitchell hit a line drive to the second baseman. Wamby stepped on second to double-off Pete Kilduff and then tagged a stunned Otto Miller arriving from first. Tribe pitching really took charge at the end, blanking Brooklyn for the final 18 innings of the Series. Mails hurled a 1–0 shutout in the sixth game and Coveleski tied the Series record with his third victory, a 3–0 shutout on October 12 to make the Cleveland Indians World Champions of baseball.

Another pennant would not be raised by the Indians for 28 years, covering the remaining years of the Dunn family ownership and the entire reign of club president Alva Bradley (1928 to 1946), until a baseball pied piper arrived on the shores of Lake Erie. A baseball renaissance dawned in Cleveland on June 21, 1946, when Bill Veeck purchased the Indians from the estate of Alva Bradley. Cleveland had never, and has never since, seen the likes of one Bill Veeck. Cleveland Municipal Stadium became center stage for wild fan promotions and a carnival-like atmosphere. The Veeck approach put people in the seats, but Veeck was also an experienced baseball man and set out to end the pennantless drought in Cleveland. "The sportshirt" (Veeck) brought second baseman Joe Gordon and pitcher Gene Bearden to the Indians in separate deals with the Yankees. The forward-thinking owner also first integrated the American League in 1947 by signing Larry Doby. In the best trade Veeck did not make, player-manager shortstop Lou Boudreau was not shipped to the Browns for Vern Stephens as long rumored. In 1948 Boudreau responded with one of those epic seasons that carries a player into the Hall of Fame. Having suffered their worst season of the 1940s in 1946, the Indians improved in 1947, but still finished far from first place.

Cleveland's 17-win improvement in 1948 occurred in large part because of two pitchers who had won only 11 games combined the previous season. Converted third baseman-outfielder Bob Lemon became a full-time starting pitcher and 20-game winner at age 27. A bigger surprise was 27-year-old lefty Bearden. The rookie knuckleballer set the A.L. on its ear with a 20–7 mark. The great Bob Feller had a subpar (for him) 19–15 season, but was 6–0 when it counted most during the month of September. Veeck signed pitcher Russ Christopher, a 30-year-old question mark with a heart ailment. Used judiciously by Boudreau, Christopher, a submarining righthander, saved 17 games and teamed with Eddie Klieman to give the Tribe a dependable bullpen. Offensively Boudreau, Ken Keltner, and Eddie Robinson had career seasons. The starting infield alone drove in 432 runs versus 288 the year before.

Cleveland kicked off the 1948 season with six straight wins and battled another surprise team, the Philadelphia A's, for the early A.L.

lead. The defending Yankees were a factor throughout, but never did reach first place. These three clubs were neck and neck in early July when Veeck made another controversial, historic, acquisition. Boudreau was skeptical of adding the elderly Negro League pitching legend Leroy "Satchel" Paige, until Satch convinced the player-manager with a spectacular performance in a secret tryout. The Paige signing was blasted by J.G. Taylor Spink, editor of *The Sporting News*, as exploitation, but Satch nearly copped Rookie of the Year honors with a 6–1 record and became the biggest gate attraction in baseball. Despite Paige, the Indians stumbled to a 14–15 record in July. The high-scoring Red Sox struggled early, but surged into first place in late July.

On August 1, 70,702 fans filled Cleveland Municipal Stadium to see Lemon and Sam Zoldak humble Boston in a double-header. The sweep sent Cleveland off on an 18–4 tear and a three-game lead over Boston. Paige capped the winning streak with a three-hit, 1–0 win against Chicago before 78,382 fans at the Stadium, still the biggest crowd ever to see a major league night game. Paige's whitewash was also the fourth straight by Tribe pitchers. Lemon had all but secured the fifth shutout when ninth-inning homers by Aaron Robinson and Dave Philley gave the last place White Sox a 3–2 win. The stunning loss to Chicago started a 7–11 skid which allowed the tribe to fall four and one-half games behind the Red Sox. Just when another Tribe fold seemed at hand, Cleveland rattled off seven straight victories to remain close.

Tragedy, inescapable for the Indians in the best of times, struck again on September 13. Pitcher Don Black, a starter and author of a no-hitter in 1947 but relegated to the background in 1948, made an infrequent start against St. Louis. Batting in the second inning, Black suffered a cerebral hemorrhage and entered St. Vincent Charity Hospital in critical condition. Though he recovered, Black never pitched another major league game. As in 1920, the Indians rallied from adversity for a final stretch drive. Another seven straight wins, capped by Feller's three-hitter against Boston before 76,772 fans on Don Black Night at the Stadium, pulled the Tribe into a first place tie. On September 26 it was Feller again leading the Tribe. Rapid Robert's five-hit, 4–1 win over the Tigers broke the first-place deadlock. Bearden followed with a four-hit, 11–0 win against the White Sox on Joe Early Night at the Stadium to give Cleveland a two-game edge with four games left. Early, representing the average fan, was saluted with a variety of gifts as 60,405 fans responded to another Veeck promotion, not to mention the tight pennant race.

Feller's 19th win left the Tribe needing two wins against Detroit to clinch the pennant. After the Tigers beat Lemon, Bearden clinched a tie with an 8–0 win before 56,238 at the Stadium. On the final day of the regular season, 74,181 fans packed the Stadium in hopes of celebrating Bob Feller's 20th win and an end to the 28-year drought. Instead, Feller's great 1940s rival, Hal Newhouser, handcuffed the Indians. Detroit spoiled Bill Veeck Day with a 7–1 win, and Boston routed New York 10–5. For the first time in A.L. history, a one-game playoff was necessary to determine the league champion. Keeping his starter a secret until game time, Boudreau made a somewhat surprising choice in Bearden. Boston manager Joe McCarthy was even more unpredictable, choosing 36-year-old Denny Galehouse coming off a mediocre 8–8 campaign. Boudreau capped his M.V.P. season with a pair of home runs. Keltner added a three-run, tie-breaking homer in the fourth and Cleveland was finally able to celebrate.

With the Indians remaining in Boston, an Injun World Series between Cleveland and the Braves began at Braves Field. Feller was sensational in the first game, hurling a two-hitter. Boston's Johnny Sain was also superb, and the game was still scoreless in the eighth. Bill Salkeld opened the Boston eighth with a walk and pinch runner Phil Masi took second on a sacrifice. An intentional pass to Eddie Stanky preceded one of the most controversial plays in World Series history. Boudreau and Feller executed a timed pickoff play, with the pitcher throwing to second on a predetermined count. Masi was caught off guard, and so, perhaps, was N.L. umpire Bill Stewart. Though Masi seemed clearly out, Stewart ruled safe. Feller retired Sain, but Braves batting star Tommy Holmes delivered the game's only run with a single to left. Lemon kept the Braves at bay in the second game, while Boudreau doubled home one run and scored another in a 4–1 Cleveland win. With a World Series record 70,306 fans on hand at Cleveland Municipal Stadium for Game Three, Bearden spun a five-hit, 2–0 victory.

For the pivotal fourth game, Boudreau chose valuable spot pitcher Steve Gromek to face Sain. Doby's third-inning home run made the difference as Gromek scattered seven hits in a 2–1 win. Photographs of the black Doby and white Gromek hugging each other after the game captured a significant moment in baseball's integration efforts. As with the regular season finale, Cleveland was again poised to celebrate if Bob Feller could end the Series in Game Five. With a new Series record 86,288 packed into the Stadium, Robert was rocked, however, in the highest scoring game yet between the Indians and Braves. More history was recorded that day when Paige became the first black hurler to appear in a World Series. One week after the playoff game in Fenway Park, Cleveland was back in Boston for Game Six. With Lemon pitching the Indians took a 4–1 lead as Boudreau drove in the first run and Gordon homered. When Boston rallied in the eighth, Boudreau called upon Bearden in relief. The Braves scored twice, before Gene retired the side. When Sibby Sisti bunted into a double play in the ninth and Holmes flied out to Bob Kennedy in left, the Indians were again world champions of baseball. Cleveland's Boston Massacre complete, the Indians returned home to a ticker-tape parade and heroes' welcome.

For a brief moment in 1948, Cleveland was the true capital of baseball. More fans came through the turnstiles at Cleveland in 1948 than anywhere else (2,620,627). But Casey Stengel, new manager of the Yankees, passed the word that Bearden's knuckleball was rarely in the strike zone, and began a dynasty of his own in New York. For five of the next eight years, the Indians would finish second to the Yankees. The happy exception was 1954, when a powerful offense and legendary pitching staff made baseball history. Lemon, Early Wynn, and Mike Garcia led the pitchers, followed by Art Houtteman, plus legends Feller and Newhouser, now teammates, used in spot roles. Don Mossi and Ray Narleski comprised the best relief duo in the game. Second baseman Bobby Avila led the league in hitting, Doby in homers and RBIs. First baseman Vic Wertz and third sacker Al Rosen added still more punch. After a lackluster 6–6 record in April and 13–10 start, the Indians won 11 straight games and took control of the division by June 1. While beating up on second-division clubs, Cleveland had continued trouble with Chicago and New York. Just .500 against the White Sox and Yankees (11–11 versus each), the Indians were 89–21, a staggering .809 winning percentage, against the Red Sox, Tigers, Senators, Orioles, and Athletics. When the White Sox swept four games from the Tribe to reach the All-Star break, the Indians were just a half-game ahead of the Yankees.

After the mid-season break, the Indians went 15–3, shaking the White Sox, but not the Yanks. In June and July Cleveland was 41–17, but New York was 43–17. On September 8 the Indians set a new club win record with victory number 99, as Early Wynn beat Philadelphia 9–2. Newhouser won in relief of Feller the next day as the Indians reached 100 wins for the first and only time. On September 12, 84,587 fans, the most ever to attend a doubleheader, filled Municipal Stadium to see the Indians finally dethrone New York after three straight second-place finishes. Rosen's two-run double and Lemon's six-hitter for his 22nd victory won the first game. Wynn's three-hitter and 21st victory in the nightcap gave Cleveland an insurmountable 8½-game lead. The Yankees won 103 games, their highest total under Stengel, yet finished eight games behind the Indians. Cleveland set a league standard that year with 111 wins and seemed a cinch to beat the New York Giants in the World Series.

Two legendary events in the first game of the 1954 World Series burst the Indians bubble, however. Vic Wertz started a bittersweet day with a two-run triple to give the Indians a 2–0 lead. New York tied the game, with two runs off Lemon in the third, but Cleveland rallied in the seventh. Doby walked, Rosen singled, and Wertz, three-for-three already, came up to face relief pitcher Don Liddle. Wertz hit a blast to dead center field, the deepest part of the Polo Grounds. Willie Mays ran away from home plate at full speed to make an unbelievable, over-the-shoulder catch of the 460-foot drive, then whirled and made a miraculous throw to the infield. Doby barely advanced to third, while Rosen returned to first. Reliever Marv Grissom set down shortstop George Strickland and catcher Jim Hegan without allowing a run. In the 10th inning pinch hitter James Lamar "Dusty" Rhodes batted for Monte Irvin, a move manager Leo Durocher made often in 1954. Rhodes hit a weak fly to right, an out in any other park. Yet in the Polo Grounds Rhodes was a hero with a 260-foot homer into the short right-field stands, giving the Giants a 5–2 victory.

New York pitching surprisingly dominated the Series. Al Smith's leadoff homer was Cleveland's only offense against Johnny Antonelli in a 3–1 second game loss. Rhodes hit another homer for the winners. Ruben Gomez pitched six two-hit innings in the third game and Hoyt Wilhelm closed out a 6–2 New York win at Cleveland. Cleveland scored just five runs in the first 32 innings of the Series and again trailed 7–0 in the fourth contest. Bypassing Feller and young Houtteman, Lopez had called on Lemon, who was kayoed in the fifth. The Giants held on for a 7–4 win and four-game sweep of the Tribe, sending 78,102 fans home unhappy—and also unaware that the city would still be awaiting another World Series game some 35 years later.

World Series have been the exception, high hopes, frustration, and disappointment the rule, throughout the history of Cleveland's American League club. There was no World Series, in fact no American League, when Ban Johnson contacted Charles Somers about financing a Cleveland franchise. Somers not only bankrolled the Cleveland club, he helped with finances for other clubs in the new circuit. The Cleveland Blues, so-named for their blue uniforms, played the first game in A.L. history on April 24, 1901 (the other three games were rained out). Chicago's Roy Patterson bested Bill Hoffer and Cleveland 8–2, one of 82 losses against just 55 wins for the seventh-place club. Earl Moore, Cleveland's best hurler, pitched the first no-hitter in A.L. history on May 9, but Chicago scored two tainted runs in the third inning and broke a 2–2 tie with two runs and two hits in the 10th.

On-field help for Cleveland arrived in 1902 in the person of Nap Lajoie. A star second baseman with Philadelphia in the National League, Napoleon jumped to Connie Mack's Philadelphia Athletics in 1901. When a court order barred Lajoie from playing for the A's, Mack remembered how Somers had helped him launch the new Philadelphia franchise and sent the Frenchman to Cleveland. Larry became such a fan favorite that the club was renamed the Naps in 1903. Lajoie also became player-manager in 1904. Cleveland was a boarderline contender in 1906 and 1907, before the great race of 1908, best remembered for the great pitching duel between Ed Walsh and Addie Joss.

The 1908 season produced Cleveland's first A.L. club of distinction. While the 1908 N.L. pennant race gets most of the historical attention, the A.L. battle was just as close. With Hall of Famers Lajoie at second and Joss on the mound, the Naps battled Detroit, Chicago, and St. Louis to the wire. Third baseman Bill Bradley and first baseman George Stovall were premier players at their positions. Despite injury to shortstop Terry Turner, the all-time Cleveland leader in games played, and illness to outfielder Elmer Flick, a .304 hitter and 1905 batting champ since joining Cleveland in 1902, Lajoie's men set a club record of 90 wins that would stand until 1920. Heading the best pitching staff in baseball (2.02 team ERA) were 28-year-old righthanders Joss (24–11) and Bob "Dusty" Rhoades (18–12). On September 18 against Boston, Rhoades pitched a no-hitter for Cleveland's 12th win in the last 14 games, keeping the Naps a game behind the first place Tigers. On October 2 Joss and 40-game winner Walsh met in, arguably, the greatest game ever pitched. Walsh allowed just four hits and struck out 15, but Joss retired 27 consecutive batters, a perfect game. Cleveland scored the only run when a wicked Walsh spitball eluded catcher Ossie Schreck. The 1–0 win should have vaulted Cleveland to the pennant, but was instead a final triumph. Consecutive losses to Chicago and St. Louis eliminated the Naps from contention. Cleveland finished a half-game behind the Tigers, the difference being a Detroit rainout that was not made up.

When Bradley, Stovall, and the rest of the offense struggled in 1909, Cleveland could not keep pace with the explosive Detroit, Philadelphia, and Boston clubs. Flick was finished at age 32. Joss managed a weak 14–13 record despite a brilliant 1.70 ERA. After 114 games and a 57–57 record, Lajoie gave up and surrendered his managerial duties. Deacon McGuire took the helm and Cleveland staggered home with just 14 more wins and 25 losses. A lone bright spot was the return of Cy Young. Baseball's winningest pitcher rose to fame with Cleveland's N.L. club from 1890 to 1898, winning 239 of his 511 career victories. The 42-year-old righthander led Cleveland with 19 wins during 1909, in his last victorious campaign.

The second decade of the twentieth century began with controversy and tragedy, but still became the first of many with relatively little for Cleveland baseball fans to cheer about. Joss struggled to a 5–

5 record, including his second no-hitter, and Cleveland struggled home in fifth place, despite a brilliant season by Lajoie, in 1910. The Cleveland second baseman and Detroit outfielder Ty Cobb fought for the A.L. batting title, and the Chalmers Automobile that went with it, to the last day of the season. The bare facts of the final day's fireworks appear in *The Sporting News Hall of Fame Fact Book,* alongside Ty Cobb's record. Lajoie, recipient of some charitable play by the St. Louis Browns, a group of players that joined seemingly all the rest of baseball in despising Cobb, appeared the batting champ at the close of the season. Following a records check, Cobb was declared champ, until 1981 when *The Sporting News* published clear documentation that Lajoie had indeed been robbed of the title.

Joining Cleveland in July 1910, was a young Southern outfielder who would supplant Lajoie as the greatest batsman in club history. Joseph Jefferson Jackson batted .387 in 20 games for Cleveland in 1910, having pried himself loose from the Athletics where he was made uncomfortable by the taunts of teammates from the North and East. Connie Mack, unable to get any production from Jackson, again favored Charley Somers and traded Joe to the Naps. Shoeless Joe would soon replace Lajoie as Ty Cobb's chief rival for the A.L. batting throne.

One of Cleveland's great baseball tragedies struck in 1911 when Joss was stricken with spinal meningitis. Joss' Hall of Fame career ended suddenly and the hurler was dead on April 14, just two days after his 31st birthday. Vean Gregg, chosen the lefthanded pitcher on the All-Time Indians team as selected in 1969 (which says more about the state of Cleveland's lefties than Gregg), was a bonafide star in 1911 with a 23–7 record and 1.81 ERA. McGuire was fired as skipper, however, after just 17 games. Stovall became player-manager and impressed with a third-place finish, so much so that he was traded to the Browns for pitcher Lefty George, author of a 4–9 record as a 25-year-old rookie in 1911. Lefty never won a game for Cleveland. After a miserable 54–71 start under Harry Davis, a 21–7 finish behind player-manager Joe Birmingham left the 1912 Naps in fifth place, wasting another 20-win season by Gregg. Cleveland would soon become known as the graveyard of managers, with only Lajoie, Tris Speaker, Roger Peckinpaugh, Lou Boudreau, and Al Lopez surviving four or more seasons from start to finish.

By 1913 Cleveland had the look of a coming contender. Jackson and Lajoie led the offense, Ray Chapman became the starting short-stop, 21-year-old catcher Steve O'Neill returned from a 1912 broken finger to bat .295, and 20-game winners Cy Falkenberg and Vean Gregg led a balanced pitching staff. Only the World Champion Athletics had more hits or runs scored in the junior circuit than Cleveland.

Instead of a pennant contender, Cleveland was an undisputed tailender in 1914, 18½ games out of seventh place. Falkenberg's defection to the Federal League, where he won 25 games for Indianapolis, left the pitching staff in ruins. Only Willie Mitchell topped 10 wins. Lajoie's batting average fell 77 points and Cleveland's offense went from almost first to almost worst. After setting a club record in home attendance with 541,000 in 1913, just 185,997 fans entered League Park to see the Naps in 1914, launching the first of many financial crises for Cleveland's major league club. An era ended in 1914, as Nap Lajoie's 13-year association with Cleveland was severed. Nap was released to finish out his major league career back in Philadelphia. The Naps were consequently left needing both a new leader and a new nickname.

Cleveland's attendance was even worse in 1915, forcing a trade that forever altered baseball history. Batting star Joe Jackson was dealt to the White Sox for outfielders Braggo Roth and Larry Chappell, and pitcher Ed Klepfer plus cash. Though the deal is considered perhaps the worst in club history, the money obtained by Somers kept the club in business. Roth hit four homers with Cleveland and became the club's first home run leader with seven total circuit blasts in 1915. He hit just six homers the next three seasons combined and became more important as part of a 1919 trade to Philadelphia.

When Lajoie left, the name Naps no longer suited the Cleveland franchise. Standing out among submissions by fans was the name Indians, suggested in honor of former Cleveland Spiders (NL) player Luis Soxalexis, then thought to be the first native American to play in the major leagues, who had died in 1913. Cleveland's American League club has been the Indians continuously since 1915. That the new name was christened amid the two worst seasons in franchise history might be considered a dreary harbinger of things to come for modern Tribe fans.

Another great player-manager arrived on the scene to fill the leadership void left by Lajoie. Tristram Speaker, disgruntled after seven full seasons with the Red Sox, was snapped up by the Indians, but not easily. According to *The Cleveland Indians* by Franklin Lewis, Speaker would not consider a trade to Cleveland. Lewis quotes Speaker, "I think you've got a bad ball club, for one thing. You finished seventh and eighth in two years. Cleveland isn't a good baseball town either. I don't want to go to Cleveland and wind up in the second division." When Speaker demanded, and received, $10,000 of the purchase price, however, he did come to Cleveland after all.

Led by new manager Lee Fohl and field general Speaker, considered the best outfielder of his era, and perhaps any era, the Indians moved 30 games closer to first place in 1916, but still finished sixth.

The Somers ownership was also finished. The bankers whose loans enabled Somers to keep the team now demanded he concentrate on his failing coal mining interests. Jim Dunn headed up a group that purchased the ballclub in 1916.

Dunn's Indians rose to third place in 1917 and became genuine contenders the following season. With dependable starters Coveleski and Bagby, the 1918 Indians fought Boston and Washington to the wire in a season ending on Labor Day due to World War I. Running out of time, Cleveland's faint pennant hopes were crushed on August 28 when Speaker was suspended for arguing with an umpire. The frustrated Tribesmen skipped a final-day doubleheader at St. Louis, but still finished second, 2½ games behind the Red Sox.

Two major events in 1919 shaped the 1920 championship club. In March the Indians acquired outfielder Charlie Jamieson, third baseman Larry Gardner, and pitcher Elmer Myers from the A's for Braggo Roth. Gardner plugged a gaping hole at third and Jamieson became one of Cleveland's greatest outfielders. The improved Indians were fighting for first place when Boston visited Cleveland in mid-July. The Red Sox had tumbled to also-ran status and had lost nine straight games to the Indians. They also trailed Cleveland 7–4 on July 18 at League Park as Myers faced Babe Ruth with the bases loaded. As the great slugger prepared to hit, Speaker, Fohl's on-field captain, signaled for a righthander to relieve Myers. For whatever reason, Fohl brought in Fritz Coumbe, a junkballer. Ruth blasted Coumbe's second slow curve far beyond the right-field fence to give Boston an 8–7 win. Fohl immediately resigned as manager and Speaker took the helm. The consensus of Cleveland fans for some time had been that Speaker should be running the club. Though the Tribe could not seriously challenge Chicago, Cleveland finished a strong second for the second straight year with a late-season surge.

Cleveland's 1920 club was the finest yet put forth by the franchise. The Indians led the A.L. in runs scored, doubles, triples, runs batted in, walks, and batting (.303). Speaker led the league with 50 two-base hits and led the team in batting average (.388), runs (137), and hits (214). Speaker, Elmer Smith, and Larry Gardner each drove in over 100 runs. Bagby enjoyed one of the great pitching seasons in baseball history, leading the A.L. in wins, winning percentage (.721), games, starts, complete games, and innings pitched. Coveleski became Cleveland's first strikeout leader with 133. Cleveland could also boast three 20-game winners for the second of five different seasons. Regardless of any shenanigans pulled by the White Sox, the 1920 Indians deserve recognition as one of baseball's great teams.

For the second straight year Cleveland and New York were the offensive powers in the A.L. in 1921, while Chicago collapsed under the weight of the Black Sox scandal. Bagby and Caldwell won just 20 games between them, but Coveleski, Mails, 22-year old George Uhle, Guy Morton, and waiver acquisition Allen Sothoron comprised a fine pitching corps. Donning new uniforms that proclaimed World Champions across the chest, the Indians survived injuries to Speaker, Wambsganss, and O'Neill to remain in contention. New York, led by Ruth and Bob Meusel on offense, Carl Mays and Waite Hoyt on the mound, and Miller Huggins in the dugout, was rising, while Cleveland had peaked. The Indians took a slim lead on September 16 when Uhle beat Washington. The Yankees won 13 of 22 games with the Indians, including three of four games in a late-September set that decided the issue. New York edged the Tribe by 4½ games for its first A.L. pennant.

The death of Jim Dunn in 1922 preceded a four-year dry spell for an aging Indians squad. A brilliant season by Uhle (26–16) in 1923 rallied Cleveland to third place. Hall-of-Famers Speaker and Joe Sewell gave local fans some excitement in 1924 and 1925. A huge pitching improvement brought Cleveland back toward the top in 1926. Uhle shook off two poor seasons with league highs in wins (27), winning percentage (.711), complete games (32), and innings pitched (318). The club shaved a full run off its team ERA of 1925. Emil "Dutch" Levsen, a 16-game winner, made baseball history by pitching complete-game victories in both games of a twin-bill against Boston on August 28, becoming the last pitcher to do so. Levsen's heroics came in the midst of a nine-game winning streak. Cleveland's surge gave the Tribe a glimmer of hope as the Yankees came to town in mid-September for six games. New York won the first but Levsen, 240-pound Garland Buckeye, Joe Shaute, and Uhle posted consecutive wins, the fourth before 26,782 fans squeezed into Dunn Field. With 29,726 fans packing Cleveland's park at East 66th Street and Lexington Avenue, the Tribe magic wore off as Ruth and Lou Gehrig hit home runs off Levsen in New York's 8–3 win. Cleveland first baseman Sewell capped a phenomenal season with a record 64th double, but the Indians finished second, three games behind the Yankees.

From Jim Dunn's death in 1922, until 1927, the Indians were in need of new ownership. On November 17, 1927, a syndicate led by John Sherwin and Alva Bradley purchased the club from Dunn's widow. Though Bradley put forth only a small part of the purchase price, he was made president of the Indians and is generally recognized as club owner from 1927 to 1946. Among his first decisions was hiring umpire and sports reporter Billy Evans as general manager. Evans was already a legendary umpire and was later inducted into the Hall of Fame. Evans began building Cleveland's farm system, but soon encountered financial difficulties with the stock market crash of 1929.

Billy left the general manager post following the 1935 season, replaced by Tribe superscout Cy Slapnicka.

Tris Speaker left the Indians in a cloud after the 1926 season, caught in a betting scandal with Ty Cobb, Joe Wood, and Dutch Leonard. There was never positive proof of the charges, but Speaker was gone and so too was Cleveland from contention. The Tribe collapsed completely in 1927. For the next 13 years the Indians finished no closer than a distant third under managers Jack McAlister, Roger Peckinpaugh, Walter Johnson, and Ossie Vitt. Lew Fonseca's batting title and Wes Ferrell's first of four straight 20-win seasons highlighted the 1929 campaign. That season also saw a 19-year-old righthander from Beemer, Nebraska earn the first of 223 wins with Cleveland, a club record until 1951. Melvin Leroy Harder would pitch in more games than anyone for the Indians and spend 35 years with the organization as a pitcher and pitching coach. Earl Averill began a Hall-of-Fame career, including an Indians-record 226 home runs, with an outstanding rookie campaign in 1929 after three great seasons in the Pacific Coast League. The Earl of Snohomish (Washington) debuted as the first A.L. player ever to hit a home run in his first at-bat on April 16. Cleveland sandlot star Joe Vosmik joined Averill as an outfield regular in 1931. Big Hal Trosky had one of the greatest rookie seasons ever in 1934. The 21-year-old lefthanded first baseman hit .330 with 35 homers and 142 RBIs. Overshadowed by the likes of Hank Greenberg, Lou Gehrig, and Jimmie Foxx, Trosky deserves inclusion as well among the great first basemen of the 1930s. A regrettable trade, on May 25, 1934, sent Ferrell and outfielder Dick Porter to the Red Sox for pitcher Bob Weiland, outfielder Bob Seeds, and cash. Wes won 59 games the next three seasons at Boston.

In hopes of luring the 1932 Summer Olympic Games to Cleveland, the city constructed a gigantic facility that would also become home to the Indians. Cleveland Municipal Stadium was a massive structure with a seating capacity above 78,000. Built primarily for track and field events, the Stadium was the original circular, multipurpose park, without the intimacy and unique features of League Park and similar big league fields. While the enormous seating capacity was a plus in accommodating huge crowds, it proved a drawback to season ticket sales and left even good crowds of 20,000 and 30,000 rattling around a seemingly empty park. On July 31, 1932, Mel Harder faced Lefty Grove before 80,184 fans (76,979 paid) in the first major league game at the new stadium. Grove and the Athletics bested Harder 1–0. The Indians played all home games at Municipal Stadium until 1934, then moving all but Sunday and holiday games back to League Park. Lights were installed at the Stadium in 1939, where all night games would be played. On June 27, 1939, Bob Feller pitched a one-hitter in the first night game in Cleveland.

After four years of little team success, Bradley replaced Peckinpaugh as manager 51 games into the 1933 season. Walter Johnson brought an A.L. record 416 wins to Cleveland, but those were as a pitcher. The Big Train was not so successful a skipper. His Senators had been competitive from 1930 to 1932, but rose to the pennant only under Joe Cronin in 1933. Johnson was not a big hit with the fans or several players. After 348 games Walter was replaced by Tribe catching great and coach Steve O'Neill in 1935. Illness again rocked the Tribe in 1935 when outfielder Bruce Campbell contracted spinal meningitis. Campbell recovered, relapsed in 1936, then bounced back again in 1937. One of Cleveland's most colorful characters arrived following the 1935 season by way of a trade with the Yankees. Johnny Allen's temper outmatched his pitching ability, although Allen was a 20-game winner in 1936! Also joining the Tribe in 1936 was a 17-year-old righthander who would rewrite baseball history.

Cy Slapnicka discovered Robert William Andrew Feller in Van Meter, Iowa, where he had gone to look at future big-league pitcher Claude Passeau. Slapnicka forgot Passeau when he saw the high-kicking, hard-throwing Feller. Cy quickly signed young Feller to a handwritten contract for a bonus of one dollar and a baseball. Unfortunately the signing was technically illegal. As a sandlot pitcher, Feller was eligible to be signed only by a minor league team. After one outing with a Cleveland sandlot team, the Rosenblums, Bob Feller made his big-league debut in an exhibition contest against the St. Louis Cardinals on July 6. The wild youngster overmatched the Gashouse Gang (those that were willing to face the kid) with eight strikeouts in three innings. Bob made 14 regular-season appearances, with five wins and three losses, including 15 strikeouts against the Browns and a major-league-record-tying 17 against the A's.

Bob Feller was nearly freed from the Indians by Commissioner Landis when Cleveland was ruled to have acted illegally in moving Feller through its minor league system. When Feller, and his father, indicated a desire to stay with the Indians, Landis agreed. While Slapnicka was fortunate enough to keep Feller, he lost Tommy Henrich, also declared a free agent by Landis, who became "Old Reliable" for the Yankees. Then the priceless Feller suddenly became suspect with a sore arm. He won just nine games in 26 appearances. Johnny Allen produced the highlight of 1937 with a 15-game winning streak. Gunning for an 18th straight triumph, dating back to 1936, Allen was stopped when Detroit's Jake Wood edged Cleveland 1–0 with a one-hitter.

Allen's fierce style was the exception for the O'Neill Indians. Looking for a scrappier manager, the Tribe chose Ossie Vitt, the pivotal figure in Cleveland's return to the pennant race in 1940. Vitt made his reputation as manager of the New York Yankees' farm club at Newark which featured stars such as Joe Gordon, Charley Keller, Babe Dahlgren, and others. The former Detroit infielder led Newark to the 1937 International League pennant by 25½ games, sufficient evidence to Cleveland that Vitt was a winner. As in Newark, Vitt also had the horses in Cleveland. Newcomers Ken Keltner at third base and Jeff Heath in the outfield aided the offense. A healthy Feller won 17 games and led the A.L. with 240 strikeouts, including a new record 18 against the Tigers, stealing the spotlight from Hank Greenberg's bid to break Babe Ruth's record of 60 homers on October 2.

Johnny Allen took the spotlight again on June 7. Allen had made a practice of cutting slits in his right-arm uniform sleeve. Originally for ventilation, Allen soon realized a tattered sleeve would distract batters and work to his advantage. Umpire Bill McGowan demanded Allen change t-shirts, then ejected the pitcher when he refused. Vitt then fined Allen $250 for his actions. Owner Bradley pacified Allen by having the now-infamous t-shirt purchased for $250 and displayed at Higbee's department store in Cleveland. From there the t-shirt was sent off for display at the Hall of Fame in Cooperstown. Unfortunately Allen injured his arm and was never as big a winner afterward. Despite the further emergence of Feller in 1939, Cleveland was a distant third. Feller, however, closed the decade with a 24–9 record, leading the A.L. in wins, strikeouts (246), innings pitched (297), and complete games (24).

A veteran Cleveland team was joined by two rookie infielders that thrust the Tribe back into contention in 1940. Second baseman Ray Mack was a product of the Cleveland sandlots. Shortstop Lou Boudreau was a baseball and basketball star in Illinois. Both came to Cleveland from the farm club at Buffalo as rookies in 1940. Only Bobby Doerr and Joe Cronin at Boston drove in more runs as a keystone combination than Mack and Boudreau in 1940. Their defense helped the Indians lead the A.L. in fielding percentage and helped the pitchers post the best ERA in the circuit. Feller, Harder, Al Milnar, Al Smith, and Allen led the pitching staff. His contending club notwithstanding, Vitt seemed constantly dissatisfied with his players. Some players had already rebelled, but a full-scale uprising failed to materialize in 1939 or early 1940. Sniping aside, the Indians started brilliantly when Feller no-hit Chicago on Opening Day.

Snide remarks, criticisms, and a poor road trip finally drove Cleveland players to action in mid-June. A group excluding the newest and youngest players went to owner Bradley and demanded Vitt's ouster.

Bradley refused to dismiss Vitt and the rebellion became front-page news when Hall-of-Fame sportswriter Gordon Cobbledick broke the story. The 1940 Indians became forever labeled as the Crybabies. In the *Cleveland Plain Dealer* the players' revolt was bigger news than the fall of Paris to the Germans. The mismatched manager and players soon continued past the controversy, however, and took command of the A.L. race.

Wins by Feller and Harry Eisenstat against the Tigers and Al Smith's one-hitter against Chicago in front of 59,068, a night-game record at the time, gave the Indians a three-game lead over second-place Detroit. The lead was four games when Cleveland invaded Detroit on September 4. The hard-hitting Tigers routed the Indians in three straight games and moved into a virtual tie for the lead by beating St. Louis on September 7. Returning to Tigertown on September 20, Vitt sent Harder to the mound. For seven innings, Mel was magnificent and led 4–1 in the eighth. With two runners on and big Hank Greenberg coming to bat, Vitt brought Feller into the game. Bob had pitched two complete games in the previous five games and needed rest. Three hits later, Feller was gone. Detroit scored five runs and won 6–5. Detroit won again, before Feller salvaged a final game with his 27th win. By the last weekend of the season, Cleveland was in the throes of a team batting slump and needed a three-game sweep of the Tigers to win the pennant. Feller faced unknown Floyd Gibell in the first game. Rapid Robert dominated, but the Indians could not score against Gibell. Rudy York hit a two-run homer that gave Detroit the pennant. The weekend series against Detroit was Vitt's last major league managerial assignment.

Roger Peckinpaugh returned to the Cleveland helm and presided over a 1941 collapse that soon had Bradley looking for new, fresh leadership. The surprise choice to replace Peckinpaugh was shortstop Boudreau, just 24 years old. Upon accepting the Indians' helm, Boudreau lost ace pitcher Feller who joined the U.S. Navy immediately after the bombing of Pearl Harbor. Cleveland also lost the services of Trosky. Big Hal suffered from severe migraine headaches that ended his career prematurely. Cleveland floundered through the war years in the middle of the American League. Boudreau's 1944 batting title and a strikeout crown won by 28-year-old rookie righthander Allie Reynolds were singular high points of the war period.

Despite Feller's return in 1945 and big seasons by Gromek (19–9) and Reynolds (18–12), the Tribe struggled. Only the last-place Athletics scored fewer runs than the Indians. Cleveland was in search of offense and Bill Veeck was in search of a ballclub. Setting his sites on the Sherwin brothers, anxious to leave the baseball arena, Veeck negotiated purchase of the franchise for $1.6 million. Bringing with him a reputation for antics far removed from basic baseball, Veeck set out to make baseball fun in Cleveland and put a winner back on the field. On-field improvement would take awhile, but immediate results were seen in the stands of Municipal Stadium. Baseball comedians Max Patkin and Johnny Price were added to the coaching staff and an orchestra added music to the festivities. Veeck also had two big playing attractions, Feller and Boudreau. Rapid Robert had pitched his second no-hitter against the Yankees on April 30. He also struck out batters at a record pace, finishing up with an A.L-record 348 strikeouts.[2] Boudreau continued his outstanding all-around play and developed the Ted Williams shift, moving his entire defense toward right field with the Boston slugger batting and daring him to hit to the opposite field.

The Veeck years were, attendance-wise, the best ever in Cleveland. Cleveland had a booming economy. Although the Indians dropped in the standings, attendance shot to a club record 1,057,289 as League Park gave way to full-time play at the huge Municipal Stadium. With post-war prosperity, more night games, and increased promotion, the Indians were the hottest attraction in baseball.

Bill Veeck's wheeling and dealing in 1946 and 1947 built the 1948 champions. Immediately after the 1946 campaign, Veeck sent Reynolds to the Yankees for slugging second baseman Joe Gordon and third baseman Eddie Bockman. Just before Christmas Mack and catcher Sherman Lollar went to New York for three unknowns, outfielder Hal Peck, and pitchers Al Gettel and Gene Bearden. Gordon became Cleveland's home run and RBI leader, Gettel the club's second winningest pitcher, but the Indians were a distant fourth. Still another club record audience, 1,521,978 visited the Stadium. Following the 1947 campaign outfielders Allie Clark, Walt Judnich, and Thurman Tucker, pitchers Bob Muncrief and Russ Christopher, and second baseman Johnny Berardino entered the Cleveland fold.

Because Cleveland can boast just three championship teams in nearly 90 years, its two World Champion teams do not receive the recognition properly due them. The 1948 Indians were a truly great team, if only for one year. Hall-of-Famers Feller and Lemon anchored the pitching staff, with one-year-wonder Bearden and Gromek. An All-Star cast of everyday players included Boudreau, Gordon, Keltner, and Doby. The 1948 Indians led the A.L. in batting average, home runs, hits, ERA, shutouts, and fielding percentage. They were also a colorful team, more so than the 1954 record setters and far different from the faceless congregations that have represented Cleveland since 1960.

From the perspective of the 1980s, 1948 seems to be a magical moment that defies duplication. Cleveland was one of the biggest markets in the country, booming with post-war prosperity. Matched with the greatest promoter in modern baseball history, the Indians achieved successes on the field and at the turnstiles that have never been remotely approached by another Indians club, including the 1954 unit.

So great was 1948 in Cleveland that the arrival of a baseball legend was largely overshadowed. Hank Greenberg, major league baseball's first true Jewish superstar, had been brought into the Tribe front office as a vice president by Veeck, fresh from his retirement as an active player after the 1947 season. Though Greenberg did little in 1948, he made a sudden and brilliant rise to the top of the Tribe organization, becoming farm director, then general manager.

The Bill Veeck era in Cleveland was far too brief. The Indians were in contention much of 1949, before falling to third place with 89 wins, at the time matching the fifth highest total in club history, despite the end of Bearden's success and huge drops in performance by Boudreau and Keltner. Joining the starting rotation were two pitchers soon to make their mark, Early Wynn and Mike Garcia. Attendance remained high, with 2,233,771 fans filing through the turnstiles. Veeck, however, needed cash to settle a divorce. In November sale of the Indians to a group headed by 45-year-old insurance executive Ellis Ryan was finalized as local ownership again held the Tribe.

When Boston and New York surpassed Cleveland in 1949 and 1950, Boudreau could no longer escape his often-rumored dismissal as manager. Rather than stay on as a player only, Lou moved on to Fenway Park where he would become manager of the Red Sox in 1952. Al Lopez took the reins at Cleveland and began a career of Yankee chasing.

The past was bright, the future brighter for the Indians after a half-century of American League baseball. At Cleveland Stadium, a museum housing the new Indians Hall of Fame was planned to honor and preserve the proud heritage of baseball in the Forest City. The Indians Hall of Fame was the forerunner of future stadium museums at St. Louis, Pittsburgh, and elsewhere. Fan balloting in the *Cleveland Plain Dealer, Press,* and *News* selected the Indians all-time team. Voting on retired players only, the fans selected first baseman Trosky, second baseman Lajoie, shortstop Sewell, third baseman Keltner, outfielders Speaker, Averill, and Jackson, catcher O'Neill, and pitchers Harder and Young. Jackson was a controversial choice. Some media members felt Shoeless Joe should be omitted from the ballot due to his role in the Black Sox scandal. Over the next 20 years Bill Bradley, Lou Boudreau, Stan Coveleski, Larry Doby, Elmer Flick, Jim Hegan, Bob Lemon, Satchel Paige, and Early Wynn doubled the ranks of the Hall of Fame.

In a sad episode of Tribe history, but telling in the perception of club history, the Hall of Fame at the Stadium was sacrificed in the early 1970s when the space was taken over for television purposes. The Indians ceased inducting players into their Hall of Fame, though the 20 inductees remain listed in the Indians annual Media Guide. On the field 43-year-old Al Lopez became the 16th manager in club history and embarked on one of the greatest managerial careers in baseball history. The Lopez-led Indians averaged 95 wins per season and never finished lower than second. Thanks to far-sighted leadership, the Indians, with their lead in the integration movement, benefited from the talents of players like Doby, Luke Easter, Bobby Avila, and others.

The Indians of the 1950s boasted one of the great pitching staffs of all time. In 1951 Feller, Garcia, and Wynn were all 20-game winners, Lemon added 17, and the Indians led the league in ERA and complete games, but the offense was subpar and Cleveland finished five games behind New York. The 1952 Indians led the A.L. in runs scored, but still finished two games behind the Yankees. The 1953 Tribe out-homered the Yankees, but finished 8½ games behind the Bronx Bombers. Ownership changed again in 1953 when a feud broke out among the board of directors. Half the board felt Ryan was wielding too much power and should be replaced. Ryan consented when long-time friend, insurance executive Myron "Mike" Wilson, became the compromise choice for club president. The leadership change also gave Hank Greenberg full control of Cleveland's baseball operation.

By 1954 Clevelanders and the rest of the baseball world felt that no matter what advantage the Indians might grab early in a season, they would inevitably finish behind the mighty Yankees. Such an attitude must be part of the explanation for Cleveland's 1954 attendance of just 1.3 million fans. And the 1954 Indians were not, although deadly efficient on the field, the stuff legends are made of. Finally, the 1954 Indians laid claim to baseball glory by carrying an old baseball axiom beyond the extreme. They really clobbered the poorer teams of the American League but barely held their own with the Yankees and White Sox, the only other clubs in the league with above-.500 records.

Like the 1906 Cubs, the winningest team in N.L. history, the 1954 Indians took a backseat in big-league history by losing the World Series. Paced by Doby and Rosen, the Indians led the A.L. in home runs for the fifth straight year (tied with New York in 1951) and trailed only the Yankees in runs scored. That was plenty of offense for a club with a 2.78 ERA, best in the A.L. since Washington's 2.14 in 1918. In all, Cleveland's 1954 performance should have vindicated a club that must be ranked a close second to the Yankees from 1948 to 1956.

That it has not says something about Cleveland and the "winning is everything" mentality.

Bob Feller's apparent successor blazed his way to rookie-of-the-year honors in 1955. A young, lefthanded native of New York, Herb Score set a major league rookie record with 245 strikeouts while winning 16 games. Score was one of three Cleveland 20-game winners in 1956, but they could serve only as bridesmaids for the Yankees both seasons. Developing the front-runner image now entrenched in Cleveland, baseball fans stayed away from Municipal Stadium in droves. Apparently a pitching staff featuring the brilliant Score and three future Hall of Famers, 20-game winners Lemon, Score, and Bob Feller in a winless final season, could not compensate for an offense last in the A.L. in batting average, even though it was second in home runs. Just 865,467 fans attended Indians home games in 1956. From 1956 to 1958 only the Washington Senators, soon to be the Minnesota Twins, kept the Indians from trailing all A.L. clubs in attendance.[3]

Tragedy struck Cleveland again on May 7, 1957. That night Score faced the Yankees and was in his usual, defenseless position following a pitch to Gil McDougald of the Yankees. The off-balance hurler was struck squarely in the right eye by McDougald's liner. Narrowly escaping with his life, Score missed the remainder of the season. A subsequent arm injury, incurred when Score pitched hurt rather than miss more action, finished his mound career three seasons later. Wynn and Lemon were both past 35 years old and the elderly Indians fell from contention. There were two bright spots in the outfield in Score's friend, 23-year-old Rocky Colavito, and 22-year-old Roger Maris. More youth joined the pitchers in 1958 with the addition of Gary Bell and Jim "Mudcat" Grant, but attendance sagged to a post-war low 663,805. The winningest era in Indians history was overshadowed by the bridesmaid role the club played to the Yankees in all but two seasons. A group headed by William R. Daley purchased the Indians in 1957. Lopez, then Greenberg, were soon dismissed, ushering in the pivotal years preceding the drought that was soon to follow.

In his posthumous autobiography, *Hank Greenberg: The Story of My Life,* edited by Ira Berkow, Greenberg makes no attempt to hide his disdain for Cleveland as a baseball city, the local media, and the ownerships that followed the Veeck era. The unmistakeable conclusion is that Cleveland would no longer have the Indians if it were up to Greenberg. Following the 1957 season Hank says, ". . . finally the board of directors decided that maybe it would be better to move Hank Greenberg out of the general manager's role than to move the team to another city. I had been pleading with them, because of the constant pressure we had from the press, to move because it was difficult to win in Cleveland." Greenberg also says he fired Al Lopez as Tribe manager because of constant criticism and, "I thought I would be doing him a favor if I released him." When Greenberg sold his stock in the Indians in 1958, he was called "one of the most controversial figures in Cleveland's sports history" in a *Cleveland Plain Dealer* article. While no doubt true, Hank pales in modern memory to his successor as general manager of the Indians.

When Frank Lane replaced Greenberg as general manager, he came with a reputation for making things happen. As general manager of the White Sox from 1949 to 1955, Lane revived what had been a financial and artistic failure since 1919. What followed was a record-setting attendance and a return to respectability. With the St. Louis Cardinals from 1955 to 1957, Frantic Frankie oversaw a Redbird renaissance featuring a climb from seventh place to second. His brief tenure in Cleveland, however, would forever shape the Frank Lane mystique.

According to the 1960 *Indians Pressbook,* Lane made 60 separate deals from December 2, 1957, to December 15, 1959. His first blockbuster, December 4, 1957, sent 38-year-old Wynn and 30-year-old Al Smith to the White Sox for 35-year-old Minoso and Fred Hatfield. Another seemingly nostalgic move brought 34-year-old Larry Doby back, sending 35-year-old Gene Woodling, Bud Daley, and Dick Williams to Baltimore. Seeking youth at first base and shortstop, Lane grabbed two versatile infielders, Vic Power and Woodie Held, from Kansas City, but paid a huge price, trading Maris, Dick Tomanek, and Preston Ward to the Athletics. (The thought of a long-reigning Tribe outfield of Maris, Minoso, and Colavito brings tears to the eyes of Tribe fans.) Veterans Hegan, Woodling, Chico Carrasquel, Hoyt Wilhelm, Mossi, Narleski, Avila, Wertz, and Doby would be gone by Opening Day 1959. Replacing these aged warriors were firebrands that, oh so briefly, changed the Wahoo image.

Excitement returned to Cleveland baseball in 1959. The old, lumbering Indians were replaced with a hustling, dynamic club featuring dynamos like second baseman Billy Martin and outfielders Jimmy Piersall, Colavito, and Minoso. The Indians led the A.L. in home runs (167), runs scored (745), batting average (.263), and slugging percentage (.408). Cal McLish was second in the league in wins, Score fourth in strikeouts and first in fewest hits allowed per nine innings. Cleveland chased the White Sox—led by owner Veeck, Vice President Greenberg, manager Lopez and a rejuvenated Early Wynn—throughout the season before finishing a close second. Chicago's sweep of a four-game series in Cleveland at the end of August gave the Sox an edge they never relinquished. Tribe attendance was up 125 percent, trailing only the Yankees in the A.L. and the new N.L. baseball meccas at Los Angeles and Milwaukee. But the young Tribe was not close enough for general manager Frank Lane. The impetuous executive fired manager Joe Gordon on September 22. Expected to announce Leo Durocher as new manager at a press conference on the 23rd, Lane introduced Gordon, suddenly rehired for two years. Then Lane set about dismantling the 1959 Indians. Minoso and three other players went to the White Sox for third baseman Bubba Phillips, catcher John Romano, and first baseman Norm Cash. Martin, McLish, and Gordy Coleman were shipped to the Reds for second baseman Johnny Temple. Trader Lane was just warming up.

Frantic Frank Lane cut the soul out of the Indians on April 17, 1960, by trading Colavito, A.L. co-home-run champ in 1959, to the Tigers for 1959 A.L. batting champ Harvey Kuenn. While arguments might be made to justify the deal, the impact of trading the popular Rock was devastating.[4] The 25-year-old rightfielder was an unparalleled fan favorite, displaying great flair both at-bat and in the field. With 108 homers in three seasons, Rocky most probably would have become Cleveland's all-time home run leader before he was reacquired by the club on January 20, 1965. Another retrospective disaster of a deal sent newly acquired Norm Cash to Detroit for third baseman Steve Demeter. Cleveland needed a third baseman, but Demeter hardly got a chance and Cash became a fixture in Detroit. As the Indians fell in the A.L. standings, so did attendance at Municipal Stadium.

With the dawn of a new decade, a black cloud settled over Cleveland baseball. The 1960 Indians, a viable contender only a year earlier, finished two games below .500 and 21 games out of first place. Frank Lane's last flourish, with the help of Detroit's Bill DeWitt, was an unprecedented trade of managers, Gordon to the Tigers for Jimmy Dykes. With that the Tribe embarked on a journey through the wilderness of baseball that is unequalled in the expansion era. A late-season slump in 1989, common to modern Tribe baseball, assured a third consecutive decade without a legitimate contender. Excluding the 1981 strike season, not one Cleveland team in the 1960s, 1970s, or 1980s finished within 10 games of first place. Even the 1981 Indians, with their 103-game record extended over 162 games, would have finished 11 games behind the A.L. East leader. Only the 1968 Indians finished higher than fourth during the drought and that was a distant third.

Lane's resignation on January 3, 1961, was followed by the acquisition of Gabe Paul on April 27. Paul had been in baseball since 1928, becoming publicity director of the Reds in 1936 and rising to general manager at Cincinnati in 1951. Paul left for the new N.L. franchise in

Houston in 1960, then came to Cleveland. Though he was continually saddled with underfinanced ownership, the losing legacy of the Indians since 1959 must be largely attributed to Gabe Paul.

If there was a Cleveland constant in the 1960s, besides mediocrity, it was pitching prowess—such quality hurlers as Sam McDowell, Luis Tiant, Sonny Siebert, Stan Williams, Eddie Fisher, and others. McDowell was A.L. strikeout leader five times from 1965 to 1970, topping 300 Ks in 1965 and 1970. Sudden Sam might have been truly great if not for his troubles with alcohol. Early Wynn made a brief return in 1963 to notch his 300th victory, then supplanted long-time pitching coach Mel Harder. After 35 years with the organization, Harder was rudely dismissed, getting the word from Gabe Paul after the fact and over the telephone. Such treatment is evident of a franchise that has recently made little effort to respect its heritage. The sixties were hardly sensational for Cleveland managers. The Tribe went through seven skippers during the decade (Gordon, Dykes, Mel McGaha, Birdie Tebbetts, George Strickland, Joe Adcock, and Al Dark). Ownership remained unstable, with three different regimes in the 10 years. Bill Daley's effort to move the Indians to Seattle was thwarted when Paul formed a syndicate to buy the club in 1963. Paul's group was short on funds and sold out in 1967 to frozen food magnate Vernon Stouffer who lost his financial strength through some poor business decisions. Stouffer rejected a bid from Clevelander George Steinbrenner and sold out to a group headed by sports entrepreneur Nick Mileti in 1972. Like Paul, Mileti was the front for a cash-poor group that was soon looking for help. Cleveland businessman Alva "Ted" Bonda bailed out Mileti.

With an underfinanced farm system, trades became Cleveland's only avenue for improvement. Unfortunately, the revolving door policy left fans unable to identify with the transient Indians. Pitchers Jim Perry and Mudcat Grant found fame at Minnesota. Outfielder Joe Rudi, who never played a game for the Indians, became a fixture at Oakland. Even the reacquisition of Colavito in 1965 cost Cleveland pitcher Tommy John and outfielder Tommie Agee, both future stars, plus all-star catcher John Romano. Rocky led the A.L. in RBIs in 1965, but he was traded again in 1967.

After a seven-year run of abject mediocrity (1960–1966), the Indians began a roller-coaster ride of frustration in 1967, the first year of the Stouffer ownership, with their worst team since 1946. The slightest glimmer of hope was followed by worse failure. (The light at the end of the tunnel was always an oncoming train.) The promise of 1968, when 21-game winner Luis Tiant led the A.L. with a 1.60 ERA (best for the Indians since the stat became official in 1913) and the Indians led the A.L. with a 2.66 ERA and 1,157 strikeouts, vanished with the beginning of divisional play in 1969. Tiant suffered a sore arm and 20 losses. A trade for 1968 A.L. RBI champ Ken Harrelson, nearly cancelled when The Hawk briefly retired rather than come to Cleveland, cost the club Siebert, pitcher Vicente Romo, and catcher Joe Azcue. The club ERA swelled to 3.94 in 1969. The Indians ended an A.L. record 54 straight seasons (1915–1968) without recording the worst winning percentage in the circuit. Cleveland's first last-place finish since 1914 was the first of six in the next two decades. Seven times from 1968 to 1989, the Indians improved their won-loss record by 10 or more wins. Six times the club lost 10 or more games than they had the prior year. For the Indians, consistency was inconsistency. Youth movements were followed by the acquisition of veterans. Teams based on hitting were followed by teams based on pitching. Poor fundamentals were routine.

The dark cloud remained in the 1970s. Harrelson broke his foot in 1970 and retired. Catcher Ray Fosse was a rising star until blocking the plate during the 1970 All-Star Game at Cincinnati. When Pete Rose came barreling home, Fosse was on the receiving end of a jarring collision. Rose missed the next several games. Fosse returned to action immediately, but was later found to have suffered severe shoulder damage. An outstanding hitter before the accident, the Mule was never a great offensive threat again, though his catching prowess helped Oakland's championship teams from 1973 to 1975. Dark convinced Stouffer that he should run the entire baseball operation and nearly ran it to New Orleans. Gabe Paul regained control and Dark was fired in 1971. Ken Aspromonte then became Indians' manager in 1972.

Aspromonte benefited from one of the greatest trades in Tribe history. Unpredictable Sam McDowell was traded to the Giants for veteran righthander Gaylord Perry and shortstop Frank Duffy. Sudden Sam won just 19 more games for three different teams in four years. Perry, with or without his alleged spitball, promptly registered a league-high 24 wins and a 1.92 ERA for the fifth-place Indians to win the Cy Young Award. Throw-in Duffy was Cleveland's starting shortstop from 1972 to 1977. Still, trades could not compensate for a farm system in ruins.

Baseball in Cleveland, like Cleveland itself, was without vision and thus floundering in the 1970s. Nick Mileti's purchase of the club soon sent George Steinbrenner off to purchase the Yankees. George took along several Clevelanders, including Gabe Paul and major stockholder F. J. "Steve" O'Neill.[5] Also heading East were two players that might have led Cleveland out of the wilderness. Star third baseman Graig Nettles, obtained in a brilliant 1969 deal with the Twins, went to the Yankees with catcher Gerry Moses for four players, most notably catcher John Ellis and outfield prospect Charlie Spikes. After some initial success, Spikes proved to be merely another unfulfilled talent. That the trade occurred just five weeks before Paul went to New York raised some eyebrows, but is perhaps best considered a mere coincidence. On April 27, 1974 Paul acquired 1971 Rookie-of-the-Year Chris Chambliss and 1972 Rookie-Pitcher-of-the-Year Dick Tidrow from Cleveland for four pitchers. Nettles, Chambliss, and Tidrow became cornerstones of World Championship teams in 1977 and 1978 at New York. With briefly fortified pitching, the 1974 Indians, paced by Gaylord Perry's 21 wins and Jim Perry's 17, were contenders until September, then stumbled to fourth place, costing Aspromonte his job as manager. Cleveland baseball suffered another black eye on June 6 as 25,134 fans turned out for 10-cent beer night. When the Indians forged a 5–5 ninth-inning tie with the Texas Rangers, drunken fans stormed the field and the game was forfeited to Texas.

Ted Bonda brought Cleveland back to the forefront of baseball's integration achievements with the decision to hire Frank Robinson as major league baseball's first black manager on October 3, 1974. As player-manager, Robinson slammed a home run in his first 1975 regular season at-bat, a moment deemed the most memorable in Indians history by short-sighted Tribe fan voting in conjunction with the American League's 75th anniversary in 1976. The stormy Robinson era featured battles with Gaylord Perry, John Ellis, Rico Carty, and others. Though the Indians showed significant improvement under Robinson, including their first winning season of the decade (1976), Bonda, now controlling owner of the club, was persuaded to fire Frank Robinson after a poor start in 1977. F.J. O'Neill returned in 1978, buying the club from Bonda, but only on the condition that Gabe Paul return as club president.

By any measurement Gabe Paul's second tenure with the Indians (1978–84) has to be considered one of the darkest eras in franchise history. The Indians were 504–565 (.471) and, with the exception of the 1981 strike season, never finished closer than within 17 games of first place. Cleveland's failure was magnified by the success of the expansion Toronto Blue Jays and firmly illustrated when the six-year-old Jays tied the 82-year-old Indians for sixth place on the final day of the 1982 season. While the Blue Jays quickly rose to pennant contention, the Indians continued to flounder on the South Side of Lake Erie. From 1978 to 1981, only the Blue Jays kept Cleveland out of the cellar. The Tribe tumbled back into the basement in 1983, the first of three seventh-place finishes, all in odd-numbered years, from 1983 to 1987. Attendance also suffered during the Paul-II years. The Indians averaged less than 900,000 fans in home attendance from 1978 to 1984 (excluding 1981), drawing fewer than 800,000 in both 1983 and 1984. With the increasing costs of running a major league franchise, and prior to increased television revenues, the Indians were truly in financial trouble.

While players continued to come and go, one constant was Andre Thornton. Stolen from the Montreal Expos by general manager Phil Seghi in 1976, "Thunder" remained with the Indians until his retirement in 1987. His 214 home runs with Cleveland rank fourth in club history. Mike Hargrove arrived in 1979 to perfect his act as "The Human Rain Delay" and Len Barker pitched a perfect game against Toronto in 1981. A disastrous deal sent no-hit pitcher Dennis Eckersley to Boston, where he won 20 games, in 1978. Fan-favorite Buddy Bell was shipped to Texas where he became a perennial all-star at third base. In a nutshell, the wheels kept spinning.

When Steve O'Neill died in 1983, loss of the franchise became a clear and present danger once again. Steve's nephew Pat O'Neill became chairman of the board, indicated he had no desire to run the club, but would sell only to a group dedicated to keeping the Indians in Cleveland. While still in search of a buyer, O'Neill hired Peter Bavasi to replace Gabe Paul and run the Indians.[6] Bavasi, an executive in the early days of the Blue Jays, took over in Cleveland, cleaning out the front office and promising a clear vision for the future. He brought in Joe Klein, who fortified the farm system with pitching prospects, and Dan O'Brien, whose salary battle with Joe Carter in 1987 established ill feelings between the slugger and front office for several years after. (Carter eventually departed to free-agency at the close of the 1989 season.) Since Bavasi was once hired to bring baseball to St. Petersburg, Florida, suspicion arose that Peter was simply maneuvering to move the Indians south. His decision to take the "C" for Cleveland off Tribe caps and replace it with the more generic (if more traditional) Chief Wahoo logo only accelerated the rumors. Though far short of a championship, Bavasi announced in 1987 that he had completed his mission, turned the Indians in the right direction, and would leave to pursue new challenges.

The third decade of the drought, the 1980s, intensified the frustrated baseball climate in Cleveland. Grandfatherly Dave Garcia, manager from mid-1979 to 1982, seemed perfect for an Indians team that seemed content to drift through one baseball season after another. Young Mike Ferraro, hired as a departure from the laid-back approach of Garcia, suffered a bout with cancer during spring training in 1983, apparently losing his tough edge, and lasted just 100 games into the campaign. Even though Pat Corrales was found wanting by the Phillies and fired with that club in first place in 1983, the Indians felt the tough ex-catcher could light a fire in the teepee. Despite a poor season in 1984 and a club-record-tying 102 losses in 1985, Corrales was given a "perpetual" contract by Bavasi.

An unexpected Indians uprising took place in 1986 as Carter, A.L. RBI champ, and Julio Franco led the highest scoring offense in the league. Pat Tabler, unparalleled bases-loaded hitter, and Tony Bernazard had career seasons, leadoff man Brett Butler set the table, and Brook Jacoby, Mel Hall, Thornton, and Olympian Cory Snyder provided power. Almost 1.5 million fans attended Tribe home games, the best Cleveland attendance since 1959. With expectations that the dry spell would end (the Indians were the only team in a seven-year period that had not won the A.L. East) in 1987, Cleveland sank back to its 1985 level. The 1986 offense was part mirage, part inflation (all batting stats were up in 1986), part surprise (expectations for the Indians had been dismal), and part the fact that teams would just as soon beat Cleveland 10–9 as 2–1. "Perpetual Pat" Corrales was replaced by another ex-catcher, Doc Edwards. Edwards, like so many before him, seemed a well-meaning man without the tools or genius to reverse the growing tide of Tribe troubles.

With Cleveland's baseball existence nearly terminal, brothers Richard and David Jacobs came to the rescue. The Jacobs brothers had made millions developing shopping malls and were on the verge of reshaping downtown Cleveland with several ambitious building projects. They had developed a reputation for quiet but effective business success. In a city where project after project was announced, never to see the light of day, the Jacobs did not go public unless success was assured. They consummated purchase of the Indians on December 9, 1986, bringing financially stable ownership to the Tribe for the first time in decades.

Just as Steve O'Neill turned to Cleveland's past for a new leader, so did Dick Jacobs. Hank Peters, head of the farm clubs for Cleveland in 1966 and director of player development from 1967 to 1971, rejoined the Tribe as Chief Operating Officer on November 2, 1987. Peters was an executive with the Athletics from 1961 to 1965, when the beginnings of their 1970s dynasty were formed. When Cleveland's minor league system was forsaken, Peters left to become president of the National Association. His reign as chief executive of the Baltimore Orioles (November 1975 to October 5, 1987) yielded a pair of A.L. champions, a World Championship in 1983, and Major-League-Executive-of-the-Year honors from *The Sporting News* in 1979 and 1983. Peters sought to bring Baltimore-like stability to Cleveland. The early transition period was hardly a success. Peters was criticized for cautious management and his assistant, Tom Giordano, was the focal figure in a drafting fiasco when Cleveland's number one choice in 1989, Calvin Murray, turned his back on the Indians to attend college.

A surprising pronouncement from Dick Jacobs came midway through the 1989 season when he announced the desire for the Indians to play in a new and smaller stadium, one more suited to baseball than huge Cleveland Stadium. As in other cities with old facilities, a new baseball stadium for Cleveland had been talked about for decades. In the early 1980s the Greater Cleveland Domed Stadium Corporation, a non-profit venture, was formed. Cleveland taxpayers, however, were unwilling to support public financing for the project. When County Commissioner Vince Campanella was soundly defeated in a re-election bid after supporting the Domed Stadium, no politician would unconditionally support a new stadium. The Domed Stadium Corporation became the New Stadium Corporation and joined forces with the Jacobs brothers in announcing a desire to build a 45,000-50,000-seat stadium, with an option of adding convertible seating that would increase capacity to 72,000 fans for football. This facility supposedly would be located at what is known as the Central Market site in downtown Cleveland. Art Modell, owner of the National Football League Cleveland Browns and Cleveland Stadium Corporation, the Indians landlords, was unwilling to leave behind 8,000 seats and control of the Stadium to join the Indians in a new house. As the Cleveland Indians ended play in a third straight decade without seriously challenging for a pennant (1960 to 1989), the fate of the Tribe seemed hinged on the ability of Jacobs, Modell, and the politicians and citizens of Cleveland to compromise on the stadium issue.

Cleveland's stadium issue also drew the attention of the two biggest Tribe stars in the 1980s. The comments of Andre Thornton and Joe Carter, several years apart, are indicative of the recent baseball atmosphere in Cleveland. Chapter Seven of *A Baseball Winter* is titled "Andre," referring to Thornton. A free agent following the 1984 season, Thornton spoke out on baseball in Cleveland. "This team needs a vision. It begins with the stadium. Something must be done to make baseball in this town an attractive package. The team itself is just a part of that package. It is important, but not everything. The stadium is a dull old park," Thornton concluded. As if carrying on in Thornton's footsteps as a spokesman like he did as the big-run-producing bat in the Indians' lineup, Joe Carter echoed Thornton's comments with eerie similarity in 1989. Carter said flat out that no free agent would ever choose Cleveland as a place to play so long as the Indians toiled in the antiquated lakefront stadium. Carter's ballpark comments, following his publicized thinking that family members should travel with the team (opposed to current Tribe policy), and preceding his perhaps naive stance regarding fickle fans that boo a player for striking out in one at-bat and cheer his home run the next, all but assured that Carter would be the next in a series of unhappy stars such as Jim Bibby, Bert Blyleven, Rick Sutcliffe, Brett Butler, and others that forced an escape from the Wigwam. And as expected, Carter was traded away to the San Diego Padres for talented young catcher Sandy Alomar, Jr. at season's end.

As the city, a victim of industrial decline and a population exodus to the South and West, climbed back to respectability, Cleveland slowly shed its earlier image as a loser—exemplified by the default of the city in 1979. The Browns and National Basketball Association Cleveland Cavaliers joined the revival in the latter 1980s, but the Indians continued to flounder. As losing season followed losing season, a perceptible anger mounted among Cleveland's fans. In the opinion of many a championship team, and nothing less, would return the Tribe to a warm place in the hearts of Clevelanders.

Fittingly the 1980s ended with a managerial change in Cleveland, the 15th in 30 years. Hank Peters claimed the 1989 Indians had become too comfortable with losing, a charge loyal Indians fans would no doubt also attribute to a variety of players, ownerships, and managements in recent Indians history. John Hart, another Baltimore refugee, replaced Doc Edwards on an interim basis September 12, 1989. Once again Tribe fans had been teased into believing the long dry spell might end in 1989, as strong pitching, led by Greg Swindell, Tom Candiotti, Bud Black, and ace reliever Doug Jones, and mediocre competition kept the Indians close to the top well into August. The mirage vanished with a free-fall slump that left the club fighting to finish above sixth place for only the second time in the decade. For Cleveland baseball fans, the 1980s mercifully ended with the Indians fighting Texas and Atlanta for the second worst won-loss record of the decade, ahead of only the Seattle Mariners.

As a new decade unfolded there were still no first division finishes in sight. Yet the Tribe did boast more respectability as it marched to a fourth-place slot in 1990, then repeated the act two summers later. And there were some shining new stars on the horizon: Charles Nagy provided evidence that he was as capable a starter as almost any in the junior circuit, while Sandy Alomar matured from hyped-rookie into a solid everyday receiver. And with slugging second sacker Carlos Baerga (.312 BA and 299 total bases in 1992) the Indians now possessed one of the league's most exciting youngsters at the plate and in the field. With a new ballpark on line for 1994, Tribe fans could now legitimately dream of finally escaping a curse so long draped over the huge arc of an ancient ballpark that had withstood so many summertime disappointments on the windy shores of Lake Erie.

Notes

1. Rumors persist that the series between the Indians and White Sox was not on the up-and-up. In the February 1963 *Baseball Digest*, an article by Ritter Collett quotes Duster Mails as suspecting that the White Sox might not have given 100 percent when he shut them out during the final week of the season.

2. Research conducted after Feller racked up his 348 strikeouts revealed that Waddell actually struck out 349 batters in his record-setting season. To deny Feller the record (since broken twice) because of after-the-fact research is like changing the rules during the game. Feller broke the accepted existing record and was certainly capable of passing the revised record.

3. In fairness to Tribe fans of the day, there were four fewer home games prior to expansion and even fewer home dates due to doubleheaders. The Indians had 12 scheduled twin-bills in 1956. With the exception of new major league markets in Milwaukee, Kansas City, and Baltimore, attendance was on a downward trend. The Giants and Cubs drew even fewer fans than the Indians in 1956 and 1957, while the outstanding Brooklyn teams hovered around the one million attendance mark throughout the 1950s before accompanying the Giants to California in 1958.

4. Kuenn actually had more runs-created than Colavito in 1959, a brilliant example of the sometimes misleading nature of statistics. Colavito was the heart and soul of Cleveland's offense. Without the Rock, Cleveland went from first to second in team batting average, but first to fifth in runs scored. In the *Bill James Baseball Abstract 1982,* James' article on the Indians discusses the everlasting effects of the Colavito trade.

5. Dan Coughlin's article "Cleveland, Siberia" in the December 1983 issue of *Inside Sports* magazine is an insightful capsule look at recent Indians ownership.

6. See *A Baseball Winter* (Pluto and Neuman) for the embarrassing details of the non-sale of the Indians to a group headed by David LeFevre during the winter of 1984–1985.

References

Collett, Ritter. 1965. "Did Black Sox Throw 1920 Flag, Too?" *Baseball Digest* (February).

Greenberg, Hank, and Ira Berkow. 1989. *Hank Greenberg: The Story of My Life.* New York: Times Books. Pp. 196–226.

James, Bill. 1982. *The Bill James Baseball Abstract 1982.* New York: Ballantine Books (Random House Publishers), "Cleveland Indians" on pp. 50ff.

Lewis, Franklin. 1949. *The Cleveland Indians.* New York: G. P. Putnam's Sons.

MacFarland, Paul. 1983. *The Sporting News Hall of Fame Fact Book.* St. Louis, Mo.: The Sporting News. Pp. 32ff.

Pluto, Terry, and Jeffrey Neuman. 1986. *A Baseball Winter.* New York: Macmillan Publishing Company.

Wallack, Nate. 1960. *Cleveland Indians 1960 Press Book.* Cleveland, Ohio: Cleveland Indians Baseball Company. Pp. 42–43.

Annotated Bibliography

Berkow, Ira. *Hank Greenberg: The Story of My Life.* New York: Times Books, 1989. 311 pp.

Berkow posthumously edited Greenberg's memoirs into a compelling narrative of his life, including his days as an executive with the Indians. Greenberg's feelings toward Cleveland as a baseball city are most revealing. Though Hank presided over much of the most glorious era in Tribe history, he seems to have cared little for the franchise and its native city.

Boudreau, Lou, with Ed Fitzgerald. *Player-Manager.* Boston: Little, Brown, 1949, 256 pp.

The season of a lifetime is the basis for Boudreau's autobiography, published immediately after the Indians' 1948 World Championship. Lou's career, to that point, is well covered.

Cobbledick, Gordon. *Don't Knock The Rock.* Cleveland, Ohio: World Publishing Company, 1966. 158 pp.

Rocky Colavito is, without debate, the most charismatic and memorable figure in recent Indians history (1955–present). Colavito's life and career is described by Cobbledick, the dean of Cleveland sportswriters for many years, up until the Rock's triumphant return season with the Indians in 1965.

Eckhouse, Morris. *Day by Day in Cleveland Indians History.* New York: Leisure Press, 1983. 400 pp.

One of a series of day-by-day books, the Indians volume features its day-by-day section, statistics, trades, post-season history, nicknames, and features. The book is the first since Franklin Lewis' *The Cleveland Indians* to focus exclusively on Indians history and emphasizes highlights since the publication of the Lewis book in 1949.

Feller, Bob. *Strikeout Story.* New York: A.S. Barnes, 1947. 258 pp.

Bob Feller remains the brightest star in Indians history and his autobiography is a well-told account of his life through the 1946 season, mostly devoted to Bob's professional career. By covering Feller in detail, the book also sheds considerable light on the Indians from 1936 to 1941, including the Crybabies incident of 1940.

Hano, Arnold. *A Day in the Bleachers.* New York: Crowell, 1955. 152 pp.

Many consider Hano's account of the first game of the 1954 World Series to be one of the best baseball books ever written. From a Cleveland perspective, it can also be viewed as an agonizing look at a huge turning point in club history.

Lewis, Franklin. *Cleveland Indians.* New York: G.P. Putnam's Sons, 1949. 276 pp.

One of the Putnam series, Lewis' book tells the story of baseball in Cleveland up through the triumphant 1948 campaign. Entertaining and relatively comprehensive, Lewis' *Cleveland Indians* is a fine starting point for learning about the club.

Moore, Joseph Thomas. *Pride Against Prejudice.* New York: Praeger Publishers, 1988.

Several books dealt with Jackie Robinson and the modern integration of major league baseball, but none focused on Larry Doby, the first black in the American League, until Moore's scholarly study. Well researched and notated, Moore's book depicts a complicated man whose place in baseball history had been significantly overlooked.

Murphy, J.M. *The National Pastime—Nap Lajoie.* Kansas City, Mo.: The Society for American Baseball Research, 1988. 80 pp.

The Society for American Baseball Research deserves credit for devoting an entire issue of its magazine, *The National Pastime*, to Murphy's biography of Lajoie. Napoleon is one of the first superstars of modern major league baseball (since 1901) and remains one of the greatest stars in Cleveland baseball history. Murphy provides a solid look at Nap and his career in Cleveland.

Paige, Satchel, as told to David Lipman. *Maybe I'll Pitch Forever.* Garden City, NY: Doubleday, 1962. 285 pp.

One of the most controversial episodes in Tribe history was the signing of Paige in 1948. Satch's colorful biography tells the story of his days in

Cleveland, including becoming the first black to pitch in the World Series.
. . . *Forever* has an advantage over *Pitchin' Man* (the other important Paige
biography) in that it covers Satch's entire career with the Indians.

Phillips, John. *Cleveland Baseball Winners.* Cabin John, Md: Capital Publishing
Company, 1987.
Cleveland Baseball Winners refers to members of the Indians from 1946 to
1956, the golden age of major league baseball in Cleveland. Phillips
furnishes a brief biography of each Indians player during that time
period. A self-published work, spiral bound and computer generated,
CBW still represents a useful reference regarding Indians history.

———. *96 Years of Hope.* Cabin John, Md: Capital Publishing Company,
1987.
This self-published work by Phillips is a comprehensive listing of all the
trades in club history. Trades are listed chronologically and an index lists
transactions alphabetically according to the Cleveland player involved.

Schoor, Gene. *Bob Feller—Hall of Fame Strikeout Star.* Garden, City, NY: Doubleday, 1962. 191 pp.
Though basically a juvenile account of Feller's life and career, Schoor's
effort improves on Feller's own *Strikeout Story* with an unbiased approach,
including discussion of Feller's surprising lack of popularity during a
portion of his Cleveland career. Schoor's volume also has the advantage
of covering Feller's complete major league career, ending with his induction into baseball's Hall of Fame.

Sowell, Mike. *The Pitch That Killed.* New York: Macmillan Publishing Company,
1989.
One of the most memorable single events in baseball history finally gets
full-scale written treatment. Sowell tracks the careers of New York pitcher
Carl Mays and Cleveland shortstop Ray Chapman, both players who
might have been destined for the Hall of Fame until fate intervened in
1920. A well-researched, though somewhat dry, presentation of Chapman's fatal beaning and the principal characters involved.

Veeck, Bill, and Ed Linn. *Veeck as in Wreck.* New York: G.P. Putnam, 1962.
380 pp.
Because the Indians have suffered so many seasons without a championship since 1948, Bill Veeck remains a revered and mythical figure in local
baseball lore. His biography, then, is necessary reading to understand the
brief, brilliant, phenomenon of the Veeck years in Cleveland.

Year-by-Year Standings and Season Summaries

Year	Pos.	Record	Pct.	GB	Manager	Player	BA	Player	HR	Player	W-L	ERA
1901	7th	54–82	.397	28.5	McAleer	McCarthy	.321	Beck	6	Moore	16–14	2.90
1902	5th	69–67	.507	14	Armour	Hickman	.379	Bradley	11	Bernhard	17–5	2.20
1903	3rd	77–63	.550	15	Armour	Lajoie	.355	Hickman	12	Moore	19–9	1.77
1904	4th	86–85	.570	7.5	Armour / Lajoie	Lajoie	.355	Lajoie / Flick	6 / 6	Bernhard	23–13	2.13
1905	5th	76–78	.494	19	Lajoie	Flick	.306	Flick	4	Joss	20–12	2.01
1906	3rd	89–64	.582	5	Lajoie	Lajoie	.355	Congalton / Bemis / Turner / Bradley	2 / 2 / 2 / 2	Rhoades	22–10	1.80
1907	4th	85–67	.559	8	Lajoie	Flick	.302	Flick	3	Joss	27–11	1.83
1908	2nd	90–64	.584	.5	Lajoie	Stovall	.292	Hinchman	6	Joss	24–11	1.16
1909	6th	71–82	.464	27.5	Lajoie / McGuire	Lajoie	.324	Hinchman / Stovall	6 / 6	Young	19–15	2.26
1910	5th	71–81	.467	32	McGuire	Lajoie	.384	Lajoie	4	Falkenberg	14–13	2.94
1911	3rd	80–73	.523	22	McGuire / Stovall	Jackson	.408	Jackson	7	Gregg	23–7	1.81
1912	5th	75–78	.490	30.5	Davis / Birmingham	Jackson	.395	Jackson	3	Gregg	20–13	2.59
1913	3rd	86–66	.566	9.5	Birmingham	Jackson	.373	Jackson	7	Falkenberg	23–10	2.22
1914	8th	51–102	.333	48.5	Birmingham	Jackson	.338	Jackson	3	Mitchell	12–17	3.19
1915	7th	57–95	.375	44.5	Birmingham / Fohl	Jackson	.331	Roth	4	Morton	16–15	2.14
1916	6th	77–77	.500	14	Fohl	Speaker	.386	Graney	5	Bagby	16–16	2.55
1917	3rd	88–66	.571	12	Fohl	Speaker	.352	Graney / Smith	3 / 3	Bagby	23–13	1.96
1918	2nd	73–56	.566	2.5	Fohl	Speaker	.381	Wood	5	Coveleski	22–13	1.82
1919	2nd	84–55	.604	3.5	Fohl / Speaker	Johnston	.305	Smith	9	Coveleski	24–12	2.52

134

Year	Pos.	Record	Pct.	GB	Manager	Player	BA	Player	HR	Player	W-L	ERA
1920	1st	98–56	.636	+2	Speaker	Speaker	.388	Smith	12	Bagby	31–12	2.89
1921	2nd	94–60	.610	4.5	Speaker	Speaker	.362	Smith	16	Coveleski	23–13	3.36
1922	4th	78–76	.507	16	Speaker	Speaker	.378	Speaker	11	Uhle	22–16	4.08
1923	3rd	82–71	.536	16.5	Speaker	Speaker	.380	Speaker	17	Uhle	26–16	3.77
1924	6th	67–86	.438	24.5	Speaker	Jamieson	.358	Speaker / Myatt	8 / 8	Shaute	20–17	3.75
1925	6th	70–84	.455	27.5	Speaker	Speaker	.389	Speaker	12	Buckeye	13–8	3.65
1926	2nd	88–66	.571	3	Speaker	Burns	.358	Speaker	7	Uhle	27–11	2.83
1927	6th	66–86	.431	43.5	McAllister	Burns	.319	Hodapp	5	Hudlin	18–12	4.01
1928	7th	62–92	.403	39	Peckinpaugh	Sewell	.323	Burns	5	Hudlin	14–14	4.05
1929	3rd	81–71	.533	24	Peckinpaugh	Fonseca	.369	Averill	18	Ferrell	21–10	3.59
1930	4th	81–73	.526	21	Peckinpaugh	Hodapp	.354	Morgan	26	Ferrell	25–13	3.30
1931	4th	78–76	.506	30	Peckinpaugh	Morgan	.351	Averill	32	Ferrell	22–12	3.75
1932	4th	87–65	.572	19	Peckinpaugh	Cisell	.315	Averill	32	Ferrell	23–13	3.65
1933	4th	75–76	.497	23.5	Peckinpaugh / Johnson	Averill	.301	Averill	11	Hildebrand	16–11	3.76
1934	3rd	85–69	.552	16	Johnson	Vosmik	.341	Trosky	35	Harder	20–12	2.61
1935	3rd	82–71	.536	12	Johnson / O'Neill	Vosmik	.348	Trosky	26	Harder	22–11	3.29
1936	5th	80–74	.519	22.5	O'Neill	Averill	.378	Trosky	42	Allen	20–12	3.44
1937	4th	83–71	.539	19	O'Neill	Solters	.323	Trosky	32	Allen	15–1	2.55
1938	3rd	86–66	.566	13	Vitt	Heath	.343	Keltner	26	Harder	17–10	3.83
1939	3rd	87–67	.565	20.5	Vitt	Trosky	.335	Trosky	25	Feller	24–9	2.85
1940	2nd	89–65	.578	1	Vitt	Weatherly	.303	Trosky	25	Feller	27–11	2.62
1941	4th	75–79	.487	26	Peckinpaugh	Heath	.340	Heath	24	Feller	25–13	3.15
1942	4th	75–79	.487	28	Boudreau	Fleming	.292	Fleming	14	Bagby, Jr.	17–9	2.96
1943	3rd	82–71	.536	15.5	Boudreau	Cullenbine	.289	Heath	18	Smith	17–7	2.55
1944	5th	72–82	.468	17	Boudreau	Boudreau	.327	Cullenbine	16	Harder	12–10	3.72
1945	5th	73–72	.503	11	Boudreau	Meyer	.292	Heath	15	Gromek	19–9	2.55
1946	6th	68–86	.442	36	Boudreau	Edwards	.301	Seerey	26	Feller	26–15	2.18
1947	4th	80–74	.519	17	Boudreau	Mitchell	.316	Gordon	29	Feller	20–11	2.68

135

Year	Pos.	Record	Pct.	GB	Manager	Player	BA	Player	HR	Player	W-L	ERA
1948	1st	97–58	.626	+1	Boudreau	Boudreau	.355	Gordon	32	Bearden	20–7	2.43
1949	3rd	89–65	.578	8	Boudreau	Mitchell	.317	Doby	24	Lemon	22–10	2.99
1950	4th	92–62	.597	6	Boudreau	Doby	.326	Rosen	37	Lemon	23–11	3.84
1951	2nd	93–61	.604	5	Lopez	Avila	.305	Easter	27	Feller	22–8	3.49
1952	2nd	93–61	.604	2	Lopez	Mitchell	.323	Doby	32	Wynn	23–12	2.90
1953	2nd	92–62	.597	8.5	Lopez	Rosen	.336	Rosen	43	Lemon	21–15	3.36
1954	1st	111–43	.721	+8	Lopez	Avila	.341	Doby	32	Lemon	23–7	2.72
1955	2nd	93–61	.604	3	Lopez	Smith	.306	Doby	26	Lemon	18–10	3.88
1956	2nd	88–66	.571	9	Lopez	Smith	.274	Wertz	32	Score	20–9	2.53
1957	6th	76–77	.497	21.5	Farrell	Woodling	.321	Wertz	28	Wynn	14–17	4.31
1958	4th	77–76	.503	14.5	Bragan / Gordon	Colavito	.303	Colavito	41	McLish	16–8	2.99
1959	2nd	89–65	.578	5	Gordon	Francona	.363	Colavito	42	McLish	19–8	3.64
1960	4th	76–78	.494	21	Gordon / Dykes	Kuenn	.308	Held	21	J. Perry	18–10	3.62
1961	5th	78–83	.484	30.5	Dykes	Piersall	.322	Kirkland	27	Grant	15–9	3.86
1962	6th	80–82	.494	16	McGaha	Francona	.272	Romano	25	Donovan	20–10	3.59
1963	5th	79–83	.488	25.5	Tebbetts	Alvis	.274	Alvis	22	Kralick	13–9	2.92
1964	6th	79–83	.488	20	Tebbetts	Chance	.279	Wagner	31	Kralick	12–7	3.20
1965	5th	87–75	.537	15	Tebbetts	Davalillo	.301	McDowell	28	McDowell	17–11	2.18
1966	5th	81–81	.500	17	Tebbetts / Strickland	Wagner	.279	Siebert	30	Siebert	16–8	2.80
1967	8th	75–87	.463	17	Adcock	Davalillo	.287	Alvis	21	Hargan	14–13	2.62
1968	3rd	86–75	.534	16.5	Dark	Maye	.281	Horton	14	Tiant	21–9	1.60
1969	6th	62–99	.385	46.5	Dark	Horton	.278	Harrelson / Horton	27 / 27	McDowell	18–14	2.94
1970	5th	76–86	.469	32	Dark	Fosse	.307	Nettles	26	McDowell	20–12	2.92
1971	6th	60–102	.370	43	Dark / Lipon	Uhlaender	.288	Nettles	28	McDowell	13–17	3.39
1972	5th	72–84	.462	14	Aspromonte	Chambliss	.292	Nettles	17	G. Perry	24–16	1.92
1973	6th	71–91	.438	26	Aspromonte	Chambliss	.273	Spikes	23	G. Perry	19–19	3.38

Year	Pos.	Record	Pct.	Manager	GB	Player	BA	Player	HR	Player	W-L	ERA
1974	4th	77–85	.475	Aspromonte	14	Gamble	.291	Spikes	22	G. Perry	21–13	2.52
1975	4th	79–80	.497	Robinson	15.5	Carty	.308	Powell	27	Peterson	14–8	3.95
1976	4th	81–78	.509	Robinson	16	Carty	.301	Hendrick	25	Dobson	16–12	3.48
1977	5th	71–90	.441	Robinson / Torborg	28.5	Bochte	.304	Thornton	28	Eckersley	14–13	3.53
1978	6th	69–70	.434	Torborg	29	Kuiper .283	.283	Thornton	33	Waits	13–15	3.21
1979	6th	81–80	.503	Norris / Torborg	22	Hargrove	.325	Thornton	26	Waits	16–13	4.44
1980	6th	79–81	.494	Garcia	23	Dilone	.341	Charboneau	23	Barker	19–12	4.17
1981	6th	26–24	.520	Garcia	5	Hargrove	.317	Diaz	7	Blyleven	11–7	2.89
1981*	5th	26–27	.491		5							
	6th	52–51	.505									
1982	6th	78–84	.481	Garcia	17	Harrah	.304	Thornton	32	Barker	15–11	3.90
1983	7th	70–92	.432	Ferraro / Corrales	28	Tabler	.291	Thornton Thomas	17 17	Sutcliffe	17–11	4.29
1984	6th	75–87	.463	Corrales	29.5	Vukovich	.304	Thornton	33	Blyleven	19–7	2.87
1985	7th	60–102	.370	Corrales	39.5	Butler	.311	Thornton	22	Heaton	9–17	4.90
1986	5th	84–78	.519	Corrales	11.5	Tabler	.326	Carter	29	Candiotti	16–12	3.57
1987	7th	61–101	.377	Corrales / Edwards	37	Franco	.319	Snyder	33	Bailes	7–8	4.64
1988	6th	78–84	.481	Edwards	11	Franco	.303	Carter	27	Swindell	18–14	3.20
1989	6th	73–89	.451	Edwards / Hart	16	Browne	.299	Carter	35	Candiotti	13–10	3.10
1990	4th	77–85	.475	McNamara	11	James	.299	Maldonado	22	Candiotti	15–11	3.65
1991	7th	57–105	.352	McNamara / Hargrove	34	Cole	.295	Belle	34	Nagy	10–15	4.13
1992	4th(T)	76–86	.469	Hargrove	20	Baerga	.312	Belle	34	Nagy	17–10	2.96

*Split Season Totals (Players' Union Strike).

137

All-Time Indians Career and Season Records

Career Batting Leaders (1901–1992)

Games Played	Terry Turner	1,617
At Bats	Nap Lajoie	6,037
Runs Scored	Earl Averill	1,154
Hits	Nap Lajoie	2,051
Batting Average	Joe Jackson	.375
Home Runs	Earl Averill	226
Stolen Bases	Terry Turner	254
Strikeouts	Larry Doby	805

Career Pitching Leaders (1901–1992)

Innings Pitched	Bob Feller	3,828
Earned Run Average	Addie Joss	1.88
Wins	Bob Feller	266
Losses	Mel Harder	186
Winning Percentage	Addie Joss	.623
Strikeouts	Bob Feller	2,581
Walks	Bob Feller	1,764
Games	Mel Harder	582
Shutouts	Bob Feller	46
Saves	Doug Jones	128
Complete Games	Bob Feller	279

Single-Season Batting Records (1901–1992)

Batting Average (502 ABs)	Joe Jackson	.408	1911
Home Runs	Al Rosen	43	1953
Home Runs (lefthanded)	Hal Trosky	42	1936
Runs Batted In	Hal Trosky	162	1936
Hits	Joe Jackson	233	1911
Singles	Charlie Jamieson	172	1923
Doubles	George Burns	64	1926
Triples	Joe Jackson	26	1912
Slugging Percentage	Hal Trosky	.644	1936
Extra Base Hits	Hal Trosky	96	1936
Game-Winning Hits	Andre Thornton	15	1982
Sacrifices	Ray Chapman	67	1917
Stolen Bases	Ken Lofton	66	1992
Pinch Hits	Bob Hale	19	1960
Strikeouts	Cory Snyder	166	1987
Total Bases	Hal Trosky	405	1936
Hitting Streak	Bill Bradley	29	1902
Grand Slam Home Runs	Al Rosen	4	1954
Hit by Pitch	Minnie Minoso	17	1959

All-Time Indians Career and Season Records *(continued)*

Single-Season Pitching Records (1901–1992)

ERA (150 innings)	Addie Joss	1.16	1908
Wins	Jim Bagby	31	1920
Losses	Pete Dowling	22	1901
Winning Pct. (10 decisions)	Johnny Allen	.938	1937
Strikeouts	Bob Feller	348	1946
Walks	Bob Feller	208	1936
Saves	Doug Jones	43	1990
Games	Sid Monge	76	1979
Complete Games	Bob Feller	36	1946
Games Started	George Uhle	44	1923
Shutouts	Bob Feller	10	1946
	Bob Lemon	10	1948
Innings Pitched	Bob Feller	371	1946
Home Runs Allowed	Luis Tiant	37	1969
Consecutive Games Won	Johnny Allen	15	1937
(season)	Gaylord Perry	15	1974
Consecutive Games Lost	Guy Morton	13	1914
(season)			
Wild Pitches	Sam McDowell	18	1967
Balks	Tom Candiotti	7	1988

4
Detroit Tigers
The Cornerstone of Detroit Baseball Is Stability
MORRIS A. ECKHOUSE

Conservative, stable, consistent. These are words that come to mind when describing the Detroit Tigers, a charter member of the American League. The familiar, Old English "D" graces the cap and home uniform. The familiar, comfortable confines of Tiger Stadium, the hitter's paradise, stand at the corners of Michigan and Trumbull Avenues, site of major league baseball in Detroit since the start of the 1900s. The nickname, "Tigers," has been with the club since the 1890s when newspaper man Philip J. Reid noticed the similarity between Detroit's black and yellow colors and those of Princeton University (the popular story that the club was nicknamed in honor of Ty Cobb is untrue) (Lieb, 1946, 22). The remarkable stability of ownership has a heritage that runs from Frank Navin's purchase of the franchise in 1908, to Walter Briggs, to John Fetzer, to Fetzer's hand-picked successor, Tom Monaghan.

Detroit is the only major league team that has had an extended monopoly on one state. The Tigers are Michigan's team. This unique identity has been aided by remarkable stability in the broadcast booth, that daily link between team and fans. Ty Tyson became the first voice of the Tigers when they began radio broadcasts of home games in 1927 over radio station WWJ, starting with the April 19, 1927 game between the Tigers and Indians. Tyson, born in Tyrone, Pennsylvania, described Detroit home games until 1942. Ty also inaugurated Detroit telecasts in 1947. Rival station WXYZ also broadcast Tigers games on radio from 1934 to 1942 with retired batting star Harry Heilmann at the mike. Tyson broadcast to Detroit itself, Heilmann to Michigan listeners outside the city. When the rival broadcasts merged in 1943, "Old Slug" Heilmann carried on with home and away games until stricken by cancer. Tyson returned for a year, followed by Van Patrick. The knowledgeable, somewhat overbearing Patrick teamed with Tyson, Dizzy Trout, and Mel Ott who died in a car crash in November 1958. Ott was followed by George Kell, a fixture on Detroit radio, then on TV broadcasts ever since. When Patrick went to the Mutual Network after the 1959 season, the Tigers and WKMH hired Ernie Harwell away from the Baltimore Orioles. Harwell and Tiger baseball are linked as one by many after a partnership of three decades, and since 1964 on radio station WJR.[1]

The legacy of consistency seems left by Frank J. Navin. A graduate of the Detroit College of Law, Navin entered the world of baseball when his boss, Tigers' owner Samuel Angus, added bookkeeping duties for the ballclub to Navin's work with Angus' insurance agency. When Navin rose to become the club's top executive he instituted strict, conservative financial policies. To the public, Navin was an unemotional sort, keeping his feelings in check through good times and bad. He also refused to let feelings interfere with the business of baseball. Navin's simple philosophy was that he could pay out only what came in. Though the early Tigers were highly successful on the field, attendance was limited in major league baseball's smallest market. The great players of those clubs were paid accordingly less than they were worth, giving Navin the reputation as a penny pincher.[2]

Though manager George Stallings led the 1901 Tigers to a third-place finish, 8½ games behind first place Chicago, Detroit had trouble competing with other A.L. teams that continued to raid N.L. squads for talent. Pitcher George Mullin made his debut with the 1902 Tigers. His 13–16 record gave little indication that Mullin would become a five-time 20-game winner and the first of four hurlers to win 200 games with the Tigers before 1990 (when Jack Morris was poised to become the fifth).

Concern among 1902 Detroit baseball fans was not so much would the Tigers be competitive, but would they compete in Detroit. A.L. President Ban Johnson literally kept the club afloat, but rumors during the winter of 1902–03 had Johnson moving the Tigers to Pittsburgh for direct competition with the N.L. powerhouse Pirates. Detroit's baseball fortunes were saved, narrowly perhaps, when the two leagues opted for peace. The N.L. agreed to give the A.L. equal billing and allow an A.L. club in New York with the condition that the junior circuit stay out of Pittsburgh. The Tigers prospered further when Sam Crawford, a jumper from Cincinnati to Detroit, was allowed to stay with the Michigan club. Crawford, a great all-around player, hit over .300 eight times with the Tigers and set major league records for triples (312) and most years with 20 or more triples (five) en route to the Hall of Fame. The A.L.-N.L. war was nearly re-ignited when Detroit shortstop Kid Elberfeld was traded to the New York Americans for aging shortstop Herman Long in 1903. The N.L. New York Giants, who lost Elberfeld during the peace negotiations, were infuriated, but protested to no avail.

Troubles were far from over for the 1903 Tigers. Soon after being appointed player-manager, pitcher Win Mercer committed suicide. Ed Barrow, later the phenomenally successful general manager and president of the New York Yankees, was hired in place of Mercer. Barrow was the only manager in the first half-decade of the A.L. Tigers to be rehired and lasted just 84 games into his second season (1904). Wahoo Sam Crawford, born in Wahoo, Nebraska, played left field, finished second to Nap Lajoie in the batting race, and became the only player in major league history to lead the N.L. and A.L. in triples in back-to-back seasons. His 25 three-base hits established a record broken only by Joe Jackson in 1912 and Crawford himself in 1914, both with 26. Mullin and Wild Bill Donovan paced the pitching staff with 19 and 17 wins respectively.

When Sam Angus tired of baseball in the winter of 1903–04, Frank Navin found a potential buyer in William Clyman Yawkey. Yawkey died suddenly, but his 28-year-old son William Hoover Yawkey did purchase the Tigers, retaining both Navin and Barrow as minor stockholders. Yawkey became club president and Navin secretary-treasurer. Bill was the uncle and foster father of Thomas Austin Yawkey, later the benevolent owner of the Boston Red Sox. In contrast with other Detroit owners, Bill Yawkey was a free spirit who enjoyed nightlife and camaraderie with his players.

Though Barrow was not around to lead Detroit's first championship teams, he was instrumental in their formation. His trades of 1904 brought shortstop Charley O'Leary, third baseman Bill Coughlin, and left fielder Matty McIntyre to Detroit, all key performers on the 1907–09 clubs. Rowdy Bill Coughlin later became team captain and then baseball coach at Lafayette College. The purchase of Coughlin from Washington for $8,000 was a rare instance in which Navin opened up Yawkey's pocketbook.

A clash between Barrow, willing to spend Yawkey's money freely, and the tight-fisted Navin, was destined. With the Tigers faring no better than seventh place in August 1904, Yawkey accepted Barrow's resignation. Second baseman Bobby Lowe, best known as the first major league player ever to hit four home runs in one game (with Boston on May 30, 1894), guided the Tigers for the remainder of 1904 as playing manager, with the club finishing a distant seventh.

In 1905 Bill Armour replaced Lowe as manager and Germany Schaefer took the vacant second base job. Schaefer, best known for once stealing first base, ranks with Ty Cobb as the most colorful of the early Tigers. Armour had managed Cleveland's A.L. entry since 1901 until second baseman Nap Lajoie was given the reins. Detroit topped its Great Lakes rival by hiring Armour and rising to third place. Cleveland fell from fourth to fifth place. The Tigers notched a club-record 79 wins, 17 more than 1904, but still ranked last in A.L. attendance with less than 200,000. The 1905–06 Tigers gave little evidence of the greatness that lay in store.

Arriving late in Armour's first managerial season was a righthanded throwing, lefthanded hitting outfielder whose .326 batting average led the Sally League that season. Detroit baseball fortunes were forever altered when Tyrus Raymond Cobb was purchased by the Tigers for $750 in 1905. Cobb had already begun building his reputation as a fearless player, reckless on the bases, and something of a crazed nut. The Georgia peach made his Detroit debut on August 30, 1905, at Bennett Field. In his first at-bat, Cobb doubled off Jack Chesbro, driving in two runs. Playing 41 games with the 1905 Tigers, however, Cobb batted just .240, with only seven of his 36 hits going for extra bases. Even so, Cobb was playing what would surely be now known as "Ty-ball," a style that might make world wars look like a picnic. To Cobb, baseball *was* war, sharpened spikes his most feared weapon. Cobb asked for no quarter and gave none. In fact Cobb was merely protecting his job in baseball, though doing so to an extreme unparalleled in baseball history. If any pitcher or player would try to intimidate the young Cobb, they would get more in return. Cobb's southern roots did not help in a game dominated by northerners. Even Cobb's own teammates joined in the hazing of the rookie.[3]

There was little difference in personnel between the 1906 Tigers that fell to sixth place and the 1907 club that rose to its first pennant. Outfielder Davey Jones and catcher Boss Schmidt joined the team, but the big change was at the helm, where Hughie Jennings replaced Bill Armour. Against the objections of Ban Johnson, Detroit acquired Jennings from Baltimore's Eastern League club, drafting the 36-year-old shortstop for $1,000.

Jennings inherited a team on the verge of greatness. A key addition came when first baseman Claude Rossman was purchased from Cleveland. Schaefer and Red Downs handled second, while O'Leary and Coughlin manned the left side of the infield. Cobb, Crawford, and Jones roamed the outfield and Schmidt handled a pitching staff that fell one victory short of four 20-game winners. Bill Donovan's 25–4 record achieved the best winning percentage in club history. Ed Killian also won 25, George Mullin won and lost 20, while Ed Siever added 19 wins. Those four starters accounted for 89 of Detroit's 92 wins.

Now 20 years old, Cobb became the dominant offensive player in the league, leading the circuit in batting average by 27 points over teammate Crawford, RBIs by 24 over Socks Seybold, and in steals, hits, total bases, and slugging percentage. Cobb led the Tigers with five of the club-total 11 home runs. Crawford paced the team in doubles, triples, and runs scored, leading the league with 102. Detroit led the A.L. in runs, hits, and batting average, all for the first time.

Thanks to Cobb the Tigers have won more batting championships than any other A.L. team, even though no Tiger has won the title since Norm Cash in 1961. During the first 60 years of the franchise, seven different Tigers won the batting crown. Cobb was followed by Heilmann's odd trick of titles in 1921, 1923, 1925, and 1927. Heinie Manush won in 1926. Charlie Gehringer was among the top five for five straight years, culminating with his own title in 1937. Kell was among the leaders in five of his six seasons in Motown, taking a turn at the top in 1949. Batting champs Al Kaline (1955) and Harvey Kuenn (1959) joined the top five in 1955 and were among the top A.L. hitters the rest of the decade. Besides Kaline and Cash only Willie Horton, in 1968, cracked the top five in the 1960s. Ron LeFlore was Detroit's only bat title contender (1976–77) in the 1970s. Lou Whitaker and Alan Trammell, the longest running keystone combination in major league history, were among the leaders in 1983, as was Trammell in 1984 and 1987.

Detroit was a newcomer to pennant contention in 1907. Connie Mack's A's, Fielder Jones' White Stockings, and Nap Lajoie's Cleveland club provided stiff competition for Jennings' first Detroit club. Philadelphia made the best run at the upstarts from Michigan. When Detroit visited the city of brotherly love on September 27, the Tigers and A's were in a virtual tie for the A.L. lead. Bill Donovan beat Eddie Plank to put Detroit in first place. A rainout on Saturday set up a crucial doubleheader on September 30. Jennings pitched Donovan with just two days' rest and the A's jumped to a 7–1 lead. The Tigers rallied against Jimmy Dygert and Rube Waddell, but still trailed 8–6 entering the ninth inning. Cobb's dramatic, two-run homer off Waddell tied the game. After 17 innings the contest was halted due to darkness. Proceeding to Washington, Detroit won four straight against the tailenders and clinched the pennant October 5 with a win against St. Louis. Detroit, emerging as the automotive capital of America, had its first A.L. championship. Home attendance was up by almost 120,000, but still ranked just seventh best in the circuit.

Frank Chance's N.L. champion Chicago Cubs are recognized as one of baseball's greatest teams, but they had been beaten by the "hitless wonder" Chicago White Stockings in the 1906 World Series, giving the hard-hitting Tigers plenty of confidence. Detroit, however, fared little better at the plate than their A.L. counterparts had the previous October. Cobb batted just .200, Crawford .238. Chicago forged a 3–3 tie in the first game when Boss Schmidt, victimized by seven stolen bases, enabled a run to score by dropping a third strike to Del Howard with two out in the ninth. Chicago pitching dominated the remainder of the series. Detroit managed just three runs as Jack Pfiester, Ed Reulbach, Orvie Overall, and Three Finger Brown pitched consecutive, complete game victories for four straight wins. Worse yet, only 11,306 fans turned out for Game Four in Detroit, followed by just 7,370 fans for the finale, ranking as the lowest attendance yet for a World Series game.

Following the 1907 season Navin joined Bill Yawkey as a co-owner of the Tigers and became club president, a position he would hold for 28 years. The new top executive immediately found himself in contract squabbles with Mullin, Rossman and, most noticeably, Cobb. Asking for $5,000, Cobb finally settled for $4,500 toward the end of spring training.

Though the 1908 A.L. pennant race is consistently overshadowed in hindsight by the N.L. race, it ranks as one of the greatest in baseball history. Detroit led the four-team tussle throughout, but Cleveland, Chicago, and St. Louis were never far behind. On the final day of the season, the Tigers and White Sox squared off at Comiskey Park for the pennant. Wild Bill Donovan pitched a shutout, Cobb and Crawford combined for seven of Detroit's 13 hits, and the Tigers left Chicago with a 7–0 win and second straight A.L. title. Cobb and Crawford finished one-two in the A.L. batting race for the second straight season.

With 10,812 fans on hand in Detroit, the Tigers opened the 1908 World Series against the Cubs with an instant replay of the 1907 opener. Chicago drove Ed Killian from the box, but the Tigers rallied to a 6–5 lead in the ninth. Three outs from a first-game defeat for the second straight year, Chicago rallied with seven straight hits and five runs. Three Finger Brown closed out a 10–6 win. Game One, like the fourth game in 1907, was played in steady rain that affected play on both sides. At Chicago the Cubs took a two-game lead in a pitching duel between Donovan and Overall, breaking a scoreless tie in the eighth with six runs, including Joe Tinker's controversial two-run homer into a roped-off section of fans. Mullin notched Detroit's first World Series victory in Game Three. Cobb broke loose with four hits, two steals, and two RBIs in an 8–3 decision. The return to Detroit brought 12,907 fans to Bennett Park for a duel between Brown and Summers. Chicago pitching took charge again. Brown scattered four hits and RBI hits by Harry Steinfeldt and Solly Hofman paced a 3–0 win for the Cubs. Overall surrendered just three hits in the fifth game, Evers and Chance had three hits each for the Cubs. Chicago's 2–0 win took one hour and 25 minutes, the shortest game in World Series history. It occurred before just 6,210 fans in Detroit, the smallest crowd in fall classic annals. Cobb fared better this time around, however, batting .368 with a Series-high four RBIs, but he went hitless in the final two games.

For the third straight season in 1909, Detroit laid claim to the best offense in the American League. Donie Bush, a late-season addition in 1908, back for a full season at shortstop, led the league with 88 walks. George Moriarty moved in at the hot corner and Oscar Stanage was added behind the plate. Cobb became the American League's second triple crown winner (9, 107, .377) and set a league record with 76 steals. Crawford led the league in doubles again, finished second in RBIs, third in homers, and fourth in batting average. Mullin peaked with a league-high 29 wins, Ed Willett added 21, Summers 19, Killian 11, and Donovan eight.

The complexion of the Tigers changed in mid-August with a pair of trades. Schaefer and catcher Red Killefer traveled to Washington for second baseman Jim Delahanty and Rossman was swapped to St. Louis for first baseman Tom Jones. With the right side of the infield shored up, the Tigers swept a series against the A's in late August and proceeded to win their third straight pennant by 3½ games. The club also set a home attendance record (490,490) that would last until 1916.

A large chapter in the Ty Cobb story was written on August 24 in the series with Philadelphia. Spikes flashing, Cobb spiked Baker sliding into third base. Cobb's right to the base notwithstanding, public opinion sided with Baker and Connie Mack, against the aggressive Cobb. A four-game series at Philadelphia in September brought 120,000 fans out to taunt Cobb. Detroit won just once, but that was enough to escape with a 2½ game lead, an advantage that proved too much for the Athletics.

In the senior circuit Pittsburgh outlasted the Cubs to set up a match of early baseball stars, shortstop Honus Wagner of the Pirates against Cobb of the Tigers. Both batting stars were overshadowed by rookie pitcher Babe Adams of the Pirates. Adams scattered six hits and pitched shutout ball, after Delahanty's single scored Cobb in the first inning, to win the 1909 World Series opener. Wild Bill Donovan finally tasted World Series triumph in the second game with a five-hit, 7–2 decision. The first game at Detroit brought 18,277 fans to the expanded Bennett Field in hopes of seeing the Tigers take a Series advantage for the first time, but Pittsburgh took a 6–0 lead and prevailed 8–6. The fourth game was played in wintery conditions that had little effect on the crowd (17,036) and none on George Mullin. Detroit's mound ace pitched a five-hit shutout, Stanage singled home two runs, Cobb doubled in a pair, and the Tigers coasted to a 5–0 win that evened the series.

Back in Pittsburgh, Davey Jones became the first player ever to start off a World Series game with a home run, but the Bucs scored solo tallies in the first, second, and third. Cobb started a Detroit rally in the sixth with a one-out single, scoring on Crawford's double. A wild throw by Wagner on Delahanty's grounder let Delahanty score the tying run. Pittsburgh player-manager Fred Clarke took charge in the seventh, belting a three-run homer off Summers to break the tie. Crawford's eighth inning homer was not enough to prevent Adams from an 8–4 win. Frustration again got the best of the Tiger faithful as just 10,535 showed up for the sixth game. They must have also sensed futility when Pittsburgh scored three first-inning runs off Mullin. Clarke singled home one run, Wagner two, before anyone made out. That was the Pirates scoring until the ninth inning. Meanwhile, Crawford doubled home a run in the first, Moriarty and Tom Jones drove home runs in the fourth, Delahanty doubled for another marker in the fifth and Cobb doubled home Davey Jones for a fifth run in the sixth. Things got sticky in the ninth, but Detroit withstood a Pirates rally, winning 5–4.

With 17,562 fans on hand at Bennett Field for the decisive seventh game, Tiger bats went on vacation for the third consecutive year's final World Series game. Series hero Babe Adams paced out six hits and faced real trouble in just the second inning. Wild Bill Donovan lived up to his nickname, walking six in three innings, and a tired Mullin was unable to keep the game close in relief. For the third straight year, Detroit's season ended in disappointment with a final-game World Series loss, the Tigers becoming the only team in A.L. history to lose three consecutive World Series. The Cobb-Wagner duel was also disappointing for Detroiters. Hans hit .333 with eight hits, six stolen bases, and six runs driven in. Cobb hit just .231, scored three runs, drove in none, and stole just two bases in his final World Series appearance.

Blessed with the greatest player in the game and a strong supporting cast, Detroit's 24-year absence from the World Series is puzzling. The 1910 Tigers were a carbon copy of the 1909 champs and again produced the most runs in the American League. Cobb led the league in runs scored, Crawford in runs driven in, and Bush again set the table with a league-high 78 walks. Pitching was another story. The club ERA jumped from 2.26 to 3.00. Only Bill Donovan improved on his 1909 campaign in his last stellar season. Regardless, the entire league was no match for Connie Mack's juggernaut in Philadelphia. Only Boston in 1903 had a bigger pennant-winning margin than the 1910 A's to that point. New York edged the Tigers for third place. Detroit was not up to the challenge of winning a fourth straight pennant, a feat no AL club would attain until the 1936–39 Yankees. Hughie Jennings' troops were no doubt also worn down by the friction inherent to playing with the tempestuous Cobb.

Though the Tigers were not part of the 1910 pennant race, the battle of bats between Cobb and Cleveland's Nap Lajoie is still talked about today. In addition to bragging rights, a brand new automobile, courtesy of the Chalmers Automobile Company, was at stake for the winner. Safely ahead of Lajoie entering the season's final games, Cobb chose to ride the bench. Lajoie, with the subversive help of the St. Louis Browns, went eight for eight, including seven bunt hits. St. Louis third baseman Red Corridan was instructed to play back against Lajoie, giving the Naps second baseman a wide open field for bunt hits. The Browns, and most everyone else, were rooting for Lajoie. Nap apparently finished the day with a .384 batting average, one point better than Cobb. Ty's rivals and many of his teammates congratulated the new batting champ.

A.L. President, Ban Johnson, however, ordered a check of Cobb's batting record. He also banished St. Louis manager Jack O'Connor from the game. Upon review, Cobb was given two extra hits, a .385 batting average, and the batting title. A different result appeared in almost every major newspaper, all using unofficial figures. The Chalmers company gave cars to both players. Seven decades later, on April 18, 1981, *The Sporting News* published research indicating that the official A.L. records omitted Cobb's first two games of the season, during which he went one-for-eight. In addition Cobb was given credit for the game of September 24 twice, giving Ty two extra hits. *The Sporting News* maintained that Cobb's actual 1910 batting average was .382 and Lajoie's .383. Cobb's lifetime hit total and batting average were also changed. On December 16, 1981, however, the Official Records Committee rejected the findings of *The Sporting News* and ruled that Ban Johnson's 1910 decision could not be overturned (Mac-Farlane, 1983, 32).

Though Frank Navin would fight night baseball, he did make a radical scheduling change in 1910. Sunday baseball had never been played in Detroit, but instead at Burns Park in Springwells Township. As Detroit became more industrialized, Navin brought Sunday baseball to Bennett Field to please the workers looking to enjoy Tigers games on their single day off.

The 1911 Tigers gave notice to the A's with a brilliant start of 21 wins in 23 games. Despite missing most of spring training, Cobb was off to his best season, a necessity to withstand the challenge of newcomer Joe Jackson. Cobb's attitude continued to create problems with Crawford, Bush, and others. They felt he could get away with anything. Jackson, the young Clevelander in his full-season debut, featured a phenomenal .408 batting average, highest ever that did not capture a batting title. Cobb, at 24 years old, batted a career high .420 and also led the league in runs, hits, doubles, triples, and stolen bases. The story of Cobb's refusing to talk to Jackson, a fellow Southerner, during a late-season meeting with Cleveland, has become part of baseball lore. Cobb intentionally sought to bruise the feelings of the mild-mannered Jackson. Though Joe had a sizable lead in the batting derby, Cobb rallied for another crown. Crawford's .378 batting average was a distant third in the race. Bush was the outstanding shortstop in the circuit and again led in walks. Pitching, however, slipped again. The team ERA (3.73) was second worst in the league and Detroit starters were required to complete a league-high 108 games.

There was a new Chalmers award in 1911, going to the player voted most valuable by a commission of baseball writers. Cobb was the unanimous choice in the A.L. Cobb's heroics helped increase Detroit attendance by almost 100,000 over 1910 to 484,988, second only to the 1909 total. Navin saw the possibilities of a bigger park and expanded the Detroit facilities following the season. The wooden stands were demolished and replaced with a single deck, concrete grandstand. The playing field was also altered, as home plate was moved to the southwest corner of the field. At the suggestion of many, the new plant was christened Navin Field, with formal opening ceremonies taking place April 20, 1912.

A familiar Detroit pattern of success, aging, and rebuilding began taking shape in the years 1912–14. The 1912 pitching staff was poor and the offense fell off dramatically, despite the continued success of Cobb, batting champ again with a .410 average, and Crawford. The highlight of the 1912 season was veteran George Mullin's 7–0 no-hit win against the Browns at Navin Field on the fourth of July, the first no-hitter in Tigers history. Otherwise Mullin struggled to his worst season in Detroit (12–17, 3.54) and was sold to Washington after an even worse start in 1913.

The 1912 season also featured the players' strike provoked when Cobb battled a fan in New York. When Ty was suspended indefinitely by Ban Johnson, his Detroit teammates agreed to strike unless the ban was lifted. The players were no more enamored with Cobb than in the past, but they did feel he was right to go after the heckler in New York. The May 18 Detroit-Philadelphia game featured a bootleg Tigers team including manager Jennings, coaches Jim McGuire and Joe Sugden, and a variety of amateurs. Al Travers was recruited to pitch and went the distance, despite allowing 26 hits, seven walks, and 24 runs in Detroit's 24–2 loss. Johnson met with the Detroit players and, with Cobb's help, coaxed them to give up the strike. Cobb was fined $50 and suspended 10 days. The striking players were fined $100 each.

Out of the running again in 1913, Detroit began setting the foundation for another contender. Newcomers Ossie Vitt and Bobby Veach would be mainstays for years to come. Cobb's batting average dipped to .390, still enough to best Joe Jackson for the third straight year. George "Hooks" Dauss became a full-time starter and led the staff with a 2.68 ERA. Dauss would pitch 15 big-league seasons, entirely with Detroit, and retire as the club's all-time winningest pitcher.

Detroit survived the Federal League crisis without losing any major players, though Cobb was given a big raise and Crawford received a four-year contract as the result of new bargaining power. Injuries limited Tyrus to just 97 games, but he was still awarded the batting title with a .368 average. Crawford led the league with 104 RBIs. Considerable improvement was also seen in the pitching staff. New arrival Harry Coveleski won 22 games, second only to Walter Johnson in the A.L. Coveleski, Dauss, and Jean Dubuc would pitch the Tigers back into contention in 1915.

The mighty Athletics were crippled by the Feds, leaving Boston, Detroit, and Chicago to fill the void. Leading the Tigers was a rejuvenated Cobb. The Georgia Peach matched his career high with 156 games played, led the A.L. in runs, hits, batting average, and steals with 96, breaking Clyde Milan's record (1912) by eight and setting standards for the major leagues until Maury Wills' 102 thefts in 1962 and for the A.L. until Rickey Henderson's 100 steals in 1980. Veach and Crawford tied for the league lead with 112 RBIs. Dauss won 24 games and Coveleski 22 in a league-high 50 appearances.

The 1915 Tigers were perhaps the best A.L. team, up to that time, that did not win a pennant. New second baseman Pep Young provided a spark as leadoff hitter. A trade sending outfielder Bill Jacobson to the Browns for pitchers Bill James and Grover Lowdermilk fortified the hurling corps.

A mid-September series at Fenway Park in Boston brought the top contenders together. Dauss won the first game, but Boston took the final three. Ernie Shore took the second game in a 12-inning duel with Coveleski and Babe Ruth defeated Dauss in the finale. Controversy again surrounded Cobb, who threw his bat at Boston's Carl Mays. Cobb required a police escort to leave the field. Ironically Ty almost found himself representing the Red Sox in 1915. Rumors of a swap that would send Cobb to Boston for star outfielder Tris Speaker did not come true, however. With Speaker, the Red Sox won 14 of 22 games from Detroit in 1915 and edged the Tigers by a scant one game for the A.L. pennant.

Speaker was traded instead to Cleveland, in 1916, but the Bosox were still a better ballclub than the Detroiters. Speaker also finally took the A.L. batting crown away from Cobb. These two stars of course would be linked again by much less admirable circumstances several years later. A future batting star arrived at Michigan and Trumbull in the person of Harry Heilmann, and Ossie Vitt set a hot-corner record with 593 chances that stood for 21 years until 1937.

Although Cobb regained his batting title, the Tigers slipped from contention altogether in 1917. Cobb also continued to battle off the field. A historic fistfight between Ty and Charlie Herzog took place during a barnstorming tour that spring.

The Detroit team that barely missed pennants in 1915 and 1916 barely escaped the basement in 1918, finishing seventh. Baseball in general suffered, as President Wilson's secretary of state said "work or fight" and the season was halted on Labor Day. Cobb's A.L.-high .382 batting average clashed with a club mark that was sixth in the league. Cobb himself entered the Army in the chemical warfare department.

The decade closed with peace and post-war prosperity that caught major league owners by surprise. The magnates cut 14 games off the standard schedule to 140. Detroit regained its spot among the top offensive teams with a .283 club mark, second only to the champion White Sox. Heilmann settled in at first base, and Cobb copped his final batting title, finishing one-two with Veach in the batting race and tying Bobby for the league hit lead. Dauss (21–9) paced the pitchers, but the rest of the staff was weak. Howard Ehmke (17–10), however, fared well as the baby of the corps at age 25.

The roaring twenties were anything but for Detroit's Tigers. The twenties was the only decade in which Detroit did not win, or finish within five games of, a pennant at least once. Hughie Jennings, unable to bring his club back to its 1907–09 heights, bowed out after the 1920 campaign. Jennings' inability to build a pitching staff on par with his offense was the biggest factor in the drought that followed 1909. In that light, the choice of Ty Cobb as new playing-manager is questionable. Offensive production was down in 1920, magnified by the emergence of the lively ball, and the season was a big disappointment in Detroit.

As with other great players turned managers, Cobb simply could not cope with players less skilled than himself. His six-year reign as player-manager must be classified as unimpressive. Cobb's fire as a player did not transfer to the clubs he managed.

As you might expect, Cobb's Tigers were an offensive power. The aging outfielder remained one of baseball's most feared hitters. Heilmann added his four batting titles and Manush added one. Competing against the great Yankee teams of Ruth and, later, Gehrig, Detroit still led the A.L. in batting in 1921, 1924, and 1929, while hitting .300 or better as a team in 1922, 1923, and 1925 as well. Manush replaced Veach, and Lu Blue moved Heilmann to the outfield, until Blue was replaced by Bill Sweeney in 1928 and Dale Alexander in 1929. Charlie Gehringer took over at second base in 1926, beginning a 17-year run that included a 1937 batting championship. Aside from Dauss, the pitchers came and went. Earl Whitehill moved up among the club's all-time winners, but Ehmke, Dutch Leonard, Herm Pillette, Ownie Carroll, and George Uhle, baseball's best-hitting pitcher, had only fleeting success in the Motor City.

Acquisition of pitchers Pillette and Syl Johnson in 1922, two Pacific Coast League stars, provided a one-year spark. Pillette won 19 games in 1922, but lost a league-high 19 the next year. After subpar play from the keystone combination of shortstop Bush and second baseman Young in 1921, a new pair of George Cutshaw at second and Topper Rigney at short debuted in 1922. Bob "Fat" Fothergill also debuted in 1922. Fat fit right in with the heavy hitting Tigers and ranks third on the club's all-time batting list with a .337 average that trails only Cobb and Heilmann. Fothergill's unshapely physique took its toll as he died in Detroit on March 20, 1938, at just 40 years of age.

Cobb soon became the first player in twentieth-century major league baseball to hit better than .400 three times. As usual Cobb was thrust into controversy consisting of a debate over the validity of his 1922 .401 average. The dispute is well documented in Fred Lieb's *The Detroit Tigers* (Lieb, 1946, 170–71). It was Lieb's scoring decision, as a reporter for Associated Press, that effectively gave Cobb the .401 mark, in contrast to the "official" scorer's error ruling which would have given Tyrus an average slightly below .400. The Baseball Writers' Association did, in fact, opt to recognize the sub-.400 batting mark, but the .401 average is now accepted in all record books.

Cobb was one of five future Hall of Famers to grace the Detroit baseball scene from 1901 to 1925, along with Sam Crawford, Harry Heilmann, Heinie Manush, and Hughie Jennings. Charlie Gehringer, Mickey Cochrane, Goose Goslin, and Hank Greenberg, Hall of Famers all, made up the next great era of Detroit baseball in the 1930s and 1940s. Since 1946 only George Kell and Al Kaline have made a mark in Detroit that has led to Cooperstown.

In 1923 Fred Haney became Detroit's starting second baseman, Heilmann batted .403, Hooks Dauss (21–13) returned to the 20-win circle, and the Tigers finished second, albeit a distant second, to the Yankees. Attendance rose to a club-record 911,377 and expectations rose for true pennant contention in 1924. The club fared well despite an ill-fated trade that sent Ehmke, pitcher Carl Holling, infielder Danny Clark, outfielder Babe Herman, and $25,000 to the Red Sox for second baseman Del Pratt and pitcher Rip Collins. Pratt, nearing the end of a 13-year career, and Collins were of limited help to the Bengals. Herman would bat .324 over a 13-year big league career starting in 1926 and Ehmke would win 20 games for the 1923 last-place Red Sox.

Ballpark improvements continued, with a second deck added in the winter of 1923–24 between first and third base. The additional space enabled a crowd of 42,712 fans to attend the August 3, 1924, Sunday game between the Tigers and Yankees. Whitehill outpitched Herb Pennock for a 5–2 win.

June 13, 1924, was also a memorable day in Tigers history. A King Cole pitch that hit New York's Bob Meusel ignited a brawl that soon brought 1,000 fans onto the field. The game was forfeited to the Yankees, Cole and Meusel were suspended for 10 games and fined, as was Babe Ruth. Such excitement, however, helped Tigertown break the one million mark in home attendance for the first time, a feat that would not be duplicated until 1935.

Cobb's Tigers peaked in 1924 and were not a pennant factor in either 1925 or 1926. Despite the American League's highest scoring offense in 1925, Detroit finished fourth, 16½ games behind the champion Washington Senators. The Tigers were last in doubleplays turned and generally weak on defense. Dauss won 16 games, Ken Holloway had a second straight impressive season, and Dutch Leonard was effective, but the remainder of the pitching staff struggled. The 1926 Tigers scored 110 runs fewer than the 1925 crew, despite Manush's batting title and big seasons by Fothergill and Heilmann, who together finished behind Heinie and Babe Ruth in the batting race with .367 averages. Heilmann was honored with Harry Heilmann Day on August 9, as more than 40,000 fans saw Detroit lose a 9–8 slugfest to the Yankees. Cobb was limited to just 79 games with eye and other physical problems. And still further problems lay just ahead.

In October 1926 Frank Navin announced Cobb would not return as manager, citing a demoralized attitude on the club. Rumors predicted Cobb's retirement. A week later American League umpire and former Tiger George Moriarty was announced as Cobb's managerial replacement. In a seemingly unrelated affair, Speaker was dismissed as playing-manager of the Indians. Scandal broke late in 1926 when baseball commissioner Landis announced an investigation involving Cobb, Speaker, Joe Wood, and Dutch Leonard. The investigation concerned a game played September 25, 1919. Leonard blew the whistle on betting by Cobb and Speaker. A.L. President Ban Johnson ruled against the players, but he was overruled by Judge Landis. A.L. owners stood by Landis, sending Johnson on an extended vacation and putting Frank Navin in charge of league affairs prior to reorganization. Landis further restored Cobb and Speaker to their old clubs, though neither remained with them. Speaker went to Washington and Cobb finished his glorious career playing two seasons for Connie Mack's Athletics. Another furor developed when Swede Risberg, one of the Chicago White Sox banned from baseball for taking part in a plot to throw the 1919 World Series, said that the Tigers were bribed to ease off in a 1917 series against the pennant-bound White Sox. No punishment was forthcoming based on Risberg's charges, but Landis did institute both a statute of limitations and stricter punishments against gambling.

The modern conception of Ty Cobb is of someone obsessed with baseball success, ruthless, mean, and selfish. While there is, no doubt, much truth to that perception, there are many who speak well of Cobb, including Tigers historian Fred Smith. Smith, who saw Cobb play, says, "One day, he was playing for Philadelphia and I was outside the clubhouse after the game. Cobbs got his arm around my shoulder, he signed my baseball, which I still have, and wished me 'good luck, kid.' He treated me perfect. I know he was damn nice to one little kid" (Smith, 1988).

Regardless of Cobb's reinstatement, Navin had determined that a change in course was necessary. Unfortunately, George Moriarty presided over a pair of Detroit clubs that finished out of the running. The 1927 club shone on offense, led by Heilmann, Fothergill, and Gehringer. Entering the season, the Tigers swung a seven-player deal with the Browns that proved to be of little benefit to either team. When the two teams renewed negotiations, a Detroit bid to improve two trouble spots, pitching and middle defense, backfired in a bigger trade with the Browns. Detroit sent Manush and Blue to St. Louis for veteran pitcher Elam Vangilder, veteran shortstop Chick Galloway, and outfielder Harry Rice. Rice was no match for the Hall-of-Fame-bound Manush, while Vangilder and Galloway were terrible disappointments. Worse yet, a pitching prospect named Carl Hubbell was sold by Beaumont, an affiliate of the Tigers, to the Giants. Hubbell went on to win 253 games with New York. As a result, the Tigers finished 68–86 and 33 games out of first place, spelling the end of Moriarty's tenure as manager.

Two highlights of the 1927 season focused on the two greatest hitters in Tigers history. Cobb returned to Navin Field on May 10 and received a hero's welcome. The batting race between Heilmann and Al Simmons came down to the final game. Simmons held a two-point lead, but Harry finished with a flurry of six hits in eight at-bats to bat .398, six points better than his Philadelphia rival.

The brief George Moriarty era was replaced with a forgettable five-year term as manager by Bucky Harris. Harris' first Detroit club was another offensive juggernaut, bolstered by the addition of first baseman Dale Alexander and outfielder Roy Johnson, scoring a league-high 926 runs and also leading the circuit in doubles, triples, batting average, and slugging average; the pitching staff, however, limped home with a league-high 4.96 ERA and the club finished sixth,

36 games out of first place. After the season Heilmann was sold to the Cincinnati Reds, despite hitting .344 in 1929. The 1930 season was noteworthy only for wholesale changes on the club and the very brief debuts of two players that would anchor the next several great Detroit clubs. Acquisition of two Yankees stars, pitcher Waite Hoyt and short-stop Mark Koenig, did not bring New York–type success. The nagging shortstop hole was finally filled by Billy Rogell. Huge 19-year-old first baseman Hank Greenberg had one at-bat with the big club and Tommy Bridges made eight pitching appearances. Neither gave much notice that they would soon help lead Detroit back to contention.

Bridges joined the Detroit starting rotation in 1931, but Green-berg did not make the grade until 1933, the final year of the Harris regime. In 1931 the departure of Heilmann and Fothergill, sold to the White Sox during the 1930 campaign, and injuries to Gehringer, made,for a dismal season. A mid-1932 trade that sent Alexander and Roy Johnson to the Red Sox for outfielder Earl Webb dismissed the 1932 A.L. batting champ. Alexander, built for designated hitter status, batted .372 at Boston and edged triple crown candidate Jimmy Foxx for batting honors with a .367 overall average. Alexander's replace-ment, Harry Davis, was more agile afield, but far less effective at bat. Webb made no one forget the great outfielders of Detroit's past. Bridges was erratic, turning in performances both spectacular and terrible. On August 5, 1932, Tommy retired 26 consecutive Washing-ton batters as Detroit built a 13–0 lead. One out from a perfect game and baseball immortality, he surrendered a clean single to pinch hitter Dave Harris.

While adding Greenberg in 1933, a trade with Washington sent Earl Whitehill to the Senators for relief pitching ace Fred Marberry and pitcher Carl Fischer. Pete Fox joined the outfield and 23-year-old righthander Lynwood "Schoolboy" Rowe improved the pitching staff. The Tigers had become a younger club, with more emphasis on pitching and defense, but still lacked a key ingredient necessary to rise among the A.L. clubs.

The next great era in Tigers history began December 12, 1933, when Frank Navin sent catcher Johnny Pasek and $100,000 to the Athletics for catcher Mickey Cochrane. Bucky Harris had resigned his managerial post four days prior to the end of the 1932 season, leaving coach Del Baker to run the final two games. After dismissing the thought of hiring Babe Ruth, Navin decided to go after Cochrane. Connie Mack was having another fire sale, caused in part by financial woes brought on by the 1929 stock market crash. Detroit's finances were also weak. Attendance had fallen steadily since 1924 to a rock bottom 320,972 in 1933. Navin called on Walter Briggs, then owner of 50 percent of the club after the death of John Kelsey, who agreed to advance the money necessary to get Cochrane. Veteran batting star Goose Goslin was added in another December deal that sent outfielder John Stone to Washington.

The new outfield of Pete Fox, Jo-Jo White, and Goslin, with speedy Gee Walker in reserve, was Detroit's best in years. The infield of Greenberg, Gehringer, Rogell, and third baseman Marv Owen was also solid, as was a pitching staff led by Rowe, Bridges, and Marberry. The 1934 Tigers brought ferocious offense back to Navin Field, leading the league in batting average, doubles, stolen bases, and runs scored with a club record 958. Fox was the only starter to bat less than .295. White and Cochrane set the table for the G-Men—Gehringer, Greenberg, and Goslin. Cochrane was the perfect answer to a team and town that had grown accustomed to uninspired baseball.

Not until 1968 did a Detroit team win more than the 101 victories posted in 1934. Rowe won 16 straight until August 29 and paced the champs with a 24–8 record. Bridges blossomed with a 22–11 mark, Marberry and Eldon Auker added 15 wins each. An aging Yankees team could finish no closer than seven games back as Boston pitcher John Merena's shutout of New York on September 24 gave the idle Tigers their first pennant since 1909.

Awaiting the Tigers in the 1934 World Series were the Gashouse Gang St. Louis Cardinals. Like Detroit in the A.L., St. Louis was a surprise champ in the N.L., outdistancing the frontrunning Giants on the final day of the season. Instead of playing the slugging New York club, as expected, the Tigers had to shift gears for the red-hot, down and dirty Gashouse Gang. Rather than pitting ace against ace, Cochrane started Alvin Crowder, a late-season pick-up from Washington, not Schoolboy Rowe, against 30-game winner Dizzy Dean. At least Detroit still had its best pitcher ready after St. Louis posted an easy 8–3 win in Game One at Detroit before 42,505 fans. Five Detroit errors, plus 13 St. Louis hits, gave Dean plenty of cushion.

In the second game Rowe battled Wild Bill Hallahan in a classic pitchers' duel. After allowing two runs in a shaky start, Schoolboy retired 22 straight batters. Detroit scored a run in the fourth on doubles by Rogell and Fox. In the ninth the St. Louis defense faltered as Gee Walker batted with Fox on second base. Catcher Bill DeLancey and first-baseman Rip Collins converged on the ball, but each expected the other to make the catch. Neither did. Walker lined a single to left, scoring the tying run. In the 12th inning Bill Walker lived up to his name, issuing bases on balls to Gehringer and Greenberg. Goslin drove a single to right, scoring Gehringer with the winning run to even the series.

Tommy Bridges faltered in the first game at Sportsman's Park in St. Louis, leaving in the fifth inning and trailing 4–0. Paul Dean was tougher than brother Dizzy, hurling shutout ball until a meaningless Tigers rally in the ninth made the final 4–1. Tex Carleton proved no match for Detroit's offense in Game Four. Greenberg belted a home run, two doubles, and a single, Rogell drove in four runs and Detroit rapped 13 hits off five St. Louis pitchers, and rolled to a 10–4 victory. Pepper Martin committed three errors, including one in the seventh that enabled the Tigers to take a 5–4 lead. A five-run eighth inning then broke the game open. Auker went the distance for Detroit to even the series. Game Four is best remembered for St. Louis manager Frankie Frisch's use of Dizzy Dean as a pinch runner in the fourth inning. While trying to break up a double play, Dean took a throw from Rogell square in the head. With no batting helmets for protection, Dean was knocked cold for several minutes.

Injured or not, Diz faced Bridges in Game Five at St. Louis. Tommy recovered from his third game woes and limited the Redbirds to one run. Detroit scored in the second on a walk to Greenberg and Fox's long double. In the seventh Gehringer homered, Rogell singled, went all the way to third on center fielder Chuck Fullis' error, and scored on Greenberg's sacrifice fly. The 3–1 win sent the Tigers back to Detroit needing just one victory in two home games to finally capture a World Series. Celebration began prematurely with a big homecoming welcome for the home club at the train station and a crowd of 44,551 at Navin Field for the sixth game. Despite the warnings of player-manager Cochrane, most Detroiters felt a victory over Dizzy Dean had meant sure victory for the Bengals.

The sixth game matched Paul Dean and Schoolboy Rowe. St. Louis struck first on a double by Jack Rothrock and single by Ducky Medwick. Detroit answered when Cochrane's infield single scored Jo-Jo White. Light-hitting Leo Durocher started a two-run St. Louis rally in the fifth, but Detroit evened the game again in the sixth. White walked and took third on Cochrane's single. One run scored when Dean could not handle Gehringer's grounder. One of the most controversial plays in Tigers history followed. With runners on first and second and none out, Goslin bunted. DeLancey gambled, throwing to third base. Umpire Brick Owens called Cochrane out at third. Many insist, to this day, that Cochrane was safe. Gehringer moved up on Rogell's fly and scored on Greenberg's single, but Owen grounded out to end the game-tying rally. Two unlikely offensive heroes stepped forward in the St. Louis seventh. Durocher doubled and Dean singled home what proved to be the winning run. In the Detroit seventh Fox doubled and took third on Rowe's sacrifice with one out, but Durocher threw out the potential tying run at the plate on White's grounder. In the eighth one-out singles by Gehringer and Goslin put runners on the corners, but Rogell's short fly and Greenberg's foul out killed the threat. Dean retired Detroit one-two-three in the ninth to complete a 4–3 win that knotted the Series. Though Detroit was at home, the sixth game win gave St. Louis a huge edge.

There was no doubt that Dizzy Dean would pitch the seventh game on one day's rest. Cochrane had used both Rowe and Bridges and was forced to call on fourth-game hero Auker. In each of the 1907, 1908, and 1909 World Series, Detroit failed to score in the final game. The 1934 World Series was no exception. St. Louis battered Detroit for seven runs in the third inning that removed all doubt concerning the final outcome. World Series history, however, was still ahead. In the sixth inning a Ducky Medwick triple scored Pepper Martin, making the score 8–0. Medwick slid hard into third baseman Marv Owen and a brief skirmish followed. When Medwick returned to left field in the bottom of the sixth, Tiger fans vented their frustration by hurling anything not bolted down at the St. Louis villain. Apples, oranges, score cards, and other litter showered down on Medwick. Looking on from a front row box was Commissioner Landis who summoned Medwick, Owen, and the four umpires. Judge Landis then ordered Frisch to removed Medwick from the game. The Cards proceeded to an 11–0 win as Dizzy Dean clowned his way to the finish and further into baseball immortality. Any individual heroics achieved by the Tigers, including fine performances by Gehringer and Bridges, were overshadowed by having been so close to a six-game win and yet unable to bring the championship to Detroit. Greenberg hit .321 in the Series, but struck out nine times. He was eventually dropped from fourth to sixth slot in the batting order.

The 1935 Tigers were every bit as good as the 1934 model. They again led the American League in runs scored with 919 and in batting average (.290). They did lead the league in errors, yet also led in fielding percentage. Detroit pitchers paced the circuit in complete games, shutouts, and only the Yankees had a better team ERA. Cochrane's crew took first place at the end of July, pulled away in August, and coasted in September as the Yankees closed within a deceiving three games of first place at the end of the season. Greenberg won Most Valuable Player honors with a brilliant season that included 170 RBIs and 36 homers, both league highs, and a .326 batting average. Gehringer, Fox, Cochrane, and Walker all topped .300 in batting average, while second baseman Gehringer and shortstop Rogell led their positions in fielding average. The four-man pitching rotation of Rowe, Bridges, Crowder, and Auker was the strongest in the league.

Detroit faced another N.L. surprise, the Cubs, winners of 21 straight games in September to reach a third Fall Classic in seven years. As in 1934 the Tigers again faced a red-hot team entering the Fall Classic. Worse yet, they faced Chicago without the great Greenberg after Henry was hurt in the second game. Marv Owen moved from third base to first and Flea Clifton replaced Owen.

The first game, played before 47,391 fans at Navin Field, extended Detroit's World Series shutout streak to two games as Lon Warneke surrendered just four hits. Rowe's first-inning throwing error allowed one run to score, Gabby Hartnett singled home another, and Frank Demaree homered in the ninth to give the Cubs a 3–0 win. Tiger bats quickly recovered in Game Two. In the first inning, against Charlie Root, White led off with a single, Cochrane doubled him home, Gehringer singled home Cochrane, and Greenberg hit a two-run homer into the left-field stands. Root was lifted without retiring a batter. A bases-loaded wild pitch and Gehringer's single brought home three more runs in the fourth. Bridges scattered six hits in an 8–3 Detroit win that proved costly when Greenberg suffered two broken bones in his left wrist during a collision at home plate in the seventh inning. Cochrane considered moving to first and putting Ray Hayworth behind the plate; Schoolboy Rowe volunteered to play first, but Frank Navin insisted on the shifting of Owen and insertion of Clifton.

The third game was a mess that featured the ejection of three Cubs and one Tiger. Insults had been hurled at Greenberg throughout the first two games and they continued in the third. Verbal sparring aside, the Cubs took a 3–0 lead against Auker on Demaree's homer, pitcher Bill Lee's run-producing groundout and Augie Galan's RBI single. A Goslin triple and Fox single put Detroit on the board in the sixth. Lee was five outs from a win when the Tigers rallied in the eighth. With White on first, Gehringer doubled. Goslin singled home the tying runs and Lee was lifted in favor of Warneke. Singles by Fox and Rogell gave Detroit a 4–3 lead. With runners on first and third, Rogell attempted to swipe second. Caught in a rundown, the Detroit shortstop stayed alive long enough to allow Fox to sneak home with the insurance run. That run proved crucial when Chicago rallied against Rowe in the ninth. Hits by Stan Hack and pinch hitters Chuck Klein and Ken O'Day scored one run. A sacrifice fly by Galan sent the game to extra innings. In the 11th, an error by the veteran Freddie Lindstrom at third base preceded White's run-scoring single. Rowe pitched a perfect last of the 11th to give Detroit a 6–5 win.

Alvin Crowder, pitching in his third consecutive World Series, gave Detroit a commanding 3–1 lead with a five-hitter in the fourth game. Tex Carleton, now with the Cubs, was almost as tough, but a Chicago defensive lapse ultimately cost him the game. Chicago scored first, on Hartnett's second-inning homer, but Detroit answered on Gehringer's double in the third. With two out in the sixth, Clifton reached second base when Galan dropped his fly ball. Shortstop Jurges then misplayed Crowder's grounder as Clifton scored the winning run. General Crowder allowed just one more hit until one out in the ninth. Back-to-back singles by Frank Demaree and Phil Cavaretta brought the Wrigley Field crowd of 49,350 to life, but Hack bounced to Rogell who started a six-four-three double play to end the game.

Pitching prevailed again in the fifth game. Warneke pitched six shutout innings and Chicago took a 2–0 lead in the third on Klein's home run off Rowe. Babe Herman doubled home another run in the seventh. Lee pitched two shutout innings, but faltered in the ninth. Consecutive hits by Gehringer, Goslin, and Fox gave Detroit a run and two runners with none out, but the next three batters went quietly as the Cubs escaped in Chicago with a 3–1 win.

Once again, Detroit headed home one win away from a championship. The pitching matchup of Bridges and Larry French produced one of the most dramatic endings in World Series history. With 48,420 fans crowding Navin Field, the Tigers scored in the first inning on Fox's double. Chicago responded with Herman's run-scoring hit in the third. Bridges got a run home with a fourth-inning groundout, but surrendered two in the fifth when Herman blasted a home run to left with French aboard. With two out in the sixth, Rogell delivered a ground-rule double. As Bridges waited on deck, Owen carried a .000 batting average (no hits in 19 at-bats) to the plate. Marv came through with the biggest hit of his life, a single to left that tied the game. The tie was jeopardized in the ninth when Hack led off for Chicago with a triple over Walker's head. After Jurges struck out, Grimm elected to stay with pitcher French who bounced back to the mound. Galan flied out to end the threat. With one out in the ninth, Cochrane singled off Herman's glove and took second on Gehringer's bounce out. Goslin ripped a single to right, sending manager Cochrane happily home, jumping up and down on home plate with the winning run that gave Detroit its first World Championship. The victory celebration that followed was fitting tribute to Cochrane and Navin, and a well-deserved party for the city of Detroit.

The official end of Detroit's second great baseball era is dated November 13, 1935. Just over a month after seeing his beloved club finally bring ultimate victory to Detroit, club president Frank Navin was dead of a heart attack. Walter O. Briggs stepped out of the background to become sole owner of the Tigers. He made Cochrane vice president of the club and son Walter O. "Spike" Briggs, Jr. treasurer and assistant secretary. Cochrane proceeded to purchase his old A's teammate, Al Simmons, from the White Sox for $75,000. Simmons replaced Pete Fox in the outfield and helped give Detroit another formidable offense, despite the absence of Greenberg, out the entire season with a fractured left wrist. Detroit still had the best defense in the league, but there was little in the pitching department past Bridges, the top winner in the league, plus Rowe and Auker. General Crowder retired in July with stomach trouble. The Yankees, featuring rookie Joe DiMaggio, were by far the class of the league and finished 19½ games up on the second-place Tigers.

Inability to remain in the hunt for a third straight pennant took its toll on Cochrane. Portending the troubles of another successful Detroit manager, Mickey left the club in mid-June of 1936, suffering from exhaustion. Del Baker took the reins until late July.

Despite the best team batting in the majors, with home run and runs scored totals second only to the Yankees, the 1937 Tigers finished 13 games behind the Bronx Bombers. Only the St. Louis Browns had a higher team ERA than the Detroiters. Rowe left the team after just 10 appearances with arm troubles. Rowe would come back, but Cochrane would not, after a beaning that ranks among the worst in baseball history. On May 25 Detroit visited Yankee Stadium, using a battery of Rowe and Cochrane. Schoolboy was coming off a 10-day suspension for not being in condition to pitch. In the fifth inning Cochrane faced New York pitcher Irving "Bump" Hadley. Hadley's pitch struck the player-manager over the left temple. The unconscious Cochrane was carried off the field and rushed to St. Elizabeth's Hospital where he remained for days with a triple fracture of the skull. Mickey spent six weeks at Henry Ford Hospital in Detroit, before returning as manager. Heeding medical advice, Cochrane retired as a player at age 34. Gehringer's batting title and Most Valuable Player award, Greenberg's 183 RBIs (one short of Lou Gehrig's American League record), and Gee Walker's 27-game hitting streak (including hitting for the cycle on opening day), plus the emergence of slugger Rudy York, could not conquer the Yankees.

York, a burly slugger, taxed Detroit management to find him a position. He began the season at third base, was found wanting and optioned to Toledo (American Association), only to be recalled when Marv Owen was hurt. Following Cochrane's injury, York settled in behind the plate and belted 35 homers as a rookie. Rudy really took off in August, slamming 18 homers in the month, a major league record.

The new Briggs regime made its mark in 1938. The ballpark at Michigan and Trumbull was expanded to 56,000 seats and renamed Briggs Stadium. Gee Walker, Owen, and Mike Tresh were traded to the White Sox for pitcher Vern Kennedy, outfielder Dixie Walker, and infielder Tony Piet. A terribly unpopular trade, the Walker deal was further criticized when Kennedy struggled after a blazing start. Briggs, Sr. made a stunning move on August 6, firing manager Cochrane. Del Baker took over the club once again. The big story in 1938 Detroit baseball, however, was Hank Greenberg's challenge to Babe

Ruth's single-season home run record. Hammerin' Henry socked 58 homers. His final bid to beat Ruth was stifled when Bob Feller struck out 18 Tigers on the final day of the season, even though Detroit and Harry Eisenstat beat the Iowa fastballer 4–1.

There were deals aplenty in 1939, but none that immediately brought Detroit back to contention. Yet the addition of third baseman Mike Higgins, outfielder Barney McCosky, and pitchers Bobo Newsom, Dizzy Trout, Hal Newhouser, and Fred Hutchinson made Del Baker's club ready for a pennant run in 1940. Schoolboy Rowe, winner of one game in 1937–1938, won 10 games for a pitching staff that now ranked behind only New York and Cleveland in team ERA. Future success was jeopardized, however, when Judge Landis made 91 members of the Detroit farm system free agents and provided compensation for 15 others. Roy Cullenbine and Benny McCoy were lost, but York and Bridges were allowed to remain with the Tigers. Jack Zeller, general manager since Cochrane's dismissal, had run the Detroit farm system since 1926. He felt it was responsible for success in 1934 and 1935, but later lobbied against the farm system concept.

Two major changes fortified Detroit for its 1940 pennant battle with Cleveland. In a swap of shortstops Rogell went to the Cubs for Dick Bartell. Bartell, an old-time player in the tradition of John McGraw and Hughie Jennings, added fire to the Tigers. Hank Greenberg was moved to left field so Rudy York could play first base and Birdie Tebbetts could catch full time. Detroit hurlers led the A.L. in strikeouts and strikeout/walk ratio. The offense led in runs, batting average, on-base percentage, doubles, and walks. Newsom's 21 wins, Rowe's league-high .842 winning percentage (16–3), and Al Benton's 17 saves paced the pitchers.

Cleveland's pitching staff had the best ERA in 1940 and kept the Indians atop the A.L. much of the season, until Detroit took charge late in the campaign. The pennant race climaxed when an unknown, unheralded, rookie Detroit hurler took his one and only step into the major league spotlight. On September 27 Detroit began a three-game, season-ending series in Cleveland, needing one win to eliminate the Tribe and clinch the pennant. Knowing that the Tribe would use fireballing ace Feller, Baker held back his own aces. As Feller was nearly unbeatable, the Detroit manager decided not to waste a top pitcher against him. Young Floyd Giebel, a rookie up from Buffalo and ineligible for World Series play, was chosen to face Rapid Robert. In one brief moment of glory, Giebel pitched a six-hit shutout. Feller allowed just three hits, but one was York's two-run homer. Detroit forged its return to the World Series with a 2–0 victory. Giebel would never win another major league game.

Cincinnati coasted to its second straight N.L. pennant, well rested and ready to avenge a 4–0 sweep at the hands of the Yankees in the 1939 World Series. The more tired Tigers, nonetheless, never trailed in the Series, winning Games One, Three, and Five, until the final contest. As was the case in four previous fall classics, Detroit bats fell silent at the most critical time. Bucky Walters pitched a five-hit shutout in the sixth game, setting up a classic duel between Newsom and Paul Derringer in the seventh. Just 26,854 fans were at Crosley Field for the finale. Heads up baserunning by Billy Sullivan, scoring from second on an infield out, gave Detroit its only run in the second inning. Newsom, a shutout winner in the fifth game, held the 1–0 lead through six frames. Frank McCormick led off the Cincinnati seventh with a double. Jim Ripple also doubled, but McCormick, thinking the ball might be caught, got a poor jump off second. Bruce Campbell hit cutoff man Bartell, who inexplicably held the ball while McCormick scored. After a sacrifice, Ernie Lombardi was walked, bringing .130 hitting Billy Myers up. Myers, playing his final game for the Reds, hit a tie-breaking sacrifice fly. A 2–1 loss sent Detroit to its fifth Series loss in six tries, but last for the next five decades.

The 1940 Tigers were, to an extent, a one-year wonder. In 1941 Greenberg was lost to the military draft. Bartell was released in the spring. Newsom lost a league-high 20 games and Detroit fell back to its 1939 level, 26 games behind the rejuvenated Yankees, while attendance also fell almost 50 percent.

Detroit's worst finish in a decade prompted the dismissal of manager Baker following the 1942 season. The poor finish, 30 games behind the Yankees, was not indicative of an upcoming pitching staff. Dizzy Trout, Hal Newhouser, Tommy Bridges, and Virgil Trucks gave the Tigers four solid starters.

Under new manager Steve O'Neill, the Tigers showed marked improvement in 1943, prior to another tight pennant race in 1944. The 1943 pitching staff led the A.L. in strikeouts for the fifth consecutive year as Newhouser, Bridges, and Trucks finished second, fourth, and fifth, respectively, among the individual leaders. Only the Yankees had a better team ERA. Dick Wakefield's bid to join the Detroit circle of batting champs ended in a late-season slump that saw Chicago's Luke Appling overtake the Tiger star. Dick was, however, the only A.L. player with 200 hits in 1943.

A war-weakened league and the best pitching staff in the A.L. kept Detroit abreast of the surprise team of the decade, the St. Louis Browns. Tigers' hurlers led the circuit in complete games, shutouts, ERA, and fewest homers allowed. Newhouser (29–9) and Trout (27–14) formed the winningest one-two pitching punch since Walter Johnson and Bob Groom with the 1912 Senators. Newhouser and Trout were the only 20-game winners in the A.L. They also finished one-two in ERA (Diz 2.12, Hal 2.22), innings pitched (Diz 352, Hal 312), and strikeouts (Hal 187, Diz 144). On offense, no Detroit regular (100 or more games) hit .300 for the second time in three years. The absence of Bridges and Trucks, both in military service, left little help for the two mound workhorses. On the final day of the season, Trout lost to Washington knuckleballer Dutch Leonard and St. Louis beat New York, giving the Browns their only A.L. pennant ever.

Some strange scheduling made for another dramatic finish to the 1945 A.L. pennant race. Washington finished its season a week before Detroit. With destiny in their own hands, the Tigers faced St. Louis in a season-ending doubleheader, needing one win to clinch the pennant. The 1945 Tigers were hoisted into contention by the return of slugging Hank Greenberg. His batting tear over the second half of the season powered an otherwise average offense. Newhouser, A.L. MVP for the second straight year, and Dizzy Trout again paced the pitchers. Prince Hal led the league in wins (25), ERA (1.81), innings pitched (313), winning percentage (.735), complete games (29), shutouts (8), and strikeouts (212). He also won the decisive game of the season, in relief of Trucks, when Greenberg's grand slam beat the Browns. The second game of that twinbill was cancelled by rain, leaving Detroit with the worst winning percentage yet (.575) for a major league pennant winner.

The 1945 World Series was another that had Detroit leading after five games. With wartime restrictions, the first three games were played in Detroit, the next four in Chicago. After Hank Borowy blanked the Tigers, 9–0, in the first game, war vet Trucks evened the Series with a 4–1 win as Greenberg homered. Claude Passeau overwhelmed Detroit with a one-hit, 3–0 win in the third contest. Back-to-back wins by Trout and Newhouser at Wrigley Field gave Detroit the edge. Game Six was one of the wildest in Series history. The Cubs squandered a 7–3 lead and needed four shutout innings of relief from Borowy and Stan Hack's RBI double for a 12-inning, 8–7 win. Two days later, Borowy trudged out for his third straight appearance. Consecutive singles by Skeeter Webb, Eddie Mayo, and Doc Cramer sent Borowy to the showers trailing 1–0. Paul Derringer gave up a bases-loaded walk to Jim Outlaw and a three-run double to Paul Richards. With two days rest and a five-run cushion, Newhouser coasted to a 9–3 win. Detroit, a champion of the war effort through the automotive industry, was again champion of baseball as well with its second World Championship in 10 years.

Memories of a glorious decade would have to sustain Detroit baseball fans for much of the next two decades. The 1946 Tigers were no match for a new offensive juggernaut in Boston, led by Ted Williams. Though Greenberg led the A.L. in homers and RBIs, and Newhouser led in wins again, the Tigers finished a distant second to the boys from Beantown. Then Greenberg was waived to the Pirates, a puzzling move to this day in that no A.L. club claimed Greenberg off the waiver list. Greenberg was always a tough negotiator and his demand for $75,000 in 1947 was too much for Walter Briggs. A picture of Greenberg admiring the Yankee pinstripes and an article by Dan Daniel stating demands that Hank would play first base for the Yanks but only the outfield for Detroit greased the skids that sent Henry to Pittsburgh (Berkow, 1989, 173). The post-Greenberg parade at first base included Roy Cullenbine, George Vico, Don Kolloway, Paul Campbell, Dick Kryhoski, Walt Dropo, Wayne Belardi, Ferris Fain, Earl Torgeson, J.D. Phillips, Ray Boone, Gail Harris, Bobo Osborne, and Steve Bilko, until Norm Cash settled in for a 14-year run beginning in 1960. With Hank gone only newly arrived George Kell, acquired in a steal that sent Barney McCoskey to the Athletics (the second best trade in Tigers history according to *The Baseball Trade Register*), kept up the proud offensive tradition of the Tigers (Reichler, 1984, 329). Detroit closed out the decade with an aging, slipping team. Red Rolfe replaced O'Neill as manager after the 1948 season.

Robinson's Rock was the key play in a decade that was anything but fabulous for Detroit baseball—the 1950s. After four years out of the running, the Tigers relied on aging arms and improved offense to battle the Yankees for first place. Defending batting champ Kell turned in another lusty season, hitting .340, and joined Vic Wertz and Hoot Evers in the 100 RBI Club. The mirage vanished on September 24, 1950. Heavy smoke from Canadian forest fires set the scene for a pitching duel between Ted Gray and Bob Lemon of the Indians. Cleveland threatened a 1–1 tie with the bases loaded in the 10th inning. With one out, Luke Easter grounded to first baseman Kolloway who stepped on first, then threw home. Catcher Aaron Robinson never saw Kolloway touch first, so he simply tagged home plate as Lemon slid across with the winning run. Detroit fell 2½ games behind the first-place Yankees and never recovered. For the next decade (1951–60), the Tigers finished no closer than within 15 games of first place. Seven different managers (Rolfe, Fred Hutchinson, Bucky Harris, Jack Tighe, Bill Norman, Jimmie Dykes, and Joe Gordon) were the most ever in a 10-year period in Tigertown. Only 13 skippers had been employed in the first 50 years of the franchise.

By 1952 the Tigers were a last-place club, suffering the only eighth-place finish in franchise history. Detroit also suffered the loss of owner Walter Briggs, Sr. who died on January 17. Spike Briggs succeeded his father as club president and presided over a dismal

chapter in Tigers lore. The ensuing house-cleaning and youth movement featured the addition of 1953 Rookie of the Year Harvey Kuenn,
the A.L. hit leader that season.

The premier player to land at Briggs Stadium in the fifties was a
kid from Baltimore. Al Kaline joined the Tigers in 1953, won the
batting title in 1955, his first gold glove in 1957, and was the last Hall
of Famer (as of 1989) to play the majority of his career for Detroit.
Kaline joined Kuenn to form the K kids combination. One, or the
other, led the club in batting average each year from 1953 to 1959
when Kuenn paced the A.L. with a .353 mark. Key additions to the
pitching staff in the fifties were Frank Lary, Jim Bunning, Paul Foy-
tack, Billy Hoeft, Hank Aguirre, and Don Mossi, building a nucleus
for the sixties.

The trustees owning the Tigers since the death of Briggs, Sr.
decided to sell the club in 1956. Bidding was fierce, with Bill Veeck,
Jack Kent Cooke, Jerry Hoffberger, Charlie Finley, and Briggs, Jr.
vying for ownership. Briggs was ineligible to buy the club, but used his
influence on behalf of an 11-man Michigan group led by broadcasting
magnates Fred Knorr and John Fetzer. The Knorr-Fetzer group narrowly outbid Veeck to capture the prize. Briggs, Jr. was retained as
executive vice-president and general manager.

The Briggs, Jr. era ended in 1957. Poor performance and ill-
timed remarks about the ownership syndicate and Kaline's demand
for a better contract preceded his departure on April 26. Assistant
General Manager John McHale replaced Briggs, Jr. Ozzie Virgil became the first non-white player to don the Tiger flannels, joining the
team in 1958. Only the Red Sox took longer to integrate than the
Tigers. McHale resigned to join the Braves in 1959, replaced by Rick
Ferrell, but only until Bill DeWitt was hired following the 1959 campaign. Despite improved talent, Detroit had been unable to escape the
middle of the A.L. pack. DeWitt was consequently expected to shake
things up.

Wheeling and dealing Bill DeWitt made trade after trade in 1960,
including three that will never fail to generate discussion. First, and
best, he sent Steve Demeter to Cleveland for Norm Cash (Detroit's
best deal ever according to *The Baseball Trade Register*) (Reichler, 1984,
329). Tribe general manager Frank Lane had just acquired Cash, who
never played a game for Cleveland, from the White Sox. DeWitt and
Lane then made the first of two moves yet to be duplicated in baseball.
First they swapped the defending batting champ for the co-leader in
homers. Kuenn's four A.L. hit titles, six seasons over .300, and .314
career average over seven years went to Cleveland. Rocky Colavito
and his slugging prowess, tailor-made for cozy Briggs Stadium, joined
the Bengals. Though controversial, and still considered the death knell

of the Cleveland franchise by some (Kuenn spent just one season with the Indians), that trade proved of no immediate benefit for either club. With both teams floundering, DeWitt and Lane decided new managers were in order, so Detroit skipper Dykes went to Cleveland for Tribe pilot Joe Gordon, the first and last time major league managers were swapped. Gordon had been a Detroit coach until resigning after a Spike Briggs tirade. The results were far less dramatic than the deals themselves. Both Cleveland and Detroit were out of the running in 1960.

John Fetzer had a lineup with pennant potential and had a championship manager pegged to lead the Tigers out of the wilderness. Casey Stengel, unceremoniously dumped by the Yankees after losing the 1960 World Series, was Fetzer's choice. Stengel was ready to take the job, until a physical exam and medical advice vetoed the move. Bob Scheffing, a coach with the Braves in 1960, replaced Gordon as manager.

When expansion came to major league baseball in 1961, profound changes came to the Tigers as well. The home run was in, and a team that had led the A.L. in batting average 16 times since 1907 won its last team batting title in 1961. Two clubs—the Yankees, perhaps the greatest club in major league history, and the expansion Los Angeles Angels, playing in little Wrigley Field, hit more homers than the 1961 Tigers. Ironically, though the 1961 Yanks are famed for their powerful offense, the 1961 Tigers scored more runs. From 1961 to 1988, no A.L. club led the league in homers more often than the Tigers, even though no Tiger led the league until aging Darrell Evans hit 40 in 1985, becoming the first player in major league history with 40-homer seasons in the A.L. and N.L., and the oldest A.L. home run leader ever.

Cash and Colavito were the power punch of the surprising 1961 Tigers. Norm and Rocky were one of the first two duos with more than 40 homers in one season since 1931. Of course Rocky's 45 and Norm's 41 were overshadowed by the 61 of Roger Maris and 54 of Mickey Mantle that same season. With five players (Colavito, Cash, Kaline, Jake Wood, and Billy Bruton) scoring more than 95 runs, and with a staff comprised of Yankee Killer Frank Lary (23–9), Jim Bunning (17 wins), and Don Mossi (15 wins), the Tigers kept pace with New York until September. The month opened with a three-game series between the leaders at Yankee Stadium. A record 171,503 fans turned out for a New York sweep that finished off Detroit. Individual honors, however, went to Cash (batting title), Kaline (comeback player of the year), and Scheffing (manager of the year).

Like the 1950 Tigers the 1961 team was something of a one-year wonder. Only Kaline, Cash, and McAuliffe would be part of Detroit's next great team, the 1967–72 model. In the interim, a youth movement and managerial tragedy were the big news of the early sixties. Local prospects Bill Freehan and Willie Horton would anchor the offense. Denny McLain, Mickey Lolich, Joe Sparma, and Earl Wilson succeeded the Bunning-Lary staff. Building the next championship team was left to James Arthur Campbell, an employee of the Detroit organization since 1949, named general manager in 1962. With minor exceptions, the Tigers would bear the stamp of Jim Campbell ever after.

The youth movement began under Charlie Dressen, one of three Detroit helmsmen that did not see the fruits of their labor. At 65 years old, Dressen replaced the mild-mannered Scheffing in 1963 to toughen the Tigers. Dressen left the club in March 1965 with a heart attack, replaced by coach Bob Swift. Charlie returned in 1966, only to suffer another attack. Swift took over again, only to enter the hospital himself after the All-Star Game. Coach Frank Skaff became Detroit's third manager of 1966. Dressen re-entered the hospital on August 5 with a kidney infection and died August 10. Swift, suffering from cancer, died October 17.

Emerging as the pitching leader of the Dressen Tigers was young righthander and part-time organ player Dennis Dale McLain. Acquired on waivers from the White Sox in 1963, Denny won 16 games in 1965, 20 in 1966, and looked to be the anchor of a Detroit contender in 1967.

Campbell named Mayo Smith, former manager of the Reds and Phillies, to run the Tigers in 1967. The Smith selection could hardy be inspiring. His 299–326 managerial record included not one season above .500. Smith inherited an offense second only to World Champion Baltimore's and an able pitching staff. Mayo improved his defense by moving McAuliffe to second and putting Ray Oyler at short. Only luck of timing kept the dividing line of major leaguers that can and cannot hit from being called the Oyler line instead of the (Mario) Mendoza line.

Experience gained in 1966 made the 1967 Tigers a bona fide contender. Joe Sparma's rebound gave Detroit four solid starters and the offense ranked with Boston's as best in the league. They looked destined by defeating the Orioles on April 30 without a hit. They also brought momentary joy to a city torn by violence. One game against Baltimore was moved out of Detroit after riots broke out in the downtown area. A rare outburst by Kaline, slamming his bat after striking out against Cleveland's Sam McDowell, resulted in a broken finger and a long absence, a crippling blow to the Tigers. McLain suffered a mysterious foot injury (a result of his gambling connections, some say) and was winless in September. Still, Detroit could win the pennant with back-to-back doubleheader sweeps against the Angels on the final two days of the season. Not until the last out of the season, when McAuliffe hit into his first double play of the year, were the Tigers eliminated. Frustrated fans tore into Tiger Stadium after the final out, vandalizing the park that was now 22 years without a pennant winner.

To a man, the Tigers felt they were the best team in 1967 and determined to prove so in 1968. Not only did Detroit coast to the 1968 American League title, it did so in a magical way. Late-inning heroics were commonplace for a team that harkened back to Detroit's 1934 nemesis, the Gashouse Gang of St. Louis. The first win of the year came on Gates Brown's ninth-inning, pinch-hit homer against Boston. Jim Northrup hit three grand slams in five days in June, two in one game. Brown won two games with pinch-hits on August 11. Like the 1934 Cards, the 1968 Tigers were led by a devilish pitcher having the season of a lifetime. "Denny McLain, Denny McLain, there's never been any like Denny McLain," went the song that blared over Detroit radios in 1968. McLain became the first 30-game winner since Dizzy Dean, another number 17, for the 1934 Cards. The dramatic 30th came after McLain had been lifted from the September. 14 game against Oakland when Horton singled home Mickey Stanley in the bottom of the ninth. Despite injuries to Kaline and McAuliffe, Detroit led the A.L. for all but 15 days and won the pennant by 12 games, clinching the banner on September 17.

The Year of the Tiger in Detroit was a year of further violence and racial turmoil throughout America. While baseball in Detroit could not take credit as a cure for the troubles of the community, it did give many people a rallying point, a display of racial harmony, and a champion.

A rematch of the 1934 World Series pitted the Tigers against the defending champion Cardinals. In a brilliant strategical move, Mayo Smith moved Stanley from outfield to shortstop so that Kaline, out much of the year with a broken arm, together with Horton and Jim Northrup could man the outfield and increase the offense. That did not stop Bob Gibson from a record-setting 17 strikeouts in a first-game win. St. Louis took a 3–1 lead as Gibson beat McLain twice. Game Six was St. Louis' for the taking as Lou Brock sped toward home in the fifth inning. But Brock elected to come in standing, not sliding, and was retired on Horton's throw to Freehan. Instead of a 4–2 deficit, Detroit trailed by a run. Kaline's bases loaded single in the seventh paced a three-run rally that gave the Tigers and Lolich a 5–3 win. McLain breezed to a 13–1 win in Game Six. A seventh game classic between Lolich and Gibson was scoreless until a St. Louis defensive breakdown in the seventh. Centerfielder Curt Flood's error helped

Detroit to three runs. Lolich, the surprising series hero, went on to a 4–1 win, his third victory of the Series, and the city of Detroit went wild.

Like many champs, the Tigers encountered plenty of troubles trying to repeat. McLain's selfish behavior became a problem, Horton struggled, and a feud between Mayo Smith and pitching coach Johnny Sain climaxed with Sain's firing during the 1969 season. Detroit was no match for baseball's new dynasty, the Baltimore Orioles, in the new Eastern Division of the expanded American League.

As part of the baseball centennial celebration in 1969, an all-time Tigers team was chosen by the fans. The selected squad was 1B Hank Greenberg, 2B Charlie Gehringer, SS Billy Rogell, 3B George Kell, outfielders Ty Cobb, Harry Heilmann, Al Kaline, LHP Hal Newhouser and RHP Denny McLain, the youngster of the dream team. Voters could have no idea that McLain would win only three games for the Tigers after the centennial season.

Denny suffered three suspensions in 1970 and a disorganized Detroit team never contended. Breaking with tradition, the Tigers chose a flamboyant manager to replace Mayo Smith in hopes of harnessing another championship effort from a now veteran Detroit club. Billy Martin returned to Detroit, where he played in 1958, and drew every last effort from baseball's version of the over-the-hill gang. Besides Martin, Jim Campbell also landed a great trade with Washington. McLain, Don Wert, Elliot Maddox, and Norm McRae went to Washington for pitcher Joe Coleman, third baseman Aurelio Rodriguez, shortstop Ed Brinkman, and pitcher Jim Hannan. In one brilliant stroke, Campbell rebuilt his inner defense and put the Tigers back in contention. The 1971 Tigers were still no match for the Orioles, but the 1972 Tigers were. Along with veteran holdovers, role players such as Tony Taylor, Frank Howard, and Duke Sims kept Detroit close. Woody Fryman (10–3) was the pitching surprise. Thanks to a strike and imbalanced schedule, the Tigers captured the A.L. East by a half-game over the Red Sox. Detroit surprised another budding dynasty, the Oakland A's, by pushing the League Championship Series the full distance before bowing to Vida Blue in the fifth game.

The 1972 pennant was costly. As often happens with a team that stays together a year too long, the collapse was swift and total. Martin was fired in 1973 and another ex-Yankee would oversee the rebuilding years. Ralph Houk, the Major, became manager of the Tigers in 1974 and initiated a five-year plan that would pave the way for the team of the 1980s. The 1974–75 Tigers were the first ever with back-to-back last-place finishes.

For a season in which Detroit never threatened for a pennant, 1976 was one of the most memorable in club history. It was "The Year of the Bird." Mark Fidrych was the lead character, but Ron LeFlore, Rusty Staub, and Jason Thompson formed a stellar supporting cast. Fidrych was a rare baseball commodity, a character so unique that none like him had been seen before. The Bird packed Tiger Stadium and parks around the league. He talked to the ball, played with the dirt on the mound, ran around the field congratulating teammates after good plays, and he won ballgames as well. His 19–9 record as a rookie included league bests in complete games (24) and ERA (2.34). Unfortunately, Fidrych was a one-year wonder, suffering arm trouble in 1977 and winning just 10 more major league games.

Two other unique Tigers of the 1970s were LeFlore and John Hiller. Without formal baseball training, LeFlore came to the Tigers from Jackson Prison. Ron was the first Tiger since 1962 with more than 20 steals in a season, led the A.L. with 68 steals in 1978, and became the first Tiger with more than 250 career steals since 1926. Hiller, a starter-reliever with Detroit since 1965, missed the 1971 season after suffering a heart attack. He bounced back in 1972 to lead the A.L. with 38 saves and 65 appearances. Hiller's 545 games pitched for Detroit are a club record.

Jim Campbell broke with Tiger tradition again in 1979, making perhaps the most significant move in the modern history of the club. Campbell had replaced Houk with veteran minor league skipper Les Moss. The club played well, but a chance-of-a-lifetime opportunity tempted the Detroit general manager. Sparky Anderson, manager of the team of the 1970s, the Cincinnati Reds, sat idle after being unceremoniously fired following the 1978 season. Despite a commitment to Moss, Campbell gambled on Anderson. Detroit actually won one game less than in 1978, but Anderson would leave an unmistakable imprint on the Tigers in the next decade.

From 1980 to 1982, Jim Campbell methodically built the next great Tigers team, then turned the general manager reins over to Bill Lajoie. The middle infield was already set with catcher Lance Parrish, second baseman Whitaker, shortstop Trammell, and pitchers Jack Morris, Milt Wilcox, Dan Petry, and Aurelio Lopez. Michigan State University's Kirk Gibson was a rising superstar. Key 1982 trades brought Chet Lemon and Larry Herndon into the outfield, while rookies Howard Johnson and Glenn Wilson made an impact. In 1983 Detroit placed second, its best finish since 1972 (excluding the second half of the 1981 split season).

As the 1967 season sparked Detroit in 1968, so was the 1983 season a platform that launched the 1984 Tigers, the winningest A.L. team (matched by Oakland in 1988) of the decade. After 40 games the Tigers were 35–5, the best 40-game start in major league history, including Morris' no-hitter at Chicago on April 7. The injury-prone

Gibson finally put in a full season, Parrish belted 33 homers, and the club jelled behind them. Reliever Willie Hernandez enjoyed a dream season with 32 saves in 33 chances, copping both MVP and Cy Young honors, matching McLain's 1968 effort. Detroit led the A.L. in runs scored, homers, on-base percentage, ERA, and fewest runs allowed. Evidence of Detroit superiority came in the post-season. Kansas City was vanquished in three games and San Diego managed just one win in the World Series. Morris won Games One and Four with complete-game efforts, Wilcox won the third, and Lopez took the fifth when Gibson socked two electrifying homers before 51,901 fans at Tiger Stadium, where a club-record 2,704,794 spectators attended during the regular season. Trammell won MVP honors for the Series and Sparky Anderson became the first manager ever to guide World Champions in both the American and National Leagues.

The dynastic expectations that always accompany a team like the 1984 Tigers never materialized. First Parrish, then Gibson, left the club when Detroit management continued its stance against wild bidding on free agents. The 1985 and 1986 Tigers were respectable, non-contending teams.

As with the 1972 club, the 1987 Tigers were bolstered with veterans that brought immediate success while jeopardizing the future. Former batting champ Bill Madlock anchored third base and pitcher Doyle Alexander caught fire down the stretch. Brilliant play in the final week enabled Detroit to catch and pass the late-season leaders— Toronto Blue Jays. Favored to beat the Minnesota Twins, champs of the weaker A.L. West, the tired Tigers were quickly and surprisingly disposed of.

For a time in 1988, the Tigers seemed poised to win the greatest fight of all, the fight against time. The veteran club took an early lead in the A.L. East, only to be swept aside by Boston. Both teams faltered down the stretch, but the Red Sox survived by one game. Detroit was 52–33 prior to the All-Star Game, leading the division by three games. Sparky's gang was 36–41 down the back stretch, 15–24 after building a four-game lead on August 21.

Detroit entered the 1989 season needing more wins than the Yankees to be the team of the decade, needing just a .500 season for the best decade (by winning percentage) in club history. But, like other great Tigers teams, total collapse came to a proud, but aged, group of players. Sparky Anderson, overwhelmed by a losing club and a non-stop schedule of benefit appearances, left the club with mental exhaustion. Detroit trailed the field from start to finish. A rebuilding program seemed imminent at the end of the decade. Perhaps the 1990s, like the 1950s and 1970s, would tax the loyalty of faithful fans. Most likely, patience would be rewarded with future success, as it had been in the 1960s and 1980s and throughout club history.

Of course that success would not come overnight, at least not if measured by pennants and game victories. A brief climb into the division's third slot in 1990 and a surprising second-place tie in 1991 were followed by an immediate tumble to sixth in 1992, and only once in this stretch (1991 at 84–78) did the club play .500 ball. Yet it has to be observed that Sparky's Tigers could provide plenty of excitement by filling the air with flying baseballs. Cecil Fielder emerged as a major power force with 51 trippers in 1990, adding three consecutive RBI crowns and thus becoming the first to reach such a plateau in either league since Ruth. And Fielder had plenty of longball help as Rob Deer and Mickey Tettleton contributed to an AL best 209 homers in 1991. The trouble was that those same free swingers also amassed that summer the second highest club strikeout total (1,185) in big-league annals, narrowly failing to supplant the 1968 Mets in a hallmark category for futility. And as keystone duo Alan Trammell and Lou Whitaker logged their record 15th tandem season, it could only be said that the mid-1990s Detroiters were hamstrung by a surplus of old age and torpedoed by a scarcity of sound pitching.

Notes

1. Two sources provide information on the history of Tigers Radio and TV broadcasts. Curt Smith's exhaustive work, *Voices of the Game,* breaks the history of broadcasting into different eras, with Detroit announcers covered in each. Some of the great play-by-play moments are also included. The *Detroit Tigers Press Guide* gives a brief, but complete, rundown of the club's proud broadcast history.

2. The primary reference source for early Tigers history is *The Detroit Tigers* by Fred Lieb. Part of the Putnam series, Lieb's Tigers history might seem dated in style, but the substance is there and largely corroborated by more recent team histories.

3. Ty Cobb is one of the most discussed figures in baseball history. No fewer than five biographies about Cobb exist, and many feel *Ty Cobb,* by Charles Alexander, is the best of these.

References

Berkow, Ira. 1989. *Hank Greenberg: The Story of My Life.* New York: Times Books.

Ewald, Dan. 1989. *Detroit Tigers Press Guide (1989).* Detroit: Detroit Tigers.

Lieb, Frederick, G. 1946. *The Detroit Tigers.* New York: G. P. Putnam's Sons.

MacFarlane, Paul. 1983. *The Sporting News Hall of Fame Fact Book.* St. Louis, Mo.: The Sporting News.

Reichler, Joe. 1984. *The Baseball Trade Register.* New York: Collier Books.

Smith, Curt. 1987. *Voices of the Game*. South Bend, Ind.: Diamond Communications.

Smith, Fred T. 1988. *Tiger Tales and Trivia*. Lathrup Village, Mich.: Fred T. Smith, Russ Entwisle, and John Duffy.

Annotated Bibliography

Alexander, Charles C. *Ty Cobb*. New York: Oxford University Press, 1984. 272 pp.
> Of the many Cobb biographies, Alexander's might be the best. The Ohio University professor's work is painstakingly researched, with numerous sources and interviews, giving a detailed account of Cobb's life and times. *Ty Cobb* is included in the mythological "Essential Baseball Library" as listed in *The SABR Review of Books*, Volume II, Number 1.

Anderson, Sparky, and Dan Ewald. *Bless You Boys: Diary of the Detroit Tigers' 1984 Season*. Chicago: Contemporary Books, 1984. 264 pp.
> The winningest season in Tigers history receives day-by-day treatment, along with the comments of manager Sparky Anderson. Each day includes the game box score and Sparky's colorful commentary. A special World Series edition includes playoff and World Series coverage as well. Ewald is the public relations director of the Tigers.

Berkow, Ira. *Hank Greenberg: The Story of My Life*. New York: Times Books, 1989. 311 pp.
> Finished after Greenberg's death, this is a work for which Berkow took the notes of baseball's first Jewish superstar and connected them to form a posthumous autobiography. Although Greenberg takes a surprising backseat to Cobb, Cochrane, and Kaline, his career in Detroit is an important chapter of club history. The details of his contract squabbles and departure from Detroit are especially illuminating.

Butler, Hal. *Al Kaline and the Detroit Tigers*. Chicago: Henry Regnery Company, 1973. 273 pp.
> Detroit's 1972 divisional championship provided Butler an opportunity to tell the story of the man who exemplifies the modern Tigers better than anyone. Kaline's career is chronicled from his rookie season through the 1972 campaign. As Kaline spent his entire career in Detroit, the book is also an effective history of the Tigers from 1953 to 1972. Butler's book is the better of two Kaline biographies, the other being Al Hirshberg's *The Al Kaline Story*, published in 1964.

Cobb, Ty, with Al Stump. *My Life in Baseball: The True Record*. Garden City, NY: Doubleday, 1961. 283 pp.
> Cobb's autobiography, published just after his death in 1961, is faithful to the spirit of one of baseball's most controversial figures. The book also acts, literally and figuratively, as the final chapter in Cobb's life; as though once he had committed his side of the story of his life to a permanent record, he could move on to final rest.

Falls, Joe. *Detroit Tigers*. New York: Collier Books, 1975. 192 pp.
> One of a brief series published by a trade division of Macmillan, *Detroit Tigers* is broken down into an introductory section (Play Ball), Beginnings, Milestones, Great Years, Moments to Remember, Managers, Players, Off The Wall (humorous moments), and Linescore (statistics). Well-written and well-illustrated, the book is a capsulized look at the franchise and a fine introduction to club history.

————. *The Detroit Tigers: An Illustrated History*. New York: Walker & Company, 1989. 212 pp.

For a team as rich in history as the Tigers, a pictorial treatment was long overdue. With photo selections by Gerald Astor, *The Detroit Tigers* recovers much of the ground of Falls' earlier work, but in a less compartmentalized fashion. Jim Campbell calls *The Detroit Tigers* the best written history of the club.

Fidrych, Mark, and Tom Clark. *No Big Deal*. New York: J. B. Lippincott, 1977. 251 pp.

With everyone else capitalizing on the Fidrych phenomenon, Mark himself teamed with poet and baseball fan Clark in what could also be called "The Fidrych Interviews." Using a question and answer format, Fidrych discusses his youth, his early baseball career, and his remarkable rookie season of 1976. The candid format gives a clearer look at "The Bird" than a more traditional biography might provide.

Freehan, Bill. *Behind the Mask*. New York: The World Publishing Company, 1970. 225 pp.

An early example of the player diary, in this case Freehan's view of Detroit's 1969 season. Most significantly, Freehan describes the demise of the 1968 World Champions, including the All-Star Game exploits of Denny McLain who left teammate Mickey Lolich high and dry when Lolich expected to fly with McLain back to Detroit. The breakdown between manager Mayo Smith and pitching coach Johnny Sain is also discussed in some detail.

Green, Jerry. *Year of the Tiger*. New York: Coward-McCann, 1969, 249 pp.

The day-by-day story of perhaps the greatest season in Tigers history is well-told by Green, baseball beat writer for the *Detroit News*. *Year of the Tiger* is especially helpful in light of the 1968 newspaper strike in Detroit that suspended local baseball print coverage for several weeks.

Hawkins, John C. *This Date in Detroit Tigers History*. Briarcliff Manor, NY: Stein and Day, 1981. 239 pp.

One of a series of "This Date" books, the Detroit version is similar to the other volumes, including a day-by-day section, nicknames, statistical information, a post-season section, an interview with Jim Campbell, noteworthy box scores, and other odds and ends.

Hill, Art. *I Don't Care If I Never Come Back*. New York: Simon and Schuster, 1980. 283 pp.

The late Art Hill combined the passion of a true baseball fan with exceptional writing skill. Born in northern Michigan, Hill touches on various aspects of Tigers history: the broadcasters, the writers, the heroes. His witty writing makes for an entertaining and informative book throughout.

Lieb, Frederick G. *The Detroit Tigers*. New York: G.P. Putnam's Sons, 1946. 276 pp.

Dated by 1980s standards, the Putnam series remains one of the best sources on the early histories of the teams covered. The Detroit volume, one of six of the Putnam team histories penned by Lieb, covers the club from its inception through the 1945 World Championship.

McLain, Denny, with Dave Diles. *Nobody's Perfect*. New York: The Dial Press, 1975. 208 pp.

Within a decade prior to the publication of his biography, McLain went from unknown to superstar to suspended troublemaker to ex-ballplayer. The rise and fall of McLain from 1966 to 1970 directly parallels the fortunes of the Tigers themselves.

Smith, Fred T. *Tiger Facts.* Lathrup Village, Mich.: Fred T. Smith, Russ
Entwisle, and John Duffy, 1986. 288 pp.
    Smith gives a capsule review of each Tigers season beginning with Mickey
    Cochrane's first Detroit club in 1934. Each season summary includes the
    American League standings and individual batting and pitching records.
    Special sections are included for post-season play.
————. *Tiger Tales and Trivia.* Lathrup Village, Mich.: Fred T. Smith, Russ
Entwisle, and John Duffy, 1988. 288 pp.
    The Detroit chapter of the Society For American Baseball Research is
    named after Fred Smith who has spent the majority of his life watching
    and chronicling the history of the Tigers. The book contains a brief sketch
    of every player in Tigers history.
Sullivan, George, and David Cataneo. *Detroit Tigers: The Complete Record of
Detroit Tigers Baseball.* New York: Macmillan Publishing Company, 1985.
410 pp.
    One of a series of books published by Macmillan extracting the statistical
    histories of individual teams from *The Baseball Encyclopedia. Detroit Tigers*
    includes brief written summaries on each season and gives a more com-
    plete statistical look at each Detroit club than that available within the Big
    Mac. An interesting graphic section and complete career playing records
    for everyone to wear the Tigers uniform are also featured.

Year-by-Year Standings and Season Summaries

Year	Pos.	Record	Pct.	GB	Manager	Player	BA	Player	HR	Player	W-L	ERA
1901	3rd	74–61	.548	8.5	Stallings	Elberfeld	.310	Barrett	4	Miller	23–13	2.95
								Holmes	4			
1902	7th	52–83	.385	30.5	Dwyer	Barrett	.303	Casey	3	Mercer	15–18	3.03
1903	5th	65–71	.478	25.0	Barrow	Crawford	.335	Crawford	4	Mullin	19–15	2.25
1904	7th	62–90	.408	32.0	Barrow	Barrett	.268	Crawford	2	Donovan	17–16	2.46
					Lowe			Hickman	2			
								McIntyre	2			
1905	3rd	79–74	.516	15.5	Armour	Crawford	.297	Crawford	6	Killan	23–14	2.27
1906	6th	71–78	.477	21.0	Armour	Crawford	.295	Coughlin	2	Mullin	21–18	2.78
								Crawford	2			
								O'Leary	2			
								Schaefer	2			
1907	1st	92–58	.613	+1.5	Jennings	Cobb	.350	Cobb	5	Donovan	25–4	2.19
1908	1st	90–63	.588	+0.5	Jennings	Cobb	.324	Crawford	7	Summers	24–12	1.64
1909	1st	98–54	.645	+3.5	Jennings	Cobb	.377	Cobb	9	Mullin	29–9	2.22
1910	3rd	86–68	.558	18.0	Jennings	Cobb	.385	Cobb	8	Mullin	21–12	2.87
1911	2nd	89–65	.578	13.5	Jennings	Cobb	.420	Cobb	8	Mullin	18–10	3.08
1912	6th	69–84	.451	36.5	Jennings	Cobb	.410	Cobb	7	Dubuc	17–10	2.77
1913	6th	66–87	.431	30.0	Jennings	Cobb	.390	Crawford	9	Dubuc	15–14	2.89
1914	4th	80–73	.523	19.5	Jennings	Cobb	.368	Crawford	8	Coveleski	22–12	2.50
1915	2nd	100–54	.649	2.5	Jennings	Cobb	.369	Burns	5	Dauss	24–13	2.50
1916	3rd	87–67	.565	4.0	Jennings	Cobb	.371	Cobb	5	Coveleski	21–11	1.97
1917	4th	78–75	.510	21.5	Jennings	Cobb	.383	Veach	8	Dauss	17–14	2.42
1918	7th	55–71	.437	20.0	Jennings	Cobb	.382	Heilmann	5	Boland	14–10	2.65
1919	4th	80–60	.571	8.0	Jennings	Cobb	.384	Heilmann	8	Dauss	21–9	3.55
1920	7th	61–93	.396	37.0	Jennings	Cobb	.334	Veach	11	Ehmke	15–18	3.29
1921	6th	71–82	.464	27.0	Cobb	Heilmann	.394	Heilmann	19	Ehmke	13–14	4.55

Year	Pos.	Record	Pct.	GB	Manager	Player	BA	Player	HR	Player	W-L	ERA
1922	3rd	79–75	.513	15.0	Cobb	Cobb	.401	Heilmann	21	Pillette	19–12	2.84
1923	2nd	83–71	.539	16.0	Cobb	Heilmann	.403	Heilmann	18	Dauss	21–13	3.62
1924	3rd	86–68	.558	6.0	Cobb	Heilmann	.346	Heilmann	10	Whitehill	17–9	3.86
1925	4th	81–73	.526	16.5	Cobb	Heilmann	.393	Heilmann	13	Dauss	16–11	3.16
1926	6th	79–75	.513	12.0	Cobb	Manush	.378	Manush	14	Whitehill	16–13	4.00
1927	4th	82–71	.536	27.5	Moriarty	Heilmann	.398	Heilmann	14	Whitehill	16–14	3.36
1928	6th	68–86	.442	33.0	Moriarty	Heilmann	.328	Heilmann	14	Carroll	16–12	3.27
1929	6th	70–84	.455	36.0	Harris	Heilmann	.344	Alexander	25	Uhle	15–11	4.08
1930	5th	75–79	.487	27.0	Harris	Gehringer	.330	Alexander	20	Whitehill	17–13	4.24
1931	7th	61–93	.396	47.0	Harris	Stone	.327	Stone	10	Sorrell	13–14	4.12
1932	5th	76–75	.503	29.5	Harris	Walker	.323	Gehringer	19	Whitehill	16–12	4.54
1933	5th	75–79	.487	25.0	Harris / Baker	Gehringer	.325	Greenberg	12	Marberry	16–11	3.29
1934	1st	101–53	.656	+7.0	Cochrane	Gehringer	.356	Greenberg	26	Rowe	24–8	3.45
1935	1st	93–58	.616	+3.0	Cochrane	Gehringer	.330	Greenberg	36	Bridges	21–10	3.51
1936	2nd	83–71	.539	19.5	Cochrane	Gehringer	.354	Goslin	24	Bridges	23–11	3.60
1937	2nd	89–65	.578	13.0	Cochrane	Gehringer	.371	Greenberg	40	Lawson	18–7	5.27
1938	4th	84–70	.545	16.0	Cochrane / Baker	Greenberg	.315	Greenberg	58	Bridges	13–9	4.59
1939	5th	81–73	.526	26.5	Baker	Gehringer	.325	Greenberg	33	Newsom	17–10	3.37
1940	1st	90–64	.584	+1.0	Baker	Greenberg	.340	Greenberg	41	Newsom	21–5	2.83
1941	T4th	75–79	.487	26.0	Baker	McCosky	.324	York	27	Benton	15–6	2.96
1942	5th	73–81	.474	30.0	Baker	McCosky	.293	York	21	Trucks	14–8	2.73
1943	5th	78–76	.506	20.0	O'Neill	Wakefield	.316	York	34	Trout	20–11	2.48
1944	2nd	88–66	.571	1.0	O'Neill	Higgins	.297	York	18	Newhouser	29–9	2.22
1945	1st	88–65	.575	+1.5	O'Neill	Mayo	.285	Cullenbine	18	Newhouser	25–9	1.81
1946	2nd	92–62	.597	12.0	O'Neill	Kell	.327	Greenberg	44	Newhouser	26–9	1.94
1947	2nd	85–69	.552	12.0	O'Neill	Kell	.320	Cullenbine	24	Hutchinson	18–10	3.03

Year	Pos.	Record	Pct.	GB	Manager	Player	BA	Player	HR	Player	W-L	ERA
1948	5th	78–76	.506	18.5	O'Neill	Evers	.314	Mullin	23	Newhouser	21–12	3.01
1949	4th	87–67	.565	10.0	Rolfe	Kell	.343	Wertz	20	Trucks	19–11	2.81
1950	2nd	95–59	.617	3.0	Rolfe	Kell	.340	Wertz	27	Houtteman	19–12	3.53
1951	5th	73–81	.474	25.0	Rolfe	Kell	.319	Wertz	27	Trucks	13–8	4.32
1952	8th	50–104	.325	45.0	Rolfe-Hutchinson	Groth	.284	Dropo	23	Gray	12–17	4.14
1953	6th	60–94	.390	40.5	Hutchinson	Kuenn	.308	Boone	22	Garver	11–11	4.45
1954	5th	68–86	.442	43.0	Hutchinson	Kuenn	.306	Boone	20	Gromek	18–16	2.74
1955	5th	79–75	.513	17.0	Harris	Kaline	.340	Kaline	27	Hoeft	16–7	2.99
1956	5th	82–72	.532	15.0	Harris	Kuenn	.332	Maxwell	28	Lary	21–13	3.15
1957	4th	78–76	.506	20.0	Tighe	Kaline	.295	Maxwell	24	Bunning	20–8	2.70
1958	5th	77–77	.500	15.0	Tighe-Norman	Kuenn	.319	Harris	20	Lary	16–15	2.91
1959	4th	76–78	.494	18.0	Norman-Dykes	Kuenn	.353	Maxwell	31	Mossi	17–9	3.36
1960	6th	71–83	.461	26.0	Dykes-Gordon	Kaline	.278	Colavito	35	Lary	15–15	3.51
1961	2nd	101–61	.623	8.0	Scheffing	Cash	.361	Colavito	45	Lary	23–9	3.24
1962	4th	85–76	.528	10.5	Scheffing	Bruton	.278	Cash	39	Bunning	19–10	3.59
1963	T5th	79–83	.488	25.5	Scheffing-Dressen	Kaline	.312	Kaline	27	Regan	15–9	3.86
1964	4th	85–77	.525	14.0	Dressen	Freehan	.300	McAuliffe	24	Wickersham	19–12	3.44
1965	4th	89–73	.549	13.0	Dressen-Swift	Horton	.273	Cash	30	McLain	16–6	2.62
1966	3rd	88–74	.543	10.0	Dressen-Swift-Skaff	Kaline	.288	Cash	32	McLain	20–14	3.92
1967	T2nd	91–71	.562	1.0	Smith	Kaline	.308	Kaline	25	Wilson	22–11	3.27
1968	1st	103–59	.636	+12.0	Smith	Horton	.285	Horton	36	McLain	31–6	1.96
1969	2nd	90–72	.556	19.0	Smith	Northrup	.295	Horton	28	McLain	24–9	2.80

Year	Pos.	Record	Pct.	GB	Manager	Player	BA	Player	HR	Player	W-L	ERA
1970	4th	79–83	.488	29.0	Smith	Kaline	.278	Northrup	24	Lolich	14–19	3.79
1971	2nd	91–71	.562	12.0	Martin	Kaline	.294	Cash	32	Lolich	25–14	2.92
1972	1st	86–70	.551	+0.5	Martin	Northrup	.261	Cash	22	Lolich	22–14	2.50
1973	3rd	85–77	.525	12.0	Martin Schultz	Horton	.316	Cash	19	Coleman	23–15	3.53
1974	6th	72–90	.444	19.0	Houk	Freehan	.297	Freehan	18	Hiller	17–14	2.64
1975	6th	57–102	.358	37.5	Houk	Horton	.275	Horton	25	Lolich	12–18	3.77
1976	5th	74–87	.460	24.0	Houk	LeFlore	.316	Thompson	17	Fidrych	19–9	2.34
1977	5th	74–88	.457	26.0	Houk	LeFlore	.325	Thompson	31	Rozema	15–7	3.10
1978	5th	86–76	.531	13.5	Houk	LeFlore	.297	Thompson	26	Slaton	17–11	4.12
1979	5th	85–76	.528	18.0	Moss Anderson	Kemp	.318	Kemp	26	Morris	17–7	3.28
1980	5th	84–78	.519	19.0	Anderson	Trammell	.300	Parrish	24	Morris	16–15	4.18
1981	4th	31–26	.544	3.5	Anderson	Gibson	.328	Parrish	10	Morris	14–7	3.05
	T2nd	29–23	.558	1.5								
1981*	4th	60–49	.550	2.0								
1982	4th	83–79	.512	12.0	Anderson	Herndon	.292	Parrish	32	Morris	17–16	4.06
1983	2nd	92–70	.568	6.0	Anderson	Whitaker	.320	Parrish	27	Morris	20–13	3.34
1984	1st	104–58	.642	+15.0	Anderson	Trammell	.314	Parrish	33	Morris	19–11	3.65
1985	3rd	84–77	.522	15.0	Anderson	Gibson	.287	Evans	40	Morris	16–11	3.33
1986	3rd	87–75	.537	8.5	Anderson	Trammell	.277	Evans	29	Morris	21–8	3.27
1987	1st	98–64	.605	+2.0	Anderson	Trammell	.343	Evans	34	Morris	18–11	3.38
1988	wnd	88–74	.543	1.0	Anderson	Trammell	.311	Evans	22	Morris	15–13	3.94
1989	7th	59–103	.364	30.0	Anderson	Bergman	.268	Whitaker	28	Henneman	11–4	3.70
1990	3rd	79–83	.488	9.0	Anderson	Trammell	.304	Fielder	51	Morris	15–18	4.51
1991	2nd(T)	84–78	.519	7.0	Anderson	Phillips	.284	Fielder	44	Gullickson	20–9	3.90
1992	6th	75–87	.463	21.0	Anderson	Whitaker	.278	Fielder	35	Gullickson	14–13	4.34

*Split Season Totals (Players' Union Strike).

All-Time Tigers Career and Season Records

Career Batting Leaders (1901–1992)

Games Played	Al Kaline	2,834
At Bats	Ty Cobb	10,586
Runs Scored	Ty Cobb	2,087
Hits	Ty Cobb	3,902
Batting Average	Ty Cobb	.369
Home Runs	Al Kaline	399
Runs Batted In	Ty Cobb	1,828
Stolen Bases	Ty Cobb	865

Career Pitching Leaders (1901–1992)

Innings Pitched	George Mullin	3,394
Earned Run Average	Harry Coveleski	2.33
Wins	Hooks Dauss	221
Losses	Hooks Dauss	183
Winning Percentage	Denny McLain	.654
Strikeouts	Mickey Lolich	2,679
Walks	Hal Newhouser	1,227
Games	John Hiller	545
Shutouts	Mickey Lolich	39
Saves	John Hiller	125
Games Started	Mickey Lolich	459
Complete Games	George Mullin	336

Single-Season Batting Records (1901–1992)

Batting Average	Ty Cobb	.420	1911
Home Runs	Hank Greenberg	58	1938
Home Runs (lefthanded)	Norm Cash	41	1961
Runs Batted In	Hank Greenberg	183	1937
Hits	Ty Cobb	248	1911
Singles	Ty Cobb	169	1911
Doubles	Hank Greenberg	63	1934
Triples	Sam Crawford	26	1914
Stolen Bases	Ty Cobb	96	1915
Strikeouts	Cecil Fielder	182	1990
Total Bases	Hank Greenberg	397	1937
Hitting Streak	Ty Cobb	40	1911
Grand Slam Home Runs	Rudy York	4	1938
	Ray Boone	4	1953
	Jim Northrup	4	1968
Hit by Pitch	Bill Freehan	24	1968

All-Time Tigers Career and Season Records *(continued)*

Single-Season Pitching Records (1901–1992)
ERA

Wins	Denny McLain	31	1968
Losses	George Mullin	23	1904
Winning Pct.	Bill Donovan	.862	1907
Strikeouts	Mickey Lolich	308	1971
Walks	Joe Coleman	158	1974
Saves	John Hiller	38	1974
Games	Willie Hernandez	80	1984
Complete Games	George Mullin	42	1904
Games Started	Mickey Lolich	45	1971
Shutouts	Denny McLain	9	1969
Innings Pitched	George Mullin	381	1904
Home Runs Allowed	Denny McLain	42	1966
Consecutive Games Won (season)	Schoolboy Rowe	16	1934
Wild Pitches	Jack Morris	24	1987

5
Kansas City Royals
Building a Champion from Scratch in America's Heartland

BILL CARLE

1968! It was a year of turmoil throughout the United States of America. The Vietnam War was raging at its most fierce. Martin Luther King and Robert Kennedy were to be eliminated by pointless assassinations. There were riots on college campuses throughout the land. The drug culture was in its first flowering as young people looked to escape the grim realities of mid-twentieth-century life. But in Kansas City, 1968 will be remembered simply as the year the home city was without professional baseball.

Baseball made its debut in Kansas City as early as 1884, with a team in the Union Association. Since that time—more than a century ago—the city has held franchises in seven different leagues, and in some years Kansas City even fielded two teams. But on October 18, 1967, those dreams of everlasting summers, sitting out at the ballpark munching hot dogs, drinking beer, and cheering a Kansas City team to victory, went up in smoke when the American League gave Charlie Finley permission to pack up his team, his green and gold uniforms, and his mule and move west to Oakland in sunny California.

But Kansas City had never felt that the A's belonged to them in the first place. In 1955, when Arnold Johnson, a Chicago industrialist, bought the Philadelphia A's from the Mack family and moved them to Kansas City, Missouri acquired a team which had long been little more than an American League doormat, having finished in the first division only twice in the preceding 20 years and in the cellar 11 times. Johnson did his best to continue that tradition by making a series of inept trades with the New York Yankees, trading away much of the A's talent and getting next to nothing in return. Kansas City fans suspected that Johnson, a former owner of Yankee Stadium, secretly wore pinstriped underwear.

Then in 1960 the A's were sold to Charles O. Finley, another Chicago-based businessman. One of his first moves as owner was an attempt to move the team to Dallas, a ploy which was rebuffed by the

American League. Despite efforts made by the Kansas City govern-ment to appease Finley and amazingly good fan support of a woeful team that never finished higher than sixth, Finley made repeated efforts to move until finally being granted permission on that fateful day in 1967.

The American League owners met in Chicago to discuss Finley's bid to move and were aware that there could be serious repercussions as a result of their decision. When the Milwaukee Braves were granted permission to move to Atlanta in 1965, the city of Milwaukee had sued the National League in an effort to keep their franchise. Although the lawsuit was unsuccessful, the American League wanted to avoid legal action and was ready to consider expansion as a compromise solution.

Kansas City town fathers knew that they had a good case for keeping their ballclub. In June voters had approved a $42 million bond issue for the construction of the Jackson County Sports Complex, a facility which would house both a baseball and football stadium. The city had also been very actively promoting the team despite constant threats by Finley to depart. Representing Kansas City at the meeting were Mayor Ilus Davis, Missouri Senator Stuart Symington, Judge Charles Curry, and Dutton Brookfield, chairman of the Jackson County Sports Authority.

After hearing both sides, the American League voted to allow Finley to move to Oakland and to place expansion teams in Kansas City and Seattle no later than 1971. Senator Symington was outraged. Kansas City had hoped to have uninterrupted baseball and the thought of three years without baseball was unconscionable. Symington imme-diately confronted the owners and stated that unless Kansas City was awarded an expansion franchise no later than 1969, he would initiate congressional action to remove baseball's antitrust exemption. The owners hurriedly reconvened and awarded expansion franchises to Kansas City and Seattle beginning in 1969.

So while 1968 marked a year Kansas City would have to suffer through a summer without baseball, it also signalled a new beginning. But in order to begin play in 1969 a considerable amount of work had to be done. An owner needed to be found, an organization formed, a team nickname selected, a manager hired, and players signed, all in the short span of a year. 1968 was to be a busy year for Kansas City baseball.

Four Kansas City businessmen submitted bids to become the new owner of the fledgling franchise: Ewing Kauffman, president of Mar-ion Laboratories, Alex Barket, president of Civic Plaza National Bank, Richard Stern of Stern Brothers Investment Company, and R. Crosby Kemper, retired chairman of the City National Bank. In December of 1967 a screening committee from the American League visited Kansas

City to meet with the prospective owners. And on January 11, 1968, Joe Cronin, the president of the American League, announced that the new franchise had been awarded to Ewing Kauffman.

Kauffman, 51, was a self-made millionaire who began his pharmaceutical firm by producing pills in the basement of his house. His talent for marketing built the company into one of the leading drug companies in the United States and Kauffman became one of Kansas City's richest and most influential citizens. Upon being awarded the franchise, Kauffman vowed to hire knowledgeable baseball people to run the club while he provided the financial support necessary to produce a winner.

The first man Kauffman hired was Cedric Tallis as executive vice president. Tallis had 20 years of front office experience and had most recently served as vice president of the California Angels. Tallis picked Lou Gorman, Baltimore's director of minor league clubs, as director of player development and Charley Metro, a longtime scout, as director of player procurement. It was an experienced front office that was fully dedicated to developing a competitive ballclub.

In March a contest was held to choose the team's nickname. More than 17,000 entries were received with such selections as Eagles, Mo-Kans, Hearts, and Zoomers. But the clear-cut winner was the name Royals, chosen in honor of the American Royal, a national livestock show held annually in Kansas City.

The summer of 1968 was a busy one for Tallis, Metro, and Gorman. Gorman and Tallis worked at building a farm system and deciding upon a manager while Metro was scouting all 20 major league clubs to prepare for the expansion draft to be held on October 16. On September 9 Joe Gordon was chosen as the Royals' first manager. Gordon had previously managed the Indians, Tigers, and A's, leading Cleveland to a second-place finish in 1959.

The days leading up to the expansion draft were exciting ones in Kansas City as fans eagerly waited to see who would be the first players to wear the Royal blue. The accent was on youth as the Royals drafted promising young players such as pitchers Roger Nelson, Jim Rooker, and Dick Drago, infielders Joe Foy, Paul Schaal, and Mike Fiore, outfielders Joe Keough and Pat Kelly, and catchers Ellie Rodriguez and Fran Healy. Veterans Moe Drabowsky, Hoyt Wilhelm, and Jerry Adair were chosen to provide stability for the youthful club. Many of these players would later become trade bait for the key members of the division championship clubs of the mid-seventies.

As spring training opened in 1969, the long empty summer of 1968 became a distant memory. Kansas City fans looked forward to the renewal of baseball with the same eager anticipation generally reserved for a bridegroom on his wedding night.

Just prior to the opening of the season the Royals made a key trade, swapping outfielder Steve Whitaker and pitcher John Gelnar to their expansion counterparts, the Seattle Pilots, for outfielder Lou Piniella. This was to be the first in a long series of clever trades engineered by Cedric Tallis.

The opening game April 8 was a precursor to the types of games patrons of Municipal Stadium would relish that first year. The Royals squeaked by the Minnesota Twins 4–3 in 12 innings as Lou Piniella collected four hits and Joe Keough drove in the winning run. The next night the Royals again took the Twins to overtime, this time winning in 17 innings by the same 4–3 score. Many of Kansas City's victories were tough hard-fought decisions, some of which were won in thrilling fashion.

On May 6 the Royals trailed the Tigers and eventual Cy Young Award winner Denny McLain 6–1 after six innings but later rallied for five runs in the ninth and a 7–6 victory when Bob "Hawk" Taylor lashed a two-out three-run homer. Earlier in the year Taylor had given the Royals another come-from-behind triumph with a three-run eighth-inning homer against Oakland.

The 1969 season featured some fine individual performances, paced by Piniella, who hit .282 and captured the American League Rookie of the Year Award. On May 4 Bob Oliver became the first American Leaguer in seven years to get six hits in a game when he went 6-for-6 against the California Angels. Wally Bunker led the team with 12 victories while Drabowsky notched 11 out of the bullpen. But most important, the 1969 Royals instilled a new sense of pride in Kansas City baseball.

Although the 1970 club produced an abysmal 65–97 record, the year was marked by two exceptional trades. Prior to the season the Royals pulled off the greatest trade in their history when Joe Foy was shipped to the Mets for outfielder Amos Otis and pitcher Bob Johnson. Johnson had the best year of any Royals starter in 1970 going 8–13 and striking out 206 men. But it was Otis who would go on to become one of the Royals' all-time greats. AO, as he would come to be known, hit .284, led the league with 36 doubles, stole 33 bases while being caught only twice, and played stellar defense in center field.

A third promising player was obtained in June when veteran second baseman Cookie Rojas was acquired from the Cardinals for little-used outfielder Fred Rico. Rojas hit .260 and dazzled Royals fans with spectacular plays around the second base bag. Both Rojas and Otis, of course, would go on to earn well-deserved spots in the Royals Hall of Fame.

Cedric Tallis was a man who was not satisfied by mediocrity. The 1970 season so angered Tallis that he made another daring trade during the winter of 1970. Tallis packaged Jackie Hernandez, Bob

Johnson, and Jim Campanis off to Pittsburgh for shortstop Fred Patek, pitcher Bruce Dal Canton, and catcher Jerry May. The key to the trade was Patek, who already had a growing reputation as an excellent glove man, but was not highly regarded as a hitter due to his diminutive size.

The Royals entered spring training in 1971 expected to finish fifth. But new manager Bob Lemon's easygoing style set the tone for an exciting team characterized by pitching, speed, and defense.

The pitching staff was led by Dick Drago, who notched a fine 17–11 record. Mike Hedlund was right behind him with 15 wins and Tom Burgmeier established himself as a quality reliever winning nine, saving 17, and posting a 1.74 ERA. In the field Amos Otis showed himself to be an emerging star, winning a Gold Glove, leading the league in stolen bases with 52, and hitting .301. New shortstop Fred Patek swiped 49 bases, led the league in triples, and teamed with Cookie Rojas to form the best double play combination in the league. Rojas and Patek perfected a spectacular play where on a ground ball up the middle, Rojas would backhand the ball, and in one motion flip it to Patek out of his glove hand, then Patek would throw the runner out at first.

The 1971 Royals enjoyed the most successful season to date in Kansas City major league history, finishing 85–71 and capturing second place. Cedric Tallis was named Executive of the Year by the *Sporting News* for his clever trades and Bob Lemon finished second in the Manager of the Year voting. What's more, Kansas City was finally out of the second division and out from under the cloud of mediocrity that had plagued the city during all its previous major league campaigns.

The success of the 1971 season caused the Royals to look toward the 1972 season with visions of a pennant dancing in their heads. Cedric Tallis was busy again in the off-season pulling off two more outstanding deals. First he purchased minor league outfielder Richie Scheinblum from the Texas Rangers, as the Rangers incredibly let the promising prospect go after he had won the American Association batting title by hitting .388 and driving in 108 runs in only 106 games. Then he traded reliever Jim York and young lefthander Lance Clemons to the Houston Astros for John Mayberry, a slugging 22-year-old first baseman.

Mayberry had a brilliant first season in a Royals uniform. He became the first Royal to drive in 100 runs, belting 25 home runs in the process. He also surprised the Royals with his defense at first base, showing outstanding agility for a big man, and proving himself especially adroit at scooping errant throws out of the dirt.

The starting outfield helped the Royals lead the league in hitting as all three outfielders finished in the top 10 in batting. Piniella came back from an off-year in 1971 to hit .312 and lead the league in doubles, while Scheinblum hit .300 and Otis .293. Otis dropped off in his stolen base total to only 28, probably as a result of fatigue from covering extra ground in the outfield for the lead-footed Scheinblum in right and the equally slow Piniella in left.

But largely due to poor pitching, the 1972 Royals could not even top the .500 mark, finishing 76–78 and in fourth place. It was an extremely disappointing year that had begun with such promise. At the end of the season, an unhappy Ewing Kauffman fired Bob Lemon and replaced him with Jack McKeon, who had been managing the Omaha Royals.

Tallis spent the winter in his usual way, by making another outstanding trade. He swapped Roger Nelson and Richie Scheinblum to the Reds for pitcher Wayne Simpson and outfielder Hal McRae. Simpson proved a failure, but McRae would eventually become a star.

The Royals had a new home for the 1973 season as they moved into Royals Stadium at the Harry S. Truman Sports Complex. Royals Stadium featured a 12-story scoreboard and a multicolored water spectacular that extended from the right-field foul pole to left-center field. The Royals inaugurated the new stadium with a 12–1 thrashing of the Texas Rangers on April 10. The new stadium and a successful season enabled the team to set a Kansas City attendance record as they drew 1,345,341 fans. The 1973 Royals also posted their best record to date by winning 88, losing 74, and finishing just six games behind the front-running Oakland A's.

Several Royals had fine seasons in 1973, led by John Mayberry and Amos Otis. Each had 26 home runs, while Mayberry drove in 100 runs for the second straight year and led the league in walks with 122. Otis hit .300 and drove in 93 runs. Third baseman Paul Schaal posted the best average of his career at a respectable .288.

In the pitching department lefthander Paul Splittorff became the Royals' first 20-game winner as he won an even 20 and lost only 11. Steve Busby, a promising rookie from the University of Southern California, won 16 and pitched the first no-hitter thrown by a Kansas City major league pitcher since 1915, when he no-hit the Detroit Tigers on April 27. Doug Bird came up from Omaha to shine as the Royals' bullpen stopper.

But Hal McRae's first season in a Royals uniform was a disaster. He hit only .234 and continually failed to produce with men on base. The other problem was the starting pitching. Splittorff and Busby pitched well but the other starters were plagued by control problems, and the Royals were doomed to another second-place finish.

The Royals followed up their fine 1973 performance with a terrible season in 1974. They finished in fifth place with a 77–85 mark and won only nine of their final 36 games. Virtually every player on the team had a bad year and only the performances of Hal McRae, Steve Busby, and rookie third baseman George Brett kept the Royals out of the cellar.

Busby had a terrific 22-win sophomore season and pitched another no-hitter on June 19. In fact he narrowly missed a perfect game, allowing only a second-inning walk to George Scott as the Royals beat the Milwaukee Brewers 2–0. Hal McRae rebounded from an awful season in 1973 to hit .310 and drive in 88 runs. And George Brett showed sparks of the greatness that was to come as he hit .282 and made numerous spectacular plays in the field.

But as disappointing as 1974 was on the field, it was an off-the-field move that left Kansas City fans in a state of shock. It occurred in mid-June when Royals owner Ewing Kauffman inexplicably fired General Manager Cedric Tallis and replaced him with Business Manager Joe Burke. Tallis had been the architect of some of the best trades in baseball over the previous five years and the reasons for his dismissal were never made clear by Kauffman. But Tallis' legacy would be felt in Kansas City for several years to come.

The Royals opened 1975 determined to rebound from the debacle of the previous season. They got out of the gate quickly winning nine of their first 11 games. But they swiftly reversed themselves and dropped 14 of their next 20. An undercurrent of discontent swept through the Royals camp as the players openly feuded with manager Jack McKeon. The problems had begun toward the end of the prior season when McKeon dismissed popular hitting coach Charlie Lau. The player's grumbling continued throughout the winter and in May the dispute reached a head when pitcher Steve Busby threatened to jump the team in New York. Busby was convinced to stay but McKeon was on thin ice from that moment on.

Finally, on July 24 with the Royals trailing the Oakland A's by 11 games, the Royals fired McKeon and replaced him with former Texas skipper Whitey Herzog. Herzog was a popular choice with the fans as he had been a favorite during his playing days with the Kansas City A's. The Royals rallied under Herzog going 30–15, but it was too little too late and they couldn't quite overtake the powerful A's.

Despite the disappointment of finishing second for the third time in five years the Royals had enjoyed an extremely successful season. They finished with the best record in their history at 91–71, going 41–25 with Herzog at the helm. John Mayberry had an outstanding year and finished second to Boston rookie sensation Fred Lynn in the league's Most Valuable Player voting. Mayberry clouted 34 home runs, drove in 106, also drawing a league-leading 119 walks.

George Brett lived up to the promise he had shown during his fine 1974 rookie campaign by hitting .308 and leading the league in at-bats, hits, and triples. Hal McRae posted a .306 mark and proved to be an inspirational leader with his aggressive base-running style.

The Royal pitching was solid all season, led primarily by Steve Busby with 18 wins. Al Fitzmorris was right behind him with 16, while rookie righthander Dennis Leonard loomed as a star of the future while going 15–7.

But all of these fine performances could not overcome the anguish of again losing to the Oakland A's. It was a gut-wrenching experience for Royals fans to see Charley Finley, certainly a *persona non grata* in Kansas City, guzzling champagne on the dugout roof while celebrating consecutive Oakland World Series victories. Even so, these were tremendous Oakland teams and at the end of the 1975 season, it seemed as if the Royals would be destined to play second fiddle to the hated West Coast A's forever.

The 1976 season began with two significant changes in the Royals' lineup. The first occurred at second base where Frank White replaced aging Cookie Rojas. White, a Kansas City native, had a reputation as a weak hitter but a good fielder. It seemed to be a relatively trifling move at the time, but White would go on to become one of the best fielding second basemen in baseball history, winning a total of eight Gold Gloves during the next decade.

The other move was the shifting of Hal McRae from left field to the designated hitter role. Royal manager Whitey Herzog made this move for McRae's own protection. McRae was an extremely aggressive outfielder who let nothing get in his way when chasing a fly ball, whether it be the left-field wall or pint-sized shortstop Freddie Patek. So to keep McRae from getting hurt and Patek from getting killed, Herzog moved McRae to designated hitter and installed Tom Poquette in left field. McRae became the prototype designated hitter and channeled his aggressiveness onto the base paths. When breaking up a double play, he would often bury an enemy second baseman with a roll block, a move which would later be outlawed in a rule known as the "McRae Rule."

The Royals wobbled to a poor start, finishing April with a shoddy 5–7 record. But as May began, the Royals improved noticeably as both their hitting and pitching rounded into shape and they reeled off 16 wins in their first 19 games of the month. The Royals' fine play continued throughout the summer. Brett and McRae's duel for the batting lead fueled the Royals' attack and Tom Poquette provided extra support by consistently flirting with the .300 mark. The Royals also used their fine speed to great advantage, eventually finishing the season with seven players copping at least 20 stolen bases. On August 28 the Royals led the Western Division by nine games and it seemed that only a total collapse could prevent the Royals from claiming their first Western Division crown.

That collapse very nearly did occur. The Royals suddenly stopped hitting and lost 12 of their next 17 games. The A's kept the pressure on with a 10–7 record over the same period and pulled to within four games of the struggling Royals. A five-game winning streak gave the Royals a little more of a cushion, but then they promptly lost four out of five and held a shaky 4½ game lead as they traveled to Oakland for a crucial final week three-game series. One victory over the A's would clinch a tie for the division title.

The first game of the series was captured by the A's when home runs by Ron Fairly and Sal Bando led Oakland to an 8–3 win. The second game featured a brilliant pitching duel between the Royal's Marty Pattin and Oakland's Mike Torrez. The game was scoreless until the seventh when Bando hit his second homer in as many nights. That proved to be all the A's needed as Torrez allowed the Royals only two singles in the A's 1–0 win. The Royals were reeling as they took the field for the finale of the series. Herzog gambled by sending little-used southpaw Larry Gura to the mound in the Royals' most important game of the year. Gura came through with a four-hit shutout and Amos Otis knocked in two runs with a homer and double to lead the Royals to the needed 4–0 win.

The Royals now required only one victory in their last three games or an Oakland loss to clinch the coveted title. The Royals did not get that one victory but fortunately the A's fell to the Angels on October 1 and the Royals were finally able to claim their first division championship.

As spine-tingling as the pennant race had been, a secondary drama was developing during the final days of the 1976 season. George Brett and Hal McRae of the Royals and Rod Carew and Lyman Bostock of the Minnesota Twins were battling neck-and-neck for the American League batting crown. And as fate would have it the Royals were playing the Twins in the final series of the season. The series opened with McRae leading at .333, followed by Brett at .329, Carew at .326, and Bostock at .325. As the series wound down to the ninth inning of the final game of the season, Carew and Bostock had fallen out of the race leaving Brett and McRae to duel for the title. McRae held a narrow .333 to .332 lead over Brett, but both were scheduled to bat in the ninth.

Brett was up first and hit what appeared to be an ordinary fly to left field. But Twin leftfielder Steve Brye misjudged the ball and it bounded over his head as Brett circled the bases with an inside-the-park home run. A hit by McRae would wrest the title away from Brett but he grounded to short to finish at .332 while Brett copped the title at .333. As McRae walked back to the dugout he screamed angrily at Twin manager Gene Mauch accusing him of ordering Brye to let the ball drop so Brett could win the title. The accusation tainted what otherwise was a tremendously exciting batting race.

The playoffs were somewhat anticlimactic as the Royals were just happy to make their first trip into post-season play. Kansas City seemed at a disadvantage from the outset as their leadoff batter in Game One, Amos Otis, hit the first base bag wrong on an infield grounder and sprained his left ankle, putting him out of commission for the rest of the playoffs. Despite Otis's loss the Royals battled the Yankees to the wire and were tied two games apiece as they headed to a fifth and deciding game in New York. The Yankees jumped out to an early 6–3 lead until George Brett launched a three-run homer in the eighth to knot the score at 6–6. But in the bottom of the ninth the end came quickly as Chris Chambliss hit a leadoff homer off Mark Littell to give the Yankees the American League pennant.

Even with the playoff loss, 1976 was a highly successful year for the Kansas City Royals. The team finally gained the needed confidence that they were a ball club that truly could win it all. But Kansas City also refused to stand pat. Catching problems had plagued the Royals since their inception and prompted Joe Burke to make a deal that sent outfielder Jim Wohlford, infielder Jamie Quirk, and reliever Bob McClure to the Milwaukee Brewers for catcher Darrell Porter and pitcher Jim Colborn.

The 1977 season featured a different type of team than the one which had struggled to a narrow victory the previous season. The Royals were a confident club determined to storm away with the American League pennant. And storm away they did!

The season started fairly slowly as it took the Royals a couple of months to get their bearings. Newly acquired Jim Colborn tossed a no-hitter May 14 against the Texas Rangers becoming the first Royal to achieve perfection in Royals Stadium. But on June 16 Kansas City had an unimpressive 28–31 record. Then the Royals got hot. They finished June by winning 10 out of their last 14 games. An eight-game winning streak helped them to an 18–8 record in July. August featured a 10-game streak as they closed out the month with a 20–11 record.

But on August 31 the Royals began one of the greatest stretch drives in baseball history. The victory on August 31 began a 16-game winning streak, the longest seen in baseball in over 24 years. Only a 4–1 loss to Seattle September 16 prevented a 25-game streak, as the Royals obliterated the rest of the Western Division and captured the title with a team record 102–60 mark.

Many Royals had fine seasons in 1977. Right fielder Al Cowens hit .312 with 23 homers and 112 RBIs and finished second in the MVP voting to Rod Carew; thus the Royals had the MVP runner-up for the third straight year. George Brett compiled statistics very similar to Cowens as he also hit .312 and poked 22 home runs. Hal McRae checked in at .298 with 21 roundtrippers and led the league in doubles as well with a staggering total of 54, the most in the major leagues since 1950. Fred Patek provided the speed and led the league in stolen bases with 53.

The Royals' pitching was the best in the league and was led by Dennis Leonard who notched 20 victories and fanned 244 batters. Jim Colborn contributed 18 wins and Paul Splittorff chipped in with 16. Such a fine season allowed the Royals to set a team attendance mark as they drew 1,852,603 fans through the turnstiles of Royals Stadium. Herzog's team entered the playoffs bursting with confidence that they would bury the Yankees and give Kansas City their first American League pennant.

And had the series been one inning shorter that would have been what transpired. The Royals and Yankees had traded victories for the first four games as the Royals won Games One and Three, and the Yankees captured Games Two and Four. The fifth game was a tense struggle spiced by a fight between George Brett and Yankee third sacker Graig Nettles after Brett slid hard into Nettles on a first-inning triple. The Royals held a narrow 3–2 lead as the game entered the ninth. Then Whitey Herzog made a move which would be second-guessed all winter. Herzog inserted Dennis Leonard, who had pitched a complete game only two days before, to pitch the ninth.

Paul Blair greeted Leonard with a single. Then Roy White, a long-time Royal nemesis, drew a walk. Herzog pulled Leonard and put in Larry Gura who had started only the day before. Mickey Rivers promptly laced a single to right to tie the game. Mark Littell came in to yield a sacrifice fly to Willie Randolph to give the Yankees the lead. An error by Brett allowed the final run in a 5–3 Yankee win which proved to be the most heartbreaking loss in Royals' history.

The Royals made it a charmed three in a row in 1978 as excellent pitching, speed, and defense led them to their third straight Western Division crown. And for the third straight time they lost to the Yankees in the playoffs. Despite the success of those three seasons, Whitey Herzog was beginning to wear out his welcome in Kansas City. Herzog was very opinionated and would often criticize his players through the media. He blamed the 1977 playoff loss on John Mayberry, implying that Mayberry was on drugs, and stated that "either Mayberry goes or I go." Mayberry was shipped to Toronto just prior to the 1978 season. After the 1978 playoffs featured more questionable moves by Herzog, fans wondered if the Royals management had kept the wrong man. Herzog even stated, "The first time we don't win it, I'm gone."

Herzog proved to be a prophet. The 1979 Royals finished second to the California Angels and Whitey was given the boot at season's end and replaced by Baltimore coach Jim Frey. The Royals did enjoy a fabulous offensive season in 1979. George Brett became only the fifth player ever to post at least 20 doubles, 20 triples, and 20 home runs in the same season and hit a rousing .329 to boot. Darrell Porter became only the second catcher to have 100 runs scored, 100 RBIs, and 100 walks in the same season. Willie Wilson emerged as the regular center fielder and hit .315 with 83 stolen bases. But as good as the offense was, the pitching was woeful. No Royal starter had a good year in a season where any pitching at all would have enabled the Royals to overtake the Angels for another first place finish.

The summer of 1980 will not be remembered for solid pitching in Kansas City either. Rather, 1980 will be recalled for the hitting of George Brett. Brett had a phenomenal season, flirting with the .400 mark all year before finishing at .390, the highest batting average in 39 years of big league baseball. Along the way, Brett fashioned a 30-game hitting streak. He had 118 RBIs in only 117 games, becoming the first man in 30 years to drive in more than one run per game. He hit 24 home runs and struck out only 22 times. It boggles the mind to think what his statistics would have been had he not missed 26 games with a severe foot injury.

Brett's MVP year also overshadowed a great season by his outfield mate Willie Wilson. The switch-hitting Wilson set a major league record with 705 at bats and banged out a league-leading 230 hits, including 100-plus from each side of the plate. He also scored 133 runs and stole 79 bases.

Dennis Leonard was back in form for the 1980 Royals as he again won 20 games. Larry Gura chipped in with 18 victories and Dan Quisenberry became the top relief pitcher in the American League, leading the Junior Circuit with 33 saves. The Royals ran away with the Western Division this time around by a 14-game margin over the second place Oakland Athletics. Looming ahead was none other than the New York Yankees, who had themselves won 103 games to again capture the Eastern Division crown.

The 1980 A.L.C.S. action opened in Kansas City with Larry Gura besting Ron Guidry by a 7–2 count as Brett smacked a homer and a double to lead the Kansas City offensive surge. The Royals also took the second game, 3–2, behind Dennis Leonard. The key play of this second game occurred in the eighth inning when Brett's relay throw cut down Willie Randolph attempting to score from first on Bob

Watson's double, a play which incurred the wrath of high-strung Yankees owner George Steinbrenner.

The Royals arrived in New York needing only one victory to nail down their first American League pennant. But the Royals also knew only too well how elusive that final victory could be. Kansas City sent Paul Splittorff to the mound to face the Yankees' Tommy John. The game was scoreless until the fifth when Frank White's home run staked Jim Frey's men to a 1–0 lead. The Yankees came back with two runs in the bottom of the sixth, and in the seventh, John gave up a two-out double to Willie Wilson. Shortstop U. L. Washington followed by beating out an infield hit. That brought up George Brett. Yankee manager Dick Howser pulled John and brought in ace reliever Goose Gossage. Gossage reared back and threw his best 98-mile-per-hour fastball. Brett launched it deep into the upper deck for a three-run homer that put the final nail in the Yankee coffin. Quisenberry shut out the Yankees the rest of the way to propel the jubilant Royals into their first World Series.

The 1980 Fall Classic featured two teams that were striving for their first world championship. The National League champion Philadelphia Phillies had never won the World Series despite being in the league since series play began way back in 1903. The Phillies exorcised that 77-year-old demon by vanquishing the Royals in six games as Willie Wilson struck out a record 12 times and George Brett became inflicted with the baseball world's most famous case of hemorrhoids which incapacitated him throughout much of the Series. As Brett later quipped, "My ailment will go down in the anals of World Series history."

But the high of 1980 soon turned into the low of 1981. The Royals got off to a dreadful start losing 30 of their first 48 games before the ill-timed players' strike suspended play until August. After play resumed the Royals continued to play uninspired ball until manager Jim Frey was given the heave-ho in August and replaced by former Yankee manager Dick Howser. Howser lit a large enough fire under the team that the Royals were able to capture the second half title of the ludicrous split season format. But the Royals were quickly disposed of in three makeshift playoff games by the Oakland A's to determine the full-season divisional winner, and a dark season in baseball history was mercifully put to rest.

The success that the Royals enjoyed during the preceding six years had been the result of an uncanny ability by Cedric Tallis and, to a lesser degree, Joe Burke, to evaluate other teams' young talent and to acquire emerging stars just as they were ready to blossom into bona fide major league talent. Through the 1981 season it is difficult to identify a trade made by the Royals that proved entirely unsuccessful. But prior to the 1981 season the Royals hired inexperienced John Schuerholz as their general manager. Schuerholz adopted a different philosophy on trades. In a disastrous reversal of form, he attempted to acquire experienced major league players in exchange for Kansas City's young unproven talent. Hence, Schuerholz's first trade of 1982 sent promising young pitchers Rich Gale, Bill Laskey, Craig Chamberlain, Renie Martin, and Atlee Hammaker to the Giants for outfielder Jerry Martin and pitcher Vida Blue, a deal which quickly proved dreadful for the Royals.

But thanks to Willie Wilson's league-leading .332 batting average, Hal McRae's team-record 133 runs batted in, and the patient guidance of manager Dick Howser, the 1982 Royals very nearly captured another Western Division crown. They won 90 games and finished only three behind the Oakland A's.

At least in Kansas City, 1983 will be remembered more for events which took place off the baseball field than on it. In May, Ewing Kauffman, anticipating the day he would step down as Royals owner, sold 49 percent of the team to Memphis real estate tycoon Avron Fogelman. This came as a surprise to most Kansas City fans who assumed (and hoped) that "Mr. K" would be around forever. Then in July came the shocking news that Royals players Willie Aikens, Willie Wilson, Jerry Martin, and Vida Blue were being implicated in a federal drug investigation. All four were later convicted of attempting to possess cocaine and sentenced to three months in prison. Aikens, Martin, and Blue were all ex-Royals by the time spring training of 1984 rolled around.

On the field, the headlines were made by reliever Dan Quisenberry who set a major league record with 45 saves, as well as by the single game that became the most famous in Royals' history. That game took place July 24 in Yankee Stadium. The Yankees were leading the Royals 4–3 with two out in the ninth inning and a runner at first when New York brought in Goose Gossage from the bullpen to face George Brett. Brett promptly drilled a Gossage fastball into the upper deck in right field to give the Royals what appeared to be a 5–4 lead. As Brett sat in the dugout accepting congratulations from his teammates, he noticed that his bat had been confiscated by Yankee manager Billy Martin who was discussing the lumber with home plate umpire Tim McClelland. Brett watched with amusement as McClelland laid the bat on the ground and measured it against home plate. But when McClelland approached the Royals' dugout and signalled Brett out, Brett charged out of the dugout in rage and had to be restrained by his teammates. "I've never been that mad in my whole life," Brett later explained. It seems that the pine tar on Brett's bat extended more than the allowable 18 inches along the bat handle.

Manager Dick Howser protested the game claiming that the rule-book had no provision for calling a batter out for having applied too much pine tar. Surprisingly, American League President Lee MacPhail upheld the Royals' protest and ordered the game resumed on August 18. Only 1,245 fans showed up to see Dan Quisenberry dispatch the Yankees in 1-2-3 order to complete the zaniest game in a decade and a half of Royals' history.

But the team was never in the race in 1983 as they finished a distant second, 20 games behind the pace-setting Chicago White Sox. The uncertainty of the status of the players convicted in the drug scandal left the outlook rather bleak for 1984. And it got bleaker as the season opened, with Willie Wilson serving a month's suspension and George Brett on the disabled list. But thanks to fine performances by the Royals' young pitching staff and a league-leading 44 saves by Dan Quisenberry, the Royals once again outdistanced a very weak Western Division and qualified for post-season play for the sixth time in nine years.

The playoffs figured to be a mismatch as the Royals met the powerful Detroit Tigers who had led the Eastern Division from wire to wire and finished with 104 wins. It was indeed no contest as the Tigers demolished the Royals in three straight games to capture the American League pennant. But considering the problems the Royals had endured in 1984, it was a very satisfying year and one that under-scored the managerial acumen of Dick Howser.

Two off-season events played major roles in the shaping of the eventual 1985 World Champion Kansas City Royals. One was the hard work of George Brett. Brett had suffered through one of his worst seasons in 1984 and was determined to report to camp in the best shape of his career and to remain injury-free as well. The other was the acquisition of veteran catcher Jim Sundberg from the Milwaukee Brewers to help guide the Royals' young pitching staff. This trade, in fact, proved to be one of John Schuerholz's shrewdest yet most underrated moves.

Ultimately it was the Royals' pitching staff that was brilliant in 1985. Kansas City hurlers were led by 21-year-old Bret Saberhagen, who finished 20–6 and won the Cy Young Award. Charlie Leibrandt, 28, posted a 17–9 mark and was runner-up for the ERA crown. And Mark Gubicza and Danny Jackson, both 23, contributed 14 wins each.

Offensively, George Brett showed the merits of his winter fitness program and enjoyed one of the best seasons of his career. Brett hit .335 with 30 home runs, 112 runs batted in, 108 runs scored, 103 walks, and still found time to win a Gold Glove award for his play at third base. Steve Balboni also provided offensive firepower by clubbing a team-record 36 home runs.

The playoff series against the Toronto Blue Jays was a true A.L.C.S. classic. After falling behind in the series two games to none it looked as if the Royals were doomed to suffer yet another playoff defeat. But Game Three was vintage George Brett. Brett went 4-for-4 with two home runs, a double, and a single and made several terrific defensive plays to lead the Royals to a 6–5 win. After a tough 3–1 loss in Game Four, Danny Jackson hurled a 2–0 shutout to send the series back to Toronto. Jackson's outstanding pitching performance spurred the Royals on to victories in Games Six and Seven and a first-ever meeting in the World Series with their cross-state rivals, the St. Louis Cardinals.

The I-70 series was perhaps the most exciting sporting event in the history of Missouri. For 10 days, it seemed as if every citizen in the state was dressed in either Royal blue or Cardinal red. Governor John Ashcroft, in the spirit of neutrality, sported a red and blue hat with the Cardinal logo on one half and the Royal logo on the other.

The series itself was almost a carbon copy of the playoffs. The Royals trailed three games to one and Howser again turned to Danny Jackson to reverse the Royals' fortunes. Jackson came through with a masterful performance allowing just five hits as the Royals cruised to a 6–1 win.

The turning point of the series occurred in Game Six. The Royals trailed 1–0 entering the ninth when Jorge Orta hit a grounder to Jack Clark at first. Clark underhanded a toss to pitcher Todd Worrell who was covering first. Although television replays seemed to show otherwise, umpire Don Denkinger called Orta safe, a call which so incensed the Cardinals that they were unable to recover. The next hitter, Steve Balboni, given new life by Clark's blunder of his foul pop near the Royals' dugout, lined a single to left to send Orta to second. Jim Sundberg then attempted to sacrifice and in the process forced Orta at third. After a passed ball by ex-Royal Darrell Porter, Hal McRae drew an intentional walk. Howser sent up Dan Iorg, himself a former Cardinal, to pinch hit. Iorg lined a single to right to score two runs and give the Royals the victory in the most thrilling game in Royals' history.

The seventh game was no contest from the start. The Royals buried the Cardinals 11–0 behind the five-hit pitching of Series MVP Bret Saberhagen, who was already on cloud nine after his wife had given birth to their first child only the day before. The Royals had reached the top of the baseball world and Kansas City basked in the glow of their first World Championship.

But the feelings of exhilaration and euphoria that Kansas City felt in October of 1985 turned to shock and despair in July of 1986 when it was discovered that respected manager Dick Howser had developed a cancerous brain tumor. Howser underwent several brain surgeries and even made a courageous attempt to return as manager in the spring exhibition season of 1987. But gaunt and weakened from the surgeries and the radiation treatments he had undergone, he had to call it quits after only one day on the job. Howser returned to Royals Stadium for the final time on opening day of 1987. Introduced to the crowd, he received a lengthy standing ovation but was too weak to stay for the game. He died on June 17 and the grief was felt throughout the baseball world. The popular manager's number 10 became the first uniform number ever retired by the Royals and Howser was also posthumously inducted into the Royals Hall of Fame.

The Royals pulled off a surprise in 1986 by signing former Heisman trophy winner Bo Jackson to a baseball contract after everyone assumed he would sign a contract with the National Football league. However, Jackson's 1987 announcement that he would play football with the Los Angeles Raiders as a winter "hobby" coupled with the distraction of Howser's death made it difficult for the team to concentrate on simply winning ball games. The turmoil eventually led to manager Billy Gardner's dismissal in August and the announcement of his replacement by Omaha AAA pilot John Wathan. Rookie Kevin Seitzer lashed out 207 hits in 1987 including six in one game, and newly acquired Danny Tartabull clubbed 34 home runs and knocked in 101 runs. But the off-the-field distractions were simply too much for the team to overcome.

Distractions of a different kind struck the Royals in 1988. The team was loaded with talent but never seemed to gel into a contender. Rumors of racial tension swirled around the team as there were several altercations between black and white players. While the racial aspects were exploited by the media, the root of the problem was the retirement of Hal McRae. McRae had been a quiet leader for a number of years and no one had emerged to take his place. Thus despite Mark Gubicza's 20-win season, the Royals could manage only a third-place finish.

For a young franchise, the Kansas City Royals have experienced more than their share of memorable moments. There was the excitement of six division titles, two American League pennants, and one World's Championship, the disappointment of several playoff losses to the Yankees, the awe-inspiring performances of George Brett, particularly that fabulous .390 season in 1980, and the tragedies of the 1983 drug scandal and the death of manager Dick Howser. The Royals had two promising pitching careers cut short by injury: Steve Busby with a torn rotator cuff and Dennis Leonard with a devastating knee injury. Busby made several unsuccessful attempts at a comeback before finally hanging it up, but few fans can forget the game of April 12, 1986, when Leonard, after 2½ years of rehabilitation, made his comeback with a three-hit shutout of Toronto.

The success of the Kansas City Royals is the result of relentless hard work in the team's front office and the vision of Ewing Kauffman. One of Kauffman's most unique ideas was the Royals Baseball Academy which opened its doors in 1970. The idea behind the Academy was to take undrafted players with rudimentary baseball skills, provide room and board and a junior college education, and teach them the finer points of the game. During its four years of operation, 10 percent of its players made the major leagues compared with six percent of drafted players. Royal regulars Frank White and U.L. Washington were among the graduates of the Academy, whose only entrance requirements were good speed and an average major league arm. The Academy closed in 1974 due to its astronomical expense, but its eye-testing kits and coordination tests are used by most major league teams today.

Perhaps the most thrilling moment of Royals franchise history, however, was to come at the end of 1992's season. As the campaign played out its final days in September, George Brett would become only the 18th player in big-league history to garner 3,000 base hits, reaching 3,005 by season's end. Brett's performance was a singular highlight of the first three summers of the 1990s, a three-year span which saw several lame second-division finishes and the break-up of a once-promising ballclub of the late 1980s. Saberhagen was now gone to the NL Mets and Hal McRae was back on board as the new field skipper. But George Brett was still around, and his presence captured all that was best in Royals history.

Annotated Bibliography

Bordman, Sid. *Expansion to Excellence: An Intimate Portrait of the Kansas City Royals.* Marceline, Miss: Walsworth Publishing Company, 1981. 182 pp.
    A difficult to locate small press collectors item, this volume provides the only true extensive history of the Kansas City expansion franchise. Bordman covers the details of the first 12 seasons with the Royals, focusing on the four divisional championships of the late 1970s and the World Series defeat at the hands of the Phillies in 1980. Valuable for its portraits of stars and journeyman players with the Royals over the first decade of franchise history.
Eskew, Alan. *A Royal Finish—The Celebration of the 1985 Kansas City Royals.* Chicago: Contemporary Books, 1985.

In a predictable spinoff book inspired by the 1985 championship season, Eskew focuses on the Royals of the mid-1980s and on details of the exciting 1985 pennant drive. The result is a useful supplement for, but not a replacement for, Bordman's more detailed history of the first decade of the expansion Kansas City ballclub.

Garrity, John. *The George Brett Story*. New York: Coward, McCann and Geoghegan Publishing Company, 1981.

This is a surprisingly enjoyable biography on the Royals' popular third baseman, concentrating on his carefree lifestyle and his relationships with his Kansas City teammates. The book also provides an excellent insight into the Kansas City Royals of the 1975–1980 divisional championship era.

James, Bill. *The Bill James Baseball Abstract 1986*. New York: Ballantine Books (Random House Publishers), 1986 ("Kansas City Royals—A History of Being a Kansas City Baseball Fan" on pp. 39–71).

Fine accounts from a fan's perspective of what it was like to be a Kansas City baseball fan growing up in the 1960s. Told in James' wonderful irrevervent style, this essay contrasts the inept front office of the Kansas City Athletics under Arnold Johnson with the fine brain trust of the Kansas City Royals over the past two decades, a talented management team whose exceptional performance was to culminate in the Royals' surprising 1985 World Series triumph.

Martin, Mollie. *Kansas City Royals*. Mankato, Minn: Creative Education Publishing Company, 1982. 48 pp.

A heavily illustrated team history designed and written for a juvenile market. The photographs are entertaining here, but there is little in the text of interest to the serious baseball reader.

Year-by-Year Standings and Season Summaries

Year	Pos.	Record	Pct.	GB	Manager	Player	BA	Player	HR	Player	W-L	ERA
1969	4th	69–93	.426	28.0	Gordon	Piniella	.282	Kirkpatrick	14	Bunker	12–11	3.23
1970	4th	65–97	.401	33.0	Metro	Piniella	.301	Oliver	27	Abernathy	9–3	2.57
					Lemon							
1971	2nd	85–76	.528	16.0	Lemon	Otis	.301	Otis	15	Drago	17–11	2.99
1972	4th	76–78	.494	16.5	Lemon	Piniella	.312	Mayberry	25	Nelson	11–6	2.08
1973	2nd	88–74	.543	6.0	McKeon	Otis	.300	Mayberry	26	Splittorff	20–11	3.98
								Otis	26			
1974	5th	77–85	.475	13.0	McKeon	McRae	.310	Mayberry	22	Busby	22–14	3.39
1975	2nd	91–71	.562	7.0	McKeon	Brett	.308	Mayberry	34	Busby	18–12	3.08
					Herzog							
1976	1st	90–72	.556	+2.5	Herzog	Brett	.333*	Otis	18	Leonard	17–10	3.51
1977	1st	102–60	.630	+8.0	Herzog	Brett	.312	Mayberry	23	Leonard	20–12	3.04
						Cowens	.312	Cowens	23			
1978	1st	92–70	.568	+5.0	Herzog	Otis	.298	Otis	22	Leonard	21–17	3.33
1979	2nd	85–77	.525	3.0	Herzog	Brett	.329	Brett	23	Leonard	14–12	4.08
1980	1st	97–65	.599	+14.0	Frey	Brett	.390*	Brett	24	Leonard	20–11	3.79
1981	5th	20–30	.400	12.0	Frey	Brett	.314	Aikens	17	Leonard	13–11	2.99
	1st	30–23	.566	+1.0	Howser							
1981**	4th	50–53	.485									
1982	2nd	90–72	.556	3.0	Howser	Wilson	.332	McRae	27	Gura	18–12	4.03
1983	2nd	79–83	.488	20.0	Howser	McRae	.311	Brett	25	Splittorff	13–8	3.63
1984	1st	84–78	.519	+3.0	Howser	Wilson	.301	Balboni	28	Black	17–12	3.12
1985	1st	91–71	.562	+1.0	Howser	brett	.335	Balboni	36	Saberhagen	20–6	2.87
1986	3rd	76–86	.469	16.0	Howser	Brett	.290	Balboni	29	Leibrandt	14–11	4.09
					Ferraro							
1987	2nd	83–79	.512	2.0	Gardner	Seitzer	.323	Tartabull	34	Saberhagen	18–10	3.36
					Wathan							
1988	3rd	84–77	.522	19.5	Wathan	Brett	.306	Tartabull	26	Gubicza	20–8	2.70
1989	2nd	92–70	.568	7.0	Wathan	Eisenreich	.293	Jackson	32	Saberhagen	23*–6	2.16
1990	6th	75–86	.466	27.5	Wathan	Brett	.329*	B. Jackson	28	Farr	13–7	1.98
1991	6th	82–80	.506	13.0	Wathan/McRae	Tartabull	.316	Tartabull	31	Saberhagen	13–8	3.07
1992	5th(T)	72–90	.444	24.0	McRae	Brett	.285	Macfarlane	17	Appier	15–8	2.46

*Led American League.
**Split Season Totals (Players' Union Strike).

All-Time Royals Career and Season Records

Career Batting Leaders (1969–1992)

Games Played	George Brett	2,562
At Bats	George Brett	9,789
Runs Scored	George Brett	1,514
Hits	George Brett	3,005
Batting Average	George Brett	.307
Home Runs	George Brett	298
Runs Batted In	George Brett	1,520
Stolen Bases	Willie Wilson	612
Sacrifice Hits	Frank White	101
Strikeouts	Frank White	1,003

Career Pitching Leaders (1969–1992)

Innings Pitched	Paul Splittorff	2,555
Earned Run Average	Dan Quisenberry	2.56
Wins	Paul Splittorff	166
Losses	Paul Splittorff	143
Winning Percentage	Bret Saberhagen	.585
Strikeouts	Dennis Leonard	1,323
Walks	Paul Splittorff	780
Games	Dan Quisenberry	573
Shutouts	Dennis Leonard	23
Saves	Dan Quisenberry	238
Games Started	Paul Splittorff	392
Complete Games	Dennis Leonard	103
Hit Batsmen	Dennis Leonard	52
Wild Pitches	Dennis Leonard	73

Single-Season Batting Records (1969–1992)

Batting Average	George Brett	.390	1980
Home Runs	Steve Balboni	36	1985
Home Runs (lefthanded)	John Mayberry	34	1975
Runs Batted In	Hal McRae	133	1982
Hits	Willie Wilson	230	1980
Singles	Willie Wilson	184	1980
Doubles	Hal McRae	54	1977
Triples	Willie Wilson	21	1985
Slugging Percentage	George Brett	.664	1980
Extra Base Hits	Hal McRae	86	1977
Game-Winning RBIs	Danny Tartabull	21	1987
Sacrifices	Frank White	18	1976
Stolen Bases	Willie Wilson	83	1979
Pinch Hits	Hal McRae	15	1986
Strikeouts	Bo Jackson	172	1989
Total Bases	George Brett	363	1979
Hitting Streak	George Brett	30	1980
Grand Slam Home Runs	Danny Tartabull	3	1988
On-Base Percentage	George Brett	.461	1980
Hit by Pitch	Hal McRae	13	1977

All-Time Royals Career and Season Records *(continued)*

Single-Season Pitching Records (1969–1992)

ERA (150 innings)	Roger Nelson	2.08	1972
ERA (100 innings)	Dan Quisenberry	1.94	1983
Wins	Bret Saberhagen	23	1989
Losses	Paul Splittorff	19	1974
Winning Pct. (10 decisions)	Larry Gura	.800	1978
Strikeouts	Dennis Leonard	244	1977
Walks	Mark Gubicza	120	1987
Saves	Dan Quisenberry	45	1983
Games	Dan Quisenberry	84	1985
Complete Games	Dennis Leonard	21	1977
Games Started	Dennis Leonard	40	1978
Shutouts	Roger Nelson	6	1972
Innings Pitched	Dennis Leonard	295	1978
Home Runs Allowed	Dennis Leonard	33	1979
Consecutive Games Won (season)	Rich Gale	11	1980
Consecutive Games Lost (season)	Dick Drago	8	1970
	Wally Bunker	8	1970
	Bill Butler	8	1970
Consecutive Complete Games	Dennis Leonard	7	1977
Wild Pitches	Bruce Dal Canton	16	1974
Balks	Jeff Montgomery	6	1988

6

Los Angeles Angels- California Angels
A Cowboy's Search for Another Champion
RICHARD E. BEVERAGE

If the California Angels could be depicted as a comic strip character, they would be Joe Btfsplk. The little man in the Li'l Abner cartoon strip always traveled under a black cloud and brought bad luck with him wherever he went. So it has been with the Angels.

The Angels have been cursed with an inordinate amount of tragedy (in the true sense) and just plain ordinary misfortune in their short existence in the American League. From the career-ending arm injury suffered by pitcher Johnny James in 1961, through the untimely deaths of pitchers Dick Wantz, Jim McGlothin and Bruce Heimbechner, shortstops Mike Miley and Chico Ruiz, and outfielder Lyman Bostock, and finally the tragic suicide of relief pitcher Donnie Moore during the summer of 1989, the Angels have had more than their share of lost careers. And bad luck has struck at strategic intervals. The infamous home run by Dave Henderson in the 1986 League Championship playoffs is the most painful example. But despite the unhappiness, or partly because of it, perhaps, the Angels have had an interesting history.

In a sense, the Angels owe their very being to Walter O'Malley. The owner of the Brooklyn Dodgers took a calculated risk when he moved his team to Los Angeles in 1958, but soon reaped incredible riches from his venture. By 1960 his Los Angeles Dodgers were defending World Champions, were drawing the biggest crowds in the majors, and had a magnificent new ballpark under construction. The American League, which would have moved the St. Louis Browns to Los Angeles in 1941 were it not for World War II, was profoundly interested in sharing the riches of the Southern California market.

Expansion of the major leagues had been a serious topic of discussion since the end of the war. The Pacific Coast League (PCL) had petitioned for major league status to no avail, and finally the blueprint for a new Continental League under the auspices of Branch Rickey seemed to move the leagues to action. Accordingly, the American League voted to expand to 10 teams no later than December 1, 1961, at a special league meeting on August 30, 1960. But when the National League voted six weeks later to expand for the 1962 season while awarding franchises to New York and Houston, the Americans accelerated their move on October 26. The Washington franchise was transferred to the Twin Cities of Minnesota, and new franchises would be placed in Washington and Los Angeles.

The leagues nearly went to war over this move. O'Malley was probably the most powerful figure in the game, and he was not overjoyed to share the Los Angeles market with a rival from the other league. He certainly didn't want a new club to be controlled by a group headed by Bill Veeck and Hank Greenberg; they were said to be the favorites to acquire the franchise. Eventually, a compromise was worked out. O'Malley conceded to a new American League club in Los Angeles, provided it played in the city-owned Wrigley Field in 1961 and agreed to play in the new Chavez Ravine park that O'Malley was building to be opened in 1962 under a four-year lease. In addition, he was to be paid $350,000 for his rights to the territory. The ownership of the new franchise was awarded to a group headed by Gene Autry and Robert Reynolds, Autry's partner in the Golden West Broadcasting Company. The new club would bear a traditional and appropriate name for Los Angeles baseball clubs, one going back to 1903 when the first Pacific Coast League team took the field—the Angels.

At the beginning, Reynolds was president of the club and Autry chairman of the board, but eventually Autry bought out Reynolds' interest and the club became identified as his own. Gene Autry's career as a singing cowboy is well known, and he made millions as a performer. Yet he made significantly more as a businessman with major interests in real estate and broadcasting, the latter being the foundation of his wealth. At its peak Autry's Golden West Broadcasters owned flagship radio station KMPC and TV station KTLA in Los Angeles as well as AM stations and cable TV stations in other markets. But Autry had been a baseball fan all his life and enjoyed the opportunity to mingle with the athletic greats whenever he could. The ownership of a major league club was the dream of a lifetime for him.

The expansion franchises were to be stocked by a draft from a player-pool created by the existing clubs. The Angels would pay $2.1 million for the 28 players they were required to draft. Autry and Reynolds had less than a week to prepare for the draft selections, and they hurriedly hired Fred Haney as their general manager. Haney was a native of the Los Angeles area with a long career as a player, manager, and broadcaster. He was immensely popular in Southern California from his days as the broadcaster of the Hollywood Stars games in the Pacific Coast League and was currently doing broadcasts as a color analyst for NBC. The challenge of building a club from scratch was appealing, and the Angels had their first real baseball man.

A manager soon followed. Bill Rigney was given a three-year contract after Casey Stengel and Leo Durocher were considered. It was a fortunate choice. Rig had managed the Giants, both in New York and San Francisco, from 1956 through June 1960. He was a sound baseball man who seemed to get more out of average material than most. In addition, he was considered to be a fine teacher of young players, which would be a useful skill in the years to come.

The Angels drafted with an eye toward building for the future, but they also wanted some players with ready name identification so that they could compete with the Dodgers. The first player selected was Eli Grba, a righthanded pitching prospect, from the Yankees. In short order the Angels chose Ted Kluszewski, Bob Cerv, Eddie Yost, and Ned Garver—all prominent major league veterans who had their best years behind them. But they also drafted Bob Rodgers, Jim Fregosi, Fred Newman, and Ken McBride—all youngsters with little previous experience. Fregosi was only 20 while Rodgers was 23. These players would form the nucleus of the club during the balance of the decade. Somewhat in between these extremes were Duke Maas, Earl Averill, Jerry Casale, and Tex Clevenger—players who had some major league service but were still trying to establish themselves. Little Albie Pearson, who was American League Rookie of the Year in 1958 but had regressed since, was a selection, as was Steve Bilko, the scourge of the Pacific Coast League in 1955–57 and the most popular player in Los Angeles history up to that time. It was a mix of talent which would give the club respectability while building an organization.

The 1961 home of the Angels had last been used in 1957 by the PCL club and had gone to seed before being resurrected for its major league debut. Wrigley Field was originally built in 1925 and was long considered to be the finest minor league park in existence. It somewhat resembled its major league namesake in that a brick wall extended from the left-field line to right center with a scoreboard standing high above the wall. The park was double-decked from left field to right with the club offices located in a tower behind home plate. It seated somewhat more than 20,000 when the right-field bleachers were included, but rarely was this capacity to be taxed during the Angels' occupancy. The dimensions were 340 feet in left, 412 feet in dead center, and 338 feet to the screen in right. But a critical design flaw resulted in power alleys of only 345 feet, and with a prevailing wind blowing out to right field, easy fly balls would find their way out of the park with great regularity. Wrigley Field became a home run hitter's paradise in its only major league season. A total of 248 home runs were hit there, a total that has never been exceeded elsewhere.

Rigney's first Angel crew assembled in Palm Springs, California, and it soon became apparent that the young players chosen in the draft were nowhere near ready for major league play. The club would have to make do with the tired veterans and fringe players, at least at the beginning. Rig settled on a power-oriented lineup that included Big Klu (Ted Kluszewski) at first base and Bob Cerv in left field. These two provided what Gene Autry would call for many years "my greatest thrill in baseball."

The Angels were expected to win about a third of their games, and perhaps the experts looked at their schedule, which called for opening on the road for 11 straight games. Baltimore was the first stop, where Eli Grba was to pitch the very first Angel game. As the big crowd was still filing in, Albie Pearson walked with two out and Kluszewski and Cerv followed with back-to-back home runs. In the second inning Pearson drove in a run with a single, and with two on Klu did it again with a towering blast into the right-field bleachers. That made it 7–0, and the Angels breezed to a 7–2 win. The players reacted as if they had won the seventh game of the World Series.

That game was the highlight of the first half of the Angel season. The club proceeded to lose eight straight, falling into last place where they remained until July 4. Haney did not sit still with his original player complement and consummated many deals. During the first week the club acquired outfielder Leon Wagner, an especially valuable choice. Rigney had him in San Francisco, and when the Giants let him go to the minor leagues, the Angels were able to pick up Daddy Wags for a mere pittance. Wagner led the club with 28 home runs in 1961, increased that total to 37 the next year, and was a crowd favorite until he was dealt to Cleveland in 1963. On May 9 a major trade with the Yankees brought outfielder Lee Thomas along with pitchers Ryne Duren and Johnny James in exchange for Cerv and Clevenger. Thomas joined Wagner in pounding the fences for the next two years.

Duren, at the height of his career in mad-cap revelry before he reformed and became the respected head of the Wisconsin Drug Rehabilitation Program, was still a very effective pitcher who moved between starting and relieving. He became the cornerstone of a very capable bullpen along with Tom Morgan, Art Fowler, and Jack Spring. The group had 34 saves, second best in the league, and they combined with a new keystone combination of Billy Moran and Joe Koppe to help the club play at a .500 pace over the last 90 games. The Angels won 70 games, the most ever by a first-year expansion team, and finished in eighth place, ahead of Kansas City and Washington.

The Angels took advantage of Wrigley Field as well as anybody, hitting 122 home runs at home with five players above 20—Wagner-28; Ken Hunt-28; Lee Thomas-24; Earl Averill and Steve Bilko with 20 each. Fittingly, on the last day of the season Bilko hit the last home run at Wrigley, where he had starred for the original Angels. The Angels were very competitive at home, winning 10 more than they lost, but they were a disaster on the road with only 24 wins. Pitching was a problem all season, with Ted Bowsfield the only starter to win more than he lost with a modest 11–8 record. Rigney could not come up with a consistent rotation all year and used his bullpen extensively with Morgan and Fowler each appearing in more than 50 games.

Although the Angels were an interesting team and played many exciting games, Los Angeles did not warm up to this team. The poor start dampened any early enthusiasm, and by the time the Angels began to play better in July, the fans had lost interest. Only the Yankees attracted decent crowds. The location of the park in a deteriorating section of town with limited parking held attendance to a league low of 603,510.

The summer of 1962 would be different. The Angels moved to newly opened Dodger Stadium, and the contrast between the old and the new was remarkable. Seating capacity was more than twice as large, there was ample parking, and the park was much friendlier to pitchers. Attendance climbed to 1,114,063 as Los Angeles finished a surprising third. This is by far the best performance of a second-year expansion team, and sadly, it was to be the best year ever for the Los Angeles Angels.

The great team performance had to share top billing with the biggest character ever to wear an Angel uniform—Bo Belinsky. The glitter of Hollywood was made for this southpaw rookie who relied on a screwball for his out pitch. Acquired in the expansion draft from the Baltimore system, Belinsky exploded on the Southern California scene with five straight victories. Included in that total was the first no-hitter in Angel history, a 2–0 decision over the Orioles on May 5. After that effort, Bo owned the town. The Angels, desperate for a hero of their own to counteract the Dodger popularity, gloried in the publicity Belinsky garnered. But as Ross Newhan points out in his history of the Angels, "no major league player received more publicity for accomplishing less." Belinsky slumped to 10–11 after his great start, was 2–9 in 1963 while spending part of the year in the minor leagues, and despite a 9–8 mark and a 2.87 ERA, was gone after a fight with *Los Angeles Times* sportswriter Braven Dyer in August 1964.

But the real story was the team. The 1962 season was Rigney's most satisfying as a manager, and he was named American League Manager of the Year for his efforts. The Angels opened with a so-so

April, picked up steam in May to surge above .500, and then won 14 of 20 games, beginning on June 17, to vault into first place on July 4 when they swept a doubleheader at Washington. At that point the Angels had won 11 more than they had lost and were beneficiaries of a very close four-team pennant race. A memorable homecoming saw more than 3,000 fans greet the Angels on their return to Los Angeles that night, and the excitement carried over at least until the next game which the Angels lost to the Red Sox. They quickly fell to third place, never to lead again, but remained in contention until early September. The Yankees were making their move at this time and gradually put all of the contenders out of the race. A six-game losing streak ended the dream for the Angels, who finished at 86–76, 10 games behind New York and five games behind the Minnesota Twins.

The pitching staff improved immensely over 1961 and kept the Angels in the race. In addition to Belinsky, Ken McBride, Dean Chance, and Eli Grba were the starting pitchers. Chance was the leader with 14 victories and was by far a better pitcher than Belinsky. While Bo relied on a great screwball for his success, Chance intimidated the hitter with a great fastball thrown from an unorthodox windup. The two rookies ran together at night with country boy Dean trying to keep up with city slicker Bo. Although Chance enjoyed two marvelous years with the Angels, he was never quite the pitcher that Rigney expected him to be, and it was widely speculated that his nighttime frolics prevented him from reaching greatness.

The Angels operated with a pretty good offense but just an average defense. Leon Wagner and Lee Thomas had career years with 37 and 26 home runs, respectively, and each garnered over 100 RBIs. Other key players on this club were second baseman Billy Moran, center fielder Albie Pearson, and third baseman Felix Torres. Rigney gave credit for the improved pitching to rookie catcher Bob Rodgers, who caught 150 games and was to be a fixture behind the plate for the rest of the decade. In August 20-year-old Jim Fregosi was installed as the regular shortstop, where he would roam for the next 10 years.

In what was to become a consistent pattern over the years the Angels experienced several injuries which may have prevented them from staying on top. Pitcher Ken McBride was the best pitcher on the staff until August when he suffered a rib injury that sidelined him for virtually the rest of the season. The day before, bullpen ace Art Fowler was hit in the head by a ball during batting practice. Although it was not considered serious at the time, Fowler was through for the year and eventually lost the sight in his left eye. Earlier in the season outfielder Ken Hunt, an outstanding rookie in 1961, suffered a broken collarbone which was essentially career ending. Had these three been available down the stretch, it is likely that the Angels would have been right in the thick of it at the finish.

After the fine 1962 season the Angels began what would become a tradition for them by following a good season with a bad. The 1963 team slumped to ninth place with a 70–91 record. The Angels played winning baseball through June, but a 10-game losing streak brought them down to earth. The fine offense of the previous year virtually disappeared. Thomas fell 70 points to .220 with only nine home runs and was never to be an important Angel again. Rodgers broke a finger and missed 75 games, while Wagner lost his home run stroke at home, hitting only two of his 26 home runs there. The only bright light was Fregosi, who played 154 games in his first complete American League season and hit .287.

Attendance fell to 821,015 as the novelty of the new park wore off and the Angels began to play poorly. Only the Yankees were a consistent draw at Chavez Ravine—the Angel name for a park which everyone else called Dodger Stadium. The Dodgers won the pennant in 1963 after a four-year hiatus, and the attention of Los Angeles was focused entirely on their success. In retrospect, it appears that the fine play of the Angels in 1962 was detrimental to their future in Los Angeles. Angelenos were used to a winner; they had seen the Dodgers win after their first season in Los Angeles and when the Angels did so well in their second year, that was to be expected. When they failed in 1963, the fans turned their back on what seemed to be just an expansion club. The crowds trailed off ominously after the All-Star break.

The Angels bounced back to fifth place in 1964 with what was probably their best team in Los Angeles. They won 82 games and had a remarkable pitching staff. The pitchers tossed 28 shutouts, the most in the majors since 1909, and led the American League with a 2.91 ERA. This was also the Dean Chance year. Now a seasoned veteran, Chance was the Cy Young award winner with a 20–9 record and a league-leading 1.65 ERA. He was especially dominating at home where he recorded five 1–0 victories. From the All-Star Game on, Chance was 15–4. Among his many outstanding feats were four wins over the first-place Yankees which included 50 scoreless innings against that club. For that one year, at least, Los Angeles fans could seriously debate which local club had the better pitcher.

Offensively, it was another story. The Angels were basically a punchless lot with only 102 home runs, last in the league. Their leader was first baseman Joe Adcock, who had been acquired from Cleveland in what was a curious trade, with the Angels sending Leon Wagner to the Tribe. Daddy Wags was six years younger than Adcock and proceeded to hammer 31 home runs in his first year as an Indian.

Why the Angels traded their most popular player at a time when they needed all the colorful play they could get remains puzzling to this day.

Other personnel moves saw Bobby Knoop take over at second base where he teamed with Fregosi in as fine a double play combination as the Angels have ever had. Although Knoop would win several Golden Gloves, he was a low average hitter who struck out far too often, attributes the Angels already had an abundance of in other positions. The club got a good year from pitcher-outfielder Willie Smith, who was the best pinch hitter in the league, saw Jimmy Piersall replace Pearson in center field, sent Lee Thomas and Billy Moran to Boston and Bo Belinsky to Philadelphia. At least the Angels got some value from Bo, receiving pitcher Rudy May, who later turned in some fine work on the mound.

The Angels made headlines off the field in 1964 when they signed their first bonus babies. Outfielder Rick Reichardt, off the University of Wisconsin campus, was signed for a reported $200,000, and catcher Tom Egan, a fine high school prospect from Whittier, California, for $100,000. This was the last year before the inception of the free agent draft, and prospects were free to sign with teams of their choice. Both of these young men were said to be certain major leaguers. They eventually made the ballclub, but neither lived up to his advanced reputation, partly because of injuries.

At the beginning of 1964 Gene Autry made a critical decision when he informed the Dodgers that the Angels would not renew their lease at Dodger Stadium when it expired in 1965. The Angels were being suffocated by the Dodger presence in Los Angeles with attendance declining steadily each year. Not only that, the Dodgers were not the most generous of landlords. They never hesitated to charge the Angels for expenditures of any kind, the benefit or lack of same to the American League club notwithstanding. Perhaps the most outrageous case was a charge for parking lot repairs which was rescinded when the Dodgers were reminded that the Angels didn't share in parking revenue.

Autry naturally wanted to remain in Southern California, and after being romanced by the city of Long Beach, he found a location in Anaheim, located in Orange County approximately 35 miles from downtown Los Angeles. Although Anaheim had a population of only 150,000 at that time, it was in the center of the fastest growing county in California and almost six million people lived within 30 miles. The city of Anaheim had put together an attractive package for the Angels. They were offered a ballpark that would seat more than 43,000 fans, and it would be ready by the 1966 season. The Angels accepted the offer, signing a 35-year lease with three 10-year options to follow;

groundbreaking at the site on State College Boulevard took place on August 31, 1964, and the Angels were on their way to Anaheim.

Meanwhile, the club played out its last days in Los Angeles with a seventh-place finish in 1965. The Angel offense was anemic through most of the year, and only a reasonably effective pitching staff kept the ballclub competitive. Although Chance slumped to a 15–10 record after his banner year, rookies Marcelino Lopez and Fred Newman stepped in to provide a good starting staff. Lopez was especially effective in Chavez Ravine with a 10–3 mark, but 1965 was to be the best year of his career. The Angels played well at home, but no one wanted to see them play. Only 566,727 paid their way into American League games in LA in 1965, and as the season ground to a close, the last Angel crowds were miniscule. In their next-to-last home game the all-time low was reached when 945 fans were in attendance at a 4–2 loss in a make-up game with Baltimore. On September 2 the Angels renounced their ties to Los Angeles when the club was officially christened the California Angels.

The season of 1966 was a dramatic contrast for the new Anaheim entry. The new ballpark opened on April 19 with 31,660 on hand, a larger crowd than any the Angels had enjoyed during their last season in Chavez Ravine. The new park bore a superficial resemblance to Dodger Stadium but had certain unique characteristics. Chief among them was a giant A-frame scoreboard located just beyond the fences with an illuminated halo that blinked after an Angel victory and could be seen from the five adjacent freeways. It was less of a pitcher's park than Dodger Stadium, although the dimensions were close—foul lines of 333 feet down in right and left and 404 to center field. The ball seemed to carry better, especially in the daytime, much to the pitchers' chagrin. In their first season in Anaheim the Angels increased their home run count by 50 percent, and other clubs performed in the same fashion. The Orange County fans supported the club with 1,400,321 in attendance, but that was to be the high mark for 11 years.

On the field the Angels were undergoing a transition period. Rick Reichardt joined the club after brief minor league service and was enjoying a fine rookie season when he was stricken with a kidney ailment in mid-July. One kidney had to be removed, and Reichardt was finished for the season. He was hitting .288 when he was forced to depart and was on a pace to hit 30 home runs for the season, but Reichardt was never to return to this level. The Angels were never satisfied with his performance after that fine beginning and finally traded him to Washington in 1970.

Other changes saw rookie Ed Fitzpatrick take over in right field, giving the Angels a youthful outfield that with Reichardt and Jose Cardenal averaged 22 years. The infield was also composed of youngsters Knoop, Fregosi, and Paul Schaal. But the pitching staff was long of tooth. The young pitchers of Chavez Ravine had begun to fade from the scene. McBride was gone, his career demolished by injury, while Lopez and Newman fell off to 7–14 and 4–7, respectively, and were never to be important Angel factors again. The staff leaders were Jack Sanford, Lew Burdette, and George Brunet, veterans all with no promise for the future. Rigney did a good job in manipulating this crew, which eventually ended up only three games behind the White Sox in fourth place. A healthy Reichardt may have made the difference.

The 1967 season was perhaps the most exciting in American League history with four clubs in pennant contention down to the last week. Surprisingly, Rigney's Angels were right there with the others. They started poorly and were in 10th place as late as May 21, but a remarkable June brought them to within four games at the All-Star break. They played competitively thereafter and were within 1½ games of the top in the middle of August but never came any higher. Finally eliminated in the last week of the season, the Angels played spoiler by defeating Detroit twice on the last weekend of the season.

A major trade keyed the Angels' 1967 success. They sent Dean Chance to Minnesota in exchange for outfielder Jimmie Hall and first baseman Don Mincher. Although Chance won 20 games with the Twins, he had worn out his welcome in Anaheim. Mincher provided some badly needed power and was a good fielder to boot. For that one season the Angel infield of Mincher, Knoop, Fregosi, and Schaal was as good as any in the league. As a further endorsement, Knoop and Fregosi were Golden Glove winners. Mincher's 25 home runs led the club, and Hall had 16 homers, as well, but was not nearly the player he had been in Minnesota.

The pitching staff consisted of youngsters for the most part and missed one more when rookie Dick Wantz, who had made the club, was sidelined with a fatal brain tumor. Jim McGlothin, one of the early products of the Angel farm system, led the way with 12 wins and a 2.97 ERA. The baby-faced redhead had a period in mid-summer during which he pitched 33 consecutive scoreless innings. He never quite lived up to this promise, was traded to Cincinnati in 1970, and died of cancer at the early age of 33. Ricky Clark, another young farm product, matched McGlothin's 12 wins, but that was to be his major-league high. The star of the team was reliever Minnie Rojas, who led the league with 27 saves and was the American League Fireman of the Year, an honor he richly deserved. The Angels appeared to be set in their bullpen for years with this willing worker, but the Angel black cloud descended tragically again after the 1968 season. Rojas was the victim of an automobile accident which resulted in the loss of two of his children and left him paralyzed from the neck down.

The Angels participated in a game that year that produced one of the saddest events of the decade. On August 20 at Boston, Red Sox slugger Tony Conigliaro was almost fatally beaned by a pitch thrown by Jack Hamilton, a hard throwing right-handed starter whom the Angels had acquired from the New York Mets in June. Conigliaro lost much of the vision in his right eye, missed the entire 1968 season, and was never the great player he had been before the accident. And Hamilton, who was 9–6 in 1967, was so affected by the injury that he was never the same pitcher and was out of baseball within two years.

Expectations were high for 1968, but once again the Angels followed a good year with a bad, falling into an eighth-place tie with the White Sox. In this year of the pitcher, the Angels' promising staff saw the collapse of the fine defense of the year before and their records suffered accordingly. McGlothin dropped to 10–15 and Clark plunged to 1–11. In his final year, Rojas experienced arm problems much of the time and saw his ERA balloon to 4.25 with only six saves. Only George Brunet enjoyed anything approaching a reasonable year with a 13–17 mark and a 2.87 ERA.

The Angel jinx struck early when Don Mincher was beaned by Cleveland's Sam McDowell in the season's second game. The injury caused Mincher to miss 42 games and cut his home run production in half. His career was ruined for all practical purposes; he passed from the Angel scene the next year and retired after the 1970 season. The Angels needed his bat, for the rest of the offense was pathetic. The club scored a meager 498 runs, lowest in its history, and batted a powerless .227. Hall was a complete bust and was traded to Cleveland in June for Vic Davalillo, a singles-hitting center fielder who had a club-leading .298 average. Schaal lost his job at third to fine fielding Aurelio Rodriguez, and the club made a terrible trade by sending Jose Cardenal to the Indians for outfielder Chuck Hinton. Hinton hit a dismal .195 while Cardenal was just coming into his own and remained a fine player for another 10 years.

The 1968 Angels were exceptionally weak at home, losing 29 of their last 41 games in Anaheim with a corresponding sharp drop in attendance. Rigney came under severe criticism during this period, and Haney, too, was under fire for the failure of the Angel farm system to produce any help for the big club. In September Autry and Reynolds made a decision that was to prove disastrous when they retired Haney, offering him a job as a consultant, and hired as his replacement former Dodger Vice President Dick Walsh. Walsh had been employed by the Dodgers in various capacities and most recently had been the commissioner of the North American Soccer League. He was given a seven-year contract by the Angels who announced simultaneously that Rigney had been rehired for the next two years. The Angels were now entering a new era that was to be the most depressing in their history.

Walsh served as general manager for three years during which his cold impersonal handling of club matters managed to antagonize just about everyone in the organization as well as the officials of the city of Anaheim. Inexperienced in player personnel matters, he was responsible for several unfortunate trades that depleted the weak farm system of its best prospects in exchange for very questionable value. His legacy was a club that was barely competitive until the advent of free agency in 1976.

The American League split into Eastern and Western Divisions in 1969 with the addition of expansion teams in Kansas City and Seattle. The Angels hoped to compete for the Division title, but a terrible start ended that hope as well as the tenure of Bill Rigney. Rig was fired on May 26 after the Angels had lost 10 straight during an Eastern road trip. His replacement was pitching coach Lefty Phillips, who had been hired by Walsh as director of player personnel and then assigned to the coaching staff in the spring. The firing of Rigney was not a surprise, but the hiring of Phillips certainly was. He had been a very successful scout and coach with the Dodgers and had been in baseball for over 30 years. His knowledge of the game was vast, and he was considered a fine judge of talent. He simply wasn't able to communicate with his players, and when major personnel problems developed in 1970, Phillips was utterly lost.

The Angels won their first game under Phillips and played at a .500 pace to finish a respectable third. They enjoyed improved pitching when Andy Messersmith, Rudy May, and Tom Murphy developed into dependable starters to go along with McGlothin. Messersmith, who was the best pitcher ever developed in the Angel farm system, was given a starting spot at the beginning of the season and after losing his first five decisions, went 16–6 the rest of the way. The bullpen was also given some life with the development of Ken Tatum, who had 22 saves in 54 appearances. Phillips installed three youngsters as regulars—first baseman Jim Spencer and outfielders Jay Johnstone and Bill Voss. All were under 25, all showed great promise, and all were gone from Anaheim before much of their potential was realized. In one of the few good trades that Walsh ever made, the Angels acquired second baseman Sandy Alomar from Chicago in exchange for Bobby Knoop. Alomar proved to be a durable replacement with good range and was a fine base stealer over the next several years.

Clearly the Angels needed more offense, and Walsh thought he had provided it when he traded McGlothin and two rookie pitchers—Pedro Borbon and Vern Geishert—to Cincinnati for outfielder Alex Johnson, infielder Chico Ruiz, and pitcher Mel Queen. Johnson was a fine hitter and proved it with the Angels in 1970. He won the American League batting title and had over 200 hits. But he was a bitterly misanthropic man who disrupted the clubhouse with his constant taunting of teammates and his reluctance to hustle. Phillips didn't really know how to handle Johnson and received little support whenever he tried to impose discipline. Although Johnson's bat helped lead the Angels to a third-place finish, his presence on the team ultimately destroyed Phillips and brought down Walsh as well.

The Angels played well during Phillips' first full year as manager and finished only 12 games behind the division-leading Twins. They were only three games behind as late as September 4 before losing three straight to Minnesota in a crucial series. Johnson paced an improved offense, and he had help from Fregosi, Johnstone, Roger Repoz, and new third baseman Ken McMullen. McMullen was another ex-Dodger and had been acquired from Washington in exchange for Rick Reichardt and Aurelio Rodriguez. This was another Walsh trade that was ill advised. Although McMullen was adequate in the field and had fair power, Rodriguez was a fine fielder and remained in the league for another 10 years. In effect, the club had given Reichardt away for nothing at a time when he still had some value.

A new star of the Angel pitching staff was Clyde Wright, who enjoyed his finest year with 22 wins. He had joined the club in 1967, had a good year in 1968, but slumped to a 1–8 mark in 1969. Not blessed with exceptional speed, Wright was more of a finesse pitcher with fine control. He thrilled Anaheim Stadium fans on July 3 with the first no-hitter ever thrown there, a 4–0 defeat of Oakland. If Messersmith and May had avoided injury, the Angels might have been in closer competition with the Twins. But Messersmith slumped to 11–10 after straining his rib muscles early, and May fell to 7–13 with arm miseries along the way. The fine bullpen work of Ken Tatum came to an abrupt halt in August after he beaned Paul Blair of the Orioles. Tatum seemed reluctant to pitch inside after that and recorded only two saves for the balance of the year.

Once again the Angels were active traders, and after the winter meetings they came away with a raft of new players. Tony Conigliaro was the biggest name, and he was joined in Anaheim by catcher Gerry Moses, infielder Syd O'Brien, outfielder Ken Berry, and pitchers Billy Wynne, Ray Jarvis, and Jim Maloney. Sadly, only Berry performed well for the Angels. And to get these players they traded away Tatum,

Jay Johnstone, Doug Griffin, Tom Bradley, and the other bonus baby, Tom Egan. The Angels would have been well advised to avoid the trades; Griffin, Johnstone, and Bradley performed well for their new clubs for several years.

On the surface, however, the Angels appeared to be improved and were thought to be a legitimate contender in 1971. But the seething cauldron that was Alex Johnson boiled over, completely destroying the team morale, and the Angels fell to fourth place, finishing 25½ games behind the champion Oakland A's. The troubles with Johnson began in spring training when Phillips twice suspended him for failure to hustle. But each time he was restored to the lineup. When the regular season began, Johnson occasionally showed signs of returning to his 1970 form, but he then reverted to his lackadaisical ways. Phillips was absolutely bewildered with his play. He benched Johnson five times during the regular season and fined him a grand total of 29 times during the brief span of three months, all to no avail. After the fourth benching on May 23, Phillips announced to his team that Johnson would never again play for the Angels. But Walsh came to Johnson's defense once again, and Alex was soon back in the lineup.

A bizarre confrontation in the Angel locker room occurred between Johnson and Chico Ruiz when Ruiz reputedly threatened Johnson with a gun, and this led to the final suspension on June 26. This time it was for the balance of the season. Johnson never played for the Angels again and was traded to Cleveland on October 5. He filed an appeal for his suspension and was awarded back pay from the Angels when an arbitrator found that Johnson was emotionally incapable of playing at that time.

Conigliaro, a complete bust with the Angels, also left the club shortly afterwards. On July 11, after the Angels had lost a 20-inning marathon at Oakland, Conigliaro called an impromptu press conference at five o'clock in the morning to announce his retirement. He had never fully recovered the sight in his left eye after the beaning. Subsequently, he filed for disability instead of retirement and was paid for the balance of the season. At the time, Conigliaro was hitting .222 with only four home runs.

To compound the Angel woes of 1971, Jim Fregosi, the club's best player, developed a tumor on his foot that required surgery in July. The ailment limited his play to 107 games during which he hit a weak .233. Altogether, five Angels spent 21 or more days on the disabled list that year. The only bright spots on this team were Andy Messersmith, who won 10 of his last 12 decisions to finish 20–13, and durable Sandy Alomar, who was the leading hitter at .260 and stole 39 bases.

After the disastrous season Autry cleaned house, firing Philips and his entire coaching staff on October 7 and two weeks later informing Walsh that his contract was terminated with four years to go. The new general manager was Harry Dalton, the director of Player Personnel with the Orioles. Dalton's immediate task was to restore order in the clubhouse, but his main purpose was to build up the farm system, and he was given a five-year contract to do so. He immediately entered the trading markets, sending relief pitcher Dave LaRoche to Minnesota for shortstop Leo Cardenas. The move was made because Dalton was uncertain that Fregosi would make a complete recovery from his surgery, and on December 10, Dalton made the most important trade in club history when he sent the popular all-star to the New York Mets in exchange for four players—pitcher Nolan Ryan, outfielder Leroy Stanton, pitcher Don Rose, and catcher Francisco Estrada.

In Ryan the Angels received an extraordinary talent who had not fulfilled his promise in New York. He had four so-so years with the Mets, but he immediately blossomed with the Angels and became the greatest gate attraction the club had ever enjoyed. He won 19 games in 1972, averaged better than 10 strikeouts a game, and had a 1.07 ERA at Anaheim Stadium. During the next four years, when Angel fortunes were at their lowest, Ryan kept some attention focused on what was a very uninspiring team.

The replacement manager was Del Rice, one of the original Angels and the 1971 Minor League Manager of the Year at the Angel farm in Salt Lake City. Rice was Dalton's choice, and it was felt that he would add some stability to the chaotic Angel organization. But Rice lasted only one year. His club spent almost the entire year in fifth place, and only the miserable play of the Texas Rangers kept the Angels from ending at the bottom of the Western Division.

The 1972 campaign saw the first strike in major league history, lasting 13 days at the beginning of the season. This delay did not help the Angels, who were very unsettled. New regulars were first baseman Bob Oliver, outfielders Vada Pinson and Leroy Stanton, and shortstop Leo Cardenas. They did not contribute much offensively, placing an inordinate burden on the pitchers, who responded well by allowing the fewest hits and posting the most strikeouts in the league. Ryan was the league leader with 329 and finished with a 19–16 record, including 11 games in which he allowed four or fewer hits. Wright was the most consistent, and Rudy May won 12 games. Messersmith slumped to 8–11 but missed a month with a broken finger. During the last six weeks of the season, this foursome pitched 26 complete games, but it wasn't enough to save Rice's job. In what was to become an annual event during the Dalton regime, the Angels announced a change of managers. Bobby Winkles, a very successful college coach at Arizona State, was given the job. It was a real gamble: Winkles had no professional managerial experience and had never been on a major league club until his appointment to the Angel coaching staff in 1972.

Winkles had a fine reputation as a teacher, and this attribute was expected to serve the club well as the farm system began to produce quality players. But the situation was complicated almost immediately when the Angels made a major trade with the Dodgers. They sent Messersmith and McMullen to Los Angeles for five players—outfielder Frank Robinson, pitchers Bill Singer and Mike Strahler, and infielders Bobby Valentine and Billy Grabarkewitz. The purpose of this trade was to improve the offense, and it certainly did that. Robinson, a future Hall of Fame member, crushed 30 home runs, the most by an Angel since Anaheim Stadium opened. This was the first year of the Designated Hitter Rule in the American League, an ideal situation for Robinson. He was well past his prime at 38, but with no outfield duties, he continued to be a potent force in the Angel lineup.

The Angels improved to fourth place in 1973. They were tied for the lead as late as June 29 but collapsed in July and finished 15 games behind Oakland. The offense was somewhat improved but still needed yet further improvement. In an effort to add some punch to the lineup, the Angels traded first baseman Jim Spencer to Texas for Mike Epstein, who had enjoyed several good power years with Washington. He proved to be an utter failure, hitting a dismal .215 with only eight home runs, and was released after only 10 games in 1974. The club thought the shortstop position was settled for years with Bobby Valentine, who hit .302 over the first 32 games and fielded well. But in one of those terrible misfortunes which have dogged the Angels through their existence, he suffered what was effectively a career-ending injury on May 17 against Oakland. Playing in center field that night, Valentine raced to the wall trying to track down Dick Green's home run, leaping high and catching his spikes in the fencing. His leg was broken in two places, and he did not return that season. When he resumed play, his great speed was gone, and he drifted from club to club before ending his career in 1978.

The summer of 1973 belonged to Nolan Ryan. The flamethrower came into his own that season as a superstar with record-setting performances. He fanned 383 batters to set a new major league strikeout record, pitched two no-hitters and just missed on two others, set a record for most strikeouts in consecutive seasons with 712, and tied the major league record for most strikeouts in three consecutive seasons. He averaged over 10 strikeouts per game with a record of 21–16.

The second of the Ryan no-hitters, on July 15 at Detroit, ranks as one of the most powerful games ever pitched in the major leagues. He struck out 17 Tigers, his high for the year, and had racked up 12 after only five innings. The Angels had a prolonged eighth-inning while batting around, and Ryan's arm stiffened. As a result, he struck out only one in the last two innings to fall just short of the then-major-league record of 19. Not until the ninth inning did any Tiger hit a ball hard.

Bill Singer joined Ryan as a 20-game winner at 20–14, and if Clyde Wright had been able to equal his record of the previous three years, the Angels might have made a race of it. But he suffered through an 11–19 season and was gone to Milwaukee after the season when the Angels sent four players to the Brewers for a package that included pitcher Skip Lockwood and catcher Ellie Rodriguez. The Angels needed a catcher, and Rodriguez was adequate for the next two years. But Lockwood was the real prize, developing into a fine relief pitcher for the Mets after the Angels let him get away after one season in Anaheim.

The Winkles experiment ended abruptly in 1974 when the Angels suffered the ignominy of a last-place finish for the first time. Winkles was not around to see the climax, having been fired on June 26 with the club in fifth place, 14 games below .500. The Angels were a hopeless mixture of youth and experience which was decimated by injury and saddled with a bullpen that produced only 12 saves all year. The tone for the season was set in spring training when promising pitcher Bruce Heinbechener was killed in an automobile accident and continued with one injury after another. The most serious was Bill Singer's back, which required surgery on June 30 and put him out for the remainder of the year.

Relations between Robinson and Winkles were never good, and the strife between the established major league star and the college coach appeared to create a split between the players which was morale sapping. In spite of a reconcilatory meeting with Dalton, the situation was tenuous at best and Winkles was let go. Coach Whitey Herzog ran the club for four days, and then on July 1 Dick Williams was hired as the replacement. He had won three straight divisional championships as well as two World Series, and it was hoped that he would instill some of that winning spirit into the Angels. But California was only 36–48 under his leadership, and that record was achieved only by winning seven of the last eight games of the year.

Williams saw his club lose the first 10 games under his command, and before long he began to get rid of the veterans. By the end of the season Rudy May, Sandy Alomar, Bob Oliver, and Frank Robinson were gone, the latter on his way to Cleveland to become baseball's first black manager. Bright spots on this team were the continued fine performance of Nolan Ryan, who won 22 games and led the league in strikeouts for the third time in a row, hard throwing rookie Frank

Tanana who won 10 games over the last two months of the season to finish 14–19, and rookie shortstop Dave Chalk.

But the Angels finished in last place once again in 1975. Williams changed the offense (after getting rid of Robinson and Oliver) to a running attack. The Angels came out running on Opening Day and didn't stop until they had stolen 220 bases, the most in the major leagues since 1916. Mickey Rivers blossomed in his second full year as a regular, stealing 70 bases while leading the league in triples and hitting .284. Rookie second baseman Jerry Remy stole 34, while out-fielders Dave Collins, Leroy Stanton, and Morris Nettles all stole 18 or more. It was exciting to see the rabbits run, but they didn't score many runs and they didn't win many games.

Ryan started out as if he were going to enjoy his greatest season. He pitched his fourth no-hitter against Baltimore on June 1 and had boosted his record to 10–3 before experiencing some arm miseries which put him out of action. When he returned, he lost eight straight decisions at one stretch and missed the final month of September, finishing with a disappointing 14–12 record. Surgery was required after the season during which bone chips were removed from his arm. Frank Tanana took Ryan's place as ace of the staff, winning 16 and leading the league in strikeouts. Ed Figueroa enjoyed a fine 16–13 mark in his first regular year, but Bill Singer was not the pitcher he had been before his back problems. He slumped to 7–15 and was traded to Texas after the season.

During the off-season the Angels attempted to restore some balance to the offense, which was really not competitive with the rest of the league. In doing so, however, they continued to build on their bad trading record by sending two of their most promising young players, Mickey Rivers and Ed Figueroa, to the Yankees for outfielder Bobby Bonds. Bonds had been a great player in the past with a fine combination of speed and power. But he was entering his declining years that would see him become a migratory player, drifting to six teams in six years. Bonds had a poor season in 1976 because of injury. He suffered a broken finger in spring training that never healed properly and ultimately required surgery. His play was restricted to 99 games; still, he led this powerless club with 10 home runs. Meanwhile, Rivers and Figueroa proved to be the catalysts to the first Yankee pennant in 12 years.

Another disappointing trade saw third baseman Bill Melton arrive from the White Sox, and he was expected to provide consistent power along with Bonds. But Melton experienced severe back problems which limited his play to 118 games during which he hit only six home runs and batted .208.

The Angels rallied to finish in fourth place in spite of the disappointing Bonds and Melton, but Williams was not around to see it. He was fired on July 23 when the club had a record of 39–57 and was already out of the race. As the losses mounted, Williams ragged his players constantly. Tension built up and finally the situation climaxed on the team bus returning from a road trip. Williams and Melton had words which led to the manager suspending Melton. Nevertheless, Dalton fired his manager that day. His successor was popular coach Norm Sherry, who created a more relaxed atmosphere to play in, and the Angels responded with a 37–29 record over the balance of the season.

The best news of the 1976 season was the return to form of Nolan Ryan. There was legitimate concern that he might not be as effective after the surgery, and in truth he was not completely right when the season began. But he went 9–4 after Sherry took over to finish with a respectable 17–18 mark and a record 327 strikeouts. Tanana, too, responded to the Sherry touch and enjoyed his best season as an Angel, winning 19 games. He and Ryan finished 1–2 in strikeouts, fewest hits allowed per game, and lowest opponent's batting average.

Outside of the pitching duo, there was not much excitement at Anaheim in 1976. The offense was very weak with little evidence of power. Although the double play combination of Remy and Chalk was steady, they showed little punch; neither hit a home run that season, which perhaps epitomized the club. Attendance, which had climbed back to 1,058,163 in 1975, dropped to 1,006,774, and only the extra 5,000 or so that attended Ryan's starts kept the numbers respectable.

This was the lowest point in Angel history. But off-the-field events were taking shape which were to cause a complete turnaround in Angel fortunes. At the end of the 1975 season former Angel Andy Messersmith, who had played that year without a contract at Los Angeles, had taken the position that he was now a free agent. He filed a grievance to that effect with the Players Association, and at an arbitration hearing on December 23 Arbitrator Peter Seitz ruled that the renewal clause in a major league contract—the so-called reserve clause—was not perpetual but was good for only one year. Beyond that period a player was free to negotiate his services with any club. The era of free agency had begun.

Although the concept of total free agency was modified in agreements between the players and owners over the next several years, it remained that players would have a right to sell their services to the highest bidder under certain conditions. This would allow a weaker team with abundant resources to strengthen itself immediately without relying on a farm system to provide the talent. The Angels with their weak minor league organization were exactly in that category. Harry Dalton was quick to see the possibilities of instant improvement, and he convinced Gene Autry to authorize major expenditures for available free agents.

For those who had played the 1976 season without a contract a re-entry draft was held in November where the clubs obtained negotiating rights with the available 22 free agents. The Angels were among the most active bidders, and when the smoke had cleared, they had signed three of the best players available—second baseman Bobby Grich of the Baltimore Orioles and outfielders Don Baylor and Joe Rudi of the Oakland Athletics. Each had been signed to a long-term contract with the Angels at an estimated combined total of $5,200,000.

The signings proved to be a wise move by Autry. The immediate impact was to stimulate increased season ticket demand; the Angels saw attendance increase to 1,432,663 in 1977. That has been the low figure in the ensuing 12 years, in spite of a number of disappointing seasons of lackluster play. The Angels had acquired an identity that had escaped them during the first 16 years of their existence.

On the field, however, the Angels did not receive immediate dividends from their three new all-stars. Grich suffered a back injury in February that required surgery in June and limited his play to 52 games. Rudi started well, setting a club record for runs batted in during a single month in April; then a pitch thrown by Texas pitcher Nelson Briles broke his hand on June 26. At the time Rudi was second in the league in RBIs, and the Angels were only two games out of first place, but the combination of the two injuries together with arm problems suffered by Ryan and Tanana doomed the club to another disappointing finish. The Angels collapsed in July and eventually plunged to fifth place, 28 games behind the Kansas City Royals. They actually won two fewer games than the 1976 ballclub.

Injuries were the biggest contributor to the Angels demise. Tanana, who was on the threshold of stardom, suffered an arm injury just before the All-Star Game, and won only three games after that. With a record of 12–6 at the break, he finished 15–9 to go with his league-leading ERA of 2.54 and did not appear in a game after Labor Day. He blamed some of his arm problems on the 14 straight complete games he pitched during the first two months of the season.

Ryan's arm miseries didn't prevent him from winning 19 games and striking out 341 batters, but the rest of the staff was spotty. Dalton improved the group with mid-season trades, bringing in Ken Brett and Dave LaRoche. LaRoche came at a high price, the Angels giving up Bruce Bochte and $250,000 to Cleveland for him, but he improved the bullpen considerably, while Brett proved to be a capable starter. Both of the new additions were signed to long-term contracts.

The offense was the strongest the Angels had enjoyed in years. They hit 131 home runs, the most since 1962, and would have had more if Grich and Rudi had been available all season. Bonds was healthy for the first time in several years and had a fine season—37 home runs, 115 runs batted in, and 41 stolen bases. The RBI total represented a new club record, and the home runs tied Leon Wagner's mark set in 1962. Baylor started slowly and had only nine home runs during the first half of the season, but he finished with 25 to provide (with Bonds) the best 1-2 punch in the batting order the club had enjoyed in Anaheim. Just an average outfielder with a weak throwing arm, Baylor was the designated hitter most of the time.

The shortstop position had the traditional black cloud over it in 1977. Young Mike Miley, who had spent the last half of 1976 with the club and looked to be the shortstop of the future, was killed in an automobile accident in January. When Grich was injured, he was replaced by another rookie, 21-year-old Rance Mulliniks, who also logged time on the injury list. The unsettled nature of the position weakened the effects of an improved offense.

Norm Sherry was not able to survive the Angel misfortunes either. Dalton replaced him as manager on July 11 with coach Dave Garcia, a career minor leaguer with 14 years of managerial experience. With a record of 39–42 under Sherry, the Angels went 35–46 under Garcia, who brought in his former boss at Cleveland, Frank Robinson, to serve as hitting coach.

In spite of the improved attendance the Angels were said to have lost a record amount of money in 1977. Autry was concerned about the business side of the operation and apparently felt that controls were lacking. That as much as anything explains why he hired former Dodger general manager, Emil J. "Buzzy" Bavasi, in October. Bavasi was brought in as financial director to oversee the business side of the operation, but within a month General Manager Harry Dalton had resigned to take a similar post at Milwaukee, and Bavasi took over those duties as well. Although the Angels were to win their first two divisional championships under Bavasi's stewardship, relationships with the players were strained during his regime. He never quite understood that free agency had changed the rules of baseball and the players were almost equal partners with management.

The Angels jumped right back into the free agent market at the close of 1977, and again they came up with a prize in outfielder Lyman Bostock. Of all the many tragedies to strike the Angels in their history, Bostock was probably the saddest. Only 27, Bostock had hit .323 and .336 in back-to-back years at Minnesota. He was a slashing line-drive hitter who was a good outfielder as well. Bavasi signed Bostock to a contract estimated at $2,200,000, and it appeared to be money well spent until September 23, 1978. As Baylor had done the previous year, Bostock started slowly as he pressed to justify his big contract. But by September he had raised his average to .296 and was doing everything expected of him when, with seven games left in the season, he was shot to death as an innocent bystander in a lover's quarrel. One can only speculate on the impact of this loss on the Angels.

Shortly after the Bostock signing, Bavasi engineered his first trade, sending Bonds to the Chicago White Sox along with rookie outfielder Thad Bosley and pitcher Dick Dotson for catcher Brian Downing and pitchers Chris Knapp and Dave Frost. Although this deal was widely panned at the time, the club acquired two players in Downing and Frost who would play major roles in future Angel successes. Knapp won 14 games in 1978, but his future was clouded by a late-season back injury and he was never as good again. Other transactions saw second baseman Jerry Remy traded to Boston for pitcher Don Aase, another good move, and the signing of free agent outfielder Rick Miller of the Boston Red Sox.

The Angels were considerably improved as a result of these moves and finished in a tie for second in 1978, only five games behind the Royals, who were winning the Western Division for the third consecutive time. For the first time they had a strong outfield in all three positions in Bostock, Miller, and Joe Rudi, who made a complete recovery from his injury of the previous year. Grich bounced back to play 144 games at second base where he would remain for the balance of his career. The Angels moved Dave Chalk back to shortstop to make room for promising rookie Carney Lansford. He was another product of the Angel farm system, which was beginning to show the results of Dalton's rebuilding work. Downing took over the catching position and proved to be the best since Bob Rodgers was in his prime.

The pitching was led by Tanana, but once again he experienced arm trouble after a great start. He finished 18–12, but his ERA increased by more than a full run. It was the last good year he was to enjoy in Anaheim. Ryan had the worst year of his Angel career, finishing 10–13. He, too, had some tenderness in his arm and didn't win a game from May through July. The work of Knapp, 14–8, and Aase, 11–8, made up for Ryan's loss somewhat, and the Angels had a good stopper in LaRoche, who had 25 saves.

As usual during the seventies, the Angels experienced a change in managers. Dave Garcia was let go on May 31 at a time when the Angels record was 25–21 and right after they had been blasted, 17–2, at Chicago. Although there wasn't any single cause for Garcia's firing, it was widely known that Autry wanted a more colorful manager. After making overtures to Whitey Herzog of the Royals and Gene Mauch of the Twins, the Angels' boss chose Jim Fregosi. This was an overwhelmingly popular move. Fregosi had been everyone's favorite player during his 10-year career as an Angel player and was frequently discussed as a future managerial prospect. His active career was coming to an end at Pittsburgh, and the Pirates did not stand in his way to better himself. As a manager, Fregosi proved to be a better disciplinarian than either of his immediate predecessors and convinced Don Baylor that he would best aid the club by serving as the designated hitter full time. The Angels played at a 62–54 pace under Fregosi and were in first place as late as August 25 before a five-game losing streak knocked them back to third.

The Angels had plenty of offense in 1978. Baylor hit 34 home runs and drove in 99 runs to lead the way, and the club got good production out of Lansford, who hit .294, first baseman Ron Jackson, who hit .297, Bostock, and Rudi. The Angels now appeared to be real contenders, and it was off to the free agent market again. But circumstances had changed slightly. Knowing that they could not afford to keep their high-priced players, several clubs began offering them in trades simply to get something of value.

The Twins were unable to cope with the inflationary salary demands of outfielder Dan Ford and second baseman Rod Carew and made them both available. Although Carew had been offered to several clubs, no one had provided a satisfactory deal until finally, in February, the Angels came up with four young players to complete a deal—outfielder Ken Landreaux, pitchers Paul Hartzel and Brad Havens, and catcher Dave Engel. They had also acquired Ford two months earlier for Ron Jackson and young catcher Danny Goodwin.

The two trades made champions of the Angels. Carew was one of the finest hitters in American League history, winning seven batting titles with a career high of .388 in 1977. He was an adequate second baseman in his prime but was beginning to slow down, and the Angels resolved that problem by putting him at first base where he was more than satisfactory. Not a power hitter, Carew's job was to get on base in front of the Angel sluggers Baylor and Ford. The replacement for Bostock in left field, Ford had shown good power at Minnesota and along with Rudi gave the Angels a formidable threesome in the middle of their lineup.

The result was the finest Angel offense in history. The club hit .282, scored 866 runs to lead the American League for the only time in their history, and crashed 164 home runs, their second best total. They needed every ounce of hitting, for this year the pitching staff, which had generally kept the club at least competitive, slumped badly from its previous high level.

The 1979 Angels won only one more game than the 1978 club, but they nevertheless finished in front of the Royals by three games. They enjoyed a good start, winning 30 of their first 50 games, and actually won the pennant in July when they moved 7½ games ahead of the Royals on July 31. That gave the Angels an edge when they slumped to 11–17 in August. Never very far behind, the club took over the lead permanently on August 31 when they outslugged the Indians 9–8 to break a five-game losing streak. They immediately won eight of the next nine and were thereafter in the driver's seat. The pennant was clinched on September 25 at Anaheim when Tanana turned back the Royals, 4–1.

The Angels were distinct underdogs to the Baltimore Orioles in the best-of-five playoff series. The pitching-rich Orioles had beaten the Angels in nine of the 12 games between the two clubs during the regular season and had held the Angel power to two runs or less in each of those victories. Still, the Angels felt they had a fighting chance and opened strongly in Baltimore. The clubs were tied 3–3 in the 10th inning when pinch hitter John Lowenstein ended it with a three-run homer off bullpen ace John Montague, who had pitched a strong two innings in relief. On the next day Baltimore raced out to a 9–1 lead after three innings, hitting Dave Frost hard, but the Angels rallied to score six runs in the last three innings and had the tying run at third before losing 9–8. The series moved to Anaheim where the Angels took their only victory, 4–3, scoring two runs in the bottom of the ninth with little-used Larry Harlow driving in the winning run. But the Angels were helpless in the final game against Scott McGregor, a long-time nemesis, who shut out the Angels, 8–0. The fine Baltimore pitching had at last asserted itself.

There were plenty of Angel heroes in 1979, and the biggest of all was Don Baylor. He drove in 139 to lead the American League and blasted 36 home runs to go along with his .296 average. For his efforts he became the first Angel to be named league Most Valuable Player. He and Carew split the designated hitter duties as Baylor was forced into outfield duty because of injuries to Rudi. The two combined for a DH average of .318. Ford had his best year with 21 home runs and 101 runs batted in. Both he and Baylor scored over 100 runs. Carew batted .318 in an injury-marred year for him; when he DH'd, young Willie Aikens spelled him at first and was the fourth Angel with 20 or more home runs. Grich had a marvelous year, hitting 30 home runs and driving in 101 runs. But Brian Downing had the greatest turn-around. After a winter of heavyweight lifting, he hit .326 and increased his slugging average by over 100 points. Downing developed quite a batting eye that year, drawing 77 walks to lead the team and setting the Angel record for on-base percentage at .420.

The pitching was another story. Both Ryan and Tanana had off years. Although Ryan led the league in strikeouts for the seventh time, he finished 16–14 after being 9–2 on June 18. He won what was to be his last victory as an Angel on September 24 at Anaheim, beating Kansas City 4–3 and clinching a tie for the division championship. Again, he complained of arm problems, but they were minor compared to Tanana. The gifted southpaw was restricted to 90 innings and finished 7–5. Dave Frost filled some of the void with a 16–10 record, going 7–2 in August and September when the rest of the staff was showing effects of the long season. The bullpen was just good enough to win. Mark Clear was the leader in saves with 14, but LaRoche had lost some of his effectiveness of the past year. Bavasi made a good trade with Seattle on August 29, bringing in John Montague, who had six saves in September.

In retrospect it seems clear that the Angels won in 1979 because several players enjoyed career offensive years. When the attack collapsed in 1980 the club plunged to the lower recesses of the division. The Angels won only 65 games, the fewest in their history, and finished in sixth place. For much of July and August they occupied the cellar but managed to crawl ahead of the weak Seattle Mariners in September. Injuries decimated the club early. Don Baylor suffered a cracked wrist in the opening game of the season, played with it a month while hitting miserably and then going down for two months, while catcher Brian Downing broke his ankle in the club's ninth game and didn't return until September. Dan Ford struggled with knee problems all year and played in only 65 games. The trio batted in 213 fewer runs than in 1979. The disabled list was home for much of the Angel lineup with only Carew, Lansford, and Grich playing what could be called complete seasons.

The lack of a cohesive attack placed a heavy burden on a pitching staff, which at best was average and had been severely damaged by what has to be considered the worst off-season player decision in Angel history. All during the 1979 season the club had refused to negotiate a renewal of Nolan Ryan's contract, which was to expire at the end of the year. As time went on, Bavasi began to negotiate in the media, a decision that irked Ryan and his agent. The pitcher had made a proposal in January 1979 for a contract extension of three years and informed Bavasi that he had no intention of filing for free agency. But as the year went on with no positive response from the Angel front office Ryan decided to test the free agency waters. In his autobiography, *Throwing Heat*, the ace pitcher states that by August he had determined that as long as Bavasi was associated with the club, he would not return to Anaheim.

It turned out to be a wise decision for Ryan, who signed a long-term contract with the Houston Astros for in excess of $1 million a year. But it was a disastrous decision for the Angels. Ryan proved to be a steady if not spectacular winner for the Astros through 1988, when he once again went the free agency route and moved to the Texas Rangers after flirting briefly with a return to the Angels. Ryan twice led the National League in ERA. It does not take much imagination to believe that the Angels would have snuck into at least one World Series during that period if Nolan Ryan had remained in Anaheim.

During his eight years in Anaheim, Ryan posted a won-loss record of 138–121, not impressive on its surface, but 14 percent better than the Angels did when he wasn't on the mound. If he had a flaw while he was at Anaheim, it was a tendency to experiment too much during a game, which sometimes resulted in losses; the scouts' pet name for him was "Young Tom Edison."

After Ryan left, Bavasi attempted to minimize his loss by wise-cracking that all the Angels needed to replace Nolan were two 8–7 pitchers. Buzzy appeared to be trying to take just that approach when he signed free agent Bruce Kison before the 1980 season and then really entered the market during the winter of 1980–81. For an estimated $4 million the Angels acquired four pitchers—Bill Travers, Jesse Jefferson, John D'Acquisto, and Geoff Zahn. Of this group, only Zahn and Kison helped. Neither D'Acquisto nor Travers ever won a game for the Angels, appearing in parts of 20 games combined over the next three years, while Jefferson was strictly a mop-up man.

The signings were just a part of the Angel personnel moves that winter, as the Angels began to rebuild after the 1980 disaster. In separate trades with the Red Sox the club sent Carney Lansford, Joe Rudi, Rick Miller, Mark Clear, and Frank Tanana in exchange for Rick Burleson, Butch Hobson, and Fred Lynn. In Lynn the Angels thought they had acquired their center fielder for the balance of the decade. He had debuted with the Red Sox in 1975 and was selected both Rookie of the Year and Most Valuable Player during that glorious season in Boston. He was the 1979 American League batting champion with a .333 average and had a lifetime average of .308 when the Angels obtained him. They promptly rewarded him with a four-year contract worth an estimated $5.2 million.

In other trades the Angels sent first baseman Jason Thompson to Pittsburgh for catcher Ed Ott and shortstop Dickie Thon to Houston for pitcher Ken Forsch. When the season opened only Carew, Grich, Downing, Ford, and Baylor were remaining regulars from the 1979 championship team. Fregosi was under much pressure to make this team work. The pressure had been intensified in January when Autry hired Gene Mauch as director of player personnel. The former manager of the Twins, Mauch had managed in the majors since 1961 and had a well-deserved reputation as a master strategist. He had never won anything in his managerial stints with the Phillies, Montreal, or Minnesota, where he always seemed to be outmanned. Autry had tried to get Mauch as his manager in 1977, but Twins owner Calvin Griffith would not release him from his contract. Mauch finally quit the Twins in August 1980, and Autry persuaded him to join the Angels. Both parties denied that Mauch was there to replace Fregosi, but when the clubs started poorly once again, on May 28 the Angels did the predictable. Fregosi was fired with a 22–25 mark and was replaced by Gene Mauch.

The summer that Fregosi departed will always be remembered as the year of the strike. The major league players walked out on June 13 and remained out of action for 50 days. At the time of the walkout, the Angels had improved their record to 31–29 and were only 6½ games behind Oakland. When play resumed, the leagues agreed to a split season, and the Angels hoped that the improvement shown during Mauch's first two weeks would continue. But those hopes were quickly dashed. Lynn reinjured his bad knee during the All-Star Game and was never the same player. He finished the season with a career-low .219 average, appearing in only 76 games. This opened a large hole in center field which was only partially filled by weak-hitting Juan Beniquez. The Angels played at the .500 level through the last week of August but then began a 14-game road trip during which they utterly collapsed. They lost eight straight and 14 of 15 to fall into last where they ended the second half with a record of 20–30.

The only bright spots on the 1981 Angels were Carew and Grich, who hit .305 and .304 respectively. Grich also hit a league-leading 22 home runs. The Angel offense improved over the dismal 1980 record, and this was partially a result of the improved hitting conditions in Anaheim Stadium. The park had been enclosed following the 1979 season to accommodate the Los Angeles Rams football team, and the ball now carried better, especially during the daytime. Pitching was improved despite the failure of the free agents to produce; the Angel ERA dropped to 3.70 as Mauch reconstructed the starting pitching rotation. Forsch, Zahn, and Steve Renko carried the burden, and the Angel farm system produced Mike Witt, who debuted at 20 and won eight games. Andy Hassler and Don Aase were effective out of the bullpen.

With the structure remaining in place the Angels went out to fill the holes during the off-season and were successful beyond their wildest dreams. In December they purchased catcher Bob Boone from the Phillies. The ankle injury suffered by Downing had effectively ended his catching career, and Ed Ott had been a dismal failure. Boone was one of the premier defensive catchers in the National League and was especially durable. During 1982 he would catch 143 games and before his Angel career ended in 1988 he would establish an all-time major league record for games caught. Five days later they traded rookie outfielder Brian Harper to Pittsburgh for shortstop Tim Foli. The plan was to use Foli as a utility man, but when shortstop Rick Burleson suffered a rotator cuff injury in April after his fine 1981 season, Foli took over the post and fielded brilliantly during much of the year. Then on January 28 the Angels traded Dan Ford to Baltimore for third baseman Doug DeCinces, who was in the last year of his contract. DeCinces, who was always known as a fine fielder, had his finest year, hitting .301 and driving in 97 runs.

But the frosting on the cake had been obtained six days earlier when the Angels signed free agent Reggie Jackson to a four-year contract said to be worth a million dollars a year. Here was the first bonafide Angel superstar. Jackson had begun his career with the Athletics in 1967 and was the pivotal character on the great A's teams of the early 1970s. When free agency came into being, Jackson took full advantage of it and ended up with the Yankees, where he became the colorful "Mr. October" in leading New York to pennants in 1978 and 1981. Reggie would turn 36 during the season and was determined to show the Yankees that he was not through. He proved that with gusto, hitting 39 home runs to lead the league for the third time in his career and to set an Angel franchise record as well.

The Angels enjoyed their greatest season as a result of these moves. They won 93 games, an all-time high, and won the Western Division championship by three games over a very strong Kansas City club, while establishing a club attendance record of 2,807,360 in the process. The Angels featured the home run with Jackson, DeCinces, Downing, Baylor, and Lynn each hitting over 20. With Burleson the exception, the Angels did not lose much time to injury. All starting infielders and outfielders played at least 133 games.

The starting pitchers were again effective and also very durable with Zahn, Forsch, Renko, Witt, and Kison starting all but 28 of the Angel games. They had to be durable, for if there was a weakness on this team, it was in the bullpen. Don Aase was expected to be the stopper, but an arm injury suffered in the spring removed him from contention. The Angels then made a very questionable trade when they sent promising power hitter Tom Brunansky to Minnesota for Doug Corbett, who had performed well for Mauch. But he seemed to have lost it after an impressive first week, and the Angels were never able to satisfactorily fill the gap.

On the strength of a good April the Angels led much of the first half but fell out of first place on August 3. Kansas City then took over and was leading by two games on September 14. But the Royals subsequently collapsed, losing seven straight on the road, and the Angels moved into first place for good by sweeping Kansas City in a three-game series ending September 22. They built the lead to 4½ games on September 27, when late-season acquisition Tommy John beat the Royals 4–2 at Kansas City. But the Royals would not die easily. They beat the Angels two straight and forced the pennant race into the last weekend. Dave Goltz, in one of his infrequent Angel victories, beat the Rangers 6–4 on the next-to-last day to end the suspense.

The American League Championship Series pitted two big slugging aggregations in the Angels and Milwaukee Brewers, a series that looked dead even at the beginning. Before 64,406, the largest crowd ever to watch a game at Anaheim, the Angels opened the Series with an easy 8–3 win. A four-run rally in the third inning overcame an early Brewer lead, and the Angels coasted behind a complete game effort by the veteran Tommy John. The Angels were even more impressive the next day behind Bruce Kison, winning 4–2. Kison pitched perhaps the best game of his career, scattering five hits and inducing the Brewer sluggers to hit 14 ground ball outs. The Angels were now in the driver's seat. No team had ever come back to win the best of five series after losing the first two games, and they had their ace, Geoff Zahn, scheduled for the third game as the series moved to Milwaukee.

The Brewers had their own late-season veteran in Don Sutton, and he absolutely stifled the Angels until the eighth inning, when he had to be relieved by Pete Ladd. Behind 5–0 at that point, the Angels scored three and had the tying run at bat before Ladd retired the side with no further scoring. The fourth game was most critical, and here Mauch made a curious decision. He chose to bring back John with only three days of rest in spite of the fact that 13-game-winner Ken Forsch was available. It was a costly move. John was hit hard and was wild as well, leaving after 3⅔ innings and after giving up six runs. The Brewers evened the series with a 9–5 victory that was not really that close. That set the stage for the fifth game, and the Angel pitcher would be Kison. He staggered through five innings, then was relieved by Luis Sanchez with the Angels clinging to a 3–2 lead. After one hitless inning, Sanchez loaded the bases in the seventh with two outs. The batter was left-handed-hitting Cecil Cooper, who had experienced a poor series up to then. This was to be one of the truly eventful moments in Angel history. Mauch left Sanchez in and Cooper promptly sliced a single into left field, scoring two runs. The Brewers had the lead, and they did not relinquish it. Ladd was again the stopper, and although the Angels got the tying run to second in the ninth, they were not able to bring it in.

Unlike 1979, this evenly matched series could have been won by the Angels, and the results left much opportunity for second guessing. It is not clear why Forsch didn't start the fourth game. John had done remarkably well in September, but at his age an extra day of rest would have left him available for the money game. The weakness of the Angel bullpen during the regular season manifested itself in the final game. Without a bonafide stopper Mauch left Sanchez in one batter too long. But it remains curious why he did not bring in lefthander Andy Hassler to pitch to Cooper.

The decisions left Mauch open to much second guessing during the early winter and perhaps led to his stunning decision to resign the Angel post. The announcement indicated that he had personal problems and was just simply burned out after the pressures of managing. It was later learned that his wife had terminal cancer, and Mauch needed to be with her during her last days.

The new Angel manager was John McNamara, who had previously managed Oakland, San Diego, and Cincinnati and had won a division title in the latter city in 1979. But there would be no championship for him with the Angels in 1983. As is their custom, the Angels followed a good season with a bad, falling into a fifth-place tie with Minnesota and to a disappointing 70–92 record. The first sour note of the season had been heard in November when Don Baylor could not come to terms with the Angels and signed with the Yankees. This left a huge hole in the batting order and contributed in part to the worst season of Reggie Jackson's career. His home runs declined from 39 to 14, and he batted a weak .194 in only 116 games. Bruised ribs were the major culprit in Reggie's poor performance, but the lack of Baylor's big bat behind him didn't help.

Jackson's injury typified the Angel season. Thirteen players saw service on the disabled list in 1983 and two of them—catcher Ed Ott and pitcher Don Aase—were out the entire year. Ott's career was effectively over, while Aase made a fine comeback in 1984, only to sign with Baltimore after that year. Rick Burleson attempted to return after his rotator cuff injury of the year before, but managed only 33 games. His replacement, Tim Foli, who had played so well in 1982, missed half the season as well with injury. Only Bob Boone, who caught 142 games, had anything approaching a full season.

In spite of the plethora of injuries, the Angels played well for half a season before disappearing, losing 55 games after July 10. The pitching was a big disappointment with Kison the only starter with a winning record. Goltz and Hassler flopped dismally, neither winning a game for the Angels.

The biggest excitement that summer was Rod Carew's effort to crack the .400 mark. He was off to the fastest start of his career, hitting .500 after 96 at bats, and was still at .402 when the All-Star break came. But he, too, was plagued by injuries, and although he did not go on the disabled list, he missed 33 games and lost his early advantage.

Carew eventually finished second to Wade Boggs at .339, the highest average ever for an Angel.

The Angels bounced back from the miserable experience of 1983 to finish in a second place tie with Minnesota in 1984, only three games behind Kansas City. It was not as impressive as it might appear, for the American League West was now becoming the "American League Worst." Only the Royals won more than they lost, and any one of four teams could have won it. The Angels at 81–81 had as good a chance as any. They led the division for 52 days straight from May to July and were as much as 7½ games ahead of the Royals during this stretch. But Kansas City finished strongly in August and September to pass the Angels. Although the California team was in first place on September 15, their 75–72 mark was not impressive and they skidded thereafter. They needed two straight shutouts at Texas on the season's last weekend to tie the Twins.

This was the year that Mike Witt finally arrived as an outstanding pitcher. He finished strongly at 15–11 with 196 strikeouts and enjoyed two spectacular efforts. The first, a 16-strikeout game against Seattle on July 23, was overshadowed by his perfect game masterpiece against the Rangers on the season's final day. Witt bested knuckleballer Charlie Hough, 1–0, and did not allow anything even resembling a hit. Geoff Zahn was steady at 13–10 with five shutouts, and the club got good work from rookie Ron Romanick, who finished 12–12 in 33 starts. But the pitching was too thin behind this trio to win the division.

This year the Angels introduced two rookies to the starting lineup in shortstop Dick Schofield and center fielder Gary Pettis. They were there primarily for defense, for neither hit a lick—Schofield, .193 and Pettis, .227. Pettis covered center field better than anyone else has ever done for the Angels. He added some needed team speed to this aging veteran club, stealing 48 bases, the most since the days of Mickey Rivers. Unfortunately, Pettis had a disturbing propensity to strike out. He fanned 115 times in 1984 and would increase that number in future years.

The veteran hitters were beginning to fade. Carew fell below .300 for the first time since 1968, hitting .295. He was now 38 and played in only 93 games. Jackson hit 25 home runs to lead the team and hit the 500th homer of his career on September 17, but Brian Downing was more valuable with his 23 homers and 91 RBIs. In his final year at Anaheim the disappointing Fred Lynn had a satisfactory year with 23 home runs and a .271 average, but he frequently missed games with minor injuries.

At the end of August Buzzie Bavasi announced his retirement after more than 50 years in baseball administration. His successor as general manager was 39-year-old Mike Port, who had been the director of Player Personnel and most recently the chief administrative officer of the club. He was experienced in the negotiation of player contracts, and it was here that he would get his initial baptism. Fred Lynn's contract had expired at the end of the season, and he was much in demand. But the Angels were concerned about Lynn's durability and offered him a contract with a much smaller base but one that was heavily weighted with incentives. If Lynn produced, he would be paid; if he didn't, he would earn much less. This was not acceptable to the veteran, and he accepted an offer from Baltimore that had more guarantees. Shortly thereafter, Bruce Kison signed a guaranteed contract with Boston after refusing an Angel offer that was conditional on his performance in spring training. The era of big contracts was changing. The economy that Bavasi had supposedly preached was now being supported by Jackie Autry, Gene's second wife and his former banker. In the years ahead the Angels would take a more rigid stance in their dealings with the players, and Port would become very unpopular with fans as a result.

Once again, the Angels had a managerial change, and this time it was the return of Gene Mauch. His personal crisis now resolved, Mauch needed the Angels as much as they seemed to need him, and he resumed his former duties. McNamara had resigned at the close of 1984 to manage the Red Sox in 1985. The task facing Mauch was formidable; the club was getting old, did not appear to be improved, and in some quarters was picked for last place. But in perhaps the best managerial performance of his career, Mauch guided the Angels to a second-place finish in 1985. They won 90 games and led the division for most of the season, only to fall just short, finishing one game behind the Royals. If it was a surprisingly successful season, it was also a bittersweet one. The Angels led by one game when they went into Kansas City for a four-game series on September 30. They came out of the series one game behind and could not make up the difference.

Mauch was at his finest through much of this season. He bunted more than ever, his team walked more, they executed better in the field, and he had a better bullpen. The loss of Lynn proved to be a blessing in disguise. The Angels were entitled to compensation for his loss from the free agent pool, and they selected reliever Donnie Moore. Moore proved to be the indispensable man, appearing in 65 games and establishing a club record for saves with 31. He and rookie Stu Cliburn, 9–3 with a 2.09 ERA, propped up an otherwise undistinguished pitching staff that had only three dependable starters.

The club's offense left much to be desired. Although the Angels scored slightly more than the previous year, they lacked consistency all season. Only part-time outfielder Juan Beniquez was at the .300

mark. Carew was definitely through. Although he hit .280, he was not a useful player at that level and was slow in the field. Pettis improved to .257 and stole 56 bases, and Reggie led the team once again with 27 homers.

In spite of the obvious deficiencies the Angels roared through the first half of the season, leading the division by six games at the All-Star break. The club struggled during a long road trip in late July, but still had a comfortable lead of five games when a two-day players strike took place on August 6. This proved to be a crucial event for the Angels. They had two games at home with Seattle postponed by the strike. The games were subsequently made up but not at Anaheim, where the Angels were exceptionally formidable that year. They were part of back-to-back doubleheaders with the Mariners in Seattle, both of which were split. Quite likely, the Angels would have taken at least one of the pair at Anaheim. They were 49–30 at home.

The Angels had been remiss in past years in not picking up additional strength for the stretch drive, but not so in 1985. They acquired pitchers John Candelaria from Pittsburgh in August and Don Sutton from Oakland in September to join Mike Witt, Ron Romanick, and rookie Kirk McCaskill in the rotation. Candelaria was especially effective with a 7–3 mark, but it was Sutton who was on the mound in what was the pivotal game of the season. At Cleveland on September 28 and one game back, Sutton pitched a masterful game and led, 5–0, after seven innings. But he did not come out for the eighth, Cleveland rallied with five runs off a tired Donnie Moore, and then won it in the ninth on a two-run homer by Jerry Willard off Stu Cliburn. It proved to be a devastating blow from which the club never quite recovered.

Nevertheless, hopes were high for continued success in 1986, and the Angels lived up to them by winning the Western Division championship, finishing five games ahead of the Texas Rangers, the only other club in the division above .500. This was considered by many to be the "Last Hurrah" for a mainly veteran team. At the end of the season 12 Angels would be eligible for free agency, and many would probably not be back. The Angels made their intentions perfectly clear at the end of 1985 when they did not offer Rod Carew a new contract. The great veteran had reached the end of the line; besides, the Angels had a rookie waiting in the wings in Wally Joyner, who had recently compiled some good power numbers in the minors. The club made virtually no other changes and entered the season with a set lineup for one of the few times in its history.

After a slow start, the Angels enjoyed a red-hot June to shoot by the Rangers into first place on July 7. They never left it. The lead grew to a high of 10 games on September 26 when the pennant was clinched.

The Angels easily handled the Rangers during the year, defeating them in the first seven encounters between the teams.

The club leader was Joyner, who enjoyed a Rookie-of-the-Year season with 22 homers and 100 RBIs to go along with a .290 mark. He created "Wally's World" in Anaheim Stadium during May and June with his spectacular exploits. Joyner had 72 RBIs by the All-Star break, but he had to drive in two in the season's last game to reach 100. His relative ineffectiveness during the last half of the year may have cost him the rookie award, which went to Oakland's Jose Canseco.

Joyner had plenty of help from Downing and DeCinces, who each drove in over 90 runs, and DeCinces led the club with 26 home runs. Grich had slowed down in his last year, but was ably backed up by Rob Wilfong, while Dick Schofield improved to .249. It was his dramatic bases-loaded homer on August 29 in the last of the ninth that climaxed a seven-run rally to defeat Detroit, 13–12, in the season's most spectacular game. Reggie Jackson was the full-time designated hitter but was not much of a factor in the last half of the season.

For the first time in their history, the Angels had three 15-game winners on their pitching staff. Mike Witt was the leader at 18–10 with 208 strikeouts, and he was almost matched by Kirk McCaskill at 17–10. Don Sutton had a 15–11 mark and gave six good innings almost every time out. John Candelaria probably would have made this a quartet, but he missed most of the first half with injury and did not win his first game until July 8. Nevertheless, he finished 10–2 and gave the Angels a strong starting rotation going into the playoffs. The bullpen was somewhat shaky, although the numbers did not indicate it. Moore fell off from his 1985 record of 21 saves and 2.97 ERA. Doug Corbett and Gary Lucas provided excellent support, and veteran Terry Forster supplied five saves. But the ballclub missed Stu Cliburn, who injured his arm during spring training and was never to be effective again, and Moore had suffered some shoulder problems. By season's end he was not the durable pitcher he had been in the past, and this would have fatal consequences in the playoffs.

The Boston Red Sox were the Angels' opponent in the championship playoffs, which were now a best-of-seven-game format. The Angels had taken the season series from the Red Sox and were confident going into the series. Mike Witt was utterly dominant in the opener at Boston, scattering five hits as the Angels were easy winners, 8–1. The Red Sox evened the series the next day, 9–2, behind Bruce Hurst. The action then shifted to Anaheim for the next three games. Candelaria was a 5–3 winner in Game Three with Moore working the last two innings and getting a save. Moore was not effective, however, giving up four hits and two runs while committing a balk. The Angels rallied to tie the Red Sox with three runs in the bottom of the ninth in Game Four, and then Bobby Grich singled home Jerry Narron with the winning run in the 11th inning. All they needed was one more victory.

The next day, October 12, will be remembered in Anaheim as long as baseball is played there. Mike Witt opposed Bruce Hurst, and in the second inning he threw a home run ball to catcher Rich Gedman to give the Red Sox a 2–0 lead. But the Angels took the lead in the sixth when Grich blasted a drive to left center that bounced off Dave Henderson's glove and out of the park for a two-run homer. The Angels scored two more runs in the seventh and moved into the ninth ahead, 5–2. Witt had settled down and allowed only six hits going into the ninth, walking no one.

Bill Buckner led off with a single. After Jim Rice struck out, Don Baylor hit a home run to cut the lead to 5–4. Dwight Evans popped up on the infield for the second out. Now came the critical moment of the game, and if a little black cloud appeared on the horizon, it may have indicated that all was not well. The batter was left-hand-hitting Rich Gedman, who had three hits already off Witt. Although his ace did not appear to be tiring, Mauch decided to change pitchers. He brought in left-handed Gary Lucas to pitch to Gedman. Donnie Moore was warming up in the bullpen to pitch to the right-hand-hitting Henderson should Gedman get on. It was classic Mauchian strategy.

On his first pitch Lucas attempted to back Gedman off the plate but was in too tight and hit him on the hand. And Lucas had not hit a batter with a pitch all season. Once again, the pitching change was made, and Moore was brought in. He was in pain from the shoulder and back injuries that had not healed, but he quickly got in front of Henderson one ball and two strikes. After a low pitch and two foul balls, Moore threw Henderson a fork ball that didn't get down quite far enough. The Red Sox outfielder hit it over the left-field fence to give Boston a 6–5 lead.

But the Angels rallied back. They tied the game in the bottom of the ninth and had the bases loaded with one out. But reliever Steve Crawford retired both DeCinces and Grich without another run scoring. That turned out to be the ball game and the series. The Red Sox scored in the 11th off the tired Moore, and the Angels went out harmlessly in their half. They were done. When the series resumed in Boston the Red Sox romped, 10–4, and then won the final game, 8–1. In neither game did the Angel starter get beyond the fourth inning.

Mauch's decision to replace Witt has been second guessed widely ever since. Strategically, given the Little General's tendency to always play the percentages, it should have come as no surprise. And if Lucas, who had excellent control, had retired Gedman, it would have been another example of Mauch's genius. Witt, after all, had trouble with

Gedman all afternoon and was nearing the end of a pressure-packed game. But the key hitter was Henderson. If Gedman did get on against Witt, he would then be matched against the righthanded hitter whom he had easily handled all afternoon. At that point in the season Witt was a better pitcher than Moore, who was less than healthy.

Moore became a tragic figure in Angel history and lasted only one more year. He was roundly booed by Anaheim Stadium fans for that home run ball, but they didn't remember that the club probably wouldn't have been that close to the World Series without him. On July 18, 1989, the story reached its tragic climax when Donnie Moore took his own life. His agent said that the pitcher never got over Henderson's home run.

It was the last act for the old Angel gang. Before spring training began, Grich had announced his retirement, Burleson had signed with Baltimore, and Jackson with Oakland. Boone had declared free agency also and remained that way until May 1, when he finally re-signed.

The Angels opened the 1987 season with three new players in the lineup—second baseman Mark McLemore, third baseman Jack Howell, and outfielder Devon White. All were products of the much-maligned Angel farm system. In fact, the Angel infield of Joyner, McLemore, Schofield, and Howell was entirely home grown.

The Angels opened the season with a 7–1 victory behind Witt and won eight of their first 11 games. But then disaster struck when McCaskill required elbow surgery after winning his first two decisions. He did not return until July, did not win another game until August 12, and finished 4–6. The rest of the staff unraveled after that. Candelaria suffered severe problems of depression in the spring and was disabled for two months, slumping to 8–6 before being sold to the Mets in September. And Moore was virtually useless, appearing in only 14 games.

The losses put a major burden on the rest of the staff, and it was not up to the challenge. After McCaskill went down, the club went into a tailspin, losing 25 of its next 38 games. The Western Division was so weak that year that no team was entirely out of the race for long, and the Angels got right back into it with a good June. They remained at or above the .500 mark through August when they re-played their early miseries. Only three games behind the Twins and Athletics on September 4, the Angels proceeded to lose 10 of the next 12 and collapsed into the cellar. Only by winning two of their last three games were they able to tie the Texas Rangers for fifth place. The Angel record of 75–87 left them 10 games behind the first-place Twins.

Witt was the symbol of the late season collapse. On August 1 he was 13–6 and unquestionably the ace of the staff, but he won only three games thereafter and finished 16–14. Sutton and Willie Frazier were .500, but both were the victims of too many home run balls. The bullpen was a shambles all season, and only an unexpectedly fine performance by rookie Dewayne Buice with 17 saves made it respectable.

The bright spots amidst the gloomy Anaheim atmosphere were the fine play of Wally Joyner and rookie Devon White. Joyner improved on his 1987 rookie numbers with a team-leading 34 home runs and 117 RBIs, the first time that an Angel had enjoyed back-to-back 100 RBI years. White was a strong candidate for Rookie-of-the-Year honors with his 24 homers and team-leading 32 stolen bases. Boone had a fine year after rejoining the club in May and established a major league record when he caught his 1,919th career game on September 16.

Both Mauch and Port felt that the Angels were a much better team than they had shown. Few steps were taken to strengthen the base during the off-season, the most important being the trade of Pettis to Detroit for pitcher Dan Petry and the signing of free agent outfielder Chili Davis. Petry had been a solid pitcher for the Tigers earlier in the decade but had suffered numerous arm problems during the past two seasons. The Angels had despaired of Pettis ever improving his hitting and finally gave up on him. White would move to center, and Davis would be in right.

The 1988 spring training had begun normally, when Mauch was hospitalized for 15 days and then, nine days before the season began, announced his retirement. His successor was Cookie Rojas, the club's longtime advance scout who had never managed beyond the winter league level. Although there was concern expressed about Mauch's health, the move was generally favored by the players. Mauch managed intensely as befitting his personality; there was little lightness in the clubhouse when he was in command. It wasn't altogether bad as witnessed by his record two division championships and a winning percentage of .519, highest of all Angel skippers. Perhaps Boone summed it up best when he said, "It was great playing for Gene Mauch, as long as you didn't screw up."

Rojas was much more relaxed, and the players seemed to enjoy playing for him. But the results were almost identical to Mauch's own final year. The Angels were 75–87, this time in fourth place instead of sixth, but they were 29 games behind Oakland, who ran away with the division. This 1988 year was a season that resembled a sandwich. The club played poorly for the first two months, then enjoyed a stretch where they were as good as anyone in the league, and finally *Gotterdamerung*, when they lost 18 of their last 20, including a season-ending 12-game losing streak. It was during this period that Cookie

Rojas lost his job; Port fired him on September 22, and coach Moose Stubing guided the club during its last eight defeats.

The season was marked by many curious decisions. The club had acquired second baseman Johnny Ray from Pittsburgh in late August 1987, and his fine hitting relegated Mark McLemore to the bench. In an effort to improve the defense, however, it was announced that Ray would be moved to left field in 1988 with McLemore back at second. But Ray had never played in the outfield before and simply couldn't adjust to the move. After floundering for 47 games, he was moved back to second base, and McLemore ended up in the minors.

There was the usual spate of injuries, but the club seemed to be oblivious to their impact. When Devon White went out for six weeks in May, the Angels relied on minor league retreads Chico Walker and Junior Noboa while releasing veteran Bill Buckner, who could still swing a good bat. And the only addition to a very shaky pitching staff was rookie Terry Clark, who managed a 6–6 record but was hammered in many of his starts.

The pitching was weaker than ever. Witt regressed even further, to a 13–16 record and his worst-ever ERA of 4.15. But that was the best on the staff. The club was next to last with a 4.32 mark. Chuck Finley, Willie Frazier, and Kirk McCaskill were effective at times but not consistently, and McCaskill suffered a recurrence of his elbow problem in August. The bright spot of the pitching staff was Brian Harvey, the Rookie Pitcher of the Year, who became the bullpen ace with 17 saves. He, too, went down with elbow surgery in September, and there was no bullpen behind him.

At season's end there was general discontent among Angel fans and observers. The consensus was that the Port administration had done little to strengthen the team after the disappointment of 1986. Outside of Chili Davis, who had enjoyed a fine season at the bat but was a positive menace in the field, and Wally Joyner, the club had little offensive potential. And the pitching staff was dreadful with few outstanding prospects ready to contribute. An Angel contender was thought to be several years away. This was a gloomy picture indeed, but during the off-season, several events took place which brought the Angels back to life.

The day after the 1988 season ended, the Angels acquired catcher Lance Parrish from Philadelphia. Parrish had been an All-Star performer in Detroit but was unhappy with the Phillies, and the Angels were able to get him at a reasonable price. This proved to be an important move when Boone elected to sign with Kansas City instead of returning to Anaheim. Parrish had more power than Boone and was much younger. Although Boonie was still able to catch 122 games in 1988, there was much question how much longer he could be expected to carry the load.

Exactly one month later the Angels obtained a pitcher they had been seeking for almost 10 years. Bert Blyleven was an Orange County high school star and was very popular among the fans while pitching in Minnesota. He had suffered a poor 10–17 season with the Twins in 1988 and was thought to be at the end of his career. Port thought he would be helpful in a limited role and got him for three minor league prospects. The deal succeeded beyond anyone's expectations. Blyleven stabilized the staff and gave the club a strong performance in almost every appearance. At mid-season he was the club's ace, and perhaps more importantly had become a team leader in establishing a more relaxed and closely knit clubhouse.

The Angels traded for backup catcher Bill Schroeder in December and signed free-agent outfielder Claudell Washington in January. Again, the signing of a free agent veteran was greeted with much skepticism. But Washington was only 34, and his presence enabled the Angels to move Chili Davis to left field, where he was much better defensively. Washington had a good arm as well, and the usual pattern of 1988 when runners routinely raced from first to third on singles to right field would not repeat in 1989.

But the most important move of all had taken place in November when the Angels signed Doug Rader as their manager. He had managed the Texas Rangers in 1983–85 with undistinguished results, and as a player Rader had the reputation of something of a wild man. The hiring was met with deep skepticism by the media, who looked upon Rader as just another managerial retread. But Rader was an exceptionally intelligent man and one who learned from his mistakes. Blyleven's was one of the few voices heard to praise the decision.

In spring training Rader's approach was dramatically different from the one he used in Texas. The atmosphere was much more relaxed, but the work was well organized. The Angels came out of camp with an established pitching rotation. A surprising addition was lefthander Jim Abbott. Drafted out of the University of Michigan in 1988, Abbott had been born with only one hand. This had not hindered him in college ball, but the major leagues were another story. And yet, Rader had confidence that he could make the grade, and when the season began, Abbott was a regular starter.

Jim Abbott was about the only bright spot for an Angels organization that skipped and sputtered its way through the final seasons of the 1980s and the inaugural campaigns of the 1990s. The future seemed optimistic enough by the end of 1989 as Abbott (12–12, 3.92 ERA) ranked among the league's outstanding rookie hurlers, Rader's first seasons brought a strong 3rd place finish and a ledger 20 games over .500, and the signing of $3 million-a-year free agent pitcher Mark Langston (previously with the Montreal Expos) only seemed to brighten the already rosy picture. But the more things changed the more they remained the same for Gene Autry's destiny-bitten Halos. Rader would last but a second full season, his replacement Buck Rodgers offered few solutions for a pitching-rich ballclub cursed with dismal offense and defense, and the on-field record dipped below .500 in 1990 and then crashed to a full 18 games below the break-even point by 1992. For the former silver screen cowboy idol of three decades earlier who had so often ridden his prize horse "Champion" into a Hollywood sunset, there now seemed altogether little prospect that another champion lay anywhere around the next bend or even over the next distant hill.

Annotated Bibliography

The four expansion teams of 1961–62 have a very mixed experience as far as literature is concerned. At the extreme end of the spectrum are the New York Mets, who are rivaled only by the Yankees in number of works done on the franchise. The Angels rank a far distance behind, but there are a few books that are useful in tracking and analyzing this franchise.

Allen, Maury. *Bo—Pitching and Wooing*. New York: The Dial Press, 1973.
Who needs this? It isn't exactly a baseball book but rather a book about a playboy who happened to play baseball and had his antics publicized because he was a baseball player. *Bo* is an offspring of Jim Bouton's *Ball Four* in that it features the after-hours activities of major leaguers. The Angels of 1962–64 are prominently featured with Dean Chance one of the major players.

Bavasi, Emil J., and John Strege. *Off the Record*. Chicago: Contemporary Books, 1987.
This is Buzzy's *apologia*. The emphasis is naturally on his Dodger years, but he includes a chapter on his tenure with the Angels where he modestly takes credit for holding inflation in Angel spending in check and indirectly allows that his efforts brought the Angels their first division championships.

Coberly, Rich. *The No Hit Hall of Fame—No Hitters of the Twentieth Century*. Newport Beach, Calif: Triple Play Publications, 1985.

Dickey, Glenn. *The Great No Hitters*. Radnor, Penn: Chilton Book Company, 1976.
Dickey includes a good chapter on Ryan and a brief description of his four no-hitters as an Angel. Coberly has a game description of all the nohitters, both for and against, in which the Angels were participants, including the box scores and other bits of information.

Jackson, Reggie, and Mike Lupica. *Reggie*. New York: Villard Books, 1984.
One of the major autobiographies on the great superstar, this one has some description of his years in Anaheim and why he chose to sign with the Angels after his successful career with the Yankees.

Newhan, Ross. *The California Angels*. New York: Simon & Schuster, 1982.

This is the major work on the history of the club. Newhan is a very perceptive author who was the beat writer for the Los Angeles *Times* for many years, and as a result, he is very close to his subject. His history focuses on personalities for the most part, and somewhat unevenly. Bo Belinsky warrants almost 10 percent of the book's 191 pages while Nolan Ryan gets a paragraph here and there along with all the other good soldiers. The figure of Gene Autry overrides all else, to the point where one wonders if Autry really exists. There is an attempt here to portray Autry as the West Coast version of Tom Yawkey, that he really is a sportsman at heart, that he really loves his boys and all he wants is to have a winner. Newhan never seems to blame Autry for the major strategy errors. He clearly points out the failure to develop a good farm system as the main reason for the Angels' lack of success over the years but never really indicates where the fault for this decision lies. It is as if some mysterious committee made this decision with Mr. Autry strangely absent. This book is now clearly out of date with much water under the bridge since 1981. If Newhan were to write this book in 1991, one suspects that there would be a major shift to an emphasis on the club's performance on the field and less on the mad cap adventures of the early years.

Pluto, Terry, and Jeffrey Neuman, *A Baseball Winter*. New York: Macmillan and Company, 1986.

This is an interesting description of the inner workings of the front office of four major league clubs during the winter of 1984–85. The Angels are featured with their dealings with the free agency of Fred Lynn.

Robinson, Frank, and Berry Stainback. *Extra Innings*. New York: McGraw-Hill, 1988.

Robinson's view of his relationship with Bobby Winkles is included here, and contrary to Newhan, Frank reports innocent intentions when he joined the Angels.

Ryan, Nolan, and Harvey Frommer. *Throwing Heat*. New York: Doubleday and Company, 1988.

This is a typical baseball autobiography, not very deep and certainly not a work of literary art. But it is very readable and gives a good picture of Ryan the man and Ryan the player. He accepts his skill in a matter-of-fact way that is neither egotistical nor falsely modest. The reasons for his decision not to sign with the Angels after the 1979 season are well stated here, and they are certainly not the conventional wisdom as it appeared in the Southern California press at the time.

Year-by-Year Standings and Season Summaries

Year	Pos.	Record	Pct.	GB	Manager	Player	BA	Player	HR	Player	W-L	ERA
1961	8th	70–91	.435	38.5	Rigney	Pearson	.288	Wagner	28	Bowsfield	11–8	3.73
1962	3rd	86–76	.531	10	Rigney	L. Thomas	.290	Wagner	37	Chance	14–10	2.96
1963	9th	70–91	.435	34	Rigney	Pearson	.304	Wagner	26	McBride	13–12	3.26
1964	5th	82–80	.506	17	Rigney	Rodgers	.243	Adcock	21	Chance	20–9	1.65
1965	7th	75–87	.463	27	Rigney	Fregosi	.277	Fregosi	15	Chance	15–10	3.15
1966	6th	80–82	.494	18	Rigney	Cardenal	.276	Adcock	18	Sanford	13–7	3.83
1967	5th	84–77	.522	7.5	Rigney	Fregosi	.290	Mincher	25	Rojas	12–9	2.52
1968	8th	67–95	.414	36	Rigney	Reichardt	.255	Reichardt	21	Wright	10–6	3.94
1969	3rd	71–91	.438	26	Rigney Phillips	Johnstone	.270	Reichardt	13	Messersmith	16–11	2.52
1970	3rd	86–76	.531	12	Phillips	Johnson	.329	Fregosi	22	Wright	22–12	2.83
1971	4th	76–86	.469	25.5	Phillips	Alomar	.260	McMullen	21	Messersmith	20–13	2.99
1972	5th	75–80	.484	18	Rice	Pinson	.275	Oliver	20	Wright	18–11	2.98
1973	4th	79–83	.488	15	Winkles	Robinson	.266	Robinson	30	Singer	20–14	3.22
1974	6th	68–94	.420	22	Winkles Williams	Rivers	.285	Robinson	20	Ryan	22–16	2.89
1975	6th	72–89	.447	25.5	Williams	Rivers	.284	Stanton	14	Tanana	16–9	2.62
1976	4th	76–86	.469	14	Williams Sherry	Remy	.263	Bonds	10	Tanana	19–10	2.43
1977	5th	74–88	.457	28	Sherry Garcia	Chalk	.277	Bonds	37	Tanana	15–9	2.54
1978	2nd	87–75	.537	5	Garcia Fregosi	Bostock	.290	Baylor	34	Knapp	14–8	4.21

Year	Pos.	Record	Pct.	GB	Manager	Player	BA	Player	HR	Player	W-L	ERA
1979	1st	88–74	.543	+3	Fregosi	Downing	.326	Baylor	36	Frost	16–10	3.57
1980	6th	65–95	.406	32	Fregosi	Carew	.331	Thompson	17	Clear	11–11	3.30
1981	5th	51–59	.464	13.5	Fregosi Mauch	Carew	.305	Grich	22	Forsch	11–7	2.88
1982	1st	93–69	.574	+3	Mauch	Carew	.319	Jackson	39	Zahn	18–8	3.73
1983	6th	70–92	.432	29	McNamara	Carew	.339	Lynn	22	Kison	11–5	4.05
1984	5th	81–81	.500	3	McNamara	Downing	.275	Jackson	25	Witt	15–11	3.47
1985	2nd	90–72	.549	1	Mauch	Carew	.280	Jackson	27	Witt	15–9	3.56
1986	1st	92–70	.568	+5	Mauch	Joyner	.290	DeCinces	26	Witt	18–10	2.84
1987	6th	75–87	.463	10	Mauch	Joyner	.285	Joyner	34	Witt	16–14	4.01
1988	4th	75–87	.463	29	Rojas	Ray	.306	Downing	25	Witt	13–16	4.15
1989	3rd	91–71	.562	8	Rader	Ray	.289	Davis	22	Blyleven	17–5	2.73
1990	4th	80–82	.494	23	Rader	Ray	.277	L. Parrish	24	Finley	18–9	2.40
1991	7th	81–81	.500	14	Rader/Rodgers	Joyner	.301	Winfield	28	Abbott	18–11	2.89
1992	5th(T)	72–90	.444	24	Rodgers	Polonia	.286	Gaetti	12	Langston	13–14	3.66

All-Time Angels Career and Season Records

Career Batting Leaders (1961–1992)

Games Played	Jim Fregosi	1,429
At Bats	Jim Fregosi	5,244
Runs Scored	Brian Downing	5,027
Hits	Jim Fregosi	1,408
Batting Average	Rod Carew	.314
Home Runs	Brian Downing	208
Runs Batted In	Brian Downing	787
Stolen Bases	Gary Pettis	186
Sacrifice Hits	Jim Fregosi	74
Strikeouts	Reggie Jackson	690

Career Pitching Leaders (1961–1992)

Innings Pitched	Nolan Ryan	2,182
Earned Run Average	Bob Lee	1.99
Wins	Nolan Ryan	138
Losses	Nolan Ryan	127
Winning Percentage	Frank Tanana	.567
Strikeouts	Nolan Ryan	2,416
Walks	Nolan Ryan	1,302
Games	Dave Laroche	304
Shutouts	Nolan Ryan	40
Saves	Bryan Harvey	126
Games Started	Nolan Ryan	288
Complete Games	Nolan Ryan	156
Hit Batsmen	Nolan Ryan	56
Wild Pitches	Nolan Ryan	102

Single-Season Batting Records (1961–1992)

Batting Average (502 ABs)	Rod Carew	.339	1977
Home Runs	Reggie Jackson	39	1982
Home Runs (righthanded)	Don Baylor	36	1979
Runs Batted In	Don Baylor	139	1979
Hits	Alex Johnson	202	1970
Singles	Alex Johnson	156	1970
Doubles	Doug DeCinces	42	1982
Triples	Jim Fregosi	13	1968
	Mickey Rivers	13	1975
Slugging Percentage	Doug DeCinces	.548	1982
Extra Base Hits	Doug DeCinces	77	1982
Game-Winning RBIs	Don Baylor	21	1982
Sacrifices	Tim Foli	26	1982
Stolen Bases	Mickey Rivers	70	1975
Pinch Hits	Winston Llenas	16	1973
Strikeouts	Reggie Jackson	156	1982
Total Bases	Don Baylor	333	1979
Hitting Streak	Rod Carew	25	1982
Grand Slam Home Runs	Joe Rudi	3	1978/ 1979

All-Time Angels Career and Season Records *(continued)*

On-Base Percentage	Brian Downing	.420	1979
Hit-by-Pitch	Rick Reichardt	18	1968
	Don Baylor	18	1979

Single-Season Pitching Records (1961–1992)

ERA (150 innings)	Dean Chance	1.65	1964
ERA (100 innings)	Ken Tatum	1.36	1969
Wins	Clyde Wright	22	1970
	Nolan Ryan	22	1974
Losses	George Brunet	19	1967
	Clyde Wright	19	1973
	Frank Tanana	19	1974
Winning Pct. (10 decisions)	John Candelaria	.833	1986
Strikeouts	Nolan Ryan	383	1973
Walks	Nolan Ryan	204	1977
Saves	Bryan Harvey	46	1991
Games	Minnie Rojas	72	1967
Complete Games	Nolan Ryan	26	1973/ 1974
Games Started	Nolan Ryan	41	1974
Shutouts	Dean Chance	11	1964
Innings Pitched	Nolan Ryan	332.2	1974
Home Runs Allowed	Don Sutton	38	1987
Consecutive Games Won (season)	Ken McBride	10	1962
Consecutive Games Lost (season)	Andy Hassler	11	1975
Consecutive Games Lost	Andy Hassler	17	1975/ 1976
Wild Pitches	Nolan Ryan	21	1977
Balks	Chuck Finley	8	1988

7

New York Yankees
Pride, Tradition, and a Bit of Controversy

MARTY APPEL

To tell the history of the New York Yankees is to tell the story of the most successful and celebrated professional sports franchise in America. Its championship seasons far surpass the total for any other team in any sport, while its top players (most notably, Babe Ruth, Lou Gehrig, Joe DiMaggio, and Mickey Mantle) have transcended sports to become household names and part of the nation's social and cultural history. This success has been a product of playing in the nation's most populous city and media center, well-financed management, and the development of a certain aura to the franchise, which has made outstanding young players yearn for the chance to play in the famed pinstriped uniform, in historic Yankee Stadium.

It did not begin on such a plateau. Indeed, when the American League was enjoying its first season in 1901, there was no New York entry, a fact which kept many from considering the new circuit truly "big league." But John Brush, owner of the National League's New York Giants, and his still-involved predecessor Andrew Freedman, had strong political connections and were able to keep the American League from securing a playing site in New York.

In January 1903, after two years of player raids, during which a number of National League stars had jumped to the American League, a peace conference was held at the St. Nicholas Hotel in Cincinnati at which an agreement to coexist was hammered out, putting an end to the raids, and the inevitable higher salaries they brought. As part of the settlement, it was agreed that a New York franchise would be admitted to the American League, pending the securing of a proper playing facility and ownership. At this point, sportswriter Joe Vila introduced American League President Ban Johnson to Frank J. Farrell, 37, who had run three gambling houses and a saloon near New York's West 13th Street police station. Farrell offered cash for the moribund Baltimore franchise, which Johnson was prepared to shift to New York. He took as a partner William S. "Big Bill" Devery, a retired New York police chief, who often frequented the saloon, and who willingly accepted Farrell's payments to turn his back on the gambling operations.[1] Together, Farrell and Devery paid $18,000 for the Baltimore franchise, and managed to lease property from the New York Institute for the Blind, between 165th and 168th Streets and Eleventh Avenue and Ft. Washington Avenue in upper Manhattan, for construction of a playing field and wooden grandstand, at a cost of $300,000. While the Giants still put up a bit of an argument even over the use of that remote site, Farrell and Devery were themselves not without political connections. Thus, despite protests from Washington Heights residents that a ballpark would bring undesirables to the area, the American League landed in Manhattan, even if the subway didn't quite reach their ballpark yet. After all, the trollys did.

The first players to join New York were pitchers Jack Chesbro and Jess Tannehill, both of whom jumped from Pittsburgh before the peace agreement was reached. They had won 47 games between them for the National League champion Pirates of 1902. John McGraw, who had managed Baltimore before jumping to the Giants, took most of his good players with him, leaving Jimmy Williams, Herm McFarland, Harry Howell, and Snake Wiltse as the Oriole players who moved north to New York. Sixteen players whose contract status had been in dispute at the time of the peace agreement needed assignment, and four of them were awarded to New York: Lefty Davis, Dave Fultz, Wid Conroy, and "Wee Willie" Keeler. At 31, Keeler was clearly the "pick of the litter," as he brought a .377 lifetime batting average with him after 11 National League seasons. He was a Brooklyn native, famous for "hittin' 'em where they ain't." He was paid $10,000 a year, tops in the league. Keeler would spend the next seven seasons in New York, winding down a career that would take him to the Hall of Fame.

Another longtime National League star (with Boston) awarded to New York was 37-year-old shortstop Herman Long. Long then figured in the first trade made by the franchise, when, on June 10, 1903, he went to Detroit for Norm "The Tabasco Kid" Elberfeld.

To manage the team, Ban Johnson arranged for Clark Griffith to move over from Chicago, where he had piloted the White Sox the previous two years. A 200-game winner, Griffith, 33, would also take his turn on the mound for New York on occasion, but his greatest fame lie ahead, when he would become owner of the Washington Senators (1920–1955).

Farrell and Devery hired Joseph W. Gordon, a coal dealer, former state assemblyman and, 20 years earlier, the president of the New York Metropolitans of the American Association, to serve as the team's first president, although in fact, he was a mere front figure for the owners. Nevertheless, when Ban Johnson introduced the New York

"Americans" to the press, it was Gordon he introduced. Farrell and Devery were not present.

The team was nicknamed the Highlanders, in part because its wooden ballpark, hastily erected in three months, was at the point of highest elevation in Manhattan (and was nicknamed Hilltop Park), and partly because a famed British Army regiment of the time was called The Gordon Highlanders. The name "Yankees," full of patriotic pride, was used on occasion in that first decade by newspaper editors desperate to find a shorter word than "Highlanders" for headlines. (The name did not formally change to Yankees until 1913 when Hilltop Park was abandoned.) There is a record of the use of "Yankees" in newspapers as early as 1904.[2] The team's uniform was at first black with N and Y on the breasts, and changed frequently. The Y over the N design on shirts and caps was a variation of the Giants design, and pinstripes first appeared in 1915. The current home uniform design, with the NY on the left breast, appeared for good in 1935.

Hilltop Park's center-field fence measured an imposing 542 feet, while it was 365 and 400 down the left and right field lines respectively. Fans in the upper rows, seated on yellow pine, had a fine view of the New Jersey Palisades and the Hudson River, or of a Deaf and Dumb Asylum across the street. There was a scoreboard in left field and an oversized advertising billboard of a bull (for Bull Durham tobacco) dominating the right-field fence.

The Highlanders played their first game on April 22, 1903, losing at Washington 3–1. Their home opener, on May 1, resulted in a 6–2 victory over Washington, with Chesbro getting the victory before a reported overflow crowd of 16,243. The players carried small American flags as they marched onto the field, led by the 69th Regiment Band. Fans, including Ban Johnson, the contractors, the owners of the Senators and the Athletics, and Gordon, waved larger flags, a tribute to the will of the American working man to construct the park in only six weeks time. Johnson threw out the first ball, and umpire Tom Connolly made a short speech.

Hilltop Park (officially, "New York American League Ball Park"), seated only 16,000 and attendance figures were often padded to help capture public attention away from the mighty Giants, but the team claimed an attendance of 211,808 in 1903, while finishing fourth. The Giants, 10 blocks south, announced 579,530 for the year.

While this franchise would go on to enormous success, it would also go 18 seasons before its first pennant, a remarkable dry spell in the eight-team league. In fairness, neither the Browns, Senators, nor Indians fared much better. Its only real run at the title came in 1904, when Chesbro, their 30-year-old spitballing righthander, won 41 games, a twentieth-century record unlikely to be equalled under current conditions. Ironically, a wild pitch on the final day of the season cost Chesbro and the Highlanders the pennant. The loss came at the hands of Boston, which over the years would become the keenest league rival of New York. For nearly two decades, the spitball that got past catcher Jack Kleinow would be the most memorable moment in the franchise's unfolding history. An announced crowd of 28,540 fans jammed Hilltop Park for that first pennant-deciding clash between the two rivals.

The 1905 season saw the arrival of 20-year-old Hal Chase, a heralded first baseman purchased from Los Angeles. Chase was a gifted fielder, still rated one of the best ever at that position, and he became the darling of the fans almost at once. His .323 average in 1906, coupled with Al Orth's 27 victories, gave the Highlanders another second-place finish.

Farrell and Devery dismissed Gordon in 1907, Farrell taking the title of president, and the two owners took a very active role in the daily running of the club. The two would sit by the bench and shout suggestions to Griffith, who, having had enough, resigned in July 1908. Thus began a period of great instability and frequent managerial changes, with little success on the field or at the gate to show for it.

Kid Elberfeld was Griffith's successor, but the team finished last in 1908, and Chase quit the team in September and returned to California to play in an outlaw league. To help woo their star first baseman back, Farrell and Devery dismissed Elberfeld and hired George Stallings for the 1909 season. Stallings hadn't managed in the major leagues in eight years and was ill-prepared for his tempestuous new bosses. Although he had the team in second place in 1910, he resigned with 11 games remaining in the season, and Chase was given the job. (Stallings would go on to manage the "Miracle Braves" to the 1914 National League pennant.) A bright spot in 1910 was the performance of rookie righthander Russ Ford, considered the "Father of the Emory Ball." Ford was 26–6 with eight shutouts that season, and then 22–11 in 1911. Although earned run average was not an official statistic in this era, Ford's computed to 2.54 over his Yankee career, still a team record.

Chase was not cut out to be a manager. He had traits of irresponsibility and recklessness, and was certainly no example for his players. The accepted wisdom of the time was that he was not beyond placing an occasional bet against his own team, and in all likelihood may have attempted to throw more than a game or two over the years. Farrell and Devery, no strangers to gambling themselves, perhaps found a certain charm in this rogue. His name would emerge often during the investigations of gambling in baseball which followed the Black Sox scandal of 1919, and in fact, after that season, Chase never played again. It was felt that Commissioner Landis, while never formally banning Chase, in effect blacklisted him from organized baseball.

Chase managed the team to a sixth-place finish in 1911, a year in which the Highlanders generously shared Hilltop Park with the Giants for six weeks, following a fire at the Polo Grounds. The following year, Chase shed his managerial duties and returned full-time to first base.

By 1913 the team had officially become the Yankees, and, having made peace with the Giants, was now welcomed to the Polo Grounds as a tenant, the 10-year lease having expired at Hilltop. The Hilltop Park era ended with the team having averaged just over 345,000 fans a year, hardly a success and certainly not profitable, unless Farrell and Devery bet against them often enough. The Giants averaged 529,000 during that period and were still the toast of New York, with John McGraw, Christy Mathewson, et al.

To begin their new era in the Polo Grounds, Farrell and Devery reached out to the National League to hire Frank Chance as manager. Chance, part of the legendary Tinker-to-Evers-to-Chance double play combo of the Chicago Cubs, had resigned as Cubs' manager following the 1912 campaign with the intention of retiring. He was persuaded by Yankee ownership to do otherwise.

By 1914 the situation had again deteriorated. Tension grew between Chance and his bosses, while Hal Chase ridiculed Chance behind his back. Chance finally insisted on a trade which sent Chase to the White Sox—it proved to be a terrible deal—and then, in September, tried to slug Devery after a ball game. That night, Chance quit and went home. To finish out the season Roger Peckinpaugh, the 23-year-old shortstop, was given the job. Peck remains the youngest man to ever manage a major league club, although his reign lasted only 17 games.

Chase's own Yankee career lasted eight and a half seasons. His 248 stolen bases remained a team record for 74 years until broken by both Rickey Henderson and Willie Randolph in 1988. The team's single season record of 74 steals was set in 1914 by third baseman Fritz Maisel, and it also stood until Henderson stole 80 in 1985.

The Farrell and Devery era was drawing rapidly to a close. They had given life to a new franchise, but little else. Their 12 seasons of ownership produced an overall record of 861–937 with eight second-division seasons. After weeks of public rumors, they sold the Yankees on December 31, 1914, to Colonel Jacob Ruppert, 47, and Captain Tillinghast L'Hommedieu Huston, 45, for $460,000. Lawyers finalized the final agreement on January 11, and Ban Johnson, tired of a losing franchise in New York, helped to engineer the sale. Ruppert and Huston, equal partners, moved immediately, hiring "Wild Bill" Donovan as manager, acquiring first baseman Wally Pipp from the Tiger organization, and snaring Business Manager Harry Sparrow away from the Giants. Donovan, ironically, had managed rookie Babe Ruth at Providence in 1914. Farrell and Devery went their separate ways, seldom speaking to each other. Devery died virtually penniless on June 20, 1919. Farrell, also broke, died on February 10, 1926.

In Ruppert, the Yankees had a true sportsman at the helm. Inheritor of his father's brewery in Manhattan, Ruppert was a yachtsman, breeder of trotters and St. Bernards, owner of a racing stable, financier of expeditions, and a frequent patron of the Polo Grounds. A lifelong bachelor, he headed his brewery for 42 years, including the period of prohibition when he produced non-alcoholic near beer. He had been appointed a colonel by Governor David Hill of New York in 1889, whom he served as an aide de camp. In 1896 he was elected to his first of four terms in Congress. His real estate holdings were sizable, he was a millionaire many times over, and he was already considering a new ballpark for the Yankees when he bought the team. He had asked to be introduced to Huston when he read in the New York press of Huston's similar interest in purchasing a team.

Huston, a Cincinnati native and close friend of John McGraw, was a civil engineer. He was a captain in the Spanish American War, and headed a construction company in Cuba at war's end. When World War I erupted in 1917, Huston would return to uniform, serving in France and rising to the rank of colonel, joining Ruppert with that title. His absence, however, would give Ruppert strong control over the fortunes of the team and inevitably lead to a parting of the ways between the two strong-willed co-owners.

In three seasons as Yankee manager, Donovan finished no higher than fourth. Still, Pipp emerged as the league's leading home run hitter (with 12 and nine in 1916 and 1917 respectively), and two former Athletics—third baseman Frank "Home Run" Baker and pitcher Bob Shawkey—became strong contributors. Impatient with the lack of pennant contention, Ruppert decided to replace Donovan after the 1917 season. Huston, from France, urged the hiring of Wilbert Robinson, 54, the old Baltimore Orioles player and Brooklyn "Robins" manager, who had won the National League pennant in 1916, but had fallen to seventh in 1917.

Ruppert, however, preferred Miller Huggins, 39, who had finished last managing the Cardinals in 1916, but third in 1917. At only 5'4", "Hug" was diminutive but assertive, and had the backing of Ban Johnson as well. Ruppert signed Huggins and the rift between the two owners never healed. Hug remained a sore point whenever the team faltered, and Huston finally sold his half of the club to Ruppert on May 21, 1923 for $1.5 million, nearly a 650 percent profit in seven years.

A fourth-place finish in the war-shortened season of 1918 produced little promise, but in July 1919, Ruppert obtained pitcher Carl Mays from the Red Sox. This was a deal that wound up all the way in New York State Supreme Court. Mays, who had stormed off the mound in a fit of temper over a perceived lack of support from his teammates, had been suspended by Ban Johnson, who also forbade the Red Sox to trade him. Nonetheless, Boston owner Harry Frazee dealt him to the Yankees. When Johnson halted the deal, the Yankees went to court, receiving an injunction which permitted Mays to play and badly undermined Johnson's power. Although Johnson remained president until 1927, many felt his influence was never again the same after the Mays incident.

While Mays would twice top 25 victories for the Yankees, the real significance of his arrival was that it heralded a period in which Ruppert would entice Frazee to part with Waite Hoyt, Joe Bush, Sam Jones, Everett Scott, Joe Dugan, George Pipgras, Herb Pennock, and Babe Ruth, all key players in the formation of the Yankee dynasty of the 1920s. The fortunes of the two franchises were never again the same, and the "Rape of the Red Sox" still causes Boston loyalists to loathe Frazee.

Of all the trades and sales in baseball history, none was as monumental as the one that brought George Herman Ruth to New York. It was announced on January 5, 1920, with a purchase price variously reported as between $100,000 and $139,000. The previous record sale price had reportedly been $50,000, paid first for Tris Speaker by Cleveland and again for Eddie Collins by Chicago. In addition to the purchase price Ruppert also lent Frazee $350,000 and assumed the mortgage on Fenway Park.

So upset was Boston manager Ed Barrow over this sale, he personally defected to the Yankees on October 29, 1920, following the death of Yankee Business Manager Harry Sparrow. As Ruth's manager in Boston, Barrow had taken the dramatic step of converting him from one of the league's best pitchers to an everyday outfielder. So awesome was Babe's prowess at hitting the long ball, even in a dead ball era, the shift proved too tempting to resist.

Ruth had hit a record 29 home runs in 1919, his first full season in the outfield, nearly triple the runner-up total. The product of an orphanage upbringing, his devil-may-care lifestyle, gregarious personality, insatiable appetite, and barrel-chested physical presence made him a darling of newspapers and newsreels, children and adults. And oh, could he play the game of baseball. In short order, he won over New York, all of baseball, and all of America. He became the most famous of all American athletes, and remains so today, more than a half-century after his playing career ended.

While his arrival would help turn the Yankees into champions, on a larger scale it helped save baseball itself. The game had been tarnished by the rumors of a fix in the 1919 World Series, and the new commissioner, Federal Judge Kenesaw Mountain Landis, had banned eight White Sox players after details were revealed in court the following year. The taint of gamblers mixing with crooked players could have halted America's love affair with professional baseball forever. The stern Judge Landis restored confidence in the game; the Babe restored the fun.

In 1920 Ruth hit 54 home runs, drove in 137 runs, scored 158, and batted .376 with an .847 slugging percentage. In 1921 he homered 59 times, drove in 171, scored 177, batted .378, and had an .846 slugging percentage. Never has a player put together two more spectacular seasons in relationship to the rest of the league.

Ruth's first year with the Yankees did not produce a pennant, but they were only three games out of first and clearly a strong contender. In addition, the arrival of Ruth made the Yankees the first team in baseball history to draw over a million fans in one season, packing 1,289,422 into the Polo Grounds, some 360,000 more than their landlords, the Giants, and more than they would draw into Yankee Stadium to see their other great teams of the 1920s and 1930s. The attendance total stood as an American League record until the Yankees broke it themselves when they topped two million in 1946.

If there was a blemish on the 1920 season, it would be the pitch Carl Mays threw that beaned Cleveland's Ray Chapman on August 16 at the Polo Grounds. Chapman died the next day, the only death in major league history caused by a pitched ball. The Yankees spent much of the remaining weeks of the season defending Mays.

The stage was set in 1921 for the Yankees' first pennant. Barrow obtained Waite Hoyt from Boston as part of an eight-player deal just weeks after replacing Sparrow, and his 19 victories, combined with 18 from Shawkey and 27 from Mays, gave the Yanks a formidable starting rotation. Hoyt, just 21, was a Brooklyn-born product of Erasmus Hall High School, who had originally been signed by the Giants in 1916.

Huggins had an infield of Pipp at first, Aaron Ward at second, Peckinpaugh at short, and Home Run Baker at third. The rifle-armed Bob Meusel, who joined the club in 1920, was joined by Ruth and an assortment of journeymen in the outfield. Wally Schang was behind the plate. This was not quite Murderers Row, but it was the start of the Yankee dynasty. In late September the Yanks hosted the defending-champion Indians, virtually tied for first. Hoyt won the first game, the Yanks rocked the Indians 21–7 in the second, but lost the third 9–0 to slip back to a one-game lead. Huggins started Jack Quinn in the final game of the series, but was forced to bring in Hoyt and Mays in relief. Mays, working with a 4–3 lead in the ninth, loaded the bases and faced Steve O'Neill. Ruppert moved from his box seat to sit in the Yankee bullpen and watch from afar. O'Neill went down on strikes, and the Yanks won. The formality of wrapping up their first flag followed a few days later, and the Yanks prepared to face the Giants in the first World Series ever to be staged with all games in the same park.

Although Ruth's sensational season had made the Yankees the favorites to win easily, it did not turn out that way. Mays and Hoyt hurled identical 3–0 shutout victories to open the best-of-nine Series, but the Giants came back to win Games Three and Four. Hoyt won Game Five, but the Yankees lost Ruth to a bad knee and infected arm, and were without his services for the next three games. They lost them all, and the Polo Grounds would fly the World Championship flag on Giant home games in 1922. It was a blow to the Yanks, but it emphasized the need to build up their supporting cast around Ruth.

Before the 1922 season was a month old, Giants' owner Charles Stoneham sent a letter to Ruppert and Huston indicating that he wished to occupy the Polo Grounds alone, and asking them to find an alternate place for the Yankees to play. Releasing the request to the newspapers, he emphasized that in separate parks the teams would have more attractive Sunday dates available, but clearly, the Yankee popularity had made them unwelcome tenants. And although Ruppert and Huston expressed dismay at the tone of the letter, their sights had been set on a place of their own anyway. In 1920 they had taken an option on a tract of land across the Harlem River in the borough of The Bronx, walking distance from the Polo Grounds, at 161st Street and River Avenue. It covered 10 acres of vacant land, and was formally purchased on February 5, 1921, from the estate of William Waldorf Astor for $600,000.

Osborn Engineering Company of Cleveland was hired to design the new stadium, and White Construction Company did the labor. Ground was broken on May 5, 1922, giving the project less than one year to be completed. What was constructed would become the most famous sports arena in America. Some 2,200 tons of structural steel helped to form a majestic, three-deck ballpark with a copper frieze 16 feet deep from the top of the roof. That handsome "facade" gave the park an architectural distinctness and grandeur. It was promptly named The Yankee Stadium. ("The" was finally dropped by newspapers in the late 1950s.) The total construction cost was estimated to be $2.5 million.

The original plans called for a fully enclosed park, but that idea was abandoned midway through the project. The triple decks ended near the foul poles, with a single deck of wooden bleachers stretching

the length of the massive outfield. The seating capacity was assumed
to be about 80,000, although no one really knew how many could be
packed into those long wooden planks that formed the bleachers.
During the winter of 1927–28, second and third decks would be added
in left center field, with right field to be completed during the 1937
season. Lights were not added until 1946.

The original dimensions of the park were 280 down the left-field
line and 294 to right, but 490 to dead center, 457 to "deep center,"
and 395 to left center, a pasture that came to be known as "death
valley" for the difficulty it posed to right-handed sluggers.[3] The short
fence in right helped create the nickname "The House that Ruth
Built," for it was well tailored to the Babe's power. Of course, Ruth
also "helped build it" because his soaring popularity was a factor in
getting the Giants to send the Yankees packing.

While construction on the new ballpark proceeded, the 1922 season was proving a carbon copy of 1921, at least in terms of the eventual
pennant winners. The Yankees and Giants again came out on top,
although the Yanks margin was just one game over the Browns. Contributing to the closeness of the race was the suspension of Ruth,
Meusel, and Schang by Commissioner Landis for illegal barnstorming
after the 1921 season. They were unable to play in the first 34 games of
the schedule. Further, upon returning, a less than cordial relationship
between Ruth and Huggins began, one which would never totally heal.
It doubtless had to do with Ruth's general feeling toward rules and
authority, and with Huggins' intense desire to maintain unwavering
respect from his charges.

Joe Dugan joined the club in July to take over at third base from
Home Run Baker, and Bullet Joe Bush had a 26–7 record to lead the
American League. But in the Series, the final time the Yankees would
wear home uniforms in the Polo Grounds, the Giants triumphed again,
this time in just five games, with Ruth hitting a disappointing .118.

Opening Day at the new Yankee Stadium was April 18, 1923.
The announced attendance was 74,200, with police estimating that an
additional 25,000 had been turned away. It was by far the largest
crowd ever to witness a baseball game, the previous record considered
to be 42,000 for a 1916 World Series game in Boston. The fans
marvelled at the magnificent three-deck skyscraper of a ballpark,
which would be the last privately financed stadium the major leagues
would know.

Tom Connolly, who umpired the first Highlanders game in 1903,
was assigned to the plate. The pre-game ceremonies included John
Philip Sousa conducting his band, a procession to the flagpole led by
the two colonels, the raising of the American League pennant by
Commissioner Landis (Ban Johnson was said to have the flu), the

first ball ceremony by Governor Al Smith, and the first pitch by Bob Shawkey, bedecked in his trademark red sweatshirt beneath his white pinstripe uniform.

But the day's heroics belonged to Babe Ruth, who properly christened "The House That Ruth Built" with a mighty third-inning home run off Boston's Howard Ehmke, the first in Yankee Stadium history. Prior to the game Ruth had told the press he would "give a year of my life" to hit a homer in the first game at the new stadium. His flair for the dramatic was becoming legendary, and the Yankees won 4–1.

The Yankees' inaugural season in their new home was by all measures a success. The team won its third straight pennant, this one by 16 games, with Ruth hitting a career-high .393, and with newly acquired Herb Pennock going 19–6 to post the top record in the league. Pennock, Sad Sam Jones (21–8), Bush, Hoyt, and Shawkey won 92 of the team's 98 victories. The World Series was a third straight matchup with the Giants, but this time, the Yankees prevailed in six, Ruth belting three homers. The most memorable scene in the series was the sight of 32-year-old Casey Stengel, a Giants' outfielder, racing around the bases (and losing a shoe in the process), to make the first World Series home run in Yankee Stadium an inside-the-park job.

The World Championship established the Yankees as the game's most valuable franchise, a position they would hold for the next four decades. They played in the largest city, had the most dazzling stadium, the game's biggest drawing card, and now, the World Championship. From here on, it would be "Break Up the Yankees!" by fans of the other A.L. cities, although rival owners certainly relished the 11 visits a year the Yankees would pay.

The 1924 Yankees missed a pennant by just two games, but the 1925 Yankees tumbled to seventh. This was also the season in which the team established a spring training base in St. Petersburg, Florida, where they would train through 1961. (They moved to Ft. Lauderdale, Florida, in 1962.) Barnstorming north that year, Babe Ruth became ill with what the New York press called a bellyache. What the overindulgent Bambino actually caught remained whispered gossip for years, but he did in fact undergo surgery for an intestinal abscess, and was out of the lineup until June 1.

That very day (June 1, 1924), a 22-year-old first baseman named Lou Gehrig made a pinch-hitting appearance for the Yankees. A day later Wally Pipp, the team's veteran first baseman, begged out of the lineup, claiming illness. Huggins wrote in Gehrig's name as a replacement. Lou had been signed off the campus of Columbia University by scout Paul Krichell. He was a New York City kid, strong, handsome, and shy. He lived with his parents and had had brief trials with the team in 1923 and 1924. On June 1 he had failed as a pinch-hitter, but on the 2nd, he went three for five with a double, and Huggins put him back in the next day, and the next . . . and the next.

Lou Gehrig would become "The Iron Horse," playing 2,130 consecutive games, on into the 1939 season. Gehrig's streak is today considered baseball's most unbreakable record. Pipp never returned to the Yankee lineup, and Babe Ruth had a cleanup hitter behind him who would help form the game's most prodigious one-two punch ever. They would be the nucleus of "Murderer's Row," the nickname of a lineup that dominated baseball in the 1920s.

The lost season of 1925 ended with Ruth fined an incredible $5,000 by the out-of-patience Huggins, an enormous sum for a man with an increasingly enormous salary. (Ruth's salary would reach $80,000 a year by the decade's end.) Babe had broken training once too often. He was relieved of his duties as team captain after five days and out of respect for his manager, Colonel Ruppert did not rescind the fine until after Huggins' death several years later.

The 1926 season was the first real coming together of the Murderer's Row lineup, now that Mark Koenig was inserted at short and Tony Lazzeri at second. The team roared back to win another pennant, Ruth hitting .372 with 47 homers. The 1926 World Series is best remembered for aging Grover Cleveland Alexander of the Cardinals striking out rookie Lazzeri in a relief appearance in the final game with the bases loaded and the Yanks down by one. Then in the ninth, the score still 3–2 in favor of the Cardinals, Ruth (who hit four homers in the Series) incredulously tried to steal second. St. Louis catcher Bob O'Farrell cut him down, and the Cards prevailed.

This set the stage for the 1927 Yankees, still considered by most to be the greatest team in baseball history. They won 110 games, losing only 44, to finish 19 games ahead of second-place Philadelphia. They went through the entire season without a roster change, using only 25 men. Ruth broke his home run record by belting his 60th on the last day of the season off Washington's Tom Zachery in Yankee Stadium. Gehrig batted .373, adding 47 homers and 175 RBIs, the latter figure tops in the league. (Gehrig's all-time high would be 184 in 1931, a league record.) Leadoff hitter Earle Combs had 231 hits, and like Ruth, hit .356. Combs would soon be the first major leaguer to get 1,000 hits in his first five seasons. The team batting average was .307.

Hoyt led the pitching staff with a 22–7 record, while Pennock and rookie Wilcy Moore each won 19, 13 of Moore's coming in relief. The team never spent a day out of first place.

Legend has it that in the World Series, the Yankees simply stunned the Pittsburgh Pirates while taking batting practice, but true or not, they did beat them in four straight for their second World Championship.

The following season brought Huggins his sixth pennant in eight years, although the New Yorkers blew a 13½ game lead over the Athletics and barely hung on to win by 2½. But Ruth batted .625 and Gehrig .545 (with four homers) in the World Series rematch against the Cardinals, as the Yankees made it two sweeps in a row.

The 1928 season was saddened by the September 9 death of spitballer Urban Shocker, who had gone 18–6 for the great 1927 club. Shocker, only 38, developed heart disease, missed most of the season, and passed away in Denver on a recuperative trip. But the season also produced the debut of a rookie catcher named Bill Dickey, who would form the first link in a succession of great Yankee catchers.

As the Highlanders era had passed into the Polo Grounds era, the first Yankee dynasty period ended in 1929. It ended with the Athletics breaking their streak of pennants, but mostly it ended with the death of Miller Huggins. The little manager had commanded the mightiest and most renowned lineup in the game. They were an undisciplined bunch, but he led them to greatness in spite of themselves. On September 20 a red blemish appeared under his left eye. Unable to manage, he turned over the team to coach Art Fletcher. Five days later, he was dead of blood poisoning at the age of 50.

"A great little guy was Hug," said Ruth at the funeral. Three years later, a monument to Huggins was erected in deep center field in Yankee Stadium. It would later be followed by monuments to Ruth and Gehrig, and then surrounded by plaques honoring other great Yankees. The "Memorial Park" section, as it came to be called in the rebuilt Yankee Stadium of the 1970s, would add even more nostalgia and history to the already majestic ballpark.

Shawkey managed the team in 1930, but for the 1931 campaign, Ruppert and Barrow reached into the National League, and signed Joe McCarthy, recently fired by the Cubs a year after winning the 1929 pennant for them.

What McCarthy brought to the Yankees, aside from another glorious period of championship play, was a discipline and dignity which would brand the organization as one of business-like precision. He made his players wear ties and jackets and had them carry themselves in a strong silent manner with heads held high and the image of Yankee greatness ingrained on all arrivals. Eventually, this would be seen as a cold arrogance by detractors, who would come to see rooting for the Yankees "like rooting for U.S. Steel." But for those who liked the style, it was rewarded by repeated success.

McCarthy won his first Yankee flag in 1932. It marked the last pennant winner for Babe Ruth who, in the World Series, hit his "called shot" home run off Charlie Root of the Cubs in Wrigley Field. The question of whether he actually pointed to the bleachers before homering will be forever debated, although a home movie of the game does seem to indicate that the gesture was made. The Yanks swept the Cubs in four.

Ruth, not really one to embrace McCarthy's hard line of discipline, wound down his Yankee career in 1934. He was released in February of 1935 and signed by the Braves. His dream of managing the Yankees never came to pass, and in fact, he was never offered any position in the organization, save for minor league manager (which he turned down). If it produced a lingering sadness, he did not let it produce bitterness. His two emotional farewell appearances at Yankee Stadium—in 1947 for the retirement of his uniform number 3, and in 1948, shortly before his death from cancer at age 53—were moments that few Americans could watch without a tear.

The Babe hit 659 of his 714 homers as a Yankee, and in 1936 became one of the five charter members of the new Hall of Fame. (Through 1990, 27 men who spent significant portions of their careers with the Yankees had been enshrined in Cooperstown, more than any other team.)

As part of the new top-to-bottom discipline of the Yankee organization in the 1930s, Barrow hired taciturn George Weiss as the team's farm director to build a minor league and scouting system in a fashion developed by the Cardinals' Branch Rickey. Weiss's successes began at Newark, a farm team so strong it was often considered better than some major league teams. The Yankees operated the Newark Bears from 1932–1949. Over the years, other franchises operated by the Yankees provided similar fundamental training, particularly Kansas City, Denver, and Richmond. Emphasis was placed on instruction, and the Yankees were always able to regenerate either by advancing players up the ladder, or by trading a batch of highly rated prospects for a key major leaguer from another club. Prospects were always anxious to sign with the Yankees, not because their salaries were especially higher, but because the promise of a World Series share was always great. In the days before free agency, that could increase a yearly paycheck by around 33 percent.

The McCarthy Yankees were a new looking team in their familiar pinstripes (which, since 1929, bore numbers on the backs, another Yankee "first"). The pitching staff was headed by Red Ruffing and Lefty Gomez. Ruffing, another acquisition from Boston, was only 39–96 lifetime when the Yankees traded Cedric Durst and $50,000 for him in May of 1930. One would hardly figure he could still make the Hall of Fame with that start, but his Yankee record over the next 15 years would be 231–124, and he would win seven of nine World Series decisions. Gomez, a fun-loving southpaw, was purchased from the Pacific Coast League in 1930, and went 189–101 in 13 seasons with a perfect 6–0 record in the World Series, and a 3–1 mark in All-Star Games.

Frank Crosetti in turn came from the Pacific Coast League in 1932 to take over the shortstop position, which he played into 1948. Crosetti then coached for the Yankees through 1968, picking up 23 World Series checks. Red Rolfe arrived in 1934 to assume third base for the next decade, and Johnny Murphy came up the same year and became one of the first great relief specialists in baseball.

But it was the arrival of Joe DiMaggio in 1936 that truly heralded in the next great Yankee dynasty. Indeed, Gehrig had spent only one season out of Babe Ruth's shadow before this most graceful of athletes became a teammate, and in short order, the new standard by which players would be measured.

DiMaggio, a San Francisco native who played minor league ball in his home town, was one of three brothers with big league talent. All clubs were aware of his 61–game hitting streak in 1933. But in 1934, he suffered a knee injury, and interest in him had fallen off. The Yankees' West Coast scouts, Bill Essick and Joe Devine, did not lose hope, however. Essick, particularly, urged Barrow to sign the thin center fielder. For a bargain price of $25,000, the devalued DiMaggio joined the Yanks. He remained at San Francisco in 1935, hitting .398. With Combs ready to retire, the center field job was handed to Joe DiMaggio in 1936.

At 21, DiMaggio debuted with one of the biggest seasons any rookie has ever enjoyed. He batted .323 with 29 homers, 125 RBIs, and 206 hits. He displayed a sure-handedness in vast center field that became classic. His batting eye, especially for a slugger, was amazing. He would go on to hit 361 home runs while striking out only 369 times. His home run total would surely have been much greater had he not been forced to play half his games in Yankee Stadium, where left-field dimensions made it especially nightmarish for right-hand hitters.

The 1936 Yankees rate among the greatest teams of all time. Gehrig belted 49 homers and hit .354. The team average was .300 and they finished 19½ ahead of Detroit. Dickey batted .362, Crosetti scored 137 runs, and Ruffing won 20 games. They faced the Giants in the World Series, and beat them in six, as outfielder Jake Powell batted .455.

DiMaggio hit 46 homers and drove in 167 runs in 1937, outdoing Gehrig's 37 roundtrippers and 159 RBIs, as the Yanks won again in the A.L., before besting the Giants in five for another World Championship. Yet another title came in 1938 as the Yanks swept the Cubs in four after another easy triumph in the regular season.

Jacob Ruppert died of phlebitis on January 13, 1939, at the age of 71. His will left the Yankees to three women—two nieces and a friend, and named his brother George, his nephew, his lawyer, and Barrow as trustees. Barrow was elected club president.

On the field, Gehrig was the story. He had batted only .295 in 1938, and now, in the early days of the 1939 season, his performance was lackluster, his physique withering. Those who knew him well knew something was wrong.

On May 2 in Detroit, having hit only four singles in eight games, Gehrig went to McCarthy and asked to be benched. "It's for the good of the team," he told Marse Joe. Babe Dahlgren was penciled into the lineup, and after 2,130 consecutive games, Gehrig rode the bench. On June 20 the Mayo Clinic in Rochester, Minnesota, issued a report diagnosing Gehrig's illness as a form of polio. It was actually a deterioration of the central nervous system—amyotrophic lateral sclerosis, which came to be called Lou Gehrig's Disease.

On July 4, 1939, the Yankees staged Lou Gehrig Appreciation Day at Yankee Stadium. More than 61,000 fans, plus his 1927 Yankee teammates, assembled to hear Lou say "Today, I consider myself the luckiest man on the face of the earth," as he saw his number four retired, the first such ceremony in baseball history. Ruth, with whom he had at times had a strained relationship, embraced him warmly. The 1927 pennant was raised. Mayor Fiorello LaGuardia spoke, as did Postmaster General James Farley, one of the Yankees' biggest fans, and rumored as a potential buyer of the club.

Gehrig, as team captain, remained with the ballclub the rest of the year in a non-playing capacity. Despite his absence, the Yankees became the first team in history to win four consecutive World Championships, besting Cincinnati in four straight after winning the pennant by 17 games.

By 1940 Gehrig became wheelchair bound, and he passed away on June 2, 1941, at the age of 37. A movie of his life, "The Pride of the Yankees," starring Gary Cooper, is now considered a Hollywood classic.

The 1939 season was the first heard on radio in New York, and the Yankees hired a young Southerner named Mel Allen to assist with the broadcasts.[4] Mel would go on to become the "Voice of the Yankees" through 1964, becoming as famous as the men he described, and himself a Yankee legend. Such was the power of the franchise, many who worked for the team became known and respected by fans: the quiet and efficient clubhouse man Pete Sheehy, who served from 1927 until his death in 1985; the authoritative public address announcer Bob Sheppard, who joined the team in 1951; 20-year public relations director Bob Fishel; team physician Dr. Sidney Gaynor; trainers Doc Woods, Doc Painter, Gus Mauch, Joe Soares, and Gene Monahan; traveling secretaries Mark Roth, Bill McCorry, and Bruce Henry; speaker's bureau director Jackie Farrell; and groundskeeper Jimmy Esposito.

As the Yankees had continued to thrive even during the nation's Great Depression, so too did they enter the ominous days leading to World War II in high style. Local boy Phil Rizzuto was signed to succeed Crosetti at shortstop, and slugging outfielders Charlie Keller and Tommy Henrich came along to flank DiMaggio. Keller, up from Newark, hit .334 in his rookie season of 1939 and batted .438 with three homers in that year's World Series. Henrich, declared a free agent after writing to Commissioner Landis following the 1936 season, was snared by Weiss and brought to the big leagues in 1937. Rizzuto, only 5'6", became baseball's best bunter and the sparkplug of 10 pennant-winning teams.

Joe Gordon, also up from Newark, took over at second from Lazzeri in 1938; Spud Chandler, Atley Donald, and Ernie Bonham joined the pitching staff, and a young Yankee team was prepared to enter the 1940s.

Although their pennant streak ended in 1940, it resumed in 1941, with rookie Rizzuto hitting .307, Keller hitting 33 homers, and Henrich, "Ol' Reliable," belting 31. But the story of the year was the sensational 56-game hitting streak assembled by DiMaggio, beginning May 15 and running through July 17 when Indian pitchers Jim Bagby and Al Smith finally stopped DiMaggio in Cleveland. (He then hit in the next 16 straight for 72 out of 73.) The streak had "Joltin' Joe" the talk of the nation, and although Ted Williams batted .406, DiMag won the league's MVP award.

The 1941 World Series provided the first matchup between the Yankees and the Brooklyn Dodgers. The most memorable moment of the pairing was an apparent strikeout by Henrich which would have given the Dodgers a victory and tied up the Series. Instead, it was a passed ball for catcher Mickey Owen; Henrich reached first safely, and the Yankees rallied for four runs and a 7–4 win. They won the next day for their 9th World Championship.

With the war beginning to deplete major league rosters, the Yankees still won again in both 1942 and 1943. In 1942, basically at full strength, they won the pennant by nine games but lost the Series to St. Louis, their only Series loss under McCarthy. In 1943 they were without such stars as DiMaggio, Rizzuto, Henrich, George Selkirk (Ruth's successor), and Ruffing, but still managed to win by 13½ games. Chandler was 20–4 with a 1.64 ERA; Nick Etten led the team with 107 RBIs as the new first baseman; Billy Johnson at third and

Johnny Lindell in the outfield were strong new additions, and Keller hit 31 homers. Dickey, at age 36, batted .351 in 85 games. The Yanks avenged their Series loss of 1942 with a five-game triumph over the Cardinals. Etten led the league in homers in 1944 and in RBIs in 1945, but these were wartime seasons while baseball awaited the return of the soldiers.

On January 25, 1945, ownership of the team passed from the Ruppert estate to a three-man group of Larry MacPhail, Dan Topping, and Del Webb for $2.8 million. MacPhail, 53, was the best known of the trio, having headed teams in Cincinnati and Brooklyn. Flamboyant and innovative, he believed strongly in promotion. He made Old Timers Day an annual Yankee Stadium event. Topping, just 30, was a wealthy young sportsman who had owned the Brooklyn Dodgers and New York Yankees football teams of the All-America Conference. Webb, 45, was owner of a major construction and real estate development company.

McCarthy and MacPhail did not hit it off well from the first. The manager resented the 1945 sale of Hank Borowy, one of his best wartime pitchers, to the Cubs. Claiming that his nerves were acting up, McCarthy took an unusual three-week sabbatical to his Buffalo farm. He offered his resignation after the season, but MacPhail convinced him to return.

Barely had the 1946 season begun when McCarthy did resign. Claiming that his gallbladder was acting up and on the advice of his doctor, he went home 35 games into the campaign, eight pennants and seven world championships behind him. Most players who passed his way during his 16 Yankee seasons claimed he was the best they had ever played for.

Dickey managed the team for the next 105 games, but resigned when he wasn't offered a longer deal. Coach Johnny Neun finished out the lackluster season, which was a success only at the gate. The post-war attendance boom and MacPhail's promotions, including the first night games at Yankee Stadium, had brought 2,265,512 to the Bronx, the first time a big-league team ever reached two million.

MacPhail, clearly the controlling partner, hired 50-year-old Bucky Harris to manage the Yanks in 1947. Harris, as the "Boy Wonder" playing-manager of the Washington Senators, had won pennants in 1924 and 1925, but his 20 seasons of managing since that time had been decidedly mediocre, with few first-division finishes. He was being handed the plum assignment in all of baseball, but most experts figured he was not up to it. "Nice guy, but in over his head," went the wisdom.

Instead, Harris brought the Yankees back to the top, finishing 12 ahead of Detroit. George McQuinn, playing first, hit .304, bettered only by DiMaggio's .315, and Joe Page, starring in relief, won 14 and saved 17 (a statistic not yet officially recorded). The season produced three new faces who figured to stick around for awhile—Yogi Berra, Allie Reynolds, and Vic Raschi.

Berra, 22, was an unlikely looking but extremely gifted athlete. Just 5'7" and 185 pounds, with a propensity to make contact with bad pitches, he had a great Yankee Stadium swing and the tutelage of Bill Dickey to learn catching. Just out of the Navy, Berra hit 11 homers in 83 games, dividing time between the outfield and home plate.

Reynolds, 32, came to the Yankees from Cleveland for Joe Gordon, whom the Yanks successfully replaced at second with Snuffy Stirnweiss. Reynolds was 19–8 in his first Yankee season. Raschi, 28, had been on option to Portland when he was called up in 1947. A year later, they would be joined by slow-pitching lefty Ed Lopat, 30, obtained in a trade with the White Sox. Reynolds, Raschi, and Lopat would be to this era what Hoyt, Pennock, and Shawkey had been to Murderer's Row.

The Yanks met the Dodgers in the 1947 World Series, a Series distinguished by Berra hitting the first World Series pinch-hit homer; by Al Gionfriddo making a sensational catch off DiMaggio in deepest left center; by Bill Bevens, a 7–13 regular season pitcher, coming within one out of the first World Series no-hitter (Cookie Lavagetto's pinch double foiled the bid, as well as the victory); but in the end, the Series was memorable because of another World Championship for New York, their 11th.

And the fireworks were not over. At the party celebrating the new title, the fiery MacPhail belted both Weiss and Topping, firing the former, and announcing to the press that he was quitting baseball. He was true to his word; he sold his one-third interest to Topping and Webb for $2 million, and never returned to the game.

As for Weiss, he was immediately rehired as general manager and given more authority than ever. Barrow retired at 79, and basically, the team was Weiss' to run. Topping oversaw the business from a quiet office at 745 5th Avenue; Webb showed up only at World Series time. This put the handwriting on the wall for Harris, MacPhail's man. A third-place finish in 1948, despite staying in contention into the final weekend, effectively meant he was gone, and Weiss would choose his own man.

The man turned out to be Charles Dillon "Casey" Stengel, who was about 60; no one knew his age for sure. Many saw this as some sort of joke. Weiss was the embodiment of the cold, corporate image of the overly successful Bronx Bombers. Now he was hiring a man who had let a bird fly out from under his cap; a man who had played for the Daffyness Boys of Uncle Robbie (Wilbert Robinson) in Brooklyn; a man with a long history of second-division finishes as a National League manager. Yes, he had won the Pacific Coast League pennant in 1948 at Oakland, but it was seen as insignificant, given the task before him.

Off the field, Stengel did nothing to dampen the clownish image he had cultivated, speaking a doubletalk the press called "Stengelese." But in the dugout, his new genius took hold. Given the talent, he proved to be a master at getting the best out of everyone. He developed a "two-platoon system," rotating lefties and righties in and out of the lineup, recharging castoffs from other teams into useful roles, and coaxing along young, talented, but undisciplined prospects with a fatherly touch.

All he did, in the glare of the national spotlight, in the face of incredible pressure to win or be fired, was to lead the Yankees to an unprecedented five consecutive World Championships in his first five seasons, 1949–1953.

Almost at once, using outfielders Gene Woodling and Hank Bauer as his prime examples of platooning, he began to work wonders with unpredictable lineups. He took Johnny Mize from the Giants and got five years of pinch-hitting excellence from him. He added New York-bred Whitey Ford to the rotation of Raschi, Reynolds, and Lopat, and then turned Reynolds into a solid relief man. He played Jerry Coleman and Gil McDougald at all the infield spots, brought Billy Martin from Oakland to play second, sampled Jackie Jensen, Bobby Brown, Joe Collins, and Henrich in and out of the lineup, and turned Berra into an everyday player.

The 1949 season was exemplified by DiMaggio's return to the lineup in July after missing 65 games following heel surgery. He hadn't faced live pitching in nine months, save for one tuneup exhibition against the Giants, but he belted four homers in three big games at Fenway Park to lead a key mid-season sweep of the Red Sox, who were now managed by Joe McCarthy. The Yanks, slowed by 71 injuries during the year, wrapped it up at season's end by beating Boston twice more at Yankee Stadium, when a loss in either game would have meant a Red Sox pennant. The first crucial contest was played on Joe DiMaggio Day before 69,551 fans, with New York overcoming a 4–0 deficit to win 5–4. The next day Raschi beat Ellis Kinder 5–3 for the pennant-clincher. Then Stengel's men beat Brooklyn again in the World Series.

In 1950 Rizzuto batted .324 and won the MVP award, and Whitey Ford won nine straight when called up from Binghamton, in late June. Ford also won the fourth and deciding game of a World Series sweep over Philadelphia. Whitey Ford was already proving to be one cool customer.

In 1951 Reynolds hurled two no-hitters, Raschi won 21 for the third straight season, Berra won his first of three MVP awards, and the Yanks stopped the Giants in the Series, despite the euphoria surrounding Bobby Thomson's pennant-winning homer at the Polo Grounds. Rizzuto's bases-loaded squeeze bunt on September 17 against the Indians was the season's big hit, while Reynolds' second no-hitter clinched a tie for the pennant 11 days later, with Raschi winning the pennant-sealer in the nightcap.

Stengel's biggest task was overseeing the transition of Yankee glory from Joe DiMaggio to Mickey Mantle in 1951. DiMaggio was no admirer of Stengel, but he gave him his all until a painful heel spur forced his retirement after the 1951 season. He had been the league's first $100,000 player (1949), and could have kept going, but his pride refused to allow him to play at less than 100 percent.

Mantle, signed out of Commerce (Oklahoma) High School as a shortstop by scout Tom Greenwade, reached the majors at 19, with a combination of speed and switch-hitting power never before seen. He was moved to the outfield in spring training of 1951 and groomed as DiMaggio's successor, no easy burden for a teenager. Indeed, he had to go back to the minors for a time during his rookie season. And then in the 1951 World Series, he fell on a drain in right field, wrecked his knee, and was destined to spend the rest of his playing-days fighting off career-threatening injuries. Mantle's father died that year, and Stengel became like a father to him, although not so strict as to cut down on his after-hours escapades with Ford and Martin.

Reynolds was 20–8 in 1952, Berra's 30 homers set a record for A.L. catchers, and the Yanks won 15 of their last 18 to win their fourth pennant in a row. Mantle answered the challenge of replacing DiMaggio with a .311 season, and then batted .345 in the World Series. The Yanks faced the Dodgers again, beating them in seven when Billy Martin made a circus catch in the seventh inning of the final game on a little popup by Jackie Robinson.

The 1953 season brought with it an 18-game winning streak, and a 12-hit performance by Martin in the World Series victory over the fortune-wracked "wait 'til next year" Dodgers. That made it five in a row, breaking the Yankee record of four straight world championships set in 1936–37–38–39.

When the streak ended in 1954, there were few recriminations for the Yanks. After all, Cleveland set a record of 111 victories, and the Yanks, in finishing second, won 103, their high-water mark under Stengel. After the season, the Yanks and Orioles pulled off a record 17-player trade, which brought pitchers Bob Turley and Don Larsen to New York.

Occasionally during the 1954 season, civil rights activists would form picket lines around Yankee Stadium, protesting the lack of a black face on the Yankee roster. The Dodgers had integrated in 1947, the Giants in 1949. The Yankees claimed no prejudice, but were clearly dragging their feet on this issue. Vic Power, a genuine prospect owned by the Yanks, was considered "too flashy" to be the first black Yankee, although it was never the Yankee style to seek out anyone too flashy, black or white.

At last in 1955, the club was integrated by the addition of Elston Howard to the roster. A gifted outfielder-catcher, Howard had batted .330 at Toronto in 1954 and earned the shot. He would make the most of it, eventually winning an MVP award, replacing Berra at catcher, and playing for nine pennant winners.

The 1955 season was the Yanks' first without the Reynolds-Raschi-Lopat pitching staff, but Ford won 18 and Turley 17, while Mantle led the league with 37 homers, and Berra's 108 RBIs helped him snare another MVP award. Sophomore first baseman Bill "Moose" Skowron contributed a .319 average. That season also represented the sixth "Subway Series" meeting between the Yankees and Dodgers. This time, after five setbacks, the Dodgers triumphed, Johnny Podres winning the seventh game, and Brooklyn could at last celebrate a World Championship.

The campaign of 1956 was the season in which Mantle finally put it all together. He won the triple crown, threatening Ruth's homer record (he wound up with 52 homers), took his first MVP award, and became baseball's unquestioned "pinup boy." His .353 average and .705 slugging percentage captivated the nation. He hit three homers in the World Series, again against Brooklyn, but this time the October stage belonged to Don Larsen. A rather ordinary pitcher by statistical standards, Larsen merely pitched the most celebrated game in baseball history in Game Five, on October 8. Not only was it the first no-hitter in World Series history, it was in fact a perfect game, the first in baseball in 34 years. Johnny Kucks' shutout in Game Seven, to gain revenge for the 1955 final-game loss, would be overshadowed in memory by Larsen's amazing fling with perfection.

Thus the last Subway Series was played, with the Dodgers and Giants bound for California after the 1957 season, leaving the Yankees as the lone New York club until the formation of the Mets in 1962. The great fall matchups between the Dodgers (later named the "Boys of Summer") and the Stengel-led Yankees, and to another extent, the three-team New York rivalry which showcased three future Hall of Fame center fielders named Willie Mays (of the Giants), Duke Snider (of the Dodgers), and Mickey Mantle (of the Yankees), made the 1950s a very special time to be a baseball fan in New York. There was, after all, a World Series in New York in every year between 1949–1958.

The Yanks won pennants in both 1957 (Mantle hitting .365) and 1958, facing the Milwaukee Braves in both World Series. They lost three times to Lew Burdette in 1957 as the Braves won in seven, and then came back from a 3–1 deficit to recapture the World Championship in 1958. Bob Turley, that year's Cy Young Award winner, won two and saved one to become the Series hero as well.

The 1959 season was really the only disappointing one Stengel had. The team finished third, but only four games over .500. After the season the Yanks made one of their many trades with the Kansas City Athletics and obtained Roger Maris to play right field. Maris hit 39 homers in 1960 and edged Mantle for MVP honors. But in the thrilling 1960 World Series, Stengel's 10th in 12 seasons, a bottom-of-the-ninth-inning homer in Game Seven by Pittsburgh's Bill Mazeroski sent the Yanks to defeat, despite the fact that New York outscored the Pirates 55–27, and out-hit them .338 to .256.

Topping and Webb, generally "hands-off" owners, called a press conference five days after the 1960 Series and stunned the baseball world by announcing that Stengel was retiring. In point of fact, he was being fired. It was said he was too old, and that he had managed poorly in the Series. It was said also that the Yankees would lose his heir apparent, coach Ralph Houk, to the Red Sox if they didn't act quickly. Stengel went out bitter over his treatment, and the cold, corporate stuffiness of the Yankee image reared its ugly head. A month later, Weiss would be gone as well, replaced by Roy Hamey. These two, of course, would gain revenge in the worst way: they would be hired to run the Mets when that franchise began operations. And they would turn the Mets into loveable losers, winning over the old Dodger and Giant fans when the Yankees could have "owned" the city. By their third season, the Mets even outdrew the Yanks.

Houk, one of many catchers in the organization who had played a mere backup role to Berra, had been a successful minor league manager and Yankee coach, but was pretty much an unknown quantity when he took over in 1961. Little did he know, especially when the team went 9–19 in spring training, that he had before him a team which would take its place among the great Yankee teams of all time.

The 1961 season was marked by expansion to 10 teams, and with it, a schedule increase from 154 games to 162. Houk's first major action was to move Whitey Ford into a regular four-day pitching rotation. Whereas Stengel had used Ford more cautiously, picking his spots, Ford was now the focal point of the staff. Elston Howard nicknamed him "The Chairman of the Board," and he responded with not only his first 20-victory season, but a 25–4 record, 209 strikeouts, and the Cy Young Award. Luis Arroyo was the league's best relief pitcher (15 wins, 29 saves), and Ralph Terry was 16–3. Houk took a chance on two unproven youngsters, Bill Stafford and Rollie Sheldon, and they added 25 victories to what would total 109 in all.

Houk also earned the support of three gifted infielders—second baseman Bobby Richardson, shortstop Tony Kubek, and the brilliant-fielding third baseman Clete Boyer. Richardson and Boyer had felt particularly short-shifted under Stengel's platoon system. Now, as everyday players, they shone.

But it was power that distinguished the 1961 Yankees. Six players topped 20 homers, including three catchers—Berra (22), Howard (21), and Johnny Blanchard (21)—although by now Howard had become the regular (he batted .348) and Berra played 87 games in the outfield. Skowron, the number seven hitter in the lineup, belted 28 homers and drove in 89 runs.

The team hit a record 240 home runs in 1961, with Maris and Mantle combining for 115 of them, the most ever belted by two team-mates. All summer long, the "M & M Boys" waged an assault on the sacred record of 60 by Babe Ruth. The whole nation followed their progress, watching daily newspapers which charted how many games ahead of Ruth's pace they were.

Mantle, the 11-year veteran, was the popular choice, if someone had to break the mark. Indeed, the season marked the end of the occasional booing he would suffer at the Stadium, never quite measuring up to DiMaggio in some fans' eyes. He would now become the game's most popular player for the remainder of his career, both in New York and on the road.

Maris, only 26, and only a second-year Yankee, could be surly with the press and unsmiling on the field as he went about his pursuit of the record under incredible pressure. With each passing day, the press corps would mount, testing his patience with their need for daily interviews. The fans not only supported Mantle, but rooted against this newcomer taking on The Babe. To top it off, Commissioner Ford Frick, a one-time ghost writer for Ruth, ruled that if the record was to be broken, it would have to come in 154 games, not 162.

Against all of these odds, Maris persisted. By the end of July, he had 40 (one other had been rained out), Mantle 39. In September injuries finally slowed Mantle, who wound up with a career-high 54. But Maris pressed on, hitting his 59th in game 154, his 60th in game 159, and his record 61st on the season's final day, October 1, game 162, in Yankee Stadium off Boston's Tracy Stallard. His mark would be listed separately from Ruth's, a decision which grew increasingly unpopular over the years, as no one, even with the benefit of eight extra games, would challenge the record for more than the next quarter-century. By the time Maris died of cancer in 1985, he had at last earned a beloved hero image among Yankee fans.

The five-game victory in the World Series over Cincinnati was considered anti-climactic. As if Ruth didn't have a bad enough year, Ford broke his Series record for consecutive scoreless innings, 29⅔ (which Ruth had set while with the Red Sox), running his streak to 32.

There was really no encore which could match the success of 1961. In 1962 Maris "slumped" to 33 homers and was called the "Flop of the Year" by a wire-service. He never recaptured the magic of that home run stroke of 1961, but remained a very good player, particularly in right field. Led by Terry's 23 victories, Richardson's 209 hits, and Mantle's third MVP season, the Yanks won their 27th pennant and 20th World Championship. (Richardson's catch of Willie McCovey's liner for the last out of the seventh game set the Giants down.) Four rather flamboyant rookies made the club that year—Joe Pepitone, Phil Linz, Jim Bouton, and Tom Tresh—players who might have previously been passed by as not in the "Yankee image." Things were changing, but little did anyone realize that the next World Championship would be 15 years in coming.

The first shock wave hit in 1963. Skowron was traded to the Dodgers to accommodate Pepitone at first, and the Yankees won the pennant easily. But behind the pitching of Sandy Koufax, Don Drysdale, and Johnny Podres, the Dodgers (now based in Los Angeles) stopped the Yankees in four straight in the World Series. It was a humbling setback.

With three pennants in three years, Houk moved up to become general manager in 1964, and named Berra to manage. Yogi, popular with fans, was also popular with his teammates, and he found discipline difficult. With the pennant slipping away from them in September, he finally lashed out on a team bus, slapping a harmonica out of Linz's hands after a tough loss. The Yanks were 22–6 in September and edged the White Sox by one game, but then lost the Series in seven to St. Louis. In what was almost a repeat of the callous Stengel firing, the Yankees then fired Berra, and replaced him with Johnny Keane, the winning St. Louis manager. This outraged the fans, given that Berra had won everything but the seventh game, and was, of course, a Yankee hero.

There was more big news coming. After 20 seasons and 15 pennants, Topping and Webb were getting out. On November 2 they announced the sale of 80 percent of the team to Columbia Broadcasting System, CBS, the broadcasting company operated by William Paley, for $11.2 million. Webb sold his remaining 10 percent on March 1, 1965, for $1.4 million, and Topping yielded his 10 percent on September 19, 1966, to make the total sale price $14 million. This would mark the first time in which a corporation, rather than a wealthy "sportsman," would own a major league team, although many of the individual owners had amassed fortunes through corporate ownership.

Not only were Topping, Webb, and Berra now gone, Mel Allen was fired as the team's top announcer, long-time sponsor Ballantine Beer dropped out, and the great players somehow all seemed to get old overnight, with no replacements in sight.

Mantle's last great season, at age 32, was behind him. Maris, with a painful hand injury, was out much of the time. Keane had walked into a team that was about to collapse around him. The farm system had dried up. The 1965 institution of the free-agent draft of amateur player had brought to a close the Yankees' ability to sign anyone they chose to.

The team finished sixth in 1965, and dead last in 1966, their first cellar finish since 1912. Keane was fired in May; Houk returning to the field to manage. But it was to no avail; this team would now become an occasionally mediocre, occasionally bad ballclub, for the next decade.

Kubek retired after 1965, Richardson after 1966, the Yanks getting nothing for them. Boyer, Howard, and Maris were traded, with little in return; Ford retired in 1967, and finally, after the 1968 season, Mantle quit. He had batted only .254 with 82 homers in his last four seasons, the final two spent at first base. While he had spent his career battling injuries, he had played more games than any Yankee in history, 2,401. But he was only 36 when he retired, and when he saw his contemporaries—Mays, Hank Aaron, and others, play into their 40s, he came to regret not taking better care of himself. Still, he enjoyed enormous popularity, and his "Day," in 1969, was an emotional outpouring of love. His 536 home runs were the most ever by a switch-hitter, and his 18 Series homers were a record as well.

Presiding over these glum years were erudite Mike Burke, a dashing CBS executive put in charge of this division of the company, and Lee MacPhail, the son of Larry, a former Yankee farm director, and most recently, general manager of the Orioles and an aide to the commissioner. Burke was president, MacPhail general manager. If nothing else, Burke's mod style eased much of the club's longstanding stuffy image. The Stadium got a coat of white paint, promotion days covered the home schedule, and occasionally, a good player would appear. Mel Stottlemyre was as good as any Yankee pitcher during the glory days, and a three-time 20-game winner. Bobby Murcer and Roy White were solid outfielders.

Horace Clarke was a much maligned second baseman, mostly for his longevity during this dry spell. No one better came along, and Horace, an average player, became the familiar symbol of a team going nowhere. The club finished a distant second in 1968, and challenged into September of both 1972 and 1973, but by then, expectations were low, and the Mets were the more popular club in town. The Mets outdrew the Yankees each season between 1964–1975, spanning the opening of Shea Stadium to the opening of the new Yankee Stadium.

The low point for the franchise had to be September 22, 1966, when the cellar-dwelling team drew 413 fans to a weekday makeup game at the Stadium. Announcer Red Barber's insistence that the cameras show the empty seats helped cost him his job at season's end.

Not only was the team crumbling, so was Yankee Stadium. From a distance it still looked majestic, but up close it was decaying along with the neighborhood. Burke had a good rapport with New York Mayor John Lindsay, and together, they devised a plan to purchase the land and the structure (owned respectively by the Knights of Columbus and Rice University), condemn it, and spend $24 million to modernize it and the surrounding highways and parking areas. The cost would actually soar to over $100 million, and it would become a municipally owned facility, leased to the Yankees.

CBS executives were not unwilling to spend the money for star players. It was an entertainment company that understood the star system. The demise of the Yankee empire was a source of great embarrassment to it. CBS had purchased the team for the prestige of owning the most celebrated sports franchise in America.

By 1973 they were prepared to swallow their pride and unload the team, even at a loss. If a team had ever been sold at a depreciated value, there was no record of it. For a price of just $10 million, CBS sold the team to a group of investors headed by Burke himself, and George M. Steinbrenner III, 42, a Cleveland shipbuilder who had been an assistant college football coach at Purdue and Northwestern universities, and a part owner of the Chicago Bulls basketball team. He had entered his family-owned business in 1957 and built it into the American Shipbuilding Company (which he later moved to Tampa).

Burke, told he could buy the club, had sought a group to back him, and was introduced to Steinbrenner by Gabe Paul, general manager of the Indians. What was not anticipated was that Steinbrenner would bring Paul along as one of the limited partners, with the obvious intention of letting him run the team. Somehow, in the haste to consummate the deal, Burke never did understand this. When the so-called "limited partners" were introduced a week after the sale announcement, Burke was in shock. Within 12 weeks he resigned, leaving with a nice percentage of ownership for his troubles, but without ever achieving any success on the field with the team.[5]

Steinbrenner, at the press conference of January 3, 1973, backed the leadership of Burke, MacPhail, and Houk, and told reporters "I'll stick to building ships." That phrase often came back to haunt him, for in fact, he became the most active owner in the game, and certainly in the franchise's history. While at various times different people would hold the title of general manager or even president, "The Boss" was always clearly in charge.

Houk, unaccustomed to an involved owner he considered "not a baseball person," resigned after the 1973 season. His second reign with the Yankees had been a failure, and he was constantly booed by the fans in his final year.

MacPhail became American League President in 1974, clearing the way for Gabe Paul to become general manager. This also coincided with a two-season suspension of Steinbrenner by Commissioner Bowie Kuhn, related to a conviction for making illegal contributions to Richard Nixon's 1972 presidential campaign.[6]

Paul, nearly a 40-year major league executive, had never had a lot of money to work with. Now he had an owner with deep pockets and a mandate to build a winner. Although the league had long sought to "break up the Yankees" during their glory years, it actually missed having a big New York attraction with superstars and box office might. The Yankees remained a top road draw all during the CBS years, but it was the uniform drawing the customers, not the men wearing it.

Besides White, Murcer, and Stottlemyre, the rebuilding of the Yankees began with the drafting of catcher Thurman Munson in 1968. In 1972 MacPhail obtained the flamboyant relief ace Sparky Lyle from Boston, and at season's end, third baseman Graig Nettles from Cleveland. These were the six key players he passed on to Paul, who had actually sent Nettles to New York as his last act in Cleveland.

After the 1974 season, in which the Yankees went down to the final weekend before elimination, they traded Murcer, their most popular player, to San Francisco for the gifted Bobby Bonds. After just one season, Bonds went to the Angels for speedy center fielder Mickey Rivers and starting pitcher Ed Figueroa.

If there was a single moment in which the fortunes of the team changed for the better, however, it would have to be New Year's Eve of 1974. That night, the great chase for Jim "Catfish" Hunter ended. He was the first of the millionaire free agents, cut loose by an arbitrator who ruled that Oakland owner Charles Finley breached his contract by making late payments. Every club went after Hunter, but the Yankees won him, signing him to a record five-year contract worth some $3.5 million.

Hunter had just helped the Athletics to three straight World Championships, winning over 20 games each time. He "knew how to win," had leadership qualities, and demonstrated that the Yankees now meant business. While Hunter would have only one 20-win season of his five in New York, his presence seemed to turn the team around. The players saw Hunter, and they believed in themselves.

Paul continued making sound trades. He got Lou Piniella from Kansas City, Chris Chambliss from Cleveland, Willie Randolph from Pittsburgh, and Bucky Dent from Chicago. Many accused the Yankees of playing checkbook baseball, but they ignored Paul's skills at spinning deals. And in truth, Steinbrenner was not among the wealthiest owners in the game; he was just more willing to pay whatever the price tag seemed to be in his desire to win.

The minor leagues ceased to serve as a development arm for the Yankees. Rather, players were developed there to be bundled off to other organizations for established players. A long exception who slipped through in the 1970s was a thin lefthander named Ron Guidry, but termed "Louisiana Lightning."

After two seasons as tenants of the Mets in Shea Stadium, the new Yankee lineup came together by the time the new Yankee Stadium was dedicated on April 15, 1976.

The "new" Yankee Stadium retained its outer shell, but lost all of the pillars which obstructed views. The upper deck went higher and deeper, making it even more difficult to hit a fair ball out of the park, something which had never been done. The famous facade design was retained as the border of the scoreboard and advertising behind the bleachers. Right field went from 296 feet to 310; center field came in from 461 to 417, and left field went from 301 to 312. "Death Valley" went from 457 to 430, then in 1985 was shortened to 411, and in 1988, came down to 399.

Eighty-five-year-old Bob Shawkey returned to throw out the first ball; Mrs. Babe Ruth and Mrs. Lou Gehrig were on hand, as were DiMaggio and Mantle, fixtures at any nostalgic day in Yankee Stadium. (DiMaggio had made every Old Timers Day gathering between 1952 and 1987, finally missing one during recuperation from a hospital stay.)

The new manager was Billy Martin, 47, who had taken over the club late in the 1975 season from Bill Virdon. Martin, a pet of Stengel's in the 1950s, had been traded from New York in 1957 following a nightclub brawl. More than anyone who ever played for the Yankees, Martin wore the uniform like a college fraternity jacket. Although nearly 20 years had passed, he had never stopped loving the uniform or the team. He had managed, and been fired, at Minnesota, Detroit, and Texas, but his dugout skills were unquestioned, and he always carried the Yankees in his heart. To Steinbrenner, who equally embraced the team's mystique, Martin was a perfect choice.

Martin was also a brilliant tactician, and he wound up leading the Yankees to a rather easy Eastern Division title in 1976, with the team drawing over two million, with Nettles leading the league in homers, and with Munson winning the MVP award in his first year as Yankee captain. (He was the first captain since Gehrig.) A dramatic, last-of-the-ninth pennant-winning homer by Chambliss against Kansas City in the League Championship Series gave the team its first pennant in 12 years, setting off a near-riot on the field among jubilant fans. But the "Big Red Machine" of Cincinnati proved too much in the World Series, which the Yanks lost in an embarrassing four straight games.

The opening of the new stadium, and the return of the Yankees to the World Series, coincided with a new surge of popularity felt by major league baseball, during which attendance records would regularly fall and network television revenues soared. The Yankees were not the sole factor for this, but the coincidence was hard to ignore. Baseball seemed to need a strong Yankee franchise.

Free agency was now officially in place, and it was open season on stars. No one bid harder or played this game with more desire than Steinbrenner. In his first shot out of the box, he signed Reggie Jackson, the muscular outfielder who had been Hunter's teammate at Oakland and who, by his own admission, "was the straw that stirred the drink."

That remark, made in 1977 at his first Yankee spring training camp, was intended to demean the leadership abilities of Munson, and it launched an era of enormous feuding and bickering between players, managers, owners, and general managers. The principle players in this drama seemed always to be Martin, Jackson, and Steinbrenner, but others could be drawn in as well. The feuding led some to label the team "The Bronx Zoo," which became the title of a best-selling exposé of the team by pitcher Sparky Lyle.

Jackson had a stormy 1977 with the Yankees, and almost came to blows with Martin during a nationally televised game in Boston, when Martin berated him in the dugout. But the team was laden with talent, getting an especially strong year from Lyle, who won the Cy Young Award, and they took another Eastern Division title, then another pennant over Kansas City. In the World Series against the Dodgers, Jackson shattered all slugging records for Series play, hitting five home runs in the six games, with 25 total bases in 20 at bats. In the deciding sixth game, he homered three times (for four in a row over two games), each clout travelling farther than the one before. He would forever be known as "Mr. October" after that Series.

The 1978 season had a similar ending but a much different plot. Rich "Goose" Gossage was signed as a free agent, effectively making Lyle expendable just days after he'd won the Cy Young Award. By the end of the year he would be gone, while Gossage became a demon relief pitcher over the next six years, saving 150 games.

The 1978 team did not get off well. Martin, weary of his battles with Jackson, fighting his own vices, and watching his team fall 14 games behind Boston after the All-Star break, let his dream job slip away with a slip of the tongue. Against Kansas City Jackson defied Martin's sign to remove a bunt, and the Yankees lost another game. He suspended Jackson, and by the time the suspension was lifted five days later, Billy uttered his fatal words to reporters, "One's a born liar, the other's convicted." The latter referred to Steinbrenner, and Billy "resigned" the next day.

The team was turned over to Bob Lemon, a calming influence who was further helped by a sudden New York newspaper strike which took the daily controversies and feuds out of everyone's focus. Lemon led the Yankees to a 48–20 finish, including a sensational four-game sweep of the Red Sox at Fenway Park in September in which they outscored Boston 42–9. The "Boston Massacre" almost finished the Sox, but the season wound up with a first-place tie, and the two squared off again in Boston on October 2. Trailing 2–0 in the seventh, the Yanks got a three-run homer from shortstop Bucky Dent, who had hit only four all season. Jackson added a solo blast, and the Yankees had the Eastern Division title.

They beat the Royals again for their third straight pennant, and then came back once more, after losing the first two games of the World Series, to beat the Dodgers in seven for their 22nd World Championship.

The hero of the season was the 160-pound southpaw, Ron Guidry, who had nearly the best season of any pitcher in the twentieth century. "Gator" was 25–3 with nine shutouts and a 1.74 ERA. He fanned 18 in one game, and 248 for the season, both Yankee records, and won the Cy Young Award.

As for Billy Martin, he was such a popular manager with the fans that the outcry over his firing led Steinbrenner to announce, just days later (on Old Timers Day), that he would return to manage in 1980, at which time Lemon would become general manager. Lemon never got that job, but Martin did return—a year early in fact, and then three more times after that, covering five different terms in all. He always managed to find himself in some mischief that caused a firing, but the fans loved a guy who battled the boss, and Billy could always be hired again, until he died in an automobile accident on Christmas Day 1989, at age 61.

This was the beginning of managerial musical chairs on the Yankees. "They know what the bottom line is," Steinbrenner would say, and that meant a World Championship. Dick Howser would win 103 games in 1980, but got fired when the Yankees lost the League Championship Series to Kansas City. Gene Michael took two turns, Lemon had another one, Clyde King had a brief tenure, and even Yogi Berra, who rejoined the team as a coach in 1976, returned to manage in 1984, only to be fired once more in 1985. Lou Piniella took two tries, before Dallas Green, the former Phillies manager and Cubs general manager, was hired in 1989. The Yankee manager's job was the hottest seat in baseball, with the possible exception of the Yankee pitching coach job, which turned over even more frequently.

The team continued to take chances on free agents. Some worked out well, like Dave Winfield, Tommy John, Phil Niekro, and Don Baylor, but many had trouble handling the pressure in New York and the adjustment to the win-or-else mentality. Win or lose, the Yankees were media delights, and were forever grabbing the public's attention.

The mini-dynasty of 1976–77–78 ended in 1979, the year Thurman Munson died while piloting his own private jet. The crash occurred at his home airport in Canton, Ohio, on August 2nd. Munson's drive for excellence on the field helped propel the Yankees into champions, and he batted .300 five times while continuing the catching tradition which ran from Dickey to Berra to Howard to himself. The entire team went to Canton for the tearful funeral, with Murcer and Piniella reading eulogies. The club and its fans shared an incredible sense of loss. Never did Yankee Stadium witness a scene like the moment of silence for Munson at the next home game, when the catcher's position was left vacant, and the other eight players stood with heads bowed in a misty rain, the fans breaking the silence to yell "Thurman, Thurman, Thurman." He died at 32, five years younger than the last captain before him, Lou Gehrig.

There would be another pennant in strike-shortened 1981, when the Yankees got to the Series by being champions of the first half, on a shortened makeshift schedule. This time the Dodgers got the better of them, as first-year free agent Dave Winfield, fresh from a 10-year, $20 million contract, went only 1-for-22, and Steinbrenner outraged his players by apologizing to the fans for the humiliating defeat.

As 1981 was Winfield's first year with the Yankees, it was Jackson's last. Later calling it a big mistake, Steinbrenner let the charismatic but controversial slugger go the free agent route to California. Had Jackson's career lasted longer than five seasons, he would likely have been considered a legitimate extension of the Ruth-Gehrig-DiMaggio-Mantle tradition. He was arguably the most exciting player of his time.

Winfield had a no-trade clause which wound up infuriating Steinbrenner, because the two never hit it off, and despite great statistical accomplishments (six 100-RBI seasons in his first nine Yankee seasons), he was unable to lead the team to a World Championship. "Mr. May," he was called sarcastically by Steinbrenner. Winfield, 6'6" and blessed with speed, power, and great defensive ability, never seemed affected by the owners's criticisms, and always vetoed proposed trades, until he was shipped to the Angels in 1990.

The greatest find of the 1980s turned out to be a homegrown farm system product out of Evansville, Indiana, Don Mattingly. A 19th-round selection in the June 1979 free agent draft, Mattingly was of unimposing size and, given the success rate of Yankee farmhands moving up, he was barely noticed. He was shuttled between New York and Columbus in 1983, playing some first base and some outfield; a fringe player on the roster. In 1984 Berra put Mattingly at first base full time. Don stunned baseball by leading the league with a .343 average, edging out Winfield on the last day by three points, and becoming the first Yankee league batting champion since Mantle in 1956. He was also the first Yankee in 22 years to get 200 hits.

The following year Mattingly won the league's MVP award, driving in 145 runs, the most by a Yankee since DiMaggio in 1948. In 1986 he had a Yankee record of 238 hits, batted .352, and belted 53 doubles, this time breaking Gehrig's Yankee record. In 1987 he homered in eight consecutive games to tie a major league mark, and belted six grand slam homers to set another. Many considered him baseball's current best player.

Two other key Yankees of the 1980s were Dave Righetti and Rickey Henderson. Righetti, obtained in a trade with Texas for Sparky Lyle, was the league's Rookie of the Year in 1981, and on July 4, 1983, no-hit the Red Sox in 95° heat before a sellout crowd at Yankee Stadium, fanning Wade Boggs for the final out. It was the first Yankee no-hitter since Larsen's perfect game in the 1956 World Series.[7]

Moved to the bullpen following the departure of Gossage in 1984, Righetti became the league's best relief pitcher, topping out with a major league record of 46 saves in 1986.

Henderson, obtained in a trade with Oakland in 1984, was the all-time single-season base stealing champion with 130, and seemed well on the way toward breaking Lou Brock's career record. He gave the Yankees a speed factor they'd never had, stealing a high of 93 in 1988, and twice leading the league in runs scored.

Still, even with stars like Mattingly, Winfield, and Henderson in the lineup, the 1980s were a frustrating time for the Yankees. Always in contention, always attention-getting, the team entered another long dry spell after 1981 without any championships, despite winning more games than anyone else during the decade.

Financially the Yankees were an enormous success. The value of the team was said to be 15 times what Steinbrenner had first paid for it, even before they signed a cable-TV contract in late 1988 guaranteeing a half-billion dollars over the next dozen years. The team continued to draw well over two million fans a year to Yankee Stadium, although Steinbrenner would occasionally make gestures indicating that one day he might entertain thoughts of moving 15 miles southeast to the Meadowlands Sports Complex in New Jersey.

On July 30, 1990, the day the cover of *Newsweek* magazine proclaimed him "The Most Hated Man in Baseball," George Steinbrenner's reign ended when Commissioner Fay Vincent removed him as the team's chief executive. Steinbrenner had paid $40,000 to a confessed gambler, Howard Spira, seeking information to discredit Dave Winfield and the Winfield Foundation, a charitable organization. He was the first owner in American League history to be removed through disciplinary action. News of his ousting, announced during a night game at Yankee Stadium, was greeted by a standing ovation from the fans. Steinbrenner remained a limited partner and was replaced by Robert Nederlander, 57, another limited partner, whose family operated a theatre organization. Left open was the possibility that a Steinbrenner heir could still one day emerge in a top position.

Love them or hate them—and most did feel one way or the other—the Yankees remained the best-known sports franchise in the country. The words on a Yankee World Series ring summed it up best: Pride/Tradition. No team carried more.

Notes

1. Devery, a huge, likeable rogue, had in his earlier days on the force been brought up on corruption charges no fewer than seven times. In the days of accepted police corruption by New York's Tammany Hall political machine, Devery had escaped dismissal, his worst penalty being assignment on an outpost in Harlem where the opportunity for bribery was slim. But he had returned as chief of police to personally preside over corruption trials. Wrote journalist Lincoln Steffens, he "was made Chief of Police to reform not the department, but the system of police graft," and he turned corruption into an art form. At last turned away by Tammany, he was preparing to run for Mayor of New York as a third-party candidate in the 1903 election. (He would receive less than one percent of the vote.)

2. The team was incorporated in New York State as the "Greater New York Baseball Association.

3. The outfield alterations brought about by new seating caused the left-field line to extend to 301 feet by 1928, when death valley reached 402. In 1937 center field retreated from 490 to 461, and two years later, right field was measured out at 296. These would become the park's famous and unusual dimensions until it was finally remodeled after the 1973 season. By then, the capacity, more strictly enforced by fire codes, was 67,000.

4. The Yankees began televising in 1947, and cablecasting in 1979. Other long-term Yankee announcers included Red Barber, 1957–65; Phil Rizzuto, 1957–present; Frank Messer, 1968–84; and Bill White, 1971–88, who resigned to become National League President.

5. He went on to run Madison Square Garden before retiring to Ireland, where he died in 1987.

6. Steinbrenner was fined $15,000 for the crime, but received a presidential pardon from Ronald Reagan in 1989.

7. An amazing streak was that of the Yankees success in avoiding no-hitters. Relief great Hoyt Wilhelm, in a rare start for Baltimore in 1958, stopped the Yanks cold; there was not another no-hitter against them through 1989.

Annotated Bibliography

Allen, Maury. *Damn Yankee*. New York: Times Books, 1980. 302 pp.
    The ups and downs of Billy Martin through his first two stints as Yankee manager, plus his reckless playing career of the 1950s.
Anderson, Dave, Murray Chass, Robert Creamer, and Harold Rosenthal. *The Yankees: The Four Fabulous Eras of Baseball's Most Famous Team*. New York: Random House, 1979. 227 pp.
    Four of New York's top journalists/authors examine the Ruth and Gehrig Era; the Joe DiMaggio Years; Mickey Mantle and Casey Stengel; and the Money Players. This is the only published book to which Chass contributed, and he was the top journalistic chronicler of the Steinbrenner years.
Barrow, Edward, and James Kahn. *My Fifty Years in Baseball*. New York: Coward and McCann, 1951. 216 pp.
    Memoirs of the Huggins and McCarthy eras by the general manager of those great teams.
Berra, Yogi, and Tom Horton. *Yogi: It Ain't Over*. New York: McGraw-Hill Book Company, 1989. 273 pp.
    Captures Yogi's unique speech pattern with surprising insight into his days as a player for Stengel and a manager for Steinbrenner.
Creamer, Robert. *Babe: The Legend Comes to Life*. New York: Simon and Schuster, 1974. 443 pp.
    Candid profile of The Bambino for all his highs and lows on and off the field.
———. *Stengel: His Life and Times*. New York: Simon and Schuster, 1984. 349 pp.
    Similar to the Ruth treatment, and a warts-and-all look at Casey Stengel.
Durant, John. *The Yankees*. New York: Hastings House, 1949. 122 pp.
    Light history of the first 45 years, but excellent photos seldom seen today.
Durso, Joseph. *Yankee Stadium: Fifty Years of Drama*. Boston: Houghton Mifflin Company, 1972. 155 pp.
    Heavily illustrated study of the Stadium, including non-baseball, but emphasis on the great Yankee teams that played there.
Fleming, G. H. *Murderer's Row*. New York: William Morrow & Company, 1985. 399 pp.
    Newspaper coverage of the 1927 campaign.
Ford, Whitey, and Phil Pepe. *Slick: My Life in and Around Baseball*. New York: William Morrow & Company, 1987. 256 pp.
    Ford's unabashed memoirs.
Forker, Dom. *The Men of Autumn*. Dallas: Taylor Publishing, 1989. 228 pp.
    Oral history of 23 Yankees of 1949–53.
Frommer, Harvey. *Baseball's Greatest Rivalry*. New York: Atheneum, 1982. 194 pp.
    Traces the Yankee–Red Sox rivalry since its origins.
Gallagher, Mark. *The Yankee Encyclopedia*. West Point, N.Y.: Leisure Press, 1982. 640 pp.
    Excellent for biographies of off-the-field personnel, year-by-year summaries.
Golenbock, Peter. *Dynasty: The New York Yankees 1949–1964*. Englewood Cliffs, N.J.: Prentice-Hall, 1975. 394 pp.

Interviews with many people from that era, including a bitter Roger Maris who talks about 1961.

Graham, Frank. *Lou Gehrig: A Quiet Hero*. New York: G. P. Putnam's Sons, 1941. 250 pp.

Established the Gehrig legend for three generations of readers. The ultimate hero worship biography, in a very common writing style when baseball was innocent.

————. *The New York Yankees*. New York: G. P. Putnam's Sons, 1943. 282 pp.

The best history of the team to that point, culled from conversations with Mark Roth, writer and road secretary from the Highlander days, and Waite Hoyt. Later team histories all stole from this one in the interest of accuracy. Revised and updated as late as 1958.

Halberstam, David. *Summer of '49*. New York: William Morrow & Company, 1989. 304 pp.

Pulitzer-Prize winning author examines the classic pennant race of 1949 between the Yankees and Boston.

Honig, Donald. *The New York Yankees*. New York: Crown, 1987. 344 pp.

Borrows heavily from Graham, but adds beautiful photos for a splendid illustrated history.

Houk, Ralph, and Robert Creamer. *Season of Glory*. New York: G. P. Putnam's Sons, 1988. 320 pp.

The 1961 season through the memories of the manager.

Jackson, Reggie, and Mike Lupica. *Reggie*. New York: Villard, 1984. 333 pp.

Autobiography of "Mr. October."

Kubek, Tony, and Terry Pluto. *Sixty-One*. New York: Macmillan, 1987. 269 pp.

More on 1961, as Kubek revisits his old teammates for their recollections.

Lally, Dick. *Pinstripped Summers*. New York: Arbor House, 1985. 272 pp.

Good history from 1965–1982, the CBS slump to the Steinbrenner triumphs and down again.

Lyle, Sparky, and Peter Golenbock. *The Bronx Zoo*. New York: Crown, 1979. 248 pp.

Best-selling diary of 1978 madness. Revealing look at the players' lives under Steinbrenner ownership.

MacPhail, Lee. *My 9 Innings*. Westport, Conn.: Meckler Corporation, 1989. 253 pp.

Memoirs of long-time Yankee front-office official.

Mann, Jack. *The Decline and Fall of the New York Yankees*. New York: Simon and Schuster, 1967. 256 pp.

First study of how the dynasty collapsed in 1965.

Mantle, Mickey, and Herb Gluck. *The Mick*. New York: Doubleday, 1985. 248 pp.

Revealing autobiography by the always-honest hero of the 1950s and 1960s.

Meany, Tom. *The Magnificent Yankees*. New York: Grosset & Dunlop, 1952. 214 pp.

Biographies of the Yankees of the 1950s. Expanded edition published 1957.

Moore, Jack. *Joe DiMaggio: Baseball's Yankee Clipper*. New York: Praeger, 1986. 253 pp.

A "bio-bibliography," and the most complete study of DiMaggio's life, all taken from other credited sources.

Mosedale, John. *The Greatest of Them All*. New York: Dial, 1974. 220 pp.
    Study of the 1927 Murderer's Row team.
Ruth, Babe, and Bob Considine. *The Babe Ruth Story*. New York: Dutton, 1948.
    250 pp.
    A good chance Ruth never even read this, but he did tell his story to
    Considine, at least as he wanted it known.
Schaap, Dick. *Steinbrenner!* New York: G. P. Putnam's Sons, 1982. 314 pp.
    Well-researched biography of "The Boss."
Seidel, Michael. *Streak: Joe DiMaggio and the Summer of '41*. New York: McGraw
    Hill, 1988. 260 pp.
    Diary of the remarkable season in which Joe hit in 56 straight.
Smelser, Marshall. *The Life That Ruth Built*. New York: Quadrangle, 1975. 592
    pp.
    Outstanding, heavily footnoted Ruth biography.
Sullivan, George, and John Powers. *Yankees: An Illustrated History*. Englewood
    Cliffs, N.J.: Prentice Hall. 312 pp.
    Season-by-season recap, 1903–1981.
Tullius, John. *I'd Rather Be a Yankee*. New York: Macmillan, 1986. 364 pp.
    Assembling quotes from Yankees in previously published sources into an
    interesting oral history.
Winfield, Dave, and Tom Parker. *Winfield: A Player's Life*. New York: W. W.
    Norton, 1988. 314 pp.
    The troubled times of the star and the owner in the 1980s.

Year-by-Year Standings and Season Summaries

Year	Pos.	Record	Pct.	GB	Manager	Player	BA	Player	HR	Player	W-L	ERA
1903	4th	72–62	.537	17.0	Griffith	Keeler	.318	McFarland	5	Chesbro	21–15	2.77
1904	2nd	92–59	.609	1.5	Griffith	Keeler	.343	Ganzel	6	Chesbro	41–12	1.82
1905	6th	71–78	.477	21.5	Griffith	Keeler	.302	Williams	6	Chesbro	20–15	2.20
1906	2nd	90–61	.596	3.0	Griffith	Chase	.323	Conroy	4	Orth	27–17	2.34
1907	5th	70–78	.473	21.0	Griffith	Chase	.287	Hoffman	5	Orth	14–21	2.60
1908	8th	51–103	.331	39.5	Griffith Elberfeld	Hemphill	.297	Niles	4	Chesbro	14–20	2.93
1909	5th	74–77	.490	23.5	Stallings	LaPorte	.298	Chase Demmitt	4 4	Lake	14–11	1.88
1910	2nd	88–63	.583	14.5	Stallings Chase	Knight	.312	Wolter Cree	4 4	Ford	26–6	1.65
1911	6th	76–76	.500	25.5	Chase	Cree	.348	Wolter Cree	4 4	Ford	22–11	2.28
1912	8th	50–102	.329	55.0	Wolverton	Paddock	.288	Zinn	6	Ford	13–21	3.54
1913	7th	57–94	.377	38.0	Chance	Cree	.272	Wolter	2	Fisher	11–17	3.18
1914	6th	70–84	.455	30.0	Chance Peckinpaugh	Cook	.283	Sweeney Peckinpaugh	2 3	Ford Caldwell	11–18 17–9	2.66 1.94
1915	5th	69–83	.454	32.5	Donovan	Maisel	.281	Peckinpaugh	5	Caldwell	19–16	2.89
1916	4th	80–74	.519	11.0	Donovan	Pipp	.262	Pipp	12	Shawkey	23–14	2.21
1917	6th	71–82	.464	28.5	Donovan	Baker	.282	Pipp	9	Shawkey	13–13	2.44
1918	4th	60–63	.488	13.5	Huggins	Baker	.306	Baker	6	Mogridge	16–13	2.27
1919	3rd	80–59	.576	7.5	Huggins	Peckinpaugh	.305	Baker	10	Shawkey	20–11	2.72
1920	3rd	95–59	.617	3.0	Huggins	Ruth	.376	Ruth	54	Mays	26–11	3.06
1921	1st	98–55	.641	+4.5	Huggins	Ruth	.378	Ruth	59	Mays	27–9	3.04
1922	1st	94–60	.610	+1.0	Huggins	Pipp	.329	Ruth	35	Bush	26–7	3.32
1923	1st	98–54	.645	+16.0	Huggins	Ruth	.393	Ruth	41	Jones	21–8	3.63
1924	2nd	89–63	.586	2.0	Huggins	Ruth	.378	Ruth	46	Pennock	21–9	2.83
1925	7th	69–85	.448	28.5	Huggins	Combs	.343	Meusel	33	Pennock	16–17	2.96

Year	Pos.	Record	Pct.	GB	Manager	Player	BA	Player	HR	Player	W-L	ERA
1926	1st	91–63	.591	+3.0	Huggins	Ruth	.372	Ruth	47	Pennock	23–11	3.62
1927	1st	110–44	.714	+19.0	Huggins	Gehrig	.373	Ruth	60	Hoyt	22–7	2.64
1928	1st	101–53	.656	+2.5	Huggins	Gehrig	.374	Ruth	54	Pipgras	24–13	3.38
1929	2nd	88–66	.571	18.0	Huggins Fletcher	Lazzeri	.354	Ruth	46	Pipgras	18–12	4.24
1930	3rd	86–68	.558	16.0	Shawkey	Gehrig	.379	Ruth	49	Pipgras	15–15	4.11
										Ruffing	15–5	4.14
1931	2nd	94–59	.614	13.5	McCarthy	Ruth	.373	Ruth	46	Gomez	21–9	2.63
								Gehrig	46			
1932	1st	107–47	.695	+13.0	McCarthy	Gehrig	.349	Ruth	41	Gomez	24–7	4.21
1933	2nd	91–59	.607	7.0	McCarthy	Gehrig	.334	Ruth	34	Gomez	16–10	3.18
1934	2nd	94–60	.610	7.0	McCarthy	Gehrig	.363	Gehrig	49	Gomez	26–5	2.33
1935	2nd	89–60	.597	3.0	McCarthy	Gehrig	.329	Gehrig	30	Ruffing	16–11	3.12
1936	1st	102–51	.667	+19.5	McCarthy	Dickey	.362	Gehrig	49	Ruffing	20–12	3.85
1937	1st	102–52	.662	+13.0	McCarthy	Gehrig	.351	Gehrig	46	Gomez	21–11	2.33
1938	1st	99–53	.651	+9.5	McCarthy	DiMaggio	.324	DiMaggio	32	Ruffing	21–7	3.32
1939	1st	106–45	.702	+17.0	McCarthy	DiMaggio	.381	DiMaggio	30	Ruffing	21–7	2.94
1940	3rd	88–66	.571	2.0	McCarthy	DiMaggio	.352	DiMaggio	31	Ruffing	15–12	3.38
1941	1st	101–53	.656	+17.0	McCarthy	DiMaggio	.357	Keller	33	Ruffing	15–6	3.53
										Gomez	15–5	3.75
1942	1st	103–51	.669	+9.0	McCarthy	Gordon	.322	Keller	26	Bonham	21–5	2.27
1943	1st	98–56	.636	+13.5	McCarthy	Johnson	.280	Keller	31	Chandler	20–4	1.64
1944	3rd	83–71	.539	6.0	McCarthy	Stirnweiss	.319	Etten	22	Borowy	17–12	2.63
1945	4th	81–71	.533	6.5	McCarthy	Stirnweiss	.309	Etten	18	Bevens	13–9	3.67
1946	3rd	87–67	.565	17.0	McCarthy Dickey Neun	DiMaggio	.290	Keller	30	Chandler	20–8	2.10
1947	1st	97–57	.630	+12.0	Harris	DiMaggio	.315	DiMaggio	20	Reynolds	19–8	3.20
1948	3rd	94–60	.610	2.5	Harris	DiMaggio	.320	DiMaggio	39	Raschi	19–8	3.83
1949	1st	97–57	.630	+1.0	Stengel	Henrich	.287	Henrich	24	Raschi	21–10	3.34
1950	1st	98–56	.636	+3.0	Stengel	Rizzuto	.324	DiMaggio	32	Raschi	21–8	3.99

Year	Pos.	Record	Pct.	GB	Manager	Player	BA	Player	HR	Player	W-L	ERA
1951	1st	98–56	.636	+5.0	Stengel	McDougald	.306	Berra	27	Raschi	21–10	3.28
										Lopat	21–9	2.91
1952	1st	95–59	.617	+2.0	Stengel	Mantle	.311	Berra	30	Reynolds	20–8	2.07
1953	1st	99–52	.656	+8.5	Stengel	Bauer	.304	Berra	27	Ford	18–6	3.00
1954	2nd	103–51	.669	8.0	Stengel	Noren	.319	Mantle	27	Grim	20–6	3.26
1955	1st	96–58	.623	+3.0	Stengel	Mantle	.306	Mantle	37	Ford	18–7	2.62
1956	1st	97–57	.680	+9.0	Stengel	Mantle	.353	Mantle	52	Ford	19–6	2.47
1957	1st	98–56	.636	+8.0	Stengel	Mantle	.365	Mantle	34	Sturdivant	16–6	2.54
1958	1st	92–62	.597	+10.0	Stengel	Mantle	.304	Mantle	42	Turley	21–7	2.98
1959	3rd	79–75	.513	15.0	Stengel	Richardson	.301	Mantle	31	Ford	16–10	3.04
1960	1st	97–57	.630	+8.0	Stengel	Skowron	.309	Mantle	40	Ditmar	15–9	3.06
1961	1st	109–53	.673	+8.0	Houk	Howard	.348	Maris	61	Ford	25–4	3.21
1962	1st	96–66	.593	+5.0	Houk	Mantle	.321	Maris	33	Terry	23–12	3.19
1963	1st	104–57	.646	+10.5	Houk	Howard	.287	Howard	28	Ford	24–7	2.74
1964	1st	99–63	.611	+1.0	Berra	Howard	.318	Mantle	35	Bouton	18–13	3.02
1965	6th	77–85	.475	27.0	Keane	Tresh	.279	Tresh	26	Stottlemyre	20–9	2.63
1966	10th	70–89	.440	26.5	Keane	Mantle	.288	Pepitone	31	Stottlemyre	12–20	3.80
					Houk					Peterson	12–11	3.31
1967	9th	72–90	.444	20.0	Houk	Clarke	2.72	Mantle	22	Stottlemyre	15–15	2.96
1968	5th	83–79	.512	20.0	Houk	White	.267	Mantle	18	Stottlemyre	21–12	2.45
1969	5th	80–81	.497	28.5	Houk	White	.290	Pepitone	27	Stottlemyre	20–14	2.82
1970	2nd	93–69	.574	15.0	Houk	Munson	.302	Murcer	23	Peterson	20–11	2.91
1971	4th	82–80	.506	21.0	Houk	Murcer	.331	Murcer	25	Stottlemyre	16–12	2.87
1972	4th	79–76	.510	6.5	Houk	Murcer	.292	Murcer	33	Peterson	17–15	3.24
1973	4th	80–82	.494	17.0	Houk	Murcer	.304	Murcer	22	Stottlemyre	16–16	3.07
								Nettles	22			
1974	2nd	89–73	.549	2.0	Virdon	Piniella	.305	Nettles	22	Dobson	19–15	3.07
										Medich	19–15	3.60
1975	3rd	83–77	.519	12.0	Virdon	Munson	.318	Bonds	32	Hunter	23–14	2.58
					Martin							

Year	Pos.	Record	Pct.	GB	Manager	Player	BA	Player	HR	Player	W-L	ERA
1976	1st	97–62	.610	+10.5	Martin	Rivers	.312	Nettles	32	Figueroa	19–10	3.01
1977	1st	100–62	.617	+2.5	Martin	Ribers	.326	Nettles	37	Guidry	16–7	2.82
										Figueroa	16–11	3.58
1978	1st	100–63	.613	+1.0	Martin Lemon	Piniella	.314	Jackson	27	Guidry	25–3	1.74
1979	4th	89–71	.556	13.5	Lemon Martin	Piniella Jackson	.297 .297	Jackson	29	John	21–9	2.97
1980	1st	103–59	.636	+3.0	Howser	Watson	.307	Jackson	41	John	22–9	3.43
1981	1st	34–22	.607	+2.0	Michael	Mumphrey	.307	Jackson Nettles	15 15	Guidry	11–5	2.76
1981*	6th 3rd	25–26 59–48	.490 .551	5.0	Michael							
1982	5th	79–83	.488	16.0	Lemon Michael King	Mumphrey	.300	Winfield	37	Guidry	14–8	3.81
1983	3rd	91–71	.562	7.0	Martin	Baylor	.303	Winfield	32	Guidry	21–9	3.42
1984	3rd	87–75	.537	18.0	Berra	Mattingly	.343	Baylor	27	Niekro	16–8	3.09
1985	2nd	97–64	.602	2.0	Berra Martin	Mattingly	.324	Mattingly	35	Guidry	22–6	3.27
1986	2nd	90–72	.556	5.5	Piniella	Mattingly	.352	Mattingly	31	Rasmussen	18–6	3.88
1987	4th	89–73	.549	9.0	Piniella	Mattingly	.327	Pagliarulo	32	Rhoden	16–10	3.86
1988	5th	85–76	.528	3.5	Martin Piniella Green	Winfield	.322	Clark	27	Candaleria	13–7	3.38
1989	5th	74–87	.460	14.5	Green-Dent	Sax	.316	Mattingly	23	Hawkins	15–15	4.80
1990	7th	67–95	.414	21.0	Dent/Merrill	R. Kelly	.285	Barfield	25	Guetterman	11–7	3.39
1991	5th	71–91	.438	20.0	Merrill	Sax	.304	Nokes	24	Sanderson	16–10	3.81
1992	4th(T)	76–86	.469	20.0	Showalter	Mattingly	.288	Tartabull	25	M. Perez	13–16	2.87

*Split Season Totals (Players' Union Strike).

All-Time Yankees Career and Season Records

Career Batting Leaders (1903–1992)

Games Played	Mickey Mantle	2,401
At Bats	Mickey Mantle	8,102
Runs Scored	Babe Ruth	1,959
Hits	Lou Gehrig	2,721
Batting Average	Babe Ruth	.349
Home Runs	Babe Ruth	659
Runs Batted In	Lou Gehrig	1,991
Stolen Bases	Rickey Henderson	326
Strikeouts	Mickey Mantle	1,710

Career Pitching Leaders (1903–1992)

Innings Pitched	Whitey Ford	3,171
Earned Run Average	Russ Ford	2.54
Wins	Whitey Ford	236
Losses	Mel Stottlemyre	139
Winning Percentage	Spud Chandler	.717
Strikeouts	Whitey Ford	1,956
Walks	Lefty Gomez	1,090
Games	Whitey Ford	498
Shutouts	Whitey Ford	45
Saves	Dave Righetti	188
Games Started	Whitey Ford	438
Complete Games	Red Ruffing	261

Single-Season Batting Records (1903–1992)

Batting Average (502 ABs)	Babe Ruth	.393	1923
Home Runs	Roger Maris	61	1961
Home Runs (righthanded)	Joe DiMaggio	46	1937
Runs Batted In	Lou Gehrig	184	1931
Hits	Don Mattingly	238	1986
Singles	Willie Keeler	166	1906
	Earle Combs	166	1927
Doubles	Don Mattingly	53	1986
Triples	Earle Combs	23	1927
Slugging Percentage	Babe Ruth	.847	1920
Extra Base Hits	Babe Ruth	119	1921
Game Winning RBIs	Dave Winfield	21	1983
	Don Mattingly	21	1985
Sacrifices	Willie Keeler	42	1905
Stolen Bases	Rickey Henderson	93	1988
Pinch Hits	Johnny Mize	19	1953
Strikeouts	Jack Clark	141	1988
Total Bases	Babe Ruth	457	1921
Hitting Streak	Joe DiMaggio	56	1941
Grand Slam Home Runs	Don Mattingly	6	1987
On-Base Percentage	Babe Ruth	.545	1923
Hit by Pitch	Don Baylor	24	1985

All-Time Yankees Career and Season Records *(continued)*

Single-Season Pitching Records (1903–1992)

ERA	Spud Chandler	1.64	1943
Wins	Jack Chesbro	41	1904
Losses	Al Orth	21	1907
	Joe Lake	21	1908
	Russ Ford	21	1912
	Sam Jones	21	1925
Winning Pct. (10 decisions)	Tom Zachary (12–0)	1.000	1929
Winning Pct. (20 decisions)	Ron Guidry (25–3)	.893	1978
Strikeouts	Ron Guidry	248	1978
Walks	Tommy Byrne	179	1949
Saves	Dave Righetti	46	1986
Games	Dave Righetti	74	1985
Complete Games	Jack Chesbro	48	1904
Games Started	Jack Chesbro	51	1904
Shutouts	Ron Guidry	9	1978
Innings Pitched	Jack Chesbro	454	1904
Home Runs Allowed	Ralph Terry	40	1962
Consecutive Games Won (season)	Jack Chesbro	14	1904
	Whitey Ford	14	1961
Consecutive Games Lost (season)	Bill Hogg	9	1908
	Thad Tillotson	9	1967
Wild Pitches	Al Downing	14	1964
Balks	John Candaleria	12	1988

(Photo courtesy National Baseball Library, Cooperstown, NY)

Ted Williams, Boston Red Sox (1939–1960)

Here was the game's purest natural hitter, its most dedicated craftsman, and also one of its most moody and distant stars who was given to temper tantrums and running battles with the Boston press which shaded his entire brilliant career. But as humorists Brendan Boyd and Fred Harris have reminded us, "in 1955 there were 77,263,127 male American human beings . . . and every one of them in his heart of hearts would have given two arms, a leg, and his collection of Davy Crockett iron-ons just to be Teddy Ballgame."

(Photo courtesy National Baseball Library, Cooperstown, NY)

Reggie Jackson, California Angels (1982–1986)

For some he was a showboat and hotdog, for others a mercenary who took his roving bat each few summers to the newest high bidder—the Orioles, Yankees, Angels, and then back to the Athletics where he started. He was also the biggest drawing card of his era, the man for whom a candy bar was named, an outrageous self-promoter and thus a sportswriter's dream. But above all the hype he was also the sixth leading home-run slugger of all-time, surpassed only by Ruth among baseball's portside swingers.

Ty Cobb, Detroit Tigers (1905–1926)

Detroit fortunes were forever altered when Tyrus Raymond Cobb was purchased by the Tigers for a mere $750 in 1905. A twelve-time league batting champion and owner of baseball's highest lifetime batting mark (.387), this Georgia Peach built an unsurpassed legend for vicious uncompromising play and unmatched competitive spirit. And while no longer baseball's all-time base-hit leader, Cobb remains unchallenged still as the greatest all-around hitter ever to set foot inside a big league ballpark.

(Photo courtesy National Baseball Library, Cooperstown, NY)

George Brett, Kansas City Royals (1973–1992)

His indelible image is frozen forever in the fit of home plate rage which followed the infamous pine tar batting incident; his crown jewel achievement remains the 1980 .390 average which stands as the best in four decades. He is today remembered as much for injury-proneness, which has plagued his career and demoted him to the disabled list for more than 32 weeks between 1978 and 1989. Yet if ever a modern ballplayer could lay legitimate claim to the mythical title of "The Franchise" it would be Brett in Kansas City.

Shoeless Joe Jackson, Chicago White Sox (1915–1920)

He could perhaps have been the greatest outfielder ever; he was certainly the most talented natural batsman in the game before Ted Williams arrived. But in the end he left baseball prematurely and tragically, banned for life from the only true showcase for his rare athletic talents. And so it was, too, with the sad-faced franchise whose uniform he last wore, itself condemned to wander decade upon decade outside the mainstream baseball world of pennant races and spirited World Series play—seemingly a cursed team adrift forever in a century of second-division finishes and inept diamond play.

(Photo courtesy National Baseball Library, Cooperstown, NY)

Bob Feller, Cleveland Indians (1934–1956)

The winningest pitcher in Cleveland franchise history, Feller's fastball was legendary and his curve was unhittable. Yet despite six 20-victory campaigns, lost wartime seasons cost him his shot at 300 victories, 3,000 strikeouts, and perhaps a half-dozen more 20-victory ledgers. At the dawn of baseball's Golden Post-War Age, however, his was the most feared fastball in big-league play. To this very day old-timers still contend that only Walter "Big Train" Johnson was perhaps as fast, and none was ever any faster.

(Photo courtesy National Baseball Library, Cooperstown, NY)

Joe DiMaggio, New York Yankees (1936–1951)

While DiMaggio's legend may not stand up well in an age devoted so fanatically to revisionist statistics like clutch-hitting index, total average and runs produced, the Yankee Clipper nonetheless remains unrivalled as baseball icon. "Joltin' Joe" was, after all, the kind of player you had to see to appreciate, one who roamed the outfield with matchless grace and style and stroked a baseball with the craft and ease of legend. This was the truest, most invincible, most noble New York Yankee of them all.

Robert "Lefty" Grove, Philadelphia Athletics (1925–1933)

Lefty Grove's fiery temper was matched only by his blazing fastball and his scorching statistics: 300 career victories, American League strikeout leader for seven consecutive seasons, ERA leader a record nine times, and league pacesetter in winning percentage on five occasions. Legend has it that this hotheaded bad boy of the Connie Mack era also set unmatched Junior Circuit standards for shredded uniforms, cracked bats, trashed hotel rooms, smashed lockers, kicked buckets, and alienated teammates.

8

Philadelphia Athletics–
Kansas City Athletics–
Oakland A's
Three Families and
Three Baseball Epochs
Norman L. Macht

One of the most poignant moments in baseball history occurred between playing seasons, far from a ballpark, with nobody present to witness it. On a November day in 1954, a tall, spare 91-year-old man meticulously signed his name in a bold Spencerian hand—Cornelius McGillicuddy—on the back of a stock certificate, thus deporting out of the city and out of the family a business he had started in Philadelphia almost to the day 54 years before. As has happened in many family businesses, a lack of harmony among the younger generations, combined with the overstaying in power of the founder as his faculties declined, caused the franchise to wither and die in its birthplace. Its sale was inevitable; its exile was not.

Connie Mack and the Philadelphia Athletics

Unlike any other team in history, the story of the Philadelphia Athletics is the story of one man. Although other teams were owner-operated for long periods—Barney Dreyfuss at Louisville and Pittsburgh for more than 30 years, for example—no man ever has, or ever will, carry all the responsibilities of the front office as general manager, president or whatever title, and the duties of field manager at the same time, as Connie Mack did for exactly 50 years in Philadelphia.

Worshipped for his saintliness, castigated for his stinginess, he deserved neither label. Recognized for his ability to lead men, to teach, to position his players on the field for every batter and every pitch, to adapt as the style of the game changed, to build winners—this he did richly deserve.

Mr. Mack, as he was always addressed by his players, learned early that no business can long survive by spending more than it takes in.

Despite what the U.S. Supreme Court said in 1922, he knew that baseball was, first and last, a business. With no other capital or source of income, he had to depend solely on gate receipts and concession-stand sales to make a living and pay the players. Unlike his western competitors in the American League, he was denied by Pennsylvania law the chance to play before big Sunday crowds, and there was no beer sold at his ballpark.

Most fans today associate the old Athletics with the American League cellar. The team finished last seven years in a row after winning the 1914 pennant, and 10 more times after that. In 1916 they lost a modern record 117 games. They finished last in Connie Mack's fare-well season, and last again in their final year in Philadelphia.

But the Athletics were the most successful new start-from-scratch franchise in baseball history, winning six of the fledgling American League's first 14 pennants, with three runners-up. And Connie Mack built two of the greatest teams the game has ever seen, winning four flags from 1910 to 1914 and sweeping three straight in 1929–1931. Some would argue his last champions surpassed the 1927 Yankees for total talent. Mr. Mack maintained his 1912 team, which finished third, was his best.

When Connie Mack, 37, arrived in Philadelphia in the fall of 1900, he had a little more in his pockets than Ben Franklin, who got off the boat and strolled the city's streets with two rolls to fend off hunger. Mack had the proceeds from the sale of his 25 percent interest in the Milwaukee club of the Western League (renamed the American League in 1900) where he had managed for the past four years. He had the blessing of American League president Ban Johnson to launch the Philadelphia club, with a 25 percent stake in it. He had $10,000 to work with, three-fourths of it put up by Charles W. Somers, owner of the Cleveland club, who would also supply the initial bankroll to get the Boston club started.

Mack also had the active and vocal opposition of Colonel John I. Rogers, owner of the Phillies, who had finished third in the National League in 1900, and boasted such popular powerhouses at the plate as Napoleon Lajoie, Ed Delahanty, and Elmer Flick. In fact, the only things Connie Mack lacked were an office, a ballpark, a local backer, a team name, and players.

There was no committee of civic boosters to greet him. No head-lines announced his presence in town. Philadelphia had been a mem-ber of the National League since it began. Another major league, the American Association, had come and gone with a Philadelphia entry, the Athletics. In 1890 the Players League had put a third team on the city's fields. So if anybody else wanted to field another new team in another new league in the city, it was old news.

Connie Mack had quickly established himself as a leader of the new league by some shrewd early moves. On a tip from Hugh Duffy, who succeeded him as Milwaukee manager, Mack went to Boston and closed a 10-year lease on grounds for the new Boston club. Back in Philadelphia he lined up the support of baseball writers Frank Hough and Samuel H. Jones by giving them 25 percent of the club. He signed Billy Sharsig, former owner and manager of the original Athletics, as his business manager. Sharsig enjoyed a huge circle of friends and was synonymous with baseball in the Quaker city.

Having found a home for the Bostons, Mack was still homeless himself. His first choice was a city-owned playground, adjacent to a school, that had been used by the Athletics. Frank Hough appeared before a city parks board requesting a lease on the grounds; after weeks of delays he was turned down. Mack then looked at grounds in South Philadelphia, but was persuaded by Hough that a more central location was needed.

Colonel Rogers of the Phillies inadvertently solved their problem. The National League was trying to revive the old American Association as a major league rival to squelch the upstart American League by having three teams in Boston and Philadelphia. Rogers insisted that an American Association club use his ballpark as tenants. But the potential local backers had an option on grounds at Columbia Avenue. To protect himself (he had other problems with rival National League owners), Rogers demanded that his friend, Hezekiah Niles, who still held the original Athletics charter, be awarded the franchise, providing he used Rogers' park. When Rogers' demands were met, the Columbia Avenue grounds became available and Mack snapped it up, signing a 10-year lease.

The demise of the American Association, which failed to find enough backers, left the name Athletics, previously ruled to be a trademark of the old team, up for grabs. It gradually became attached to the Philadelphia American League Baseball Club, but was never formally adopted.

"So long as our team performs to suit the fans," said Mack, "I don't care what name they use."

At last they had an empty field to play on, but with just over two months until opening day, that's all they had. Displaying no shortage of money, but still refusing to identify his local backers, Mack hired a contractor and deposited $20,000 in the bank to begin construction of grandstands and bleachers that would hold 12,000 seated and standing, at a total cost of $35,000.

Meanwhile Mack was busy scouting for players. The American League made no bones about approaching and signing National League players. They did not believe the reserve or option clause used by the Nationals would hold up in court, and did not intend to use it in their own contracts. Mack made overtures to several Phillies stars, and traveled extensively during February and March to line up players. But the American League was playing it close to the vest; no captures of National League prizes were announced, leaving rumors running freely.

The guessing game over the identity of the local backer was ended on February 20, 1901, when Benjamin H. Shibe was revealed as half owner and president of the club. His connection with the game went back to his ownership of a piece of the old Athletics, in association with Colonel Rogers. He had refused to pay an assessment levied by Rogers years ago and had washed his hands of the whole thing. Shibe was a partner with A. J. Reach (who was also part owner of the Phillies) in the manufacture of baseballs and other sporting equipment. But of greatest importance to Mack and the Athletics, his reputation for unquestioned honesty and integrity boosted the new club's standing in the community and enhanced Mack's ability to persuade National League players to jump.

By the first week of March the grandstand and fences were in place at Columbia Park, and Mack had rounded up 12 of the 14 players he would sign. But no names were revealed; some signings would prove temporary as players seesawed back and forth, and some signed more than one contract.

When the league finally released its team rosters on March 20th, it was confirmed that Mack had spirited away second baseman Nap Lajoie, a .337 hitter, whom he named his captain, and pitchers Chick Fraser, 16–9, and Bill Bernhard, 15–10, from the Phillies. For about six weeks Mack also had Christy Mathewson under contract, but the Giants rookie righthander jumped back to New York.

Colonel Rogers quickly took the Athletics and the three players to court, touching off similar suits in several cities, all claiming the jumpers had to play for their 1900 teams or not at all. When a local judge ruled the Phillies' option clause not legally binding, Rogers appealed to the state supreme court.

Opening day at Columbia Park was rained out, as was the next day's game. When they finally had a chance to play, on April 26th, Washington defeated the home team, 5–1. Lajoie went three for four and drove in the only run for the losers. Chick Fraser took the loss. But the crowd of 10,524 overflowed onto the outfield, while the rival Phillies were losing to the Boston Beaneaters before a meager 779 patrons.

Despite injuries, defections, and a variety of players tried and found wanting, the Athletics were never far from the top in the pennant race. They jousted with Detroit for third place most of the year, finishing a half-game behind the Tigers at 74–62. The funeral of President McKinley and September rains cut four dates from the 140-game schedule.

Lajoie set a personal and team high with a league-leading .422 BA, still the American League record. He swept the triple crown with 14 home runs and 125 RBIs, and led the league with 229 hits, 48 doubles, and 145 runs scored. This performance did little to support his later courtroom testimony that he didn't think of himself as "so unique a player."

Chick Fraser won 20 and lost 15, Bernhard was 17–11. (Despite their loss, the Phillies finished second.) First baseman Harry Davis, an old teammate of Mack's from Pittsburgh, hit .306, right fielder Socks Seybold, .334, and third baseman Lave Cross, .324. Rookie lefthander Eddie Plank won 17 and lost 11.

Throughout the 1901 season the Americans continued to sign National League players secretly to 1902 contracts, which were rumored to be stored in Connie Mack's safe. In the fall Mack disclosed that he had lured lighthitting shortstop Monte Cross, outfielder Elmer Flick, a .336 hitter, and righthander Bill Duggleby, 16–12, from the Phillies, who were picked so clean by American League raiders they finished seventh or eighth for the next three years. Mack also pried outfielder Topsy Hartsel from Chicago. With outfielders Dave Fultz and Matty McIntyre, and lefty Snake Wiltse, a 13-game winner after coming over from Pittsburgh during the season, he went to the winter meetings confident his team was as strong as any in the league.

That confidence was shattered two days before opening day when the Pennsylvania Supreme Court overturned the lower court and ruled that Lajoie, Fraser, and Bernhard could not play for the Athletics. The judges wrote that National League option clauses were legal and binding. The decision did not force the three to play for the Phillies, nor did it have jurisdiction outside the state, but it threw the American League into an uproar. If used as a precedent, as many as 64 players could be affected.

Bernhard pitched the opener at Baltimore, beating the Orioles, 8–1. Lajoie played and had one hit, but was benched when Colonel Rogers obtained an injunction against his playing with any team but the Phillies. Although Duggleby was not named in the suit, he jumped back to the Phillies after two games, and Connie Mack suddenly found his star batter and half his pitching staff banned from the field. There was plenty of bluster on both sides. The Americans vowed to take the case to a higher court. The Nationals pronounced the infant league doomed.

In the end Fraser returned to the Phillies, but Lajoie and Bernhard refused. As a favor to Charles Somers, who had helped the league get started and whose weak Cleveland club needed boosting, the American League let Somers have Lajoie, Bernhard, and Elmer Flick. The three had to stay out of Pennsylvania and did not play in Philadelphia until the two leagues signed a peace treaty in 1903.

Undaunted, Mack went up to Norwich, Connecticut, and brought back Danny Murphy to play second base. Murphy, a Philadelphia native, had played briefly for the Giants, batting .186 in 28 games the year before. At 26, he was batting .426 for the Norwich club in the Connecticut State League. The day he reported to the Athletics he arrived too late for batting practice, but made six hits in six times at bat. He batted .313 for the year and stayed for 11 more.

Monte Cross, a 32-year-old veteran who had batted .197 for the Phillies in 1901, crossed over unchallenged by Colonel Rogers, and led all shortstops in putouts and total chances per game while hitting .231. Harry Davis's .307 and Lave Cross at .342 gave the Athletics the hardest hitting infield in the league. The outfield of Seybold, who led with 16 home runs, Fultz, and Hartsel hit a combined .300.

To replace his lost pitchers Mack signed Bert Husting, a righthander who had played for him at Milwaukee, then went to a great deal of trouble to lure lefty Rube Waddell from Los Angeles where he was pitching for the Looloos. Too eccentric and unbridled for the management of Pittsburgh or Chicago to handle, Waddell had impressed Mack while pitching for and against Milwaukee on loan from the Pirates. Waddell was as fast as any pitcher in the days before radar guns, and probably had as much speed as anyone after. Though he pitched his first game for the Athletics on June 26, losing 7–3, he won 25 and lost seven with a 2.05 ERA and a league-high 210 strikeouts, the first of six straight years he would lead in whiffs.

Until Waddell's arrival, Eddie Plank and Husting had been a two-man staff. Overworked, Plank was 6–13. But given more rest, he won 14 of his last 16. After leading the pack in the early going, the Athletics slipped to 7½ games back in July. With the strutting, blazing Waddell on the scene, they regained first place on August 15 and won by five over the Milwaukee-transplanted St. Louis Browns.

Waddell was also a hit at the box office, a prototype of the Dizzy Dean and Babe Ruth to come. Whenever he worked, the stands were packed at home or away. The club drew 411,329, tops in the majors, and outdrew the Phillies by more than two to one.

Connie Mack had overcome the loss, just after opening day, of half his offensive power (Lajoie again led the league, at .378) and three pitchers who had won 53 games in 1901. Thousands lined the streets of Philadelphia to cheer the champions on their return home after the last game of the season at Washington.

The war between the leagues ended during the winter of 1902–03; the legal and financial news departed from the sporting pages and left them free to concentrate on the action on the field. It was also the beginning of the dead ball era in the American League. Team batting averages dropped 20 points in 1903. Even though Connie Mack had added righthander Albert "Chief" Bender, and he and Waddell and Plank won 62 games among them, everybody else had good pitching, too. The Athletics finished a distant second to Boston, 14½ games back, only a half-game ahead of Cleveland. Waddell fanned 302 while winning 22 games.

Mack stood pat in 1904, and it cost him. Although two games closer to the repeating champion Bostons at the end of the year, the Mackmen were pushed into the second division by New York, Chicago, and Cleveland. All five teams were in the race until mid-August, but two injuries to Harry Davis, prolonged batting slumps (Monte Cross batted .189 and Schreck .186), and a slowdown on the basepaths sank them in the last month of the season. Waddell at 25–18 and Plank, 26–16, were the only winning pitchers.

The young league continued its run of prosperity in 1905, topping three million attendance, 385,000 over its rival. From the start four teams were evenly matched; the Athletics pulled away in August, but the White Sox closed the gap to come within three percentage points as they arrived in Philadelphia on September 28 for a three-game series. The Mackmen took two of the three before a record 64,899 for the three games, with thousands more turned away. They clinched the pennant in the final series in Washington, and were greeted by a huge throng in a victory parade on returning home. They had set a city attendance record of 554,576, second in the league to Chicago.

The primary changes from the decline of 1904 were a healthy Harry Davis, stronger bench in rookie shortstop Jack Knight and outfielder Bris Lord, the return to form of Monte Cross (.270) and catcher Ossee Schreck (.272), and a rookie pitcher from Holy Cross, Andy Coakley, who was 20–6 with a 1.84 ERA. It was Rube Waddell's finest season, with a 26–11 record and 1.48 ERA. He had one 10-game winning streak and on July 4 battled Cy Young for 20 innings for a 4–2 win over Boston. On July 22 Weldon Henley pitched a no-hitter but won only five games all year.

After a one-year break in the World Series, the first official Series matched the A's against the New York Giants and here is where history began to be affected by the jumping jack antics of Christy Mathewson in 1901. Had he stayed with the Athletics at that time, the unique all-shutouts 1905 World Series might still have happened, but Mathewson would not have pitched three of them for the Giants. And had Rube

Waddell not lunged for Andy Coakley's straw hat on a train station platform during the fall straw-busting fiesta, he and Matty might have staged the greatest pitching exhibitions the game would ever see. But Rube's sore shoulder deprived him of his only shot at a World Series appearance. Chief Bender's second game 3–0 victory was the only one the Athletics won. It was the first of three encounters between Mack and John McGraw, whose parting shot in calling the Philadelphia franchise a white elephant for the league as he departed Baltimore for the Giants in 1902 gave the Athletics the symbol they wore proudly all their life (it has since been reincarnated by the Oakland Athletics). Many years later Connie Mack confided that the most profitable situation for a ballclub was a strong contender that did not win the pennant. The close race kept the turnstiles spinning, while runners-up did not command the high salaries that champions expected.

For the next three years that formula brought such prosperity and optimism to the Philadelphia front office they drew up plans to build the first modern steel and concrete ball park in the country, one that would offer seats to the thousands who regularly overflowed the little wooden grandstands of Columbia Park onto the outfield grass, while many more were frequently turned away. Despite cold, wet springs that forced 69 postponements in the major leagues in April and May each year, and a dismal sixth-place finish in 1908, when attendance was boosted by the unequalled four-team race that went down to the final week, the Athletics showed large profits.

In 1906 they were out in front until August, when injuries and a White Sox 19-game winning streak sank them to fourth. In 1907 they battled the Tigers down to the last day, trailing by 1½ games at the close. In 1908 they led the league as late as June, when the entire pitching staff came down with lame arms (a plague that would also cost Mack his last chance for a pennant exactly 40 years later) and the infield, creaking with age, began to leak.

Throughout these years Mack was rebuilding, signing rookies off the farms and college campuses. Eddie Collins, a student at Columbia, got into six games in 1906 under the name of Sullivan. It took a few years for Mack to find the right position for Collins, a so-so shortstop before becoming the best second baseman of them all. In July of that year Jack Coombs, after graduating from Colby College, shut out Washington, 3–0, in his first start. On September 1 Coombs pitched the American League's longest game, a 24-inning duel against Boston's Jack Harris, won by the A's, 4–1. Coombs struck out 18 and gave up 14 hits. The next year he was hampered by arm trouble; that and bouts of wildness kept him a .500 pitcher until 1910, when he became Mack's first 30-game winner. Whether the 4 hour 47 minute marathon on September 1 caused the arm ailments remains unknown.

After selling Lave Cross at the end of 1905, Mack tried to plug third base with Jack Knight, signed out of a local high school. But Knight barely hit his weight (he was not very heavy). Then Mack bought the veteran Jimmy Collins, whom he had tried to sign in 1901, from Boston. But the future Hall of Famer was well past his prime at 37. Mack brought up righthander Jimmy Dygert and got a 20–10 season out of him in 1907, but Rube Waddell was becoming more erratic and less reliable (he started 33 games and completed only 20) and was sold to the St. Louis Browns in 1908. Ossee Schreck was sold as well to the White Sox. Plank and Bender continued to win when they weren't overworked, but they, too, collapsed in the general swoon of late 1908.

Out of the pennant race by July, Mack did something else he was good at—experimenting. He tried another Holy Cross student, Jack Barry, at second, signed an 18-year-old shortstop, Stuffy McInnis, out of a Massachusetts high school, and bought a 22-year-old third baseman, John Franklin Baker, from Reading.

Mack also signed the greatest of all his greats in 1908, but let him get away. Well, let him get away is not accurate—gave him away is more to the point. Tipped off by one of his widespread unofficial scouts, Mack bought Joe Jackson from the Greenville Spinners of the South Atlantic League, for $900. Jackson arrived in Philadelphia in the fall of 1908, didn't like the city, didn't like the other players—the feeling may have been mutual—and went home. He spent another year in the minor leagues close to home, and Mack tried to bring him north again. Again he went home.

Mack recognized a great natural hitter when he saw one, and knew what he was doing. He also knew Jackson would not be happy and therefore would not produce in Philadelphia. Jackson would rather play semipro ball in South Carolina. Mack could have held Jackson's contract, suspended him, and denied him a chance to play in the major leagues or anywhere else. But he didn't. He decided he would rather see Jackson go to a competitor than lose him to the National League, so he traded Shoeless Joe to the Cleveland Naps for Bris Lord.

Even without Jackson, Mack was ready to unveil the new edition of his Athletics on April 12, 1909, as he opened Shibe Park, the world's most modern baseball stadium. Built on a site close to downtown on Lehigh Avenue between 20th and 21st Streets, the new plant cost more than $1 million. The grandstand had 10,000 seats, the bleachers 13,000. Reinforced concrete and steel construction made it fireproof, an important consideration at a time when wooden grandstands had been known to burn down, leaving teams homeless overnight.

The pavilion was of French Renaissance style brick walls and terra cotta trimmings, topped by a green slate mansard roof. At the entrance on the corner of Lehigh and 21st rose a tall, ornate round tower where the team's offices were housed. An elevator reached Mr. Mack's office on the top floor. There were modern restrooms with neat, uniformed attendants, and a garage for 200 automobiles. It was the last word in ballparks but only the first of a new wave, soon to be followed by new structures in Detroit, Pittsburgh, Chicago, Boston, Brooklyn, and a rebuilt Polo Grounds. As *Baseball Magazine* noted in October 1908, "Ball-stands, as the game is, are growing bigger each year. But, no doubt, in another year some other city will outdistance Philadelphia."

In the building of ballparks, perhaps, but not on the diamond would another city outdistance the Athletics for long over the next six years. A record crowd of 31,160—with another 10,000 banging on the gates—turned out for the grand opening of Shibe Park. The Athletics beat Boston, 8–1, but the day ended in tragedy. Veteran catcher Mike "Doc" Powers, one of the most popular players in the game and a team leader whose .216 career BA belied his value to the team, had been with the club from their first game in 1901, except for 11 games with New York in 1905. Catching the opener, he was hit with sharp abdominal pains late in the game. He caught the last pitch, then collapsed. The illness was diagnosed as gangrene of the bowel. He was operated on twice and died two weeks later, at 39. In June the Athletics played an exhibition game for his family.

Baseball fans saw the debut of most of the $100,000 infield that day, but not as they would recognize it later. Mack had switched Collins to second to stay. Baker was on third, with McInnis at shortstop and Harry Davis on first. Jack Barry soon replaced McInnis at short and three-fourths of the famed inner unit was set. It would take two years and trials at second and third, plus some teaching by Davis, before McInnis took his place at first base in 1911. Davis, 36, played the full year and hit .268. Collins hit .346 and Baker .305. Both led their positions in putouts and assists.

The duo of Barry and Collins was quick, wideranging, and smart, devising plays and strategies that others may have thought of but couldn't execute. They pulled double and triple steals, and came up with ways to stop other teams from doing the same. Fans turned out early to watch them cut up during fielding practice the way later generations would show up to watch Babe Ruth take his practice swings. Barry is sometimes cited as being overrated because of a .243 lifetime BA, but he won many a game, series, and pennant with his glove in ways that are not apparent from box scores or the agate type of statistics.

To make room for Collins at second, Mack moved Danny Murphy to right field. With Rube Oldring and Topsy Hartsel, this gave him a balance of youth and experience in every department. To handle the catching Mack bought Ira Thomas from Detroit, beginning a 40-year relationship that lasted as long as the Athletics remained in Philadelphia. (One of the most telling descriptives of Mr. Mack was the number of players who stayed with him or returned to him as coaches for long spans of time.) It was a team that, given a year of experience, would be ready to challenge the Tigers, who looked like sure winners of their third straight pennant.

To back up Bender, Plank, and Coombs, Mack bought right-hander Cy Morgan from Boston and brought up rookie Harry Krause. Krause put together a 10-game midseason winning streak en route to an 18–8 year, the best he'd ever have, with a 1.39 ERA. Morgan was a surprising 16–9. Plank and Bender won 19 each, Coombs was 12–12, and the entire staff posted a 1.92 ERA which, even in the deadball era, was 0.55 under the league average. So the young team stayed in the thick of the fight. On August 10 they beat the Tigers, 3–1, and tied for the lead, but a 14-game win streak put the Tigers back on top.

On September 18 35,409, the largest paid attendance ever to crowd into a ballpark at the time, jammed Shibe Park to watch Chief Bender outpitch Bill Donovan, 2–0. Two days later Plank was a 4–3 victor, giving the Mackmen three of the four games. The series drew 117,208, about one-fifth of the season's total of 615,000. The A's stayed on the heels of the leaders until a double loss to the White Sox on September 30 eliminated them. They won 95 games and came within 3½ games of launching one of baseball's dominant dynasties a year ahead of schedule.

Collins and Barry were 22, Baker 23, McInnis 18. Bender and Coombs were 26. Young teams make mistakes, and Connie Mack at 46 was a patient, thorough teacher. He never scolded or corrected a player in front of others or on the spur of the moment. He preferred to wait until the next day, then quietly approach the player and offer suggestions or advice. He had last worn a uniform in 1900 at Milwaukee, and seldom visited the clubhouse after a game.

But there were so many days when there were so many mistakes to talk over with so many players, it occurred to him early in the 1909 season that it would be easier, and more beneficial to all the players, if he called them all together for a skull session. One afternoon during early batting practice he gathered them all on the right-field bleacher seats and went over what was on his mind. He then added some general tips on subjects like evading a tag, where to play for certain hitters, how to wait out a nervous pitcher. The young players began asking questions and showed so much interest it became a regular occurrence. Thus was born the clubhouse meeting.

When Connie Mack began to break up his second great team, in 1932, one of the reasons advanced was that attendance falls off when a team is too good and wins the pennant too easily. Mack's critics brayed at that one, but Mack knew what he was talking about. New York fans may be front runners, and the farther they were in front the better, but he learned that Philadelphians would rather see a losing fight for the flag than a coaster by an overwhelmingly superior team. The 1910 Athletics were a superb team. Except for a lapse by the 1912 team, the one Mack described as the best of all, they would have been the first to win five straight pennants. The 1910 margin was 14½ games. Leading by six games over Boston in August, the pitching staff almost disintegrated. Bender and Plank were ill, the sophomore jinx caught up with Harry Krause, and Dygert's spitball dried up. But Jack Coombs won 18 of 19 starts in three months to finish with a 31–9 record and 1.30 ERA. His 13 shutouts are still the league record. In September nobody scored off him for 53 innings. In 12 other games he gave up just one run. In what he called his best game, he got no decision; he and Ed Walsh went 16 innings in a 0–0 tie. The introduction of the cork center ball ended the dead ball days; they were the only pitching staff in either league to post an ERA under 2.00, at 1.79. Bender was 23–5.

The Reach Official American League Guide of 1911 referred to ". . . a steady concert of action which made the whole team appear to be working like a well-oiled piece of machinery . . . Harry Davis's clever captaining deserves a word of praise, and last, but not least, is to be commended Manager Mack's skillful handling of the machine he had built—and it is not every manager who can direct as well as construct."

In his 17th year as a manager, Mack was probably at the peak of his teaching, innovating, developing, and directing skills. His second great team would be equally dominating but different: older, more powerful, less dependent on clever inside work than on sluggers and hard throwing pitchers. And Mack would be 66.

But for now they were baseball's best, and they proved it by soundly outclassing the National League Champion Chicago Cubs in a five-game World Series, using only two pitchers, Bender and Coombs. Coombs turned in three complete-game victories in six days. The Athletics' .316 team batting average remains a World Series record. Four days after the Series ended the new World Champions were honored at a big civic banquet. But Connie Mack was not present. He had been married that day (his first wife died in 1892) and was on his way to Europe. So the city threw another party for the team when he returned.

The World Champion Athletics were on top of the world in spring training of 1911 and they acted like they knew it. They coasted through the training exercises, then ran into a fierce Tiger club they had deposed after three straight pennants, and six other clubs eager to knock them off. Bender and Coombs were slow to get into shape.

Plank found himself carrying the early-season load with Morgan and Krause. Captain Harry Davis, nearing 38, had slowed drastically in the field and was struggling at the plate. In June Mack told Stuffy McInnis to hang up his shortstop's glove and get himself a first baseman's mitt.

They broke last and trailed through May before starting to climb. On June 23 they stumbled briefly, losing the only doubleheader out of 18 played that year (they swept 10) and on July 4 took the lead. They slipped again when a collision between Murphy and Collins sidelined them both, Collins for three weeks. Once he was back in the lineup, and Bender and Coombs regained their stride, there was no stopping the white elephants. They pulled away to a 13½-game final margin.

Adapting to the livelier ball, this time the Athletics won it with the bat more than defense. The team batting average jumped 30 points, to .296, while the staff ERA went from 1.79 to 3.01. Coombs closed strong to win 28 against 12 losses. Plank won 23, Bender was 17–5. Morgan won 15 and Krause 12. Everybody but Davis had a good year at the plate, led by Collins' .365. Frank Baker led the league with 11 home runs. Despite the early season slump and mid-season injuries they made it look easy again.

Facing the New York Giants in the World Series for the first time since the 1905 whitewash series, the Athletics overcame an opening-game 2–1 loss to Mathewson and took four of the next five, including two sweet triumphs over their old nemesis, Matty. Bender, Coombs, and Plank did all the pitching and Frank Baker caused future fans to believe his given name was Home Run. He earned that tag not just because he hit two home runs in the Series, but because of when he hit them. The first won Game Two for the A's, 3–1. The second tied Game Three 1–1 in the ninth, enabling the Athletics to beat Mathewson, 3–2, in 11 innings. The dramatics, and the ease with which they finished off McGraw, 13–2, in the final game, made them cockier and more convinced of their invincibility.

Everybody, including Connie Mack, rated the Athletics a shoo-in to repeat. Poor weather and a lackadaisical attitude left them unhoned in the spring. They thought they could move into high gear when they had to, but the team never put it all together. They topped the league in hitting again, and fielding stats were impressive. But whenever they ran up the score, the fielding and pitching were weak. Behind good pitching and tight fielding the hitting wasn't there. A back injury suffered in his last World Series appearance benched Jack Coombs for two months; he still won 21 and lost 10. Bender was often out of shape and finished 13–8. Morgan and Krause were of no benefit. The load fell again on a game Eddie Plank. He was 26–6, one of his losses a 19-inning 5–4 defeat by Washington. The A's tied it with a three-run rally in the ninth that brought in Walter Johnson in relief. It then became a nine-inning 1–0 battle between Plank and Johnson.

Collins had arm trouble, Barry hurt his shoulder, Murphy was injured in June and lost for the rest of the year. One bright spot was the development of Amos Strunk, a young left fielder who batted .289 and made just three errors in 118 games. Two young pitchers showed some promise. Carroll Brown, a fastball and spitter artist, won 13, Byron Houck, 8. Late in the year Mack signed a tall, thin 18-year-old lefthander off the local sandlots, but illnesses delayed Herb Pennock's taking a regular turn until 1914.

The team didn't collapse; they won 90 games. Baker hit .347, tied for the lead with 10 home runs and led with 133 RBIs. Their woes were compounded by greatly improved Boston and Washington teams, each led by pitchers having their finest years. Joe Wood was 34–5 for Boston, Johnson 32–12 for the Senators. Still, it was a disappointing year for Mack, on the field and at the gate, as they were out of the race for the last two months. For the second time Mack took his team to Cuba in the fall, where they played their best ball of the year, beating the Cubans so regularly that the fans quit coming and the jaunt was a financial disaster.

Mack didn't panic. He knew his infield was still the best in the business. He knew Danny Murphy, at 35, was over the hill, and his pitching needed shoring up. Patching, not rebuilding, was all the situation required. He felt he had the young players to do the job. When they returned from Cuba he bought outfielders Jimmy Walsh and Eddie Murphy from Baltimore of the International League. He had a 19-year-old righthander, Joe Bush, who had one minor league season behind him, and Bob Shawkey, a Pennsylvania boy. With Ira Thomas near the end of his playing days, Mack bought Buffalo's rookie sensation Wally Schang to back up Jack Lapp behind the plate.

It was a chastened and determined group of Athletics that took its spring practice seriously in 1913. Taking nothing for granted, they went into the lead on April 24 and were never headed. With Jack Coombs sidelined by typhoid and a back ailment that would idle him for two years, Mack adapted his strategy to his young mound staff. Three years earlier he had gone with his starters for 123 complete games. This time he worked the youthful Bush, Brown, Houck, and later Shawkey into the starting rotation, and used the veterans Bender and Plank to relieve them as well as start. Plank was 17–10, including seven shutouts, and relieved in 12 games. Bender started 22 and relieved in 26, with six of his 21 wins plus 12 saves in relief. Eddie Murphy, Walsh, and Strunk revitalized the outfield with speed, but the big bats were still in the marvelous infield quartet. Even Jack Barry hit his peak at .275 while the others were well above .300.

The Giants made it to their third straight World Series and promptly lost their third straight, this one in five. Their only win: a reminder of times past, a 10-inning 3–0 win for Mathewson over Plank, who beat Matty in the finale, 3–1. In 21 World Series games Mack had made only one pitching change, and that when Coombs was forced out by an injury in the fifth game of the 1911 set.

The 1913 season was a success financially. The A's were expected to win, but it was no runaway. Washington and Cleveland stayed close enough to retain fans' interest; the final margin was 6½ games. Profits were boosted by a rise in ticket prices from 25 to 50 cents for grandstand seats. Bleachers remained a quarter. The increased tariff did not discourage the fans. Championship teams had raised the payroll, and Mr. Mack always looked to the business side of the game: you had to take in more money than you spent in order to survive.

Connie Mack and his team were once again the acknowledged kings of the baseball world. He was the first manager to win three World Series. He had proven again that he could overcome the loss of key players—as he had when the courts took Napoleon Lajoie away from him in 1902—and still win. The maneuvering of his uneven pitching staff in 1913 was perhaps the finest job of managing he would ever do. His team was young, smart, and talented, and looked like it could go on winning indefinitely.

But behind this idyllic scene of success and contentment, war drums were being tuned up and lightly thumped in several places. In Europe suspicious politicians and restless generals were snapping at each other. In the United States a promoter tried to put together a new baseball league, the Federal League. After putting in a half season in 1913 the would-be major league was laughed off. Its future was regarded as deader than the last such effort, the United States League of a few years back, which had crumpled in June. Though Connie Mack would win his fourth pennant in five years in 1914, no manager ever enjoyed a winning season less. Before the spring was over both wars had broken out.

Battlefield reports filled the front pages; court battles and dollar signs dominated the sports pages. Every team in the American League lost money on the year, for a combination of reasons. One was the predominance of the Athletics, a factor sometimes ridiculed as a deterrent to attendance but one that was cited at the time as a very real influence. Everyone conceded the pennant to them, and, true to form, they led all the way, finishing 8½ games ahead of Boston, 19 over third-place Washington. The Athletics outhit the league in batting average by 24 points. They had the deepest pitching staff in the game, augmented by the addition of two young, strong right arms from local playing fields: John Wyckoff, 11–7 for the year, and Rube Bressler, who won 10 and lost 4. Chief Bender turned in the highest winning percentage of his career, .850 on 17 wins and 3 losses. Plank was 15–5. Seven pitchers won 10 or more; none had a losing year.

The general caliber of play suffered in both leagues as most teams lost top players to the Feds, and those that stayed were distracted by Federal League scouts and bounty hunters, who followed them all season, big money contracts and ink-filled pens in hand. Fans became fed up with the bickering between the rival owners and the jumping of players chasing the highest bids. It all coincided with an explosion in competitive pastimes and amusements: the movies, amateur and semipro games, golf, and the automobile. The war news put an added damper on fan enthusiasm.

None of the Athletics deserted in 1914, but they talked about it all season. How much was loyalty worth? How much was Eddie Plank's 39-year-old arm, or Chief Bender's at 31, worth? The team was divided. Some refused to consider any offers, either because they thought the Feds wouldn't last, or they placed a higher value on loyalty and were content to stay in Philadelphia. Others saw it as strictly business, nothing personal. They should make whatever they could during the limited time they could play the game. To the first group they were seen as traitors, ingrates, opportunists. How could they give their best on the Philadelphia diamond while considering offers to play on somebody else's grounds? And when might they depart? Tomorrow? Next week?

With all the turmoil, the Athletics knew they had another World Series check waiting for them. They stayed and played, and played well. But Connie Mack was disturbed. He could not merely sit back and enjoy his team's success on the field. He was looking ahead to next year. He had no illusions of the war clouds in Europe blowing over or the Federal League's bankrolls giving out. Everybody on every front was digging in for a long, wearing war.

Mack felt the crunch of a rising payroll and falling income. Forget 1912. His players had won three World Championships in four years. They might make it four in a row this fall. Nobody had done that. They wanted to be paid accordingly. But Mack was not about to compete with the Feds. His winning teams weren't drawing enough at the gate to support themselves and break even as it was. There was no prospect of a quick end to the wars and no guarantee of closer pennant races in the future. The club had survived economic panics and uncertainties in the past, thanks to suspenseful pennant races. But the Athletics were living proof that a team could be too good for its own financial welfare. When the books were closed for the year, they were $60,000 in the red.

It was money problems that forced Mack to let another great hitter get away in the middle of the 1914 season. At the time he thought he was just passing up a promising lefthanded pitcher. Jack Dunn, owner of the Baltimore club in the International League, was taking a beating at the gate by a Federal League club, which to the fans represented major league baseball. Dunn preferred to hold on to his prospects for a few years before selling them but he needed cash. He put his two rookie pitchers, Babe Ruth and Ernie Shore, on the block, offering them first to his close friend, Connie Mack. "I don't have the money," Mack said. "Sell them to somebody who can pay you a good price for them." They went to the Boston Red Sox with their catcher, Ben Egan, for under $10,000.

The National League was saved at the gate by the sensational late season spurt of the Boston Braves, who overtook the heavily favored Giants in September and won their first pennant. Despite their heroics, the Braves were underdogs to the mighty Athletics. But had he been a betting man, Connie Mack wouldn't have given you any odds. He knew his team had lost their cohesiveness, their teamness, long before the Series opened. They had won the American League pennant only because they were so much better than the rest of the league, even half-trying. He was not surprised when they were outplayed, out-pitched, and outhustled by the Braves in the first World Series sweep.

When the World Series was over, Mack took stock. New money had come into the Federal League. The stakes had been raised. He knew Chief Bender and Eddie Plank, and probably the recovered but weakened Jack Coombs, were going over. He asked waivers on them in an effort to salvage something; maybe another club would buy them and pay them what they wanted. But nobody did. Bender and Plank signed with the Feds. Coombs, now a free agent, signed with Brooklyn in the National League.

At the start of the war, Mack had signed Collins and Baker to three-year contracts. But now Collins came to him and openly told him what he was being offered. Mack couldn't match it. To save Collins for the American League, and to recoup some cash, Mack contacted Charles Comiskey. Comiskey had the money and the determination to fight the north side Chicago Whales by building a winner. He was willing to match the Feds' offer and satisfy Collins, and held out the possibility of Collins managing the team. The White Sox bought Collins for $50,000.

Baker was another matter. He wanted his contract reopened. Or maybe he would accept an offer from the Feds. Or maybe he'd just rather stay home on the farm in Trappe, Maryland. He'd made noises like that before, and never did like the traveling or being away from the farm all summer. But Mack was in no mood to tear up the old contract and give him a raise. So Baker sat out the year, playing semipro ball instead.

Connie Mack never thought he was breaking up his great team, as these moves have often been described. He'd lost stars before and won. He still had half his famed infield; there was no way he could retain the other half. His outfield and catchers were intact. And he had the young pitching staff that had matured so effectively the past two years, with a raft of rookies to look over in the spring.

In January he bought Nap Lajoie back from Cleveland. Lajoie was 39, but he'd been a manager for five years and would help steady the younger infielders. So Mack headed for Jacksonville in the spring of 1915 with a vacancy at third base, a partially refilled hole in his bank account, and no sense of disaster. The dynasty's days might be over, but a strong first-division team was a definite prospect.

If Connie Mack was given to looking for omens at the start of the 1915 season, he probably would have latched onto the wrong one: Herb Pennock's near no hitter, broken up with two out in the ninth by Harry Hooper's scratch single. Mack would have overlooked the graceful Nap Lajoie's five errors at second base eight days later.

On opening day the third base vacancy was filled by Eddie Murphy. It didn't work. Catcher Wally Schang took over. That was worse. Schang spent more time in the outfield than he did catching. Only McInnis and Strunk were hitting. The pitching was awful. In May the team slid to seventh; by July they were cellarbound to stay. They went on to lose 109 games. The players gave up on themselves early, and the fans caught on and gave up coming to the ballpark. Mack still had too many former World Champions on the payroll at inflated salaries. With the turnstiles rusting, the "for sale" sign went up. In the first two weeks of July he sold Jack Barry, batting .222, to the Red Sox for $8,000, Bob Shawkey to the Yankees for $18,000, and Eddie Murphy to the White Sox for $13,500.

Perhaps peeved by the whole patch of shambles he found himself in, perhaps goaded by what he considered an indifference to the game by his opening day hero, Herb Pennock, Mack watched the slim lefty win two more while losing six, then sent the 20-year-old prospect to Boston on waivers. Pennock pitched another 19 years, winning 240 games and a place in the Hall of Fame. It was, Mack admitted later, the biggest mistake of his career. He had let Joe Jackson get away, not because he misjudged Joe's ability, but because he was convinced Jackson would never play in Philadelphia. He had passed up Babe Ruth because he couldn't afford him at the time. But Pennock—that was an atypical lapse of patience and character assessment.

No matter, for now. Even a Walter Johnson in his prime couldn't salvage this season. Mack began experimenting halfway through the summer. He signed sandlotters, high school students, semipros. In all, 27 pitchers took the mound for him, a record at the time.

Could things get worse? They could. The Athletics lost 117 games in 1916. Somehow Joe Bush won 15 and Elmer Myers 14; the rest of the pitchers won just seven. The roommates' futility award was permanently retired by pitchers Tom Sheehan and Johnnie Nabors; they won one game each and lost 37 between them. The only highlight of the year was Joe Bush's 5–0 no-hitter on August 26 against Cleveland. It was also Nap Lajoie's last game.

The outfield stayed together all season, but everybody had a tryout at third base. Convinced that Baker would not play in Philadelphia again, Mack succumbed to the pressing requests of the Yankees and accepted $37,500 for Baker's contract. Only Stuffy McInnis remained of the great infield.

The Federal League war was settled, but it didn't cause a ripple in Shibe Park. For seven straight years the Athletics occupied the American League basement. Connie Mack kept signing youngsters, and throwing them into immediate action. Along the way he did sign some good ones: speedy center fielder Whitey Witt, who grew tired of life in the cellar and talked his way into being peddled to the Yankees in 1922; Jimmy Dykes, a local boy who became a key player in Mack's next dynasty; Joe Dugan, a third baseman from Holy Cross whose future lay elsewhere but was valuable trading material.

Mack had greatly reduced his payroll, but America's entry into the war in Europe and the damper it put on attendance kept him operating on a shoestring. In December 1917 Boston's Harry Frazee showed up at the winter meetings with a big bankroll and returned home with Wally Schang, Amos Strunk, and Joe Bush. Mack had relieved Frazee of $60,000 and the rights to a veteran but lame southpaw Vean Gregg, catcher Chet Thomas, and outfielder Merlin Kopp.

A month later Stuffy McInnis also headed for Boston for cash and players to be named later. Amid howls of scorn from the usually sympathetic press, Mack later came up with a full payment of players for McInnis: third baseman Larry Gardner, outfielder Tilly Walker, and catcher Forrest Cady, all firstline experienced men. For the war-shortened 1918 season Walker tied Babe Ruth for the home run lead with 11. Gardner hit .294. Gregg won 9, lost 14. The Athletics were still last but they won 52 games and finished just 24 from the top. They were improving, or so it seemed. Players, old and young, came and went as Mack sought a winning combination without spending any money. They lost 104 in 1919, trailing the seventh-place Senators by 20 games. They lost 106 in 1920, 100 in 1921.

But a few of the pieces were beginning to fit. Jimmy Dykes came back from a year in Atlanta ready to become the most versatile player in the game, a key interchangeable part of the next super team. Dykes eventually would be tapped to succeed Mr. Mack as manager. Eddie Rommel, knuckleball pitcher, came up in 1920 and stayed 13 years, winning 171 games. Cy Perkins, signed at 19, became the first-string catcher in 1919 and remained on the club another dozen years. Outfielder Bing Miller hit .288 in his rookie year at Washington in 1921; Mack traded Joe Dugan to Boston; Boston sent shortstop Roger Peckinpaugh to Washington, which completed the deal by sending Miller to Philadelphia, where he would hit .312 for 16 years. Mack also bought first baseman Joe Hauser from Milwaukee. A longball hitter, Hauser became the cleanup man, but two freak knee injuries cut him out of the majors before the next pennants waved over Shibe Park.

Connie Mack watched Babe Ruth hit a phenomenal 59 home runs in 1921 and he knew the game had changed forever. His first great team had been built on the strategy of score a run and hold that lead. It relied on smart infielders and pitchers you could depend on to put the ball where they wanted it. Now he would have to build a new winner on a power base. Tilly Walker hit 37 homers, two more than Ruth in 1922; Miller hit 21, Dykes and Hauser and outfielder Frank Welch 32 among them as the Athletics led the league with 111. Rommel's knuckler tied the sluggers in knots and he won 27 of the club's 65 victories. It was enough to lift them out of the cellar at last, four games over Boston.

On January 14, 1922, Ben Shibe died at 84. Known affectionately as Uncle Ben to baseball fans throughout the city, he had been an ideal partner for Connie Mack, who now owned 50 percent of the club. Shibe had never second guessed his manager, never interfered with Mack's decisions on or off the field. The same harmony that existed among the players carried through the front office. His son, Tom, became president; another son, John, was vice president.

With Babe Ruth firmly established as a gate attraction, the Yankees always drew a full house wherever they played. They literally meant the difference between a profit or loss on the season for many American League clubs, the Athletics included. Emboldened by a rise to sixth place in 1923 and the return of prosperity to the economy and customers to the ballpark, Mack decided he had enough of a nucleus to go out and buy what he needed.

Tilly Walker was through at 35. The only home run threats were Hauser and Miller. Sammy Hale was a steady hitter at third, but Mack was becoming disenchanted with the work of Chick Galloway at shortstop. Of course Dykes could play anywhere, but only one position at a time. Except for Miller, the outfield was not championship caliber. The pitching staff needed restocking, and Cy Perkins couldn't carry the catching load alone.

It was time to stop sifting the sandlots for future stars. In December he went to the bank, then went shopping. Out in the Pacific Coast League a one-time pitching prospect turned outfielder had torn the league apart playing for Salt Lake City. Paul Strand batted .394, racking up 325 hits in 194 games, including 66 doubles, 13 triples, and 43 home runs. He scored 180 runs and drove in 187. Mack went west to look him over, liked what he saw and bought him. The price was reported at $70,000, but was actually around $40,000, still a big price for a minor leaguer.

For a tiny fraction of that amount Mack bought a rookie outfielder, Al Simmons, who had signed with his hometown team, Milwaukee, when no major league club would pay his expenses for a tryout. Simmons was farmed out to Shreveport. Mack bought him for delivery at the end of the 1923 season. Simmons finished the year at Milwaukee, where he hit .398 in 24 games.

In Baltimore Jack Dunn had an experienced second baseman, a perfect leadoff man who could wangle 100 walks a year while batting .270. Mack bought Max Bishop for about the same price he paid for Paul Strand. He picked up Rube Walberg, a big lefthander in the Giants system, drafted a righthander, Sam Gray, from Beaumont, and signed a former Phillies pitcher, Stan Baumgartner.

It was an optimistic Connie Mack who went to spring training in 1924, confident he had put together a strong contender. All the early publicity focused on the phenom, Strand. Was he overrated? Did the pressure affect him? Was the air really so thin out in the desert to make his numbers suspect? Whatever it was, Strand was a flop. He hit .228 with nary a homer in 47 games, at which point Mack cut his losses and shipped him to Toledo for a former Yankee playboy, Broadway Bill Lamar. Lamar could hit the ball by day—.356 in 1925—and the bars by night with equal regularity. His night games cost him his job before the A's became a hit.

The sweet smell of success in the spring air in 1924 turned to the odor of compost in a hurry. The Athletics fell into the cellar on May 5 and stayed there for three months. Mack made a few switches in the lineup and they began to wake up. Over the last two months they played the best ball in the league and climbed to fifth. Hauser hit 27 home runs, second to Ruth, with 115 RBIs. The outfield trio hit over .300. The pitching was ragged. Despite the rainout of the last two games with the Yankees, attendance was up and it was a profitable year.

When Connie Mack had the money he spent it. He bought control of the Portland club in the Pacific Coast league to nail down the rights to catcher Mickey Cochrane, a graduate of Boston University, then shelled out $50,000 for him. The hottest property in the minor leagues was pitcher Lefty Grove. The star of Jack Dunn's perennial pennant winners in Baltimore, Grove was well paid and content in Baltimore. Dunn was in no hurry to sell his stars, but it was time for Grove to move up. Dunn and Mack had done business together for years, and quickly closed a deal: $100,600, payable in 10 annual installments for the fireballer, whose temper was as hard to control as his fastball.

At the age of 62, when men in more mundane occupations were thinking of retirement, Connie Mack was at Ft. Myers, Florida, looking over the new spring training facilities he would occupy for 15 years. There had been little permanence in spring training arrangements for most clubs. They went wherever they could get the best deal each year. Mack became a close friend of members of the Kiwanis club who had promoted the winter home of Thomas Edison, Henry Ford, and other industrialists as a training camp.

It was a young team blended with experience that took the field for an exhibition game against the Phillies in the spring of 1925. With Simmons and Cochrane not yet tested, their most dangerous hitter was Joe Hauser. On a routine grounder to short, Hauser turned to cover first when his left kneecap fell apart. The splintered knee had to be wired together and he was out for the year. Once again Mack had an early loss to overcome. He needed a first baseman in a hurry. The Portland club had a journeyman minor leaguer, Jim Poole, 30 years old with no major league experience. He was holding out and missed spring training. Mack signed him and he opened the season at first base. Lacking Hauser's power, he proved adequate and batted .298.

One week after the injury to Hauser Grove made his first big league start. He was not impressive against the Red Sox, walking four and hitting one batter before leaving in the fourth. He had struck out nobody. The A's eventually won the game, 9–8. Grove became the first pitcher to lead the league in both strikeouts and walks, winning 10 against 13 losses on a 4.75 ERA. He worked too fast, blew up too quickly.

In the eighth inning of the opener Mickey Cochrane made his debut; pinch hitting for Cy Perkins he singled, then stayed in the game. Al Simmons emerged as a longball threat, hitting 24 homers among his 253 hits for a .385 average in his second year. Mack could make out a batting order that put seven men at the plate who would bat .318 or better. Ed Rommel led the pitchers with a 21–10 record, Sam Gray was 16–8. When Gray was out for a month with a broken finger, Mack bought 40-year-old spitballer John Quinn from the Red Sox. Quinn, acquired as a temporary replacement, stayed five years.

It had taken Connie Mack 10 years to create another winner. For four months he battled the World Champion Senators, opening a five-game lead. Then, in a reversal of last year's torrid finish, they went west for the last time and lost 12 in a row and the pennant. Back home for a morning-afternoon Labor Day doubleheader, they dropped a pair to Washington. Almost 70,000 fans filled Shibe Park for the two games to cap a successful season at the gate, albeit a disappointing one in the standings.

Frank Baker was managing Easton in the Eastern Shore League. Baker told Mack he had a 17-year-old catcher who could play every other position and hit a ball as hard as Babe Ruth. Mack paid a few hundred dollars for Jimmie Foxx, farmed him out to Providence for the rest of the season, then brought him to Philadelphia for the last few weeks. Used as a pinch hitter nine times, Foxx made six hits.

The Athletics were favored to win the 1926 pennant, with good reason, Mack thought. He had proven depth on the mound, a hard hitting lineup, and Joe Hauser was back. But the season proved as vexing as the opening game, when Ed Rommel matched Walter Johnson through 14 scoreless innings before the Senators pushed over the winning run in the 15th. It was that kind of year. In the age of the slugger, their team ERA of 3.00 was the best in the league. But the pitchers couldn't hold leads or win the close ones. Within six weeks Mack knew he did not have a winner. Hauser was slow to get back in the groove and Jim Poole went back to first. The infield was weak, except for Bishop at second and wherever Dykes was playing. Everybody's hitting was off 30 to 40 points. If a pitcher won two in a row, he lost the next two.

Mack began to deal. He sent Bing Miller to St. Louis for heavy-hitting outfielder Baby Doll Jacobson, then sent Jake on to Boston with pitchers Harriss and Heimach for Howard Ehmke, who came through with 12 late-season wins against four losses. He bought a veteran minor league southpaw, Joe Pate, from the Texas League. In 47 games, all but two in relief, Pate was 9–0, and never won another big league game.

The Florida land boom was on, everybody was making money in the stock market, there were plenty of entertainment dollars to be spent, and the Athletics had a good, though not great, team for the fans to watch. In May 38,000 turned out to watch Grove blank Detroit, 8–0. Grove's control was improving. On June 12 he went 11 innings without giving up a walk, then walked two that cost him a 1–0 loss to the Indians. He finished 13–13, cut his walks to 101, while fanning 194 to lead the league for the second of seven straight years.

In July of 1926 a municipal fair, honoring the 150th anniversary of independence, was in financial trouble. The summer-long party included all the attractions of a carnival midway. When the mayor went to court and won approval to remain open on Sundays, Mack and Tom Shibe concluded they couldn't see anything more educational and uplifting about an amusement park than a baseball game. Over the howls of the mayor and the city's clergymen, the Athletics obtained an injunction preventing the police from interfering with a Sunday game as long as there was no public disturbance. After three games with the Tigers, including a Saturday, were rained out, the A's announced they would play the White Sox on Sunday, September 22. A light but steady rain kept the crowd down to about 10,000 as Lefty Grove set down Chicago, 3–2, without incident. It was the last Sunday at home for the year, and before the next season started the state supreme court declared Sunday games were still illegal. It would remain that way until 1934. The Athletics would have been happy to pay the $400 fine imposed by the law, but the court ruled they would forfeit their franchise to do business if they played on Sunday again.

Connie Mack was a shrewd showman and expert public relations practitioner. In addition to a hustling, winning team, he knew that individual stars were solid gate attractions. Grove was developing into a star, but he couldn't pitch every day. With an eye on the box office Mack departed from his policy of developing young teams and signed three free agents for 1927 whose ages totalled 118 and ball playing experience equalled 61 years. After two years as player-manager for the White Sox, Eddie Collins returned as a part-time second baseman and coach. Zack Wheat, released by the Dodgers after 18 years, signed on for one more season. Ty Cobb, who with Tris Speaker was cleared by Commissioner Landis of betting and game fixing charges, agreed to a $40,000 salary to play for Connie Mack.

Mack didn't need any help for Max Bishop at second base—he needed help at the other infield positions—and he knew Cobb and Wheat had slowed up in the field, but the three future Hall of Famers brought baseball savvy, example, and dependable bats. All three hit well over .300. Mack tried to sign Speaker also, but lost him to Washington (he would close out his career with the A's in 1928). With Foxx on first and Grove pitching, Mack could field a lineup of seven future Hall of Fame residents.

The Yankees' 1926 World Series victory did not make believers of the experts; 29 writers touring the training camps picked the Athletics to win the 1927 pennant, only nine favored New York. Mack stood pat with his pitching but plugged what he saw as his last weak spot by buying another Baltimore star, shortstop Joe Boley, for $65,000. Then disaster struck again. Joe Hauser was guarding first base, unmenaced by ball or baserunner, when he suddenly fell to the ground. This time it was his right knee that disintegrated and he was out for the year. Mack handed a first baseman's mitt to Jimmy Dykes. When Dykes was needed elsewhere (he played second, short, third, and the outfield and pitched on two occasions), the young catcher, Foxx, filled in at first.

No matter who was in the lineup there were always seven or eight .300 hitters on the card. Simmons missed 40 games but hit .392. Grove started and relieved and was 20–12. Walberg won 17, Quinn, 15. Rommel was 11–3. The Mackmen won 91 games but the 1927 Yankees ran away from everybody and won a record 110. They outscored the Athletics by 134 runs, outhomered them by 98.

Mack had assembled a winning team, but not yet a great one. Cobb (who collected his 4,000th hit in 1927 against his old Detroit teammates) signed for one more year, but Wheat retired and Collins would play very little in 1928. Mack signed Speaker for one last tour of the circuit. Having regretted the trading away of Bing Miller, he sent Sam Gray to St. Louis and brought Miller back to cover center field. Knowing Cobb and Speaker were not everyday players, he bought outfielder Mule Haas from Atlanta. In midseason he went back to Baltimore and bought the big strong righthander he was missing, George Earnshaw. A college graduate and socialite like Pennock, Earnshaw was 28—no raw rookie—but Mack would not make the same mistake and turn the 6'4", 200-pounder loose too quickly.

He still had not found a permanent place for Jimmie Foxx in the lineup. Foxx got into 61 games at third, 30 at first, and 20 behind the plate in 1928, batting .328 with 13 home runs. With Foxx, Dykes, Cobb, Speaker, and Haas on the bench, nobody ever had bench strength like the 1928 Athletics.

Still the Yankees looked unbeatable. By the end of June they were 50–16 and led by 11½ games. After July 4 it was 13½. Fan interest was waning. The swan song of Mack's superstars wasn't enough to reverse the lagging attendance. Mack decided to limit Cobb and Speaker to pinch hitting roles. He turned Bing Miller and Mule Haas loose in the outfield with Simmons and the Athletics began to move. They were 25–8 in July and the Yankees lead began, slowly, to melt. On August 10 John Quinn won his 15th, a four-hitter over Washington. By the end of August the lead was down to two games, and Shibe Park's turnstiles were humming again. On September 7 and 8 Mack's boys swept two doubleheaders in Boston and took a half-game lead into New York for a four-game series. But the Yankees took three of the four and the A's left town down by 1½. That's the way it ended. It was a two-team race, with the third-place Browns 19 games out. The paycheck from the Sunday doubleheader in New York for the visitor's share of 85,265 was small consolation.

The Athletics were closing in on the high-stakes, high-payroll ranks again, but they still weren't champions. Reminiscent of 1908 and 1909, they had enjoyed four straight years of Connie Mack's formula for maximum profitability: a contender but nonwinner, keeping attendance high while limiting players' salary demands. But Mack had spent a lot of money to build a winner, not a runner-up. Businessman that he was, he was a baseball man first, and wanted to win as much as anybody. Four times he thought he had the right combination, but freak injuries to Joe Hauser and the sudden emergence of the great Yankee juggernaut had so far thwarted him. With the over-the-hill Hall of Fame gang gone from the roster, Mack decided he had only one problem for 1929: how to get Jimmie Foxx's bat into the lineup every day. There was only one place: first base.

For Connie Mack the next three years were very sharply etched examples of the best of times and the worst of times. The days of frantic experimenting and rebuilding were over. The only changes he would make involved secondary players. The Athletics dominated the American League as no team had ever done in either league, winning 313 games over three years. They won pennants by margins of 18, 8, and 13½ games. Mack's only concern during this stretch was occasional fits of complacency and overconfidence among his players.

Championship teams demand higher salaries, and Mr. Mack had the bad fortune to flatten the field while the Great Depression was steamrolling the nation. Rising payrolls clashed with falling attendance. Philadelphia fans were not front runners. They turned out to watch a team fight for a pennant, but were turned off when it was too easy. In 1929 the Athletics led from start to finish, won by 18 games, and drew fewer fans than their up-and-coming young team that had fought for the lead in 1925. And this was before the Depression really hit. Philadelphia was an industrial city. In 1930 and 1931 unemployment lines were longer than box office lines. And Connie Mack and several of his players were also among the losers in the stock market.

When Mack began selling off players after a disappointing 1932 campaign, the Athletics had the highest payroll in the game's history. Mack had spent over a half million dollars for players. Shibe Park had been enlarged, but only in the $1 grandstand seats. It still had a smaller proportion of box seats than any other park. The club had borrowed $700,000 from the bank, and the bank needed the cash.

But all that was yet to come as the Athletics went into the 1929 World Series against the Cubs. Mack's first great champions had exemplified speed, cunning, and brains. The new edition was the epitome of the new game: power. Simmons hit .365 and missed the batting title by four points; he led in RBIs with 157 and hit 34 home runs. Foxx hit 33. Six regulars were well over .300. Grove, 20–6, Earnshaw, 24–8, and Walberg, 18–11, were all power pitchers. Rommel's slow stuff won him 12 against 2 losses with a 2.85 ERA.

Howard Ehmke, 35, a 6–3 sidearming righthander, was effective early in the season as an occasional starter and reliever, winning 7 with 2 losses. But he'd seen little activity in the second half and when he was left at home on the last road trip he wasn't missed. Before that trip Ehmke, a .500 pitcher over 13 years with second-division clubs, was advised by Mack that he would be released. Ehmke asked for a shot at one World Series start before calling it quits. This was the reaction Mack was fishing for. He was hoping Ehmke would display the heart and desire needed for the challenge he had in mind. He had already decided that Ehmke's delivery wheeling by way of third base out of a white-shirted Wrigley Field bleacher background would be the toughest for the Cubs predominantly righthanded-hitting lineup to cope with. Using a strategy that had worked for him before, he had also decided not to start Lefty Grove at all, but reserve him for relief.

So Mr. Mack told Ehmke to stay home, scout the Cubs when they came to town, and be ready to start the World Series opener. Most of the players were as shocked as the writers and broadcasters when Ehmke warmed up before the game. But Mack's analysis was on the mark. Ehmke had that one more game in his right arm, the last he ever won. He gave up eight hits, walked one and struck out 13 for a World Series record, holding the Cubs scoreless until the ninth in a 3–1 victory. Foxx hit a home run in the seventh and Miller drove in the winning runs in the ninth.

Earnshaw, who was rocked in Game Two, came back two days later and went the route, but was outpitched by Guy Bush, 3–1, for the Cubs' only win of the Series. But it looked more like the Series would be tied at two-all when the Cubs took an 8–0 lead into the last of the seventh of Game Four on Saturday, October 12. Charlie Root was breezing along with a three-hitter and Mack was ready to rest his regulars and give the subs a chance to play.

Simmons led off and hit a home run to mild applause for the futile blow. Foxx and Miller singled and Mack put off sending in the benchwarmers. When Dykes made it 8–2 with another single, Mack told Joe Boley, "This fellow is losing his stuff. Hit the first good pitch." Boley singled in a run. After George Burns batted for Rommel and popped out, Bishop singled to make it 8–4. Lefty Art Nehf relieved Root and Haas drove a liner to center where Hack Wilson misjudged it, lost it in the sun, and saw it bounce behind him while Haas followed

two other A's across the plate. This tainted home run evoked a hysterical uproar from the fans and the Philadelphia players. Jimmy Dykes
whacked his neighbor on the back and watched his manager tumble
into the bats. Mr. Mack picked himself up and told Lefty Grove to
warm up.

Nehf soon walked Cochrane. Cubs manager Joe McCarthy
brought in righthander Sheriff Blake, who gave up singles to Foxx
and Simmons and the score was tied. McCarthy called in Pat Malone
and Jimmy Dykes, thinking they still needed a hit to tie it, lined a
double to left and the Athletics led, 10–8. Boley and Burns then struck
out. Grove came in and fanned four in two perfect innings. The bench
bunch had seen no action afield but they had witnessed more action
in that half-inning than any World Series had produced before or
since.

McCarthy came back with Pat Malone on Monday and he held
the confident but weary Athletics to two hits for eight innings. Mack
gave Howard Ehmke another start, but without Wrigley Field's helpful
background, the Cubs nicked him for two runs in the fourth and Rube
Walberg came in to put out the fire, blanking them on two hits the
rest of the way. In the ninth Walter French pinch hit for Walberg and
struck out. Bishop singled and Mule Haas homered over the right-
field wall to tie the game. Cochrane grounded out but Simmons almost
cleared the scoreboard in right with a double. Foxx walked, and Miller
doubled off the scoreboard and the Cubs were finished. Game-winning
rallies late in the last two games made it the most dramatic five-game
Series in the books.

The only way the Athletics could lose in 1930 was to beat themselves, and that's the way they began the season. Only when Connie
Mack walked into the clubhouse after a game and told off his stars,
one by one, for living off their press clippings, did the team begin to
play according to form. It was the year Al Simmons finally won a
batting crown, at .381 with 36 home runs and 165 RBIs. Foxx poled
37 and drove in 156 while hitting .335. Together they were almost as
destructive a one-two punch as Ruth and Gehrig, racking up 750 total
bases to the New York duo's 798.

It was the first of two superlative years for Lefty Grove as well. In
the time of the sluggers, when three American League teams batted
over .300, Grove won 28 and lost 5. He also saved 9, led with 209
strikeouts and a 2.54 ERA (vs. the league's 4.64).

The late-charging Cardinals had come from fourth place on August 1, 11 games behind Brooklyn, to win the tight NL race by two.
In the World Series neither team batted over .200, but the Athletics
made the most of their 35 hits in six games with 18 extra base blows,

six of them homers. Simmons and Cochrane hit two each. Dykes had 5 RBIs. This time Grove started twice, winning the opener, 5–2, and losing Game Four, 3–1. But he picked up another victory relieving Earnshaw in the eighth inning of a scoreless duel against Burleigh Grimes. Foxx promptly won it with a home run in the ninth. Earnshaw came back two days later and pitched a 7–1 victory to make the Athletics the first team to win two straight World Series twice, repeating their 1910–1911 triumphs. Connie Mack, at 67, had won five World Championships, the first to do so.

After a slow April start, Mack's team made it look easy again in 1931, coasting to 107 wins and a 13½-game lead. The lineup stayed the same, with more talented youngsters filling in: Dib Williams and Eric McNair in the infield, Doc Cramer and Lou Finney in the outfield. Al Simmons, working on a three-year, $100,000 contract, led the league again at .390, hit 22 home runs, and drove in 128 runs. Foxx slipped to .291 but was good for 30 homers and 120 RBIs. Haas and Cochrane had solid years with the bat.

But the highest laurels of 1931 belonged to Lefty Grove. With a 31–4 record, including a 16-game winning streak, and a 2.06 ERA that was well below the team's league-leading 3.47, Grove became the only pitcher to put together two straight years of over .800 winning percentage. He worked 27 complete games and relieved in 11 more. Earnshaw was 21–7, Walberg, 20–12, Roy Mahaffey, 15–4, and the aging Waite Hoyt, 10–5.

The Cardinals ran away from the field in the National League, closing 13 games ahead of the Giants. They had added a rawboned rookie outfielder (though at 27 no unshaven lad)—Pepper Martin. Martin batted .300, fifth among St. Louis regulars, and stole just 16 of the Cardinals' league-leading 114 pilfered bases (the Athletics stole 27, lowest in either league).

In the seven-game World Series, both pitching staffs turned in an ERA under 3.00. The A's didn't hit. Two home runs by Simmons and one by Foxx were the only power they displayed. Cochrane, Bishop, and Haas failed to hit their weight. The big bats in the Cards lineup were Frank Frisch, Jim Bottomley, and Chick Hafey, but before the Series opened Connie Mack voiced his greatest concern: Pepper Martin. In the first five games Martin batted .667 with four doubles, a homer, five runs scored, five RBIs, and four stolen bases. Hitless in the last two games, he stole one more base and finished with a .500 BA.

There were rumors that catcher Mickey Cochrane was despondent over stock market losses and distracted by critical mail he received. Cochrane blamed Grove and Earnshaw for not holding runners on first. Grove tied the Series in Game Six with his second win, an 8–1 five-hitter. Earnshaw had lost a 2–0 six-hitter, then won a 3–0 two-hitter.

After drawing a crowd of 39,401 for the sixth game at St. Louis, the teams played the finale on a Saturday before just 20,805, the smallest Series crowd since World War I. The old spitballer, Burleigh Grimes, held a 4–0 lead in the ninth, when the Athletics threatened to repeat their spectacular finish of 1929. Pinch hitter Jim Moore hit a two-out single with the bases loaded to make it 4–2. In came lefty Bill Hallahan and Max Bishop lined to center where Pepper Martin appropriately made the catch. It was the only seven-game World Series in Connie Mack's eight appearances, and it was the last out the Philadelphia Athletics would ever make in a World Series.

The Athletics won 94 games in 1932, but it wasn't enough. Joe Boley, whose long stay in Baltimore had made him a 30-year-old rookie in 1927, finished the year in Cleveland. Eric McNair replaced him. Jimmy Dykes enjoyed the rare privilege of playing 141 games at one position: third base. Bing Miller shared right-field duties with Doc Cramer, a riflearmed consistent hitter who lacked only power. For power there was Simmons with 35 homers, Cochrane with 23, McNair with 16. But offensively the year belonged to Jimmie Foxx. He blasted 58 home runs, a record for righthanded batters later tied by Hank Greenberg. Some of his blows were stopped from going into the stands by a screen in St. Louis that had not been there in 1927. They had to make longer tapes to measure some of Foxx's drives. He topped the league with 169 RBIs and, batting .364, would have won the triple crown under later rules. Boston first baseman Dale Alexander hit .367 but had only 376 times at bat.

On the mound Ed Rommel was on the decline, but the Athletics bought a little lefty from the Pacific Coast League, Tony Freitas. He was a fifth infielder and won 12 against 5 losses. Grove was 25–10. Earnshaw and Walberg won 36 between them. But New York's pitching was a little better, as Lefty Gomez, Ruffing, and Pipgras were joined by rookie Johnny Allen who won 17 and lost 4. It was another runaway race, which didn't help the gate, but this time it was the Yankees who finished 13 in front. The Athletics nosed out a strong and improving Washington team for second place by one game.

In any other business, when you're operating at a loss and the bank is calling in your $400,000 note, you try to stay in business by selling off some assets and cutting overhead. If the business survives you're applauded for your prudent management. But when the business is baseball, and the assets sold are named Simmons, Haas, Dykes, Cochrane, Grove, Walberg, Bishop, and Earnshaw, the press and public heat up the tar and pluck the feathers to escort you out of town.

During the World Series in Chicago Mack met with Charles Comiskey, who wanted Simmons and Haas, but insisted that Dykes be included in the deal. Mack relented and accepted $150,000 for the trio. Dykes, who had been assured by the old man that he would never be traded, was outraged. Not until two years later did Dykes learn what Mr. Mack had known all along: that Dykes would become the next White Sox manager.

It was not a wholesale team wrecking. The rest of the stars remained for 1933, and Mack believed he had adequate replacements in Cramer, Finney, and third baseman Pinky Higgins. Led by Foxx, who swept all honors with 48 home runs, 163 RBIs, and a .356 BA, they could match the sluggers of New York and Washington. It was the pitching that collapsed. They gave up more runs than any team in either league, but managed a third-place finish. Only Grove, 24–8 with a 3.20 ERA, was effective on the mound.

If he couldn't win with his remaining stars, and couldn't take in enough at the gate to pay their salaries, Mack felt it was time to sell them off and start over. He was 71, but had no doubt he could build another winner. He would sell only those who would be 30 or older next season, while they still commanded some respect and a good price. Foxx was 26; he remained.

The Tigers paid $100,000 for Mickey Cochrane and made him their manager. Grove, Bishop, and Walberg went to Boston for $125,000. The White Sox paid $20,000 for Earnshaw. Connie Mack paid off the bank, and none of the money from player sales ever went into his own pocket.

Unlike 1915, the Athletics did not instantly dissolve. This time it took four years to go from top to bottom. Mack was confident he had a winner in 1935. His young outfield of Cramer, Wally Moses, and Bob Johnson was as fast and strongarmed as any in the game, and all hit over .300. Led by Foxx, Johnson, and Higgins, they topped the league in home runs. But the pitching was weak and the revamped Mackmen lost 91 games. For the next 15 years, Mack assembled good defensive clubs and strong batting orders, yet weak pitching. Philadelphia would have only two 20-game winners in the next 20 years: lefties Alex Kellner in 1949 and Bobby Shantz in 1952.

While the Athletics became perennial second-division dwellers until after World War II, there were some personal highlights for Connie Mack. He was named manager of the American League team for the first All-Star Game in 1933, and for the last time met his old rival, John McGraw. In 1934 he took his team to East Brookfield, Massachusetts, where he was born and raised, for a day in his honor. He was serenaded by boyhood chum George M. Cohan and sat in the hot sun all afternoon signing autographs while watching his Athletics lose to a local nine, 9–5. That winter he led a team of American League stars to Japan. In 1937 he was among the first select group elected to baseball's Hall of Fame.

When John Shibe died in 1937 Connie Mack became the principal owner of the Athletics. Some of the Shibe heirs retained some shares. Mack transferred some to his wife and sons Earle, a coach for him, Roy, who was in the front office, and Connie, Jr., who ran the concessions. Mack assumed the president's title, and continued as general manager and manager as he passed 80.

In 1944 Mack was honored in every ballpark in the American League to commemorate his 50 years as a manager. He was the grand old man of baseball, still loved, and respected by everyone who knew him or had ever heard of him—even the players who squawked about their meager salaries and demanded to be traded. The last of these great players, Jimmie Foxx, was sold after the 1935 season with pitcher Johnny Marcum to the Red Sox for $150,000. Foxx was 28 and would continue to terrorize pitchers for six more years in Boston.

For all the labels of tightwad pasted on him, Connie Mack had always spent big when he had the money to buy top quality talent. As Philadelphia's economy began to pick up in the late 1930s, the Athletics bank account put on a little weight. He now had one of the lowest payrolls. When Judge Landis declared 91 Detroit farmhands free agents in 1940, the top prospect was infielder Benny McCoy. While other clubs were bombarding him with offers, Mack told McCoy he would top whatever the highest bid turned out to be by $5,000. When the bidding topped out at $40,000, Earle Mack carried a check for $45,000 to Grandville, Michigan, and handed it to McCoy. It was the largest bonus ever paid a free agent at the time. McCoy, 24, got off to a slow start in 1940, improved in 1941, then, like many others, lost four years in the service and never got back into a major league lineup.

Connie Mack and the Athletics rose to the challenge of a pennant race one more time, in 1948. His eyesight weakened, his concentration occasionally lapsing at 85, Mack relied heavily on his coaches, Al Simmons and Lena Blackburn. But he made the player decisions and one, in a rare fit of spiteful anger, may have cost him that one last pennant.

The climb began in 1947 when rookie first baseman Ferriss Fain arrived. Anyone who remembered Hal Chase, George Sisler, or Bill Terry put Fain in the same class with the glove. He was a fearless charger who fielded bunts along the third-base line as regularly as those toward first. A steady hitter, he would lead the league twice, in 1951–52. With Pete Suder at second, the veteran Eddie Joost, brought back from the minor leagues, at short, and surehanded Hank Majeski at third, the Athletics had as good an inner defense as anybody. Mack felt secure enough with Majeski to trade a good-looking prospect, George Kell, to Detroit for Barney McCoskey, a solid .300 hitter back from the service. With Elmer Valo and Sam Chapman in the outfield and Buddy Rosar catching, it was not a great team, but solid enough to climb over the .500 mark into fifth place. The pitching staff was led by Canadian war veterans Phil Marchildon, 19–9, and Dick Fowler, 12–11. On September 3 rookie Bill McCahan pitched a no-hitter against Washington. There were enough strong arms to make the Mackmen optimistic that a new wave was rising.

Well into August of 1948 they stayed in the thick of a four-way pennant race with Cleveland, Boston, and New York. Lefty Lou Brissie, Joe Coleman, Fowler, and Carl Scheib were winning 14 or 15 games each. Nelson Potter, 19-game winner for the St. Louis Browns 1944 pennant winners, was added as a relief pitcher. The staff had depth and, more important, nobody else was running away from the pack.

Then a plague of sore and dead arms swept the staff. In the midst of the crisis, Potter blew a lead to the Browns and Mr. Mack blew up at him, berating Potter in front of his teammates. Inexplicably, Mack released Potter at a time when he needed healthy pitchers the most (Potter signed with the Braves and wound up in the World Series).

The Athletics fell out of the race and finished fourth, 12½ games back. The following year they finished a respectable fifth with an 81–73 record. Connie Mack made his last bad deal when he traded Majeski to the White Sox and paid $100,000 and four players for third baseman Bob Dillinger of the Browns. A .300 hitter and three-time leading base stealer (when 20 stolen bases usually led the league), Dillinger was a temperamental, howdy-do third baseman who brought far more dissension than winning attitude with him. Before the 1950 season ended he was waived to Pittsburgh. The Athletics tumbled back into the cellar and were all but vanquished from the sports pages by the Phillies's Whiz Kids who captured their first National League pennant in 35 years.

Connie Mack had now completed 50 years as the Athletics' only manager. At the end of the season he quietly announced his retirement at 88. There was no staged clubhouse meeting, no nostalgic farewell. His players read about it in the newspapers. Mack picked Jimmy Dykes, who had returned to Philadelphia as a coach, to replace him, and promised not to meddle or look over his shoulder, a promise he solemnly kept. Mack remained on as president, and traveled the circuit by automobile to follow the team. For the first time a general manager, Arthur Ehlers, was brought in to handle the front office duties.

Roy Mack and his half brother, Connie Jr., had different ideas about the direction the club should now take. Mickey Cochrane was brought into the operation, but was soon ousted. It became difficult to tell who was in charge. Longtime coaches Earle Brucker and Al Simmons were fired, apparently over Connie Mack's objections. There was a showdown within the family. Roy and Earle mortgaged the ballpark and borrowed the money to buy out Connie, Jr., his mother, and the remaining Shibe heirs. They limped along with the aid of advances from Sportservice, the concessions operators. Interest and mortgage payments came due.

On the field Ferriss Fain supplied the hitting, outfielder Gus Zernial the power, Eddie Joost the infield glue. Bobby Shantz, a local hero like so many of Mack's stars, turned in a 24–7 MVP performance to pull them into fourth place in 1952. But it was a deathbed rally. Fain was dealt to the White Sox. Joost saw limited action and Shantz came up with a sore arm that crippled him for two years. The club just as promptly slipped to seventh. When the St. Louis Browns moved to Baltimore in 1954, Dykes followed them to Maryland.

Eddie Joost took over in 1954, but there was hardly a familiar name in the lineup for what was fast becoming one of the most exclusive clubs in America, the Philadelphia American League baseball fans. Only 304,666 of them came to the season-long wake, fewer than Mack's original team had drawn to Columbia Park in 1902.

Like antiques dealers hoping to buy the family treasures as soon as the deceased is laid to rest, potential buyers hovered around the Athletics throughout the 1954 season. Los Angeles interests made a pitch. Dallas was heard from. Insurance executive Charles O. Finley made an offer; Connie Mack refused to consider it. Inspired by Connie Mack's public wish that the club remain in Philadelphia, various local groups popped up.

One of the most ardent bidders was Arnold Johnson, a Chicago vending machine executive, whose extensive real estate holdings included Yankee Stadium. He was ready to finance the purchase, but it was Kansas City business and civic leaders who wanted the team. Johnson agreed to move the team to Kansas City if he bought it, and became the front man for the midwestern group.

Earle Mack was ready to accept Johnson's offer; Roy was not. The two brothers held an option on their father's stock, but could only act together. The league's directors were divided. Some smelled a fish decaying in the moonlight because of Johnson's close ties to the Yankees' owners, Del Webb and Dan Topping. Others eyed the West Coast as the place with the most potential. Some felt an obligation to honor Connie Mack's wishes and give the Philadelphia group a chance to make a go of it.

In September and October there were several meetings. Connie Mack, sick and frail, went to one in New York to plead for the Philadelphia group. Johnson meanwhile signed an agreement with Earle and Roy and apparently had the league's approval for the transfer, helped by a sympathetic league president, Will Harridge. When the deal seemed settled, Roy Mack then asked for more time to consider the offer of a group of eight Philadelphia businessmen, and the circus moved back to the Shibe Park big top.

On October 18, 1954, Earle and Roy signed an agreement to sell the Athletics to the Philadelphians. Local papers gave the story front page spreads. Little mention was made of the need for the approval of a majority of the league's club owners. Johnson threatened to sue. The league met again on October 28. Johnson kept up the pressure on the Mack brothers, especially Roy, offering him and his sons jobs with the Kansas City Athletics and a chance to retain some stock in the club. Earle reluctantly agreed to sell to Johnson, but only if his father consented. At the end of the day the league directors turned down the Philadelphia buyers. No vote was announced, no reasons were given.

The scene shifted to the bedroom of the small Germantown apartment of Mr. and Mrs. Mack. Mr. Mack was worn down by all the bickering and was resigned to the demise of the club in Philadelphia. On the morning of November 4, 1954, Arnold Johnson came to see him with the A's attorney, Frank O. Schillp. Johnson borrowed a check from Schillp, made it payable to Cornelius McGillicuddy for $604,000 for his 302 shares of stock, and they shook hands, Mr. Mack's word was enough.

In Kansas City enthusiasm waxed again. Advance ticket sales passed $2 million. There were still a few hurdles: expansion of the stadium had not been started; there were questions about the Yankees connection; and six votes were needed to approve the transfer. Washington's Clark Griffith was adamantly against the move. Every time he made a statement knocking Kansas City as being too small, the Missourians became more determined. Griffith thought the league should finance the team in Philadelphia until a better home could be found. Hank Greenberg of Cleveland and Spike Briggs of Detroit agreed.

On November 8 the league met in New York. All morning they batted the question around with no decision. In the afternoon session Johnson was invited in to make his pitch. He cited the success of the Milwaukee transfer the year before in the National League, and of Baltimore in the American. He announced that unless they drew at least one million for each of the first three years, he would not be held to the Kansas City lease. Clark Griffith asked Johnson why he couldn't make a success of the team in Philadelphia. Johnson replied that he had given his word to the Kansas City people to move the club there if he bought it. Will Harridge asked him if he would be willing to sell Yankee Stadium. After conferring outside with his partners, Johnson agreed. This was the key to winning Spike Briggs' vote. Briggs moved the approval, Chuck Comiskey seconded it, and the transfer was approved, 6 to 2. Griffith and Greenberg cast the two negative ballots.

A few days later the stock certificates for the 302 shares were taken from a safe deposit box and brought to Mr. Mack's apartment, and it was then that the scene with which this account began—and this episode ends—was enacted.

Arnold Johnson and the Kansas City Athletics

When the movers packed up the crates of files and photos and white elephants and assorted papers at Shibe Park and carried them west to Kansas City, they carried with them the virus of second-division baseball. Only once in their 13-year sojourn in Kansas City would the Athletics finish a season as high as sixth place, and that lofty perch they accomplished in their maiden campaign.

But first the new owners had to renovate the ballpark used for many years by the Kansas City Blues of the American Association. Johnson had made some big claims to win the franchise ownership; now the promises had to be fulfilled. Working through severe winter weather, construction crews blasted and replaced 300 old footings, and had the first steel column in place with 90 days still to go before the home opener. They added a second deck of seats and a new roof and barely met the deadline—at a cost of nearly $80 per seat.

Arnold Johnson picked Lou Boudreau, recently deposed by the Red Sox, to manage his A's. He put together a front office team of Parke Carroll, Ray Kennedy, and Bill MacPhail. Roy Mack was now in charge of spring training arrangements at West Palm Beach; he made sure his father was present for the first exhibition game. Connie Mack, Roy's son, was in charge of ticket operations.

A pre-season gala party and Opening Day parade brought Connie Mack, former president Harry Truman, comedian Joe E. Brown, and former Athletics stars Frank Baker and Jimmie Foxx before the cheering thousands.

The enthusiasm was there. All they needed were players. Unlike a new expansion team starting from zero, they had inherited a team that had lost 103 games. Johnson quickly spent $35,000 in the minor league draft for three pitchers who won a total of nine games. Before the year was out he spent another $700,000 on shopworn major leaguers and top minor leaguers, but the Athletics never improved in the standings.

On April 12, 1955, Kansas City won its home opener, beating Detroit, 6–2, before 32,147. Alex Kellner started and was lifted for a pinch hitter during a sixth-inning rally which put his team in the lead. Ewell Blackwell pitched the last three innings to save the victory. Connie Mack was in the stands for his last opening day. On February 8, 1956, he died at age 93.

Two weeks later the relocated A's played before their largest single-game crowd, 33,471, Bobby Shantz shut out the Yankees on three hits, 6–0; yet he won only four more games that year. KC had a pretty good hitting lineup in the early years, but the defense and pitching usually let in more runs than the team could score. Vic Power, Enos Slaughter, and Harry Simpson batted over .300. Playing part time, Elmer Valo hit .364. Gus Zernial socked 30 home runs. The A's lost 91 games but drew 1,393,054—more than the Reds, White Sox, Orioles, Senators, Phillies, or Athletics had ever attracted up to that time. The next year KC drew just over a million while finishing dead last. From then on attendance stayed under a million. Arnold Johnson could have broken the lease after the 1957 season, but he chose to remain.

Lou Boudreau was already out during the third year. Harry Craft lasted just over two seasons, followed by Bob Elliott.

The A's never developed their own productive farm system, but for the first five years the transplanted franchise seemed to confirm what some early opponents of the transfer had feared: they were a steady supplier of talent to the Yankees, accepting in return batches of players the Yankees had no further use for. New York sent young righthander Ralph Terry to KC in 1957. After he matured for two years they brought him back and he helped New York win five straight pennants. Enos Slaughter was sent down in 1955 and returned the next year, in time to get into three World Series. Pitchers Ryne Duren, Bobby Shantz, Art Ditmar, Duke Maas, and Virgil Trucks moved to New York. In 1960 KC passed along Roger Maris for his date with destiny. In all Johnson turned 16 deals with New York involving 67 players. Of all the platoons of players the A's received, outfielder Bob Cerv gave them the best return, banging out 38 home runs in 1958 with 104 RBIs while batting .305. A parade of players long on memories and accomplishments but short on futures meandered through the lineup as well.

On March 10, 1960, Arnold Johnson suffered a fatal heart attack. His heirs ran the team for a year, but it was a dismal experience, the team finishing last yet again. The novelty had worn off; attendance dropped to 774,944. Kansas City fans were used to better teams when they were an official farm team of the Yankees. Soon after Johnson's death, Roy Mack also died. The Johnson heirs sold their 52 percent interest in the club to Charles O. Finley in December for a reported $1,975,000. Mrs. Roy Mack sold Finley the Mack family's shares, as well, over the bitter objections of her two sons, ending the Mack presence in baseball after 72 years.

He was called by some Charles Outrageous Finley. He said the "O" stood for Owner, and let nobody forget it. A farmboy who worked five years in the steel mills of Gary, Indiana, Finley was a selfmade millionaire who, as writer Jim Murray put it, "worshipped his maker." Stitched into every monologue or conversation was his slogan: S Plus S Equals S, which translates into Sweat Plus Sacrifice Equals Success. He let nobody forget that, either.

He was loud, brash, persistent, foulmouthed, and a nonstop talker who had all the sensitivity of a steamroller. He was full of ideas that major league baseball magnates did not want to hear, and he never stopped pushing them, a style which had made him a millionaire selling insurance. A semipro player, he had tried for years to buy into baseball, attending American League meetings regularly. Club owners ducked when they saw him coming. Whenever he tried to buy a team that was for sale, they hustled to find another buyer to shut him out. He bid for the Tigers, White Sox, and Indians. When the league expanded to Los Angeles, he bid for that. The league lassoed Gene Autry, who had come to town just to buy the radio rights.

When Finley got to the widow Johnson before they could cut him off at the pass, he had more than his nose in the tent. Two months later he paid another $1.9 million for the rest of the Kansas City stock, and became the only solo club owner except Tom Yawkey.

There may have been major league club owners who were bigger egomaniacs, had more radical ideas, were more hated by their players, fellow owners, and customers, had a worse press, ran a cheaper operation, made more attempts to move a team, or build a team good enough to win three World Series in a row, but none ever combined all these attributes to the extent or perfection that Charlie Finley did.

Never had any club owner craved or gained so much more publicity than his team and players, even when he had winning teams and star players with outsized egos of their own. He fought with everybody, lived on the telephone around the clock, and ran his show his way. His first act was to hire veteran baseball man Frank Lane as his general manager; within a year Lane was fired, and Finley became his own general manager. In the 21 years he owned the team he had 19 managers (three of them twice), more than 30 coaches, and dozens of office employees and broadcasters. He usually had no ticket operation, and employed more high school students to run the office than McDonalds.

Like any baseball man, he wanted to win. But he wanted even more for his players to display daily evidence of their gratitude for being paid to play a game, and for the fans to show their thanks for his putting a team on the field. Any team. Finley promised Kansas City a winner; they sank to ninth in the newly expanded league. They finished ninth, eighth, 10th, 10th, seventh, 10th. Finley promised to keep the team in Kansas City while he was trying to move it to Dallas, to Louisville, to Seattle, to San Diego. Every time he asked the league to approve a transfer they turned him down. The vote was always 9–1.

He did not hesitate to ridicule league president Joe Cronin publicly, nor to brand the Lords of Baseball, as Dick Young called the owners, for their stupidity in watching business slip away and doing nothing about it.

He threw novel ideas around like rice at a bride; not all of them were too radical to ignore. He thought a yellow or orange ball would be more visible at night than a white one. He wanted interleague games on the schedule. He thought the leagues should be realigned geographically, to take advantage of natural rivalries like the two New York and Chicago teams, or Oakland and San Francisco. He said baseball was behind the times; the fans wanted games speeded up and more offense. He pushed for a three-ball walk. Some of his ideas were adopted, e.g., playing World Series and All-Star Games at night. He pushed hard for the Designated Hitter Rule and saw it happen. He saw merit in offensive and defensive specialists as in pro football, and pushed as hard for a designated runner. He even hired one himself, a man who left the most amazing footprints in the sands of the game. Herb Washington got into 104 games in 1974 and 1975 and never held a bat, touched a ball, or wore a glove, yet he scored 33 runs, stole 30 bases, and got into three World Series games.

Finley hired ball girls and put lights in the dugout so the fans could see what was happening. He set up a picnic grounds and petting zoo outside the outfield fence, and installed a scoreboard that exploded fireworks when a home player hit a home run. He staged an elaborate contest to find the best Missouri mule, bought it, named it "Charlie O," and made it the team mascot. The mule appeared on the field, sometimes with a player on its back, in the dugout, in the parking lot, and on the owner's charter flight to the World Series—wherever and whenever its owner wanted it to go. Some players felt the mule was better treated than they were, and was at least on a par with them in their owner's estimation.

If his players asked for more money Finley refused; if they didn't ask he gave them bonuses and raises. It had to be his idea, to his credit and glory. When it came to paying out bonuses to young players, he was willing, but he had the stingiest feedbox on the circuit for the working writers and scouts and hangers-on at the ballpark. Perhaps reflecting his resentment at Connie Mack's refusal to consider him worthy to buy the Philadelphia Athletics in 1954, Finley issued a proclamation that henceforth and forevermore the Kansas City team would be known as the A's. After six decades, the Athletics were no more.

Finley's first move after hiring Frank Lane was to get league approval to replace the traditional home whites and road grays with suits of kelly green and bright gold and white shoes. He bought jerseys and pants and socks in various combinations of the two colors and posted a sartorial schedule for the players to follow. Some complained the garb made them resemble parrots. Other teams ridiculed them, but gradually other owners got away from the drab traditional costumes as well.

At a civic gathering Finley made a show of burning the contract that allowed him to cancel his lease if the team drew under 850,000. He pledged his eternal troth to the city. But he had burned a blank piece of paper instead. Every time he announced how much he loved Kansas City, he left town and went to the league directors to ask for a divorce. Attendance lagged. Season ticket sales dried up. Even if someone wanted to buy one, it was hard to find anyone in the office who knew how to sell them or where they were. He tried many promotions, most of which were ignored by the fans, all of which had been tried first by Bill Veeck in one form or another, but were claimed by Finley as products of his own genius.

The A's did have some players who had an occasional good year. Norm Siebern, who came with Don Larsen, Hank Bauer, and Marv Throneberry in the Roger Maris deal, hit .308 with 25 home runs and 117 RBIs in 1962. He was then swapped to Baltimore for Jim Gentile, who chipped in 28 homers. Rocky Colavito arrived in 1964 and delivered 34 home runs and 102 RBIs. But .300 hitters were as scarce as friends of Finley.

On taking over the A's Finley had promised to end their life as a Yankee farm team. A week later he traded the club's best pitcher, lefty Bud Daley, who had won 16 each of the last two years, to New York for Art Ditmar and Deron Johnson. Ditmar was 2–3 at the time; Johnson, a rookie of no permanent address on the field, was batting .105.

But gradually Charlie Finley, the general manager, was beginning to harvest the plums he'd signed from the farms and college campuses. It cost him $500 for a Cuban shortstop, Bert Campaneris, who began a 19-year career in 1964. Second baseman Dick Green arrived in 1963. Finley drove into Hertford, North Carolina, with a motorcycle escort and paid a 19-year-old farmboy, Jim Hunter, $75,000 to sign a contract (the name Catfish was tagged on him by Finley, who liked colorful nicknames; it stuck). Hunter was 8–8 in 1965.

Finley signed Rick Monday from Arizona State for $105,000, and drafted Sal Bando from the same campus, giving him $35,000. He next went to Blue Moon Odom's high school graduation in Macon, Georgia, then drove a truckful of food to Odom's home and cooked dinner himself. He could be as charming as a snakeoil salesman. Odom's mother urged her son to accept the man's $75,000 to sign. Odom was 5–5 and 3–8 in the A's last two years in Kansas City. Local boy Chuck Dobson signed for $25,000, won 4 and lost 6 in 1966. Finley went back to Arizona State and shelled out $80,000 for young Reggie Jackson's autograph. Jackson got into 35 games at the end of 1967 and batted .178. Among his 21 hits was his first home run, yet his striking out average was .390.

None of these young talents broke in with a bang. But while fielding losing teams in Kansas City—deliberately, some said, to turn off fans' interest, cultivate a bad press, and strengthen his case for moving—he was putting together a colorful, brawling, and winning team to take to the pot of gold on the other side of San Francisco Bay.

Acting often on hearsay, Finley did not hesitate to criticize, berate, castigate, demean, and denounce his players and managers in public. And they popped off right back at him. There was more dirty laundry surrounding the Kansas City A's than the stockyard workers hung out in a month of Mondays. It came to a head in 1967 when somebody said that on a flight home from Boston some players had gotten a little boisterous after a few drinks. Without asking any questions, Finley issued a statement that no alcoholic drinks would be served players on commercial flights because of the deplorable actions of a few of them. Manager Alvin Dark said he had seen nothing. The players asked for a meeting with Finley before the statement was made public. Finley refused. Pitcher Lew Krausse, 7–17 for the year, was singled out, fined $500, and suspended.

Between the A's performance on the field and Finley's antics off it (although the lines were blurred, as he was telling his managers who to play and how to manage), Kansas City baseball fans were finding other things to do on their summer evenings. They wanted baseball, but not if it meant having Finley, too. Visiting clubs were leaving town with pickings as slim as they'd had in Shibe Park, Philadelphia. Finley had lost money for seven years, too, but he had finally worn them all down. He went to the American League meeting in October with an Oakland agreement in his pocket and asked for a green light to move. On the second ballot the Yankees switched their vote and the A's were headed west. Said Missouri Senator Stuart Symington, "Oakland is the luckiest city since Hiroshima."

Charlie Finley and the Oakland A's

The city fathers of Oakland desperately wanted a major league team. A blue-collar town living in the shadow of a glamorous neighbor, San Francisco, they had supported a team in the Pacific Coast League until the Giants came west in 1958 and the Oakland Oaks had disappeared. The Oakland Coliseum had been built to keep the Oakland Raiders football team in town as well as to attract a big league baseball franchise. But it had not been proven that the Bay Area could support even one team, much less two.

Finley arrived in Oakland in 1968 full of optimism, and with the makings of a winning team in tow. He sang that his heart was in Oakland, promised to live there as well, and predicted his A's would soon contend for the pennant and draw a million and a half customers. He signed a $5 million radio and TV contract for five seasons, a sharp contrast to the $56,000 he had received in Kansas City.

More than 50,000 people filled the Oakland Coliseum to see the A's opener; the next night about 5,000 showed up, and that soon became the average. Finley did give the fans plenty in the way of stadium promotions. He gave away bats, caps, T-shirts, helmets, and even hot pants. His players milked cows, chased greased pigs, rode the mule before games. He gave them fan appreciation days, but very few came out to be appreciated. While Finley never could put across the three-ball walk with his fellow owners, he had launched the era of colorful uniforms. He also changed the facial appearance of the game. For Mustache Day, he promised a bonus to every player who grew one. They all did, and some liked it so much they kept them, even adding beards in some cases. The unwritten rule against unshaven players, adhered to since the early days of the century, soon became a relic of the past.

On May 8, 1968, Finley gave the fans Catfish Hunter performing the rarest feat in the game, a 4–0 perfect game over the Twins. It was the first perfect game in the American League since 1922. Only 6,300 were there to see it, however, and Finley was not one of them; he had not yet moved to Oakland. He listened to the game by telephone in Chicago, and called announcer Al Helfer during the game, exhorting him to make it more exciting on the air. The next night attendance dropped to 4,062. Finley gave Hunter a $5,000 bonus. The catcher, Jim Paglioroni, got a $1,000 raise. Finley could be generous when you didn't ask him for anything.

The A's finished sixth in 1968 and drew 837,000. Finley got a break one Saturday in September that put them over the 800,000 mark. The Tigers' Denny McLain started in Oakland in quest of his 30th win; that pulled in 44,000 paying customers. Finley had developed an exciting, colorful team. Jackson hit .250 but knocked out 29 home runs. Bert Campaneris led the league with 62 stolen bases. Hunter and Jim Nash were 13–13, Odom 16–10.

Fans thought they had the pennant won in the team's second year by the bay. Jackson emerged as a magnetic star. He started out hitting home runs at a Ruthian pace, with 37 by the All-Star break. Odom had won 14 games. But Jackson hit just 10 more after that and a sore arm limited Odom to one more win. Oakland finished second, 9 games behind the Twins in the west division of the newly split league. Sal Bando hit 31 homers and three others hit 10 or more. Campaneris stole 62 bases again. Hunter had not yet found his stride; he was 12–15. Dobson was 15–13. Rollie Fingers also made 52 relief appearances and started eight times.

It was the kind of season that fit the Philadelphia profile for profitability: a nonwinning contender with a low payroll. For all the excitement, attendance fell below 780,000. And Oakland continued to be profitable for Finley. As runners-up again in 1970, then winners of five straight division titles and three straight World Championships, his A's still couldn't top a million at the gate. But Finley battled his players hard at the negotiating table. His rent was $125,000. He received a large chunk of the concessions and parking revenues. His front office overhead was nil. He showed a profit every year of at least $500,000.

In 1970 the A's improved by one game, but so did Minnesota. Hunter led the pitchers at 18–14. Eight players hit 10 or more home runs, although Jackson slipped to 23.

Managers came and went. Bob Kennedy, Hank Bauer, and John McNamara lasted a year each. Then Dick Williams came along and remained with Charlie O as his co-pilot for three winning years before crying, "Enough."

The ragtag dustmen of Kansas City had been transformed into Cinderella and should have collected all the headlines with their play on the field. But Charlie Owner hadn't changed. He still fought with everybody in sight and muscled in on every column of copy and bite of sports news on the tube. As the young stars put a few good years behind them, they began to demand more money. Led by Jackson, they were a proud, outspoken, temperamental, intelligent bunch, not about to lick the boots of the plantation overseer. They goaded each other for below-par performances, brawled among themselves before a game, had their wounds stitched up and went out and clobbered the opposition, then took on their club owner in the press and on the air after the game. The bickering, the holdouts, the sniping crossfire between the owner and his players heated up. And it would remain that way for the rest of Finley's days in baseball.

In 1967 Vida Blue, a high school football and baseball star in Mansfield, Alabama, was signed for $25,000. Called up at the end of 1970, he pitched a 6–0 no-hitter against Minnesota on September 21, and a one-hitter as well. In 1971 he had one of those incredible years. He won 24 and lost 8 with a 1.82 ERA and eight shutouts. Suddenly he was dogged by writers from national magazines and TV cameras were everywhere. After every game he pitched he was surrounded by strangers asking questions. He made the cover of *Time*. Finley tried to get him to change his name to "True." He packed the stands wherever he pitched, made TV commercials, and doubled his salary for a day's work. The team was invited to the White House, where President Nixon remarked that Blue was the most underpaid player in baseball. Amid speculation that he would win 30, he won only one game in September. Yet he walked off with the Cy Young Award and league Most Valuable Player Award as well.

Meanwhile Catfish Hunter was winning 21 and Dobson was 15–5. The A's didn't have a .300 hitter in the regular lineup, but their power was spread throughout the batting order. Seven players hit 10 or more home runs, led by Jackson's 32. They cruised to a 16-game lead over Kansas City in the west, but the Orioles took three close ones from them in the league playoffs and ended their dream season.

During the winter of 1971 Blue got himself an agent. Into the spring they played hardball with Finley, every rap and retort reported and broadcast in detail. There was a brief player strike that delayed the start of the 1972 season. Blue missed spring training, finally signing for $50,000 and a $13,000 bonus. He reported three weeks into the season, never got into the groove, and finished at 6–10. Nobody bothered him for photos and interviews that year.

It was Hunter, 21–7, Ken Holtzman, 19–11, Odom, 15–6, and Rollie Fingers of the fancy waxed mustache with 11 wins and 21 saves, and a strong defense that won for Oakland in 1972. Joe Rudi hit .305, high for the team. Jackson had an ordinary year for him: 25 home runs, 75 RBIs, and a .265 BA. They picked on each other, then picked each other up. They mixed antagonism with teamwork and eventually won by 5½ games over Chicago's surprising White Sox. This time Finley's battlers faced off against the Tigers in the playoffs. Only 23 runs were scored in five games. Odom won two, combining with Blue on a 2–1 five-hitter in the deciding final contest.

The 1972 World Series against the Reds was a classic; six games were decided by but one run. Like many Series, this one produced an unlikely hero. Catcher Gene Tenace, a .225 hitter with only five home runs, became the first player to hit home runs in his first two World Series at bats. Tenace drove in all the Oakland runs in a 3–2 win for Holtzman, saved by Fingers and Blue, before a record Cincinnati crowd of 52,913.

The next day it was Joe Rudi's turn for heroics—a home run and game-saving catch in the ninth—and this was enough to give Hunter a 2–1 win, with Fingers mopping up once more. In Game Three Odom fanned 11 and gave up three hits in seven innings, yet lost, 1–0. Tenace hit another homer in the fourth game and added one of four singles in a two-run ninth-inning rally that pulled out a 3–2 win for Fingers in relief.

The A's needed one more victory to wrap it up but it took them three games to eventually get it. Tenace's three-run homer in the second inning of Game Five looked like enough for Hunter, but the Reds chipped away and Pete Rose drove in the lead run in the top of the ninth to tag Fingers with a 5–4 loss. The A's took it down to the last out, as the Reds nipped the tying run on a play at home plate.

Cincinnati bruised Blue in an 8–1 breeze in Game Six, giving Tenace one last chance to complete his destined hero's role for 1972. His two hits and two RBIs made the difference in a 3–2 game in which Odom, Hunter, Holtzman, and durable Rollie Fingers held the Reds to four hits. The dramatic result was the first World Series title for a team wearing the old script A since 1930. Charlie Finley was named major league executive of the year while the Lords of Baseball choked on their congratulations.

The 1972 World Champions were an exciting team to watch, but season ticket sales went up only 400, to 1,400 for 1973. Finley began making noises about moving the team. Seattle, New Orleans, even Toronto, were mentioned. None of this served to increase fans' enthusiasm. It took the defending champs time to get it together. Odom was 1–9. Hunter was winless in six starts. Reggie Jackson wanted to be the best, the highest paid, the leader, the most valuable, the most respected—and said so. But Jackson's play was spotty. They fussed with each other, and with their coaches and manager Dick Williams. They didn't need Finley to fight with, as long as they had each other. They didn't really need Finley at all, they said.

Gene Tenace had developed into a longball hitter and was playing first base while hitting 24 roundtrippers. Bando hit 29 and tied for the league lead with 32 doubles and 98 RBIs. DH Deron Johnson hit 19 roundtrippers. Bill North stole 53 bases and trailed Jackson's league-best 99 runs scored by one. Jackson got untracked and led the league with 32 home runs; his 117 RBIs and .293 BA also earned him MVP honors. Blue recovered and won 20 against 9 losses, Hunter was 21–5, and Holtzman won 21. Fingers had become the top reliever in the game. And in the end the A's finished six games ahead of Kansas City.

Finley never hesitated to go into the marketplace for players he needed to win. To bolster his bench he bought Jesus Alou and Vic Davalillo, and signed free agent Mike Andrews, who would make more headlines than any other .200 hitter in the game before the year was over. In the playoff against Baltimore, Blue was kayoed twice. But Hunter won the second and fifth games, the last a 3–0 five-hitter.

Catfish was as good as he had to be in a game, and never minded giving up runs as long as he gave up one less than the A's scored. When he had to be overpowering, he could be. Bert Campaneris hit two home runs, which was not expected; one was a game-winner in the 11th inning. The last three games were played in Oakland. Attendance was below 30,000 for the first, a 2–1 three-hitter by Holtzman. The crowd was under 25,000 for the last game also.

But they showed up in large numbers—46,021—for the first game of the World Series against the New York Mets, won by Holtzman who scored the winning run in a 2–1 squeaker. In the year that Finley finally pushed his designated hitter idea through in the American League, it was ironic that Holtzman, who hadn't batted all year, had his team's only extra base hit in the opener and was 2 for 3 in the Series.

Due to injuries the A's had gone into the World Series with only 24 players. A last-minute request to add infielder Manny Trillo to the roster had been rejected by the Mets. Finley intended to make that known to the fans at the opening game. The commissioner's office said it was okay to tell the press, but no public address announcement. Finley announced it anyhow. Commissioner Bowie Kuhn called it a deliberate act to embarrass the Mets, and later fined Finley.

When it grew dark during the second game, Finley ignored the rule that allowed lights to be turned on only at the start of an inning, and pulled the switch after the Mets had batted. Kuhn turned the lights off until the next inning started, and fined Finley for that, too. Meanwhile Blue was hit hard again, but it was Fingers who was roughed up for four runs in the top of the 12th and took the loss, 10–7, in the four-hour 13-minute game, longest in Series history. Only one of the runs off Fingers was earned.

With two second basemen retired for pinch hitters, Dick Williams sent Mike Andrews out to play second in the top of the 12th. Andrews had been in 15 games at second all season. With the bases loaded, two outs, and a run in, the Mets John Milner hit a grounder to Andrews; it went through his legs and two runs scored. The next man up, Jerry Grote, hit another one to Andrews, who threw wide to first as the fourth run scored, to make it 10–6.

Finley was furious. Andrews had no excuses, no physical problems. But Finley ordered the team physician to pronounce Andrews disabled by a recurrence of an old shoulder injury and unable to play. Andrews, under pressure, signed the statement and went home as the team went to New York. The players were angry over the obvious firing of Andrews in the middle of the Series. They threatened, blustered, uttered mutinous mutterings, made a number 17—Andrews' number—out of tape and stuck it on their uniforms. Finley asked Kuhn to allow Trillo to play. Kuhn not only said no, he ordered Andrews reinstated. In a team meeting manager Dick Williams told the A's he had had enough and would not be back next year.

The Mets jumped on Hunter for two runs in the first but that's all they got. The A's tied it against Tom Seaver, who fanned 12 in eight innings, and won it in the 11th. In Game Four New York beat Holtzman easily, 6–1. The A's only highlight came when Williams, against Finley's orders, sent Andrews in to pinch hit, to a roaring ovation from the New York crowd. But on the infielder's last time at bat in the major leagues he grounded out.

The A's were blanked on three hits in Game Five, Blue taking the loss, 2–0. Back in Oakland Hunter outduelled Seaver, 3–1. Their power stymied for the first six games, the A's finally erupted, with two-run homers by Campaneris and Jackson in the third inning giving Holtzman and Fingers & Co. all the runs they needed for a 5–2 finale. They had repeated as World Champions, but not without more bitterness and turmoil. Said Reggie Jackson, "Finley takes all the fun out of winning."

The 1973 A's drew only about one million fans despite a winning team and a fairly close race. Almost every other team in baseball outdrew them. There was no extra money to be made for the players in Oakland, no demands for personal appearances or commercial pitches. Either Oakland was not and would never be a baseball town or the fans loved the game but hated Finley so much they stayed away because of him. The latter theory gained some credibility when, during one game of the World Series at the Coliseum, fans unfurled a bed-sheet banner not entirely inspired by the mule: "Finley, Get Your Ass Out of Town."

Meanwhile Finley had suffered a heart attack, but was unwilling to follow his doctor's advice to take it easy. He let it be known the A's were for sale, and had plenty of offers, but he was only fishing. He raised the price whenever anybody offered to pay it. Just as he had in Kansas City, he seemed to be letting the organization deteriorate to pressure the league into letting him move. He cut costs, cut employees, cut ticket plans and promotions. Equipment was old. He cut back even more on the already meager press accommodations and seemed to relish whatever small indignities and inconveniences he could find to antagonize the media. He did not pursue radio or TV deals, and had a constant turnover of broadcasters. He finally had no bidders for the radio rights and couldn't sell air time, so he brought in a college kid to narrate the games.

With Williams gone, Finley found Alvin Dark playing golf in Florida and resurrected him for yet another tour of duty as manager of the A's. There was little that Finley could do to the players by now, and they probably didn't need Dark, either, to keep winning. They took the division again by five games in 1974 without a .300 hitter in the lineup. But four of them hit 22 home runs or better, led by Jackson's 29. Rudi and Bando drove in the most runs, Rudi leading the league in doubles and total bases. Bill North stole 54. Hunter was 25–12 with the league's best ERA, 2.49. Blue was 17–15, Holtzman 19–17, and the ever-ready Fingers got into 76 games. Almost predictably, attendance dropped below 900,000.

After dropping the opening 1974 playoff game to Baltimore, Oakland took the next three. Holtzman and Blue shut out the Orioles, Blue winning his first post-season game on a two-hitter, 1–0, on Bando's second home run in two days. Hunter and Fingers combined for a 2–1 win to wrap it up.

As usual, the A's were still making more headlines off the field than on it. Before the start of the World Series against the Los Angeles Dodgers, Fingers and Odom fought in the clubhouse. Fingers took a cut on his head, then went out and pitched 4 1/3 innings in relief of Holtzman to earn a 3–2 win. Jackson's second-inning homer launched the scoring. The Dodgers beat Blue, 3–2, for their only win of the Series. Hunter and Fingers beat them by the same score in Game Three, Holtzman and Fingers in Game Four, in which Holtzman himself hit a home run. Blue started Game Five but left with the score knotted 2–2. The 3–2 win went to Odom who pitched to one batter before Fingers saved it. Fingers was named the Series MVP.

They were World Champions for the third year in a row, but it was the last World Series appearance for the A's until 1988. They won the west again in 1975 using the same balanced attack—six players clouting 10 or more homers. Jackson led the league with 36; Tenace had 29. Vida Blue had his last 20-game season with a 22–11 record. Holtzman was 18–14. Fingers appeared in 75 games and Paul Lindblad, 9–1, was in 68. But the Red Sox swept them in the playoff for the pennant, Holtzman starting and losing twice. Only Jackson hit one out.

Where was Catfish Hunter?

It was the first year that arbitration was in effect in 1974; nine of the A's had used it. Five won big raises while four lost their cases and settled for smaller increases. Finley, like Connie Mack, was faced with soaring salary demands with no commensurate increase at the gate. There was no Depression to cope with, but Finley was having troubles with the IRS and a recently divorced wife. Mike Andrews was suing him for slander.

Hunter had not gone to arbitration. Finley met his demand for $100,000, payable half in salary and half to go into an annuity. Before the 1974 World Series Hunter had announced that the annuity pay-ment had not been made and he intended to file for free agency. An arbitrator agreed with him, at which point there must have been a dozen players who wished that Finley had reneged on one of their paychecks, too. Hunter, emancipated from the plantation, signed with the Yankees for over $3 million.

At the end of the 1975 season Charlie Finley tried to emulate Connie Mack by selling off his star players, but not because he needed the money to pay off the banks. Finley had enjoyed his winners and was prepared to dismantle the team, cut back to a minimal payroll on and off the field, and let the team disintegrate. As for the fans, who never showed their appreciation adequately, they could go to the devil. There was also some justification in his holding a fire sale. For the rules of the game had changed. Players could play out their option years without signing a contract and walk away. Finley knew as many of them as could would do so. He tried to salvage something by trading or selling them before the 1976 season ended.

In April he traded Ken Holtzman and Reggie Jackson to Balti-more for Don Baylor, Mike Torrez, and Paul Mitchell. As the June 15th trading deadline neared, he had seven unsigned players remain-ing. On the 15th he got Vida Blue to sign a contract, and that night sold him to the Yankees for $1.5 million. At the same time he sold Joe Rudi and Rollie Fingers to the visiting Red Sox for $1 million each. They sat on the Boston bench that night but did not play. The next day Commissioner Kuhn suspended the three sales and two days later nullified them "in the best interests of baseball," whatever that meant. Finley squawked and threatened to go to court, but the veto stood.

Despite the turmoil the A's, under Chuck Tanner, trailed Kansas City by just 2½ games in the west. Bando and Tenace led the home run hitters. Paced by Billy North's league-leading 75, they chalked up 341 stolen bases, making the most of a .246 team BA. Blue was 18–13, Torrez 16–12. Fingers was 13–11 with 20 saves in 70 games.

As Finley expected, at the end of the 1976 season Joe Rudi signed with California, Fingers and Tenace with San Diego. Bando left for Milwaukee. Campaneris went to Texas. Reggie Jackson played out his year with Baltimore, then signed with the Yankees, where Holtzman had been traded in June. The only asset Finley salvaged was Vida Blue. After a 14–19 1977 season, Blue was traded across the bay to the Giants for seven players and $390,000. In February 1977 Charlie O. also sold Paul Lindblad, to Texas for $400,000.

Not all of Finley's moves weakened the team. In March 1977 he acquired pitchers Doc Medich, Doug Bair, and Rick Langford, in-fielder Mitchell Page and a rookie outfielder, Tony Armas, from Pittsburgh for Phil Garner, Tommy Helms, and Chris Batton. Page and Armas soon developed into the longball threats the A's depended upon.

In 1978 Dwayne Murphy arrived, followed a year later by Rickey Henderson, and the A's had in place the three best outfield arms in baseball, the biggest one-man offensive threat in Henderson, and the nucleus of another winner. In 1975 Finley had signed a San Francisco youngster, righthander Mike Norris, who pitched one complete game victory, a shutout, that year. He had pitched one complete game each year until 1979, when he finished three starts, winning 5 against 8 losses.

But Oakland finished last in 1977, then sixth in 1978 as Bobby Winkles and Jack McKeon took turns running the club. They were last again in 1979 under Jim Marshall. Attendance slumped to 300,000, no more than the dying Philadelphia Athletics had attracted to Shibe Park in 1954, fewer than the newborn Athletics had drawn to Columbia Park in 1902. The sick franchise had been moved twice in search of a cure, and was still a chronic invalid.

Acting more like a man trying to build another dynasty than a man on his way out of the game, Charlie Finley brought the fans back into the Coliseum by hiring Billy Martin as his manager for 1980. Martin had produced winners at Minnesota, Detroit, Texas, and Yankee Stadium while fighting with players, fans, owners, and occasional bystanders. He was in and out of trouble as often as he was in and out of first place for 12 years. He lifted the A's to second place and fans turned out to watch leadoff man Henderson hit .303 and steal 100 bases. The old balance was back. Nobody else hit .300 but six players clouted 13 or more home runs. Armas hit 35 and accounted for 109 RBIs. Martin had four strong young right arms working for him. Mike Norris blossomed and won 22 against 9 losses. Rick Langford was 19–12, Matt Keogh, 16–13, and Steve McCatty, 14–14.

But Finley was in poor health and tired, and not interested in sticking around for another winner. Near the end of the season he sold the club for $12.7 million to the Haas family, heirs to the long-established community business, Levi Strauss, the jeansmakers. The change in ownership was as great a contrast as if Charlie Finley had immediately succeeded Connie Mack without the Arnold Johnson years as a buffer. It was a Shakespearean actor following the Marx Brothers, the New York Philharmonic following Hee Haw. Walter Haas, chairman of Levi Strauss, his son, Wally, and son-in-law, Roy Eisenhardt, bought the club to make it a community-oriented organization that would contribute something to the city. Eisenhardt, an Ivy League attorney and law professor, was named president. They brought to the business no ego trips, but sound and imaginative management. It was a public relations man's dream. Following the Charlie O. act, they had no way to go but up. They found more cobwebs than fingerprints in the club's offices and began rebuilding. They would soon find out if it was only anti-Finley feelings that kept the fans away.

One night in September they were heartened when, after the sale was announced but before it was official, a record 49,300 packed the stands for a Yankees game. They were inheriting a better team than they knew, but nothing behind it. There were no scouts, no farm organization. As people with good intentions and sound business backgrounds, the Haas family knew little about baseball. They kept Billy Martin as manager and learned a lot.

Their first full season in business was disrupted by the strike that resulted in the major leagues' only split season. The A's broke fast, winning their first 11 games, and held on to top Texas by 1½ games when the first half ended. Kansas City nosed them out for the second half title by one game, but the A's swept the makeshift division title playoff in three games, then lost three in a row to the Yankees for the pennant. Rickey Henderson led the 1981 A's at .319 and stole 56 bases in the brief 109-game season. With a thin bullpen, the four starters turned in 56 complete games. The A's 60 complete games was almost double the next highest total in the league.

Amid accusations that overwork had ruined their arms, the A's pitching staff was plagued by sore arms in 1982. For the four mound mainstays it became a chronic condition and they were never the same. The club slipped to fifth, but the fans poured out to watch Billyball, as the A's TV commercials called the hustling brand of baseball Billy Martin's crew put out. Rickey Henderson set a record with 130 stolen bases. Attendance soared to 1,735,489, settling for good the question of Oakland's interest in the A's, and apparently confirming that a fifth-place team owned by the local pantsmakers would get far more support than World Champions owned by Charlie O.

By now there was a scouting staff at work, a six-team minor league organization winning pennants, a marketing and promotion department, and public relations programs in high gear. Haas had set out to make the fans forget Finley in two years, and he had succeeded. It was a buttoned-down operation, a group that did not seek the spotlight, where never was heard a disparaging word about players, managers, press, or fellow lodge members among the Lords of Baseball.

Improvements were made to the stadium. Records and ticket orders were computerized. The club spent over $5 million more than they took in during the first two years to transform the operation from a one-man absentee boss to a staff of 50 who felt comfortable, respected, secure.

But pugnacious Billy Martin did not fit the image they were trying to promote. He was replaced by a man with no managing experience, an intellectual who not only read books but actually was writing one, Steve Boros. The A's finished fourth two years in a row; Boros was relieved midway through the 1984 season by coach Jackie Moore.

By the end of 1984 two-thirds of the best outfield in the league had departed. In 1982 Tony Armas went to the Red Sox for Carney Lansford and two others. The 1984 season convinced the front office that pitching was their greatest need, so they sent Rickey Henderson, a moody player who sometimes seemed indifferent about playing after Martin left, with some cash to the Yankees for pitchers Tim Birtsus, Eric Plunk, Jay Howell, and Jose Rijo and outfielder Stan Javier. Plunk developed into an effective reliever and eventually returned to the Yankees. Howell was the top A's reliever until he was traded to the Dodgers and came back to haunt the A's—but that comes later.

The A's signed the much-travelled longball threat Dave Kingman as a DH, but could do no better than tie for fourth with Minnesota with a 77–85 record in 1985. About this time Oakland fans began to read familiar headlines: "A's Bay Area Future Shaky." Roy Eisenhardt was quoted as saying the team might be gone by the time Opening Day 1986 came along. But this time it was not a rap at the fans nor a squeeze play for a new stadium. What it was was an echo from the past, a replay of the words of Connie Mack 50 years before.

"I see my revenues staying the same and my expenses going up," Eisenhardt said in an interview in the San Francisco *Chronicle*. "I have to do something, and I can't sit with the status quo." He questioned whether the Bay Area was a one-team market, much less a two-team one, and figured they needed almost two million to break even at the gate.

But there was a new factor in the situation, one far beyond Connie Mack's vision a half century earlier: television. By 1986 television revenue had surpassed ticket sales as a source of income. The measure of a good place to put a team was the TV market, not the potential attendance. The A's had signed a deal worth $1.5 million. The Yankees would rake in almost 10 times that amount, enough to cover their entire payroll, something clubs in "minor markets" like the Bay Area could never hope to match.

The Lords of Baseball were about to learn that young businessmen and attorneys, inexperienced in baseball, could also shock them with radical ideas, more basic to the structure of the game than the color of the ball or the uniforms. Eisenhardt put forth the idea that all television revenues, not just network money, should be shared equally. It was not adopted.

The A's had lost a reported $33 million since 1981. But they stayed in Oakland, signing a new 15-year lease on the Coliseum. Early in the 1986 season they were limping along with the worst performance in the league. But that didn't put them out of sight of the leaders in the western division, generally considered the weakest of the four big league segments.

Mike Davis in right field, a seven-year veteran at 27, had still not bloomed as expected. Dwayne Murphy, a nine-year fixture in center, struggled to stay above .250, though he hit an occasional home run when it was needed. Still, there were some bright spots. In left field was the rookie Jose Canseco, 6'3", 220 pounds, strong as an ox. He would hit 33 home runs to Kingman's 35, but he struck out 175 times. His 117 RBIs led the club. Alfredo Griffin at short and Lansford at third gave them half an infield. Lefty Curt Young's 13–9 topped a weak pitching staff.

Jackie Moore was not the field leader the team needed. The rookie club owner, Eisenhardt, was concerned over his two straight disappointing choices of managers. That, too, made him an oddity: taking the blame for picking the wrong managers. Then, in the middle of the year, the White Sox fired their manager, Tony LaRussa, after seven years and a division title in 1983. LaRussa had played for Charlie Finley briefly in Kansas City and Oakland; he hit .199 as an infielder. A law school graduate, he was a quiet person who combined the moderate temperament and the experience the A's were looking for. They grabbed him. With Sandy Alderson, Eisnehardt's former law partner, as general manager, the A's had a unique lineup off the field: three top men who could win in the courtroom as well as on the diamond.

The 1986 club improved some, but finished 10 games under .500 in a tie for third with Kansas City, 16 games out. As a gesture of support, 17,235 fans came out for the last game, a 6–0 win over the Royals for Curt Young.

The 1987 A's improved by only five games, to 81–81, but in an evenly balanced division it was good enough to finish third, just four games back of the Twins, who won the title with the worst record ever and went on to win the World Series. But the biggest noise was made by the A's second rookie sensation, first baseman Mark McGwire, signed out of USC. McGwire set a rookie record with a league-leading 49 home runs, batting .291 with 118 RBIs. Canseco hit 31 dingers, drove in 113, but hit .257 and fanned 157 times. Carney Lansford hit .290 with 19 homers and 76 RBIs. Dave Stewart, a journeyman pitcher, learned how to pitch at 30 and tied Roger Clemens with 20 wins against 13 losses. He struck out 205. Dennis Eckersley, a starter for 12 years, signed as a free agent and reluctantly agreed to become the closer; he had 16 saves, as did Jay Howell. The fans came out to cheer them on as the team looked better and played better than at any time since the pennant winners of a dozen years back. Sandy Alderson, his baseball legs firmly under him now, waded aggressively into the marketplace. From mid-1987 to the end of 1988 there were eight new faces in the 24-man roster.

With confidence in another rookie, Walt Weiss, to fill the shortstop post, the A's traded Griffin and Jay Howell to Los Angeles for veteran starter Bob Welch. They gave up on Mike Davis and cut him loose; he signed with the Dodgers. The Red Sox gave up on outfielder Dave Henderson and traded him to the Giants, who then gave up on him as well and let him become a free agent. The A's signed him in December, and moved Canseco to right field. They then swapped young righthander Tim Belcher to the Dodgers for veteran starter Rick Honeycutt and made him a middle reliever. They added Glenn Hubbard, a 10-year second baseman from the National League.

It was a young team; to add some savvy, leadership, and experience in winning they signed Don Baylor and Dave Parker. A 13-game winning streak in midseason pulled them away from the pack and the A's won going away, finishing 13 games ahead of the Twins with a 104–58 record. They won 54 at home, most in the majors. Jose Canseco worked with batting coach Bob Watson and cut down on his strikeouts by learning to hit to right field on an 0–2 count. The righthanded batter became the Big Broadcast of 1988, hitting .307 with a league-leading 40 home runs and 124 RBIs. He established the 40–40 club by stealing 40 bases, and was an easy choice for MVP. McGwire added 32 homers and 99 RBIs, batting .260. Walt Weiss hit .250 and was Rookie of the Year. Don Baylor and Dave Parker, splitting DH duties, combined for 19 home runs and 89 RBIs. The surprise of the year was the double castoff, Dave Henderson, who batted .304 with 24 home runs and 94 RBIs. He led the league with 38 doubles, playing on his fourth team in three years.

Dave Stewart became the only pitcher to put two 20-game years together in 1987–88, with a 21–12 record and 3.23 ERA. He worked 276 innings and 14 complete games. Welch was 17–9 and worked 245 innings. On the last day of the season he shut out Milwaukee before 43,148 appreciative fans.

Storm Davis, young heir apparent to Jim Palmer at Baltimore, had gone to San Diego in 1987, where he was ineffective. The A's picked him up and he won 16 and lost 7. Curt Young had a spell of arm miseries in July and August but finished 11–8. The bullpen was outstanding. Rick Honeycutt and Gene Nelson were the middle men.

Eckersley, 5–2 with a 2.89 ERA, and lefty Greg Cadaret were in almost every game between them. Eckersley had 45 saves.

The Red Sox were eastern division champions, and that didn't bother the A's, who had beaten them six times at home. The playoff opened in Boston and Bruce Hurst, almost invincible in Fenway with an 18–6 overall record, took a 2–1 loss on Canseco's home run in the fourth and Dave Henderson's RBI single in the eighth. A diving grab by Walt Weiss cut off a Boston run. Eckersley saved the win for Stewart by fanning Wade Boggs with two on in the ninth.

Behind Roger Clemens, the Red Sox took a 2–0 lead in the second game when Henderson dropped a fly ball in the sixth. In the seventh Henderson singled ahead of Canseco, who hit an 0–2 pitch over the green monster. Two more hits and a walk produced a 3–2 lead. When Cadaret relieved Storm Davis in the seventh, Rich Gedman homered to tie it. Walt Weiss, who had batted over .400 at Fenway during the season, drove in the winning run in the ninth. Eckersley shut down the home team in the last of the ninth.

Before 49,261—a far cry from the 25,000 who showed up for playoff games in Oakland 15 years before—the A's finished off the Red Sox, 10–6. Home runs by Henderson, McGwire, Lansford, and Hassey overcame a 5–0 Boston lead in which Welch was kayoed in the second. Nelson was the winning pitcher; Eckersley chalked up his third save, earning him playoff MVP honors. For Don Baylor it meant he was playing in an unprecedented third World Series in three years on three different teams.

And then the A's stopped hitting. Credit Dodger pitching, which had beaten the Mets for the National League pennant, if you wish. Oakland batted .177, scored 11 runs in the five games. Jose Canseco hit a grand slam home run in the first game, the only runs Oakland scored all night. McGwire hit a home run in Game Three. Those were the only two hits the big guns could make in 36 at bats. Walt Weiss was 1 for 16.

In the ninth frame of the Series opener the A's led, 4–3, when Eckersley walked Mike Davis. Kirk Gibson, out of the lineup with a leg injury, hobbled up to the plate and lofted a home run over the right-field fence.

In Los Angeles, it was the year of the Hershiser. In Game Two he pitched the eighth shutout in his last 10 games, 6–0. Back home another sellout crowd of 49,316 enjoyed McGwire's lone blow; it came in the ninth and gave the A's a 2–1 win, as Welch and the bullpen held the Dodgers at bay. But that was their last bright moment. The Dodgers beat Stewart, 4–3, as the erstwhile A's stopper, Jay Howell, came in and got McGwire to pop up with the bases loaded in the seventh, then mowed down the forlorn A's to the end.

In the finale former A's outfielder Mike Davis and newborn Dodger star Mickey Hatcher hit two-run homers and that's all Orel Hershiser needed for a 5–2 clincher. He fanned nine and gave up four hits in taming the tabby Athletics.

The link to the past was reforged in 1988 when Oakland reactivated the Athletics' elephant. Associated with the team in Philadelphia since 1902, the symbol had first appeared on Athletics uniforms in 1918, and appeared somewhere on the jerseys for the next 10 years. An elephant patch appeared on the left sleeves when the team moved to Kansas City in 1955, but when Charlie O. and his mule came in, the pachyderm departed. And the Oakland Athletics, in the newfound prudence and sobriety of their business conduct, and their renewed winning ways on the field, had now again come to resemble the Athletics of Connie Mack like a grandson who takes after his noble grandfather.

Winning had returned in the summer of 1988 under the capable field leadership of Tony LaRussa and the fence-bashing heroics of young sluggers Canseco and McGwire, but the World Series debacle against the pitching-rich Los Angeles Dodgers (in the second all-West-Coast World Series ever) had been a humbling setback that left a bitter taste for the organization as well as for Bay Area fans. It also left the 1989 Athletics team with a mission and a point to prove. And that point was not long in being established, as LaRussa's team (strengthened especially by the off-season acquisition of pitching star Mike Moore from Seattle) raced to 99 victories and an exceptionally easy second-straight western division crown, this time by seven games over runner-up Kansas City.

Post-season play in 1989 was rich in self-justification for the Oakland Athletics, if genuinely void of exciting or dramatic fall championship-style play. An easy five-game romp past Eastern Division title-holder Toronto was followed by an even easier four-game sweep against neighborhood rivals, the San Francisco Giants, in the first-ever Bay Area World Series. But what had been long anticipated by Bay Area fans as an ultimate baseball dream quickly disintegrated in the nightmare of a dull one-sided diamond encounter, made almost insignificant by a devastating earthquake which rocked Candlestick Park moments before Game Three. Postponed for more than a week, the 1989 World Series resumed with listless play and little fan interest for its final two uninspired games.

The Athletics took the pennant again in 1990 and battled the Cincinnati Reds in the A's third straight World Series. It is perhaps the beginning of a new dynasty, one to equal the A's powerhouse of the 1970s, or Connie Mack's Philadelphia Champions of 80 years ago.

Annotated Bibliography

Bergman, Ron. *The Moustache Gang: The Swaggering Saga of Oakland's A's.* New York: Dell Publishing Company, 1973. 255 pp.

Catfish, Reggie, Rollie, Vida, and (of course) Charlie O. A hastily written and sensationalized portrait of baseball's hottest team of the moment.

Clark, Tom. *Champagne and Baloney: A History of Finley's A's.* New York: Harper and Row Publishers, 1976. 432 pp.

Perhaps the cleverest and also the most outrageous of the half-dozen exploitation books which followed the successes of the Oakland team during the memorable period of Catfish Hunter and Reggie Jackson.

Heimerdinger, Debra. *Baseball Rhythms: Photography of the Oakland A's.* Richmond, CA: North Atlantic Books, 1982. 220 pp.

One of two pictorial essays released by this publisher on the favored hometown team after the 1981 season.

———. *Waiting Game: Photographs of the Oakland A's.* Richmond, CA: North Atlantic Books, 1982. 80 pp.

Shorter version and companion volume to the above photographic essay. Features excellent photography of the Oakland ballpark and early 1980s ballplayers.

Lieb, Fred. *Connie Mack: Grand Old Man of Baseball.* New York: G.P. Putnam's Sons, 1945. 276 pp.

The standard biography on Connie Mack, with rich details on his several powerhouse Philadelphia Athletics teams of the early era (1901–1940).

McGillicuddy, Cornelius A. (Connie Mack). *My 66 Years in Baseball.* New York: Winston Publishers, 1950. 246 pp.

The grand old man of baseball tells all in one of baseball's best-loved early autobiographies. An intimate portrait of baseball in the age when "the grass was real" and the sky was still blue and undomed.

Meany, Thomas. "Lefty Grove," in: *Baseball's Greatest Pitchers.* New York: A.S. Barnes, 1951. pp. 87–98.

One of the most detailed portraits of the spectacular playing career of this all-time greatest among Athletics pitchers of the Connie Mack era.

———. "Connie's Bull Elephants: The 1929 Athletics," in: *Baseball's Greatest Teams.* New York: A.S. Barnes, 1949. pp. 45–60.

The delightful details surrounding the greatest of all Connie Mack's championship teams, and one of the best-ever in American League history.

Mehl, Ernest. *The Kansas City Athletics.* New York: Holt, 1956.

The only existing book-length treatment of the Athletics sojourn in Kansas City, written immediately after the team's first season in Missouri and thus offering an exceedingly limited historical perspective.

Year-by-Year Standings and Season Summaries
Philadelphia Athletics (1901–1954)

Year	Pos.	Record	Pct.	GB	Manager	Player	BA	Player	HR	Player	W-L	ERA
1901	4th	74–62	.544	9.0	Mack	Lajoie	.422	Lajoie	14	Fraser	22–16	3.81
1902	1st	83–53	.610	+5.0	Mack	L. Cross	.342	Seybold	16	Waddell	24–7	2.05
1903	2nd	75–60	.556	14.5	Mack	Hartsel	.311	Seybold	8	Plank	23–16	2.38
1904	5th	81–70	.536	12.5	Mack	H. Davis	.309	Plank	10	Plank	26–16	2.14
1905	1st	92–56	.622	+2.0	Mack	H. Davis	.284	Waddell	8	Waddell	26–11	1.48
1906	4th	78–67	.538	12.0	Mack	Seybold	.316	Plank	12	Plank	19–6	2.25
1907	2nd	88–57	.607	1.5	Mack	Nicholls	.302	Plank	8	Plank	24–16	2.20
1908	6th	68–85	.444	22.0	Mack	E. Collins	.273	H. Davis	5	Vickers	18–19	2.34
1909	2nd	95–58	.621	3.5	Mack	E. Collins	.346	D. Murphy	5	Plank	19–10	1.70
1910	1st	102–48	.680	+14.5	Mack	E. Collins	.322	Oldring Murphy	4 4	Coombs	31–9	1.30
1911	1st	101–50	.669	+13.5	Mack	E. Collins	.365	Baker	11	Coombs	28–12	3.53
1912	3rd	90–62	.592	15.0	Mack	E. Collins	.348	Baker	10	Plank	26–6	2.22
1913	1st	96–57	.627	+6.5	Mack	E. Collins	.345	Baker	12	Bender	21–10	2.21
1914	1st	99–53	.651	+8.5	Mack	E. Collins	.344	Baker	9	Bender	17–3	2.26
1915	8th	43–109	.283	58.5	Mack	McInnis	.314	Oldring	6	Wyckoff	10–22	3.52
1916	8th	36–117	.235	54.5	Mack	Strunk	.316	Schang	7	Bush	15–24	2.57
1917	8th	55–98	.359	44.5	Mack	McInnis	.303	Bodie	7	Bush	11–17	2.47
1918	8th	52–76	.406	24.0	Mack	Burns	.352	T. Walker	11	Perry	21–19	1.98
1919	8th	36–104	.257	52.0	Mack	Burns	.296	T. Walker	10	Johnson	9–15	3.61
1920	8th	48–106	.312	50.0	Mack	Dugan	.322	T. Walker	17	Perry	11–25	3.62
1921	8th	53–100	.346	45.0	Mack	Witt	.315	T. Walker	23	Rommel	16–23	3.94
1922	7th	65–89	.422	29.0	Mack	B. Miller	.336	T. Walker	37	Rommel	27–13	3.28
1923	6th	69–83	.454	29.0	Mack	Hauser	.307	Hauser	16	Rommel	18–19	3.27
1924	5th	71–81	.467	20.0	Mack	B. Miller	.342	Hauser	27	Rommel	18–15	3.95
1925	2nd	88–64	.579	8.5	Mack	Simmons	.384	Simmons	24	Rommel	21–10	2.84
1926	3rd	83–67	.553	6.0	Mack	Simmons	.343	Simmons	19	Grove	13–13	2.51

Year	Pos.	Record	Pct.	GB	Manager	Player	BA	Player	HR	Player	W-L	ERA
1927	2nd	91–63	.591	19.0	Mack	Simmons	.392	Simmons	15	Grove	20–12	3.19
1928	2nd	98–55	.641	2.5	Mack	Simmons	.351	Hauser	16	Grove	24–8	2.58
1929	1st	104–46	.693	+18.0	Mack	Simmons	.365	Simmons	34	Earnshaw	24–8	3.29
1930	1st	102–52	.662	+8.0	Mack	Simmons	.381	Foxx	37	Grove	28–5	2.54
1931	1st	107–45	.704	+13.5	Mack	Simmons	.390	Foxx	30	Grove	31–4	2.06
1932	2nd	94–60	.610	13.0	Mack	Foxx	.364	Foxx	58	Grove	25–10	2.84
1933	3rd	79–72	.523	19.5	Mack	Foxx	.356	Foxx	48	Grove	24–8	3.20
1934	5th	68–82	.453	31.0	Mack	Foxx	.334	Foxx	44	Marcum	14–11	4.50
1935	8th	58–91	.389	34.0	Mack	Foxx	.346	Foxx	36	Marcum	17–12	4.08
1936	8th	53–100	.346	49.0	Mack	Moses	.345	B. Johnson	25	Kelley	15–12	3.86
1937	7th	54–97	.358	46.5	Mack	Moses	.330	Johnson	25	Kelley	13–21	5.36
								Moses	25			
1938	8th	53–99	.349	46.0	Mack	B. Johnson	.313	B. Johnson	30	Caster	16–20	4.37
1939	7th	55–97	.362	31.5	Mack	B. Johnson	.338	B. Johnson	23	Nelson	10–13	4.78
1940	8th	54–100	.351	36.0	Mack	Moses	.309	B. Johnson	31	Babich	14–13	3.73
1941	8th	64–90	.416	37.0	Mack	Siebert	.334	Chapman	25	Knott	13–11	4.40
1942	8th	55–99	.357	48.0	Mack	B. Johnson	.291	B. Johnson	13	Marchildon	17–14	4.20
1943	8th	49–105	.318	49.0	Mack	Estalella	.259	Estalella	11	Flores	12–14	3.11
1944	5th	72–82	.468	17.0	Mack	Siebert	.306	Hayes	13	Christopher	14–14	2.97
1945	8th	52–98	.347	34.5	Mack	Estalella	.299	Estalella	8	Christopher	13–13	3.17
1946	8th	49–105	.318	55.0	Mack	McCosky	.354	Chapman	20	Marchildon	13–16	3.49
1947	5th	78–76	.506	19.0	Mack	McCosky	.328	Chapman	14	Marchildon	19–9	3.22
1948	4th	84–70	.545	12.5	Mack	McCosky	.326	Joost	16	Fowler	15–8	3.78
1949	5th	81–73	.526	16.0	Mack	Valo	.283	Chapman	24	Kellner	20–12	3.75
1950	8th	52–102	.338	46.0	Mack	Dillinger	.309	Chapman	23	Hooper	15–10	5.02
						Lehner	.309					
1951	6th	70–84	.455	28.0	Dykes	Fain	.344	Zernial	33	Shantz	18–10	3.94
1952	4th	79–75	.513	16.0	Dykes	Fain	.327	Zernial	29	Shantz	24–7	2.48
1953	7th	59–95	.383	41.5	Dykes	Philley	.303	Zernial	42	Kellner	11–12	3.93
1954	8th	51–103	.331	60.0	Joost	Finigan	.302	B. Wilson	15	Portocarrero	9–18	4.06

Kansas City Athletics (1955–1967)

Year	Pos.	Record	Pct.	GB	Manager	Player	BA	Player	HR	Player	W-L	ERA
1955	6th	63–91	.409	33.0	Boudreau	Power	.319	Zernial	30	Kellner	11–8	4.20
1956	8th	52–102	.338	45.0	Boudreau	Power	.309	Simpson	21	Ditmar	12–22	4.42
1957	7th	59–94	.386	38.5	Boudreau Craft	Smith	.303	Zemial	27	Trucks	9–7	3.03
1958	7th	73–81	.474	19.0	Craft	Cerv	.305	Cerv	38	Garver	12–11	4.03
1959	7th	66–88	.429	28.0	Craft	Tuttle	.300	Cerv	20	Daley	16–13	3.16
1960	8th	58–96	.377	39.0	Elliott	D. Williams	.288	Siebern	19	Daley	16–16	4.56
1961	9th	61–100	.379	47.5	Gordon Bauer	Siebern	.296	Siebern	18	Bass	11–11	4.69
1962	9th	72–90	.444	24.0	Bauer	Siebern	.308	Siebern	25	Rakow	14–17	4.25
1963	8th	73–89	.451	31.5	Lopat	Causey	.280	Siebern	16	Wickersham	12–15	4.09
1964	10th	57–105	.352	42.0	Lopat McGaha	Causey	.281	Colavito	34	Pena	12–14	4.43
1965	10th	59–103	.364	43.0	McGaha Sullivan	Campaneris	.270	Harrelson	23	Sheldon	10–8	3.95
1966	7th	74–86	.463	23.0	Dark	Cater	.292	Repoz	11	Krausse	14–9	2.99
1967	10th	62–99	.385	29.5	Dark Appling	Donaldson	.276	Monday	14	Hunter	13–17	2.81

Oakland Athletics (1968–1992)

Year	Pos.	Record	Pct.	GB	Manager	Player	BA	Player	HR	Player	W-L	ERA
1968	6th	82–80	.506	21.0	Kennedy	Cater	.290	Jackson	29	Odom	16–10	2.45
1969	2nd*	88–74	.543	9.0	Bauer McNamara	Bando	.281	Jackson	47	Odom	15–6	2.92
1970	2nd	89–73	.549	9.0	McNamara	Rudi	.309	Mincher	27	Hunter	18–14	3.81

Year	Pos.	Record	Pct.	GB	Manager	Player	BA	Player	HR	Player	W-L	ERA
1971	1st	101–60	.627	+16.0	Williams	Jackson	.277	Jackson	32	Blue	24–8	1.82
1972	1st	93–62	.600	+5.5	Williams	Rudi	.305	Epstein	26	Hunter	21–7	2.04
†1973	1st	94–68	.580	+6.0	Williams	Jackson	.293	Jackson	32	Hunter	21–5	3.34
1974	1st	90–72	.556	+5.0	Dark	Rudi	.293	Jackson	29	Hunter	25–12	2.49
1975	1st	98–64	.605	+7.0	Dark	Washington	.308	Jackson	36	Blue	22–11	3.01
1976	2nd	87–74	.540	2.5	Tanner	North	.276	Bando	27	Blue	18–13	2.36
1977	7th	63–98	.391	38.5	McKeon / Winkles	Page	.307	Gross	22	Blue	14–19	3.83
1978	6th	69–93	.426	23.0	Winkles / McKeon	Page	.285	Page	17	Johnson	11–10	3.39
1979	7th	54–108	.333	34.0	Marshall	Revering	.288	Newman	22	Langford	12–16	427
1980	2nd	83–79	.512	14.0	Martin	R. Henderson	.303	Armas	35	Norris	22–9	2.54
1981	1st	37–23	.617	+1.5	Martin	R. Henderson	.319	Armas	22	McCatty	14–7	2.32
	2nd	27–22	.551	1.0								
1981**	1st	64–45	.587	+5.0								
1982	5th	69–84	.420	25.0	Martin	R. Henderson	.267	Armas	28	Langford	11–16	4.21
1983	4th	74–88	.457	25.0	Boros	Lansford	.308	Lopes	17	Codiroli	12–12	4.46
								Murphy	17			
1984	4th	77–85	.475	7.0	Boros / Moore	Lansford	.300	Murphy	33	Burril	3–10	3.15
1985	4th	77–85	.475	14.0	Moore	Bochte	.295	Kingman	30	Corddiroli	14–14	4.46
1986	3rd	76–86	.469	16.0	Moore / LaRussa	Griffin	.285	Kingman	35	Young	13–9	3.45
1987	3rd	81–81	.500	4.0	LaRussa	McGwire / Lansford	.289	McGwire	49	Stewart	20–13	3.68
1988	1st	104–58	.642	+13.0	LaRussa	Canseco	.307	Canseco	40	Stewart	21–12	3.23
1989	1st	99–63	.611	+7.0	LaRussa	Lansford	.336	McGwire	32	Stewart	21–9	3.32
1990	1st	103–59	.543	+9.0	LaRussa	R. Henderson	.325	McGwire	39	Welch	27–6	3.06
1991	4th	84–78	.519	11.0	LaRussa	Baines	.295	Canesco	44	Moore	17–8	2.96
1992	1st	96–66	.593	+6.0	LaRussa	Bordick	.300	McGwire	42	Moore	17–12	4.12

* American League West (first season of divisional play).**Split Season Totals (Players' Union Strike).

All-Time Athletics Career and Season Records

Philadelphia Athletics Career Batting Leaders (1901–1954)

Games Played	Jimmy Dykes	1,702
At Bats	Jimmy Dykes	6,023
Runs Scored	Bob Johnson	977
Hits	Al Simmons	1,827
Batting Average (300 or more games)	Al Simmons	.356
Home Runs	Jimmie Foxx	302
Runs Batted In	Al Simmons	1,178
Stolen Bases	Eddie Collins	375
Strikeouts	Jimmie Dykes	705

Kansas City Athletics Career Batting Leaders (1955–1967)

Games Played	Ed Charles	726
At Bats	Jerry Lumpe	2,782
Runs Scored	Jerry Lumpe	361
Hits	Jerry Lumpe	775
Batting Average (300 or more games)	Vic Power	.297
Home Runs	Norm Siebern	78
Runs Batted In	Norm Siebern	367
Stolen Bases	Bert Campaneris	168
Strikeouts	Ed Charles	379

Oakland Athletics Career Batting Leaders (1968–1992)

Games Played	Sal Bando	1,410
At Bats	Bert Campaneris	5,159
Runs Scored	Rickey Henderson	910
Hits	Bert Campaneris	1,355
Batting Average (300 or more games)	Rickey Henderson	.294
Home Runs	Reggie Jackson	268
Runs Batted In	Sal Bando	789
Stolen Bases	Rickey Henderson	664
Strikeouts	Reggie Jackson	1,180

Philadephia Athletics Career Pitching Leaders (1901–1954)

Innings Pitched	Eddie Plank	3,870.1
Earned Run Average (400-plus innings)	Rube Waddell	1.99
Wins	Eddie Plank	285
Losses	Eddie Plank	161
Winning Percentage (50 decisions)	Lefty Grove	.712 (195–79)
Strikeouts	Eddie Plank	1,985
Walks	Eddie Plank	913
Games	Eddie Plank	523
Shutouts	Eddie Plank	59
Saves	Lefty Grove	55
Games Started	Eddie Plank	457
Complete Games	Eddie Plank	362

All-Time Athletics Career and Season Records *(continued)*

Kansas City Athletics Career Pitching Leaders (1955–1967)

Innings Pitched	Ray Herbert	748
Wins	Bud Daley	39
Losses	Ray Herbert	48
Strikeouts	Diego Segui	573
Walks	Diego Segui	280
Games	John Wyatt	292
Shutouts	Ned Garver	8
Saves	John Wyatt	71
Games Started	Ray Herbert	98
Complete Games	Ray Herbert	32

Oakland Athletics Career Pitching Leaders (1968–1992)

Innings Pitched	Vida Blue	1,946
Wins	Catfish Hunter	131
Losses	Rick Langford	90
Strikeouts	Vida Blue	1,315
Walks	Vida Blue	617
Games	Rollie Fingers	502
Shutouts	Vida Blue	28
Saves	Dennis Eckersley	236
Games Started	Vida Blue	262
Complete Games	Catfish Hunter	96

Philadelphia Athletics Single-Season Batting Records (1901–1954)

Batting Average (350 ABs)	Nap Lajoie	422	1901
Home Runs	Jimmie Foxx	58	1932
Runs Batted In	Jimmie Foxx	169	1932
Hits	Al Simmons	253	1925
Doubles	Al Simmons	53	1926
Triples	Home Run Baker	21	1912
Slugging Percentage	Jimmie Foxx	.749	1932
Extra Base Hits	Jimmie Foxx	100	1932
Stolen Bases	Eddie Collins	81	1910
Pinch Hits	Bing Miller	10	1934
Strikeouts	Eddie Joost	110	1947
Total Bases	Jimmie Foxx	438	1932
Hitting Streak	Bill Lamar	29	1925

Kansas City Athletics Single-Season Batting Records (1955–1967)

Batting Average (350 ABs)	Vic Power	.319	1955
Home Runs	Bob Cerv	38	1958
Runs Batted In	Norm Siebern	117	1962
Hits	Jerry Lumpe	193	1956
Doubles	Norm Siebern	36	1961
Triples	Gino Cimoli	15	1962
Slugging Percentage	Bob Cerv	.592	1958
Extra Base Hits	Rocky Colavito	67	1964
Sacrifices	Dick Williams	11	1959
Stolen Bases	Bert Campaneris	55	1967
Pinch Hits	Bob Cerv	9	1957

All-Time Athletics Career and Season Records *(continued)*

Strikeouts	Nelson Matthews	143	1964
Total Bases	Bob Cerv	305	1958
Hitting Streak	Hector Lopez	22	1957
	Vic Power	22	1958
Grand Slam Home Runs	Roger Maris	2	1958

Oakland Athletics Single-Season Batting Records (1968–1992)

Batting Average (350 ABs)	Carney Lansford	.336	1989
Home Runs	Mark McGwire	49	1987
Runs Batted In	Jose Canseco	124	1988
Hits	Jose Canseco	187	1988
Doubles	Joe Rudi	39	1974
	Reggie Jackson	39	1975
Triples	Phil Garner	12	1976
Slugging Percentage	Mark McGwire	.618	1987
Extra Base Hits	Reggie Jackson	86	1969
Sacrifices	Dwayne Murphy	22	1980
Stolen Bases	Rickey Henderson	130	1982
Strikeouts	Jose Canseco	175	1986
Total Bases	Jose Canseco	347	1988
Hitting Streak	Carney Lansford	24	1984
Grand Slam Home Runs	Gene Tenace	3	1974
	Dave Kingman	3	1984

Philadelphia Athletics Single-Season Pitching Records (1901–1954)

ERA (150 innings)	Jack Coombs	1.30	1910
Wins	Jack Coombs	31	1910
	Lefty Grove	31	1931
Losses	Scott Perry	25	1920
Winning Pct. (10 decisions)	Lefty Grove	.886	1931
		(31–4)	
Strikeouts	Rube Waddell	349	1904
Walks	Elmer Myers	168	1916
Saves	Chief Bender	13	1913
	Russ Christopher	13	1947
Games	Eddie Rommel	56	1923
Complete Games	Rube Waddell	39	1904
Games Started	Rube Waddell	46	1904
Shutouts	Jack Coombs	13	1910
Innings Pitched	Rube Waddell	384	1904
Home Runs Allowed	Alex Kellner	28	1950
Consecutive Games Won	Lefty Grove	16	1931

All-Time Athletics Career and Season Records *(continued)*

Kansas City Athletics Single-Season Pitching Records (1955–1967)

ERA (150 innings)	Catfish Hunter	2.81	1967
Wins	Bud Daley	16	1959,1960
Losses	Art Ditmar	22	1956
Winning Pct. (10 decisions)	Bud Daley	.552	1959
		(16–13)	
Strikeouts	Catfish Hunter	196	1967
Walks	Art Ditmar	108	1956
Saves	Tom Aker	32	1966
Games	John Wyatt	81	1964
Complete Games	Art Ditmar	14	1956
	Ray Herbert	14	1960
Shutouts	Catfish Hunter	5	1967
Home Runs Allowed	Orlando Pena	40	1964
Consecutive Games Won	Bud Daley	9	1960

Oakland Athletics Single-Season Pitching Records (1968–1992)

ERA (150 innings)	Vida Blue	1.82	1971
Wins	Catfish Hunter	25	1974
Losses	Brian Kingman	20	1980
Winning Pct. (10 decisions)	Catfish Hunter	.808	1973
		(21–5)	
Strikeouts	Vida Blue	301	1971
Walks	Blue Moon Odom	112	1969
Saves	Dennis Eckersley	51	1992
Games	Rollie Fingers	76	1974
Complete Games	Rick Langford	28	1980
Games Started	Catfish Hunter	41	1974
Shutouts	Vida Blue	8	1971
Home Runs Allowed	Catfish Hunter	39	1973
Consecutive Games Won	Catfish Hunter	13	1973

9

St. Louis Browns-
Baltimore Orioles
One of the Very Worst, and
One of the Very Best
BILL FELBER

Their nominal roots lay in two of the legendary teams of nine-teenth-century baseball, the storied four-time 1880s champion St. Louis Browns of Charles Comiskey and Chris von Der Ahe, and the equally fabled thrice-crowned 1890s Baltimore Orioles of Willie Keeler. But in the shared history of the twentieth-century descendant of those epochal clubs, only one legacy brought with it unparalleled success; the ghost of the other conjured up unmatched incompetence.

It would be difficult to find a professional sports franchise with fortunes so diverse, and which changed in so comparatively short a time, as those of the baseball club presently headquartered in Balti-more. For five decades as the St. Louis-based Browns, this team suf-fered virtually interminable humiliation. But since its move east in 1954, the franchise's aggregate record ranks among baseball's elite.

After entering the newly formed American League as the Milwau-kee Brewers in 1901—they won only 48 of 137 games and finished last—the franchise was transferred to St. Louis the following spring and rechristened as the Browns. The name was borrowed from the fabled St. Louis team of the American Association, a one-generation-removed rival to the National League, which was the role the American League envisioned for itself at the turn of the century.

Those 1880s St. Louis Browns of yore had won four pennants and also compiled the best record of any club in the American Associa-tion's 10 short years of existence. Unfortunately, the magic of the legendary name failed to attach to the new Browns, who managed only two first-division finishes (in 1902 and 1908) over the next 18 seasons, while finishing last four times. And on the rare occasions when the Browns coalesced into an earnest contender for the Ameri-can League championship—such as in 1922—they ran into the formi-dable presence of Babe Ruth at the height of his abilities. That season the best team in Browns history compiled a .604 winning percentage, but ran second, one game in back of the Yankees.

Even after 1922, such modest achievements as reaching the first division remained fleeting occurrences for Browns fans. For the next 22 seasons the club never placed higher than third, only five times reached the first division, and never concluded a season closer than 15 games behind the victors. And when, in 1944, the Browns finally did win a pennant—their only one—it was universally dismissed as a fluke occurrence attributable to the war-imposed absence of "real talent" on other American League rosters.

Finally, after a decade more of sustained incompetence that included seven finishes in either seventh or eighth place, the team was sold in 1953 to a Baltimore-based syndicate and moved to that city. As the St. Louis Browns, the franchise had compiled an abysmal record .433 winning percentage, the worst among any of the 16 teams at that time, claiming only, 3,416 victories in 53 years. (The New York Yankees won that many between 1921 and the mid 1950s.) But as the Orioles—again christened after a famous nineteenth-century team from the host city—Baltimore's challenge to the league's elite budded. The Orioles finished second in 1960, the first of six first-division placings in the next seven seasons, leading to the 1966 World Championship. By 1969 the Orioles were on the verge of three consecutive American League pennants, and of gaining recognition as one of baseball's best teams ever. The club finished out of the first division only twice between 1960 and 1983, winning a total of eight league or divisional pennants, and appearing in the World Series six times. And once it gained a measure of respectability, this franchise went from having the very worst long-term record to having the very best, leading the majors in winning percentage (.558) between 1957 and 1987. In the wake of 1988 results, the Orioles no longer can lay claim to that distinction—they rank second behind the Yankees—but their winning percentage since the onset of divisional play in 1969 remains the game's best.

This franchise, so lowly and then so mighty, was conceived as a by-product of the baseball war that spawned the American League in 1901. Emboldened a year later by the comparative success of his eight-club circuit's challenge to the reigning National League, AL President Ban Johnson ordered all-out warfare, and signalled it by instructing Matt Killea, owner of the Milwaukee Brewers franchise, to transfer his team to St. Louis, then the nation's fourth largest city. In St. Louis, Killea's club not only adopted the nickname of the fabled Browns, but also appropriated the team's home playing field, Sportman's Park, at the intersection of Grand Avenue and Dodier. He raided the cross-town Cardinals' roster for six players, including the popular shortstop

Bobby Wallace. Wallace, who had batted .322 with the Cardinals in 1901 but whose prospects for recognition were limited in a league that measured shortstops by the imposing presence of Pittsburgh's Honus Wagner, received not only a substantial salary increase but the satisfaction of acclaim as the AL's best at his position over his decade as a regular. The team's first hallmark star compiled a .267 career batting average, served as Browns manager for two seasons, and lived to see himself elected to the Hall of Fame in 1953.

Wallace was one of four men who formed the core of the Browns franchise during the first decade of its existence; the others were pitchers Harry Howell and Jack Powell and the team's manager, Jimmy McAleer. Powell, who came with Wallace in the 1902 player raid, had won 59 games over three seasons for the Cardinals, and he won 22 more that first season with the Browns. Following a 15–19 season in 1903, the Browns traded him to the New York American League club in February 1904 for Howell. He was reacquired by the Browns late in the 1905 season, pitching through 1912 and winning 79 more games, with 16 victories in the best of those years, 1908.

Howell, who pitched for the Browns from 1904 through 1908, won only 77 of 168 decisions, but that record is as much a reflection of the quality of support as his own ability. His earned run average for the period never ranged above 2.19, and he averaged 300 innings per season, completing a league-leading 35 games in 1905.

The transfusion provided by the six ex-Cardinals gave the new Browns an immediate and noticeable boost. Under the direction of McAleer—who would remain as manager through 1909—the Browns gained 30 games in the standings in 1902, leaping to second place, five games behind the champion Philadelphia Athletics. Jess Burkett, who accompanied Wallace and Powell from the Cardinals, batted .306, while outfielder Charlie Hemphill, acquired from Cleveland in May, batted a team-high .317. Powell won 22 games, a total matched by Red Donahue.

The arrival of the Browns in St. Louis did not herald the onset of a dynasty. Far from it. In 1903 the team gave back 13 games on its won-lost record and four places in the standings, falling to sixth. The Browns' initial exposure to last place occurred in 1905 when they finished 54–99 and 40½ games behind the champion Athletics. Probably the best Browns team of the first two decades, the 1908 club, remained in pennant contention through mid-September, thanks in some measure to the acquisition the previous winter of the brilliant but goofy left handed pitcher, Rube Waddell. Waddell jumped the team once that summer over McAleer's refusal to pay salary Rube had coming so he could engage in a drinking spree. But his one-man strike was short-lived, and he went to the mound often enough to win 19 games in 43 appearances for a team that finished fourth, just 6½ games back of champion Detroit.

Following the comparatively close miss of 1908, the Browns' fortunes quickly flagged. The franchise opened a brand new Sportsman's Park in 1909. But with Howell, Powell, and Wallace all beyond their prime, the club slipped to seventh, then to last again in 1910. The Browns that year played a supporting role in one of baseball's strangest scandals, an apparent effort to fix the race for the league's batting championship between Cleveland's Nap Lajoie and Detroit's Ty Cobb.

The schedule called for the Indians to conclude the season with a doubleheader in St. Louis while the Tigers played Chicago. Cobb, hated across the league for his combative temperament, led the beloved Lajoie by several points when the afternoon started, and benched himself so as to ensure not losing ground. Apparently Browns manager Jack O'Connor, who had succeeded McAleer that year, instructed rookie third baseman Red Corriden to play unusually deep, prompting Lajoie to lay down a succession of safe bunts. As a result, Lajoie finished the doubleheader eight-for-eight, prompting a league investigation into the roles of both O'Connor and Howell, by then a player-coach who was reported to have made repeated trips to the press box to ascertain how the bunts were scored. League President Johnson insisted to team owner Robert Hodges that both the manager and coach be released, and neither ever donned a major league uniform again.

The Browns finished seventh or last again in 1911, 1912, and 1913. But although St. Louis failed to develop enough prospects to contend for a title, the Browns did feature several players who deserved individual recognition. Two were third baseman Jimmy Austin and outfielder Burt Shotton.

Austin, 31 years old when he was acquired in a trade with the Yankees, played third regularly through 1919, and did not play his last game until 1929 at age 50. No heavyweight as a batter—he never hit over .270—Austin is best remembered today for his flashy fielding. He led his position in double plays several times, and also was a league-leader in total chances and fielding average. Shotton, later to gain some fame as manager of the 1947 and 1949 pennant-winning Brooklyn Dodgers, was a rookie outfielder in 1911, a fleet runner who four times in his career stole 40 bases or more. An excellent leadoff man, he twice led the league in drawing bases on balls.

Del Pratt joined the Browns as a rookie second baseman in 1912, batting .302 that first season on his way to a lifetime .292 average. Pratt spent six seasons with the Browns before being traded to New York, and in 1916 drove in a league-leading 103 runs. The team even got a new owner in 1915 when, in the wake of the collapse of the Federal League, that organization's Phil Ball purchased controlling interest in the club. But the most important arrival in 1915 was that of the man who ultimately became the team's greatest star.

George Sisler, only 22, was a sought-after prospect from the University of Michigan who had actually signed his first professional contract four years earlier, obligating himself to Pittsburgh. But Sisler quickly repudiated that agreement, citing his status as a minor, and as his reputation as a college player grew he offered his services to other teams. The deal he struck with St. Louis in the spring of 1915 included a $400 monthly salary and $5,000 signing bonus, significant figures for the day. In college Sisler had been a pitcher, but he proved only so-so at that skill in the majors, winning five and losing six in 18 appearances in 1915 and 1916. But as a batter Sisler was something special. Playing first base when not on the mound, he hit .285 that rookie season, and .305 the next. Converted to first base full time for the 1917 season, he further blossomed, batting .353 to trail only Cobb among all American League hitters. He followed that up with averages of .341 and .352, then in 1920 won his first of two batting titles with a remarkable .407 average and a total of 257 hits that still stands today as the major league single-season record.

But the Browns of the mid-teens never wandered out of the second division, largely because of a distinct lack of pitching. One of the comparatively few bright moments on the mound occurred in 1917, when on successive days (May 5–6) Browns teammates Ernie Koob and Bob Groom threw no-hitters against the Chicago White Sox. The achievement was in retribution—and then some—for a no-hitter fired at the Browns by Sox master Ed Cicotte just three weeks before. The no-hitters were only the second and third in the club's history, Earl Hamilton having thrown one five seasons before. The next would be 17 years in waiting.

Signs of progress could be seen in the emergence of Sisler, and in the development of several hitters who complemented him. Shotton was traded to Washington in 1918 to make room for Johnny Tobin. A youngster with the unlikely handle of William "Baby Doll" Jacobson arrived as a regular a year later, belying any prissiness implied by his nickname with a .323 average. When outfielder Ken Williams emerged as an offensive threat in 1920, the last piece of a significant batting order was in place. And when in 1922 second-year manager Leo Fohl molded an acceptable rotation of starters around veteran Urban Shocker and young Elam Vangilder, the Browns for the first time in decades faced the start of the race with a firm belief in their own abilities to contend for a championship.

Today the 1922 Browns are often mentioned in listings of the best non-pennant winners of all time. Their offensive statistics are imposing: Sisler batted .420 for his second title, while Williams slugged

39 home runs and drove in 155 runs, both league highs. Tobin (.331), second baseman Marty McManus (.312), Jacobson (.317), and catcher Hank Severeid (.321) all bettered .300, and the team averaged a league-leading .313, the second-highest average in the long history of the American League. The Browns scored 867 runs that season, slugged for a .455 average, and hit 94 triples, all league-highs. They also stole a league-leading 132 bases—Sisler (51) and Williams (37) were one-two—and Browns pitchers compiled the best earned run average, at 3.38, while striking out a pacesetting 534 opponents. Shocker won 24 games, and led in both fewest hits allowed and in fewest walks allowed per nine innings. The club won a team-record 93 games and lost just 61 for a .604 percentage that is unmatched in all St. Louis Browns history.

In the face of that imposing statistical log, it may seem surprising that the Browns did not win the pennant. They bowed ultimately to the defending champion Yankees and Babe Ruth in an outcome that turned on the final inning of a bitterly fought three-game series between the contenders played in St. Louis in mid-September. Sisler, toward the tail end of a 41-game down-the-stretch batting streak, carried a severely strained shoulder muscle into the series. The injury limited him to just two hits in 11 at bats for the three games. Still, the Browns split the first two games, losing 2–1 and then winning 5–1, each game played before record St. Louis crowds in excess of 30,000. Striving to move within a half game of first place, St. Louis led the finale—which was witnessed by a city-record 32,000—2–1 entering the ninth. But Whitey Witt's bases-loaded single off Shocker rallied the New Yorkers to victory. The following day the Browns wasted a 3–1 eighth-inning lead versus sixth-place Washington, losing 4–3. Absent those two collapses, the Browns—who finished just one game behind New York—likely would have won their first pennant.

No St. Louis Browns team ever again won as many as 90 games. An eye injury sidelined Sisler for all of 1923, and removed the heart of the Browns' attack. St. Louis fell to fifth. And while there were sporadic instances of passably played ball throughout the remainder of the 1920s and 1930s—notably third-place finishes in 1925 and again in 1928—even those teams were not seriously in the pennant race. By 1930 St. Louis had returned to a comfortable position in the second division, where this time the Browns stayed for a solid 12 seasons, including three sentences in the cellar.

Those were perhaps the most forlorn years in the history of any major league franchise. Fewer than a million fans attended Browns home games during the entire decade of the 1930s! The attendance for several of those Depression-era seasons was not much more than the 93,000 who had flocked to Sportman's Park that one weekend in

1922 to watch their heroes and the Yanks contest for the championship. For one afternoon home game in 1934, the official paid attendance was 34. The club drew only about 84,000 for all of 1935. Longtime club owner Ball, however, was not around to see the worst of it; he had died in 1933. Ball's estate sold the club to Bill DeWitt and Donald Barnes, who sold stock to the public in order to raise working capital.

Without a doubt one of the best of the Browns of those hapless years—and one of the few with legitimate major league ability—was third baseman Harland Clift. A 1934 rookie, Clift performed for nine long seasons with the Browns, who only once in that span were a better than .500 team. He was traded away in 1943, the year before the Browns won their only pennant. But during his stay in St. Louis Clift demonstrated that he could both hit and field. He slugged 20 home runs while batting .302 in 1936, and followed that with two seasons that were even better. In 1937 Clift struck 29 homers and drove in 118 runs while batting .306. In 1938 he hit 34 homers, added another 118 RBIs, and hit .290.

In September of 1934 Bobo Newsom pitched the franchise's first nine-inning no-hitter since Koob and Groom 17 years earlier. But all he had to show for it was a 1–1 tie, which matured into a 2–1 defeat in the 10th, one of 20 losses suffered by Newsom that season. He was rewarded the following May by being sold to Washington for $40,000 in franchise survival money.

So uniformly starless were the Browns of the 1930s that for the entire decade, they placed only one man in the top five in any year's Most Valuable Player voting. That singular standout was the self-same Newsom, reacquired prior to 1938, who finished fifth in balloting that same year by the Baseball Writers of America on the strength of 20 victories. The 1938 St. Louis team won only 55 and finished seventh. For the entire decade, no Brownie batter led the league in any offensive category of consequence.

Perhaps as has been often written, it did take a world war to make champions out of the Browns. Certainly there were few outward signs during the early 1940s that the club was on the upswing. St. Louis finished sixth in 1941, although winning 55 of 110 games played under mid-season managerial replacement Luke Sewell. The team's best players were first baseman George McQuinn and outfielder Chet Laabs. In 1942, with many of the most prominent major leaguers called to military duty, St. Louis climbed to third place on the strength of 82 victories. A powerful rookie, Vern Stephens, drove in 92 runs, but demonstrated the need for defensive polish, committing 42 errors at shortstop.

At least Stephens could be counted on for availability; like McQuinn, he flunked several draft physicals. By 1944 the American

League was bereft of most of its stars. Men like Ted Williams, Joe DiMaggio, Bob Feller, and Phil Rizzuto had gone into military service. For their part, the Browns on Opening Day rostered 18 players who were listed by the military as 4F, and 13 of them stayed most of the year. In addition to Stephens and McQuinn, they included second baseman Don Gutteridge, catcher Ray Hayworth, and pitchers Jack Kramer, Sig Jakucki, and Nelson Potter. Those 4Fs may not have been able to fight, but for that one summer they could play a little ball. The Browns won their first nine games, remained at or near the top all year, and came to the season's final weekend series of four games at home against New York trailing the front-running Tigers by only one-half game. Kramer won his 17th, a 4–1 victory in the first game of a Friday doubleheader, then Potter blanked the Yanks 1–0 for his team-high 19th victory as Detroit split a doubleheader with Washington. The following day righthander Denny Galehouse shut out New York 2–0, but Detroit also won. On the final Sunday Washington's Dutch Leonard defeated Detroit 4–1, giving the Browns a chance that they, for once, did not fumble. With more than 35,000 fans in attendance and an estimated 15,000 more turned away, Laabs struck two home runs, the second a two-run blow in the fifth that broke a 2–2 tie. Jakucki shut out New York from that point on and Stephens homered, his 20th and his league-leading 109th RBI, to clinch the season's 89th victory, and the first and only pennant the Browns would ever win.

The ensuing World Series may have been viewed by some of the Browns as anti-climactic, but it was bitterly contested, more so because the opponents were the cross-town rival Cardinals. Flushed by their pennant, the Browns won the first game 2–1 behind Galehouse, with McQuinn's two-run homer in the fourth inning the decisive blow. Kramer won the third game 6–2, but the Cardinals took the second, fourth, fifth, and sixth, and thus the Series. McQuinn was marvelous in defeat, batting .438 with five RBIs. But 10 fielding errors allowed the Cardinals to score a decisive seven unearned runs among their total of 16 runs for the six-game Series.

Pete Gray came to the Browns in 1945. Gray, the one-armed outfielder signed in the depths of the war-imposed scarcity of players, played in 61 games and batted .218. A brave bid for a second successive pennant faltered in the season's final weeks, and the Browns finished with 81 victories, although Stephens did lead the league in homers with 34. He was the first Brownie to lead in home runs since Ken Williams in 1922.

With the post-war return of stars like Feller and DiMaggio to other teams' rosters, the Browns in 1946 renewed their acquaintance with hard times, falling all the way to seventh place. DeWitt, by this time the club's sole owner, applied an old strategy in the face both of declining revenues and fortunes; he sold stars. Within a two-month stretch of 1947 alone, Laabs was sent to Philadelphia, third baseman Mark Christman to Washington, and Galehouse to Boston, all for cash. In November of that year DeWitt authored three deals sending six players including Stephens and Kramer to two clubs in exchange for 12 inconsequential players and a total of $400,000. One month later slugging outfielder Jeff Heath was traded to the Boston Braves for more operating funds. With Boston, Heath played a key role in the team's 1948 pennant drive, batting .319 and stroking 20 home runs.

Meanwhile, the Browns' own efforts ranged from the routinely futile to the bizarrely futile. In 1950 the club hired a psychologist to hypnotize players and thus bring out their best efforts. The Browns finished seventh. In 1951 DeWitt sold the team to a syndicate headed by Bill Veeck. Veeck already was famed as a showman from his days operating the Cleveland franchise. Among his stunts: formally "burying" the 1948 pennant in mock funeral services on the day in September of 1949 when the Indians were eliminated from contention, staging "nights" replete with gift giveaways for selected fans, and offering female fans free orchids or nylon hosiery.

Veeck had been wildly successful in Cleveland, where his promotions drew fans in record numbers. He tried some of the same frolics in St. Louis, none more legendary than the one he staged on the afternoon of August 19, 1951, against the Detroit Tigers in St. Louis. Frank Saucier, a rookie, was to have led off, but instead Veeck sent to the plate Eddie Gaedel, a three foot, six inch midget, to face Tiger starter Bob Cain. Naturally, Gaedel walked. Naturally, also, the Browns lost, 6–2 to Detroit. On the following day American League President William Harridge issued an order disqualifying the contract Gaedel had signed with the Browns and barring the further use of midgets as contrary to the best interests of the game.

A few days later Veeck set up a special section in the grandstands where he allowed fans to manage the team by holding up cards to indicate whether to sacrifice, steal, warm up a relief pitcher, and make all the other decisions a manager normally is called on to make. The Browns won that day, breaking a four-game losing streak. Regular manager Zack Taylor resumed control the next day, and the team lost five of its next six.

By 1953 Veeck was broke and the team was once again a pitiful eighth, losers of 100 games or more in three of the previous five seasons. Amid rampant rumors, which Veeck made no attempt to deny, that efforts were afoot to move the team to Baltimore, attendance dwindled again to a trickle. On-field highlights were few, but they did occur. On May 6th of that year Bobo Holloman, making his first major league start, no-hit the Philadelphia Athletics 6–0 in what proved to be his only complete game of an otherwise undistinguished career that lasted just 65 innings that summer. Other than that one game, Holloman was simply awful, with a 3–7 record and a 5.23 earned run average. His was the fourth and final no-hitter in Browns' history; opponents had no-hit the Browns nine times.

On September 29, 1953, Veeck sold the team to a Baltimore-based syndicate led by Mayor Tommy D'Alesandro and attorney Clarence Miles, who was promptly named club president. The ballclub moved into recently renovated and expanded Memorial Stadium, which would remain their home for almost four decades. But even rechristened as the Baltimore Orioles and ensconced in new surroundings, the 1954 club fared little better than the Browns, losing an even 100 games and finishing seventh, ahead only of the equally decimated Athletics. Moves, however, were at hand to change the long run of futility. The first occurred on September 14, 1954, when Paul Richards was hired to be both general manager and field manager. With a talent for player development and player relations, the patient Richards presided for six seasons over a careful restructuring that laid the foundation for a two-decades-long period of sustained success.

Although some of Richards' later deals were more consequential, his first ranked among the most dramatic. In a 17-player trade completed over two stages in November and December 1954, Richards gave up some talent—notably pitchers Bob Turley and Don Larsen. But this time the Orioles also acquired quality players in return in the persons of Gus Triandos—who would anchor the catching duties for most of the next decade—and shortstop Willie Miranda, a four-year regular. In May of 1956 Richards obtained outfielder Bob Nieman and three other players from the White Sox. Nieman developed into a quality slugger, stroking 50 home runs between 1957 and 1959. Richards secured knuckleball pitcher Hoyt Wilhelm from Cleveland in 1958 for the waiver price. Wilhelm won 15 games and led the league in earned run average as a starter in 1959, then went to the bullpen, where he consistently ranked among the league leaders in saves. When catcher Triandos found it difficult to cleanly catch Wilhelm's knuckler, former catcher Richards devised the famed "pancake" mitt, which was about 50 inches in circumference, roughly twice the size of the normal catcher's mitt. The rulebook has since been amended to ban mitts of such size, but catchers are allowed to use mitts of up to 38 inches in circumference, very much a vestige of the Richards-Wilhelm influence.

But if Paul Richards was a slick trader, he proved even more a master at player development. In the late 1950s the Orioles minor league system began to produce youngsters who would be the stars of the coming era. Easily the forerunner was third baseman Brooks Robinson, who made his first appearance as an 18-year-old in 1955. Not until 1958 did Robinson succeed in retiring George Kell from the

regular position, but he fast gained recognition as a superb fielder and
capable batsman. As early as 1960—only his second complete season—
he placed third in voting as the league's Most Valuable Player, batting
.294 with 14 home runs and 88 runs batted in. In 1964 he hit .317
with 28 home runs and a league-leading 118 runs batted in and won
the coveted MVP Award in a runaway. On three subsequent occasions
during a 23-year career with the Orioles his name could be found
among the top five MVP vote-getters.

But Robinson's name was an even surer bet to be found atop the
fielding statistics. He led the league in 1960 in putouts, assists, total
chances per game, and fielding average, repeated as fielding average
champion in 1961, and over the course of his career led 11 times in
fielding average, eight times in assists, twice in putouts, and twice
in chances per game. Even without his impressive career offensive
statistics, Robinson would have been a certainty for induction into the
Hall of Fame—to which he was elected in 1983—on the strength of
his glovework alone.

Richards and Lee MacPhail, his successor in 1958 as general manager, focused their rebuilding efforts most closely on developing a
strong young pitching staff. By 1959 they had assembled a coterie of
powerful juvenile arms that came to be known as the "Kiddie Corps."
Youngsters like Milt Pappas (18), Jerry Walker (18), Chuck Estrada
(22), Steve Barber (21), and Jack Fisher (20) were brought to the major
leagues with little or no professional experience, but with fireballing
credentials. The emphasis on young arms didn't always work—the
Orioles tried mightily to refine the obvious talents of a prospect named
Steve Dalkowski. His fastball was the stuff of legend: In 1957 he
fanned nearly two batters per inning for a Baltimore minor league
affiliate. But he also walked better than two per inning. Dalkowski
never made it to the majors.

But he was not missed. By 1960 Barber, Estrada, Fisher, and
Pappas won 55 games for the Orioles. The following season the same
foursome won 56 games as Baltimore led the league in earned run
average and captured a franchise-record 95 victories.

The Orioles' progression toward contention—and ultimately toward recognition as one of the great teams of all time—took most of
a decade and several changes both at the general managerial and
managerial levels to bring to fruition. But by the onset of the 1960s,
the club could legitimately be viewed as a realistic contender. Those
years were a succession of near-misses for Orioles fans in a league still
dominated by the sunset years of the game's greatest dynasty, the
Yankees. Between 1961 and 1964, for instance, Jim Gentile, a powerful
210-pound first baseman acquired from the Dodger system, slugged
124 home runs and averaged nearly 100 RBIs. His average climbed

as high as .302 in 1961. But the Orioles, although averaging 89 wins per season, rose no higher than second in the standings. Despite a 78–57 record, Richards was let go as manager late in the 1961 season, replaced on an interim basis by Lum Harris, and the following year by Billy Hitchcock. But Hitchcock lasted only two seasons before he was replaced by Hank Bauer.

A former Yankee outfielder, Bauer was used to winning—he had been a regular on nine league champions and seven world titleists. Further, he knew how to get the most from his players. It had been obvious virtually from the moment of 20-year-old outfielder John "Boog" Powell's arrival in 1962 that he possessed exceptional ability. Powell was tall, muscular, and had a quick bat that produced 15 home runs that initial season. But he batted just .243 with 53 RBIs. Bauer groomed Powell almost into a remake of Bauer himself: In 1964, Bauer's first season with the Orioles, Powell raised his home run output to 39, driving in 99 runs, and compiling a league-leading .606 slugging percentage while batting .290. And when it became obvious that Powell lacked the speed or range necessary to play the outfield to the level the Orioles needed, Bauer converted him into a first baseman.

At almost the same time Bauer installed 21-year-old rookie Paul Blair as the new center fielder. Blair batted only .234 that first year, but he was a whirlwind afield, consistently ranking among the league's best center fielders in range, and pacing all of them in fielding average that very first season. Meanwhile he improved his eye at the plate, raising his average to .277 by 1965, and to .293 in 1966.

MacPhail assisted from the front office, plugging a gap at short-stop by obtaining 29-year-old All-Star Luis Aparicio from the White Sox in 1963. Aparicio contributed not only his fielding wizardry but his base-stealing daring as well. Oriole players, who had stolen a trifling 45 bases in 1962, accumulated a league-leading 97 in 1963, Aparicio getting 40 of them to lead the league as well. With Brooks Robinson at third and Powell comfortable at first, the Baltimore infield of the mid-1960s suddenly possessed three-quarters of a championship look.

This team posted respectable third-place finishes in 1964 and 1965, but it was not yet either mature enough or deep enough to capture a pennant. As the 1965 season concluded, legitimate questions could be raised about the pitching, second base play, and the lack of a power hitter. On the mound MacPhail placed his faith in a sort of second generation "Kiddie Corps" that was in the process of being brought in full force to the majors. Lefthander Dave McNally, at age 23 approaching his fourth full season, had a 28–25 record, but was coming off an encouraging 11–6 season in 1965 in which he posted a 2.85 ERA. Fastballing righthander Wally Bunker, 21, was a two-year veteran (29–13) whose .792 winning percentage had led the league in

1964. Pappas and Barber remained from the original "Kiddie Corps," but they were being pushed hard by a brilliant 20-year-old prospect named Jim Palmer, who had gone 5–4 in 27 appearances mostly in relief in 1965. MacPhail, gambling on Palmer's development into a reliable rotation starter, traded the popular and consistent Pappas— who had won at least 10 games for eight straight seasons—to Cincinnati for outfielder Frank Robinson, a proven slugger but a ballplayer with a reputation for moodiness. It was one of MacPhail's last transactions before resigning as general manager to join the staff of the commissioner of baseball, and one of his most shrewd. Far from becoming a clubhouse problem, Robinson proved to be a team leader off the field in 1966. On the field he won the triple crown, batting .316 with 49 home runs and 122 runs batted in. He provided power such that Orioles partisans had never before seen; in a game on May 8 of that year he smacked the first and still the only ball ever driven completely out of Memorial Stadium, a home run off Luis Tiant that cleared the back of the left-field bleachers.

Meanwhile, rookie Dave Johnson took over at second, and a veteran bullpen headed by Moe Drabowsky, Eddie Fisher, and Dick Hall bailed out the young Oriole pitchers whenever necessary. The so-called "Baby Birds" needed plenty of bailing out, pitching only 32 complete games—no team in American League history had ever won a pennant with fewer. But the Orioles did win, soaring to the title by eight games over the defending champion Minnesota Twins.

The 1966 Orioles excelled at bat, on the mound, and in the field. Powered by Robinson's triple crown year, they led in runs scored (755), batting average (.258), and slugging average (.409). Powell added 109 RBIs and Brooks Robinson 100 to Frank Robinson's 122, making the Orioles the first AL champion with three 100-RBI men since the Cleveland Indians of 1948. The team committed a league-low 115 errors, with Aparicio contributing only 17 of those at shortstop and Brooks Robinson just 12 at third base. Palmer won 15 games while McNally added 13, Bunker and Barber 10 each. And the Baltimore bullpen piled up 51 saves, easily leading the league. The bullpen of Drabowsky, Fisher, Eddie Watt, and Hall were looked on as the club's only hope in the World Series that autumn, but as it turned out they were used only to protect the first victory. After that Palmer, Bunker, and McNally threw successive shutouts of the National League champion Los Angeles Dodgers as the Orioles scored a stunning four-game sweep, the first 4–0 victory by any American League club other than the Yankees in the history of the Series. The two closing victories were dramatic bookend 1–0 decisions settled in Baltimore on home runs by Blair and Frank Robinson.

The franchise's first World Championship topped Bauer's 4½-year career as manager—he was fired after the team failed to repeat in either 1967 or 1968. But it proved only an auspicious debut for new owner Jerry Hoffberger, who had purchased the club the previous winter, and only the first milestone in the team's development to dynastic status. That development was completed by Hoffberger and Harry Dalton, his appointee to succeed MacPhail as general manager, and a new Oriole era may be marked from the day in the summer of 1968 when Dalton replaced Bauer with Earl Weaver, a product of Baltimore's minor league managerial system. For with the appointment of Weaver, the Orioles had made their last managerial decision for 15 years.

Weaver inherited field responsibility for a team that could not rally in time to overcome Detroit in 1968, although under his direction the club did win 48 of 82 games. But only a few key moves remained to restore the Orioles to the primacy they had held in 1966. One of those moves preceded Weaver; following the 1967 season, the 33-year-Aparicio was traded to Chicago with Russ Snyder in return for outfielder Don Buford. Bauer had replaced Aparicio at short with young Mark Belanger, a hitter of no special consequence but considered already to be Aparicio's peer or better in the field. But the most substantive deal came that December when Dalton and Weaver traded outfielder Curt Blefary and a minor leaguer for two youngsters and Mike Cuellar, a lefthanded screwball pitcher who had won 36 games and lost 32 the previous three seasons with the Astros.

The acquisition of Cuellar in the rotation and Buford leading off and playing the outfield transformed Baltimore into one of the best-balanced baseball aggregations in the game's history. The club that took the field in 1969 literally had no weaknesses, as was evidenced by the way it dominated the race in the American League East that first year of divisional play. The Orioles won 109 games, a total surpassed in all of American League history only by the 1927 Yankees and 1954 Indians. They limited opponents to a league-low 517 runs, about 3.2 per game. Their team .265 batting average ranked second, as did their .414 slugging percentage. Frank Robinson and Boog Powell both placed among the league's top five batters, with Powell also present in slugging average and RBIs. Powell hit 37 home runs, Frank Robinson, 32, Blair, 26, and Brooks Robinson, 23. In a league that batted .246 every regular except Brooks Robinson and catcher Elrod Hendricks hit .280 or better.

Afield, the Orioles led both in percentage (.984) and fewest errors (101). Johnson committed just 12 at second base, Brooks Robinson only 13 at third. Blair handled 421 chances in center field and committed just five errors.

On the mound Cuellar piled up 23 victories while McNally added 20. Palmer won 16 or 20 decisions and his 2.34 ERA barely edged Cuellar (2.38) for second in the league. The two also were second and third in fewest hits per nine innings of work. As a staff, the Orioles pitched a league-high 20 shutouts, allowed fewer walks than any team, and presented the American League's best earned run average, 2.83. Watt came out of the bullpen 56 times for a 1.56 ERA, while Hall posted a 1.92 mark in 39 appearances. Lefthanded reliever Pete Richert pitched in 44 games with a 2.20 ERA.

This is the record of the team that has been ranked among the finest in major league history. In his 1982 book, *Baseball's 10 Greatest Teams,* Donald Honig included the 1969 Orioles, and wrote that, "for the best overall balance of pitching, hitting, defense and running speed, one might have to select the 1969 Orioles" as the finest ever.

Baltimore pulled away to a 15-game lead by August and clinched the pennant on September 13, nearly three weeks prior to the season's end. Astonishingly, after easily dismissing the Twins three games to none in the first divisional playoff and opening the World Series with a 4–1 victory over the moonstruck New York Mets on Cuellar's six-hitter, the Orioles lost four straight.

Such a stunning fall might have rattled the composure of the American League champions, but there was no lingering impact visible in 1970. In some respects, in fact, the Orioles were even better. There could hardly have been a more formidable trio of starters than Palmer (20–10), Cuellar (24–8), and McNally (24–9), who averaged almost exactly 300 innings of work each. Palmer ranked second in earned run average, Cuellar and McNally shared the lead in victories, and the trio delivered 54 complete games, Cuellar producing a league-high 21 of them. As they had done the previous year, Oriole pitchers proved the league's stingiest, allowing just 574 runs on a 3.15 earned run average.

Powell led the devastating offense, which generated 792 runs, nearly five per game. The hefty first baseman rapped 35 home runs and drove in 114 runs on a .297 batting average. Frank Robinson edged him out in batting honors with a .305 mark while driving 25 home runs and 78 RBIs. Brooks Robinson provided 94 more RBIs and another 18 homers, the latter total matched by Blair. In fact, eight different Orioles hit at least 10 home runs, including reserve outfielder Merv Rettenmund. In 1970 Baltimore did not have the best fielding in the league—at least not statistically, since Washington edged the Orioles by one percentage point—but it hardly mattered. This race was not a runaway from the start, Baltimore leading by a relatively modest five games on the Fourth of July. But Weaver's team went 32–14 between August 1 and mid-September to build a final 15-game margin and a 108–54 record, failing by one game to equal the prodigious victory total of the previous year.

In 1970, however, the Orioles not only added three more victories in the divisional playoffs—again defeating Minnesota—they also claimed the World Series. That set of games today is generally recalled as the "Brooks Robinson Series" because of the phenomenal play of the veteran third baseman, who was named Most Valuable Player in the five-game victory over the National League champion Cincinnati Reds.

Robinson starred in every capacity those five games. He drove nine hits in 21 at bats for a .429 average and included two doubles and two home runs for a series-high six RBIs. But had he gone hitless, Robinson might still have won the MVP honor for his defensive play alone. With the score of the first game tied at 3–3 in the sixth inning, Lee May drove a one-hopper barely inside third base, an apparent sure double. Robinson ranged behind third and well into foul territory to field the ball, then whirled and threw May out. The play proved vital, for the next two batters reached on a walk and single that would have combined to produce the go-ahead run but for Robinson's thievery. It almost did anyway when, with Bernie Carbo at third and one out, pinch hitter Ty Cline chopped a bouncer high in front of the plate. Hendricks snagged the ball and lunged for Carbo, who was called out by plate umpire Ken Burkhart despite the fact that Burkhart had been sent sprawling by Hendricks' lunge, and appeared unable to see the play. As it was, Cincinnati did not score and Robinson himself struck the decisive blow an inning later, homering to provide the final margin in a 4–3 Orioles win.

The Orioles won the second game as well, 6–5, then Robinson stroked three more hits in the first, second, and sixth innings of the third game. He also drove in the first two runs with a double. Robinson's four-for-four performance in the fourth game might have presaged a Baltimore sweep, but the usually reliable bullpen let a 5–3 lead slip away in the eighth inning, delaying the championship celebration by one day. On the strength of Cuellar's six-hitter, Baltimore won the decisive fifth game, 9–3, as Blair delivered three hits and Frank Robinson and Rettenmund each homered and drove in two runs.

If the test of a great team is its ability to repeat as champions, the Orioles established their greatness in 1970, then underlined it in 1971. For the third successive year they breezed to an embarrassingly easy pennant, this time by 10 games over the Tigers. General Manager Dalton deserved credit for improving the powerhouse over the winter. Recognizing that his rotation of Palmer, McNally, and Cuellar, while brilliant, was in danger of being overworked, he obtained veteran Pat Dobson from San Diego for Tom Phoebus. Dobson, a mediocre 14–15 with the Padres, more than justified Dalton's faith in him, delivering

18 complete games and posting a 20–8 record. Even so, he remained only the fourth best arm on the staff that summer: Cuellar and Palmer each matched his 20 victories and McNally added 21, giving Baltimore the first 20-victory quartet in the league in more than a half century. Frank Robinson delivered 28 home runs and 99 RBIs, while Powell added 22 and 92, Brooks Robinson 20 and 92. As was becoming routine, the Orioles led the league both in most runs scored (742) and fewest allowed (530), a certain formula for victory. They also led in batting average (.261), and earned run average (3.00). But as in 1969, they faltered in October, losing a seven-game World Series to the Pittsburgh Pirates after defeating Oakland in three straight games in the divisional playoff. Once again Brooks Robinson was masterful in the post-season, combining a .364 average against the Athletics with a .318 performance versus Pittsburgh. But Powell hit only .111, and the team as a whole batted a disappointing .205, collecting just 21 hits in the final five games after decisively winning the first two.

The years 1969–71 were the apex of glory for the Orioles. The Robinson-Robinson-Weaver-Palmer-Cuellar team won at a .654 clip, a pace bettered for even a single season by only a handful of teams in baseball history. Never in the interim have they—or any other club— so dominated the league. But if the dynasty eventually cracked, it did not crumble. In fact, even in gradual transition the Orioles remained factors in the American League pennant contest through most of the 1970s.

The first evidence of that transition was provided shortly after the World Series when Dalton resigned to become general manager of the California Angels. Frank Cashen, the team's executive vice president, assumed responsibility for player personnel, and caused virtually immediate impact that December by trading Frank Robinson, still powerful but at age 36 slowing up, along with Richert to the Los Angeles Dodgers for pitching prospect Doyle Alexander and three other youngsters. Merv Rettenmund was tabbed to be Robinson's replacement, but Rettenmund unfortunately was unable to replicate his predecessor's offensive production, contributing just six home runs and 21 RBIs with a .233 average in 1972. Power production fell off everywhere that season: Johnson, who had hit 18 home runs in 1971, got just five. Brooks Robinson, who hit 20 the year before, delivered eight. Only Powell among the old faces produced his expected statistics, socking 21 home runs and driving home 81 runs. On the mound Palmer was brilliant as usual, with a 21–10 record and 2.07 ERA. Cuellar won 18 and lost just 12. But McNally slipped to 13–17, Dobson to 16–18, and Alexander yielded only six victories. The Orioles ceded the AL East pennant for the first time in four seasons—to Detroit— finishing third, five games behind.

But even in the lackluster wake of third place, new stars gave promise that the sag would be only temporary. Twenty-three-year-old Bobby Grich looked so smooth in the infield, so steady at the plate, that Cashen felt comfortable including the veteran Johnson in a multi-player trade with Atlanta. Grich took over at second base in 1973 and immediately led the league in every significant fielding category, committing just five errors in nearly 1,000 chances for a remarkable .995 fielding average.

Meanwhile, Don Baylor came up from the farm system to suggest himself as an eventual replacement for the departed Robinson. Baylor batted just .254 in 1972, his rookie year, but stole 24 bases and hit 11 home runs. Installed as a regular in 1973, he raised his average to .286 while maintaining his power. Catcher Earl Williams, acquired in the trade that sent Johnson to Atlanta, batted only .237, but slugged 22 home runs and drove in 83 runs. Another rookie, left-fielder Rich Coggins, hit .319 with 17 stolen bases and sent Buford to the bench. Veteran Tommy Davis, secured the previous season from the Chicago Cubs, never had been a defensive asset. But Davis could still bat, and he took full advantage of the new Designated Hitter Rule, posting a .306 average and a team-leading 89 RBIs.

But it was the pitchers who played the major role in returning Baltimore to the top level of the American League East. Palmer paced all pitchers in earned run average at 2.40 on his way to a 22–9 record. Cuellar contributed 18 more victories, and the staff allowed just 561 runs, low for the league for the fifth straight year. On the strength of a 97–65 record Baltimore pulled away to an eight-game victory over second-place Boston for the divisional title. Unlike their previous three ventures at that level, however, the 1973 Orioles failed to qualify for the World Series, losing 3 games to 2 to the Oakland Athletics in ALCS play . . . despite victories in the first and fourth games by Palmer.

The Orioles repeated as divisional champions again in 1974 at the culmination of the best race in the six-year history of the A.L. eastern division. With a month to play, Baltimore stood fourth, eight games behind the Red Sox. But Weaver drove his team to a 28–6 finish to overtake Boston by eight games and finish two games in front of the second-place New York Yankees. A critical factor all season was lefthander Ross Grimsley, obtained from Cincinnati for Rettenmund the previous December. Grimsley, whose father had pitched briefly in the major leagues a quarter century earlier, won 18 games and more than compensated for Palmer's unusually poor 7–12 year. Cuellar led the team with 22 victories, and Davis again paced the offense with a .289 average and 84 RBIs. Once again, however, the Orioles could not get past the Athletics in the divisional playoff, losing three straight after home runs by Grich, Blair, and Brooks Robinson secured a 6–3 victory in the opener. Pitching dominated both sides of that series: the Orioles allowed just 11 runs in the four games, but the Baltimore offense generated merely a single run in the three defeats, and batted only .177 for the four games. Veterans Robinson, Powell, and Belanger were particularly hamstrung, delivering the sum of just two hits in a cumulative 29 trips to the plate.

Evidence of the need for more changes was manifest. Cuellar, Robinson, and Powell were well into their 30s. McNally, one of the principals in the free agency dispute that rocked baseball in the mid-1970s, played without a contract in 1974 and declared his unwillingness to return for another season. Buford had retired, and Coggins, his replacement, failed to live up to expectations. The Orioles moved frenetically to rebuild a team that slipped behind Boston in 1975, and remained in a runner-up spot for two more seasons.

Cashen sent the recalcitrant McNally to Montreal in December of 1974 along with Coggins for fleet and powerful outfielder Ken Singleton and a young pitcher, Mike Torrez. A day earlier he had traded two prospects to Houston for first baseman Lee May. Powell was sent to Cleveland prior to spring training in 1975. But the two most notable moves in the multi-year restructuring program were made by Hank Peters, who became general manager when Cashen resigned to return to private business in 1976. In April Peters obtained the game's most glamorous star, outfielder Reggie Jackson, from Oakland along with pitcher Ken Holtzman for Baylor and Torrez. Peters knew he might not be able to retain Jackson, who was to become a free agent at year's end. But such unparalleled star quality was considered certain to prove valuable as a gate attraction, even if Jackson did not pan out as a long-term investment. (He didn't, moving to the New York Yankees that November.) Two months after the Jackson deal Peters engineered a second swap, this one with New York. Although the players involved did not have Jackson's marquee value, that trade would in the long run prove far more meaningful to the Orioles. They got pitchers Scott McGregor, Tippy Martinez, and Rudy May, along with catcher Rick Dempsey in exchange for Holtzman, Alexander, long-time catcher Ellie Hendricks, and two other players.

Jackson batted .277 with 27 home runs and 91 RBIs in his brief stopover in Baltimore, but his loss to free agency was only one of several suffered by the Orioles that winter. Pitcher Wayne Garland, a journeyman who developed into a 20-game winner that year, signed with Cleveland in November. Five days later Grich accepted an offer from the California Angels. The following winter Grimsley signed as a free agent with Montreal. When Peters traded Blair to the Yankees in 1977, and Robinson announced his retirement amid fanfare that same summer, it left only Belanger and Palmer to rally memories of the dynastic days of the turn of the decade.

The Oriole lineup that opened the 1978 season was replete with talented youngsters in their first, second, or third seasons. Eddie Murray arrived from the minor leagues to launch a decade-long career as the club's all-time home run hitter, taking over first base and permitting the veteran Lee May to devote his primary efforts to being the designated hitter. At third base 27-year-old Doug DeCinces was beginning to establish himself as something more than the successor to the legendary Robinson. Although he had essentially been the regular third baseman for two seasons, it was in 1978 that DeCinces matured at bat, with a .286 average and 28 home runs.

On the mound second-year lefthander Mike Flanagan—also a farm-system product—won 19 games in a league-leading 40 starts. McGregor, in his first full season as a starter, showed promise with 15 victories while 23-year-old Dennis Martinez won 16. Dempsey, a sub during his years in New York, became the regular catcher.

This revamped club realized its potential in 1979, driven by Weaver to 102 victories and a seven-game winning margin over the runner-up Brewers. The Orioles won that summer with two weapons Weaver-led teams seemed always to favor: pitching and home runs. Singleton slugged 35 of the longballs, accounting for 111 runs, but he was not alone in power production. Murray and left-fielder Gary Roenicke added 25 each, May contributed 19, and DeCinces, 16. Roenicke's total is especially noteworthy because he divided playing time with John Lowenstein and Pat Kelly. The three combined for an even more impressive 45 home runs. As a team the Orioles walloped 181 longballs, third highest total in the league.

Baltimore pitchers dominated batters with a 3.26 ERA that was an exceptional half-point better than the runner-up Yankees. Flanagan led the league in wins with 23, and ranked among leaders as well in winning percentage, earned run average, strikeouts, and shutouts. Six different Baltimore pitchers contributed at least 10 wins. When one of the starters needed help, Weaver usually called on Don Stanhouse, a curly-haired thrower who produced 21 saves. In the divisional playoffs that year Murray batted .417 and Singleton .375 as the Orioles outclassed the western division champion California Angels in four games, the finale a 6–0 shutout tossed by McGregor. Baltimore appeared bound for a third world title in the World Series after victories in three of the first four games against Pittsburgh. Even after Flanagan lost the fifth game, the Orioles still needed only one victory in the concluding two contests, both to be played in Baltimore. But the home team's bats failed to produce. Palmer was riddled for 10 hits in a 4–

0 Pirate victory in the sixth game, then Pittsburgh overcame McGregor, 4–1, in the seventh to claim the World Championship.

The Series disappointment came virtually concurrent with the end of the Hoffberger ownership of the franchise. Shortly after the Series concluded, Washington attorney Edward Bennett Williams purchased the team. The Orioles nearly presented their new owner with a debut pennant, winning 100 games but finishing three games short of the champion Yankees in 1980. It could not be said to be the fault of pitcher Steve Stone, a journeyman righthander signed as a free agent prior to the 1979 season whose career record to that time showed 67 victories, 72 defeats. Stone rolled up 25 victories in 1980 against only seven losses on his way to the Cy Young Award. Excitement was so high in Baltimore that summer that nearly a quarter-million spectators paid to attend a single five-game series with New York, a franchise record. The 1981 Orioles compiled a 59–46 strike-shortened record that was just percentage points worse than the Brewers, who had the division's best chart. But under the unique split-season format, Baltimore finished second to the Yankees by two games for the first-half title, then slipped to fourth, although just two games down to Milwaukee, during the second-half competition. One of the year's highlights was the initial appearance in the lineup of Cal Ripken Jr., a touted shortstop from the farm system who appeared in 23 games. Ripken returned to take over the position on a full-time basis in 1982, slugging 28 home runs. On June 5 of that year in Minnesota, he began a streak of consecutive innings played that ultimately spanned more than five seasons. Ripken did not miss a play on the field from that date on, for 8,243 straight innings, until September 14, 1987, when Ron Washington replaced him at shortstop in the late innings of a game in Toronto. His streak of consecutive games played, which began May 30, 1982, stood as of the end of the 1989 season at 1,251, the third longest in baseball history, trailing only Lou Gehrig and Everett Scott, and Scott was also passed, by mid-season 1990.

The disappointments of 1981 were forgotten in the back-to-back dramas of 1982–83. Weaver announced his intention early in 1982 to retire at the season's conclusion, and his farewell race was a doozy.

The Orioles opened an early advantage over the touted Brewers, but midseason managerial appointee Harvey Kuenn rallied Milwaukee into a tie by the Fourth of July, and into the lead soon after that. The Orioles, who might have wilted, instead rallied themselves, winning 30 of 39 games down the stretch to arrive at a season-ending four-game series with the Brewers in position to win. But the Orioles needed all four victories; even one defeat would give Milwaukee the title. Fifty-two thousand fans saw the first two games, played as a Friday doubleheader. Singleton's home run helped Dennis Martinez win the first, 8–3, then Murray homered in the first inning of the second game to open an eventual 7–1 Baltimore victory. The next day Sammy Stewart cooled the Brewers in an 11–3 Orioles win that made the race a flat tie. That meant that whichever team won the season's last game— which also would be Weaver's last—captured the flag. No team in history had ever won a pennant by sweeping a four-game season-ending series from its chief competition. Unfortunately for the Orioles and their fans, the Birds were not up this climactic bit of drama. Robin Yount hit two home runs and the Brewers pulled away to defeat Palmer 10–2 for the title. Even so, the crowd of 51,642 remained for a full 45 minutes following the game to salute Weaver into his retirement with a succession of standing ovations.

Peters selected Joe Altobelli, a former Orioles coach, as the new manager, and Altobelli assumed control of a veteran club at the peak of its talents. Already capable of carrying the burden as offensive leader, Ripken in 1983 batted .318 with 27 homers and 102 RBIs, a performance good enough to win the Most Valuable Player Award, the first Oriole so honored since Boog Powell in 1970. But Murray was virtually as good, with a .306 average, 33 home runs, and 111 RBIs. He finished a close second in the MVP vote, the same position he had occupied the previous season. Palmer, at age 37, yielded the staff's starring role to McGregor, who won 18 games, and to rookie Mike Boddicker, 16–8. Baltimore eliminated the Chicago White Sox in the divisional playoffs 3 games to 1 that year when part-time out-fielder Tito Landrum broke up a scoreless tie in the 10th inning of the final game with a home run. Baltimore lost the first game of the World Series to Philadelphia, but Boddicker's three-hitter in the second game squared matters, and the Orioles proceeded to win three straight in Philadelpia for the world's title. In the deciding fifth game, Murray homered twice and Dempsey—the Series MVP—added a third homer to support McGregor's five-hit shutout.

What has transpired since has given Baltimore fans a hint of how life with the old Browns must have been. In 1984 Boddicker won 20 games and Murray and Ripken combined for 56 home runs, but the defending champions posted an 85–77 record and finished well behind the World Champion Detroit Tigers. The decline continued in 1985, leading to Altobelli's mid-season firing and replacement by, of all people, Earl Weaver. This time the Orioles concluded play at 83–77, trailing the champion Toronto Blue Jays. Weaver resigned for a second time following that brief return, and was succeeded by his third base coach, Cal Ripken, Sr. But under the elder Ripken the club lost 10 more games in the standings in 1986, tumbling to Baltimore's first losing record in two decades. The 1987 season brought further setbacks: a 67–95 record and an inglorious last-place finish in the

A.L. East. That caused Williams to replace GM Peters with Roland Hemond, and to shift other front-office responsibilities. Still the Orioles opened winless through the first week of play in 1988, leading to Ripken's firing and replacement by former slugging star Frank Robinson. Not even Robinson, though, could turn around a season-opening skid that eventually reached an American League record 21 games, sealing Baltimore's last place fate again virtually before interest in the season had really developed. Their final .335 winning percentage (54–107) not only was the franchise's worst since the move to Baltimore, but the worst since the 1939 team stumbled to just 43 wins and 111 defeats for a typically Brownish .279 performance.

In the wake of that kind of disappointment, sweeping changes were at work. The most visible, although it had nothing to do with the performance of the team itself, focused on the playing field. Plans were approved for the 1992 opening of a 47,000 seat stadium, supported by Maryland Governor William Schaefer and funded by the state's legislature, to be built in the city's Inner Harbor area. Groundbreaking was held in June of 1989. The as-yet unnamed stadium, which carried a pricetag of more than $105 million, will replace Memorial Stadium, home of the Orioles since their move from St. Louis in 1954.

The personnel changes were highlighted by the mid-winter trade of Murray—discontented by the years of losing—to Los Angeles for Mike Devereaux and yet another pitching prospect, Brian Holton. The Orioles' front office had already sent Boddicker to Boston in midseason 1988 for Brady Anderson, an outfielder with speed, a touted glove, and exceptional minor league batting credentials. Devereaux and first baseman Randy Milligan, acquired from Pittsburgh, joined Cal Ripkin and his brother Billy, a 1987 rookie at second, comprising the corps of the 1989 offense. Craig Worthington filled the gap at third. But perhaps of greater long-term significance, the Orioles placed their trust in a formula that had proven its value: a host of young arms. Comparative newcomers to the major leagues like Bob Milacki, Jeff Ballard, Gregg Olsen, and Pete Harnish formed the heart of the revamped staff. The changes worked better than anyone could have expected. Far from resuming their status as tailenders, the Orioles led the American League East through mid-August in an effort to do what had never been done in the history of the major leagues, leap from last place to first in a single season.

The excitement generated by the 1989 Baltimore club continued unabated as the Orioles again blended youth with experience to sustain a series of pennant challenges in the early seasons of the century's final decade. Franchise star Cal Ripken Jr. not only continued his run at Lou Gehrig's all-time ironman record (reaching 1735 consecutive games by October 1992) but enjoyed a banner offensive season in 1991 (.323 BA with 34 HRs) and a record $7-million multi-year contract the following summer. A slip into the second division during 1990 and 1991 was cancelled out by a serious 1992 run at the top (3rd place, after trailing the championship-bound Toronto Blue Jays by a nose for much of the summer). But most of 1992 excitement was generated by the celebrations surrounding inaugura-tion of baseball's newest showcase ballpark. Blending traditional ap-pearance with state-of-the-art stadium design, Orioles Park at Camden Yards was an immediate fan favorite and pulled a club-record 3 million-plus fans through the turnstiles.

Annotated Bibliography

Beard, Gordon. *Birds on the Wing: The Story of the Baltimore Orioles.* Garden City, New York: Doubleday and Company, 1967. 179 pp.
  A fond recollection of the Baltimore Orioles' first World Championship season in 1966, as told by one of the city's veteran sportswriters. All the exciting details of the surprising four-game sweep against the seemingly invincible Los Angeles Dodgers are recounted here, along with nostalgic accounts of the evolutionary process of constructing the Orioles' earliest pennant-contending teams. This is indisputably the most painstaking history of the Orioles between 1954 and 1966.

Goldstein, Richard. *Spartan Seasons: How Baseball Survived the Second World War.* New York: Macmillan Publishing Company, 1980. 280 pp.
  Another look at the impact of wartime baseball on the national pastime, with sections on the St. Louis Browns' surprising American League pen-nant chase in 1944, and on the brief major league appearance of one-armed St. Louis outfielder Pete Gray (Gray is featured on the dust jacket cover as an appropriate symbol of wartime baseball). Only in such a story of the ineptitudes of wartime baseball could the erstwhile St. Louis Browns be expected to play a featured role.

Hawkins, John C. *This Date in Baltimore Orioles-St. Louis Browns History.* New York: Stein and Day, 1982.
  Day-by-day recounting of highlights and lowlights through the eight decades of American League baseball in St. Louis and Baltimore. This volume is part of a familiar series of baseball team chronologies from the same publisher, and thus follows the same format as its companion volumes.

Honig, Donald. *Baseball's Ten Greatest Teams.* New York: Macmillan Publishing Company, 1982.
  These fine brief anecdotal histories of some of baseball's strongest teams features a chapter on the Baltimore Orioles dynasty team of 1969, 1970, and 1971. Historian Honig considers the Earl Weaver-led 1969 Baltimore team (despite a shocking World Series loss to the Miracle Mets) as being perhaps the finest team ever assembled on a major league diamond.

Lieb, Frederick G. *The Baltimore Orioles: The History of a Colorful Team in Baltimore and St. Louis.* New York: G.P. Putnam's Sons, 1955. 246 pp.
  The first standard history of the Browns-Orioles franchise, written just five years after the Orioles became a modern-day American League reality in the city of Baltimore. This volume is most noteworthy for Lieb's engag-ing prose, as well as his immense knowledge of baseball history.

Mead, William B. *Even the Browns*. Chicago: Contemporary Books, 1978. 240 pp. (republished as *Baseball Goes to War*. New York: Farragut Publishing Company, 1985).

    Another anecdotal history of baseball as a refuge for 4Fs and youngsters during the World War II years, this time with a special focus on the author's own childhood favorite—the lowly yet loveable St. Louis Browns. This volume contains the most detailed chapter available anywhere on the dramatic 1944 pennant race in St. Louis, and that town's single intra-city World Series rivalry. There is no other book providing a more loving look at the St. Louis Browns of the 1940s.

Patterson, Ted. *Day by Day in Orioles History*. West Point, New York: Leisure Press, 1984. 304 pp.

    Another day-by-day Orioles history, this one covering exclusively the Baltimore years of the franchise (1954–1983). A similar format to that of all other standard team chronologies, this book updates by only two seasons Hawkins' competing volume in the Stein and Day team series.

Robinson, Brooks (with Fred Bauer). *Putting It All Together*. New York: Hawthorn Books, 1971. 166 pp.

    The gripping story of the 1970 World Championship Orioles season, as seen here through the eyes of the club's Hall-of-Fame third baseman. Graphic game-by-game details are featured for the three-game A.L.C.S. sweep of the Minnesota Twins, as well as for the lopsided World Series romp in five games over the outmanned Cincinnati Reds of Pete Rose, Tony Perez, and Johnny Bench.

Veeck, Bill (with Ed Linn). *Veeck, as in Wreck*. New York: G.P. Putnam's Sons, 1962. 380 pp. (with several reprint editions).

    The classic autobiography of baseball's most colorful and literary big-time showman-turned-baseball owner, including several chapters on the Eddie Gaedel promotion and on Veeck's colorful years in St. Louis with the Browns. This is a delightful and honest book which focuses more on Veeck's Cleveland years, but also provides fine insider details on the St. Louis Browns as well.

Year-by-Year Standings and Season Summaries
St. Louis Browns (1901–1953)

Year	Pos.	Record	Pct.	GB	Manager	Player	BA	Player	HR	Player	W-L	ERA
1901*	8th	48–89	.350	35.5	Duffy	Anderson	.330	Anderson	8	Reidy	16–20	4.21
1902	2nd	78–58	.574	5.0	McAleer	Hemphill	.317	Hemphill	6	Donahue	22–11	2.76
1903	6th	65–74	.468	26.5	McAleer	Burkett	.296	Burkett	3	Sudhoff	21–15	2.27
								Hemphill	3			
1904	6th	65–87	.428	29.0	McAleer	Burkett	.273	several	2	Glade	18–15	2.27
						Wallace	.273					
1905	8th	54–99	.354	40.5	McAleer	Stone	.296	Howell	7	Howell	15–22	1.98
1906	5th	76–73	.510	16.0	McAleer	Stone	.358**	Stone	6	Pelty	16–11	1.59
1907	6th	69–83	.454	24.0	McAleer	Stone	.320	Howell	4	Howell	16–15	1.93
1908	4th	83–69	.546	6.5	McAleer	Stone	.281	Waddell	5	Waddell	19–14	1.89
1909	7th	61–89	.407	36.0	McAleer	Stone	.287	Powell	3	Powell	12–16	2.11
						Ferris			3			
						Stephens						
1910	8th	47–107	.305	57.0	O'Connor	Wallace	.258	several	2	Lake	11–17	2.20
1911	8th	45–107	.296	56.5	Wallace	LaPorte	.314	Meloan	3	Lake	10–15	3.30
1912	7th	53–101	.344	53.0	Wallace	Pratt	.302	Hamilton	5	Hamilton	11–14	3.24
					Stovall							
1913	8th	57–96	.373	39.0	Stovall	Shotton	.297	Williams	5	Hamilton	13–12	2.57
					Rickey							
1914	5th	71–82	.464	28.5	Rickey	Walker	.298	Walker	6	Weilman	18–13	2.08
1915	6th	63–91	.409	39.5	Rickey	Pratt	.291	Walker	5	Weilman	18–19	2.34
1916	5th	79–75	.513	12.0	Jones	Sisler	.305	Pratt	5	Weilman	17–18	2.15
1917	7th	57–97	.370	43.0	Jones	Sisler	.353	Jacobson	4	Davenport	17–17	3.08
1918	5th	58–64	.475	15.0	Jones	Sisler	.341	Sisler	2	Sothoron	12–12	1.94
					Austin							
					Burke							
1919	5th	67–72	.482	20.5	Burke	Sisler	.352	Sisler	10	Sothoron	20–13	2.20
1920	4th	76–77	.497	21.5	Burke	Sisler	.407**	Sisler	19	Shocker	20–10	2.71
1921	3rd	81–73	.526	17.5	Fohl	Sisler	.371	Williams	24	Shocker	27*–12	3.55
1922	2nd	93–61	.604	1.0	Fohl	Sisler	.420**	Williams	39**	Shocker	24–17	2.97

Year	Pos.	Record	Pct.	GB	Manager	Player	BA	Player	HR	Player	W-L	ERA
1923	5th	74–78	.487	24.0	Fohl Austin	Williams	.357	Williams	29	Shocker	20–12	3.41
1924	4th	74–78	.487	17.0	Sisler	McManus	.333	Jacobson	19	Shocker	16–13	4.17
1925	3rd	82–71	.536	15.0	Sisler	Rice	.359	Williams	25	Gaston	15–14	4.41
1926	7th	62–92	.403	29.0	Sisler	Miller	.331	Williams	17	Zachery	14–15	3.60
1927	7th	59–94	.336	50.5	Howley	Sisler	.327	Williams	17	Gaston	13–17	5.00
1928	3rd	82–72	.532	19.0	Howley	Manush	.378	Blue	14	Crowder	21–5	3.69
1929	4th	79–73	.520	26.0	Howley	Manush	.355	Kress	9	Gray	18–15	3.72
1930	6th	64–90	.416	38.0	Killefer	Goslin	.325	Goslin	30	Stewart	20–12	3.45
1931	5th	63–91	.409	45.0	Killefer	Goslin	.326	Goslin	24	Stewart	14–17	4.40
1932	6th	63–91	.409	44.0	Killefer	Ferrell	.315	Goslin	17	Stewart	14–19	4.61
1933	8th	55–96	.364	43.5	Killefer Sothoron Hornsby	West	.300	Campbell	16	Hadley	15–20	3.92
1934	6th	67–85	.441	33.0	Hornsby	West	.326	Clift	14	Newsom	16–20**	4.01
1935	7th	65–87	.428	28.5	Hornsby	Solters	.330	Solters	18	Andrews	13–7	3.54
1936	7th	57–95	.375	44.5	Hornsby	Bell	.344	Clift	20	Thomas	11–9	5.26
1937	8th	46–108	.299	56.0	Hornsby Bottomley	Bell	.340	Clift	29	Knott	8–18	4.89
1938	7th	55–97	.362	44.0	Street	Almada	.342	Clift	34	Newsom	20–16	5.08
1939	8th	43–111	.279	64.5	Haney	McQuinn	.316	McQuinn	20	Kennedy	9–17	5.73
1940	6th	67–87	.435	23.0	Haney	Radcliff	.342	Judnich	24	Auker	16–11	3.96
1941	6th	70–84	.455	31.0	Haney Sewell	Cullenbine	.317	McQuinn	18	Muncrief	13–9	3.65
1942	3rd	82–69	.543	19.5	Sewell	Judnich	.313	Laabs	27	Niggeling	15–11	2.66
1943	6th	72–80	.474	25.0	Sewell	Stephens	.289	Stephens	22	Sundra	15–11	3.25
1944	1st	89–65	.578	+1.0	Sewell	Kreevich	.301	Stephens	20	Kramer	17–13	2.49
1945	3rd	81–70	.536	6.0	Sewell	Stephens	.289	Stephens	24**	Potter	15–11	2.47
1946	7th	66–88	.429	38.0	Sewell Taylor	Stephens	.307	Laabs	16	Kramer	13–11	3.19

Year	Pos.	Record	Pct.	GB	Manager	Player	BA	Player	HR	Player	W-L	ERA
1947	8th	59–95	.383	38.0	Ruel	Dillinger	.294	Heath	27	Sanford	7–16	3.71
1948	6th	59–94	.386	37.0	Taylor	Zarilla	.329	Coan	14	Sanford	12–21**	4.64
1949	7th	53–101	.344	44.0	Taylor	Dillinger	.324	Graham	24	Garver	12–17**	3.98
1950	7th	58–96	.377	40.0	Taylor	Lollar	.280	Lenhardt	22	Garver	13–18	3.39
1951	8th	52–102	.338	46.0	Taylor	Coleman	.282	Wood	15	Garver	20–12	3.73
1952	7th	64–90	.416	31.0	Hornsby / Marion	Nieman	.289	Nieman	18	Paige	12–10	3.07
1953	8th	54–100	.351	46.5	Marion	Lenhardt	.317	Wertz	19	Larsen	7–12	4.16

Baltimore Orioles (1954–1992)

Year	Pos.	Record	Pct.	GB	Manager	Player	BA	Player	HR	Player	W-L	ERA
1954	7th	54–100	.351	57.0	Dykes	Abrams	.293	Stephens	8	Turley	14–15	3.46
1955	7th	57–97	.370	39.0	Richards	Philley	.299	Triandos	12	Wilson	12–18	3.45
1956	6th	69–85	.448	28.0	Richards	Nieman	.322	Triandos	21	Moore	12–7	4.18
1957	5th	76–76	.500	21.0	Richards	Boyd	.318	Triandos	19	Johnson	14–11	3.20
1958	6th	74–79	.484	17.5	Richards	Boyd	.309	Triandos	30	O'Dell	14–11	2.97
1959	6th	74–80	.481	20.0	Richards	Woodling	.300	Triandos	25	Wilhelm	15–11	2.19**
1960	2nd	89–65	.578	8.0	Richards	B. Robinson	.294	Hansen	22	Estrada	18*–11	3.58
1961	3rd	95–67	.586	14.0	Richards / Harris	Gentile	.302	Gentile	46	Barber	18–12	3.33
1962	7th	77–85	.475	19.0	Hitchcock	Snyder	.305	Gentile	33	Pappas	12–10	4.03
1963	4th	86–76	.531	18.5	Hitchcock	Orsino	.272	Powell	25	Barber	20–13	2.75
1964	3rd	97–65	.599	2.0	Bauer	B. Robinson	.317	Powell	39	Bunker	19–5	2.69
1965	3rd	94–68	.580	8.0	Bauer	B. Robinson	.297	Blefary	22	Miller	14–7	1.89

Year	Pos.	Record	Pct.	GB	Manager	Player	BA	Player	HR	Player	W-L	ERA
1966	1st	97–63	.606	+9.0	Bauer	F. Robinson	.316**	F. Robinson	49**	McNally	13–6	3.17
1967	6th	76–85	.472	15.5	Bauer	F. Robinson	.311	F. Robinson	30	Phoebus	14–9	3.33
1968	2nd	91–71	.562	12.0	Bauer / Weaver	Buford	.282	Powell	22	McNally	22–10	1.95
1969	1st***	109–53	.673	+19.0	Weaver	F. Robinson	.308	Powell	37	Cuellar†	23–11	2.38
1970	1st	108–54	.667	+15.0	Weaver	F. Robinson	.306	Powell	35	McNally	24**–9	3.22
1971	1st	101–57	.639	+12.0	Weaver	Rettenmund	.318	F. Robinson	28	McNally	21–5	2.89
1972	3rd	80–74	.519	5.0	Weaver	Grich	.271	Powell	21	Palmer	21–10	2.07
1973	1st	97–65	.599	+8.0	Weaver	T. Davis	.306	Williams	22	Palmer†	22–9	2.40**
1974	1st	91–71	.562	+2.0	Weaver	T. Davis	.289	Grich	19	Cuellar	22–10	3.11
1975	2nd	90–69	.566	4.5	Weaver	Singleton	.300	Baylor	25	Palmer†	23**–11	2.09**
1976	2nd	88–74	.543	10.5	Weaver	Singleton	.278	Jackson	27	Palmer†	22**–13	2.51
1977	2nd	97–64	.602	2.5	Weaver	Singleton	.328	Murray	27	Palmer	20**–11	2.91
								May	27			
1978	4th	90–71	.559	9.0	Weaver	Singleton	.293	DeCinces	28	Palmer	21–12	2.46
1979	1st	102–57	.642	+8.0	Weaver	Singleton	.295	Singleton	35	Flanagan†	23–9	3.08
						Murray	.295					
1980	2nd	100–62	.617	3.0	Weaver	Bumbry	.318	Murray	32	Stone†	25**–7	3.23

Year	Pos.	Record	Pct.	GB	Manager	Player	BA	Player	HR	Player	W-L	ERA
1981	2nd	31–23	.574	2.0	Weaver	Murray	.294	Murray	22**	D. Martinez	14**–5	3.32
	4th	28–23	.549	2.0								
1981‡	2nd	59–46	.562	1.0								
1982	2nd	94–68	.580	1.0	Weaver	Murray	.316	Murray	32	D. Martinez	16–12	4.21
1983	1st	98–64	.605	+6.0	Atobelli	C. Ripken	.318	Murray	33	McGregor	18–7	3.18
1984	5th	85–77	.525	19.0	Altobelli	Murray	.306	Murray	29	Boddicker	20**–11	2.79**
1985	4th	83–78	.516	16.0	Altobelli Ripken Weaver	Murray	.297	Murray	31	Aase	10–6	3.78
1986	7th	73–89	.451	22.5	Weaver	Murray	.305	C. Ripken	25	Boddicker	14–12	4.70
1987	6th	67–95	.414	31.0	Ripken	Sheets	.316	Sheets	31	Schmidt	10–5	3.77
1988	7th	54–107	.335	34.5	Ripken Robinson	Orsulak	.288	Murray	28	Ballard	8–12	4.40
1989	2nd	87–75	.537	2.0	Robinson	Bradley	.277	Tettleton	26	Ballard	18–8	3.43
1990	5th	76–85	.472	11.5	Robinson	B. Ripken	.291	C. Ripken	21	D. Johnson	13–9	4.10
1991	6th	67–95	.414	24.0	Robinson/Oates	C. Ripken	.323	C. Ripken	34	Milacki	10–9	4.01
1992	3rd	89–73	.549	7.0	Oates	Devereaux	.276	Devereaux	24	Mussina	18–5	2.54

* Milwaukee Brewers.
**Led the American League.
***American League East (first season of divisional play).
†Cy Young Award Winner
‡Split Season Totals (Players' Union Strike).

All-Time Baltimore Orioles-St. Louis Browns Career and Season Records

Orioles-Browns Career Batting Leaders (1901–1992)

Games Played	Brooks Robinson	2,986
At Bats	Brooks Robinson	10,654
Runs Scored	Brooks Robinson	1,232
Hits	Brooks Robinson	2,848
Batting Average (1,000 or more at bats)	George Sisler	.344
Batting Average (Baltimore)	Bob Nieman	.303
Home Runs	Eddie Murray	333
Doubles	Brooks Robinson	482
Triples	Brooks Robinson	68
Runs Batted In	Brooks Robinson	1,357
Stolen Bases	George Sisler	351
Stolen Bases (Baltimore)	Al Bumbry	252

Orioles-Browns Career Pitching Leaders (1901–1992)

Innings Pitched	Jim Palmer	3,947.2
Earned Run Average (400-plus innings)	Stu Miller	2.37
Wins	Jim Palmer	268
Losses	Jim Palmer	152
Winning Pct. (50 decisions)	Steve Stone	.656 (40–21)
Strikeouts	Jim Palmer	2,212
Games	Jim Palmer	558
Shutouts	Jim Palmer	53
Saves	Tippy Martinez	105
Complete Games	Jim Palmer	211

Orioles-Browns Single-Season Batting Records (1901–1992)

Batting Average (500 ABs)	George Sisler	.420	1922
Batting Average (Baltimore)	Ken Singleton	.328	1977
Home Runs	Frank Robinson	49	1966
Home Runs (lefthanded)	Jim Gentile	46	1961
Runs Batted In	Ken Williams	155	1922
Runs Batted In (Baltimore)	Jim Gentile	141	1961
Runs	Frank Robinson	122	1966
Hits	George Sisler	257	1920
Hits (Baltimore)	Cal Ripken	211	1983
Singles	George Sisler	178	1922
Singles (Baltimore)	Al Bumbry	158	1980
Doubles	George Sisler	49	1920
Doubles (Baltimore)	Cal Ripken	47	1983
Triples	George Sisler	18	1920–21–22
Triples (Baltimore)	Paul Blair	12	1967

All-Time Baltimore Orioles-St. Louis Browns Career and Season Records
(continued)

Slugging Percentage	Jim Gentile	.646	1961
Extra Base Hits	George Sisler	86	1920
Extra Base Hits (Baltimore)	Frank Robinson	85	1966
Game-Winning RBIs	Jim Gentile	21	1961
Sacrifice Bunts	Mark Belanger	23	1975
Stolen Bases	Luis Aparacio	57	1964
Strikeouts	Boog Powell	125	1966
Total Bases	George Sisler	389	1920
Total Bases (Baltimore)	Frank Robinson	367	1966
Hitting Streak	George Sisler	41	1922
Grand Slam Home Runs	Jim Gentile	5	1961
On-Base Percentage	George Sisler	.467	1922
On-Base Percentage (Baltimore)	Ken Singleton	.438	1977
Hit by Pitch	Bobby Grich	20	1974

Orioles-Browns Single-Season Pitching Records (1901–1992)

ERA (150 innings)	Dave McNally	1.95	1968
Wins	Steve Stone	25	1980
Losses	Ned Garver	24	1951
Winning Pct. (10 decisions)	Dave McNally	.808 (21–5)	1971
Strikeouts	Bobo Newsom	226	1938
Strikeouts (Baltimore)	Dave McNally	202	1968
Walks	Bobo Newsom	192	1938
Walks (Baltimore)	Bob Turley	181	1954
Saves	Don Aase	34	1986
Games	Tippy Martinez	76	1982
Complete Games	Jack Powell	36	1902
Complete Games (Baltimore)	Jim Palmer	25	1975
Games Started	Bobo Newsom	40	1938
	Dave McNally	40	1969, 1970
	Mike Cuellar	40	1970
Shutouts	Jim Palmer	10	1975
Innings Pitched	Urban Shocker	348	1922
Innings Pitched (Baltimore)	Jim Palmer	323	1975
Home Runs Allowed	Robin Roberts	35	1963
	Scott McGregor	35	1986
Consecutive Games Won (season)	Dave McNally	15	1968
Consecutive Games Won (overall)	Dave McNally	17	1968–1969

10
Seattle Mariners
Waiting for a Winner in Baseball's Forgotten City
James O'Donnell

The Seattle Mariners probably have the smallest following of all the major league baseball teams. Only the most stalwart baseball fans could endure the disappointments of such a commitment, and then only those who could overlook the lack of a comparable commitment by the franchise ownership. From their inaugural season in 1977, through 1989, the Mariners have yet to complete a .500 season or to see as many as 1.5 million fans any year at home. An appropriate emblem for the perseverance of Mariners fans might well be the cement sculpture that graces the Fremont District of Seattle, a monument depicting a half-dozen huddled commuters stoically awaiting an absent train that stopped running long ago. "Waiting for the Interurban" seems to appropriately capture the bleak stolidity of major league baseball in Seattle, and also to complement that grey mausoleum several miles to its south where the Mariners play baseball—the King County Kingdome.

To some a drab and soulless place, the Kingdome has few admirers despite its $60 million price tag—a bargain among modern day ballparks. Some baseball purists disdain even to set foot inside the building, and yet the oft-maligned Kingdome has not been a major obstacle in the hapless Mariners' road to popularity. Not only have domes been successful sites for major league baseball in Houston and Minneapolis, but in Seattle itself the Kingdome is nearly always sold out when professional football is the venue. No matter how frequently one hears complaints about the Kingdome, it is clear nonetheless that the majority of abstainers from Mariners' baseball are, like the less populous Mariners' faithful, simply waiting for a winner.

Why haven't the Mariners won? Certainly no one expects expansion teams to win at first. The talent is never there. What is hoped is that gifted players will be drafted, developed, and retained, that trades and acquisitions will be made continuously, and that consistent plans for on-field progress will be followed. Success for the Toronto Blue Jays, the Mariners' 1977 expansion cousins, has borne out the effect of prudent management and substantial financial investment. Whereas the Blue Jays have employed a single general manager, Pat Gillick, and only five field managers in 13 seasons, the Mariners have made frequent changes in both positions and thus have lacked continuity.[1] The original sextet of Mariner owners were unprepared to meet the financial demands of a major league operation and unable to agree on the course to be steered. Over $7 million in debt by the third season, the owners put the club up for sale and, after a year or so of rumors, California real estate developer George Argyros purchased the club in 1981 for a reported $13.1 million. Argyros's avowed commitment to winning and his much-publicized wealth were welcome signs of a turnaround in the team's fortunes, but serious doubts subsequently arose about his willingness to spend money on player salaries. In short, Argyros appeared more interested in running his organization "in the black" each year, building up its net worth, than in paying for superior players. Exulting in his role as a hard-nosed businessman, he carried on open hostilities with the executives of King County, leaseholder for the Kingdome, creating the impression that the Seattle Mariners were a local team in name only. To the relief of most fans, Argyros sold the team in August 1989 for a whopping $77 million to a group headed by Jeff Smulyan and Michael Browning of Indianapolis.[2]

Seattle fans were prepared to be patient concerning the field performance of the Mariners as the team embarked on its first season. The city had lost one major league franchise, the Pilots, after the 1969 maiden season, and everyone was eager to see the Mariners succeed. Within two years, though, the Mariner organization appeared to be sabotaging its own cause, committing some major blunders in public relations. Before the 1978 season began, the bleacher seats in left field were reclassified and upped in price several dollars, the $1.50 bargain seats shifting to the upper decks around the cavernous ballpark, the worst seats in right field, from which vantage point the right fielder could not be seen. The mistake here was that the most exuberant fans in the park and also the ones least able to afford a price jump were alienated. These were the fans, mostly young, who greeted the Mariner outfielders each game with yells of support, the most popular cry being "Rupe! Rupe! Rupe!" for centerfielder Ruppert Jones, the considered prize of the expansion draft. For an expansion club attempting to establish its fan base among the next generation of reserved seat ticket buyers, the move was pure folly.

Seat pricing has been in a state of flux much of the club's history and poor initial planning about pricing has gradually been giving way to reason. Together with 2-for-1 price tickets for members of the team's fan club and a similar deal for all fans on Mondays, pricing restraint has resulted in fewer complaints about seating in more recent years.

Another series of blunders involved the organization's refusal to negotiate on the use of the Kingdome by the Seattle Supersonics during the playoffs of the National Basketball Association in both 1979 and 1980, as well as its refusal to give up some pre-season practice dates so that the National Collegiate Athletic Association could hold its championships (the Final Four) at the Kingdome in April 1984. The Sonics were on their way to their first NBA championship in 1979 and the city was awash in playoff frenzy, but the Mariners insisted on their rights as primary tenants of the Kingdome and ended up in head-to-head competition for sports fans with the Sonics, who had to play some playoff games in a much smaller facility at the University of Washington. It was no contest in the eyes of the sports fan. The Mariners were vilified, particularly young Kip Horsburgh, the executive officer who had replaced Dick Vertlieb in 1979. Horsburgh and the Mariners came off as arrogant in the media and the feeling that one could no longer be both a Sonics fan and a Mariners fan hurt the Mariners at the gate.

The Mariners' gaffes served only to make a difficult task more difficult. The market for major league baseball in Seattle has been relatively small, with some rapid growth in the last decade bringing the Puget Sound region up to a population of 2.3 million, about the same as Minneapolis and San Diego. It is probable that there is a greater percentage of fans at a given game in the Kingdome rooting for the visiting team than at any other major league park. The cheering is particularly noticeable when the Yankees and Blue Jays are visiting, the proximity of British Columbia accounting for the Toronto fans. While an interest in the visiting team helps attendance for that time period, for the long term it is better to have enthusiastic interest in the local team when fans come to the park no matter who is playing the locals. Unlike fans in the Midwest who will drive hours to see their team, only a few fans from eastern Washington, Idaho, and Oregon will make the drive to Seattle. A winning season or two could change this situation, particularly if the Mariners retain their bright young stars, instead of losing them to free agency or even to the threat of free agency.

As lonely as the Mariners fan can be and as grim as the season records have been, the wait for better times has been made bearable by a colorful cast and some exciting, if erratic, baseball. First in the heart of loyal Mariners fans are the first-year heroes: tall Glenn Abbott, the only starter who could be counted upon to pitch into the middle innings; Danny Meyer, whose characteristic neck twitch made his batting style a fan favorite; Lee Stanton, who had a career year at the plate only one year before bowing out of the major leagues; and Ruppert Jones, the only player in that first year around whose neck the garland of greatness appeared to lie—a sweet illusion in 1977. In these early years journeymen were in the majority, with infielders like Larry Milbourne (who spent two separate terms as a Mariner and holds the single-season pinch hit record), Bill Stein, Pat Putnam, Jose Baez, Rick Auerbach, and two who still bring a smile to the chroniclers of egregious play, Mario Mendoza and Lenny Randle. Mendoza gave baseball its term "the Mendoza line" by falling two points shy of batting .200 in 148 games in 1979.[3] Randle, in a role antithetic to the brute who assaulted Rangers manager Frank Lucchesi in 1976, did on one occasion in the Kingdome what many third baseman must have dreamed of doing when, in fielding a sure bunt single down the line, he dropped to his knees to blow the ball foul. In contrast, there was the Mariners' first *legitimate* defensive star, Julio Cruz, who made playing second base look like the most fun in the world. Offensive stars included Leon Roberts, Bruce Bochte (he of the foot-in-the-bucket swing), Tom Paciorek (the hitter of Seattle's most dramatic pair of home runs), and Willie Horton, who had waited 13 years before reproducing a 100-RBI year. Seattle also provided late-career stints for pitchers Jim Colborn, Milt Wilcox, and the infamous Gaylor Perry, the latter winning his 300th game in the Kingdome; as well as giving similar opportunities to sluggers Richie Zisk, Jeff Burroughs, and Gorman Thomas. Three distinguished catchers—Ray Fosse, Jim Essian, and Steve Yeager—showed waning talents in Seattle. And in the bullpen the M's enjoyed remarkable years from Enrique Romo, John Montague, Ed Vande Berg, Mike Stanton, and (especially) Bill Caudill, who charged to the mound for 26 saves in two consecutive seasons and kept the team loose posing as "The Inspector," a practical joker in a deerstalker.

While showmen like Cruz and Caudill gave the impression that the Kingdome was a perfect stage for their talents, few Mariners in fact have expressed pleasure in playing there. Periodically there have been complaints about protruding seams in the turf (a danger to sprinting outfielders), inadequate lighting, and what is now a prevalent concern among modern ballplayers, the cement-based field that is hard on a player's legs and may shorten a career. An added nuisance has been the occasional carom of a batted ball from the speakers or wires suspended from the dome's roof. Several otherwise certain home runs have been rebuffed in this manner including what would have been Willie Horton's 300th homer in 1979. Pitchers, knowing that the ball carries well, never have liked pitching in the Kingdome. In four different years, more home runs have been hit there than in any other major league park.

Not surprisingly, the Seattle team ERA averages out over 12 seasons to a dismal figure—4.42. Granted that Mariner pitching has never been a strong team asset, but pitchers who survive to pitch for other teams have fared pretty well. During the 1989 season a dozen or so former Mariner hurlers were still pitching in the major leagues, and one, Mike Moore, was leading the American League in ERA as late as August, yielding barely two earned runs per nine innings after averaging over four runs in seven seasons with the Mariners. One August 1989 game in the Kingdome brought back the bad times for three former Mariner pitchers—Moore, Matt Young, and Gene Nelson—as they were belted for 11 runs including four homers. Vengeful fans were calling for the appearance as well of Rick Honeycutt, a fourth ex-Mariner on the Oakland A's staff. In 1987 Mark Langston, the best pitcher that the Mariners have developed, was 7–8 in the Kingdome with a 4.29 ERA; on the road he was 12–5 with a 3.45 ERA. Ballplayers certainly enjoy hitting in the Kingdome, but that hasn't worked out to be a Mariner advantage in most seasons. The Mariners haven't had many young power hitters who could capitalize on the favorable conditions. In only two of their first 12 seasons have the M's outhomered the opposition in the Kingdome.

Seattle fans and players alike have had to learn to live with the Kingdome, and a few appear to realize that, were it not for the construction of the multi-purpose stadium, major league baseball would not exist in Seattle. Indeed, the one-year existence of the Seattle Pilots depended upon the voters of King County approving funding for the dome in 1968 after two earlier ballot tries in 1962 and 1966 failed. As it turned out, the Pilots were rushed into operation a year earlier than the American League's master plan recommended and played their single home season in Sicks' Stadium, a facility ill-equipped for large crowds, before leaving for Milwaukee. The construction of the Kingdome was held up for several years with public wrangling about the proposed site and a court challenge to the construction that was finally placed aside in 1972. At long last, ground was broken on a convenient site near the railroad station and Pioneer Square in downtown Seattle. The date was November 2, 1972, and it would be several more years before the Kingdome would see its first major league tenant, the expansion Seattle Seahawks of the NFL, kick off the 1976 season.

Baseball returned to Seattle as a result of an out-of-court settlement between the city and the American League, a victory for the fans who felt that the Pilots had been stolen from them by the league. On February 6, 1976, the American League formally agreed to grant a franchise to a group of six men: Stanley Golub, Walter Schoenfeld, Lester Smith, James Stillwell, Jr., James Walsh, and comedian Danny Kaye. A few months later the nickname "Mariners" was chosen from among 15,000 contest entries, and on September 30 pitcher Dave Johnson was purchased from Baltimore, becoming the Mariners' first player acquisition. The expansion draft followed in November and Ruppert Jones became the first pick in the draft after Seattle won a coin toss with Toronto. Each team selected 30 players with General Manager Lou Gorman expressing the opinion that Seattle's picks were better, with only shortstop Bob Bailor, Toronto's first pick, eluding them. Of the Mariners' 30 choices, 16 were pitchers. No one can say that the Mariners had not foreseen that need.

The inaugural season opened with many unresolved questions about the quality of the fledgling team and the character of the indoor ballpark. One misconception was that the ball would not carry well, simply because it did not carry in the Astrodome, the only other domed park in 1977. By the end of the season there had been 178 home runs hit, 103 of them by the opposition, unfortunately. Had the Mariners been able to test their park, they may have pursued the acquisition of additional power hitters. As for worries about attendance, they faded relatively soon. While the Pilots had drawn only 677,944 fans at Sicks' Stadium (capacity: 28,500) in 1969, the Mariners drew 1,338,511, which turned out to be their highest mark in their first 12 seasons. People apparently *would* attend indoor baseball games in Seattle. The Kingdome's capacity of 58,850 was virtually matched by the Opening Night crowd that got to experience the constant 72° environment. Seattle's reputation for rain has obscured the more serious natural detriment to night baseball in Seattle—cold temperatures. If major league baseball were still played exclusively during the day, Seattle's climate would be among the best in the country. Summers, even if short and late arriving, are typically dry with moderate heat. Thunderstorms are rare. People, though, who think that large crowds will consistently attend night games outdoors in Seattle, where even August night temperatures are often in the lower 50s, are most likely influenced by memories of baseball nights in other cities than by firsthand experience in Seattle. A more realistic scenario for Seattle's baseball future—distant, not near—would include a stadium with a retractable roof. To get public support for such a project, the Mariners will need to win greater favor through improved play on the field and improved public relations.

On the field in 1977 the Mariners were as good as could be expected. Much of the fans' attention focused on Ruppert Jones, the center fielder, who posted a .263 batting average with 24 home runs and 76 RBIs while playing fine defense. At age 22, Jones represented the future of the Mariners, and he added excitement to the less dramatic play of offensive stars Lee Stanton and Danny Meyer. Stanton, the Mariner MVP that year, hit 29 home runs and drove in 90 runs while leading the team in average as well at .275. These totals were career bests for Stanton, who left the major leagues the following year at 32 after batting .182. Meyer tied Stanton for leadership in RBIs at 90 and hit 22 home runs, both career highs. Meyer's smooth swing from the left side gave the Mariners another potent bat in addition to Jones' that could test the right-field fence. Originally, the height of the outfield walls was a uniform 11 feet, 6 inches from line to line. In 1982 the right-field wall was rebuilt to a height of 22 feet, and in 1988 several feet of plexiglass was added to the left-field wall to prevent bleacher fans from reaching over and obstructing play. The fact that it was only 316 feet down the lines made pull-hitting especially dangerous for pitchers. The Mariners were unable to supply much punch other than Stanton's, from the righthanded side, thus the power discrepancy in the first season's totals at the Kingdome.

The most glaring weakness on the Mariner team in 1977, however, was pitching. The opening night Mariner pitcher was Diego Segui, the sentimental choice as he had also pitched for the Pilots. At 39 Segui predictably received the popular epithet "The Ancient Mariner," doubly apt in the view of his critics because, like his namesake in Coleridge's poem, he usually could only "stoppeth one of three." Including the first game loss (7–0 to California), Segui was 0–7 in this, his last major league season, finishing with a 5.68 ERA. He had company. The Mariner pitching staff compiled a team ERA of 4.83, hurling only 18 complete games. The opposition outscored the Mariners, 855 to 624 as the first-year M's tallied a 64–98 record. For bright spots, Enrique Romo garnered 16 of the 31 saves and had a 2.84 ERA. While losing 13 games Glenn Abbott, the ace of the staff (also known as "The Tall Arkansan"), won 12. And for a stretch of nine days, John Montague made American League history by retiring 33 consecutive batters.

More important than the individual statistics, the Mariners showed signs of a brighter future. Manager Darrell Johnson and General Manager Lou Gorman could take satisfaction that they had not finished last in the A.L. West, having edged ahead of Oakland on the last day. Then, too, the M's had won 10 more games than the Blue Jays, their only realistic competitors. The healthy attendance certainly boosted spirits, and they had learned some things about their ballpark as well. They now knew the ball would carry and could seek out additional batting power, especially from the right side. Fly balls, particularly pop flies, were preludes to adventure because of the light background of the ceiling and the dome's inadequate lighting. Players could not afford to take their eyes off the ball. The lighting could be improved, but the ceiling would be left to discolor naturally as time went by, leaving disciplined tracking of the ball as the best defense. Pitching, of course, was the sorest need, and the Mariners acquired two promising hurlers in the off-season, Mike Parrott and Shane Rawley. For the righthanded power, they picked up Leon Roberts, an outfielder from Houston, in exchange for infielder Jimmy Sexton.

Roberts turned out to be the Mariners' most potent offensive weapon in 1978. Unfortunately, he was virtually their only power source. The broad-shouldered Roberts became the Mariners' first .300 hitter (with a point to spare) and drove in a team-high 92 runs while also leading the M's in homers with 22. Shortstop Craig Reynolds had a solid season, batting .292 and leading the team in hits, but Stanton, Meyer, and Jones were all disappointing, the latter two hampered by injuries. The trio, who had accounted for 75 homers and 256 RBIs in 1977, produced only 17 home runs and 126 RBIs among them. Signed as the Mariners' first free agent over the winter, Bruce Bochte chipped in with 11 homers, 51 RBIs, and a .263 batting average, figures he would improve upon in subsequent years. The most positive development, though, occurred at second base where speedster Julio Cruz took over and stole 59 bases, an important element in the 77 runs he scored. His defensive play was a real plus and not only because of his remarkably low total of 10 errors. Cruz was an acrobatic showman, who appeared to love performing for the crowd. His range and sure-handedness, along with his enthusiasm, made Julio a darling of the fans, who greeted him with cries of "Ju-u-u-li-o" when his name was announced on the loudspeaker. Together with Roberts, Cruz made the season more bearable, for it was a long one, with the M's taking a giant step backwards in wins (56) and finishing last in the division. Their home run production in the Kingdome dropped to an anemic 58 (their opponents had 93) and their run total decreased by 10. It was a season in which Bob Stinson, a journeyman catcher, perfected what may have been one of the M's best offensive strategies, tying a major league record by reaching base six times by route of catcher's interference.

Rawley and Parrott did not give the Mariners immediate help on the mound, winning only five games between them with a like number of saves. Glenn Abbott dropped to 7–15 and his earned run average ballooned to 5.27. While the staff ERA improved ever so little, pitching was again a major weakness. Enrique Romo appeared in 56 games, all in relief, and had more wins than saves, 11 to 10, while losing seven games. His ERA jumped to 3.69. After Romo, Paul Mitchell had the most wins (8) and the team had a major league low of 20 saves.

Not surprisingly, 1978 attendance at the Kingdome was off considerably, down to 877,440. Besides the poor play and the changes in ticket prices, some of the initial excitement accompanying the return of major league baseball had obviously worn off. Fans saw that the Mariners were a long way from being a winning team and curiosity about the Kingdome was waning. The obvious aesthetic deficiencies of the stadium were more noticeable in the absence of stellar play. Fans complained more openly about the ballpark food, finding it both unappetizing and expensive. When a spontaneous cheer arose from one sector, it was often met with surprised looks as if it were strange that someone could find pleasure in breaking the silence. In the relative quiet of the stadium, a heckler could be heard by the players quite distinctly and soon visiting players were commenting on it. While fans continued to praise the dome as a shelter from the elements earlier in the season, now more and more said that it was a shame to spend a summer day or evening watching baseball indoors. When pressed to describe the positive points of the Kingdome, more than one fan had to stop after citing the absence of cigarette and cigar smoke. The baseball honeymoon was over.

Faced with a continued deficiency in pitching, the M's management acted on the few options open to them in the trading marketplace. In December of 1978 they made two deals, giving up their stopper, Enrique Romo, a relative luxury for an expansion team, in exchange for slick-fielding shortstop Mario Mendoza, and pitchers Odell Jones and Rafael Vasquez. The acquisition of Mendoza allowed the M's to give up a successful shortstop, Craig Reynolds, for a promising young lefthander, Floyd Bannister, coveted by virtually every team in both leagues. Bannister had not been a winner in his two seasons in Houston, but he had an impressive strikeout-to-walk ratio and was just 23. An added plus was that he represented the first "home grown" Mariner, having played high school baseball in the Seattle area. The Mariners went into the 1979 season with the realistic hopes of winning more than 56 games. They had some strong arms to go with some skilled position players, nearly all of them young. One exception to youth, a big one, was Willie Horton, the slugging outfielder and designated hitter who signed with the M's as a free agent. Horton had played for three different American League teams in 1978 and had only 11 home runs and 60 RBIs. The Mariners were counting on two comebacks, his and theirs.

Willie Horton delivered the offense hoped of him, driving in 106 runs and hitting 29 homers, and the Mariners rebounded to a sixth-place finish, winning 67 games. Horton's year was marvelous and won him the Comeback Award in the American League. On June 6 he hit his 300th home run—for the second time one might say. The night before he had launched what appeared to be his 300th roundtripper only to see the ball carom off a speaker suspended from the roof in left center field. This had happened before but not at such a key time.

The double that Horton legged out—the ball is in play if it hits a speaker—was small consolation at the time. Horton, the Mariner's designated hitter in all 162 games, demonstrated what an authentic power hitter could do in the Kingdome and led to acquisitions of other aging power hitters in later years.

In 1979 Horton was joined in the limelight by Bruce Bochte, who hit .316 in his new role as the regular first baseman. That average as well as his 16 home runs and 100 RBIs constituted career bests for Bochte, whose batting stance with its odd front-leg lift belied such effectiveness. Ruppert Jones had a satisfying comeback of his own as he hit 21 homers and drove in 78 runs. He and Julio Cruz also displayed the value of team speed. Jones scored 109 runs and stole 33 bases in 162 games; Cruz scored 70 runs and stole 49 in only 107 games. In another comeback Danny Meyer hit .273 and batted safely in 21 consecutive games, contributing 20 home runs and 74 RBIs. Had Leon Roberts continued his hot hitting of 1978, the Mariners might have finished higher in the standings, but his production trailed off to a .271 BA, 15 homers, and 54 RBIs in 140 games. Of little help offensively was the full-time shortstop Mario Mendoza, who failed to hit .200 once again, having fallen short of that mark three times previously in only partial seasons of play. Mendoza managed nine walks during the year and his one home run was of the inside-the-park variety.

All in all, though, the Mariner acquisitions in trades and free-agent signings had been beneficial. GM Lou Gorman had fared well with a very limited budget and few marketable players. Dan O'Brien had become his boss in January in the new position of club president and that would prove to limit Gorman's hand in subsequent transactions. Shane Rawley and Mike Parrott paid some dividends in 1979: Rawley appeared in 48 games and had 11 saves despite missing two months with a thumb injury; Parrott put together a 14–12 record, mostly as a starter, and led the staff in ERA (3.77), innings pitched (229), and strikeouts (127). Floyd Bannister started 30 games on his way to a 10–15 record, showing promise in his two shutouts. A second lefthanded starter, Rick Honeycutt, who had been obtained as a minor leaguer in 1977 in a deal with Pittsburgh for pitcher Dave Pagan, continued to show progress, posting an 11–12 record in 33 starts. The loss of Romo was minimized by Byron McLaughlin's 14 saves, in combination with Rawley's 11. The Mariners were confident enough to sell reliever John Montague to the eventual division winners, California. (Montague won two games and saved six in 14 appearances for the Angels down the stretch.)

At the end of the 1979 season the Mariners' hopes were buoyed by their rebound from the disastrous 1978 season. They had avoided the division cellar and had pulled ahead of their expansion rival Toronto. They had showed both power and speed. Pitching was improving. The Kingdome had hosted both the All-Star Game, an exciting one-run victory by the National League, and a Willie Horton Night. On the darker side, attendance had slipped further to 844,455, the hard feelings about ticket prices and the Sonics controversy taking effect. Then, too, the Mariners appeared to be unwilling or unable to spend money needed to acquire or retain good ballplayers. This impression was reinforced when the Mariners decided to deal Ruppert Jones, their brightest hope in the early years. On November 1 Jones and pitcher Jim Lewis were traded to the Yankees for pitchers Jim Beattie and Rick Anderson, as well as catcher Jerry Narron and outfielder Juan Beniquez. In hindsight, the deal was not catastrophic. Jones played in only 83 games in 1980 before winding down his career in San Diego and Detroit, never amassing the home runs and RBIs that he had in Seattle. While Anderson, Beniquez, and Narron contributed in only minor ways to the Mariners of the early 1980s, Jim Beattie, after an initial struggle in 1980, became a reliable hurler for the M's and frequently was among the team leaders in ERA before shoulder problems forced his retirement. Had the Mariners traded Ruppert Jones because they had a capable center fielder ready to take his place, the deal might have been less discouraging. Center field prospect Dave Henderson was not yet ready for the big leagues, however, and the job was shared by several players in 1980, Joe Simpson playing there most of the time and producing little offensively.

The smallest Opening Night crowd in Mariner history (22,588) greeted the team on April 9, 1980. That was a bad omen. Although Mike Parrott managed to beat the Blue Jays that night, yielding 13 hits, he was unable to win another game the whole year and finished 1–16. The Mariners did attain their first winning record for the month of April (11–10) and were .500 at the end of May, but things went badly thereafter. Rick Honeycutt went 6–0 to start the season, made the All-Star team, and then finished 10–17 with a suspension to boot for having used a thumbtack to deface baseballs. Honeycutt was caught on the mound with the evidence protruding from a bandage around a finger. Pitching was not bad overall. Glenn Abbott had a .500 record (12–12), Floyd Bannister a decent ERA (3.47), and Shane Rawley 13 saves. The team ERA (4.38) was lower for the third consecutive year (the staff lost three 1–0 games). In 1980 it was the Mariner hitting that embarrassed the most, with league lows for batting and slugging averages, .248 and .356 respectively. The M's were outscored 793 to 610 and were outhomered in the Kingdome, 99–74. Bruce Bochte hit .300 exactly, and Julio Cruz continued his basestealing activity with 45. Tom Paciorek led the team in homers, hitting 15 in 418 at bats, but Willie Horton hit only eight and drove in a mere 36 runs. It was a year in which Mario Mendoza hit for a higher average than several of the other regulars, his .245 topping Horton, Cruz, catcher Larry Cox, and third baseman Ted Cox.

In the midst of a 12-game losing streak in August, Darrell Johnson was fired. Johnson had shown a knack for getting tossed out of games when the team had lost several in a row, but his act had worn thin by now. He had been brought in originally by Gorman because of his reputation for being good with young players, but now O'Brien was in control and, with the Mariners falling deeper and deeper into the cellar, Johnson walked the plank and Maury Wills came aboard. With Wills at the helm, the Mariners finished 20–38, worse than the 39–65 under Johnson. Their 59 wins were only three more than at their nadir in 1978 and Toronto passed them with 67. As could be expected, the attendance dropped even more, to 836,204. The Mariners could only hope that hiring Wills, an ex-star and only the third black manager in the majors, would prove a boost both to their public image and to the sagging team morale.

The off-season was a portentous one. First, Lou Gorman jumped ship and hired on with the Mets. Then the Mariners consummated the largest trade in club history. Going to Texas were Rick Honeycutt, Larry Cox, Mario Mendoza, Leon Roberts, and Willie Horton; coming to Seattle were Richie Zisk, infielder Rick Auerbach, and pitchers Brian Allard, Ken Clay, Jerry Don Gleaton, and Steve Finch. Roberts and Horton had stopped producing for the Mariners and it was thought that Zisk, bad legs and all, would give the team a more consistent bat. In his seven most recent seasons he had ranged between 17 and 30 homers and averaged over 84 RBIs. Even more momentous than this trade, though, was the January 1981 purchase of the majority interest in the club by George Argyros. Looking back on the event many Seattle fans see that transaction as the beginning of the hostage crisis, when city and club were seized by the California terrorist. At the time it was a much welcomed move. Argyros authorized a trade in March that brought another expensive slugger to the Mariners—Jeff Burroughs—and appeared to signal a willingness to invest in the team. Burroughs had just completed two injury-ridden seasons in Atlanta, in which he had hit first 11 and then 13 homers. The investment was risky, but Burroughs had just turned 30 and had demonstrated what he could do in a slugger's ballpark when in 1977 he had clobbered 41 homers and driven in 114 runs for Atlanta.

With Zisk and Burroughs, Maury Wills appeared to have much more clout in his lineup, even while his supply of AAA pitchers had increased dramatically. Wills, however, did not get to see the results. He was fired in early May after only 24 games, ending a brief and bizarre tenure as a major league manager. His 6–18 record was not likely to improve, given the long list of managerial lapses, errors, and blunders he compiled. On two different occasions he speculated aloud with the press as to how he might use a player, only to be told that the player had been traded away weeks earlier. He left a spring training game in progress without telling anyone, not even O'Brien, that he was doing so. He inserted a player into a game after having placed him on waivers before the game. He forgot to keep track of players he had available and was often caught shorthanded or unprepared. The crowning move occurred on April 25 when Wills instructed the ground crew at the Kingdome to extend the front line of the batter's box a few inches, the difference being noticed by opposing manager Billy Martin. Wills was suspended two games by the league for a violation that made little sense as batters often obliterate the lines in the first inning. On May 6 Rene Lachemann, the young manager of the Mariners' Pacific Coast League entry, took over and, under his peer-management style, the club was 15–18 until the major league strike interrupted the season in June. Immediately after Lachemann's hiring the team and, particularly, Tom Paciorek, provided some excitement. The Mariners beat the Yankees in dramatic come-from-behind fashion at the Kingdome on May 8 and 9, with Paciorek homering in the ninth both games. Paciorek's timely hitting and handsome affability made him a Seattle hero during the bizarre split season, when the Mariners attained their second highest per game attendance mark of 14,362, the best since their inaugural year. Attendance at Yankee-Mariner games was particularly good, largely because of the M's exceptional record against New York in the Kingdome over the first five seasons. Through the 1981 season, the M's were 17–9 against the Yankees in Seattle.

Paciorek led the Mariners in hitting in 1981 with a .326 average and 13 game-winning RBIs, both good for second place in the American League. Zisk had a good year as well, winning the A.L. Comeback Award with 16 homers in 357 at bats and a .311 average. Gary Gray, a veteran minor leaguer, showed good power with 13 home runs in only 208 at bats. Overall, the M's were barely outhomered in the Kingdome, 53 to 52. A notable feat was Julio Cruz's American League record of 32 consecutive stolen bases, four coming at the end of the 1980 season. The pitching staff's ERA improved for the fourth straight year, but no starter had a winning record, with the exception of Jim Beattie, who was 3–2, spending most of the season in the minors. The defense was continuing to improve, too, as the M's posted their best fielding average up to that point (.979) and Cruz was turning the double play consistently.

Both management and fans could find satisfaction in that the M's had weathered both the strike and the Wills' firing and the team had been competitive, going 23–29 in the second half of the split season and finishing fifth (sixth, by winning percentage, for the combined split-season format). Well liked by his players, Lachemann appeared to have the young M's believing in themselves. The draft was beginning to help the Mariners at last, as first-round pick (June 1977) Dave Henderson had debuted in center field and had hit with power in streaks. Lachemann knew the AAA players well and could help their transition to the big leagues. Hopes were further lifted when the team signed righthander Mike Moore, a collegian and the first pick overall in the June draft. Moore, who threw hard and well in college, represented a shift in Mariner planning, revealing a willingness to draft older players. Other Mariner choices that year included lefthander Mark Langston and outfielder Phil Bradley, also both collegians. In retrospect, the 1981 draft was the best of the M's first decade.

The Mariners should have turned the corner in 1982. They blundered, though, in their unwillingness to retain team leader Tom Paciorek. On December 9, 1981, they had traded away the sole holdover from Opening Night 1977, Danny Meyer, for Rich Bordi of the A's and minor leaguer Roy Thomas, both pitchers. As if to flaunt their callous disregard for the fans, two days later O'Brien and the M's swapped Paciorek to the White Sox for catcher Jim Essian, shortstop Todd Cruz, and minor league outfielder Rod Allen. To be fair, the trade addressed some Mariner needs, since both catcher and shortstop had continued to be "problem" positions. Essian, the fifth catcher the Mariners had dealt for in less than six years, was expected to provide leadership for the young pitching staff; Cruz, it was hoped, would combine offense and defense as no shortstop had been able to since Craig Reynolds. Besides losing Paciorek's leadership, the M's lost a key clutch hitter and front office credibility. They attempted to make amends in March when they purchased Al Cowens from Detroit and signed free agent hurler Gaylord Perry. Cowens was coming off a disappointing year while Perry, well travelled but still effective at 43, was closing in on his 300th victory. The M's were intent on making the most of the grizzled righthander's bid to reach that milestone, and they were in need of a veteran pitcher with Glenn Abbott out for the season with an injury. It was the trade on April Fool's Day that salvaged the season, though. The Mariners exchanged Shane Rawley with the Yankees for the irrepressible reliever, Bill Caudill.

Perry and Caudill gave the Mariners and their fans some reasons to overlook the loss of Paciorek. Perry's first victory in Seattle on April 20 against the Angels left California manager Gene Mauch fuming. He told reporters, "Gaylord Perry should be in the Hall of Fame, and they should nail a tube of K-Y jelly to his plaque." Perry had enough stuff on the ball to win 10 and lose 12 during the 1982 season, including

404 *Encyclopedia of Baseball Team Histories: American League*

his 300th win on May 6 when he went the distance to beat the Yankees, 7–3, in front of 27,369 fans. Caudill and fellow reliever Ed Vande Berg made frequent appearances, 70 and 78 respectively. Caudill, relying mostly on a fastball, compiled 26 saves on his way to a 12–9 record, and brought excitement to late innings at the Kingdome. Dubbed "Cuffs" and "The Inspector" for his around-the-clubhouse impersonation of a detective, the reliever made the atmosphere less pressurized. The M's played well in the first half of the season, going .500 in May and .600, their best monthly percentage ever, in June. The team's 39 saves were an all-time high but there were also 11 shutouts, primary reasons for the club-best ERA of 3.88. Floyd Bannister, 12–13, had 209 strikeouts, and Jim Beattie, as well as Mike Moore, pitched strongly at times, though neither attained a winning record. On offense Zisk had a good year with 21 homers, a .292 average, 62 RBIs, and a 21-game hitting streak within 131 games. Cowens led the club in RBIs (78) and homers (20), Bochte in average (.297), and Julio Cruz in stolen bases (46), stealing over 40 for the fifth straight year. The other Cruz—Todd—surprised some people with his 16 homers, but 25 errors offset some of this offensive help. The other principal in the Paciorek deal, Essian, played in only 48 games because of injuries. It was the improved pitching that boosted the team to its best record in its six seasons, 76–86, and its second-best attendance, 1,070,404.

A six-season comparison of the Mariners and Toronto Blue Jays shows the Mariners with 18 more wins and a better record in the odd-numbered years. In 1982 Toronto had won only two more games than Seattle. By record alone, it would appear that the two teams were close, with a slight advantage to the M's. The fortunes of the two expansion teams diverged sharply at this point however. The Jays opened the 1983 season with essentially the same team from 1982: players whom they had drafted or signed and developed through their minor league system. The M's, on the other hand, were still relying heavily on trades and other acquisitions to make up for the deficiencies in their drafts. First-round picks from 1977 through 1981 included such players as Paul Givens, Jim Maler, Tito Nanni, Mike Hood, Al Chambers, Don Freeman, and Brent McAfee. Of these, only Maler had reached the majors, having batted .226 in 64 games.

While the Mariners needed good veteran players, they were reluctant to pay high salaries to retain them. Bruce Bochte elected not to play the 1983 season rather than sign with the Mariners. His place at first base was taken by Pat Putnam, obtained in an off-season trade with Texas. The M's also traded for Steve Henderson and traded away Jim Essian. Rather than sign Floyd Bannister to a new contract, they let him escape to sign as a free agent with the White Sox. In June, on the eve of the trading deadline, they traded Julio Cruz to the White Sox for Tony Bernazard in lieu of meeting Cruz's new salary demands. (With Cruz gone and Abbott released later in the season, the M's were now without anyone from their original roster; Jim Clancy remained with Toronto through the 1988 season and Ernie Whitt was still playing for the Jays in 1989!) Even if one grants that Cruz never learned how to adapt his stroke to take advantage of the high hops on artificial turf, that Brochte didn't have great power, or that Bannister was not a consistent winner, those three players were better than any the system was developing; and they had played well for Seattle. The M's looked for inexpensive veterans to fill the bill, while waiting for the farm system to be productive, but the wait was prolonged and painful. On June 25, with a record of 26–47 weighing against him, Rene Lachemann lost his job. Simultaneously, the M's released Gaylord Perry, whose 3–10 record had reduced his worth as a gate attraction. To distract the fans from the carnage, the club promoted Spike Owen from the minors and inserted him into the lineup immediately at shortstop. What the fans remember is how George Argyros responded to probing questions about the moves at a press conference, testily asserting that he owned the Mariners and could do with them what he wanted.

While Spike Owen's cheerful demeanor and hustling play had their charms, the season was a lost cause. Del Crandall, a stern disciplinarian, fared little better than the more egalitarian Lachemann and compiled a 34–55 record, bringing the team to 60–102, 39 games behind Chicago, who won the division by 20 games with able assistance from Paciorek, Bannister, and Cruz. While Bill Caudill repeated his 26 saves, his fastball was less reliable, and he finished 2–8 with a 4.78 ERA. Without Bannister (16–10 with Chicago), the M's relied on lefthanders Matt Young and Jim Beattie as their workhorses, but both were inconsistent, 11–15 and 10–15 respectively, though Beattie's one-hitter on September 7 was the team's first ever. The staff ERA of 4.12 finally reversed the steadily improving trend maintained since the first season. Equally disappointing was the offense. The team posted its lowest average (.240) as well as its fewest runs scored (558), a 15 percent decrease from 1982. No Mariner had a fine season; Putnam's 19 homers and 67 RBIs were only respectable. Richie Zisk's bad knees allowed him to bat only 285 times, which yielded 12 home runs—a ratio typical of his total career—in this his final season. On a brighter note, the M's could cite the emergence of Dave Henderson as a major league center fielder. He demonstrated decent power with 17 homers and chased down fly balls with apparent ease. The team, though, was at its worst. In the American League East the Toronto Blue Jays had now climbed to 89–73.

Immediately following the season, Argyros appointed Chuck Armstrong, a lawyer employed by the owner's real estate firm, as the new club president and Hal Keller, the director of player development, as the general manager. Dan O'Brien was now out. Keller's first trade—Bill Caudill to the A's for catcher Bob Kearney and pitcher Dave Beard—was controversial but understandable, given the M's needs. His next deal was one of the team's best. The M's acquired designated hitter Gorman Thomas and second baseman Jack Perconte from Cleveland in exchange for Tony Bernazard. Other trades brought back Larry Milbourne and secured Barry Bonnell. While the trades looked promising, the major developments were in the farm system at last, specifically the draft choices for 1981 and 1982. Three exciting young ballplayers surfaced in Seattle: Alvin Davis, Mark Langston, and Phil Bradley. Davis was called up to the Kingdome a few weeks into the 1984 season and, after homering into the upper deck in right field off Dennis Eckersley of Boston, continued his assault on A.L. pitching, hitting safely in 22 of his first 28 major league games. Nine homers and 28 RBIs in that stretch made Davis's debut, along with Ken Griffey, Jr.'s in 1989, the most exciting days ever for Mariner baseball in Seattle. Before the season ended, Davis had 27 homers and 116 RBIs, and had garnered the Rookie of the Year Award, all accomplished without a change in his calm, self-effacing demeanor. He took adversity in stride as well when he suffered a broken nose on a bad-hop grounder and encountered his first prolonged slump. Langston pitched 225 innings with 204 strikeouts, becoming the first rookie pitcher in almost 30 years to lead the league in this department. His record of 17–10 was an all-time high for Mariner pitchers. After a slow start, Bradley went on to hit .301, including seven straight hits in a September spurt, and he gave the Mariners good speed, both on the bases and in the outfield.

To these fine rookie performances were added some better than average ones by veterans Jack Perconte (.294 with 93 runs scored and 29 stolen bases), Al Cowens (.277 with 78 RBIs), and Jim Beattie (12–16 and a 3.41 ERA). The Mariners won 74 games, an improvement of 14 over 1983, but the needs were still obvious. There were no reliable starters after Langston and Beattie, the bullpen lacked a real stopper, and the whole staff was wild, with 619 walks. The expected power from Gorman Thomas did not materialize because of a rotator cuff tear that ended the slugger's season after a mere 35 games. For the eighth consecutive season the M's were outhomered in the Kingdome. While the manager was hardly to blame, Crandall was fired and coach Chuck Cottier was appointed interim manager on September 1. The team had a winning month, due mostly to rookie performances, though Cottier's relaxed style may have been a club-house relief from Crandall's more authoritarian approach.

Because the team did finish strongly, Cottier was given a chance to continue as manager. The youthfulness of the starting lineup boosted the optimism of Mariner fans. With Thomas healthy, and some improved play from Spike Owen, Dave Henderson, and Jim Presley (another rookie in 1984), the stars of 1984 would have some support. On the mound Mike Moore and Matt Young were being looked to for further evidence of their vaunted skills. Both had pitched well at times in 1984. Hal Keller's baseball acumen was receiving praise from all quarters. Finally, the farm system was producing, but the keys, Keller thought, would be pitching and defense. The walks, in particular, had to be cut down. For a change, there was little trading over the off-season. "See It Happen" was the slogan the management chose for 1985.

The fans didn't see "it" happen in 1985, but they did see some exciting baseball. On the way to a 74–88 record (the same as in 1984), the M's exploded offensively, outhomering their opposition in the Kingdome at last and amassing their all-time high for home runs (171). Leading the way was Gorman Thomas, the A.L. Comeback Player of the Year, with 32, still the Mariner record. Jim Presley and Phil Bradley hit 28 and 26 respectively, while Alvin Davis contributed 18. The Mariners had expected figures like that from Presley and Davis, but Bradley's power was a surprise. He was without a homer in 322 at bats in 1984. Both run production and fielding percentage were improved, but Keller's worry about pitching was justified. From his 17–10 mark in 1984, Langston fell to 7–14 as his ERA ballooned to 5.47. He missed parts of the season with several injuries including an elbow injury that put him on the 21-day disabled list. Jim Beattie spent most of his season on the disabled list, and Matt Young lost 19 games. The team ERA reached 4.68, reverting to the futility of earlier years. Instead of reducing walks, the pitchers gave up a team-record 637 while setting another record of 61 wild pitches. The bright spot was the perfor-mance of Mike Moore: 17–10, a 3.46 ERA, 247 innings pitched, and 14 complete games, the latter figure attesting to his great stamina. It was not uncommon for Moore to pitch in the later innings as if he were just warmed up. Often his control would be sharper, too, than in the early innings. It was a pattern that fans would come to expect if Moore managed to survive the middle innings.

The Mariners saw signs in 1985 that public support for the team was picking up. They drew 1,128,696 fans, an increase of a quarter million over 1984. It was only the third time in nine years that atten-dance had topped one million. The bright young stars—Davis, Bradley, Presley, Langston, and Moore—were convincing fans that the Mariners were pointed in the right direction, though off the field the M's management continued to undermine the team's popularity. As the 1985 season wound down, Hal Keller, who had received much of the credit for the development of the team, was let go as the general manager and vice president for baseball operations. A holdover from Dan O'Brien's tenure, Keller was a good "baseball man," but his departure opened the door for President Chuck Armstrong's own man, Dick Balderson, the young director of player development in the Kansas City organization. Balderson was named to replace Keller on October 8.

Meanwhile, George Argyros was getting plenty of public attention, and it did nothing to win support for the Mariners. Argyros publicly warred with King County Commissioner Randy Revelle and members of the county council. Dissatisfied with the terms of his lease and his share of concessions and parking at the Kingdome, he provoked the council to renegotiate the lease, resulting in a new agreement in October that allowed Argyros to remove the team from Seattle or sell the team if the Mariners failed to draw 2.8 million fans during any two-year period. The County, if this "escape" clause was triggered, could require Argyros to offer the team for sale to local buyers during a 120-day period. Furthermore, as part of the general terms of the new lease, Argyros was required to offer for sale a minority interest in the club to a qualified local buyer, someone who would have first option to buy the club outright if Argyros ever chose to sell. The key concern for Revelle and the council members was that any Mariner owner would be committed to keeping the team in Seattle, thus stipulating a local buyer.

Argyros's commitment had become suspect. At first heralded as a savior of Seattle baseball, Argyros had not opened his pursestrings very wide since purchasing the team in 1981. The player payroll was among the lowest in the major leagues. Argyros continued to live in California, a place scorned by Seattle natives and feared as an unhealthy trendsetter in urban sprawl. He had alienated some fans when he brazenly hosted fellow Californian Richard Nixon in his private "box" at the Kingdome. His most grievous sin, though, was the aforementioned declaration that he could do anything he wanted with the M's because he owned the team, breaking a taboo among baseball owners, to avoid flaunting what is obvious on one level—the fact of legal ownership—when baseball's popularity depends so much on the perception of its continuance as a public trust. It was a public relations gaffe of great proportion in Seattle and more than likely a contributing factor in the low attendance of 1983 and 1984.

The King County Council had wanted a further stipulation in the escape clause, that it could be activated only if the Mariners played .500 ball. After nine years, public patience was wearing thin. The Mariners did have some more young players ready to move up from the minors, including two—Danny Tartabull and Harold Reynolds— at second base, where scrappy Jack Perconte, a fan favorite, was doggedly holding on. Dave Valle had not yet shown he was ready to start at catcher, so Balderson engineered his first trade: reliever Ed Vande Berg for Dodger catcher Steve Yeager. With Presley having won the third base job and starting pitching still a weakness, Balderson then swapped Darnell Coles to Detroit for pitcher Rich Monteleone. Before the 1986 season began, the M's added Milt Wilcox, Pete Ladd, and Jerry Reed to the pitching staff, counting on these veterans to provide needed experience. Of the new acquisitions, only Jerry Reed was to show any staying power with the M's. Wilcox was released during the season and, when Jim Beattie's injured shoulder sidelined him for good, the pitching staff was unable to win consistently. Neither Langston nor Moore had a winning record in 1986, though Langston posted a league-leading 245 strikeouts in 239⅓ innings, and Moore pitched 266 innings with 11 complete games and three other nine-inning stints. Matt Young proved relatively effective in the bullpen after disappointing efforts as a starter, adding 13 saves to an 8–6 record. The staff ERA of 4.65 was barely better than the year before. In all, the M's won only 67 games.

Both offense and defense fell off for the M's in 1986, some of the decline attributable to the youth of the team. Phil Bradley had another slow start—a familiar pattern now—but rebounded to hit .310. Jim Presley hit 27 homers with 107 RBIs but struck out 172 times, as pitchers began to exploit his weakness for chasing breaking pitches on the outside corner. As a club, the M's set an A.L. record striking out 1148 times and a major league mark on April 29 when they whiffed 20 times against Roger Clemens. (They improved the next day, striking out a mere 16 times.) Alvin Davis played in only 135 games and saw his average drop to .271, a career low. One year after belting 32 homers, Gorman Thomas was released, as was Jack Perconte. Harold Reynolds became the starter at second base, with Tartabull shifted permanently to the outfield. Recalled from the minors in May to replace the popular Perconte, Reynolds struggled at the plate for weeks while the fans booed. Perseverance paid off and before long everyone was cheering the youngster's fielding and base-stealing exploits. He ended the season with 30 stolen bases and a .222 batting average. In the outfield Tartabull had some expected difficulties, but at the plate he excelled, hitting 25 homers and knocking in 96 runs.

The Mariners also got remarkable offense from Ken Phelps, who in 344 at bats had 24 homers and 64 RBIs. While the team batting average was a low .253, the fielding average was even more disappointing at .975. The young M's committed a team-record 156 errors, and yet were able to tally 191 double plays and two triple plays. In nearly all facets of play, the M's were inconsistent. Matters might have been even worse were it not for a managerial change in May. Chuck Cottier was fired after a 9–19 start, and following a 0–1 interim stewardship by Marty Martinez, Dick Williams took over the ballclub. Though the team was 58–75 under Williams, they played over .500 baseball in a two-month stretch, lending credence to earlier pronouncements that the Mariners might win the A.L. West if Dick Williams were the manager.

One of the more significant occurrences during the season was an August trade with the Red Sox that sent Spike Owen and Dave Henderson to Boston in exchange for Rey Quinones, Mike Trujillo, Mike Brown, and a player to be named later (John Christensen). Owen had been the starting shortstop since the ax fell on Lachemann and Perry in June of 1983. While not a gifted player, Owen was spunky and reliable; he turned out to be a good late-season asset for the Red Sox in their successful pennant drive. Henderson *was* a gifted player with proven defensive skills in center field, going back on fly balls with confidence and grace, but his hitting was amazingly streaky. He could go weeks without a hit and then "go on a tear." Fate cast him as the improbable hero of Boston's comeback against the Angels in the A.L. playoff series when he hit a lead-reversing home run in the ninth and later the game-winning sacrifice fly in the fifth game, just as the Red Sox were about to lose the series, four games to one. Though the Mariners desperately needed pitching, the key figure for them was Rey Quinones, a thoroughly talented shortstop who could make the most difficult of plays. Buoyed by the hope of having their best-ever double-play combination, the M's overlooked some irregularities in Quinones' temperament and banked on his superior range. The trade clearly reversed the direction Hal Keller had taken, ousting two regulars, and giving Dick Williams the slick-fielding shortstop he admired.

The winter baseball meetings produced two additional trades, one the most controversial in Mariner's history. Balderson, acting on his inside knowledge of the Kansas City organization, traded for righthanded pitchers Scott Bankhead and Steve Shields, as well as outfielder Mike Kingery. He gave up minor league pitcher Rich Luecken and, shockingly, rising star Danny Tartabull. Tartabull's hard-hitting style had appeared to make him an "untouchable" on the M's roster. At the close of the season, though, he reportedly refused to acquiesce to the Mariners' request that he play winter ball to improve his defensive skills in the outfield. Whether this refusal was part of a larger "attitude" problem is unclear. More certain was that Bankhead, the key figure in the M's plans, had not yet proven his worth as a major league pitcher, having been 8–9 in 24 games with a 4.61 ERA for Kansas City. The other deal, made the same day, sent Matt Young to the Dodgers for lefthander Dennis Powell and infielder Mike Watters. Another pair of promising players developed in the M's system had departed, and the message was unambiguous: all of the Mariners were expendable.

With Balderson ready to deal and Williams ready to pilot his first full season, the players were well aware that 1987 was not going to be a relaxing season. The Mariners appeared to have greater competition for pitching spots on the roster, and the team would have to scrap to make up for the offense lost in the Tartabull deal. Defense, a Williams' benchmark, looked improved. Team speed was an asset and Williams would likely be flashing the steal sign often. Williams, who had a contract through the 1988 season, was in the spotlight. Seattle fans were eager to see more of the managerial skills that had guided three different teams to pennants.

For a change, the M's began the season well, playing above .500 in each of the first two months, with a composite record of 26–23 at the end of May. When Bankhead beat Toronto 2–0 on June 1 for his sixth win against three losses, the M's were four games above .500 and looking good. Langston was 6–4 and showing his prowess striking out batters, as 14 Blue Jays saw on May 24. Harold Reynolds was on his way to an All-Star selection, starring in the field, at bat, and on the bases. The only real disappointment was Mike Moore, who was 2–6 at the end of May (he ended the season at 7–19). The M's were running on the bases, working on a season total of 172 steals, only two short of league-leading Milwaukee. Their June record dipped slightly, 13–14, leaving them two games to the good on July 1. Called up from Calgary on May 21, lefthander Lee Guetterman stood at 8–1 on July 12. Seattle fans should have known the air would escape the balloon. On July 1 Bankhead was placed on the disabled list because of tendinitis in his right shoulder, and though activated two weeks later, he wasn't fully recovered and was dropped from the starting rotation. (He got another chance to start in September and won two games, but missed the last week and a half of the season, followed by shoulder surgery on October 15.) Langston was the only starter with a winning record in July and August—5–4—as the team dropped off to a 22–37 mark including a six-game losing streak in mid-August that steered the M's below the equator for the rest of the season. Balderson attempted to get the team some offensive support when he traded for Gary Mathews on July 10, but the righthanded designated hitter was clearly winding up his career.

In September the Mariners resurged, going 17–14 and winning eight of their last 10. Billy Wilkinson pitched well in relief at season's end, but Langston fell one game shy of winning 20. Young outfielder Mickey Brantley finished strongly, hitting .368 with seven homers and 23 RBIs in September. With the late-season improvement, the Mariners finished with their best record ever, 78–84, and only seven games behind the eventual World Champion Twins. Reynolds tallied 60 stolen bases to lead the league and Phil Bradley stole 40. The team batting average rose to .272 with both Bradley and Alvin Davis only a few points below .300. David led the team in homers and RBIs with 29 and 100, while Ken Phelps hit 27 homers in only 332 at bats and Presley, 24, after a slow start. Pitching and defense improved as a Williams' team was expected to do. Mariner pitchers allowed the fewest walks in the league, 140 fewer than the team high two years earlier. In the field, the M's committed a team-low 122 errors, 34 fewer than in 1986. Had Bankhead remained healthy and Mike Moore pitched only slightly closer to his ability, the M's would have been serious contenders in their division.

By now, though, Seattle fans had learned to temper their optimism, and the Mariners' management soon demonstrated that such caution was prudent. First of all, Dick Williams suggested that he would not manage beyond the 1988 season, the last year of his contract. Then, in December, facing the prospect of losing Phil Bradley through free agency, the M's traded him away with minor league pitcher Tim Fortugno to the Phillies for Glenn Wilson, Mike Jackson, and minor leaguer Dave Brundage. Bradley evinced little enthusiasm about playing in Seattle, appearing indifferent to the encouragement of fans. Despite good offensive and defensive skills, he was not the RBI producer the Mariners sought and was expendable, in the M's view, because of Mickey Brantley's maturity. Wilson was thought to be a more reliable RBI man, though he had slumped during the recent season. As for Jackson, he was reputed to have vast potential as a power pitcher, a 3–10 record in 1987 notwithstanding. In the public view, the Bradley trade was another indication that George Argyros did not want to pay high salaries to retain established players and was set on keeping payroll costs at the bottom of the major leagues. Other trades in the off-season did not change this view. From the Yankees came pitcher Steve Trout and outfielder Henry Cotto in return for pitchers Lee Guetterman, Clay Parker, and Wade Taylor. Few people thought that Guetterman could repeat his success of the past season, and Trout, whose high salary the Yankees would subsidize in 1988, was to be reunited with Billy Connors, the pitching coach who had shepherded him through his most successful season. The Mariners also swapped pitcher Mike Morgan for the Orioles' Ken Dixon, giving up on the inconsistent but talented Morgan.

With considerable doubts about the pitching staff (Bankhead, most notably, was still on the disabled list after his surgery), the Mariners opened the season with a loss at home against the soon-to-be-marvelous A's and, after three more games, lost sight of .500 for the rest of the season. The trades proved largely inconsequential. Dixon had been released with a sore arm before the season began. Trout had bewildering streaks of wildness during a 4–7 season (7.83 ERA), committing, for example, five balks and throwing four wild pitches in his first five games. He also spent two extended periods on the disabled list. Glenn Wilson started horrendously and was traded to Pittsburgh for Darnell Coles in July. Only Henry Cotto played to expectations, toting a .259 batting average as the regular center fielder. The established stars, Davis and Langston, had solid but unspectacular years. Davis again hit .295 and his 69 RBIs were the best on the club. Langston had four straight wins in September to compensate for a mid-season slump and led the staff in wins (15), innings pitched (231⅓), strikeouts (285), and ERA (3.34). Thanks to Langston, rookie right hander Erik Hanson, and the puzzling Mike Moore, the M's ended the season with a 14–13 record in September, but earlier deficiencies had scuttled the season. The Mariners lost 93 games and again drew just over a million fans.

The losses piling up, Dick Williams had been fired in June, the day after Langston lost a complete game in Kansas City and had words with his manager. Not a manager known for rapport with his players, Williams' parting shot was to call Langston "gutless," but it was probably his diminishing interest in dealing with young players, in general, that brought his major league managing to an end. Although he had resisted making his retirement at the end of the year official, players reported that he had appeared less absorbed by the daily routine of managing. Despite the 23–33 mark compiled by the M's during this partial season, Williams' winning percentage of .453 surpassed those of all his predecessors and that of his successor for the rest of that season, Jimmy Snyder. Under Snyder's patient eye, the more relaxed M's showed promise in September, but neither manager was able to field a cohesive team. Jim Presley, playing most of the season with a sore back, hit only .230 with 14 homers. Rey Quinones displayed his erratic temperament and was suspended for several days when he left the team without permission to attend the funeral of his wife's grandfather in Puerto Rico. He slumped badly in the last month of the season and confounded everyone with fielding lapses that marred otherwise brilliant play.

Two mid-season acquisitions by Dick Balderson did add some righthanded power. On June 1 Steve Balboni was signed as a free agent after he had been released by Kansas City; in only 97 games he hit 21 homers and made pitching "around" Alvin Davis less attractive. A trade with New York in July brought outfielder Jay Buhner and two minor leaguers in exchange for Ken Phelps. Buhner, in addition to speed and a good arm, had power for an asset (13 homers in 85 games for the M's), but also a penchant for striking out (93 times). These trades, along with the Wilson-for-Coles deal, turned out to be Balderson's parting gifts, for in late July he was replaced by Woody Woodward, who had been fired from a similar position by the Phillies earlier in the season. Woodward expressed a "wait and see" attitude about changes, but the wait was short. He knew that he had been hired to bring results and he already had some ideas.

So it was in August that Woodward attempted to sneak Mike Moore through waivers after the trading deadline, apparently to make a deal for the talented but disappointing righthander, who would be a free agent at the end of the season. The A's, wary of the Twins' interest in Moore, blocked the move, forcing the M's to withdraw Moore's name. Moore went on to pitch strongly, matching Langston in complete games (9) and shutouts (3) while compiling a 3.78 ERA that belied his 9–15 record. Fan opinion was divided on how high the Mariners should bid to retain Moore's services. 1988 was his third consecutive losing season, and in seven seasons his overall record was 66–96, not in itself a great claim for a million-dollar-a-year contract. Yet if the Mariners didn't sign Moore, they would receive only a draft choice as compensation for a pitcher who ranged between 230 and 279 innings for five consecutive seasons. Would George Argyros open his wallet and take the risk on Moore being a late bloomer who, among other things, would learn to pitch inside on batters? Unfortunately, as with Langston, Moore's temperament was often under question. While Williams had criticized Langston's will to win, Moore's problem appeared to be psychological, of feeling comfortable on the mound. Once in his rhythm, Moore could appear unhittable as the innings progressed. Some games he never found a comfortable rhythm.

Before deciding about Moore, the M's made yet another managerial change, determining that Snyder would not return in 1989. After a month's search, Jim Lefebvre was named in November as the M's eighth manager (not including Marty Martinez who guided the club for a single game in 1986). Considered to be the brightest managerial prospect around, Lefebvre was an attractive alternative to a "recycled" veteran, and his enthusiasm for the challenge in Seattle received rave reviews locally. He openly expressed his hopes for Mike Moore remaining in Seattle, but the A's soon afterward made a millionaire out of the righthander. With Moore gone, the M's turned their attention to affordable free agents and to Mark Langston, potentially a free agent at the end of the 1989 season. The affordable free agents they signed were Jeffrey Leonard and Tom Niedenfuer at $800,000 apiece, neither of whom was coming off a great season, though Niedenfuer had saved 18 games for the hapless Orioles. The doubts about these veterans and about signing Langston carried over to spring training, but something marvelous happened that made Seattle baseball exciting once more.

In June 1987, the Mariners had made Ken Griffey, Jr., the first choice in the draft. Reports were that the 17-year-old "couldn't miss" as a major league prospect, and a fine year in Bellingham (.320, 14 homers, and 40 RBIs in 53 games) corroborated those opinions. In 1988 Griffey started at San Bernardino (A level) and was leading the league in several offensive categories when he suffered a back sprain in early June. After coming off the disabled list on August 15, he was immediately promoted to Vermont (AA) where he finished the year hitting .279 in 17 games. With so little minor league experience, Griffey was thought to be still a year or two away from the major leagues, but given the chance to show his talents as a non-roster player in spring training, he allowed the M's little choice about his place on the team. Batting over .400 for much of the Cactus League season and showing great poise in the field, he began his major league career in Oakland on April 3 and doubled in his first at bat. In his first two home games back at the Kingdome he hit homers and the Seattle Mariners suddenly had their best gate attraction ever. On April 26 against the visiting Blue Jays, he played an astounding game in which he went 4 for 4, including the game-winning homer, and made a spectacular running catch that held the lead. Other early-season marvels included a dramatic three-run homer to reverse a lead and beat the Yankees before 40,563 Kingdome fans, a whirling throw from deep center field to cut down a startled Lou Whitaker at third base attempting to advance after a great Griffey catch, and a heads-up dash home with the winning run when a pitcher and a catcher left the plate unprotected. Only a broken finger in July appeared to stand in the way of a Rookie-of-the-Year season.

As Griffey was becoming a poster boy and a candy bar bearing his name and image was selling out in Seattle stores, the Mariners ended speculation about Mark Langston. On May 26, after a bizarre final offer of a three-year $7.1 million contract made over the phone to Langston during a game in Boston, the lefthander was traded to the Expos for pitchers Randy Johnson, Brian Holman, and Gene Harris. (On July 31 the Expos picked pitcher Mike Campbell from the Calgary roster to complete the deal.) Montreal's move was daring as

Langston was unlikely to sign a contract until he had tested his market value as a free agent. The M's, having lost Mike Moore in this manner, were unwilling to take the risk with Langston.

At season's end the Mariners could feel vindicated in making the Langston deal. After a fast start with the Expos, the lefthander won only two of his last eight starts, ending his National League season at 12–9 and, more important, becoming a free agent. Though the three pitchers received from Montreal finished with a combined 16–23 record, promise of better years to come showed, particularly in the strong late-season performance of Brian Holman, who lowered his ERA to 3.44. The Mariners' starting rotation, the youngest in the American League, was led by veteran Scott Bankhead, who, healthy at last, pitched over 200 innings for the first time as he put together a 14–6 record and a 3.34 ERA. Erik Hanson again pitched brilliantly in September, improving his poor early-season record to 9–5 and a 3.18 ERA. In the bullpen, Mike Schooler set a team record with 33 saves. The M's played .500 ball in September, as they did well into July, but a 12-game losing streak in August—a month in which the M's have never had a winning record—proved fatal to hopes of their first winning season. Their season mark of 73–89 was only five wins better than their disappointing 1988 season.

The major failing of the 1989 Mariners was in scoring runs in the clutch, as they lost 28 of 50 one-run games and nine games in which they had the lead after seven innings. Lefebvre used more than 110 different lineups to find the right combination of players, but none was especially successful. Jeffrey Leonard's career year of 24 homers and 93 RBIs would have been even better had he not slumped severely after the All-Star break. Early in the season Alvin Davis benefitted from having Leonard hit behind him in the lineup, and, in addition to driving in 95 runs, Davis managed to hit .305, his first time over .300. However, he dropped over 30 points in the last month and a half and drew over 100 walks again as opponents began to pitch "around" him and ply Leonard with breaking pitches. Another .300 hitter (exactly that) was Harold Reynolds, who led the team with 87 runs scored. While Ken Griffey's post-injury performance dropped off at the plate—he batted .264 overall with 16 home runs and 61 RBIs in 127 games—along with Jay Buhner and Greg Briley he demonstrated that the Mariners had great talent in the outfield. The young outfielders could look forward to playing a complete season together in 1990, barring injuries like those that limited their playing time in 1989. Their presence in 1989—particularly Griffey's—was the major reason for the second-highest attendance mark for the M's in 13 seasons—1,298,456.

The future of major league baseball in Seattle looks brighter at the end of 13 seasons than it has for several years, even though a winning season remains elusive. After initial fears that yet another baseball team was slipping away, fans have welcomed the 1989 sale of the Mariners and the departure of George Argyros. The new owners have pledged to keep the team in Seattle, and the American League has required that the pledge be in writing. The managing partner, Jeff Smulyan, has taken up residence in the Seattle area and has expressed a willingness to include an additional local buyer in the club ownership. Local ownership remains an important factor for baseball's success in a city where fears of outsiders rank ahead of volcanic eruptions and earthquakes. Will the ownership have the financial resources and clear resolve to make the M's a stable franchise? The Mariners' lease of the Kingdome expires in 1996, but in the interim the new owners will probably be seeking some revenue enhancements and improvements in the Kingdome operation. To avoid repeating the mistakes of past owners, though, the Mariners' new bosses will need to make improved public relations a top priority.

Projections of population growth in the Puget Sound area through the year 2010 are high. In polls of corporate executives, the desirability of locating businesses in Seattle has recently risen to near the top among all U.S. cities. The market for major league baseball will probably increase proportionally, but much will depend upon the Mariners' ability to obtain and retain young stars as gate attractions and the team's on-the-field performance. The salary base will have to be expanded considerably. As for the chances for construction of a more attractive facility for Seattle baseball, voters will not likely support funding for such a project until the image of the Mariners has improved. If and when a new stadium is built, it will probably have a retractable roof and, despite objections, artificial turf.

And when will the Mariners field a contending team? It has been a long wait, and the Seattle fans can expect some additional obstacles, but the 1990s will likely bring several winning seasons at least to the shores of Puget Sound. How sweet it will be!

Notes

1. Even the position of general manager has not been continuous for the Mariners. Dick Vertlieb was the first to hold the title, but Lou Gorman, as director of baseball operations, was the real GM in the sense of "baseball architect." When Vertlieb was replaced by Kip Horsburgh, Gorman's importance to the club increased even if his titles didn't. Dan O'Brien, appointed club president in 1979, subsequently minimized Gorman's power. The general manager's position became a more traditional one with the ascension of Hal Keller in 1983. He has been followed in that position by Dick Balderson and

Woody Woodward. In this chapter, Lou Gorman will be identified as a general manager in this traditional sense.

2. The sale was in cash. During the negotiations, one of the prospective owners remarked, "This isn't a Visa transaction."

3. Statistics in this chapter are taken largely from the press guides of the Seattle Mariners, but also from the Macmillan *Baseball Encyclopedia*, the *Seattle Post-Intelligencer*, and the *Seattle Times*.

Annotated Bibliography

Hinz, Bob. *Seattle Mariners*. Mankato, Minn.: Creative Education Publishing Company, 1982. 48 pp.

When the Mariners finally establish their hold on the attention of Northwest baseball fans, youngsters and oldsters (or anyone with a fourth-grade reading level) will be able to turn to this small booklet for a rosy look at the early years of the Seattle franchise. Hinz provides an altogether uninspired juvenile history of Mariners baseball through the first five seasons.

James, Bill. *The Bill James Baseball Abstract 1986*. New York: Ballantine Books (Random House Publishers), 1986 ("Seattle Mariners" on pp. 97–103).

This piece is vintage Bill James, the best and most detailed look at the Seattle Mariners by baseball's original and most famous SABRmetrician. James discusses Seattle's policies and penchant from bringing talented young players to the majors and then losing them to bad trades which only enhance rosters of American League and National League rivals. Also featured in this essay is a unique and revealing *Project Scoresheet* approach to Mariners' batting and pitching statistics for the 1985 season.

Johnson, D. Grant. *The Seattle Mariners Story*. Seattle, Wash.: Sunrise Publications, 1977.

Published before the close of the 1977 season, this little paperback resembles a low-budget media guide, containing profiles of first-year Mariners and their assorted team officials, as well as statistics for the first half of the season. This volume was obviously rushed into print to capture a market created by first-year Mariner enthusiasm. Also included is a preliminary section on the brief history and quick departure of the 1969 Seattle Pilots (a.k.a. Milwaukee Brewers).

Mungo, Raymond. *Confessions from Left Field*. New York: E.P. Dutton Company, 1983.

Subtitled "A Baseball Pilgrimage," this uneven book contains a maverick fan's personal look at the 1981 Mariners and ex-Manager Maury Wills as part of the larger baseball travelogue. Mungo chronicles the frustration of Seattle fans, though not all of them have turned (as the author apparently has) to gin-and-tonics or Thai sticks for relief from the horrors of Seattle baseball.

Ringolsby, Tracy. "Shipwrecked in Seattle." In *Sport Magazine* LXXV (March 1984): 61–71.

As a former beat writer covering the M's for the *Seattle Post-Intelligencer*, Ringolsby can claim to have viewed the team's numerous problems firsthand. This informative essay is perhaps the best account yet given of the M's disastrous front office policies and of the frustrating formative years experienced by baseball's least successful expansion franchise.

Year-by-Year Standings and Season Summaries

Year	Pos.	Record	Pct.	GB	Manager	Player	BA	Player	HR	Player	W-L	ERA
1977	6th	64–98	.395	38.0	Johnson	Stanton	.275	Stanton	27	Abbott	12–13	4.46
1978	7th	56–104	.350	35.0	Johnson	Roberts	.301	Roberts	22	Romo	11–7	3.69
1979	6th	67–95	.414	21.0	Johnson	Bochte	.319	Horton	29	Parrott	14–12	3.77
1980	7th	59–103	.364	38.0	Johnson / Wills	Bochte	.300	Paciorek	15	Abbott	12–12	4.10
1981	6th	21–36	.368	14.5	Wills / Lachemann	Paciorek	.326	Zisk	16	Bannister	9–8	4.46
1981*	5th	23–29	.442	6.5								
	6th	44–65	.404	20.0								
1982	4th	76–86	.469	17.0	Lachemann	Bochte	.297	Zisk	21	Caudill	12–8	2.35
1983	7th	60–102	.370	39.0	Lachemann / Crandall	S. Henderson	.294	Putnam	19	Young	11–15	3.27
1984	5th	74–88	.457	10.0	Crandall / Cottier	Perconte	.294	Davis	27	Langston	17–10	3.40
1985	6th	74–88	.457	17.0	Cottier	P. Bradley	.300	G. Thomas	32	Moore	17–10	3.46
1986	7th	67–95	.414	25.0	Cottier / Williams	P. Bradley	.310	Presley	27	Langston	12–14	4.85
1987	4th	78–84	.481	7.0	Williams	P. Bradley	.297	Davis	29	Langston	19–13	3.84
1988	7th	68–93	.422	35.5	Williams / Snyder	Davis	.295	Balboni	21	Langston	15–11	3.34
1989	6th	73–89	.451	26.0	Lefebvre	Davis	.305	Leonard	24	Bankhead	14–6	3.34
1990	5th	77–85	.475	26.0	Lefebvre	E. Martinez	.302	Griffey	22	Hanson	18–9	3.24
1991	5th	83–79	.512	12.0	Lefebvre	Griffey	.327	Buhner	27	Holman	13–14	3.69
1992	7th	64–98	.395	32.0	Plummer	E. Martinez	.343	Griffey	27	Fleming	17–10	3.39

*Split Season Totals (Players' Union Strike).

All-Time Mariners Career and Season Records

Career Batting Leaders (1977–1992)

Games Played	Alvin Davis	1,166
At Bats	Alvin Davis	4,136
Runs Scored	Alvin Davis	563
Hits	Alvin Davis	1,163
Batting Average	Edgar Martinez	.311
Home Runs	Alvin Davis	160
Run Batted In	Alvin Davis	667
Stolen Bases	Julio Cruz	290
Sacrifice Hits	Julio Cruz	45
Strikeouts	Jim Presley	713

Career Pitching Leaders (1977–1992)

Innings Pitched	Mike Moore	1,456.0
Earned Run Average	Bryan Clark	3.67
Wins	Mark Langston	74
Losses	Mike Moore	96
Winning Pct.	Mark Langston	.524
Strikeouts	Mark Langston	1,078
Walks	Mark Langston	575
Games	Ed Vande Berg	272
Shutouts	Mike Moore	9
Saves	Bill Caudill	52
Games Started	Mike Moore	217
Complete Games	Mike Moore	56
Hit Batsmen	Mike Moore	29
Wild Pitches	Mike Moore	42

Single-Season Batting Records (1977–1992)

Batting Average (500 ABs)	Edgar Martinez	.343	1992
Home Runs	Gorman Thomas	32	1985
Home Runs (lefthanded)	Alvin Davis	29	1987
Runs Batted In	Alvin Davis	116	1984
Hits	Phil Bradley	192	1985
Singles	Jack Perconte	152	1984
Doubles	Al Cowens	39	1982
Triples	Harold Reynolds	11	1988
Slugging Percentage	Leon Roberts	.515	1978
Extra Base Hits	Alvin Davis	68	1987
Game-Winning RBIs	Tom Paciorek	13	1982
	Alvin Davis	13	1984
	Jim Presley	13	1986
Sacrifices	Craig Reynolds	15	1978
	Larry Milbourne	15	1980
Stolen Bases	Harold Reynolds	60	1987
Pinch Hits	Larry Milbourne	12	1979
Strikeouts	Jim Presley	172	1986
Total Bases	Phil Bradley	319	1985
Hitting Streak	Dan Meyer	21	1979
	Richie Zisk	21	1982

All-Time Mariners Career and Season Records *(continued)*

Grand Slam Home Runs	Leon Roberts	2	1978
	Bob Stinson	2	1978
	Willie Horton	2	1979
	Dan Meyer	2	1979
	Alvin Davis	2	1984
	Jim Presley	2	1986
	Danny Tartabull	2	1986
On-Base Percentage	Alvin Davis	.424	1989
Hit by Pitch	Phil Bradley	12	1985
Single-Season Pitching Records (1977–1992)			
ERA (starter)	Matt Young	3.27	1983
ERA (reliever)	Bill Caudill	2.35	1982
Wins	Mark Langston	19	1987
Losses	Matt Young	19	1985
	Mike Moore	19	1987
Winning Pct. (10 decisions)	Scott Bankhead	.700 (14–6)	1989
Strikeouts	Mark Langston	262	1987
Walks	Randy Johnson	152	1991
Saves	Mike Schooler	33	1989
Games	Ed Vande Berg	78	1982
Complete Games	Mike Moore	14	1985
	Mark Langston	14	1987
Games Started	Mike Moore	37	1986
Shutouts	Floyd Bannister	3	1982
	Mark Langston	3	1987,1988
	Mike Moore	3	1988
Innings Pitched	Mark Langston	272.0	1987
Home Runs Allowed	Scott Bankhead	35	1987
Consecutive Games Won (season)	Glenn Abbott	7	1977
	Mark Langston	7	1984
	Roy Thomas	7	1985
Consecutive Games Lost (season)	Mike Parrott	16	1980
Consecutive Games Lost (overall)	Mike Parrott	18	1980–81
Consecutive Batters Retired	John Montague	33	1977
Wild Pitches	Mike Morgan	11	1987
Balks	Rod Scurry	11	1988

11
Seattle Pilots-Milwaukee Brewers
The Bombers, The Bangers, and The Burners
PAUL D. ADOMITES

The Milwaukee Brewers opened their doors for business in 1970, but the story of their birth actually began five years earlier, and even includes a one-year stopover in Seattle.

The story of the Brewers is a story of a city that refused to be minor league again. The Braves spent 13 years between Boston and Atlanta, a 13-year reign that began impossibly well. In their first eight years, they finished third once, second five times, won two pennants, and took a thrilling World Series victory from the Yankees (who had called Milwaukee "bush"). But after a fourth, sixth, and two fifth-place finishes, the Braves announced in October of 1964 that they were pulling up stakes, headed for the seemingly greener pastures of Atlanta. The city of Milwaukee was aghast. Hadn't they set the record for N.L. attendance with over two million fans in 1954, and averaged more than a million and a half fans a season overall? Legal measures to keep the Braves in Milwaukee failed, including one in which the National League was represented by an astute young lawyer named Bowie Kuhn.

With all apparent legal avenues closed, early in 1965 four leading citizens of Milwaukee founded Teams, Incorporated (later changed to Milwaukee Brewers Baseball Club, Inc.) with the sole purpose of retrieving major league status. The men involved were Edmund B. Fitzgerald, local businessman and former director of the Braves; Robert A. Uihlein, Jr., president of Schlitz Brewing; Allen "Bud" Selig, automobile executive; and Jack Winter, executive of a local clothing firm. Selig was named president. They started out with a bang: buying out County Stadium for the Opening Day of the Braves lame-duck season, they called it "Stand Up for Milwaukee Day." More than 35,000 tickets were sold, and after the Braves were paid expenses, the organization had a profit of $13,000 to use in seeking a new baseball team for Beertown.

They worked hard: they thought they won the National League expansion franchise that was awarded to Montreal; they thought they had a good shot for an A.L. expansion team; and they were close to taking the White Sox from Chicago. In fact, after a 1967 exhibition game between the Sox and Minnesota Twins drew over 50,000 in Milwaukee, Sox owner Arthur Allyn scheduled 10 games there for 1968, one with each A.L. opponent, plus an exhibition game with the Cubs. The fans turned out: the games drew over 265,000, an average of almost 30,000 per game. Chicago's biggest A.L. crowd that same year was 21,853. Milwaukee fans desperately wanted a team. *The Sporting News,* May 15, 1968 reported: "Tornado warnings and a 90% probability of rain failed to prevent 23,510 baseball-starved fans from attending the White Sox first-ever game in Milwaukee." That game occurred two days after the National League voted expansion teams to Montreal and San Diego. In 1969 11 games played in Milwaukee drew 196,684 for the White Sox; the other 70 in Comiskey Park drew only 392,682. It looked good for the Milwaukee fans to land the Sox.

There was something special about the attitude of the Milwaukeeans. All along, the men behind the hopeful team were committed to fiscal good sense—the kind that would not just land a team, but keep a team. Burned by the irreputable behavior of absentee Braves ownership, they promised to get and run a team with the people of the city. *The Sporting News* in 1967 reported that "if the Milwaukee Brewers Baseball Club, Inc., is successful in its bid for a major league baseball franchise, it will have one of the most lucrative radio-television contracts in baseball." Schlitz Brewing had a $1.1 million a year sponsorship on the table, ready to be picked up. The offer had originally been made as an incentive for the Braves to stay. In addition, the city was offering what amounted to no stadium rent for 25 years.

But when Arthur Allyn sold his Sox ownership to his brother John, the new president nixed the deal, renewed his club's commitment to Chicago, and announced they wouldn't be playing any more games in Milwaukee, either. For 1969 the American League sought new land for expansion, but Milwaukee lost out again: the A.L. choices were Seattle and Kansas City, the latter having recently been vacated by Charlie Finley's A's.

But the Seattle Pilots never really got started. Their park, the appropriately named Sicks Stadium, could hold only 25,420 fans. The largest crowd that ever showed up still left 3,500 empty seats. On the field the Pilots, with their bizarre caps and uniforms, weren't doing much to help. The Pilots also began life with a lineup loaded with retreads: Don Mincher, Ray Oyler, Jerry McNertney, and John Kennedy. There were bright spots. Mike Marshall was beginning a great career, although Seattle saw him as a starter, not a reliever. Their oldest starter, 31-year-old Mincher, supplied some power, belting 25 homers. Mike Hegan hit .292. The team scored only 639 runs, and their pitchers gave up well over 700. They deserved their last-place finish, avoiding 100 losses by only two. Total attendance was less than 700,000. The Pilots' dismal initial season over, President William Daley and the other owners sought to sell off the franchise.

During the eighth inning of the first game of the 1969 World Series between the Miracle Mets and the Baltimore Orioles, at some point between Tommy Agee being fanned by Mike Cuellar and Brooks Robinson striking out on a Ron Taylor pitch, a deal was struck. A private corporation made up of 15 Milwaukee businessmen, headed by the 35-year-old car dealer president Allen "Bud" Selig, put forward an offer of $10.8 million for the Pilots. The Seattle franchise had cost just $6 million initially.

The official announcement happened several months later. Just as had happened when the Braves sought to leave Milwaukee, desperate measures to keep the team in Seattle failed. During spring training, the team was advanced $650,000 by the American League to help defray costs. If that sounds like a lot for soaring training costs, it is. Much of the money actually went to back bills. The team had to declare bankruptcy in order to be sold.

Federal bankruptcy referee Sidney C. Volinn declared the Pilots bankrupt on March 31, 1970. The Brewers deal was approved, just one week before the season was to open, and one of the fastest franchise moves in history occurred. Allegedly the players, leaving spring training, didn't know where they were headed. "Watch whether the plane turns left or right at Denver," one wag said. It was the first time since the turn of the century a town had lost a team after just one season.

The new team just changed the letter on their caps, put Brewers instead of Seattle on the uniforms and went directly to work. The first day of season ticket sales, the faithful of Milwaukee showed how much they cared. Two thousand season plans were sold at between $150 and $375 each. In the first 10 days, more than 4,000 season tickets were sold—more than twice as well as the Braves had done their first season in Milwaukee. Twelve thousand seats were sold the first day of single-ticket sales.

On April 7 the Brewers returned to their new home after their first road trip. More than 8,000 fans were waiting in the airport terminal on a cold and windy night to welcome their new heroes. Outfielder Danny Walton said, "This is a larger crowd than we had for any game in

Seattle all last year." (Danny spoke poetically, not accurately. Seattle did have a couple of crowds better than that; in fact, they had topped 20,000 once. Dan could be forgiven; he hadn't arrived in Seattle until September first.)

The first game at home was a happening, when 37,237 showed up. Walton felt the pressure, saying "They made me so nervous it made the butterflies in my stomach feel like turkeys." Although Andy Messersmith of the Angels tossed a shutout, 12–0, the Milwaukee fans had a swell time.

It would be tough to claim that the Brewers improved on their predecessors' record. Though they finished tied for fourth instead of sixth, they won just one more game in 1970 than in 1969 and finished an identical 33 games out of first. But there was an excitement in County Stadium that hadn't been found in Seattle. The Brewers played thrilling ball under Manager Dave Bristol. They won 28 games after the sixth inning—20 in their final at bat. Three times Bristol tried a five-man infield in close games (though it worked only once). Tommy Harper became baseball's fifth 30–30 player, cracking 31 homers and swiping 38 bases. The fans took Danny Walton to their hearts, because of his early slugging feats, but also because he listed Eddie Mathews as a personal hero. Bristol was pleased. "Rome wasn't built in a day, but I'm prouder of these guys than any other club I've ever managed. We haven't been pushovers for anybody." The fans seemed pleased, too. Season attendance was 934,820. In the off-season former Milwaukee Braves favorite Del Crandall was named manager of the Brewer AAA Evansville farm team. Marvin Milkes, the team's general manager, the man they had called "a young Frank Lane," stepped down into the role of Super Scout. In his place came . . . Frank Lane.

Despite the presence of the famous "Trader," the 1971 Brewer edition returned to last place, losing 92 games. The young pitching showed promise, hurling 25 shutouts, but the hitters' average was the lowest in the majors, and only the Angels scored fewer runs. *The Sporting News* named Bill Parsons Rookie Pitcher of the Year. Ending with a 13–17 record and a 3.20 ERA, he had pitched 245 innings. Ken Sanders was chosen Fireman of the Year, his 83 appearances and 31 saves leading the league. The "highlight" of the season was probably the 10-cent beer night on June 18. A crowd of 27,474 beer-loving burghers of Milwaukee showed up, but spent more time consuming than watching the game. The long lines at the beer stands, with some fans ordering 50 or even 100 cups of the foamy liquid at a time, kept crowd involvement low. According to *The Sporting News,* "Surprisingly, only two fans wandered onto the field, and then only for brief excursions, and were ignored. They quickly went back to their seats and resumed drinking."

Although Lane was unable to alter the team's standing, he did change team personnel. By November, only one original Brewer (John Morris) was left with the club. In fact, by the end of the World Series, only two men who had started the season with Milwaukee were still around. The major deal occurred during the '79 World Series: a 10-man trade with the Boston Red Sox. Lane's Brewers swapped Tommy Harper, the team's two top pitchers, Lew Krausse and Marty Pattin, and Pat Skrable for six Bosox: George "the Boomer" Scott, Jim Lonborg, Ken Brett, Joe Lahoud, Billy Conigliaro, and Don Pavletich. Before spring training ended, Frank had swung nine more deals, also adding Jim Colborn and Brock Davis, Curt Motton and Frank Linzy. The seeds were sown for a new Brewer attack. The problem was where the league put them.

The erstwhile Pilots had spent their first two years in the weaker A.L. Western Division, but with the Washington Senators moving to Texas for 1972, the A.L. switched the Brewers to the East, where the Yankees, Red Sox, and Orioles also played. The Brewers, who had played the West to a reasonable 42–47 record in 1971, now were faced with the dreary prospect of playing most of their games against teams whom they had played 18 games below .500. However, management favored the switch because it gave the Brewers more games against the big draws in the East.

The biggest news for the future in the 1972 season happened in February, when the always-forward-thinking Brewer management applied for a cable TV franchise. The Brewers foundered in the Eastern Division. Manager Bristol got the axe in late May; Del Crandall was brought up from AAA to replace him. Crandall's first day of managing was May 30, and Skip Lockwood responded by one-hitting the Yankees. Lockwood, in fact, was involved in three one-hitters that season: on June 18 he combined with Ken Sanders for a one-hit effort against the Orioles, on August 1 the Tigers reached him for only one hit. But inconsistency was the Brewers style in 1972; Lockwood won only five games that *weren't* one-hitters to go with his 15 losses. Before Bristol was canned, the Brewers played 21 innings against the Twins and left with a suspended game tie, 3–3. When the game was resumed the next day, the Brewers quickly scored to win 4–3. Jim Colborn earned his first Brewer victory in a game that took a total of five hours and 47 minutes to complete. Then the regularly scheduled game lasted 15 innings as well.

Bad weather and the early-season players strike contributed to the drop in Brewer attendance, but neither so much as the quality of play. The highlight of the season was Jim Lonborg's impressive comeback. Winning 14, losing 12, and fashioning a 2.83 ERA, he was one bright sign. But Frank Lane was replaced in October by Jim Wilson, and a few days later Lonborg was gone, along with Ken Sanders, Ken Brett, and Earl Stephenson to the Phillies. In return the Brewers landed infielders Don Money, John Vuckovich, and pitcher Billy Champion.

According to Jeff Everson in *This Date in Milwaukee Brewers History,* the real fan turnaround came in the early part of the 1973 season. The Brewers cooked early, riding the hot pitching of Jim Colborn and the burning bats of Pedro Garcia and George Scott. Tiger manager Billy Martin felt that the Brewers were playing over their heads. He said, "If the Brewers can win with what they've got, I'm a Chinese aviator." The last time the Tigers played in Milwaukee that year, the team held a "Chinese Aviator Look-Alike Contest."

After winning nine games in a row on the road, the team returned home to face the Red Sox. The team bus was met at the ballpark by 6,000 screaming fans. Ellie Rodriguez and Pedro Garcia were lifted onto the fans' shoulders and carried into the park. The demonstration of affection lasted two hours. Everson says, "That was the day Milwaukee finally accepted the Brewers and started to forget the bitter taste left by the Braves." The Brewers won their 10th in a row that night, with manic cheering rattling Bosox hurler Don Newhauser, who walked in three runs. The next day a crowd of over 37,000 showed up, but the Brewers couldn't live up to a local restaurateur's annual prediction that the Milwaukee team would win 12 consecutive league games. They were toppled twice by the Sox, 8–4 and 4–2 in 11 innings.

By June 24 the Milwaukee Boys had cooled to 37–31. Their relief pitching, diminished by the traded Ken Sanders, damaged them. On July 4 they lost their third consecutive game in which they had held substantial leads. The cracks in their armor were showing. In late July, Texas manager Whitey Herzog openly accused Bernie Brewer, team mascot, of stealing signs from his outfield perch. "Can you imagine a team that has to cheat to beat *us?*" he said. Colborn and the Boomer kept up their good work for the whole year. Colborn took home 20 wins (the first Milwaukee player since the Braves' Tony Cloninger to do so). The colorful Scott, who said he wore a necklace of "second baseman's teeth," drove in 107 runs along with his 24 homers and .306 batting average. The team finished at 74–88, good enough for fifth. Attendance was up to a rollicking 1,092,158, nearly half a million over 1972. In the off-season the club traded away their number one reliever, 13-saver Frank Linzy.

Hopes were high for 1974. The Brewers were loaded with young talent. Garcia and Colborn had given indications of great capability. Darrell Porter and Bob Coluccio were only 21 years old. Charlie Moore and Kevin Kobel were showing strong potential in the minors.

As the 1974 season neared Opening Day, the Brewers realized they were without a real shortstop. Crandall selected a youngster, just 18 years old, and although not without criticism, gave him the job.

The Era of Robin Yount in Milwaukee had begun. In his sixth major league game, Yount made a key error in the eighth that let the Orioles tie the game. In the bottom of the eighth he slugged his first major league home run to win it, 3–2. Robin Yount has become a consistent star. Offensively, defensively, and in his quiet, reliable leadership he has been a vital member of the Brewers ever since.

They started the season with a bang again. On May 29, for example, down 4–0 to the California Angels, the Brewers unveiled some power and won 7–5. Johnny Briggs hit his 12th homer of the year and George Scott belted his 11th (Briggs had 37 RBIs already) to score four runs in the top of the ninth. On June 24 the Brewers acquired Deron Johnson from Oakland. The 35-year-old slugger immediately hit two homers in his first two games as a Brewer. The second was a grand slam, the team's third slam of the early season. The Milwaukee fans had an impact, too. Fans screamed at Oakland reliever Rollie Fingers and distracted him enough to give up a ninth-inning game-winning hit to Bobby Mitchell. Oakland announcer Monte Moore gave credit where it was due. "The crowd did it! The crowd did it" he screamed.

But the 1974 season turned out to be another half-season of good play for the Brewers. The big bats went cold; one writer called it a "power outage." The youth drive was stumbling. Garcia, who had finished second (although a distant second) in Rookie of the Year voting in 1973, hit only .199. A beaning in Minnesota damaged Bob Coluccio; his extra base hits fell from 44 to 23, his homers from 15 to six. Colborn was hurt, and finished 10–13, with an ERA over 4.00.

The season ended on somewhat of a high note, as the Brewers snapped a four-game losing streak on October 1 by beating the Yankees in 10 innings to knock the Yanks out of a chance for the Eastern Division title. But attendance fell below a million.

If 1974 was disappointing, 1975 was a disaster. Signing Hank Aaron as a designated hitter before the season started was called cynical by some. Management said, "He was the best DH available." The Brewers once again started out hot, then cooled off dramatically. In fact, "cool off" is a tender way of saying they impersonated a deep freeze. Nearly all the key players got hurt at one time or another; Champion, Rodriguez, Castro, Money, Hausmann, Darwin, and Yount. (*The Sporting News,* July 26: "Injury-ridden Brewers Place Call for Dr. Welby.") On July 4 they were 43–35 and tied with the Red Sox for the division lead. But they soon headed downward, losing 59 of their last 84 games. Del Crandall had lost control of the team.

Pedro Garcia was benched for weak hitting, and demonstrated his displeasure by challenging Crandall's authority. He stood at second during batting drills before a game with Texas and defiantly refused to take grounders. A public apology and $200 fine didn't really change

his attitude, and he continued to undermine Crandall. Some players
sided with Garcia; others were displeased with Crandall's inability to
deal decisively with the problem. Both ways, Del lost.

In late July the Brewers dropped the first game of a doubleheader
to Baltimore, then blew a six-run lead in the ninth inning of the second
game. Crandall's days were numbered. George Scott held a clubhouse
meeting in which he announced the Brewers were "the laughingstock
of baseball," but instead of the meeting firing the team up to new
heights, it just made Del Crandall even madder. Final results were a
fifth-place finish, 68–94, 28 games behind the Red Sox. The novelty
of Aaron's return resulted, however, in another Brewer attendance
record: 1,213,357.

In looking for Crandall's replacement, Brewers management
wanted someone who knew how to win. Alex Grammas, right-hand
man to Sparky Anderson of the Cincinnati Reds, was their choice. If
anything, the results were worse. Lou Chapman, veteran Milwaukee
sportswriter, borrowed a page from Mel Brooks when he called it
"The Year That Was Rotten." The second game of the season summed
it all up. Losing 9–6 to the Yanks in the last of the ninth, Don Money
hit a grand slam to win the game. But first base ump Jim McKean had
called time before the pitch. The celebration was aborted, the players
returned from the clubhouse. And lost 9–7.

Grammas's challenge was to restore the clubhouse harmony that
Crandall's battles with Garcia and Sixto Lezcano had fractured. What
Grammas did instead was miss the point. He tried to install discipline
like a third-grade teacher. He made the Brewers cut their hair, and
get rid of mustaches, mutton chops, and "other facial adornments."
Even Henry Aaron left unhappy with Grammas. Ostensibly to let him
get a standing ovation, Alex removed Aaron for a pinch runner in his
last game, thereby denying Hank the chance to break his all-time
second-place tie with Babe Ruth in runs scored. The runner, Jim
Gantner, crossed home later. In addition, according to Chapman,
Scott had "a miserable year," and Porter was "a big fat out most of the
time." The team finished two games worse than the year before, falling
off to 95 losses. For the third time in four years, their hitters led the
league in striking out.

On December 6 the Brewers made the first real move toward
creating a team that would become an A.L. Eastern power. They made
one bad trade: sending Darrell Porter and Jim Colborn to Kansas City
for Jamie Quirk and Jim Wohlford. However, on the same day, Bernie
Carbo and George Scott were sent back to Boston for a talented young
first baseman named Cecil Cooper.

After Porter left, he slammed Grammas, citing Grammas's lack
of communication with the players as the reason for the Brewers'
troubles. Mike Hegan didn't wait till he left, making his famous state-

ment about Alex: "He's a nice guy, but as a manager he makes a good third base coach." A few days later Hegan was released.

The Brewer start in 1977 was typical; they won the Cactus League handily, then took 11 wins in April. When the home opener was played in 83° sunny weather in front of 55,120, the Milwaukee faithful, used to windy, cold Aprils, should have seen it as a negative omen.

The skid was on its way. Despite good years from youngsters Cooper, Yount, and Lezcano, and quality work from oldster Money and free agent signee Sal Bando, they scored just 639 runs (only three teams scored fewer) and were third from the bottom in ERA. They lost 95 games again.

Bud Selig had been running a tight financial ship, no doubt about it. *The Sporting News* had pointed out in February that the Brewers had all of their players who counted under multi-year contracts. An editorial called them "Among the most efficiently managed clubs in baseball."

They only stank on the field!

It was time for a change. A big change. The *Milwaukee Journal* called it "The Saturday Night Massacre." On Saturday, November 19, Selig fired Grammas and director of player development Al Widmar. GM Jim Baumer, despite his canny success as a judge of talent (he drafted Yount, Molitor, and Gantner) was either fired or resigned, depending on whom you listen to. Coaches Jimmy Bragan and Hal Smith were also canned, although Frank Howard and Harvey Kuenn remained.

To find a man to run the operation, Selig's timing was perfect. Harry Dalton, the general manager who had done great work for both the Orioles and Angels, had just been pushed aside in his California job. When Angel owner Gene Autry installed Buzzie Bavasi as his chief assistant, he effectively removed much of Dalton's power. Harry was ready for another challenge, and Selig offered it. Bud explained his decision by pointing out that bad baseball management was interfering with his ability to run the other side of the team. He was spending too much time on baseball matters; he wanted someone he could trust to take charge. Selig said he had to do *something*—"I had a manager and a general manager who weren't even talking to each other, if you can believe that."

Dalton made his presence felt quickly. The Brewers reached into the free agent market for the second time, signing Larry Hisle for $3 million over six years. To add more beef to the outfield power, they swapped veteran Jim Slaton to the Tigers for Ben Oglivie. Dalton was instrumental in persuading Orioles pitching coach George Bamberger to join as manager.

"Bambi" spoke: "There are twenty-six big-league clubs, and if twenty-five of them had made me an offer, I wouldn't have taken it."

The "Baltimore Connection" with the Brewers had been established. And the Brewers were on their way.

Bamberger's managerial skills were the perfect style-match for the powerful team that Dalton had put together. In addition to getting along well with his players, Bamberger was a fan favorite, too. He could be seen joining tailgate parties before and after games, or hoisting a beer and a "brat" with fans in one of the sports bars near the Stadium. "Bambi's Bombers" were born. In that year, two vitally important members of the Brewers' future started their careers: Gorman Thomas and Paul Molitor. Molitor, the bonus baby from the University of Minnesota, was the consummately talented athlete; there was almost nothing he couldn't do, do well, and do seemingly without effort. He was the All-American shortstop, the third player chosen in the 1977 draft. Before Molitor would spend five years in the majors, he would be the Milwaukee starter at five different positions.

As Dan Okrent later put it, "If Molitor was the dreamboat that every 17-year-old girl in Milwaukee pined for, then James Gorman Thomas was the hero every 47-year-old brewery worker idolized." Gorman was a swaggering, brutish, mustachioed beer drinker, veteran of nine years in the minors, who took deep pride in his defensive ability as well as his slugging skills. The Brewers wouldn't win a pennant till four years later, but the focus of that team were the three who found themselves together for the first time in 1978: Yount, Molitor, and Thomas. Ironically, Molitor, with only 64 games of minor league experience, got his major league chance because Yount sat out the early part of the 1978 season, in frustration at the team's ineptitude, considering a pro golf career. But when the Brewers started out red hot, and Molitor looked like he had won Yount's shortstop job, the 22-year-old veteran Robin returned, re-claimed short, and moved Molitor to second.

There was a new pinstriped uniform for the Milwaukee men this year, and a new logo, designed in a fan competition, which combined the "M" and "B" of their initials into a ball and a glove.

The young Bombers led the league in runs, RBIs, and hits. New addition Hisle cracked 34 homers and set a Brewer record with 115 runs driven in. Right behind Larry in long balls was the returned Thomas. The previous regime had sent him from Spokane to Texas in the off-season to complete an August deal for Spanky Kirkpatrick. Dalton hurried to buy him back. Stormin' Gorman slugged 32 homers. Cooper and Oglivie hit .312 and .303. Both Yount and Don Money hit in the .290s; Money also cracking 14 homers while moving from position to position (five in all.)

The men from Milwaukee began the season in grand, prophetic style, winning their first five games by scoring 54 runs (scores of 11–

3, 16–3, 13–5, 9–6, and 5–0, with three grand slams in their first three games—ironically against Baltimore), and the pitching staff loved it. Even the early-season loss of Moose Haas to elbow problems didn't hurt. Mike Caldwell, picked up from the Reds for two minor leaguers the previous June, won 22 games. Perhaps best of all, he became the first pitcher since Dean Chance 14 years earlier to shut out the fearsome Yankees three times in one season. Mike set a team record with a 2.37 ERA, but only he and Larry Sorensen among the starters had ERAs below the league average. Jerry Augustine and Bill Travers won 13 and 12 games, respectively, with ERAs over 4.50. The hitting took care of it all.

A total of 1,601,406 Brewer fans came out to see this remarkable passel of hitters, who stayed close in the A.L. East, not being eliminated till the season had less than a week to go. They finished six and a half games back, winners of 93, losers of 69, the fourth-best record in the majors. The young Brewers, with four starters under 25 and Thomas still a hearty 27, were arguably the most exciting team in baseball, and destined to remain that way for several years to come.

For the 1979 season, the battling boys of Bamberger took sight on the Yankees, who had won pennants the past three years. One smart move was the free agent signing of Jim Slaton, who had been traded to get Ben Oglivie after the 1977 season. In Slaton's one year with the Tigers, he had constructed a healthy 17–11 record, but with a team that had scored 90 fewer runs than the Brewers. A smart man, Jim certainly appreciated what the Brewer bats could do for a pitcher's career.

Pre-season reports were excellent. New York sports columnist Dick Young compared the Milwaukeeans to their top competition: "The Brewers are talent-loaded, like the Yanks, but have the hunger the Yanks seems to have lost." The Brewers managed to beat out the Yanks (and Boston, too) to finish second behind the Orioles. The Brewers improved in 1979, but the hot team in the A.L. East that year was the Baltimore Orioles, who won 102 times.

Milwaukee's offensive totals were almost identical to the previous year, despite Larry Hisle's rotator cuff injury that kept him out of all but 26 games. The difference was made up by Sixto Lezcano's career year of .321, 28 homers, and 101 RBIs, and Gorman Thomas's improvement in his long ball total from 32 to 45 (which led the league, along with his 175 strikeouts). The Brew Crew slugged 12 more homers, hit three more triples, and 24 more doubles. Yet they scored only three more runs. Instead of leading the league, Boston, California, and Kansas City all outpaced them. Yet they weren't shut out until the last game of the season, completing a remarkable streak of 213 games without a whitewash. But in the light of the Orioles' strength, no one seemed to notice. Larry Hisle told the *New York Times* his team got no respect: "I can't remember anyone ever talking about us. All you hear people talk about all the time is Boston and the Yankees." Maybe that was true in Peoria and Pittsburgh, but not in Milwaukee; the Brewers drew nearly two million fans (1,918,343).

The Brewers thought they were poised for a pennant. Pre-season articles asked if they were the "Team of the '80s." But two familiar bugaboos re-appeared: injuries and inconsistent relief pitching. The health problems began early, and not just to the players. Coach Harvey Kuenn had to have his right leg amputated below the knee (veins removed for heart bypass surgery had weakened it) and the lovable manager George Bamberger had a heart attack during the first week of spring training, not to return till June 6. Hisle was quick to reinjure his already damaged shoulder; while leading the league in hitting, Molitor pulled a rib cage muscle early in June and wasn't right again until September. Don Money had, according to Tom Flaherty, "an assortment of injuries." The pitching was still up-and-down. No starter had a dominating year, no reliever had more than 10 saves.

But the hitting—wow! The Brewers led the league in doubles, homers, and RBIs, and had the individual league leader in each of those categories (Yount, Oglivie, Cooper) as well. The team slugged an outstanding .448. In 25 years, only one team had topped that figure (the Red Sox in 1977 and 1979). Cooper's .352 batting average was 11 points better than his next competitor, and 28 points higher than anyone in the National League could manage. However, a man named George Brett chose 1980 to hit .390, the highest average in baseball in nearly 40 years.

In *Sport* magazine, Jack Newcombe wrote an article titled "Wanted for Murder: The Milwaukee Gang." His description of the effectiveness of the home run is especially telling: "Nothing can spread disillusion with the enemy more abruptly." The Brewers finished the season with 203 "long taters." But somehow all that power wasn't enough to win more than 86 games, and the Brewers fell to 17 games back.

Tom Flaherty, writing in *The Sporting News Annual Guide* in 1981, noticed the first appearance in Milwaukee of an old baseball tradition: "The fans, whose hopes were high after the previous two seasons, started to boo for the first time in the franchise's history."

Then The Big Trade occurred. Dalton realized, correctly, that his offense was ready. There was no time to wait for the young pitchers from the farm system to come around. He had been searching for relief help, but had been unable to swing any major league deal for an entire year.

The action in the National League was what gave Dalton his chance. On December 8 Cardinals manager and GM Whitey Herzog had completed a swap of seven players for four from the San Diego roster, including Rollie Fingers. Fingers had joined San Diego as a free agent in 1977 after seven successful years in Oakland (where his team had won three consecutive World Championships). After 12 years of being one of the game's top relievers, some suspected his value had diminished.

Proof that Herzog shared that opinion happened the very next day when Whitey swapped three players for the Cubs' Bruce Sutter. With back-to-back years leading the National League in saves, the man with the infamous split-fingered fastball was at the peak of his career. Although Herzog had been rebuffed by Dalton earlier in the year in an offer of a straight-up swap of Larry Sorensen for Pete Vuckovich, Dalton was changing his mind. Vuckovich was no youngster, but everyone on the Milwaukee side liked his pitching variety and attitude. Herzog also wanted to be rid of his complaining catcher Ted Simmons, and, frankly, no one else but Milwaukee was interested in him. A complicated deal (explained in breathtaking detail in Dan Okrent's *Nine Innings*) was struck. The Brewers would receive Fingers, Vuckovich, and Simmons, in exchange for Sorensen, Dave LaPoint, outfielder Sixto Lezcano, and the highly rated prospect David Green (Brewer super scout Ray Poitevint: "He's got Willie Mays' physical abilities and Pete Rose's mental abilities").

And if it hadn't been for the players' strike, the Brewers might very well have been in the World Series in 1981. In the split season, the Brewers were 31–25 in the pre-strike "half season," and 31–22 to win the second "half." Most interestingly, the men from Milwaukee failed to finish first in any offensive category—a strange event for the big belting Brewers. Yet they did lead in a critical defensive category— double plays, and the deal for pitching had really paid off. Pete Vuckovich won 14 games and lost just four, best in the league. The Brewers also led the league with 35 saves, 28 of them earned by Rollie Fingers. Fingers became the first reliever to win both the Cy Young and Most Valuable Player Awards in the same season. However, the Yankees toppled them in a best-of-five playoff. Down two games to none, the Brewers battled back to tie the series, largely because of a gutty performance by Vuckovich, who left a sick bed to pitch Game Four. But Reggie Jackson, Oscar Gamble, and Rick Cerone all homered in the fifth game to earn the Yanks a 7–3 victory.

Under Buck Rodgers, who had managed the team to their "half-pennant" in 1981 (Bamberger had not returned), prospects were. bright for the 1982 season. But the usual hot start didn't happen. Players were complaining about Rodgers. As Dan Okrent described it, Rodgers' most vocal critics were also his most visible players— Simmons, Caldwell, Thomas, and Vuckovich. They told the influential

Milwaukee Journal's Tom Flaherty that the manager was guilty of "remoteness, poor communication, lack of faith, inconsistency and overmanaging." He had battles with players over dress codes. Things weren't well for the Brew Crew. The team, picked by many to win its division, languished at 23–24.

Harry Dalton found the solution in Harvey Kuenn, the amiable batting coach, and one of the few people to survive the "Saturday Night Massacre" five years earlier. Harvey said to his charges, "Let's have some fun," and the team responded. Freed from the Rodgers' brow-beating, the fun-loving Brewers went 72–43 under Kuenn to win more games than any other team in the majors.

When the Brewers had to get the job done, they did. After their slow start, the bats bellowed under Kuenn. A record crowd of 55,716 turned out on "Bat Night," July 3, as the Brewers faced the first-place Red Sox, ahead of the Brewers by just one game. Pete Vuckovich threw a three-hit shutout, Cecil Cooper hit two homers, Yount and Molitor one each for a 7–0 victory. A five-game sweep of the White Sox in mid-July got them in motion, and a victory over Cleveland on July 31 put them in first for good.

It wasn't easy, though. On August 30 Dalton tried to shore up the pitching staff by acquiring veteran Don Sutton from the Astros. Four day later Fingers' season ended with an injury, and it had an immediate impact in the standings. The Orioles put the pressure on. After losing the first game of a three-game September Boston series, sub catcher Ned Yost belted a three-run homer in the ninth to push the Brewers to a 6–3 win. They led by four with five games to go. But they lost the last game in Boston, and headed to Baltimore for four games—and the pennant decision. Earl Weaver, O's manager since 1968, had announced his retirement after the season. The Birds were running on emotion, and they took the first three games of the set. It came down to the final day of the season. And that was the day the Brewers woke up. The Boys from Milwaukee hit four homers, including two by Robin Yount, and Don Sutton won his fourth game as a Brewer to clinch the pennant by a score of 10–2. Sutton pitched that day with a bad cold, but explained the reason for his success: "I had a sore throat, so I took penicillin to get rid of the cold, cortisone to get rid of the penicillin, water to get rid of the cortisone: better pitching through chemistry."

The season was full of heroics. Paul Molitor had begun his career as a shortstop. He was sent to second because Robin Yount returned, then to center when Rodgers felt Thomas was slowing up and Jim Gantner deserved a shot at second. But when Molitor got hurt, Thomas returned to center and Paul was put in right. By 1982 Sal Bando had retired and his third-base partner Don Money was too old to play every day. So Molitor became a third baseman—his fifth regular position in five years, all at the club's request. Obviously unbothered by moving around, Paul hit .302, led the league in runs scored, and stole 41 bases. Cooper hit .313, Yount .331, to go with his league-leading 46 doubles. Gorman Thomas shared the A.L. homer title with 39, while both Oglivie and Cooper cracked more than 30, and Yount belted 29 himself. Vuckovich won the Cy Young this year, and Yount the MVP. Their hitting ability had reached the status of legend. Their 216 homers were the sixth best total in major league history. More important, only one of those other five teams also won the pennant. Goose Gossage said, "There isn't a lineup I've ever faced that's better." Allegedly, when the phone rang in the Yankees bullpen during a Brewers game, Goose put his hands over his ears and shouted "No! No!"

The League Championship Series also put the Brewers to the test. The series opened on the West Coast, and the Angels beat Mike Caldwell in the first game and Vuckovich in the second to take a two-games-to-none lead (an edge no team had ever surrendered in L.C.S. play). But when they returned to Milwaukee, Don Sutton kept his magic rolling. The Angels scored in only the eighth inning as the Brewers took Game Three 5–3. Haas started Game Four, and once again the Brewers took an early lead and held on. Mark Brouhard, subbing for a sick Oglivie, drove in three runs and scored four. The fifth game held more excitement. Down 3–2 in the bottom of the seventh, the Brewers retaliated on a two-out single by Cecil Cooper (at that point 2-for-19 in the series) that sent two runs home. A great catch by Thomas's defensive replacement Marshall Edwards, leaping against the center-field fence to rob Don Baylor of an extra-base hit, sealed the issue. Final: Milwaukee 4, California 3.

The World Series started in St. Louis, and the Brewers started off with a bang. They slammed 17 hits, Mike Caldwell allowed just three, and the final score was 10–0. Paul Molitor became the only player in major league history to have five hits in a World Series game. Leading 4–2 in the second game, the Brewers fell when former Milwaukee catcher Darrell Porter doubled in two runs to tie, and reliever Pete Ladd, trying desperately to fill Fingers' shoes, walked in the lead run in the bottom of the eighth.

The Brewers lost Game Three, 6–2. But they came back in Game Four when an error by their former pitcher Dave LaPoint opened the doors for six runs (three unearned) in the bottom of the seventh, and the Milwaukeeans escaped with a 7–5 win. The next game, as *The Sporting News* put it, "Mike Caldwell followed his nifty three-hitter of Game One with a not-so-nifty 14-hitter." The Brewers took the game 6–4. In the process, Yount got four hits for the second time in the

Series, which made him the only player ever to have two four-hit Series games in his career (much less in one Series).

With their backs to the wall, the Cardinals exploded in the sixth game. More than two and a half hours of rain delay didn't dampen the effectiveness of the Cards' rookie starter John Stuper. They scored seven runs off Sutton and six off Doc Medich (another late-season acquisition) to send the Series to a seventh contest.

The Brewers washed away an early St. Louis lead with a run in the fifth and two in the sixth. But when the Cards loaded the bases in the last half of the sixth, singles by Keith Hernandez and George Hendrick gave the Cardinals the lead they wouldn't lose.

Milwaukeeans still loved their team. When the defeated Brewers returned home, delighted fans treated them to a ticker-tape parade down Wisconsin Avenue to the Stadium. At the Stadium, the energetic Yount took a speedy turn around the track on a motorcycle, and management's pulse rates increased dangerously. The folks of Milwaukee were thrilled with the exploits of their heroes. "Bambi's Bombers" had been replaced by "Harvey's Wallbangers." The future for fans of Milwaukee baseball had never looked brighter.

Bill James said, "I think that the Brewer infield of the last two years is clearly the greatest infield of my lifetime . . . I don't know that I could name a better four-man infield ever." But even a team like the Brewers, who looked so solid, found repeating impossible.

They began 1983 shakily, but a July streak pushed them to the top. They were holding on to first place as late as August 25, but dropped six of nine on a West Coast trip, returned home to take two from the Yankees, then lost 12 of their next 13.

In retrospect, it was the year of the disabled list. Rollie Fingers, who had missed September, the 1982 L.C.S. and Series with a torn muscle in his forearm, seemed ready for a comeback, until bone chips were discovered in his elbow. He didn't throw a pitch all season. Pete Vuckovich had torn his rotator cuff severely, and he was able to appear in only three games. Without the Cy Young winners of the previous two years, the Brewers were a much weaker team.

The club slumped at the plate as well, scoring nearly 130 fewer runs and hitting 83 fewer homers; there was no chance. The dependable Cecil Cooper still managed a .307 average to go with his 30 homers and league-leading 126 RBIs, and Robin Yount slugged .503, with more than 40 doubles, 10 triples, and 17 homers to accompany his .308 batting average. But no one besides Cooper hit more than 17 homers, and only two men drove in more than 100 runs (compared to four, plus one with 97, the year before).

The Milwaukee team finished 87–75, 11 games behind Baltimore, good enough only for fifth place. The fans didn't seem to mind, though; the Brewers drew 2,397,131. But Dalton and Selig did; Harvey Kuenn was replaced by Rene Lachemann.

The 1984 season was a disaster. As Tom Flaherty described it for *The Sporting News Annual Guide:* "The Milwaukee Brewers opened the 1984 season with a new manager and high hopes. They finished it six months later with a last-place finish in the American League East and the return of an old manager. In between there were very few victories, a bundle of injuries, and a lot of grief."

It started with Vuckovich again. He seemed to have recovered from his rotator cuff problem, but a bone spur was discovered, surgery was required, and Pete didn't pitch all year. The usually healthy Molitor went down with a torn muscle in his elbow and played only 13 games. The story with Fingers was different; off to a great start, he had 23 saves by the 23rd of July. Then back problems put him on the shelf for the rest of the summer.

The fabled Brewer punch had also left for good. Everybody in the league outscored them. The 1984 team hit just 96 homers, 36 fewer than 1983, 120 less than the A.L. champs of 1982, and the largest drop in two years in American League history, according to the Elias Sports Bureau. Brewer attendance plummeted like their four-baggers: 700,000 fewer fans showed up at County Stadium. The team was a miserable 36½ games out of first. Seeing that rebuilding years lay ahead, Dalton rehired former manager George Bamberger in September, with the hope that the beloved Bambi could keep the fans interested.

The Brewers had risen and fallen, in a large hurry. Bill James pointed out, "With one more loss in 1984, the Brewers could have been the first team in history to travel from 95 losses to 95 wins and back to 95 losses in less than a decade."

The Brewers won four more games in 1985 under Bamberger, moving from last to sixth in their division. As Tom Flaherty put it, "Bambi was back, but the Brewers weren't." The only bright spots were the successful return of Paul Molitor, with a .297 batting average, and first-year hurler Ted Higuera, whose 15–8 record earned him *The Sporting News* title of Rookie Pitcher of the Year. Earnest Riles became the shortstop, and Robin Yount moved to center. Attendance was the worst in eight years.

Milwaukee baseball historian Dennis Sell remarked that the Brewers sent a message to their fans as the 1986 season began: "Be patient." It was clear the Brewers were making a move to youth. Rob Deer came over from the Giants and hit 33 homers. Dale Sveum played nearly 90 games in the infield. Highly heralded Billy Jo Robidoux made his big-league debut. Youngsters Juan Nieves, Dan Plesac, and Bill

Wegman did plenty of pitching. By the end of the season the only pitcher left from the 1985 staff was Teddy Higuera, who obligingly won 20 games. The change to youth was complete when Bamberger stepped down in September in favor of Tom Trebelhorn.

It would be hard to describe the 1987 Brewer season as anything other than "The Year of the Streak." By combining an amazing set of team and individual streak performances, Milwaukee bounced back to win 91 games, and finish third, within seven games of the Tigers. In addition, it could also be characterized as the year the Brewers grew legs. New manager Trebelhorn pushed the running game, and they set a team record with 176 successful steals, nearly 50 more than any other Brewer team.

The season began remarkably, and a bit of Milwaukee baseball legend finally came true. For years neither the Braves nor Brewers had been able to fulfill the annual prophecy of Milwaukee restaurateur George Webb: victories in 12 straight league games. Even after Mr. Webb's death, his company continued the tradition. He never said what he would do if they did, but it didn't matter, because they didn't. The Braves had won 11 in a row twice, the Brewers 10 consecutively three times.

The fans thought Mr. Webb's prediction had failed again, when, after winning their first 11 games, the Brewers were losing to Texas 4–1 in the last of the ninth on sunny Easter Sunday. But the loyal fans rose to their feet to give their team a grateful ovation for their tremendous effort. The Brew Crew responded; Rob Deer hit a 445-foot three-run homer to tie the game and Dale Sveum belted another to claim a 6–4 victory. The fans left the park chanting "George Webb! George Webb!" and marched to the Webb restaurants' corporate head-quarters. Several days later the George Webb restaurants gave away 165,000 free hamburgers as a reward for the team (finally) living up to the founder's prediction.

The Brewers won the next day, too, so their 13-game streak tied the record the Atlanta Braves set in 1982 for consecutive wins to open the season. By May 2, they were 20–3. Then they ran in reverse, losing a dozen in a row, and their 18–3 April was almost mirrored by a 6–18 May.

Paul Molitor had missed 44 games with a variety of injuries by the All-Star break, but he came back rested, to say the least. The day his season resumed, he started hitting and wouldn't stop. It wasn't until August 26, at the hands of Cleveland pitcher John Farrell, that he would be held without a hit again. In fact, Molitor was on deck when Rick Manning singled in Mike Felder to win the game for Milwaukee. For his game-winning hit, Manning was booed. Molitor's streak extended to 39 games, seventh longest in major league history. He was a winner: the Brewers were 76–41 with Paul in the lineup, 15–30 without him.

There was a great pitching streak, too. Ted Higuera hurled three shutouts in a row on his way to 32 consecutive scoreless innings. Rob Deer continued to do his Gorman Thomas impersonation—slugging hard (28 HRs) but fanning often (186 Ks, which set the A.L. record, previously held by—who else?—Gorman Thomas). Dale Sveum also tagged 25 homers and hit well in the clutch, driving in 95 runs. Rookie catcher B.J. Surhoff showed promise with a .299 average.

The 1988 season ran the other way. The Brewers enjoyed an early streak because of a strange motivation. They won 10 in a row from the end of April through May 9, because Trebelhorn said players wouldn't have to wear ties on planes if they won 10 straight. But with only 30 games left the Brewers were dead even at 66–66. Ten games back, their pennant chances were slim at best.

However, "streak" was still a key word in the Brewer vocabulary. They began to win, reminding fans of their season-opening efforts in 1987, taking 21 of 28, driving to within 2½ games of the lead with three to go. It wasn't enough. Ironically, the Brewers, who had been moved from the A.L. West to the East in 1972, were the swing team in 1988, which meant they spent the final month of the season playing Western division clubs. As Tom Flaherty put it, "The Brewers had to rely on someone else to knock off the three teams ahead of them while they watched from the West." They finished the season just two games back. They were the last team eliminated in the majors.

But the future held promise. The young pitching staff was improving, losing the team ERA title to Oakland on the final day of the season. The Brewers led the league in stolen bases again, and Teddy Higuera's 16 wins made him the first Brewer to win 15 or more in four consecutive seasons. Dan Plesac missed most of September, yet rang up 30 saves, just one less than the team record. The bullpen as a whole collected 51 saves in 58 chances. Once again, the Brewers were combining young blood with the talented experience of Molitor, Yount, and Gantner.

Those three played a large part in the Brewers' successes in 1989, and then again in 1992. In 1989 there were only 15 major leaguers who had played 10 or more years with their original team— three were the Brewer men. A six-game losing streak after the All-Star game came to a sudden halt when Molitor, Yount and Gantner held a team meeting which cleared the air and provided the needed senior leadership. Behind Yount's .318 hitting spree the veteran Trebelhorn club maintained a .500 pace throughout the balance of that summer to secure a respectable 4th-place divisional ledger. Three summers later, with rookie skipper Phil Garner now at the helm, it was still the bats of Yount (.264, but 217 total bases) and Molitor (a league fourth-best .320) that authored a surprising second-place (92–70) pennant charge, a late season rush that almost unseated the defending champion and heavily favored Toronto Blue Jays. And further glitter was added to the 1992 campaign by Robin Yount's own personal date with destiny as the all-time franchise star became but the 17th batsman ever to reach the charmed 3,000-hit circle.

Annotated Bibliography

Everson, Jeff. *This Date in Milwaukee Brewers History*. Appleton, Wis.: Everson House, 1987.

    A standard chronological review of on-field highlights during the first 18 seasons of Brewers baseball. This volume was self-published and therefore it remains most difficult to locate for the average baseball buff or baseball book collector.

James, Bill. *The Bill James Baseball Abstract 1986*. New York: Ballantine Books (Random House Publishers), 1986 ("Milwaukee Brewers" on pp. 147–153).

    The best of Bill James' annual statistical evaluations of the Brewers, as part of his long-running series of yearly team portraits of all major league clubs from the perspective of SABRmetrics. This essay contains such interesting and useful features as a statistical breakdown of Brewers team performances for the preceding decade; a discussion of the impact of County Stadium on the offensive production of the Brewers and their rivals; and much, much more.

Okrent, Daniel. *Nine Innings*. New York: Ticknor and Fields, 1985 (New York: McGraw-Hill Book Company, 1980).

    The anatomy of baseball as seen through the playing of a single game—the Milwaukee Brewers versus the Baltimore Orioles, in County Stadium on June 10, 1982. Many behind-the-scenes observations on the ballpark in Milwaukee, the front-office and on-field operations of the ballclub, and the historical background of the Milwaukee Brewers organization.

Sell, Dennis. "Twentieth Anniversary: A Collection of Brewer Memories." In *Milwaukee Brewers' 1989 Official Yearbook*, 3–14. Waukesha,. Wis.: Delser Lithograph Company, 1989.

    Colorful overview of 20 seasons of Brewer baseball in Milwaukee, including all franchise highlights, remarkable performances, and brief seasonal recaps. This article is also supplemented with an attractive collage of numerous excellent color photographs.

Skibosh, Thomas. "That Championship Season." In *Milwaukee Brewers' 1983 Official Yearbook*, 4–15. Waukesha, Wis.: Delser Lithograph Company, 1983.

    A detailed look at the exciting 1982 American League championship season, including both the narrow defeat of the Angels in A.L.C.S. play, and the action-packed seven-game World Series defeat at the hands of the Cardinals. This was the year when Harvey Kuenn took the reins in mid-season and engineered an unforgettable final-weekend triumph over Earl Weaver's Orioles in Baltimore.

Year-by-Year Standings and Season Summaries

Year	Pos.	Record	Pct.	GB	Manager	Player	BA	Player	HR	Player	W-L	ERA
1969*	6th	64–98	.395	33.0	Schultz	Mincher	.246	Mincher	25	Brabender	13–14	4.37
1970	4th	65–97	.401	33.0	Bristol	Harper	.296	Harper	31	Pattin	14–12	3.40
1971	6th	69–92	.429	32.0	Bristol / McMillan / Crandall	D. May	.277	Briggs	21	Pattin	14–14	3.12
1972	6th	65–91	.417	21.0	Crandall	Scott	.266	Briggs	21	Lonborg	14–12	2.83
1973	5th	74–88	.457	23.0	Crandall	Scott	.307	D. May	25	Colborn	20–12	3.18
1974	5th	76–86	.469	15.0	Crandall	Money	.283	Scott, Briggs	17	Slaton	13–16	3.92
1975	5th	68–94	.420	28.0	Crandall / Kuenn	Scott	.285	Scott	36	Broberg	14–16	4.28
1976	6th	66–95	.410	32.0	Grammas	Lezcano	.285	Scott	18	Travers	15–16	2.81
1977	5th	67–95	.414	33.0	Grammas	Cooper	.300	Money	25	Augustine	12–18	4.48
1978	3rd	93–69	.574	6.5	Bamberger	Cooper	.312	Hisle	34	Caldwell	22–9	2.37
1979	2nd	95–66	.590	8.0	Bamberger	Lezcano	.321	Thomas	45	Caldwell	16–6	3.29
1980	3rd	86–76	.531	17.0	Bamberger / Rodgers	Cooper	.352	Oglivie	41	Haas	16–15	3.11
1981	3rd	31–25	.554	3.0	Rodgers	Cooper	.320	Thomas	21	Vuckovich	14–4	3.54
1981**	1st	31–22	.585	+1.5								
	1st	62–47	.569	+1.0								
1982	1st	95–67	.586	+1.0	Rodgers / Kuenn	Yount	.331	Thomas	39	Vuckovich	18–6	3.54
1983	5th	87–75	.537	11.0	Kuenn	Yount, Simmons	.308	Cooper	30	Slaton	14–6	4.33
1984	7th	67–94	.416	36.5	Lachemann	Yount	.298	Cooper	16	Sutton	14–12	3.77
1985	6th	71–90	.441	28.0	Bamberger	Molitor	.297	Yount	15	Higuera	15–8	3.90
1986	6th	77–84	.478	18.0	Bamberger / Trembelhorn	Yount	.312	Deer	33	Higuera	20–11	2.79
1987	3rd	91–71	.562	7.0	Trebelhorn	Molitor	.353	Deer	28	Higuera	18–10	3.85
1988	3rd	87–75	.537	2.0	Trebelhorn	Molitor	.312	Deer	23	Higuera	16–9	2.45
1989	4th	81–81	.500	8.0	Trebelhorn	Yount	.318	Deer	26	Bosio	15–10	2.95
1990	6th	74–88	.457	14.0	Trebelhorn	Sheffield	.294	Deer	27	Robinson	12–5	2.91
1991	4th	83–79	.512	8.0	Trebelhorn	Randolph	.327	Vaughn	27	Wegman	15–7	2.84
1992	2nd	92–70	.568	4.0	Garner	Molitor	.320	Vaughn	23	Navarro	17–11	3.33

*Seattle Pilots. **Split Season Totals (Players' Union Strike).

All-Time Brewers Career and Season Records

Career Batting Leaders (1969–1992)

Games Played	Robin Yount	2,443
At Bats	Robin Yount	10,554
Runs Scored	Robin Yount	1,570
Hits	Robin Yount	3,025
Singles	Robin Yount	2,101
Doubles	Robin Yount	558
Triples	Robin Yount	123
Batting Average	Paul Molitor	.303
Home Runs	Robin Yount	243
Runs Batted In	Robin Yount	1,355
Stolen Bases	Paul Molitor	412
Strikeouts	Gorman Thomas	1,033
Extra Bases Hits	Robin Yount	924
Total Bases	Robin Yount	4,558

Career Pitching Leaders (1969–1992)

Innings Pitched	Jim Slaton	2,025
Earned Run Average	Ken Sanders	2.22
Wins	Jim Slaton	117
Losses	Jim Slaton	121
Winning Percentage	Tom Tellman	.682 (15–7)
Strikeouts	Ted Higuera	1,019
Walks	Jim Slaton	760
Games	Dan Plesac	365
Shutouts	Jim Slaton	19
Shutouts (lefthander)	Mike Caldwell	18
Saves	Dan Plesac	133
Games Started	Jim Slaton	268
Complete Games	Jim Slaton	69

Single-Season Batting Records (1969–1992)

Batting Average (500 ABs)	Paul Molitor	.353	1987
Home Runs	Gorman Thomas	45	1979
Home Runs (lefthanded)	Ben Oglivie	41	1980
Runs Batted In	Cecil Cooper	126	1983
Hits	Cecil Cooper	219	1980
Singles	Cecil Cooper	157	1980
Doubles	Robin Yount	49	1980
Triples	Paul Molitor	16	1979
Slugging Percentage	Robin Yount	.578	1982
Extra Base Hits	Robin Yount	87	1982
Stolen Bases	Pat Listash	54	1992
Strikeouts	Rob Deer	186	1987
Total Bases	Robin Yount	367	1982
Hitting Streak	Paul Molitor	39	1987
Runs Scored	Paul Molitor	136	1982

All-Time Brewers Career and Season Records *(continued)*

Single-Season Pitching Records (1969–1992)

ERA (150 innings)	Cal Eldred	1.79	1992
Wins	Mike Caldwell	22	1978
Losses	Clyde Wright	20	1974
Winning Pct. (10 decisions)	Cal Eldred	.846 (11–2)	1992
Strikeouts	Ted Higuera	240	1987
Walks	Jim Slaton	102	1974
Saves	Dan Plesac	33	1989
Games	Ken Sanders	83	1971
Complete Games	Mike Caldwell	23	1978
Games Started	Jim Slaton	38	1973,1976
Shutouts	Mike Caldwell	6	1978
Innings Pitched	Jim Colborn	314	1973

12

Toronto Blue Jays
Okay, Blue Jays! From Worst to First in a Decade

Peter C. Bjarkman

The problem is that you acquire a past. In the beginning, what needs to be done is so clear, so obvious. When you have no players you must acquire the young players that you can find. When they are ready you put them in the lineup because the people who were there before them are just a holding action, just waiting until the future is warm. When you have no past you have no loyalties, no debts. You know exactly where you are in the cycle. You have a memory of no yesterday's dreams which still might flower tomorrow, and thus there is no confusion of tomorrow with yesterday, plans with dreams, or what is right with what is best for the team. On September 20, 1987 the Toronto Blue Jays had a clean slate. They never will again!
Bill James, *The Bill James Baseball Abstract 1988.*

Loaded with talented and colorful young players, and blessed with baseball's most lavish pleasuredome stadium, the Toronto Blue Jays are today one of the premier drawing cards of North America's favorite pastime. In 1989 over 3.3 million fans crammed into Toronto's Exhibition Stadium and passed through the portals of the remarkable Toronto SkyDome, establishing the largest home attendance total in the century-long history of American League baseball. The Toronto Blue Jays story is the exciting saga of a youthful baseball franchise with an already rich and storied history—one stretching back across the past decade and a half, and encompassing some of modern baseball's most distinctive heroes and most cherished moments.

In the early franchise years of the 1970s the Jays were one of baseball's worst teams, losing 207 games in their first two seasons of big-league play. By the mid-1980s they had emerged as a talented bunch of underachievers who couldn't seem to learn how to win the big games, blowing the 1987 Eastern Division title with seven consecutive losses at season's end. Yet by the close of the 1989 campaign, these stubborn Jays (spurred by the clubhouse leadership of newcomer

Mookie Wilson and the comeback season of enigmatic George Bell) appeared to be a team that had finally lived up to its fans' longstanding expectations, and done so with a dramatic flair for come-from-behind victories and nearly flawless home field play. Winning the league's Eastern Division for the second time in four short seasons, Toronto's Blue Jays proved in 1989 that they are—and will be for some time to come—a team to be reckoned with at each new season's outbreak of pennant fever.

A baseball team doesn't have to be ancient to exude a sense of baseball tradition. It doesn't require decades of pennants won and lost to mold a big league team's colorful identity and its own rich sense of mythology. Baseball's foremost poet, Roger Angell, has embellished this theme while describing one of his own cherished teams—the New York Mets. Born in 1962, the Mets were quick to develop an unrivalled baseball mythology, one arising from the team's astonishing ineptitude and further heightened by legendary players who were tied forever to New York's rich baseball past—Duke Snider, Gil Hodges, and especially the "Old Professor" Casey Stengel. Angell lovingly chronicles the earliest mythic underpinnings of the hapless yet "amazin" New York Mets within his masterwork, *The Summer Game* (1972), marvelling at "the carefree unreality, the joyful bitterness, the self-identification with a brave but hopeless cause" which already sustained one of baseball's most colorful teams during its maiden years at the legendary Polo Grounds.[1]

Nor is an eventful diamond history any guarantee of true baseball tradition, as Angell again cogently observes about certain less-favored teams, such as the Met's New York progenitors, the Los Angeles (nee Brooklyn) Dodgers. For nostalgic fans like Roger Angell—those steeped with baseball lore and enamored of historic ballparks—the transplanted Dodgers are the classic baseball anathema, a team with little evident appreciation for their colorful Flatbush heritage. Upon abandoning historic Ebbets Field and traditional East Coast roots, Walter O'Malley's Dodgers callously discarded the familiar "Dem Bums" trappings of Brooklyn in order to cultivate a freshly polished image of wholesome All-American virtue and West Coast prosperity. And something indigenous to baseball was somehow significantly lost in the process.

Just as the lovable Mets contrast with the too-sterile latter-day Dodgers, Toronto's fledgling Blue Jays contrast dramatically with their French Canadian rivals, the National League's Montreal Expos. For one thing, baseball history in Montreal is distinguished by all-too-few "flaky" yet lovable diamond personalities—Bill "Spaceman" Lee provides perhaps the only noteworthy example. Nowhere else in baseball can stark contrasts between the colorful tradition-laden ballclub and the sterile expansion franchise be more dramatically showcased, in fact, than with Canada's two "Johnny-Come-Lately" entries into America's national pastime.

In Toronto, for example, the bizarre baseball personality has been almost a franchise trademark since the first Opening Day of April 1977. First to mind is Rick Bosetti, a talent-poor journeyman outfielder who made up in outrageous onfield behavior for his distinct lack of demonstrable diamond skills; next stands utility infielder Roy Howell, who distinguished himself by flaunting bare biceps on the most wintry Exhibition Stadium days; there is can't-miss prospect Lloyd Moseby, who sulked his way out of the hearts of Toronto fans, yet once gained baseball immortality by stealing second, then first, then second again— all on a single infamous botched baserunning play befitting the legendary Germany Schaefer. Finally there was mammoth Cliff Johnson, prototype designated hitter, who looked and hit like Paul Bunyan, yet also unfortunately fielded his first-base position (the few times he was permitted carelessly to don a glove) in the manner of an untrained lumberjack to boot. These were among the principal actors who assured that Toronto baseball would always be a top entertainment draw, even in the worst of expansion years.

The Blue Jays story, like that of the fan-rich Mets, is a tale of miraculous and equally sudden transformation from such "lovable losers" into one of baseball's premier pennant-contending teams. It is the story of a ballclub which has from the outset captured the passions of a nation of Canadian sports fanatics for whom baseball was supposedly only a secondary warm-weather sport, a team whose players have become national sporting heroes as well as symbols of community pride and rallying points for national optimism. Despite an embarrassing opening season total of just 54 victories, Blue Jays baseball attracted an unprecedented 1.7 million paying customers as enthusiasm never waned throughout the maiden 1977 summer. Overnight this team was also to become as much a marketing success as a baseball success, with $10 million in sales of souvenir toys and T-shirts reported during the earliest months of the team's inaugural campaign (Reidenbaugh, 1983, 274). These Jays were suddenly aloft and soaring far beyond the fondest hopes of Toronto baseball promoters, and the flight has yet to diminish, though 13 summers have now passed without a single World Series game yet played on Canadian soil.

The bulk of major league teams have their beginnings obscured by ravages of time, and events surrounding their earliest games are often hopelessly lost in the dim light of a bygone century. Who recalls details of the 1880s St. Louis Browns or the legendary Athletics of Philadelphia's earliest days under Connie Mack? Latter-day expansion franchises have more recently struggled through premier seasons that both fans and players alike would sooner forget. By contrast with these more normal big league scenarios, the earliest years of Blue Jays baseball are both vivid in recent memory and buoyed by colorful events and nostalgic happenstance. No team boasts a more memorable opening game. April 7, 1977, was witness to a remarkable baseball "happening" which millions of Canadians today proudly (if fallaciously) claim to have experienced first hand. Within a decade of that memorable moment the Blue Jays had arrived at the very zenith of baseball success. Their record of wins and losses (457–352, .585 pct.) today ranks first among major league teams over the past five seasons; and only three franchises (Dodgers, Mets, and Cardinals) have drawn more fans through turnstiles during that same period.

The fact that such immediate success has been tinged with compensating failures—two division flags diminished by three successive late-season failures in the race to achieve Canada's first World Series—has only added to the emotional charge of a sport where failure is commonplace and poignant defeat almost always outshines spectacular success. The season of 1989 was clearly a "year at the crossroads" for baseball fortunes in Toronto, and 1990 finds the Blue Jays still poised precariously on the brink of an uncertain if nonetheless optimistic baseball future. With a new ultra-modern downtown stadium having now undergone its spectacular baptism—perhaps the first unfortunate break with Toronto's brief yet history-laden baseball past—the Blue Jays are now prepared to wing into the heart of a second decade of major league expansion baseball. Yet the future is not entirely bright; led by a less-than-popular field manager and his stable of high-priced but disgruntled superstars, the late 1980s editions of the Toronto Blue Jays lined up among baseball's most mysterious and unpredictable ballclubs. What will the 1990s hold—one of the earliest World Championships in expansion baseball history, or perhaps only more defeats, disappointments, and failed expectations—the hallmark of all but a handful of baseball's newest and also oldest teams?

Expansion Baseball—Youthful Jays Aloft, with Talent in the Wings

The opening chapter of Blue Jays baseball transpired far from the lush diamonds of summertime play. Official birth of Toronto's fledgling major league franchise came instead amid much hoopla and ceremony in the elegant Terrace Room of New York's ancient downtown Plaza Hotel. The date was November 5, 1976, and the occasion brought together an august group of baseball dignitaries and officers from the American League's two infant expansion ballclubs. League Chairman Joe Cronin opened the morning's proceedings by presenting Blue Jays Board Chairman Howard Webster with an official certificate of membership for the league's 76th year of play. Comedian Danny Kaye, part-owner of the nascent Seattle ballclub, launched the true business of the day—the 1977 expansion draft—by selecting journeyman outfielder Ruppert Jones as the first Seattle Mariner. At exactly 10:31 a.m. Toronto vice president and general manager Peter Bavasi followed Kaye onto the rostrum to announce the choice of shortstop (and present AAA manager at Syracuse) Bob Bailor, late of the Baltimore Orioles, as the Toronto Blue Jays' first-drafted player. Over the next seven hours Bavasi and his staff selected an additional 29 players left unprotected by the existing 12 American League franchises—at a modest cost of $175,000 apiece. From this rare assemblage of failed veterans (such as Bill Singer of the Twins), not-too-promising youngsters (like Pete Vuckovich of the White Sox), and heretofore untested utility players (Jim Mason of the Yankees), an official major league roster was jerry-built. On paper the team looked at best like a mediocre entry in the AA Southern Association. But at long last Toronto was officially in the big leagues, and for Canadian patrons, this was all that ultimately mattered.

Several players (Phil Roof, Dave Roberts, John Hilton, John Henry Scott) had actually been signed weeks earlier, inked to contracts by a team which was yet unnamed and still in search of a field manager. Only Roof, who had played AAA ball in Toronto 14 years earlier, boasted previous major league experience. Perhaps the best prospects to emerge from the Jays' expansion draft were only indirect byproducts of the formal selections on draft day itself. Cleveland catcher Alan Ashby was acquired via a draft-day swap for Kansas City pitcher Al Fitzmorris; and outfielder John Lowenstein and catcher Rick Cerone came on board the following month, also from Cleveland, for outfielder Rico Carty. Carty, ironically, was later to return to the Jays from Cleveland, in time for the 1978 and 1979 seasons. Other draft-day acquisitions who eventually saw more than modest playing time in a Blue Jays uniform were pitchers Jim Clancy, Jerry Garvin, Dave Lemanczyk, Jesse Jefferson, and Mike Willis; outfielders Alvis Woods and Otto Velez; catcher Ernie Whitt; and opening day batting star Doug Ault. Only Clancy and Whitt became more than journeymen ballplayers during subsequent seasons, and both were still wearing Blue Jays uniforms 12 years later at the close of the 1988 season (Whitt, the last original Jay, was not dealt away until December of 1989).

Draft day 1976 represented an exciting fulfillment of a nearly century-long dream of bringing major league baseball to the Queen City of Toronto. Yet the true beginnings of the Toronto Blue Jays story stretch back much further, encompassing nearly five years of active campaigning by city officials bent on gaining an expansion franchise, and capping nearly three-quarters of a century of vague dreams and often vain hopes for big-time baseball. Prior to the unexpected and dramatic expansion events of March 1976, Toronto had nearly captured a major league team at least twice before, each time seemingly reaching the doorstep of big-league baseball only to have the prize snatched suddenly from its grip. In fact, Toronto had once earlier almost landed squarely in the National League, and had fate and politics taken a few different twists, today's Toronto fans might well have been loyal to the Horace Stoneham's Giants, or perhaps seen the come-lately Padres of burgermogul Ray Kroc, rather than to the fledgling American League Blue Jays.

The city of Toronto first harbored a dream of big league baseball as early as the 1880s, when Albert Goodwill Spalding reportedly visited the Canadian metropolis in mid-winter of 1886 and suggested that Toronto would be a most excellent site for a proposed National League franchise.[2] Toronto was again prominently mentioned in 1899, while Ban Johnson was scouting cities throughout the Northeast for inclusion in his nascent American League, and also reported once again in 1919 as a certain entry for the never-to-materialized New Liberty major league. Yet it was not until 1973 that serious plans emerged for renovating existing Canadian National Exhibition Stadium in hopes of capitalizing on new rumors of major league expansion. An often-repeated but perhaps only apocryphal story involves the apparent seeds of baseball's long-awaited migration northward to Ontario province. Metro (Toronto City) Chairman Paul Godfrey and Ontario Premier William Davis reputedly stood at midfield of Exhibition Stadium awaiting opening-game ceremonies of the 1973 Grey Cup Football Game and chatted informally about the shared dream of luring major league baseball. An ardent baseball fan, Godfrey is reported to have whispered to Davis, "I think we should build a baseball stadium . . . Right here." And in that single fateful moment the most momentous deal in Canadian sporting history was supposedly sealed, with little more than a handshake and a smile.

Two events which followed were also highly significant for the eventual birth of the Toronto Blue Jays, albeit not before a convoluted series of events and misadventures surrounded the efforts to bring a second big-league franchise to Canada. The first was a commitment by Metro and provincial government officials to expand Exhibition Stadium toward a seating capacity of over 40,000, an necessary step in any plan to lure a baseball tenant. The second was promotion of 36-year-old Donald J. McDougall to the presidency of powerful Labatts Breweries, one of the province's leading industrial giants. Over the course of the next three years the stadium was indeed rebuilt—albeit with taxpayers' money—though no likely team yet loomed on the horizon. During the same period McDougall joined forces with Robert

Howard Webster, chairman of *The Globe and Mail* newspaper, to form an official consortium of Toronto investors, designed explicitly for the purpose of actively seeking an expansion franchise. For nearly two years not a major league owners' meeting, World Series, or All-Star Game passed without a contingent headed by McDougall, Godfrey, and Webster in attendance to promote Toronto as a potential major league city. Success seemed nearly at hand in January 1976, when the Labatts group tentatively reached an "agreement in principle" to purchase the financially troubled San Francisco Giants for $13.5 million; but a court injunction launched by San Francisco mayor George Moscone delayed action just long enough for the entire deal to fall through by early March. Against this backdrop of blatant campaigns and backroom dealings, other Toronto investors groups soon entered the fray. As early as 1971, before joining forces with the McDougall consortium, Montreal financier Webster had made a first unsuccessful attempt to purchase and relocate the National League's San Diego Padres, an effort repeated unsuccessfully in 1972 as well.

The pursuit of the Giants had been a costly adventure for the Labatts consortium, and the group headed up by McDougall and Webster (along with the 10 percent partnership of the Canadian Imperial Bank of Commerce) had reportedly lost almost one quarter million Canadian dollars in the effort. Things looked bleak indeed, and time for reflection and regrouping seemed to be at hand. And then—when least expected—good fortune struck quite suddenly and from the most unexpected corner. Just three weeks after the disappointing announcement that local San Francisco buyers had been arranged for the Giants, the American League owners meeting in Tampa unpredictably voted 11–1 to expand to a 14-team circuit and immediately announced preparations for offering expansion franchises to both Seattle and Toronto. The entry fee was to be a tidy $7 million apiece. American League president Lee MacPhail, ignoring the overtures of several newly formed Toronto investor groups, turned to the McDougall-Webster consortium which had already been on the scene of expansion negotiations for more than five years. A last substantial hurdle had yet to be cleared, however, as Commissioner Bowie Kuhn pursued last-ditch efforts to delay American League expansion. Kuhn hoped to prompt National League bosses to honor an earlier commitment to the nation's capital by expanding into Toronto and Washington, D.C. Nothing concrete was to come of the 11th-hour Kuhn power play, however, and at long last the issue seemed settled. Ironically, the $7 million entry fee was little more than half the original proposed purchase price for the nearly moribund Giants. This was good fortune indeed, on more counts than one. Establishment of a new franchise not scheduled to compete until April 1977 promised significant departure from the disastrous path of recent expansion franchises. Such a length-ened time-frame would facilitate necessary structuring of a big-league organization and allow adequate planning for a properly designed long-range baseball operation. In the end "Lady Luck"—the true patron saint of baseball—had at long last smiled favorably on the Queen City and on Canada's millions of disenfranchised baseball fans.

While Metro government officials were busy allocating in excess of $2.8 million (Canadian)—by the lopsided vote of 27–3—for further expansion and improvements on Exhibition Stadium, the new Ameri-can League club began hiring its first payroll employees. Webster was named board chairman of Metro Baseball Ltd. (the official corporate franchise name), with Labatts vice president N.E. "Peter" Hardy pegged as vice chairman. Peter Bavasi, 34-year-old vice president and general manager of the San Diego Padres, was also tabbed for a similar slot in Toronto. In what proved the first of many astute personnel decisions, the McDougall management team selected from the finest of baseball pedigrees in hiring Bavasi. The younger Bavasi was son of Padres president (and ex-Brooklyn and Los Angeles Dodgers general manager) Buzzy Bavasi. Paul Beetson, a respected Ontario accountant, was lured as vice president for administration, while Howard Starkman (still with the club in 1990) was named public relations director, a slot he had long filled for hockey's Toronto Maple Leafs. Bavasi himself demonstrated instant baseball savvy as well, bringing on board former associate Pat Gillick, then a New York Yankees farm director, as new vice president for player personnel.

The most significant addition to the Blue Jay staff, of course, was Gillick, who in short order became the main architect—along with an able assist from super scout Epy Guerrero—of a master plan of player recruitment unparalleled in the major leagues over the next 10 years. It was Gillick, of course, with his carefully fostered Latin American connections and his patient and astute handling of the Blue Jays minor league program, to whom the lion's share of credit would later be given for Toronto's incredibly rapid ascent to the top of the baseball world (details are drawn in Bjarkman, *The Toronto Blue Jays*, Chapter 6).

By November 1976 one substantial element of a true major league team had already been put firmly in place—a roster of big-league players, albeit largely minor league hopefuls and major league has-beens. A second piece of the puzzle had also been artfully constructed through selection of a stable team of administrative staffers and on-field management personnel. At the end of the team's first 12 years (in 1988), Webster, Gillick, Hardy, and Starkman would still sit in their original management positions, with only Peter Bavasi having departed from the Blue Jays front office. (Bavasi would resign as president and chief operating officer on November 24, 1981, replaced by Board Vice Chairman Hardy.) A third essential ingredient for major league play was the ballpark, a makeshift football stadium with plenty of character and an ideal downtown location, which was already undergoing final grooming for the 1977 opener.

What remained to be settled was only the most visible component—an official team name. In a move designed to boost both civic interest and community involvement, a "Name the Team" contest was held during June and July of 1976; it drew over 30,000 individual entries and almost 4,000 different and often offbeat suggestions. Proposed monikers included such memorable possibilities as Dingbats, Blue Bats, Hogtowners, Trilliums, Blue Sox, Bootleggers, and the inevitable nationalistic choice—Maple Leafs. Ten names were ultimately drawn randomly by a panel of select judges and "Blue Jays" was announced as the popular choice on August 13, 1976. The winning team name had been submitted by no fewer than 154 different fans, necessitating a second random drawing for the promised pair of season tickets and announced all-expenses-paid trip to spring training 1977. The wealth of wild birds throughout the Ontario region was motivation enough for the chosen nickname and a logo was promptly unveiled which combined indentifiable features of the new Canadian franchise—bird profile, baseball, and patriotic maple leaf underscoring Canadian national pride. In announcing the choice of name and logo, an official team press release boasted that "the Blue Jay is a North American bird, bright blue in color, with white undercovering and black necklace . . . strong, aggressive, inquisitive . . . it dares to take on all comers, yet is down-to-earth, gutsy, and good-looking." For diehard Blue Jays fans the bird-on-baseball logo remains a point of unmatched public pride; in the view of many state-side baseball fans, however, the Toronto insignia has to be judged one of the ugliest and least traditional logos ever to grace a big-league baseball cap (though the bland bi-color cap itself was greatly improved to a snappy all-blue format for road games by 1989).

Each big-league team seems to have its own distinctive date with destiny, a unique contract with the unpredictable and the bizarre. For the Toronto Blue Jays this stroke of repeated ill-fortune has from earliest days involved the saga and pageantry of Opening Day. The very first Blue Jays game ever scheduled, a spring training encounter with New York's Mets pencilled in for Grant Field, in Dunedin, was unceremoniously and somewhat portentously rained out. Opening Day at Exhibition Stadium a month later proved equally as unfit for baseball play; yet April 7, 1977, remained a day destined for true baseball immortality. The inaugural game in Toronto American League baseball history remains (at least for the present) unquestionably the most dramatic moment of franchise history. No team—perhaps in all of baseball's considerable history—has experienced such an eventful and even legendary opening game. Certainly none has seen such an Opening Day in the expansion era of the past three decades. The game-time temperature on April 7, 1977, was an intolerable 32° fahrenheit, cold snow blew everywhere, 44,649 standing-room-only fans (300 more than official capacity) remained on their feet and screamed continuously through almost four hours of what only appeared to be the summertime pageant of baseball. Yet almost no one left before the final frigid out was made.

Authors Phillippe van Rjndt and Pat Blednick have immortalized the moment in print: "What we bore witness to that afternoon had to be the most unbelievable spectacle in the history of major-league baseball: tens of thousands of parkas, overcoats, ski-jackets, sweaters and snow suits jammed up one against other, elbows digging into ribs, lumberjack boots stomping on galoshes, eyes glaring out of ski masks as though this was a Montreal bank robbery. For a game that was traditionally southern white and warm weather it certainly had come a long way!" (van Rjndt and Blednick, 1984, 4).

Even before the opening pitch was launched, a deafening chant of "We Want Beer!" arose in unison throughout the park—an ironic joyous cry which would become a trademark of Toronto baseball for the five seasons which preceded the first official ballpark beer sales in 1981. Richie Zisk of the visiting White Sox pounded out a two-run homer in the first inning to stake the Chicagoans to a 2–0 lead, only to be answered by 27-year-old rookie Doug Ault in the bottom of the first with a blast into the covered bleachers in left. In the fifth inning, rookie Alvis Woods of the Blue Jays became only the 11th player in major league history to connect for a pinch homer in his first big-league at bat. The final tally was a come-from-behind 9–5 victory for the home team that left all 44,000-plus exhausted and overjoyed.

Baseball has always been a game of individual heroes, a saga of men momentarily made larger than life by inspired events performed upon the legendary diamonds of their youth. Thus the glory of Opening Day in Toronto fittingly belonged to just one man. He was one Douglas Reagan Ault, a journeyman infielder-outfielder from North Carolina whose career would end by 1980 and who would hit only 15 more big-league homers. Yet on April 7, 1977, Doug Ault was to find his own special encounter with baseball destiny. Again it is van Rjndt and Blednick who have immortalized the moment, one which a million or more Torontonians today falsely boast of having witnessed first-hand, ensconced in ski masks and battered by snowshowers: "Opening day, the first game, constitutes a pantheon just waiting for a hero to walk in. The man through the door was first baseman Doug Ault, who took one of Chicago starter Ken Brett's favorite pitches and laced it deep over the fence in left center . . . Because nobody expected it, the reaction rivaled the pandemonium generated by Moses's parting of the Red Sea. The bitter cold, the cached booze, the wailing kids, everything went out the window as 44,000 rose to their feet in an ovation that would have gone over well in Rome's Coliseum. It was TRIUMPH! . . . The shock was instantaneous because the last image the mind has of this man includes 44,000 hysterical fans—VICTORY! HEROISM! You can still hear the screams and the cries, feel the pounding backslapping from total strangers—TOTAL EUPHORIA!" (1984, 5, 10). A second time Ault strode to the plate in the third inning and a second home run sealed Ault's place as Toronto's first and most indelible baseball legend.

The heroism of Opening Day was later to appear (in the callousness of retrospect) as a brief moment of inspired overconfidence, and for the first five years of their existence the Toronto Blue Jays never even threatened to win a pennant. For five years Toronto baseball featured a seemingly endless supply of promising rookies, career minor-leaguers, players that nobody wanted; it was typical expansion baseball at its best, and often the most entertaining baseball of any team's maiden decade. Inaugural seasons of 1977 and 1978 saw nearly identical numbers: 54–107 (45½ games behind) followed by 59–102 (40 games behind). Yet both campaigns brought over a million fans pouring through the busy turnstiles (1,701,052 followed by 1,562,585) as baseball proved an immediate hit in the land of relentless arctic weather.

The 1977 inaugural edition of the Jays was surprisingly competitive for a ballclub which finished with a .355 won-loss percentage; 77 of its 161 games were decided by two runs or less. While Doug Ault became an immediate fan-favorite with his Opening Day heroics, there were other colorful and tenacious performers as well: Otto Velez hit .422 the opening month of the season and was American League Player of the Month for April 1977; Bob Bailor's .310 season average (496 at bats) was the highest BA ever for a first-year expansion-club player, veteran Ron Fairly, in his 20th major league season, became the first player since Stan Musial to appear in over 1,000 games at both outfield and infield positions; and Dave Lemznczyk's 13 wins in 1977 was also a record for major league first-year expansion play. The return of colorful Dominican slugger Rico Carty from Cleveland (where he had been shipped less than a month after the expansion-day draft), along with the arrival of heavy-hitting first baseman John Mayberry, formerly with Kansas City, provided the Jays with their first two 20-home-run sluggers during the summer of 1978.

The 1978 season also marked the arrival of rookies Rick Bosetti and Jim Clancy. Bosetti quickly proved to be an expansion-era fan favorite and the first of what was to become a seemingly endless parade of fleet young Toronto outfielders. Clancy was the only Jays pitcher able to win 10 games in the team's second year. But perhaps the two most portentous events of the Blue Jay's first two seasons occurred in the early summer of 1978, both actually transpiring far from the daily dramas being played out at Exhibition Stadium. The June free-agent draft that year found Toronto placed in the number two slot; here they selected a previously unheralded outfielder named Lloyd Moseby. Almost simultaneously, at the A-ball level, a struggling rookie slugger named Dave Stieb was being switched from his outfield post to the pitcher's mound in order to take full advantage of what seemed to be an uncommonly talented young throwing arm.

On-the-field progress is not always either visibly steady or outwardly measurable to the average fan, and the 1979 season witnessed a number of apparent setbacks in the Jays' gradual march toward baseball respectability. The on-field records of 109 losses and 50½ games out of first place were both franchise standards for futility, and the first phase of Blue Jay development came to an unceremonious end with the firing of manager Roy Hartsfield at the conclusion of the 1979 campaign. One pleasant surprise of the Jays' third year was the dramatic jump from A-ball to the majors by Dave Stieb, an unexpected event which transpired in early June 1979. This talented rookie righthander completed an outstanding 18–10 record (8–8 in Toronto) in a season split between A-level Dunedin, AAA Syracuse, and the parent club in Canada. Under new manager Bob Mattick (elevated to the bench from his initial role as scouting supervisor), the 1980 Blue Jays improved to 67–95 (36 games out), the ballclub's first season with under 100 losses. This certainly smacked of improvement, even if only good enough for a fourth consecutive seventh-place finish. John Mayberry was the club's first 30-homer man that year, and future pitching aces Jim Clancy (13–16) and Dave Stieb (12–15) emerged as Toronto's most consistent hurlers. Dave Stieb was an All-Star selection and also American League Player of the Month for April; Danny Ainge (later to star in basketball with the World Champion Boston Celtics) made a token appearance as utility infielder with 111 plate appearances); Ernie Whitt first took over as regular starting catcher; and Lloyd Moseby and Willie Upshaw caught on as regulars in the Blue Jays lineup by late 1980.

The campaign of 1981 witnessed not only the most bizarre summer of the first decade in Exhibition Stadium but also marked perhaps the strangest season of all baseball history. An unpopular players' union strike nearly wiped out the entire summer's play and succeeded for nearly three months in obliterating daily baseball as North American fans had always known it. The unparalleled split-season schedule format which resulted after resumption of play in mid-July was a laughingstock for traditional baseball (Cincinnati, with the season's best overall big-league record, didn't even qualify for post-season play in the revamped playoffs); yet this bizarre turn of events seemed at the same time somehow to signal an ironic improvement in Toronto baseball fortunes.

While the first half of the season had witnessed only further ignominy for Toronto (lowlighted by the major league's first perfect game in 13 seasons being thrown at the Jays by journeyman Cleveland pitcher Len Barker on May 15), after the strike the rejuvenated Blue Jays of Bob Mattick managed to play .500 ball for all but the final two weeks of the season. Signs of change were everywhere apparent: Dave Stieb (11–10) became the Jays' first winning pitcher among starting hurlers; future superstar George Bell first appeared in the regular lineup during the post-strike month of August and responded with a .310 BA; and Lloyd Moseby tied for the club lead in RBIs (with John Mayberry) in his first full season of league play. The future of the Jays seemed to be arriving right on schedule, even if not everyone attending games in Exhibition Stadium was altogether aware of this in September 1981. Even at AAA Syracuse the Jays' future was stirring; promising 19-year-old Dominican shortstop Tony Fernandez appeared on the scene by late season and drew immediate raves with his respectable .278 BA and impressive defensive range and agility.

The Blue Jays were never quite the same after the exotic split-season of 1981—a year when baseball's winningest team (Cincinnati) did not qualify for the World Series, Pete Rose did not garner 150 hits for the first time in almost two decades, and Montreal somehow emerged from the National League pack as Canada's first major league division winner. The season was full of surprises in Toronto as well, with the shortened schedule preventing a home attendance mark surpassing one million for the only time in franchise history; with Bob Mattick becoming the second Blue Jay manager to be dismissed, despite his team's marked on-field improvement; and with Bell, Barfield, and Moseby starting in the outfield together for the first time on September 3 in Chicago. This latter trio was soon to be labelled by no less an authority than baseball statistics guru Bill James as standing arguably among the best same-club outfields of all-time.[3]

With the arrival of Bobby Cox as field manager on October 15, 1981, and the departure of GM Peter Bavasi from the front office little more than a month later, expansion baseball had seemingly come to an end and respectable big-league play appeared now to loom on the horizon for Toronto. Some of the most colorful players and memorable events of franchise history had been the true legacy of the first half-decade of Blue Jays baseball in Toronto. It was perhaps inevitable that the tensions of tightly contested pennant races would all-too-soon obliterate some of the unabashed fun at the ballpark which had so enlivened those maiden years for Toronto baseball.

The Sudden and Surprising Rise of Those Amazing Jays

The year of 1982 is to be remembered as the season the Toronto Blue Jays finally escaped seventh place. And it all seemed to go according to some carefully executed master plan, plotted out with the ruthless precision of a corporate takeover or a measured military maneuver. Luck was there as well, of course: a late-season surge of 10 wins in the final 12 games and a corresponding collapse by Cleveland's Indians allowed a sixth-place tie on the season's final day.

But all the elements had already been put neatly in place over the preceding five seasons, as corporate architect Pat Gillick was to explain in a recorded 1984 interview with authors van Rjndt and Blednick. The Hartsfield era was a period, Gillick recounts, when winning was unimportant and the myopic goal was the stockpiling of as many young players as possible. ("We knew that whatever we did we would win no more than fifty or sixty games," Gillick remarked.) Scouting director Mattick had been brought in to manage the next brief phase of team restructuring. Mattick was the ideal man for accelerated player development, with his intimate first-hand knowledge of the core of young talent carefully stockpiled between 1977 and 1979. ("That was his responsibility," recalled Gillick, "to try to bring those players along, give them a good amount of instruction, more playing time than they actually deserved, so they could develop.")

The role of Bobby Cox in 1982 was to begin trying to win, and this was achieved by assigning increasingly larger roles to promising young players. Willie Upshaw was ensconced at first base as Mayberry was shipped back to Kansas City and Upshaw responded immediately with 21 home runs; Damaso Garcia showed signs of future stardom with a .310 BA at second; Jesse Barfield was platooned in right field and hit 18 homers while ranking second among American League outfielders in assists; and on the mound Dave Stieb further blossomed as one of the league's top young hurlers (17–14, 3.25 ERA). Jim Clancy rebounded from injuries with an impressive 16–14 record (3.71 ERA). The Jays stockpiled talent under Hartsfield, taught and developed young talent with Mattick, and turned the reins loose on a talented flock of youngsters under Bobby Cox. The Jays had done it by the book and had seemingly done it exactly right.

If any doubts remained among Toronto baseball watchers about Gillick's master plan, they were all but obliterated during the 1983 and 1984 seasons. The on-field improvement was almost geometrical in its progression—a fourth-place finish in 1983, but with 89 victories and only nine games behind the victorious Orioles (only three games behind second-place Detroit and two games out of third). Late August saw the club only 1½ games behind the leaders, but pennant fever was dowsed by a late-August string of heart-rending extra-inning defeats. Acquisition of Cliff Johnson (DH-1B, Oakland), Jorge Orta (OF-DH, Mets), and Dave Collins (OF, Yankees) had solidified the young Toronto outfield. Perhaps the key to the strong 1983 season showing, however, was stabilization of the youthful pitching staff (Stieb, Clancy, and Luis Leal were again the core, and Doyle Alexander was acquired for late-season strength), as well as the emergence of Lloyd Moseby as one of the finest young outfielders in the game. Moseby was the first Blue Jay to score 100 runs, Upshaw was the first to post 100 RBIs, and Damaso Garcia batted over .300 for the second consecutive year.

The 1984 season brought a strange mix of joy and foreboding to the Queen City baseball scene. The Blue Jays—far sooner than either rabid fans or skeptical experts had expected—were no longer merely expansion laughingstocks. In what was admittedly baseball's best division, the American League East, the 1983 Jays had found themselves firmly entrenched in the thick of pennant contention. Yet a pervasive sense of tragedy appeared to plague this young team, and by the spring of 1984 it had become unsettlingly apparent that baseball fortunes for Toronto might not rest solely in the hands of front office wizards like Pat Gillick nor in the bats of stellar on-field performers like Barfield, Moseby, and Bell. Other darker forces seemed at work, and one of those forces resided only a few hundred miles to the east in Detroit's Tiger Stadium. By early 1984 the Jays had significantly improved their most notable earlier weakness—the bullpen—with acquisition of the team's first significant free-agent talent, relief-ace Dennis Lamp. Yet the bullpen still faltered in crucial game situations, and despite another 89-victory season the Jays were never serious contenders in 1984. The unstoppable Tigers won a record 35 of their first 39 decisions and Toronto and the rest of the league were left far behind as Detroit bolted unharnessed from the gate. Second place was something of a hollow consolation for a Blue Jays team which finished 15 games behind the leaders and never actually tasted the thick of the pennant race it had enjoyed in 1983.

For nearly every baseball franchise (save perhaps those in Seattle and Arlington, Texas) there comes sooner or later that one ultimate dream season, that fateful summer when everything falls suddenly into place and wildest dreams of glory and victory are dramatically reached. In Philadelphia, or perhaps Chicago, fans may wait nearly five decades for such a season; in Toronto it came most miraculously after only eight campaigns of American League play. The unstoppable Tigers of 1984 slumped badly in 1985 and the door was thrust wide open for Bobby Cox and his batting young Blue Jays. Tom Henke (13 saves) had emerged from the minors and Bill Caudill (14 saves) was plucked from free agency to (at long last!) elevate the bullpen to the level of major league competency. Doyle Alexander (17–10) and newcomer Jimmy Key (14–6) supported Dave Stieb (11–10) in the starting mound assignments, and Dennis Lamp enjoyed a remarkable 1985 campaign (11–0) in his familiar middle-relief role.

The Jays moved into first place on May 13 and pennant euphoria ignited Exhibition Stadium throughout the long summer months. A record 2,468,925 fans poured through the turnstiles—a second consecutive season over the two-million figure—and nearly 47,000 crammed the Big Bird Feeder on Saturday afternoon, October 5, as pennant-fever reached epidemic proportions. None among the faithful was disappointed, as Doyle Alexander pitched a masterful 5—1 victory over the much-hated Yankees and Toronto enjoyed its first-ever championship celebration.

The pandemonium which surrounded clinching of Toronto's first division title provided a cherished moment of Canadian sporting history rivaled only by Doug Ault's heroics in the legendary opening game of April 1977. That the pennant race had come down to the season's final week only added a fitting touch of baseball drama in the finest poetic traditions of the national pastime. And this drama was still further heightened by the Jays' heartbreaking 4–3 10-inning loss the previous night of October 4, before the largest (pre-SkyDome) Toronto baseball crowd ever (47,686). But in less than 24-hours agony was replaced by ecstasy as George Bell snagged Ron Hassey's harmless fly ball to cap the ninth inning and the long-awaited celebration began. In the immediate aftermath of a first division title, the disappointing seven-game American League Championship Series defeat at the hands of Kansas City's Royals, eventual World Champions, seemed at the time to be almost anti-climatic. The Jays had arrived and there was always next year, when a World Championship seemed all but certain. The Jays now stood fast among the baseball elite, and Toronto fans (untrained by decades of shifting baseball fortunes) were inclined to pay little heed to what had just happened before their very eyes to those seemingly invincible Tigers, who had themselves reigned so supreme only a short summer earlier. But the Tigers of Detroit and the lessons of baseball's fickle fortunes would be back in all their glory in Exhibition Stadium before the next year of baseball had been played to its final out.

The most transparent reasons for the sudden on-field and off-field baseball successes enjoyed by Toronto between expansion-draft day in 1977 and the divisional title of 1985 are not hard to locate. In his detailed study of the young Toronto franchise, *Globe and Mail* sportswriter Larry Millson carefully documents (in his book *Ballpark*

Figures, 1987) the role of Pat Gillick and his staff in constructing a minor league support system and major league front office staff with few parallels in baseball's long and storied history. Gillick's contributions were fittingly acknowledged by the baseball establishment at the end of the 1985 season when the Toronto VP was tabbed as organized baseball's major league executive of the year. But perhaps the key, as Millson notes, is the degree to which the Blue Jays followed the sterling example of the Los Angeles Dodgers and painstakingly developed continuity and loyalty deep within the Toronto organization. Former players were regularly hired back into the system as scouts, coaches, and minor league managers (Ault, Mayberry, Bailor, Hector Torres, and Eddie Dennis are examples). Bob Mattick provided essential continuity throughout three phases of team development, as scouting supervisor (1977–1979), field manager (1980–1981), and vice president for baseball operations (1982–1988). The Latin American scouting and recruitment program under the astute management of Gillick and super scout Epy Guerrero has become a model unrivalled by previous major league baseball operations (see Bjarkman, *The Toronto Blue Jays,* 1990). By June 1985, Toronto employed 34 Latins (23 Dominicans) throughout its system, a league standard; during spring training of 1989 the 16 Latin players on the Blue Jays' 40-man roster was again the most in the majors by a wide margin (Pittsburgh was second with 11).

And yet for all the obvious successes there were also the inevitable storm clouds building on the horizon. Championships bring huge contract demands from star players, and winning teams are never as hungry as losing teams, especially victory-starved expansion teams. Millson underscores the paradox of the Blue Jays at the end of the 1985 season when he notes that owning a sports franchise confronts management with two distinct though not unrelated "bottom lines" as yardsticks to major league success. The fans are always aware of the first such measure—wins and losses, and championship flags joyously celebrated in the month of October. More subtle yet even more vital to franchise survival is the ledger-item of dollars and cents, and the unfortunate fact in Toronto is that it is always Canadian and not U.S. dollars and cents which count. By such a measure, the post-championship season was to become the team's worst year ever. In the face of the second largest attendance in Blue Jay history (2,455,477 paying customers), the organization lost $3 million or more. The problem here, of course, was that $14 million (Canadian) in revenue had to sustain player payrolls and other burgeoning expenses to be paid out in U.S. dollars, a losing proposition from the start. And 47,000-seat (standing-room capacity) Exhibition Stadium was already proving a burden to the overtaxed Canadian franchise. While each sellout in Yankee Stadium meant $400,000 (U.S.) to New York Yankees ownership, a sellout in Toronto would bring only $250,000 (Canadian) for Blue Jays ownership (Millson 1987, 286). The long-awaited SkyDome Stadium—scheduled to premiere by 1989 as perhaps baseball's finest facility—was now projected to be only several short seasons away. But so too was MVP slugger George Bell's $4.5 million two-year contract!

Cold Starts and Colder Finishes on the Shores of Lake Ontario

By spring training of 1986 the defending American League Eastern Division Champions seemingly had arrived at a crucial crossroads of franchise history. Had Toronto's lovable Jays arisen so suddenly to the heights of pennant contention through some kind of inexplicable fluke? Would they soon fall again in the expected rapid ebb and flow of shifting team fortunes that has distinguished baseball since the onset of free agency? (Division-play, after all, has provided 23 champions in 26 big-league cities.) Or had Toronto become a true dominant force in the American League East, the showcase product of expert long range planning by a corporate management that seemed to do everything right from the very outset in 1977? The tentative answer revealed by the subsequent 1987 and 1988 seasons seems to suggest that perhaps it was a little of both.

A 10th-anniversary season in 1986 was much anticipated as potentially heralding the Blue Jays' inevitable glory year, but it didn't quite work out that way. Over-confidence perhaps, a slow-start to be sure—these were the factors which conspired to reaffirm that old baseball adage: it is much easier to win a pennant than it is to defend one. Under a reign of new manager Jimy Williams the talented Jays did muster an impressive late-season finish which left them nine and one half games back and in fourth place. At best it was a season of individual milestones, with Clancy and Stieb becoming the club's first two career 100-game winners and with George Bell (31 homers and a club-record 108 RBIs) and Jesse Barfield (a club-record 40 homers) emerging as true major American League batting stars.

When it comes to labelling baseball summers in terms of highlight individual performances, 1987, in turn, was indisputably "The Year of George Bell"—unless it was more fittingly labelled "The Year of the Ultimate Collapse"! Ironically, Bell's season-long successes and the team's final-week failures were intricately woven together as the flamboyant Latin American slugger's MVP season tailed off into a final-week slump which many blamed in part for the seven-game season-ending slide which handed another division pennant to Detroit. Yet in the end it was as much the crucial season-ending injuries to shortstop Tony Fernandez (taken out on a rough slide by Detroit's Bill

Madlock in the season's penultimate week) and catcher Ernie Whitt (a bruised hand) during the final dramatic 10 days of September, as it was the hitting slump by Bell, which explained the Jay's inability to pull off a single needed victory in the final three-game set at Detroit. What was almost lost to Torontonians in the final week of pennant disappointment was the indelible impression for the neutral observer that this 1987 Toronto ballclub was indeed a beautiful team to watch, and that the season's final two tightly contested series with Detroit (three wins and one loss at home the final week of September, and three crucial defeats at Detroit the following weekend) provided some of the most colorful and dramatic baseball in the long annals of American League championship season play.

Perhaps the most painful irony of Toronto's brief baseball history is the depressing fact that the Jays played far better baseball during those final seven 1987 games (three at home with Milwaukee and the final three-game set at Detroit)—all which they lost—than did any of the four division champions (Detroit, Minnesota, St. Louis, and Los Angeles) during post-season play which was to follow. (This was the year a Twins team with a 29–52 road record emerged as World Champions!) But first impressions and the hindsight of memory are often as illusory in baseball as they are in all other walks of life. The Jays did not exactly collapse in the season's final month; they simply could not win the crucial close games, due mostly to impotent hitting down the stretch (only three Blue Jays hit higher than .222 during the final week of the season). Nor did Toronto lead the division for very much of the season, trailing the Yankees and Brewers as well as the Tigers for most of the summer and standing at only 14 games over .500 near the end of July. It was in August and September that the lethal Toronto bats boomed at a torrid pace and the club played nearly .700 ball; yet Toronto still trailed Detroit by a full game on September 1. The Tigers were again in first place on September 17, and it was only after sweeping three of four from Detroit in the last days of September that the Blue Jays seemed to take temporary command of the race. Yet in the end the Toronto ballclub could not avoid what it had so successfully avoided all season long—a prolonged losing slump and neutralization by strong opposition pitching. The ultimate irony about the 1987 Blue Jays, when all was said and done, was that they could not win the close well-pitched games for which their team speed and strong starting pitching should have equipped them to excel. In slugfests (games with more than 10 runs scored) the Jays were ironically the most successful team in either league, winning 37 and dropping only 17 (.685 percentage). In pitcher's duels, however, the Jays' winning percentage dropped to an anemic .417 (17–24), easily one of the year's worst marks in either league.

The late-season failures of 1987 were abated only by the high expectations for 1988. Could the Blue Jays rebound? Was this finally to be the year of Toronto's (Canada's!) first World Series? After all, the outfield of Bell, Barfield, and Moseby was still intact and potent, and the lively young arms of Stieb, Clancy, and Key were still the envy of the league. And despite the stability of the Blue Jays' roster (only 14 regular starters at the eight defensive positions over the past five seasons), this was a team featuring only one key player (Ernie Whitt) over the age of 31. Everyone's pre-season pick this time around seemed to be the ill-fated yet multi-talented Jays. Sparky Anderson's Detroit Tigers now looked depressingly over-aged and talent-thin, and no other serious challenger seemed quite equal to the task of derailing a Toronto team which appeared capable of pacing the league in almost all offensive and defensive categories.

But just as 1985 was followed by the slow start of 1986, so 1987's final disastrous week was encored by an even slower get-away in April 1988.[4] From the first days of spring training there were ominous signs. MVP George Bell feuded loudly throughout training camp with field boss Jimy Williams over his assigned role as permanent DH, a move calculated to advance promising rookie speedsters Sil Campusano and Rob Ducey into the Toronto outfield and strengthen the club measurably on the defensive front. While Campusano and Ducey had already ingloriously played their way back to Syracuse by opening week, however, malcontents Bell and Moseby were again entrenched in the Toronto outfield when the new season debuted on the road in Kansas City. Bell promptly answered his many critics by clouting three mammoth homers on Opening Day at Royals Stadium, but then just as promptly tumbled into a season-long slump from which he inevitably emerged as the biggest goat in a season filled with lost opportunities. A mid-season incident in Minnesota, where Bell was yanked from the lineup after two badly misplayed outfield balls, seemed to capsulate the erstwhile slugging star's year of total frustration, one which saw him eclipse even Rick Bosetti's lofty 1979 club standard for outfield errors.

George Bell did come on strong offensively at season's end and the Jays did finish with a sudden flurry, with six wins in a row, nine victories in the final 10 games, and 15 wins over the final 18 contests. For the last three weeks of September, in fact, Toronto was once again recognizably the best team in baseball, coming from 8½ games off the pace on September 20 to a scant two games out after the final day's play. But seasons are played out over the long summer months, and Toronto's inspired late-season heroics were once again far too little and altogether too late.

Bell's persistent sulking was not the only sign of dissension on this troubled 1988 club, however. A contingent of the team's dedicated

Christian athletes, led by group spokesmen Jesse Barfield and Tony Fernandez, had fumed over manager Williams' early-season suspension of road-trip clubhouse chapel sessions. Religion has always been as familiar as stray towels in the Jays' clubhouse, yet Williams was the first skipper to see the practice as disruptive of the club's normal baseball routine. When club officials balked as well at the idea of Fernandez and teammate Kelly Gruber wearing team-logo caps and jackets while promoting a religious fund raiser for starving third-world children, morale among activist Christian players dipped still further. Williams' managerial tenure now seemed in considerable jeopardy, in light of such dissension piled atop the ongoing feud with Bell, but at season's end front-office management made it abundantly clear just where it stood in regard to the beleaguered field manager and his unhappy players. The 45-year-old Jimy Williams was rehired in October, while George Bell remained the favored subject of continued trade rumors fed to the press throughout much of the off-season. After all, blame for the poor showing of 1988 might easily be attributed as much to repeated injuries—this time to Tony Fernandez (yet again) and Jimmy Key (who missed 13 starts due to minor arm surgery)— and to the uncooperativeness of Bell and Moseby, as to any leadership flaws of the taciturn Williams. That the Blue Jays finished 1988 by winning the final six games of the season, closing to within two games of division champion Boston, may also have had much to do with rescuing the controversial manager at the bitter conclusion of a second consecutive disappointing campaign.

Another major story of 1988 was veteran All-Star hurler Dave Stieb. Stieb, along with stellar fireballing reliever Tom Henke, seemed at times to be misused by dugout and front-office management. Both pitchers were known to have contract clauses specifying bonus payments attached to their innings pitched, and both appeared not to receive their fair share of the pitching workload in what all-too-often seemed a calculated front-office conspiracy to sabotage such bonus agreements. But whatever his motives for discontent, Stieb fought back with a banner season (16–8, 3.04 ERA), capped by two brilliant year-end mound performances which highlighted Toronto's otherwise disappointing season. On September 11, before a sparse night crowd in Cleveland, the 31-year-old righthander came within a single pitch of achieving a first franchise no-hitter. A two-strike, two-out bad hop single off the bat of Julio Franco in cavernous Municipal Stadium ruined Stieb's initial bid for baseball immortality. A mere six days later, this time at home against Baltimore, pitch-hitter Jim Traber blooped a fatal two-out ninth-inning single into right field to erase Stieb's second consecutive near-no-hit effort. While Dave Stieb thus became baseball's first pitcher ever to lose back-to-back no-hitters, each time on the potential game-final pitch, Toronto remained the only major league franchise never to enjoy a hometown hurler's no-hit effort. But there was a small consolation at least in Stieb's brilliant accomplishment itself—perhaps the finest single back-to-back pitching performance since Johnny Vander Meer successfully realized two consecutive no-hitters for the Cincinnati Reds way back in June 1938, a full half-century earlier.

Bill James seemingly put it best. On September 20, 1987, the Toronto Blue Jays began a fateful seven-game home-and-away series that mercilessly ended the 1987 season and saw the Jays unable to win even a single game which would have brought home a second division pennant. On that fateful day the Jays still held a clean baseball slate, and yet they never would again enjoy such a luxurious reprieve from the harsh judgments of baseball history. For with that final seven-game collapse against Milwaukee and Detroit an era as well as a season dramatically ended; the Blue Jays of 1987 passed into the history books, alongside the 1964 Philadelphia Phillies, as authors of baseball's most memorable late-season collapse. Whatever the team had accomplished during its first decade had always been deliciously unanticipated; it always exceeded all reasonable expectations. After the dramatic late-season foldup of September 1987, however, the team seemed to enter that true fellowship of major league franchises owning an indelible baseball history—a history of excruciating failure, of yearly frustration, and inexcusable annual loss under the most inopportune of circumstances. Like the Cubs, Red Sox, and Phillies, the Blue Jays would forevermore seem doomed always to lose the big game, the single victory needed for pennant or World Championship. Although barely a decade old, this was now a franchise with a tradition of failure cast in the same mold as some of baseball's most lovable and battle-worn franchises—the Brooklyn Dodgers of the early 1950s, the Detroit Tigers throughout 1960s, the Cubs and Red Sox of the past four decades, or the Phillies and White Sox of the entire past half-century. The future and the past would always be measured differently after that season-ending seven-game confrontation with the Brewers and Tigers. For it was precisely then that the Jays and their fans had reached the brink for the first time, and had for the first time as well been turned back in utter and unpardonable defeat.

There's No Easy Way to Get to Toronto's "Big Bird Feeder!"

Baseball tradition is forever inexorably bound up with the incomparable aura of historic baseball stadia. The stadium—a unique reflection of the urban neighborhood which houses it and site of past hometown triumphs as well as inglorious defeats—is a key element in each ballclub's historical perception of itself. Modern-day players roam the same outfield grasses and circle the very same basepaths as legendary heroes of yore; ancient ballparks link generations of old and new fans. As baseball's most literate spokesman, essayist Roger Angell also repeatedly articulates this preference, shared by most true fans, for teams instilled with rich baseball tradition—tradition fostered most effectively by legendary ballplayers and history-laden baseball stadia (Angell, 1972).

A new ballclub with little apparent claim on baseball history, Toronto's Blue Jays played out their first decade in one of baseball's most charming and unusual ballparks, a park which made up in special character for what it sorely lacked in decades of legendary event. Its first game will never be forgotten as baseball's snowiest and most drama-filled season's opener; its final contest—fittingly against the same Chicago White Sox ballclub which baptized the park a dozen seasons earlier—marked the single occasion on which a major league ballpark's very last pitch produced a game-winning homer. With George Bell's dramatic 10th-inning blast off of Sox relief ace Bobby Thigpen on May 28, 1989, Exhibition Stadium bowed out as it had lived—in a moment of unparalleled baseball drama.

While certainly not Fenway Park or Wrigley Field, Exhibition Stadium earned in only a few short seasons a permanent place in both Canadian and American baseball lore and legend. No major league park witnessed over the past decade more bizarre baseball moments. It was here that balls bounced wildly off the hidden concrete floor to float tauntingly over amazed infielders' heads; here that Yankee Dave Winfield struck down a helpless sea gull with his infamous warmup throw; that Lloyd Moseby once stole second and then first again in an unintentional modern-day re-enactment of Detroit's legendary Germany Schaefer; and that each game seemingly ended with massive invasions of hungry sea gulls befitting dark scenes from any of Alfred Hitchcock's most ominous cinematic thrillers.

Exhibition Stadium is often shortchanged by baseball fans who have not experienced its charms first-hand. To rate this ballpark as the worst in the majors—as does Bob Wood in this 1988 volume *Dodger Dogs to Fenway Franks—The Ultimate Guide to America's Top Baseball Parks*—is to judge stadiums only in terms of creature comfort. Ballpark fast-food, seating amenities, scoreboard aesthetics, ballpark employees, and stadium upkeep are among Wood's limited criteria for ranking North America's ballparks, and by these standards most of the quaint parks of an earlier age would fail miserably. To complain that Exhibition Stadium is first and foremost "a plastic baseball diamond literally rolled onto a plastic football field" is to ignore the unavoidable fact that all newer major league facilities are multi-purpose stadia, and thus always more suited to football than to the national pastime. To its credit[5] Exhibition Stadium claimed—unlike its prototypes in Cincinnati, Pittsburgh, or San Deigo—its traditionally rectangular baseball shape. And best of all, this wintry ballpark avoided from the outset that unpardonable breach of faith with fans that has marred most newly minted urban parks—it didn't remove fans hundreds of feet from the actual field of baseball play.

While Exhibition Stadium could admittedly boast a somewhat strange appearance, with its covered left-field bleachers featuring individualized contoured plastic seats, and its uncovered grandstands behind home plate and along the baselines befitting the aluminum benches of college football stadia, this uniqueness was no less colorful than the architecture of such vaunted ancient parks as Braves Field in Boston, Sportsman's Park in St. Louis, or Crosley Field in Cincinnati. While overflow crowds at sellout games left some fans at a distant vantage point (sometimes several hundred feet beyond the night-field fence), the poorest seats at the EX were no worse than the obstructed-view locations often sold at the older-style parks. The distant right-field locations of Exhibition Stadium were, in fact, no further from homeplate than the deep center-field bleachers in one of baseball's most ballyhooed ballyards—the ancient Polo Grounds, which served New York's Giants so proudly for decades and which featured a shape and construction far from consistent with the fan's notion of what an ideal ballpark should be. Among the newer parks, Exhibition Stadium was in fact distinctive in its unique oblong shape and freedom from the "oval sameness" of other multipurpose stadia; and box seat locations along the baselines provided an intimate on-field closeness matched only by the tiny spring training facilities of Florida and Arizona.

Yet it was foremost the unique character of Exhibition Stadium—nestled between ferris wheels and carnival booths within the Canadian National Exhibition grounds—which lent the park its special water-front charm.[6] No out-of-town visitor attending Blue Jays games soon forgets the ever-circling flocks of Canadian sea gulls which descend upon the popcorn-rich bleachers when fans depart in late innings of one-sided games. The "Big Bird Feeder" has been affectionately labelled by more than one Toronto baseball writer as Canada's contribution to American baseball humor. And the reputation seemed duly earned. High bounces off the concrete-like artificial playing surface often caused outfielders to wait in frustration for careening baseballs to return to earth, as runners gleefully circled the basepaths. One result of this baseball circus act was that games sometimes appeared to be played with a maple stick and a tennis ball rather than with ash bat and hardball. And Exhibition Stadium will live on in the memory of every American League and Canadian fan for its opening game of

1977, the only major league game ever played throughout its entirety in a relentless sub-arctic blizzard.

Some of the peak moments in Blue Jays history are also fast interwoven with this special ambience of Exhibition Stadium. This park has been home not only to some of the most fabled moments of Toronto sports history, but also to several of baseball's most unforgettable events of the past two decades. First was the 9–0 forfeit victory over the Baltimore Orioles on September 15, 1977, a game in which starter Jim Clancy had held the Birds scoreless on two hits over five innings before Manager Earl Weaver pulled his Orioles team off the playing field in vehement protest. Weaver's contention was that the bullpen tarps constituted an unacceptable hazard for his players in the chasing of foul balls. On June 26, 1978—again versus Baltimore and Earl Weaver—the Jays erupted for a lopsided 24–10 victory, the Canadian team's highest-scoring game ever and one of the highest in major league history. The Orioles, in fact, seemingly took special delight in playing doormat to the upstart Blue Jays in Exhibition Stadium. Thus Baltimore's Birds were again victimized on September 14, 1987, by a second unprecedented Toronto offensive uprising. In this latter game the Jays exploded for a major league record 10 home runs while pounding out an 18—3 drubbing of hapless Baltimore. On that memorable afternoon Ernie Whitt (3), George Bell (2), Rance Mulliniks (2), Fred McGriff, Rob Ducey, and Lloyd Moseby all contributed to the record-setting onslaught of Toronto roundtrippers. A second major league standard was set in this same game for most players on one team simultaneously enjoying multiple-home-run games. An irony of this 1987 slugfest, however, was that Baltimore manager Cal Ripken, Sr., seized upon the hopeless situation to replace his son, Cal, Jr., at shortstop during the eighth inning, bringing to an end iron-man Ripken's unprecedented streak of 8,243 consecutive innings played. "What the hell," quipped the senior Ripken in reference to the one-sided score, "he (Cal, Jr.) couldn't have hit a 20-run homer!"

When Exhibition Stadium hosted its final game midway through its 13th season, it had already left a legacy that some parks achieve only after decades of major league play: the unique right-field bleacher seats extending hundreds of feet beyond the field of play, as well as the equally unprecedented covered and individualized bleacher seats (the only covered seats in the ballpark) of the left-field grandstand area; the first four seasons with no beer sales allowed and the resulting almost continuous chant of "We Want Beer!" arising from the local faithful; the cheerleading aerobic instructors singing "Okay, Blue Jay!" from the dugout rooftops during the traditional seventh-inning-stretch of each game; and the circling sea gulls (lovingly called "Shit-

Hawks" by local partisans) filling the outfield skies during late innings of each nighttime contest.

Toronto's baseball establishment has remained sensitive from the beginning to the inefficiency of playing baseball in a temporary park designed primarily for the rival autumn game of football. The long-planned replacement for Exhibition Stadium, officially launched with formal groundbreaking ceremonies on October 1986, was eagerly envisioned by club and city officials as an ultimate showcase for contemporary baseball—the diamond sport's first multipurpose stadium with retractable dome roof, a true futuristic facility providing all the conveniences and luxuries of an indoor arena and yet allowing for outdoor baseball on sunbaked summer days as well. Special features of Toronto's unprecedented SkyDome would include a retractable roof capable of opening or closing in as little as 20 minutes, 100 percent uncovered playing surface (with 91 percent uncovered seats) under open-air conditions, and a 364-suite hotel complex at the north-end of the stadium featuring approximately 70 rooms overlooking the actual baseball playing field. Built at the foot of the landmark CN-Tower in the heart of downtown Toronto, baseball's newest architectural wonder held out promise as the most revolutionary ballpark in major league history—a twenty-first century edifice designed to accommodate America's indigenous nineteenth-century game. The impact of this futuristic stadium upon the game of baseball it houses promises to be the most radical ever witnessed in this modern age of multipurpose stadia. The possibility of closing or opening the stadium roof in such short time periods quickly prompted the American League rules committee to consider new standards to cover special circumstances of sudden rain-delays arising during play in the Toronto Skydome. And as might have been anticipated by the duly skeptical, the instance of such an unanticipated cloudburst (in just the third game after the SkyDome's celebrated June 1989 debut) resulted in unexpected difficulties with closing the park's hydraulic roof, a near 40-minute delay under downpour conditions, and very nearly baseball's first rain out in a roofed and protected ballpark arena.

As the 1989 season opened in wintry Toronto, the SkyDome was still two months away from becoming a baseball reality—delayed by numerous construction setbacks, plagued by astronomical cost over-runs, site of continuing labor difficulties, and recipient of bad press of every imaginable sort. Major controversies had already arisen concerning anticipated parking inadequacies and huge projected transportation gridlocks to be encountered daily when Toronto fans begin flocking to the downtown stadium by the middle months of the 1989 season. But whatever the political issues and public alarm surrounding construction of baseball's first moveable-roof stadium, the Toronto

Skydome was finally on schedule to become a reality sometime in mid-season 1989, and with it an era would end and another would begin. Indoor baseball—at least partially indoor baseball—would at last come to the one city where perhaps the normally frigid weather actually justifies such an anomaly. And civic pride had already been buoyed by late 1988 with announcements that the Queen City of Toronto—still awaiting its first World Series—would reap the honor of hosting its first Major League All-Star Game during the summer of 1991.

A Season in the Sun ... and Under the Remarkable Pleasure Dome

As baseball seasons are long and each fresh spring brings renewed pennant dreams, the agony of defeat fades quickly, even if it returns regularly and with nagging persistence. Thus the bitter final week of 1987 and the failure to get off the ground running for 1988 were both eventually swept away in the late euphoria of the action-packed 1989 season. At least the second half of the 1989 season! For at its outset, 1989 seemed destined to be merely another tiresome replay of 1986 and 1988. George Bell was still pouting about frequent if not daily DH duties. The bullpen was again in disarray, as Mark Eichhorn faltered in spring training and was dealt to Atlanta, while Tom Henke proved unproductive in early going and sank from his expected role as the traditional closer. Long-time outfield standby Jesse Barfield was traded away in April to the Yankees for promising lefthander Al Leiter, but Leiter was "damaged goods" and spent the bulk of the season wasting on the disabled list. It was an inauspicious start indeed, and by mid-May the foundering Jays were buried in last place alongside another sinking ship, Detroit, already 5½ games off the pace of the mediocre Red Sox, themselves only playing at a .500 pace. Only the ineptitude of the remainder of the league's Eastern Division kept the Jays from falling totally from sight during the earliest weeks of the 1989 campaign.

The embattled Jimy Williams seemingly had little respect from his disgruntled players during even the earliest days of spring training, and Toronto newspapers were speculating on a managerial change almost from before Opening Day. One of the few highlights was the early-season appearance of rookie Junior Felix, a 24-year-old diminutive Dominican outfielder with only three seasons of professional baseball experience. Felix poked a homer in his first big league at bat—on the very first pitch served up in his May 4 debut against the California Angels in Exhibition Stadium—in the process becoming only the 11th man in league history to accomplish this rare feat (homering on his first big-league *pitch*). Another early highlight was the hitting display of Kelly Gruber on April 16. In the season's third home game against Kansas City the popular Toronto third baseman became the first batsman in team history to hit for the cycle, stroking a single, double, triple, and homer within a single game. But while Gruber continued to hit early, maintaining a .300-plus average on into July, and Felix offered to salvage the botched Barfield trade, little else seemed to go right for the Jays throughout April or the earliest weeks of May.

The true turning point of the Jay's 13th season came precisely in mid-May, spurred by the involuntary departure of Jimy Williams and the arrival of new skipper Clarence "Cito" Gaston, the fifth manager in club history. Williams had long since worn out his welcome with the usually patient Toronto fans and certainly with his own players, and the club stood at 12–24 and mired in sixth place at the time of his firing. But dismissal of Williams on May 15 seemed at least temporarily to throw the organization into even further chaos. No clear managerial replacement immediately emerged, which fortuitously bought acting skipper Cito Gaston some extra time to get the Jays off and running once again. Ex-Yankee skipper Lou Piniella (later hired on at Cincinnati in 1990) was mentioned prominently in the press, as was announcer and ex-big-leaguer Tony Kubek, and Bob Bailor, now manager of the Jays AAA club in Syracuse. But Piniella was not freed from his existing contract as advisor to Yankees owner George Steinbrenner and was thus unavailable for serious consideration, despite his rumored favored status in the eyes of top executive Pat Gillick. In the end it was the 45-year-old batting coach, Gaston, who was tendered the permanent job, thus becoming baseball's third-ever black field boss. Gaston had taken over a sputtering flock, yet soon had them moving forward again with renewed dedication to the American League pennant chase. Under Gaston the Jays were to play at a torrid .611 pace (77–49) throughout the remaining months of the campaign. The middle of the season seemed a period doomed to a desperate and futile chase of the high-flying Orioles, however, and an exciting two-team pennant race was the unlikely scenario on tap for the final weeks of American League Eastern Divisional play.

It was in early August that the Jays finally moved into command of the American League East, a division waiting for someone to make a move as six teams sputtered behind overachieving Baltimore throughout most of the summer. Dave Stieb's third near no-hitter in slightly less than a year—this time a near-flawless masterpiece which fell just one pitch short of a 13th big-league regular-season perfect game—was a turning point against the Yankees on August 4 in Toronto. This time it was rookie Roberto Kelly of New York who slapped a double to left on a 2–0 count with two down in the ninth, making hard-luck Dave Stieb the fifth pitcher of 1989 to lose a no-hitter in the ninth inning. The game was already the 28th played in the new

SkyDome and was witnessed by a then-record Toronto crowd of 48,789.

If Gaston's elevation as manager had been a crucial change, another personnel move in early August was perhaps equally as crucial to the Jay's ultimate pennant chances. Just before the August 1 trading deadline Jeff Musselman (fresh off alcohol rehabilitation) was shipped off to the National League New York Mets for veteran speedster Mookie Wilson, while a day later reserve veteran outfielder Lee Mazzilli was claimed off waivers from the self-same floundering Mets. The popular Mookie Wilson became an instantaneous on-field leader with his hustle and experienced outfield glove play, while Lee Mazzilli provided needed late-season clubhouse leadership and part-time DH service and pinch-hitting as well. The two expatriated New York ballplayers were such instant hits with the overjoyed Toronto ballpark faithful that they quickly received the widespread joint nickname of "Mazzookie."

The 1989 season ultimately came down to a final weekend series, a true fan's delight fortuitously provided by the omniscient A.L. schedule makers. The Jays had been unable to pull away from Frank Robinson's inspired baby-faced Orioles, despite a torrid August streak which brought them from five games behind to first place before Labor Day. Baltimore was still but a single game behind when the final three-game set was launched in the SkyDome on September 29. The first few innings of the tense series opener seemed to foreshadow a replay of 1987, as the Blue Jays performed listlessly and wasted several golden scoring opportunities. But luck and spunk were with the Blue Jays in 1989, and an eighth-inning mistake by Baltimore hurler Gregg Olsen was the window of opportunity that Cito Gaston's club had sought. Olsen wild-pitched home the game-tying run in the eighth and reliever Mark Williamson yielded a game-winning single to Lloyd Moseby in the 11th to spark a come-from-behind 2–1 extra-inning victory. Friday's thrilling win was matched by similar heroics in the late-innings of Saturday's game. Williamson was again touched up for the tying and winning runs in a three-run eighth-inning rally which preserved a 4–3 pennant-clinch victory. Aided by run-producing singles from the bats of Mookie Wilson and Fred McGriff and George Bell's vital game-clinching sacrifice fly, Toronto had locked up their second division crown in half a decade. But this time it was the one that had so cruelly eluded them for three successive seasons, each one marked by late-September failures and each crammed with mid-season disappointment and a faltering team self-image. The inexplicable pennant drought was suddenly and thankfully over.

One reason for the Jay's successes in 1989 had to be the dramatic re-emergence of George Bell. Where Bell had failed down the stretch during his earlier controversial MVP year, in 1989 he unarguably carried the club when the chips were down and the pennant was on the line during late August and September play. No longer swinging exclusively for the fences, nor faltering with runners in scoring position, Bell slugged away relentlessly throughout the late summer, compiling his most impressive offensive numbers since the glory year of 1987—18 HRs, 88 runs, 104 RBIs, .297 BA. In a summer when other contenders lacked a true offensive leader—Canseco missed much of the season for Oakland, Cal Ripken hit only .257 (with 21 HRs and 93 RBIs) for Baltimore, and Minnesota's Kirby Puckett wasted a superb offensive year on a non-contending team—Bell once again seemed a legitimate candidate by year's end to capture his second league MVP award in three seasons. Despite Bell's three-month heroics at season's end, his damaged reputation with the nation's sportswriters throughout the U.S. and Canada allowed no higher than a distant fourth-place finish in League MVP balloting.

The excitement of a second pennant season in Toronto was matched throughout the final months of the summer by the hoopla surrounding baseball's newest and most luxurious stadium. For the first time modern technology could provide a welcomed combination of baseball's natural venue of outdoor play with defense against the elements and protection of creature comforts during foul-weather indoor play. At the cost of an additional $80 million (Canadian), the prototype Toronto SkyDome now boasted a moveable roof which covered 53,000 plush baseball seats in a matter of one half-hour or less when bad weather descended upon downtown Toronto. Unlike previous domed stadia, this was neither a baseball disaster nor a financial albatross. SkyDome management and Blue Jays officials projected shortly before opening night that the new dome would generate a cash flow of over $20 million for 55 home playing dates within the first partial season. Unlike the Louisiana Superdome, for example, which still loses almost $6 million (U.S.) yearly in operating expenses, Toronto's new baseball showpiece seemed guaranteed to make money from the night it opened, only partially completed, in early June (on June 4, versus Milwaukee, a 5–3 loss with Jimmy Key tossing the first pitch, Milwaukee's Paul Molitor stroking the first hit, and Fred McGriff blasting the first roundtripper). And the Jays themselves found their new surroundings conducive to inspired play as well, playing almost unbeatable baseball there the final month of the season and compiling a 12–0 mark in the first season's play during those games in which the SkyDome roof remained closed to the outside elements. At season's end, aided by 53 home dates in the popular dome, the Jays had reached a new American League attendance mark of 3,375,573, far outstripping the existing mark set only a season earlier in Minnesota by the defending World Champion Twins.

By season's end the Blue Jays had also rid themselves—at least temporarily—of the nagging loser-image that had marked the second phase of their brief franchise history. Around the corner were the powerful Oakland Athletics who had cruised through the Western Division with 99 victories and boasted the best pitching staff in baseball. Paced by Dave Stewart (21–9), Mike Moore (19–11), and Storm Davis (19–7)—as well as the league's top closer in veteran Dennis Eckersley— Manager Tony LaRussa's Athletics were a formidable final obstacle to a first-ever World Series appearance for Canada's beloved Blue Jays. But much had already been established by the conclusion of the topsy-turvy 1989 season, as the Toronto Blue Jays were finally a team that had reasonably lived up to pre-season hype and soaring fan expectations. What now remained to be written was simply the dramatic and as yet unforeseen last chapter in one of baseball's most successful expansion-era stories.

It was a different kind of Toronto team that entered the 1989. A.L.C.S., not at all like the euphoric but inexperienced bunch that bolted from the gate and then as quickly folded up against Kansas City in the 1985 post-season series. This was a team which blended raw youthful talent (Felix, McGriff, Liriano, Lee) with considerable pennant-race experience. Bell, Moseby, Stieb, Key, Gruber, Fernandez, Whitt—all were veterans of several tense seasons of trying to shake the dogged image of last-minute losers. Now a plateau had been reached and a burden had been lifted. This was a team for whom the pressure was seemingly off and World Series play would be an unexpected icing to a fine comeback season. It was a fortunate matter, also, that expectations were not too high, for the Jays realistically had little change against the talented and pennant-hungry Oakland Athletics, a team which outmanned them at nearly every position.

This was a truly awesome Oakland team that entered post-season play. Featured was the best pitching staff in baseball, including four of the season's top winners and two of baseball's most underrated pitchers. Dave Stewart (21–9, and about to draw one of baseball's highest-ever annual salaries in 1990) had led all big-league hurlers in wins over the past three summers, despite his inability to gain the Cy Young. Mike Moore (19–11) had labored in almost total obscurity in Seattle for several seasons before 1989 provided him with a luxurious opportunity to prove his talents with a winning team. Dennis Eckersley (33 saves) was still among the best short-relievers in baseball. Add to this the speed and daring of Rickey Henderson on the basepaths and the power of Mark McGwire and Jose Canseco (the only two men in baseball history to hit over 30 homers in each of their first three big-league seasons) and you had a team reminiscent of the late 1970s Yankees or the slugging 1950s Dodgers. This Oakland team was, to make matters worse, a ballclub driven by a fevered mission. Having been embarrassed in 1988 post-season play by the underdog Los Angeles Dodgers, Tony LaRussa's men were determined this year to obtain their rightful spot in the history books among baseball's strongest all-time teams.

The added dimensions that Rickey Henderson brought to the 1989 Oakland Athletics were never more apparent than in the opening innings of the 1989 A.L.C.S. playoff series. From the first Henderson seemed bent on making his initial post-season appearance a truly memorable one. Having led the American League with 77 steals (58 after returning to Oakland from the Yankees on June 20), Henderson established his baserunning dominance early in the first game, breaking up a potential double play with a hard slide into Blue Jays second baseman Nelson Liriano in the sixth inning and thus sparking Oakland's game-winning rally in a come-from-behind victory against Toronto's ill-fated starter Dave Stieb. Dave Stewart kept the Jays in check throughout, allowing just five hits, striking out six, and walking but three in eight innings of solid mound work.

In the end it was simply too much of Rickey Henderson and Dennis Eckersley for the overmatched Toronto roster as Oakland tucked away the 1989 A.L.C.S. by an almost effortless 4–1 count. The Jays had played gamely if not always well; the dormant bats which plagued Toronto throughout the Series may just as well have been attributed to the strength of Oakland pitching as to any lack of championship effort on the part of Blue Jays hitters. The defeat would not only disappoint Canadian fans, however; it would also place a very large monkey on the back of the Toronto franchise for several seasons to come. This talent-rich team pasted together by Pat Gillick seemed to be a ballclub that simply couldn't win the big one. Thus the 1990 season would see another pennant-race fade despite widespread pre-season optimism. A 1991 squad would begin with high hopes as well, then crashland yet again at post-season playoff time. This time around it would be the Twins from Minnesota who would make short work of the Jays' World Series dreams with yet another 4–1 A.L.C.S. romp, including three straight victories at the supposedly friendly SkyDome.

But despite such post-season flops, this Toronto outfit remained the premier ballclub of the junior circuit. Front office maneuvers continued to provide needed improvement. Fernandez and McGriff were shipped away to San Diego, but Joe Carter and Roberto Alomar achieved immediate star status as more than adequate replacements. Dave Winfield transported his personal quest for 400 homers and 3,000 hits to Toronto in 1992 as a high-profile free agent. And as the Jays rushed to a third division title in four years down the stretch of the 1992 campaign, NL ace David Cone was brought on board to strengthen a mound staff already cemented with the free-agent acquisition of 1991 World Series hero Jack Morris (Toronto's first-ever 20-game winner). And as the team won, the turnstiles continued to click, totalling an incredible attendance of 4 million for the second season in a row.

If the Jays had faltered in several post-season outings at the dawn of the 1990s, the 1992 club lead by aging Winfield and Morris, plus budding stars Alomar and Juan Guzman (16–5,. 2.64 ERA), would simply not be headed in their date with destiny. In a dramatic A.L.C.S. rematch against Oakland the Jays captured a crucial come-back fourth game, then ran away from LaRussa's fading A's back at the SkyDome. The World Series had finally come to Toronto, and what a Series it would be. A Toronto team that specialized in come-backs shocked the Atlanta Braves during the ninth inning of Game 2 on a dramatic game-saving homer by unheralded infielder Ed Sprague. Series MVP Pat Borders and veteran Kelly Gruber next sparked two crucial home victories. And it was the senior citizen Winfield who provided the final heroics of Game Six with an eleventh-inning single that spelled World Championship celebration. After 16 short seasons, the Toronto Blue Jays had brought Canada its first World Series triumph and national euphoria rolled thunderously from Cape Harrison to Cape Cook.

*   *   *

Travelling from their recent beginnings to an American League powerhouse in less than a decade, Toronto's Blue Jays can only be described as an outlandish success story. What is there, then, about the newborn Toronto Blue Jays team—a team that has no Hall of Famers, no legendary diamond heroes of past decades, and limited World Series glories to boast—that creates such a frenzied following? The answer, of course, is that Toronto's short yet dramatic dozen years of American League play enfolds improbable and drama-filled events supplying some of the most thrilling moments of recent baseball history. This is a team that has played in two of baseball's most unusual ballparks and has experienced some of the most unorthodox on-field events in recent memory. It is also a team that has risen from abject baseball poverty to pennant riches in a shorter span than any other post-expansion-era ball club, save the legendary New York Mets of the late 1960s.

Perhaps no other team from the Golden Age of televised baseball has been blessed with such sound front-office management and long-range planning as has the Blue Jays organization under the tutelage of Baseball Operations Director Pat Gillick. None has developed a more productive farm system or has so efficiently exploited the new fountainhead of Latin American player talent. And none has more effectively marketed its team to hometown fans or created a more rapid and loyal national baseball following. In the several eventful summers of Toronto Blue Jays baseball, this newest Canadian entry in America's national pastime has been painstakingly built over a few short years into one of the most colorful and highly successful franchises in modern baseball—perhaps in all professional sports.

Notes

This chapter could not have been completed in its present form without the assistance of unparalleled Blue Jays fan(atic) Tony Formo, rare champion of SABRmetrics, who willingly made available his extensive and unique personal Blue Jays archives. I am also indebted to Howard Starkman, Blue Jays media relations director, who cheerfully and patiently answered my every inquiry. Ronnie Wilbur (as always) provided much-needed editorial assistance; and essential contributions were also made by Bruce L. Prentice of the Canadian Baseball Hall of Fame, and William Humber, unmatched writer of Canadian baseball history.

1. Angell's discussion of "traditional" and "nontraditional" baseball franchises is one of the most insightful and memorable passages among his dozens of instructive observations on contemporary baseball. Mr. Angell's contrasts of traditional teams like the Red Sox, Tigers, and Mets—versus tradition-flouting (and thus inherently less attractive) teams such as O'Malley's Dodgers, and the present-day Cardinals and Reds—is further explored in the introductory essays to both volumes of this encyclopedia.

2. A note on sources is mandatory here. The best comprehensive account of Toronto's struggle for a major league franchise is found in the colorful history of Toronto baseball provided by Louis Cauz; Cauz is rivaled only by anonymous narrative accounts written for the unsurpassed *Toronto Blue Jays Tenth Anniversary Yearbook* (Canadian Controlled Media Communications, 1986). The most informative treatment of the business/management side of Toronto major league baseball is unquestionably Larry Millson's book (see bibliography below). An "unauthorized" and somewhat hostile examination of big-time baseball business in Toronto is also provided by van Rjndt and Blednick. While this latter paperback is both highly entertaining and informative throughout, the authors' candid efforts to identify strongly with fans and thus to rail against the baseball establishment leads to sarcastic portraits of Blue Jays administrative officials (especially Player Personnel Director Pat Gillick and Media Relations Director Howard Starkman) which are often embarrassing, usually pretentious, and in the end quite distracting from the otherwise insightful inside baseball information at hand. Those interested in statistical analysis and computerized seasonal summaries should locate David Driscoll's ongoing self-published works: *The 1985 Blue Book: A Statistical Analysis of the Toronto Blue Jays* (London, Ontario, 1985); *The 1986 Blue Book: A Statistical Analysis of the Toronto Blue Jays* (London, Ontario, 1986); *Jays Jazz*

(1987 edition); and *Blue Jays Jazz* (1988 edition). Bill James' essays on the Blue Jays in his yearly *Bill James Baseball Abstract* are also must reading on this team (as on all others), especially an insightful essay entitled "The Greatest Outfield Ever" from his 1987 annual (see note below).

3. See Bill James' essay (pp. 179–180) in *The Bill James Baseball Abstract 1987*, which offers somewhat ambiguous statistical support for this point. For those not familiar with the current literature, SABRmetrics (derived from the acronym for the Society for American Baseball Research) is often a pejorative designation for labelling fans/professionals devoted to laborious statistical analysis of the national pastime. James (through his popular annual volumes launched in 1982) has provided endless insights into the game of major league baseball, these insights usually being derived from highly technical computerized analysis of individual player performance and of team hitting, fielding, and pitching performance as well.

4. I am indebted here to yearly Blue Jays summaries written by Tony Formo for desktop publication in 1988 and 1989 issues of the underground *Left Field Baseball Extravaganza,* two entertaining radical baseball annuals compiled by SABR member Elliot Regenstein of Ithaca, New York. Formo's essays provide indepth firsthand knowledge of the Blue Jays franchise and offer refreshing overviews of recent seasons, drawn always upon Mr. Formo's novel perspective as both dedicated fan and practicing baseball SABRmetrician.

5. Wood objects to Exhibition Stadium largely because of its multipurpose stadium design and undeniable football-field appearance: "Problem is, the ball diamond doesn't cover the whole plastic rectangle. Beginning in the west end zone, it crosses midfield and pulls up at the rightfield fence. Beyond it, football markings, hidden underneath the outfield pop-up roll, take over. They run parallel with the fence all the way to the opposite end zone, every five yards, as clear and white as if they were gonna pull out the pigskin that inning" (1988, 224). But this is a multipurpose stadium with a difference, of course, and there are compensating features as well. Absent is the offensive oval shape of the typical football stadium, as well as the faint white football lines marring outfield and infield surface, often seen during August and September in other ballparks shared with NFL franchises. The Monsanto baseball covering (at 160,000 square feet, the largest in North America) is a carpeting placed directly atop the football surface; and the fact that most of the infield (including pitcher's mound, homeplate, and first base) lies outside of the football playing area allows as well for permanent installation of that part of the baseball surface.

6. Wood agrees that Exhibition Stadium has its plusses: "No major league ballpark enjoys a prettier setting. No other stroll from car to stadium is quite as inviting. Backed up against the bright blue waters of Lake Ontario, Exhibition Stadium . . . sits surrounded by the 300 acres of tidy green Exhibition Park. A few miles away a tight Toronto skyline says 'Hi.' Everything and everybody are pleasant" (1988, 223). What more do we desire of our ballparks, especially the new and too-often multipurpose monoliths built primarily to serve their interloping NFL tenants?

References

Angell, Roger. 1972. *The Summer Game.* New York: The Viking Press. (New York: Popular Library, 1972).

Bjarkman, Peter C. 1990. *The Toronto Blue Jays.* New York and Toronto, Ont.: Brompton-Bison Books (W.H. Smith of Canada).

Cauz, Louis. 1977. *Baseball's Back in Town: From the Don to the Blue Jays, A History of Baseball in Toronto.* Toronto, Ont.: Controlled Media Corporation.

Driscoll, David. 1988. *Blue Jays Jazz.* London, Ont.: Tag Communications.

Formo, Tony. 1988. "The Toronto Blue Jays." In *The 1988 Left Field Baseball Extravaganza,* 44–48. Edited by Elliot Regenstein, Ithaca, N.Y.: Mike Elliot Baseball Productions.

————. 1989. "The 1988 Toronto Boo Jays." In *The 1989 Left Field Baseball Extravaganza,* 38–51. Edited by Elliot Regenstein, Ithaca, N.Y.: Mike Elliot Baseball Productions.

James, Bill. 1987. *The Bill James Baseball Abstract 1987.* New York: Ballantine Books (Random House Publishers) ("The Greatest Outfield of All-Time" on pp. 179–180).

————. 1988. *The Bill James Baseball Abstract 1988.* New York: Ballantine Books (Random House Publishers) ("Toronto Blue Jays" on pp. 84–87).

Millson, Larry. 1987. *Ballpark Figures—The Blue Jays and The Business of Baseball.* Toronto, Ont.: McClelland and Stewart Publishers.

Reidenbaugh, Lowell. 1983. *Take Me Out to the Ball Park.* St. Louis, Mo.: Sporting News Publishing Company.

Van Rjndt, Phillippe, and Patrick Blednick, 1985. *Fungo Blues—An Uncontrolled Look at the Toronto Blue Jays.* Toronto, Ont.: McClelland and Stewart Publishers.

Wood, Bob. 1988. *Dodger Dogs to Fenway Franks—The Ultimate Guide to America's Top Baseball Parks.* New York: McGraw-Hill Book Company.

Annotated Bibliography

Bjarkman, Peter C. *The Toronto Blue Jays.* New York and Toronto, Ont.: Brompton-Bison Books (W.H. Smith of Canada), 1990.

Richly illustrated coffee-table history covering the first 13 years of Toronto Blue Jays' baseball. Chapters on such topics as year-by-year pennant races; the saga of obtaining an expansion franchise for Toronto; the Blue Jays' Latin America recruiting connection; Exhibition Stadium and the ultramodern SkyDome Stadium; and colorful personalities among popular Blue Jays players. One hundred and ten color and black-and-white photos make this one of the most handsome volumes devoted to the Toronto Blue Jays' short yet lively baseball history.

Caulfield, Jon. *Jays! A Fan's Diary.* Toronto, Ont.: McClelland and Stewart Publishers, 1985.

A delightfully written fan's diary account of the dramatic 1984 Toronto Blue Jays season—the last of the pre-championship expansion period. Excellent book for recapturing the daily tensions of an exciting summer-long American League pennant race, the emergence of George Bell as a potential superstar, the "snatching defeat from the jaws of victory" performances of the Toronto bullpen staff, the countless small moments of tension that shape each individual baseball season. Complete with 24 pages of glossy black and white game-action photographs and nine pages of team and individual season statistics which fill in details of 1984 American League play in Toronto.

Cauz, Louis. *Baseball's Back in Town: From the Don to the Blue Jays, A History of Baseball in Toronto.* Toronto, Ont.: Controlled Media Corporation, 1977. 204 pp.

This richly illustrated 204-page oversized coffee-table volume details Toronto's baseball history, from nineteenth-century Canadian origins of the game, through the unprecedented excitement which accompanied planning for Toronto's first major league game in 1977. Nine chapters explore the Toronto baseball story decade-by-decade from the 1880s through the 1960s; four final chapters recount events surrounding formation of the Blue Jays franchise and acquisition of talent via the November 1976 American League expansion draft.

Driscoll, David. *Blue Jays Jazz.* 1988 Edition. London, Ont.: Tag Communications. 128 pp.

Originating as a self-published 171-page 1985 statistical summary (*The 1985 Blue Book: A Statistical Analysis of the Toronto Blue Jays*), Driscoll's work evolves with 1987 and 1988 glossy editions into a handsome desktop publication of highest professional quality. Features month-by-month statistical summaries, individual ballplayer analyses (utilizing unique computer graphics in the production of informative individual hitting and pitching charts for each player), and essays on the farm system, umpires, and "Stolen Base Effects." Driscoll offers many entirely novel angles for assessing Blue Jays on-field performance.

Fidlin, Ken, and Fred Thornhill. *The Official Blue Jays Album—A Dozen Years of Baseball Memories.* Toronto, Ont.: Seal Books, 1989. 128 pp.

Richly illustrated yearbook-style team history scrapbook, complete through the 1988 season. Attractive color-collage glossy cover, featuring Blue Jays memorabilia, and filled throughout with approximately 100 large black-and-white and color-action photos. Each season is treated with a short narrative chapter tracing the ongoing history of the Blue Jays, from expansion doormat of the late 1970s to championship-caliber front-runner in the final years of the 1980s. A collaborative effort by the beat writer covering the Jays for *The Toronto Sun* since 1983 (Fidlin) and the same newspaper's sports photographer (Thornhill) who has long served as a staff photographer in the Blue Jays Public Relations Department as well.

Gordon, Alison. *Foul Ball! My Five Years in the American League.* New York: Dodd, Mead and Company, 1984. 204 pp.

Highly entertaining first-person accounts of the Toronto baseball scene by the city's only woman baseball beat reporter of the early 1980s. Focus is on Ms. Gordon's often off-color experiences while traveling the American League circuit with the Toronto team between 1979 and 1983. Candid observations on players, bosses, ballparks, life on the road, and the actual game of baseball itself. Many lively scenes and passages will later reappear, only quite thinly disguised, in Gordon's popular 1988 baseball mystery novel *Dead-Pull Hitter*—itself a gripping "baseball murder mystery" featuring the crudely disguised Blue Jays (rechristened as the Toronto Titans) and Gordon's alter ego (here named Katherine Henry). Gordon's accounts of the zany 1985 Toronto pennant season provide perhaps the most honest and colorful writing done to date on the highs and lows of following Toronto Blue Jays baseball.

———. *Foul Balls.* Toronto, Ont.: General Paperbacks Publishing Company, 1986. 223 pp.

A slightly altered Canadian paperback edition of the previous work, this volume was published at the conclusion of the Blue Jays' pre-pennant 1984 season and reissued to capitalize on "Blue Jays Mania" sweeping throughout Toronto and across all of Canada after the American League Eastern Division Championship summer of 1985. The text here is largely identical to the earlier 1984 edition, with some last-minute rewriting (most notably a final chapter on the 1985 campaign) to accommodate newsworthy events of a championship season.

Humber, William. *Cheering for the Home Team: The Story of Baseball in Canada.*
Toronto, Ont.: The Boston Mill Press, 1983. 150 pp.
  The most comprehensive essay available on baseball's Canadian origins
  and the Canadian history of North America's national pastime, including:
  the story of Canada's only legitimate major league championship team;
  barnstorming Japanese Canadian teams; black players in Canadian baseball, from the nineteenth century to Jackie Robinson's debut in Montreal;
  Canadian nationals in the big leagues; and finally the birth of the Blue
  Jays and Expos as the "big show" comes north of the border. Lavishly
  illustrated with rare black-and-white photos, this handsome coffee-table
  volume was once praised by reviewer George Bowering as a must for
  Canadian baseball fans: "There should be a copy in the parlour of every
  baseball fan and everyone at all interested in Canadian memorabilia over
  the past 150 years."
Martinez, Buck. *From Worst to First—The Toronto Blue Jays in 1985.* Toronto,
Ont.: Fitzhenry and Whiteside Limited, 1985. 179 pp.
  A reserve bench player's diary accounts of the 1985 championship strug-
  gle, enlivened with the most memorable moments culled from the Jay's
  "best-ever summer"—the infamous George Bell-Bruce Kison incident in
  June at Exhibition Stadium, two crucial late-season series against the arch-
  rival New York Yankees, the best game the Blue Jays ever played, and
  inning-by-inning accounts of Toronto's very first American League
  Championship series with the Kansas City Royals.
Millson, Larry. *Ballpark Figures—The Blue Jays and The Business of Baseball.*
Toronto, Ont.: McClelland and Stewart Publishers, 1987. 290 pp.
  Simply stated, this is indisputably the most fascinating and informative
  book yet written on the business side of a professional baseball franchise.
  Millson provides painstaking documentation of why the Blue Jays have
  emerged as one of baseball's most successful franchises, both on the
  field and off. A highly readable text features special insights into Latin
  American player recruitment, the marketing of "team image" within the
  Ontario corporate community, and step-by-step development of the Jays'
  outstanding minor league system.
Robertson, John. *Ok Ok, Blue Jays (The Story of the Amazing Jays—The 1983
Season).* Toronto, Ont.: Key Porter Books (*Toronto Sun* Publishing Corporation), 1983. 126 pp.
  A day-by-day account of the 1983 season, drawn from the journalistic
  files of the *Toronto Sun's* baseball beat writer. Numerous excellent game-
  action, dugout, and clubhouse photographs are featured and the ebb and
  flow of an entire season is relived precisely as it could be captured through
  scrapbook-style collection of daily newspaper accounts. A date-by-date
  diary format and journalistic writing style further enliven the unfolding
  drama of the long summer's baseball season.
———. *Those Amazing Jays.* Toronto, Ont.: Key Porter Books (*Toronto Sun*
Publishing Corporation), 1984. 96 pp.
  A spin-off replay of Robertson's 1983 scrapbook account, this time
  featuring day-by-day coverage for the 1984 season. Better color illustra-
  tions and considerably less text, but few other departures from the
  1983 format. If this version is slightly better reading it is only because
  the 1984 season itself proved somewhat more dramatic and successful
  for Blue Jays players and fans alike. In terms of production, photos,
  and narrative detail, this is hands down the best of Robertston's three
  Jays season diary books.

———. *Blue Jays 1985—How the East Was Won!* Toronto, Ont.: Key Porter
Books (*Toronto Sun* Publishing Corporation), 1985. 96 pp.
    The final installment of Robertson's seasonal highlight books, reduced to
magazine format but enhanced by the excitement of a division-winning
season. The text has been reduced still further here, but full-page color
game-action photos throughout are a true collector's delight.
Stieb, David, and Kevin Boland. *Tomorrow I'll Be Perfect.* Garden City, N.Y.:
Doubleday and Company, 1986. 167 pp.
    The "as-told-to" baseball and non-baseball life of the player who Jays'
radio announcer Tom Cheek has aptly characterized as Toronto's only
true matinee idol. Like most formula books of this type, there is little here
that the die-hard Blue Jay fan doesn't already know and little as well that
the non-fan would really care to know. Yet this book is an interesting
read, if only for Stieb's outspoken insider's views of the modern pitcher's
perspective on such lively issues as salaries, contracts, and arbitration—
and even on pitching games in Chicago's cavernous Comiskey Park.
Van Rjndt, Phillippe, and Patrick Blednick. *Fungo Blues–An Uncontrolled Look
at the Toronto Blue Jays.* Toronto, Ont.: McClelland and Stewart Publishers,
1985. 220 pp.
    From food at the ballpark (a distinct thumbs down!) to corporate manage-
ment in the front office of Labatts Breweries (with Board Chairman Peter
Hardy), this delightful book takes an unauthorized, unexpurgated, and
totally irreverent look at the Blue Jays organization just before the 1985
championship season. The collaboration of a well-known Canadian novelist (van Rjndt) and a lesser-known Canadian public relations consultant
(Blednick), this book is one of the most readable and entertaining (if not
always objective) treatises ever done on inside big-business machinations
and front-office follies found with today's pro sports franchises.
Whitt, Ernie, with Greg Cable. *Catch—A Major League Life.* Toronto, Ont.:
McGraw-Hill Ryerson, 1989. 271 pp.
    Hard-hitting, no-holds-barred biography from one of the most popular
Blue Jays players and the only remaining original member (until 1990)
of Toronto's inept expansion-era ballclub of the late 1970s. Memories of
Blue Jays seasons past are here set against outspoken month-by-month
recounting of the troubled 1988 Toronto season. Whitt comments can-
didly as well on how major league life and its relentless celebrity status
affects the individual player and strains to the breaking point his family
and personal life.

Year-by-Year Standings and Season Summaries

Year	Pos.	Record	Pct.	GB	Manager	Player	BA	Player	HR	Player	W-L	ERA
1977	7th	54-107	.335	45.5	Harsfield	Howell	.316	Fairly	19	Lemanczyk	13-16	4.25
1978	7th	59-102	.366	40.0	Harsfield	Howell	.270	Mayberry	22	Clancy	10-12	4.09
1979	7th	53-109	.327	50.5	Harsfield	Griffen	.287	Mayberry	21	Underwood	9-16	3.69
1980	7th	67-95	.414	36.0	Mattick	Woods	.300	Mayberry	30	Clancy	13-16	3.30
1981	7th	16-42	.276	19.0	Mattick	D. Garcia	.252	Mayberry	17	Stieb	11-10	3.19
	7th	21-27	.438	7.5								
1981*	7th	37-69	.349	23.5								
1982	6th	78-84	.481	17.0	Cox	D. Garcia	.310	Upshaw	21	Stieb	17-14	3.25
1983	4th	89-73	.549	9.0	Cox	Moseby	.315	Barfield	27	Stieb	17-12	3.04
								Upshaw	27			
1984	2nd	89-73	.549	15.0	Cox	Collins	.308	Bell	26	Alexander	17-6	3.13
1985	1st	99-62	.615	+2.0	Cox	Mulliniks	.295	Bell	28	Alexander	17-10	3.45
1986	4th	86-76	.531	9.5	Williams	Fernandez	.310	Barfield	40	Eichhorn	14-6	1.72
1987	2nd	96-66	.593	2.0	Williams	Fernandez	.322	Bell	47	Key	17-8	2.76
1988	3rd	87-75	.537	2.0	Williams	Mulliniks	.300	McGriff	34	Stieb	16-8	3.04
1989	1st	89-73	.549	+2.0	Williams / Gaston	Bell	.297	McGriff	36	Stieb	17-8	3.35
1990	2nd	86-76	.531	2.0	Gaston	McGriff	.300	McGriff	35	Stieb	18-6	2.93
1991	1st	91-71	.562	+7.0	Gaston	Alomar	.295	Carter	33	Key	16-12	3.05
1992	1st	96-66	.593	+4.0	Gaston	Alomar	.310	Carter	34	Morris	21-6	4.04

*Split Season Totals (Players' Union Strike).

All-Time Blue Jays Career and Season Records

Career Batting Leaders (1977–1992)

Games Played	Lloyd Moseby	1,392
At Bats	Lloyd Moseby	5,124
Runs Scored	Lloyd Moseby	768
Hits	Lloyd Moseby	1,319
Batting Average	Roberto Alomar	.302
Home Runs	George Bell	202
Runs Batted In	George Bell	740
Stolen Bases	Lloyd Moseby	255
Sacrifice Hits	Alfredo Griffin	67
Strikeouts	Lloyd Moseby	1,015

Career Pitching Leaders (1977–1992)

Innings Pitched	Dave Stieb	2,822.2
Earned Run Average	Juan Guzman	2.79
Wins	Dave Stieb	174
Losses	Jim Clancy	140
Winning Pct.	Doyle Alexander	.639
Strikeouts	Dave Stieb	1,631
Walks	Jim Clancy	814
Games	Tom Henke	446
Shutouts	Dave Stieb	30
Saves	Tom Henke	217
Games Started	Dave Stieb	405
Complete Games	Dave Stieb	102
Hit Batsmen	Dave Stieb	120
Wild Pitches	Jim Clancy	82

Single-Season Batting Records (1977–1992)

Batting Average (350 ABs)	Tony Fernandez	.322	1987
Batting Average (100 games)	Rance Mulliniks	.324	1984
Home Runs	George Bell	47	1987
Home Runs (lefthanded)	Fred McGriff	36	1989
Runs Batted In	George Bell	134	1987
Hits	Tony Fernandez	213	1986
Singles	Tony Fernandez	161	1986
Doubles	Joe Carter	42	1991
Triples	Alfredo Griffin	15	1980
	Dave Collins	15	1984
	Lloyd Moseby	15	1984
Slugging Percentage	George Bell	.605	1987
Extra Base Hits	George Bell	83	1987
Game-Winning RBIs	George Bell	16	1987
Sacrifices	Luis Gomez	22	1978
Stolen Bases	Damaso Garcia	54	1982
Pinch Hits	Wayne Nordhagen	11	1982
Strikeouts	Fred McGriff	149	1988
Total Bases	George Bell	369	1987

All-Time Blue Jays Career and Season Records *(continued)*

Hitting Streak	Damaso Garcia	21 Games	1983
	Lloyd Moseby	21 Games	1983
Grand Slam Home Runs	George Bell	2	1985, 1987
	Roy Howell	2	1979
On-Base Percentage	Cliff Johnson	.393	1984
Hit by Pitch	Damaso Garcia	9	1984
Hitting for the Cycle	Kelly Gruber	1	1989
Games	Tony Fernandez	163	1986

Single-Season Pitching records (1977–1992)

ERA (150 innings)	Dave Stieb	2.48	1985
ERA (100 innings)	Mark Eichhorn	1.72	1986
Wins	Jack Morris	21	1992
Losses	Jerry Garvin	18	1977
	Phil Huffman	18	1979
Winning Pct. (10 decisions)	Doyle Alexander	.739	1984
Strikeouts	Dave Stieb	198	1984
Walks	Jim Clancy	128	1980
Saves	Tom Henke	34	1987, 1991
Game Appearances	Mark Eichhorn	89	1987
Complete Games	Dave Stieb	19	1982
Games Started	Jim Clancy	40	1982
Shutouts	Dave Stieb	5	1982
Innings Pitched	Dave Stieb	288.1	1982
Home Runs Allowed	Jerry Garvin	33	1977
Consecutive Games Won (season)	Dennis Lamp	11	1985
Consecutive Games Lost (season)	Jerry Garvin	10	1977
	Paul Mirabella	10	1980
Consecutive Games Lost (overall)	Tom Underwood	13	1978–1979
Consecutive Complete Games	Dave Stieb	7	1980
Wild Pitches	Dave Lemanczyk	20	1977
Balks	Jimmy Key	5	1987

13

Washington Senators-
Minnesota Twins
Expansion-Era Baseball Comes to
the American League
PETER C. BJARKMAN

On the surface there seems to be altogether little dramatic or even memorable about the baseball club lately called Minnesota Twins (nee Washington Senators). This is especially true during the half-century history of the ballclub (1912–1962) which bears so indelibly the family stamp of Clark Calvin Griffith (The Old Fox) and his adopted son and successor, Calvin Griffith, Sr. What glories could possibly be recounted about a baseball franchise which so regularly made its home in the American League cellar during the first half of the present century? While residing, first, in the nation's capital, Griffith's team earned baseball's most famous epithet ("first in war, first in peace, and last in the American League"). In more recent decades (without much visible improvement in the league standings), it continued its lackluster play (forgiving two bold flurries of unanticipated greatness) while entrenched along the nation's northwestern-most baseball frontier. Senators immortals begin and end with Walter Johnson, an incomparable fastball pitcher recently lost in the shadow of modern baseball's ageless strikeout king Nolan Ryan. Minnesota has boasted four remarkable hitters over the past three decades: Killebrew, Oliva, Carew, Puckett. Just about everything else is secondary to the histories of more glory-bound franchises like the Yankees, Red Sox, or Tigers.

No other ballclub with roots in the original American League of 1901 has appeared less often in World Series play than the hapless Twins-Senators. While the laughable St. Louis Browns (one pennant only—and that during a war-ruined campaign of 1944) admittedly outdid the erstwhile Washington Senators (who themselves won but three American League flags in 1924–1925, and 1933) in pure ineptitude, their resurrection as the high-flying Baltimore Orioles was a far more profitable transfiguration than the one which the lowly Senators underwent when transported to Minnesota. The Orioles have reigned as proud American League champions a full six times, the transplanted Twins but twice—and those two brief triumphs stand almost a full quarter-century apart. Between the Twin-Cities' two league pennants lies a 22-year wasteland of uninspiring teams and lackadaisical play that often surpasses its legendary Washington ancestry for comical baseball ineptitude.

Yet decades of big-league history are as full of rare surprises as are brief innings of diamond action, and the saga of this gypsy Twins-Senators franchise does indeed provide some of the more colorful lore, larger-than-life diamond heroes, and memorable baseball drama found within accounts of any proud major league ballclub. There is the legendary presence of Clark Calvin Griffith himself, for instance, followed by the remarkable success story of his nephew (adoptive-son) and successor, Calvin Robertson Griffith, Sr.—seemingly the Branch Rickey and Walter O'Malley all-rolled-in-one of American League baseball history. Few if any sports franchises have so clearly reflected the image of one man or of one family; perhaps only the Athletics under Connie Mack come close. And no baseball franchise has more ostentatiously borne the mark of a single family in still another fashion than did the Senators under Clark Griffith from 1912 to 1955. Almost from the day he took control as manager in 1912, the senior Griffith (who bought a majority interest in the team and named himself president in 1920) kept his ballclub operating as strictly closed family business. All eight post-Griffith Washington managers down to 1955 were former members of the team Griffith had managed between 1912 and 1920 (viz., McBride, Milan, Bush, Harris, Johnson, Cronin, Bluege, Kuhel). Charlie Dressen, hired on in 1955, was the first intruder in three and a half decades to take the helm of the Washington Senators as a distinct outsider and non-crony of the irrepressible Clark Calvin Griffith.

Throughout the century's first six decades Washington baseball also enjoyed its handful of diamond heroes boasting Hall-of-Fame credentials. In flamethrowing Walter Johnson—first and foremost—there was baseball's greatest strikeout pitcher and perhaps the most intimidating fireballing hurler the national game has ever witnessed. Johnson stands alone among immortal moundsmen who came along before a modern age of super hurlers—a recent period which has seen Nolan Ryan, Tom Seaver, Steve Carlton, Gaylord Perry, Early Wynn, and Warren Spahn (aided by the expansion-era attrition of quality batsmen) rewrite virtually all the game's cherished pitching records. But even the numbers of these latter-day Hall-of-Famers pale for pure dominance when compared with those of the immortal "Big-Train" Johnson. Walter Johnson's 3,508 career strikeouts were amassed in an age untainted by free-swingers and then stood alone as the all-time standard for nearly six decades before being overhauled by the likes of Ryan, Carlton, and Seaver. His seven consecutive seasons of 25 or more victories (twice over 30) outdid even the incomparable Cy Young. And a lifetime 2.17 ERA (recorded over a span of 21 seasons and 695 big-league decisions, while pitching usually with a second-division ballclub) defies the modern imagination. Any and all discussion of baseball's greatest pitcher inevitably begins and ends with none other than Walter Perry Johnson.

During those earlier years there were great sluggers in the nation's capital, as well, behemoths who have rewritten the record books and terrorized American League pitching with their booming bats and towering circuit clouts. Throughout the late 1950s Roy Sievers, Jim Lemon, and Bob Allison clubbed A.L. pitching with awesome regularity, despite playing in baseball's most spacious longball park. The pacesetter among all American League sluggers during the modern period was Harmon Killebrew, whose brilliant career spanned both the Washington and Minnesota eras of the franchise. Count solely American League home run totals and Killebrew (with 573) stands in rare company atop the list, behind only the immortal Babe Ruth.

There have also been a half-dozen memorable Washington hitters more attuned to stroking endless singles than bashing long balls, yet unforgettable among the game's great hitters of the current century. Goose Goslin was a legitimate Hall-of-Famer whose hitting feats were largely lost in the glare of Babe Ruth and Lou Gehrig. In an 18-year big-league career split between Washington (12 seasons), St. Louis, and Detroit, Goslin pounded out an impressive .316 career average, amassed 2,735 hits, and recorded three seasons in the 1920s with a better-than-.340 BA. An even more popular Washington crowd-pleaser of the Ruthean era, teammate Edgar "Sam" Rice, today remains baseball's true forgotten man, perhaps the least-known Hall-of-Fame batsman boasting such unquestioned star status. Rice's 20-season .322 BA and 2,987 career hits remain buried in baseball obscurity, due largely to the sad fact that this brilliant slugging outfielder toiled 19 summers for usually inept Washington ballclubs and never once led the Junior Circuit in either batting or longball slugging (though he did twice pace the A.L. in total hits and once in triples).

During the latter post-World-War-II period, as well, versatile infielder James "Pete" Runnels was also a consistent batting pacesetter and two-time league batting champion (1960 and 1962, both with the Boston Red Sox) in American League play of the 1950s and 1960s. Runnel's line-drive-style hitting thrilled many a diehard bleacherite in old Griffith Stadium during those otherwise lean Eisenhower years which marked the Senators' final decade of play in Washington. A half-decade earlier, in the late forties and early fifties, popular first sacker Mickey Vernon had matched Runnels' hit-for-hit (and then some), himself garnering over 1,800 base hits and two A.L. batting crowns (1946, 1953) while in the nation's capital.

Minnesota's short-lived expansion franchise, with but three-decades lifespan, has enjoyed its own remarkable string of glorious hitters as well. Throughout the volatile 1960s there was the flamboyant Pedro Lopez "Tony" Oliva, the most remarkable of all talented Cuban batsmen to burn a lasting mark upon America's national pastime. (Oliva had borrowed a brother's birth certificate to obtain the needed passport for his first Twins tryout camp, and his illegitimate given name had eventually stuck.) Oliva was a three-time league batting champion who on five separate occasions was the league-leader in base hits as well. Early seasons of indoor baseball in the Humphrey Metrodome coincided with the emergence of colorful hitting star Kirby Puckett, perhaps the most complete ballplayer of the 1980s in either league. Puckett's 1990 notoriety as America's first three-million-dollar-a-year ballplayer only complements the considerable luster already surrounding baseball's most exciting offensive and defensive performer since the days of all-time-best center fielder Willie Mays. Comparisons with the legendary Mays are certainly not frivolous or unjustified, even at this early stage in Puckett's career, and perhaps the most overlooked fact about Kirby Puckett is the degree to which statistics amassed during his first big-league seasons compare favorably with those of the greatest slugger ever to play the center-field position.[1]

But clearly the greatest Minnesota pure batsman of all was an unassuming Panamanian singles-hitter who captured an unmatched seven American League batting titles in the decade stretching from 1969 through 1978. Rod Carew—perhaps the truest pure hitter of the modern age in the Junior Circuit, at least after Ted Williams—has left a hitting legacy matched only by Williams and the ubiquitous Tyrus Cobb among all batsmen before him. Uniquely, this certain future Hall-of-Famer is jealously claimed by both Latin Americans and the American Jewish community as their own greatest gift to the national pastime. Ironically, Carew was technically neither Jewish nor Latin American, having been born in the Panama Canal Zone (and thus a natural American citizen) and having converted to Judaism at a late age through the influence of his orthodox wife. But despite his hotly debated ethnic background and religious affiliation, Carew was for 12 glorious seasons during the sixties and seventies simply the finest hitter in Senators-Twins history and an unforgettable baseball fixture as well at Metropolitan Stadium and throughout the State of Minnesota.

Also interwoven with Senators-Twins history is the parallel saga of two of baseball's most unusual ballparks—one a glorious and eccentric park standing flush in the tradition of baseball's old-style and rapidly disappearing urban settings. The other—a space-age inflatable bubble at odds with all that is sacred in baseball tradition—provides perhaps the worst aesthetic venue for the national pastime yet devised by human ingenuity. While the Hubert H. Humphrey Metrodome admittedly proffered a huge homefield advantage for the otherwise mediocre World Champion 1987 Minnesota Twins, its "white ceiling, tacky carpet, and absolutely no extra óptions" approach to baseball is perhaps all too adequately captured in the apt phrases of ballpark critic Bob Wood—"no frills and no thrills . . . from the air-blown fabric roof to the cheap overworked scoreboard, it's obvious that the only real motive in building the thing was cost" (Wood, 1988, 65). Never has there been a baseball stadium demonstrating less of baseball's pastoral atmosphere than the Minneapolis Metrodome.

Griffith Stadium, by delightful contrast, was a pure baseball Mecca—intimate, compact, lush with spacious outfield pastures, enriched with unique layout and foul-line dimensions—a traditional ballpark, with unsurpassed diamond character. And there was an all-pervasive sense of history about the place as well. This was the ballpark that fostered, among other traditions, the original "Megaphone Man" of baseball, E. Lawrence Phillips. Phillips commenced announcing home and visiting team batteries to fans with the outset of American League play in 1901 and continued on down through the dawn of an electronic baseball age in 1928. This was also the home for more than half a century of the Opening Day presidential visit and the tradition-bound inaugural "first pitch" of baseball's springtime ritual. Established by then-manager Clark Griffith in 1912, the ceremonial Opening Day presidential toss would eventually include eight of the nation's chief executives before its demise with the death-knell of the Washington ballclub itself—Taft, Wilson, Harding, Coolidge, Hoover, Roosevelt, Truman, and finally Dwight D. Eisenhower, all pitched in (quite literally) to keep Griffith's opening day ceremonies alive. With its unbroken string of presidential visits, for one day each season at least, Washington was always briefly on top of the baseball world.

The story of the Washington Senators and Minnesota Twins, then, begins with the story of several of the most colorful personalities in baseball's long history. Clark Calvin Griffith is a story unto himself—a pitching great of the game's infant years who emerged as one of baseball's supreme executives from the old school tradition. Walter Johnson—top pitching wizard of the dead ball era—epitomizes baseball "when the grass was real" and the sky was naturally blue and still undomed. Harmon Killebrew remains the greatest fanpleaser in the history of both Griffith franchises, a home run giant of equal stature to Jimmy Foxx, Mickey Mantle, or Reggie Jackson—surpassed in four baggers only by Aaron, Mays, and Frank Robinson among righthanded swingers. Rod Carew maintains a cherished spot forever in the collective memories of Minnesota fans as a certain Hall-of-Famer who graced the first two decades of Twins baseball history. For seven short seasons in particular (1971–1978) Rod Carew *was* the Minnesota Twins. And over the past five seasons the Twins have witnessed as well the emergence of perhaps the most colorful all-around player in franchise history. Kirby Puckett is rated by almost all qualified observers as the best multifaceted player in the game today. Furthermore, he is baseball's first three-million-dollar man, a story which in itself—in this modern age of Wall Street athletes—provides a distinguished landmark of modern baseball history.

Yet despite the presence of this modest panopoly of baseball heroes and larger-than-life baseball legends, the saga of the nation's pastime in Washington and in Minnesota has also been a relentless tale of defeat and disaster plaguing one of baseball's longest suffering original franchises. It is not an exaggeration to claim that for six decades in Washington the old pun about "first in war and peace and last in the American League" was more a pragmatic assessment than a classic piece of baseball wit. And to review those decades from the hindsight of history is again to recall how truly inept Washington baseball play usually was, for summer after long summer, stretching all the way from Clyde Milan and Chick Gandil in the falsely secure pre-war era of William Howard Taft to Wayne Terwilliger and Dick Hyde during the paranoia-filled Cold War reign of Dwight David Eisenhower.

First in War and First in Peace . . . A Half-Century of Baseball in the Nation's Capital

The Washington Senators—perhaps not surprisingly—did not appear in the first-ever World Series game held at Boston in 1903. Characteristically and portentously, Washington finished a distant last that season—the year that saw the fledgling American League begin its century-long series of fall classics with the better-established Senior Circuit. The Senators had finished in sixth place both of the first two seasons of American League play. But by 1903 (with the newfangled World Series adding a novel dimension to the stature of the national pastime) they were firmly entrenched in the league's cellar. And this was a home base they would come to know quite intimately over the course of the next five baseball decades.

While the story of the Washington Nationals (as they were then known) begins officially in 1901 with formation of the upstart American League, the true history of this franchise stretches far back into baseball's dim past of the nineteenth century. Many historians of

American sport, in fact, believe this to be baseball's oldest professional organization. There was indeed big-league baseball in the nation's capital long before the advent of the American League and the commencement of fall World Series play. Yet prior to Ban Johnson's American League, there was little in the way of stability for professional baseball franchises in the nation's capital; Washington franchises were seemingly kicked across the baseball map, jumping repeatedly from one ill-fated league to another. In 1884 the Washington team had even begun its campaign in the American Association and finished out the same season in the short-lived Union Association. While the first known Washington Nationals ballclub was reputedly organized in the fall of 1859 by a group of government clerks, the first official Washington entry in an organized professional league came with the "Olympics" in the 1871 inaugural National Association season. Subsequent Washington teams (all officially known as the "Nationals" after 1873) appeared in the American Association (1884 and 1891), Union Association (1884), Eastern League (1885), and finally the better-established National League (1886–1889, and again in 1892–1899).

During its maiden decade of American League play, the Senators (as fans and journalists began calling the ballclub even in its earliest days) consistently remained at or near the bottom of the heap—last again in 1904, seventh in 1905 and 1906, last in 1907, seventh again in 1908, dead last in 1909. After 10 years of American League play the Washington entry was the only club yet to finish as high as second place; four of the original eight teams had miraculously already won a pennant—*at least twice each!*

The second decade of league play began precisely as the previous one had ended, with seventh-place finishes for Washington in 1910 and 1911. The turning-point year seemingly came the next season, however, as under new manager Clark Griffith the Washington ballclub surprisingly jumped to the head of the pack, finishing a remarkable second to Boston's powerful Red Sox, a Boston team led by the awesome hitting of Tris Speaker (trailing only Cobb and Joe Jackson in hits and BA) and the incomparable pitching of Smokey Joe Wood (34–5, 1.91 ERA). Washington, however, also had its first true contingent of superstars for the 1912 campaign as well. Walter Johnson burst upon the scene that year with his first of many remarkable pitching performances (32–12, with a league-best 1.39 ERA). Johnson was aided by fellow moundsman Bob Groom (24–13), first-baseman Chick Gandil (.305 BA), and fleet-footed outfielder Clyde Milan (.306, with a league-leading and then-record 88 stolen bases).

Clark Griffith—a former pitching great (24–7 with Chicago in the American League's opening season of 1901) and one of the founders of the new American League—was 42 at the time he took over the managerial reins in Washington for the 1912 season. Perhaps Griffith's most astute early player move was his surprise acquisition of Chick Gandil (later to gain his own lasting reputation as a member of the infamous 1919 Black Sox outfit) from the minor league franchise in Montreal. Griffith's men went on an immediate 17-game victory streak once the heavy-hitting and slick-fielding Gandil was inserted into the lineup at first base, and they remained smack in the thick of a pennant race with Boston almost until the summer's waning days. Boston eventually ran away from the pack in September, yet Washington held fast in second, barely ahead of Connie Mack's oncoming Athletics, and 14 games behind the uncatchable Boston ballclub.

The winter of 1911–1912 had also witnessed the unfortunate destruction by fire of the American League ballpark in Washington, a ballyard that had stood on the same site at the intersection of Georgia and Florida Avenues ever since Washington had first fielded a club in the old 12-team National League. By Opening Day of 1912 a partially complete concrete and steel stadium had been hastily erected that would subsequently serve the franchise (with several minor expansions and alterations) right down to the final season in Washington four decades later. While this new ballpark would be built in several sections between 1912 and 1915, there would be essentially no major alterations to the park after its 1912 rebuilding, until the additon of 1,500 bleacher seats before the 1956 season raised seating capacity to slightly over 29,000. Renamed for the colorful club owner in the 1920s, spacious Griffith Stadium soon became known around the Junior Circuit as a true paradise for pitchers. Tiger hurler Hal Newhouser once quipped: "Give any pitcher a ball-hawk in centerfield and he'll win in Washington." Ironically one of the park's longest home runs before Mickey Mantle's monstrous 565-foot blast off of Chuck Stobbs in May 1953 was hit by none other than Walter Johnson—a titanic smash which landed halfway up the sloping left-field bleachers. But the park was long to remain the most difficult in the circuit for home run hitters, due to its spacious outfield dimensions of 405 feet to the left-field corner and 423 feet to straightaway center. The Senators would, in fact, long remain the only charter member of the American League without a home run champion, until Roy Sievers turned the trick in 1957, the park's 45th year of play.

The Senators of Clark Griffith remained a first-division club for the next three seasons—1913–1915. Walter Johnson enjoyed his best year ever in 1913 when he recorded 11 shutouts, a league-leading 36 victories, and an unprecedented record 1.09 ERA. Yet the Senators could never capitalize completely on Johnson's remarkable mound mastery and thus move solidly into contention. Johnson would post 28 and 27 victories in the next two campaigns and yet the club would limp home third one season and fourth the next. In 1916 Washington slid temporarily to seventh, a game under .500 though only a surprising 14½ games in arrears of pace-setting Boston. The World War I years brought an abrupt end to Griffith's term as manager. "The Old Fox" seemingly had decided his by-then considerable financial investment in the club could be far better served by front-office employment than by field management. A stockholder and member of the board of directors from as early as his first season as field manager, Griffith frequently quibbled with his co-owners about player-personnel moves for the troubled ballclub; by 1920 he had grown altogether weary of these squabbles and simply brought the club outright, stepping up from the dugout and selecting himself as team president.

This period of front-office reshuffling at first witnessed a series of advances and declines, with finishes as high as 3rd in 1918 and as low as seventh the following year. The search for leadership at the helm of the Washington ballclub also proved rather exasperating in the years immediately following, as Griffith replaced himself as manager with a series of his veteran ballplayers—George McBride in 1921, Clyde Milan in 1922, and then Donie Bush in 1923. Three short seasons thus saw three different managers and three campaigns smack in the middle of the American League pack. But the arrival of "Boy Wonder" Bucky Harris at the conclusion of the 1923 campaign finally seemed to be precisely what was needed to solidify a rapidly improving team of veterans and potential future stars which Griffith had long been stockpiling for his heretofore lackluster Washington franchise.

The first few years under Stanley "Bucky" Harris were indisputably a high-water mark in Washington Senators history. In his boldest move to date, guileful Clark Griffith had shocked the baseball world with the appointment of his 27-year-old fifth-year second baseman as playing manager of a largely veteran team, an outfit which in 1923 had climbed back into fourth place under skipper Donie Bush and finished only three games under .500. The tenacious Harris had already earned full respect by his scrappy style of play from his mostly older teammates. The results were remarkable. Two consecutive league pennants in 1924 and 1925 quickly put to rest a quarter-century of baseball mediocrity in the nation's capital. The 1924 pennant race had been a dogfight to the bitter end with the Ruth-powered Yankees who finished a close second at the wire, two games back. Goose Goslin emerged as a full-blown star that summer, actually outstripping the mighty Ruth in RBIs (129–121) and thus blocking the Babe's near-miss triple-crown season (Ruth easily pacing the circuit with 46 homers and a .378 BA). A thrilling seven-game World Series victory over the New York Giants that autumn fueled a remarkable follow-up campaign in which Harris's now-potent Senators outstripped the field with a club-record 96 victories (later surpassed only by the 99 wins posted in 1933) and left Connie Mack's Athletics a distant 8½ games behind.

Both 1924 and 1925 World Series classics were nothing less than thrilling affairs. While it took Washington the better part of three decades to get there, the Senators certainly didn't disappoint in World Series play, stretching both classics to a dramatic seventh game in which victory hung in the balance until the closing innings. The 1924 Series with McGraw's Giants provided one of baseball's most dramatic stories of the pre-radio era, involving baseball's great pitcher, Walter "Big Train" Johnson, locked in an emotion-filled struggle to achieve the one trophy that had been denied him—a World Series victory. After 18 seasons in the majors without a single crack at October championship play, Johnson was the nation's clear sentimental favorite in World Series 1924, as well as the primary hope of the victory-starved Washington faithful. The Big Train failed over 12 innings in Game One, however, as a bases-loaded single by Ross Youngs erased the effort of 12 Johnson strikeouts. Again in Game Five Johnson was the loser, pounded for three Giant runs in the bottom of the eighth. In Game Seven Walter Johnson remained on the bench and the Senators trailed early as the Griffith Stadium partisans sensed a last chance at precious victory slipping away. And then—at the very moment when all seemed lost—a story-book finish appropriate only to Hollywood scripting brought one of baseball's greatest Series to its surprising and dramatic close.

Manager Bucky Harris singled with the bases jammed in the bottom of the eighth to knot the score; the stands erupted as Walter Johnson was brought from the bullpen to face the Giants in the ninth; Frankie Frisch tripled to greet Johnson but remained stranded at third as the Big Train fanned George Kelly and retired dangerous Bob Meusel on a harmless roller. With a runner in scoring position in the 11th frame Johnson again recorded two key strikeouts to keep the game alive for one final dramatic at-bat. And that single half-inning today remains for all-time the most famous brief episode in Washington baseball annals. It all started with weak-hitting Muddy Ruel being given a new life by a dropped foul pop-up, then doubling down the left-field line. To the crowd's delight Walter Johnson was allowed to bat for himself and reached on a second costly Giant error. And then, on one of the most legendary bad-bounce plays of Series' history (indeed, all baseball history), Earl McNeely lashed a sharp bounder at third sacker Freddy Lindstrom which skipped wildly over the amazed defender's outstretched hands for the thrilling game-winner. Forty summers later, on the eve of the destruction of old Griffith Stadium in the urban heart of the nation's capital, baseball columnist Jimmy

McCannon wrote whimsically in *The Sporting News* (June 13, 1964) about that famous small peddle of infield gravel which had so surprisingly determined the outcome of a dramatic World Series finale, and which in 1964 still lay buried somewhere out there in the long-unused infield of one of the nation's most nostalgic and now condemned ballparks.[2]

The World Series of 1925, this time played out against the surprising runaway N.L. champion Pittsburgh Pirates, was a far less fortunate affair for the men of Bucky Harris. It was again a seven-game Series, yet this time the National Leaguers prevailed in the end. Washington had again cakewalked to an A.L. crown, paced by Walter Johnson's 12th and last 20-game season and by spitballer Stan Coveleski's 20–5 mark in a solid supporting role. It was Coveleski's fifth consecutive 20-win campaign (his first in Washington); but was also only the second time in Johnson's 19-year career that he was aided by another 20-game winner on the same staff. Washington bolted to a 3–1 Series lead, then faded in the final three games, with Walter Johnson giving up 15 hits in the final contest and manager Harris being soundly criticized in the press for not pulling his tiring ace Johnson down the stretch of this final game. The criticism came from none other than League President Ban Johnson.

Harris's ballclubs slipped noticeably after 1925 and tumbled as low as fourth place in 1926 and as far out as 25 games in 1927. In the summer of 1928 the Senators were finally back under .500 for the season and the subsequent summer they were entrenched once more in the second division. By 1929 there was even a new manager in Washington, and it was an old familiar face—the "Big Train" himself. And if Walter Johnson had mastered American League hitters for nearly two decades as a moundsman with little assist from his second-rate supporting cast, his fate was hardly any different as field boss. After a slow start in 1929 (fifth place and 10 games under .500), Johnson put together three consecutive 90-win campaigns; yet he never once pulled his outmanned troops higher than second (1930) nor moved closer to the talent-laden Athletics and Yankees than eight games from the top.

Baseball in Washington in the 1920s was also not without its local color and penchant for the bizarre. Already very much the showman in his earlier seasons as club owner, Clark Griffith—who at the end of his career three decades later would hype tickets for a Sunday doubleheader by staging Cleveland's Bob Feller in a pre-game throwing contest featuring a newfangled radar device—entertained Griffith Stadium fans with several special late-season appearances by long-time coach Nick Altrock at the outset of the 1920s and 1930s. In the first of these staged events, Altrock (who had won 82 games as a turn-of-the-century pitcher) pinch hit in 1924 to become the oldest man (at 48) ever to record a base hit (a triple at that) in big-league play. In 1931 and 1933 Altrock repeated his staged cameo appearances, on the latter occasion becoming the oldest performer to date (at 57) in a major league game. It would be 1965 before Satchel Paige would hurl three innings at age 59 for the Kansas City Athletics to erase the second standard, and 1976 before Minnie Minoso of the White Sox eclipsed the first by collecting a one-base hit at age 53 and counting.

An irony of Washington baseball history remains the fact that all three Senators pennants came under raw first-time managers. Where Bucky Harris had turned the trick in 1924–1925, it was Joe Cronin's turn in 1933. A brilliant leader and eventual American League president, Cronin at the time was a skilled 27-year-old shortstop with more than a full decade of playing time still stretching out before him. While possessing similar inspirational qualities to the young playing-manager Harris, Cronin was himself aided perhaps as much by a huge Yankee collapse as by the stellar play of his own talented team. Babe Ruth (who was to hit .300 for the final time that season while outwardly expressing interest in soon managing the New Yorkers) led a contingent of Yankees who refused to speak to manager Joe McCarthy or any players loyal to him for nearly the entire season. Spurred by Yankee disharmony and the brilliant defensive play of their own veteran infield (Kuhel at first, Myer at second, Ossie Bluege at third, and Cronin himself at short), Washington cruised to a remarkable seven-game bulge over the runner-up Yankees of Ruth, Gehrig, and Lazzeri. The 99 victories that year were the most ever earned by a ballclub representing the nation's capital. Alvin "General" Crowder was the pitching star with a league-leading 24–15 record, backed up ably by Earl Whitehill with 22 wins of his own. But Heinie Manush was the batter and all-around day-in-and-day-out player that carried Cronin's club, finishing second to triple crown winner Jimmy Foxx in batting, and leading the league in hits (221) while racking up the league's third best numbers (behind Foxx and Gehrig) for total bases.

But if the Senators outdistanced one New York team with relative ease during the 1933 pennant race, they had little luck against another Gotham ballclub in the World Series that fall. The 1933 Series was a replay of the Senators-Giants matchup of eight years earlier—in terms of the opponents at least. The results were not so similar: led by Carl Hubbell, Hal Schumacher (19–12 that year), and veteran Cuban Dolph Luque, the Giants wrapped up the Series this time in five games, without breaking much of a sweat. Mel Ott hit two homers and slugged away at a .389 clip to lead all Series batters. The Nats' Heinie Manush, by contrast, was the undisputed flop of the 1933 Fall Classic with a .111 BA (on the heels of his .336 season's mark) and only two hits, both singles. Even the presence of President Franklin Delano Roosevelt in the special Chief Executive's box at Griffith Stadium for Game Three did little to help the Senators in what was to be their last World Series appearance ever.

Cronin not only enjoyed the same immediate success as Bucky Harris in the won-loss column, but also an identical rapid fall from grace. In his second year at the helm his team limped home a distant seventh, winning 33 fewer games than a season earlier. By 1935 Bucky Harris had returned as playing-manager and Cronin had been sold off to Boston for Lyn Lary and $225,000. The always cash-starved Clark Griffith had peddled away the future A.L. president (who was also his own son-in-law) in an obvious effort to gain needed operating capital which always seemed in such short supply. And this time Bucky Harris would be around for eight full seasons, the second-longest managerial tenure ever in Washington, ranking a whisker behind Griffith's own nine-season span two decades earlier. The Senators were never a serious challenger again under Harris between 1935 and 1942, finishing only once (1936) as high as fourth place. There were, however, some individual highlights in those years. Buddy Myer won the league batting championship in 1935, with four hits on the last day of the season to edge out Joe Yosmik of Cleveland. Joe Cambria began operating behind the scene in Griffith's front office as a rare talent scout with uncanny insight, early signing up such future stalwarts as George Case and Mickey Vernon, and the first success among his many Latin signees, outfielder Bobby Estalella. An overflow crowd of 35,563 witnessed a July 4, 1936, doubleheader with the Yankees, the largest throng ever to attend an American League ball game at Griffith Stadium.

The Washington Senators of the 1920s and 1930s were as familiar with the second division as they were with true pennant-race contention, yet the fans who came out to stately Griffith Stadium in these years (including a young scoreboard operator named Bowie Kuhn) saw as much fence-rattling hitting as anywhere else in American League play. Throughout the 1920s a muscular outfield duo composed of future Cooperstown immortals Goose Goslin and Sam Rice consistently rained hits upon Junior Circuit pitchers, providing one of the most fearsome batting duos in all baseball. Goslin stroked 190 or more hits four times during the 1920s and hit over .300 eight of 10 seasons in Washington, before departing for St. Louis in 1930. Even more productive, Rice enjoyed six 200-plus-hit seasons between 1920 and 1930. And in the 1930s, after Goslin's departure, there was the brief but highly productive career in Washington of Heinie Manush, a back-to-back author of 200-plus hits in 1932 and 1933 and owner of a .300-plus BA in each of his first six Washington seasons. And Cecil

Travis earned his share of accolades during the 1930s as well. Travis led the A.L. with 218 safeties in 1941 (remember, this was the year of DiMaggio's streak and the year Williams hit .406), but he also batted over .330 in 1937 and again in 1938 and authored a not-insignificant 12-year .314 careermark at the plate.

The Second World War years saw two near-misses under new field boss Ossie Bluege. With Harris out (he had elected to leave for a lucrative front-office job with minor league Buffalo) and Bluege in for 1943, the Senators rallied to a second-place finish (13½ games behind the Yankees) and then a heart-breaking game-and-a-half loss to the Tigers in 1945. But a disappointing eighth-place finish in 1944, sandwiched between two second-place summers, only indicated the sad unevenness of big-league play during those wartime seasons when bevies of near-cripples and minor leaguers filled out most major league rosters. Washington did manage to produce a few young stars on the rise in this epoch, with young Early Wynn capturing 18 victories in his second full season of 1943 and fleet George Case leading the Junior Circuit with 56 steals that same season.

June of 1947 witnessed a landmark addition to Griffith Stadium with the erection of a memorial plaque in honor of the legendary Walter Johnson. The impressive eight-foot-high bronze plaque, imbedded in solid grey granite, was unveiled at the main entrance to the first-base grandstand (it now stands at Walter Johnson High School in Bethesda, Maryland) by President Harry S. Truman with full ceremony befitting the greatest player of franchise history and one of the true immortals of Cooperstown. Such memories of by-gone glories were the sole solace for Washington fans of the post-war period, however, and the Senators soon closed out the 1940s and the first half of the century exactly as they had begun five decades earlier, with two of the poorest seasons in franchise history. One hundred and four losses in 1949 were surpassed only by the record 113 defeats of 1904 and the 110 losses of 1909. Joseph Kuhel's two-season stint as manager brought the worst composite winning percentage (.345) of all among a long string of ill-fated Washington skippers. Kuhel's tenure was therefore an understandably short one. By the end of the 1949 campaign Clark Griffith had already wearied of Kuhel and the old first-base star of the 1930s was promptly sent packing.

It was now time to bring back an all-too familiar face. At the outset of the new decade the ubiquitous Bucky Harris would return for his third turn onboard as Washington manager, his seventh tour of duty on a big-league bench. Harris was baseball's perennial "available man"—especially when the call came from Clark Griffith—and in five different decades as a major league skipper Harris would eventually accumulate the third most victories (2,159) and third most games managed (4,410 behind only Connie Mack and John McGraw). He would also lose more games (2,219) than anyone but Mack, and the bulk of those losses would eventually come during 18 seasons in Washington.

And Last in the American League ... The Colorful Nats of the Fabulous Fifties

In the decade of the fifties the Washington American League ballclub provided some of the most exciting baseball play and some of the most colorful baseball personalities ever associated with a perennial last-place franchise. To keep fans tottering on the edges of their slatted wooden grandstand seats in venerable Griffith Stadium there was always the longball threat of muscular Roy Sievers at the outset of the decade, as well as that of the fearsome outfield trio of Jim Lemon, Bob Allison, and the young Harmon Killebrew at the decade's end. And Washington was blessed with several proficient singles hitters as well. Pete Runnels irregularly stood among the league's better hitters throughout the mid-1950s, as did Mickey Vernon a few years before him. While Runnels actually hit .300 only once in Washington (.310 in 1956), when surround with a better supporting cast in Boston, Pete would soon pace the A.L. in batting in both 1960 (.320) and 1962 (.326). Vernon's 1946 batting title for Washington was repeated in 1953, and the popular first sacker hit at or near .300 for five of his six Washington years between 1950 and 1955. Durable Eddie Yost, in turn, was perhaps the most steady third baseman and consistently underrated player in the entire American League throughout this period; a several-time league All-Star, Yost had a special knack for getting on base, pacing the A.L. in bases-on-balls five different times during the 1950s. A remarkable ironman player (not missing a game between mid-1949 and late 1955, and establishing a league consecutive-game record for third sackers at the time of 838), Yost was perhaps one of the most popular players ever to don a Washington Senators uniform.

Among the hurlers, Latin American flamethrowers Camilo Pascual and Pete Ramos were widely admired around the entire league as two of best pitchers in all of baseball, equally cursed with long-term assignment to an otherwise largely untalented team. Workhorse Ramos twice (1958 and 1960) paced the Junior Circuit in games started, yet for four consecutive summers (1958–1961) lost more ball games than any other A.L. hurler to boot. With little hitting or fielding support, Camilo Pascual posted only two winning seasons in Washington (the best was a 17–10 mark in 1959); yet the move to Minnesota and increased hitting support which lay around the corner would make him a two-time 20-game winner and three-time league strikeout leader (1961–1963, with over 200 each season) during the coming decade.

And there were other strong arms in the nation's capital as well: Dick Hyde, a bespectacled sidearmer with buggy-whip delivery, was a pioneer relief specialist in an age which saw little such pitching specialization. In one remarkable year, Hyde posted a 10–3 mark in 1958 (all in relief), ranking second to the Yankees' Ryne Duren in saves (with 18) and posting the best overall numbers among league relief hurlers (based on the new classifications for such categories provided by revisionist baseball historians John Thorn and Pete Palmer in their *Total Baseball* volume of 1989).

And then there were a host of remarkable role players and colorful diamond figures as well. Bobo Newsom pitched for Washington in those years, appearing for the third different time in three different decades for the Senators when he pitched 10 Washington games in 1952. In 20 big-league seasons Newsom both won and lost over 200 games (he is one of only two big league pitchers ever to win 200-plus games and yet lose more than he won); yet Newsom is best remembered as one of the most colorful and flamboyant hurlers ever—a poor-man's American League Dizzy Dean. There was also a catcher with the improbable name of Clyde Kluttz and even less probable playing style which he seemed to derive perfectly from his name. The most infamous among dozens of totally infamous Washington outfielders of the 1950s was a Cuban slugger, Carlos Paula, whose abilities to smash a baseball never came near to compensating for his seemingly total inability to field one cleanly in the outfield. Carlos Paula hit .299 in 115 games in 1955; he also led the A.L. in errors for outfielders and was gone from baseball completely by the end of only his third season. There was a potential young superstar, Jackie Jensen, who put in nearly two full seasons (1952–1953) in Washington and showed flashes of becoming a franchise player before he was traded to Boston for outfielder Tommy Umphlett and flaky hurler Mickey McDermott. Jensen never did fulfill his bright promise, despite leading the circuit in RBIs three times while with the Red Sox. Ironically, an inordinate fear of flying cut short his big-league career after only 11 bright seasons.

And then there was that raft of memorable utility players in every Washington season of the 1950s—like the incomparable Wayne Terwilliger. Unsurpassed baseball wits Brendan Boyd and Fred Harris (*The Great American Baseball Card Flipping, Trading, and Bubble Gum Book*) cogently observe that Wayne Terwilliger, in fact, played on a whole team of Washington utility players . . . "Wayne was the perfect utility man. He couldn't hit his hat size, but he could field every position. He also looked like a utility man—he had a utility man's face, a utility man's build, and a utility man's outlook on life . . . of course, what made it better was that he played with some of the worst Washington Senators teams of the early fifties, teams consisting of entire rosters of utility men" (Boyd and Harris, 1973, 36).

But perhaps most memorable about the Washington Senators of the fifties was their distinct Latin American flavor. This was the very franchise which pioneered the now-popular movement to exploit newly discovered and seemingly immense talent pools of Latin and Caribbean ballplayers. Hispanics, making their first inroads into big-league baseball as the color barrier tumbled in the years immediately following the nation's Second World War, were of course only the latest ethnic group to find baseball an acceptable conduit for the material wealth and social mobility lining the American Dream. Any cursory search of names in Macmillans's *Baseball Encyclopedia* reveals that at the outset of baseball's professional history, ballplayers had all been largely Irish and northern European immigrant stock; then came the Slavs and Poles and other broad-shouldered eastern Europeans; eventually the Italians (with DiMaggio the first great Italian baseball hero of the period between the two great wars); and finally came the black players. Each new ethnic group found in baseball the much-sought-after entry into American privileged society and economic respectability. Beginning largely with the Washington Senators in the 1940s and 1950s, it was the turn of the Latin American ballplayer in post-World-War-II America. Of course the countries "south of the border" had long produced great baseball talent; but much of it was black and thus forced to remain hidden away in winter ball and the underground Negro Leagues. (Ironically, Black Cuban hurler Tommy de la Cruz was unceremoniously drummed out of the big leagues after one short summer in Cincinnati, due to racial intolerance, three full seasons before Robinson's pioneering debut in 1947.) But Clark Griffith and his trusted super scout Joe Cambria began changing all that in the late 1930s and early 1940s with Cambria's first serious scouting sorties throughout the untapped Caribbean region.

Latin American ballplayers began appearing in force on Washington rosters in the years immediately preceding the Second World War. Mexican Mel Almada was the first, as full-time center fielder with a .309 BA in 1937; Cuban Bobby Estalella (who first joined the club in 1935) was also an outfield fixture, while Venezuelan righthander Alex Carrasquel (winner of 50 games in eight big-league seasons) made 40 mound appearances. Other notable Latino players wearing Senators colors in the late 1940s and early 1950s included Rene Monteagudo (Cuban pitcher whose son Aurelio also pitched seven major league seasons during the sixties), Gil Torres (Cuban-born third baseman), Roberto Ortiz (Cuban outfielder), Baby Ortiz (pitcher and brother of

Robert Ortiz), Pedro (Preston) Gomez (Cuban infielder and later big-league manager), Chile (Jose) Gomez (Mexican infielder), and Mike Guerra (Cuban catcher).

An onset of wartime conditions worked to dramatically increase Griffith's growing stock of Latin players. The fact that such non-citizens were altogether free from draft call must have had a certain appeal for the financially strapped and minor-league thin Griffith, and the increased proportion of Latin players on the roster actually worked to improve the Senators' fortunes ever-so-slightly in the early forties (Vaughn, 1984).[3] While other teams inevitably faded under the exodus of top talent drained off by the war effort, Washington slid past normally stronger teams for two surprising second-place finishes in 1943 and 1945. Penurious by nature and faced with inevitable wartime falloff in ballpark attendance, Clark Griffith had trimmed the Senators already inadequate farm system to a mere six ballclubs by 1947. Seemingly as a direct result of such drastic cutbacks, by the late 1940s the Senators had begun scouting the Caribbean almost exclusively, maintaining only three full-time scouts during 1947 and 1948 whose bird dog activities were strictly limited to the nation's eastern seaboard and to the tropical climes of Havana and other unfrequented Latin ports.

The controlling reason for Clark Griffith's evident interest in Latin America as a primary source of player talent seems, therefore, to have been largely financial from the very outset. Even when a decade-long improvement in the Washington farm-system was finally launched with the 1947 appointment of former manager Ossie Bluege as farm director, maverick scout Joe Cambria (named official scout for Cuba and Puerto Rico in 1949, and then for the West Indies and South America in 1954) continued to comb Latin American soil for potential big leaguers to serve his boss Clark Griffith in Washington. Joe Cambria is even reported to have scouted and nearly signed a promising young pitching prospect of the early 1940s named Fidel Castro. While Castro was soon called to his predestined date with history by other pressing career aspirations and (perhaps most unfortunately in retrospect) never did don the Senators uniform, the following cache of Cambria signees all made appearances for the Senators in the early 1950s, and with varying degrees of big-league success: pitchers Sandy Consuegra (Cuba), Mike Fomieles (Cuba), Connie Marrero (Cuba), Julio Moreno (Cuba), Camilo Pascual (Cuba), Carlos Pascual (Camilo's older brother), and Pedro Ramos (Cuba); outfielders Francisco Campos (Cuba), Pompeyo Davalillo (Venezuela), Juan Delis (Cuba), and Carlos Paula (Cuba); infielders Ossie Alvarez (Cuba), Julio Becquer (Cuba), Willie Miranda (Cuba), and Jose Valdivielso (Cuba). If Cambria's scouting activities did not turn Clark Griffith's ballclub into an instant winner, it did supply a continual cheap supply of adequate major league talent to keep the often floundering ship barely afloat.

The considerable honor role of Latin American ballplayers resident in Washington in the 1950s begins, of course, with the solid pitching of Pete Ramos (67–92 for the Senators between 1955 and 1960) and Camilo Pascual (53–77 for the same period). Other strong-armed Latin pitchers also rounded out the bulk of the Senators usually undermanned staff throughout the fifties: Sandy Consuegra was 20–16 over three seasons, before being dealt to Chicago in 1953; Connie Marrero compiled a 39–40 career mark in the first six seasons of the decade; Mike Fomieles registered an impressive rookie 1.37 ERA in brief action before departing to the White Sox in exchange for eventual Washington ace lefthander Chuck Stobbs. And then there were utility players like Jose Valdivielso, Carlos Paula, and Julio Becquer. In all, almost two dozen Latin American-born ballplayers appeared in major league action for the Senators during the cellar-dwelling club's final topsy-turvy decade in Washington.

Of course this considerable influx of Latin American player talent didn't help the floundering Senators that much in the league standings, for all it may have done to pump vital life's blood into a nearly moribund baseball franchise. Yet when it came to winning ball games, not much changed in Washington between the end of the global hot war with V-J Day of 1945 and the thick of the cold war during the Eisenhower years of the mid-1950s. Bucky Harris was, remarkably enough, back for five more years at the start of the decade—his third tenure as Washington manager, giving him a franchise-record 18 seasons in all at the helm in Washington. This time Harris brought his teams home seventh once, sixth once, and fifth three times. The best showing by far was a single year over .500 (78–76, 17 games out) in 1952, a summer in which Harris' men finished up the campaign only a single game behind Philadelphia and the league's first division, and but a scant three games behind third-place Chicago. While 1953 brought a drop-off of only two games in the won-lost column, Washington never challenged the first division and came home a full seven-and-one-half games behind fourth-place Boston, 23½ games in arrears of the pace-setting Yankees. By 1954 the men of Bucky Harris were once more buried deep in sixth place, 11 games under .500 (66–88), locked out of their deserved home in the cellar only by the even more horrible performance of the Baltimore and Philadelphia clubs, which both lost in excess of 100 games.

Charlie Dressen (out of the major league managerial scene for a single season after his back-to-back pennant triumphs at Brooklyn in 1952–1953) was the new skipper for the 1955 season, and his ballclubs promptly lost 101 games that season and a mere 95 the following summer. Successive eighth- and seventh-place finishes quickly ended the new skipper's welcome with both the Griffith family and Washington fans, and the dour Chuck Dressen was replaced only 21 games into the 1957 campaign by unheralded Cookie Lavagetto, another Brooklyn Dodger refugee who had served as Dressen's number one lieutenant since 1951 and had accompanied Dressen from Pacific Coast League Oakland at the outset of the recent 1955 campaign. The long-standing traditional team nickname of "Senators" which had been replaced with the turn-of-the-century moniker "Nationals" at the outset of the 1950s was again restored for the 1957 baseball campaign, but no consequent change in team identity would miraculously emerge as a result. Under new field boss Lavagetto the end result of this mid-decade switch in dugout leadership was yet another eighth-place finish and a flip-flop in the standings with cellar-rival Kansas City. Then in 1958 and 1959 Cookie Lavagetto was to prove that this ineptitude was no fluke, guiding his team through two additional seasons sequestered firmly in the league basement. Yet with Roy Sievers, Jim Lemon, and newcomer Harmon Killebrew now bashing homers with regularity, and with Pascual and Ramos on the mound, this was indeed a more interesting and colorful Washington ballclub to watch than the Bucky Harris entries of a few seasons earlier. Washington ranked second to Cleveland in team homers in 1959, with young Killebrew individually leading the league (in third base errors as well as in homers, incidentally).

Perhaps the saddest aspect of the waning months of major league baseball in the nation's capital—at least in hindsight—was the widespread feeling around the baseball map that this Senators team departing for Minnesota in 1961 was finally on the verge of becoming a true American League powerhouse, as well as one of the most entertaining ballclubs in all of baseball. In their swan-song season of 1960 the Washington Senators climbed back into fifth place, only a scant three games out of the first division. This was drastic improvement for a team which still hadn't seen the first division since 1946. Jungle Jim Lemon and Harmon Killebrew were again among the league's leading sluggers, the former with 38 homers and the latter boasting 31. Earl Battey had been acquired from Chicago to shore up the catching department and had emerged as one of the A.L.'s leading receivers, pacing the Junior Circuit in putouts and assists (as well as errors) at his backstop position. Pete Ramos paced the league with 18 losses but was still coveted by most other clubs wanting a durable fireballing righthanded starter. And Camilo Pascual enjoyed perhaps his finest season to date, 12–8 with a respectable 3.03 ERA and a nearly three-to-one strikeouts (143) to walks (53) ratio. This seemed to be a team on the move. How far it was about to move (halfway across the nation's expanding professional sports landscape in point of fact!) was the terrible irony that lay hidden around the corner for the handful of remaining faithful Washington baseball supporters.

Fans of the Washington Senators during the 1950s had little to buoy their spirits by the more conventional measures of fandom. There were no first-division finishes—four fifths, four eights, two sevenths, and one sixth, for the record—certainly nothing that resembled the excitement of the home team caught in the throes of a pennant race. There were only two seasons of .500 baseball (1952 at two games over and 1953 at dead-even .500). Yet there was colorful and idyllic Griffith Stadium, perhaps the most fan-friendly park in all of baseball. Featuring one of the largest "outer pastures" in the major leagues, Griffith Stadium was long the nemesis of the league's home run hitters,with its 405-foot left-field fence and its imposing 31-foot-high right-field concrete wall. Seating only 28,669 fans after its last expansion in 1957, Washington's legendary park was the epitome of old-style open-view ballyards. A legendary location of six decades of American League play, Griffith Stadium became the most famous park in the land each April as eight presidents threw out the ceremonial first pitch to launch the new spring baseball season. Washington Senators team yearbooks of the 1950s repeatedly boasted that Griffith Stadium patrons found this the easiest park in which to view a major league game, with a majority of the park's seats located breathtakingly close to the on-field action. It was also often the nation's loneliest ballpark, with its league-low seating capacity of less than 30,000 rarely taxed by the skimpy crowds which actually attended Senators ball games during the swan-song seasons of the late 1950s. Like its cousins Ebbets Field and Shibe Park, Griffith Stadium was to hold far more charm for the nation's backward-looking ball fans as a dim nostalgic memory than it ever did as a standing concrete baseball relic.

The Senators of this period also provided a host of colorful diamond heroes far beyond the normal expectancy of a perennial cellar-dwelling ballclub. Bob Porterfield was arguably the best pitcher in baseball in 1953, compiling league-leading totals of 22 victories and 24 complete games, as well as pacing the Junior Circuit with nine shutouts. Mickey Vernon was one of the league's best hitters in the early part of the decade and brought home the excitement of his second batting title in that same 1953 season. Paced by Porterfield's moundwork, Vernon's humming bat, and Eddie Yost's stellar third-base play, the Senators rose to the .500-mark for both the 1952 and 1953 campaigns. And in the final four years of the decade there was the awesome trio of home run sluggers that took up residence in spacious Griffith Stadium and challenged for the league's home run title each season. Roy Sievers became the club's first-ever longball champion with 42 in 1957, poking 180 roundtrippers in six Washington seasons. Jim Lemon provided his own brand of terror for American League pitchers, belting 27 trippers in 1956, 33 in 1959, and 38 in 1960. Lemon also contributed 100 RBIs in each of the final two seasons in Washington, pacing the ballclub in that department as well. And by those last years of the decade a new hero had been born as well to join forces with the slugging Jim Lemon and replace the departed Roy Sievers. Harmon Killebrew—eventually the greatest home run hitter after Babe Ruth in all of American League history—was just coming into his own (after five wasted seasons as a bench-riding bonus baby) as the franchise entered its fifth decade under tutelage of the Griffith family, and as it quietly prepared to pull up stakes and surreptitiously head off to the lucrative northern climes of Minnesota.

Young Harmon Killebrew was, in fact, exactly the imposing Ruthean figure which the long-suffering fans of Washington had always coveted down through 20-odd summers of second-division baseball. This rare parallel of Killebrew and Ruth was not immediately apparent, unfortunately, as the Senators' first-ever bonus baby languished on the bench for five full seasons before bursting to stardom in his initial regular season of 1959. Finally given the opportunity to play third base after the departure of popular iron-man Eddie Yost, Killebrew posted a league-leading total of 42 homers (tied with Cleveland's Rocky Colavito) along with 105 RBIs and 98 runs scored. And Killebrew was far from a late-bloomer; despite appearing in only 113 games and socking only 11 homers in five bench-warming seasons between 1954 and 1958, Harmon Killebrew was only 23 when he emerged from obscurity to become the second Washington player ever to reign as league home run champion.

But the best all lie ahead: in the next full decade Killebrew's home run output would drop below 30 in only a single injury-plagued season of 1965. And Harmon Killebrew's unsettling parallels with the fictional Joe Hardy of baseball literature, as well as real-life sluggers like Ruth and Mantle, would certainly not pass unnoticed by diehard Washington fans. Like the dauntless hero of Douglass Wallop's popular novel *The Year The Yankees Lost the Pennant* (progenitor of the popular Broadway musical and film "Damn Yankees"), Killebrew would over a few short seasons spark a remarkable resurgence for the victory-starved Griffith-owned ballclub. This resurgence—which so ironically paralleled the plot-line of Wallop's famous novel, in which a celebrated batting phenom of mysterious origin appears on the scene to magically lead the hometown Senators in unprecedented pennant triumphs over the unbeatable New York Yankees—was fittingly destined to terminate at long last an oppressive league domination by the legendary and hated New York ballclub. But if baseball fans throughout the rest of the nation soon rejoiced at the new baseball age of American League parity which slugging Harmon Killebrew in large part represented, the final irony was that dedicated baseball fans of the nation's capital were not around to see it all happen. For Joe Hardy (alias Harmon "Killer" Killebrew, along with his supporting cast of Jim Lemon, Bob Allison, and Camilo Pascual) had already packed their pinstriped flannels and gone elsewhere by the time the new baseball decade had opened in springtime of 1961.

Hammerin' Harmon and the Age of Calvinisms

The flight of the Senators out of Washington in 1960–1961 came as a shock to many of the nation's fans, and a blow from which some Washington baseball diehards have never fully recovered. Despite the decades of poor play, baseball somehow seemed indigenous to the nation's capital—Washington was the city of Walter Johnson and Goose Goslin, home of the time-honored Opening Day presidential first pitch, site of venerable Griffith Stadium and its half-century of indelible baseball memories. But the inevitable franchise move was not at all a surprise to league insiders. Calvin Griffith had long coveted westward expansion and the anticipated flood of untold riches it seemed to promise for his attendance-poor second-division ballclub. He had repeatedly made his interest in Minneapolis publicly known almost from the day he took over the club's presidency after his uncle's death in 1955. In hindsight, it can hardly be disputed that the visionary role played by the younger Griffith, in this bold expansion of baseball's western frontiers, parallels that of Walter O'Malley in bringing live baseball to fans in the nation's western sectors. In the spring of 1961, while a few thousand broken-hearted protesters moaned in the nation's capital, millions of new baseball fans cheered wildly at the prospect of hometown baseball in Minneapolis, Houston, Los Angeles, and beyond.

Minnesotans in the fall of 1960 were inevitably thrilled at the prospect of a hometown major league club. These, after all, had been dedicated baseball fans for years, sporting one of the proudest minor league traditions found anywhere in the country. Ted Williams had once played here with the Minneapolis Millers; slugging minor-league legend Joe Hauser had thrilled Minneapolis throngs with a Herculean performance of 69 circuit clouts in a single summer. Hall-of-famers Willie Mays, Carl Yastrzemski, Duke Snider, and Roy Campanella all jumped to the big leagues from a proud baseball training ground in Minneapolis and St. Paul.

The deal that brought the Senators to Minneapolis-St. Paul was struck at New York's Savoy-Hilton Hotel in late October of 1960. This was a rather complex transaction, at face value, that was to bring with it baseball's first league expansion in a full half century. Earlier in the year National League owners had already agreed upon such expansion to ward off the planned rebel Continental League, and now with American League owners also embracing inevitable expansion, new clubs would be added in New York (N.L. Mets), Houston (N.L. Colt .45s), Los Angeles (A.L. Angels), and Washington (A.L. Senators). This was more than just a single franchise shift, as had been seen several times before—in 1953 (Boston Braves to Milwaukee), 1954 (Philadelphia Athletics to Kansas City, and St. Louis Browns to Baltimore), and 1958 (Dodgers and Giants to Los Angeles and San Francisco). This was, indeed, a radical restructuring of the organizational face of baseball that had not been attempted since Ban Johnson introduced his American League itself in 1901.

While Calvin Griffith had been outspoken often enough in the past about packing his Senators off to Minneapolis, the October 1960 owners' meetings in New York found him suddenly less than sanguine about any potential franchise shift. A surprising turn of events, however, spurred undoubtedly by the lust of American League owners for the opportunity to compete against Walter O'Malley and Horace Stoneham in the lucrative California market, miraculously began unfolding with the October 26 closed-door sessions; after much heated debate, a contentious recess, and a second narrow vote (a pre-recess vote had rejected Griffith's request), Calvin Griffith was finally granted permission to move his beleaguered ballclub. Fearing the outrage of Washington politicos, A.L. owners also saw to it that a spanking new franchise was promised the nation's capital as part and parcel of the deal. On the morning of October 27 unsuspecting Minnesotans awoke in shocked disbelief to bold oversized newspaper headlines proclaiming that the Twin Cities were now unexpectedly in the major leagues.

The team that arrived in Minnesota in 1961 was indeed a team with considerable talent: sluggers Killebrew, Lemon, and Allison; hurlers Ramos, Pascual, Kralick, and Kaat; sure-handed infielders Billy Martin (actually obtained from Milwaukee for Billy Consolo on June 1), Zoilo Versalles, and Bill Tuttle; brilliant young defensive catcher Earl Battey. It simply lacked enough overall talent and bench strength to compete on a daily basis (Mona and Jarzyna, 1986, 8).

The 1961 inaugural Twins ballclub posted 70 wins, and one of the most thrilling of these occurred on Opening Day in New York. Behind the masterful pitching of Pete Ramos, the newborn Minnesota Twins won their first-ever game by the count of 6–0 in Yankee Stadium, over the eventual champion New Yorkers and their "M and M Boys" Mantle and Maris. Such a surprising heady start was followed by more such immediate beginner's success, and the undaunted Twins returned from their inaugural road trip for their franchise home opener sporting a shocking 5–1 record. A crowd of 24,606 witnessed an inevitable tumble back to earth in the home opener staged at Metropolitan Stadium in Bloomington, however, as Minnesota suffered an embarrassing 5–3 defeat at the very hands of none other than their makeshift Washington replacements, their fledgling expansion Washington Senators (alias Texas Rangers).

The 1961 Minnesota club finished seventh, ahead of doleful Kansas City (without a .300 hitter or 20-game winner in the lineup), expansion Los Angeles, and the makeshift Washington team that had replaced them with little fanfare in Griffith Stadium. A managerial change was made 66 games into the season, with the team already faltering at 25–41, as Senators holdover Cookie Lavagetto gave way to popular coach and former outfielder Sam Mele. Harmon Killebrew slammed 46 homers (recall that this was the year Roger Maris cracked his record 61), and Killebrew was amply supported by new slugging sensation Bob Allison (with 29 circuit clouts and 105 RBIs). Earl Battey was again the leading catcher in the American League; Pete Ramos once more displayed sufficient talent to hang around just long enough to be the league's losingest pitcher at 11–20. Perhaps the best news for Calvin Griffith, however, was that his ballclub drew nearly 1.3 million fans in its first season at Metropolitan Stadium, enough to put the franchise back in the black if not into the thick of an American League pennant race. In an attempt to accomplish the latter, as well, the normally stand-pat Griffith dealt away star hurler Ramos to Cleveland in the off-season, obtaining in exchange the services of slick-fielding Puerto Rican first baseman Vic Power and promising lefthanded starter Dick Stigman.

A second season in Minnesota proved to be a year marked by dramatic reversal of form for the rapidly improving Twins. In Mele's first full year at the helm the club jumped into second place and improved 21 games in the won-loss column. The 1962 ballclub even remained a contender until late September, when they finally fell five games behind the pace-setting Yankees. As a natural fallout of these instant successes, Minnesota's new entry also led the A.L. in attendance, drawing in excess of 1.4 million to a ballpark with a seating capacity of only 39,525. And it was pitching that was the biggest difference in the Twins' dramatic turnaround. With his countryman Ramos now departed, Camilo Pascual finally emerged as star material and led the league in strikeouts (206), shutouts (5), and complete games (18). While Ramos fell to 10–12 with the Indians, the newly acquired Dick Stigman proved adequate replacement with a 12–5 record, while Jim Kaat won 18 and Jack Kralick 12. Kralick also gained sudden immortality with a first Minnesota no-hit game against Kansas City on August 26, missing a perfect game outing by virtue of an unfortunate ninth-inning walk to George Alusik of the Athletics. Killebrew was the league's top slugging star this time around, outpacing both Maris and Mantle in homers (48) and RBIs (126).

Hopes were naturally high entering the 1963 season, after the successes of 1962, and only the most unrealistic Twin Cities fans were to be disappointed by the Twins' third season. Again the Yankees had just too much firepower for either Minnesota or runner-up Chicago, as Al Lopez's White Sox edged ahead of the Twins in the final days of the campaign. Yet Minnesota won the same 91 games as the previous season; Killebrew again paced the league in homers; Pascual sported an impressive 21–9 mark and again paced the circuit in strikeouts. Earl Battey remained an all-star catcher, and a remarkable rookie, outfielder Jimmy Hall, stroked 33 homers. Hall's total was the second most (at that date) ever hit by a raw rookie during American League play. But what had cost the Twins the 1963 pennant was essentially what had also done them in during the previous three seasons— exceptionally poor defense and very little team speed. For all their fancy glovework, shortstop Zoilo Versalles and third sacker Rich Rollins both led their key positions in errors, while the entire team stole a mere 32 bases, thus besting only lead-footed Boston in that crucial offensive department among all American League ballclubs.

The 1964 Minnesota Twins again bashed the longball with remarkable authority, just like their predecessors of the previous three seasons, yet their pitching and defense were simultaneously about the worst in all of baseball. Killebrew slugged away as usual with 111 RBIs and a league-best 49 roundtrippers. Hall proved that his rookie season was no fluke by rapping 25 homers and batting .282. Unfortunately, the Twins also gave up far more runs (a league-high 737) than they produced. Kaat, Pascual, and Jim "Mudcat" Grant (acquired in mid-season from Cleveland) provided a more-than-adequate starting three-man rotation. But there were no fourth or fifth starters anywhere in sight, with Stigman falling off to a 6–15 mark and no one else even approaching 10 victories. In the end the Twins simply gave up too many runs, but they indeed had their bright spots as well. One of the brightest was a brilliant rookie rightfielder from Cuba named Tony Oliva, a runaway Rookie-of-the-Year choice who led all American Leaguers in batting (.323), total bases (374), hits (217), doubles (43), and runs scored (109). Oliva's performance was indeed one of the best first-season efforts ever recorded in almost six decades of American League history.

Four years after leaving Washington, Calvin Griffith's Twins finally put together one of the best all-around years in franchise history, achieving a club-record 102 victories, the only 100-plus victory total in 88 long years of Senators-Twins history. The prize was a first league pennant for the Twin Cities and fourth in club history for the long-suffering Griffiths. Tony Oliva remained the league batting champion for the second consecutive year and Versalles paced the Junior Circuit in total bases, though an injured Harmon Killebrew fell off to but 25 homers and the Twins dropped to fourth place in the longball department. Versalles also led the A.L. in doubles, triples, at-bats, and runs scored and was the hands-down league MVP choice. But the old adage about pitching as the key to winning also proved once more to be validated. The same Twins staff that had been rocked for a league-high run total in 1964 miraculously found new life under first-year pitching coach Johnny Sain and recorded the third-best league ERA (at 3.14). The effort also provided an American League record attendance of 1,463,258. And there were many unsung heroes on this team: Don Mincher filled in the second half of the season for Killebrew and punched 22 homers; Al Worthington had 22 saves and a 2.14 ERA; Mudcat Grant's 21–7 mark topped the circuit in both winning percentage and victories. The 1965 pennant-clincher ironically came over the lowly Senators in Washington on September 26, a 2–1 victory that was undoubtedly an especially bitter blow to most Washington diehards. A small and stunned Kennedy Stadium throng was on hand that day to watch in dismay, as their latter-day heroes posted the ultimate triumph while now wearing the altogether strange navy and red colors of the hated anachronistic Minnesota Twins.

The 1965 World Series provided a dramatic climax to what was indisputably the greatest full season of Minnesota baseball. July of 1965 had also brought the Twin Cities its first summer All-Star Classic, but nothing could match the excitement surrounding a Fall Classic featuring the hometown Twins and the awesome Los Angeles Dodgers. Los Angeles sported such diamond heroes as the incomparable pitching duo of Koufax and Drysdale and the rare base-stealing wizard Maury Wills. Minnesota had plenty of vaunted pitching of its own, and the opening two games at Metropolitan Stadium saw Sam Mele's Twins race to a two-game lead on the strength of brilliant complete-game pitching by Mudcat Grant (aided by a six-run Twins third-inning explosion) and Jim Kaat (who bested Koufax in a tight duel highlighted by Allison's remarkable sliding catch of Jim Lefebrve's sinking drive to end a crucial fourth-inning rally).

In the end, it was simply too much Los Angeles pitching by Koufax and his supporting crew, however, as the future Hall-of-Famer returned with a vengeance to silence Minnesota bats with complete-game shutouts in Games Five and Seven. Claude Osteen chipped in with a five-hit shutout in Game Three; Drysdale hurled another five-hitter in Game Four. And in the dramatic seventh game Sandy Koufax was at his most brilliant, posting a 2–0 triumph with a final spectacular three-hitter that served to abruptly end the Twins' sudden Cinderella story.

Immediately succeeding years brought two more contending teams in Minnesota, yet both were incomplete ballclubs never quite capable of seizing the ultimate prize. Both the 1966 and 1967 teams were resigned to second place, with the 1967 edition battling Detroit and the Bosox right down to the wire before ultimately losing out to the champion Red Sox on the year's final day in Boston. That same season of 1967 also saw Dean Chance perform the remarkable feat of two no-hit games within the month of August, the first a rare rain-shortened five-inning affair against Boston and the second a 2–1 squeaker at Cleveland. These two hitless masterpieces, remarkably thrown within three weeks of each other, were destined to be two of only three no-hit efforts by Minnesota Twins pitchers in 28 seasons of team play, and all three were achieved by the mid-sixties. Jack Kralick had thrown the first back in 1962, the only nine-inning feat of perfection ever tossed by a Minnesota hurler before the hometown crowd.

The Minnesota Twins of 1968 were one of those legendary teams that achieve remarkable baseball infamy by performing far below expectations. For the first time since the move to the Twin Cities, the vaunted hitting prowess of the Twins collapsed completely in 1968. The result was predictable: a team expected around the circuit to compete for a league pennant floundered throughout the summer and limped home seventh, 24 games behind the pace-setting Tigers. But the collapse proved to be a temporary one, and the succeeding two seasons provided an immediate return to glory for the men of Calvin Griffith. Baseball suddenly took on a new look as divisional play entered the picture with expansion franchises again being added in Montreal (N.L.), San Diego (N.L.), Kansas City (A.L.), and Seattle (A.L.). There was dramatic change in Minnesota, as well, as fireplug Billy Martin was brought on board for his first managerial post, and the 1969 team responded by out distancing the field in the newly created A.L. Western Division. Billy Martin brought with him a new explosive brand of baseball that featured Rod Carew's major-league-record-tying seven steals of home and even produced more than half of Harmon Killebrew's rare base thefts in his 14 seasons with the Twins. But the controversial Martin was not destined to last long in Minnesota; his personality and flamboyant style were extremely popular with fans, but not so with the staid Calvin Griffith. The club president terminated his popular field boss only days after the season-ending A.L.C.S. drubbing at the hands of Eastern Division champion Baltimore. If Martin was soon gone, the new-found Twins' success formula seemingly was not, and the performance of 1969 was quickly repeated the following summer under new skipper Bill Rigney. The 1970 Twins ballclub was, in fact, even something of an improvement— the second most successful club in Minnesota history, winning only four fewer games than the powerhouse 1965 league championship team, and falling only two victories short of the coveted century mark.

Divisional play had arrived at exactly the right moment for the Minnesota Twins. Baltimore, Boston, and Detroit were the elite teams in the American League after 1967, but all were clustered in the tightly contested Eastern Division. The Twins had little difficulty with their lackluster Western Division rivals, at least in the seasons before the emergence of the Oakland Athletics as a powerhouse in 1971. Under Billy Martin in 1969 and Bill Rigney in 1970, the Twins approached 100 victories both seasons and enjoyed identical nine-game margins over the distant second-place Athletics. But the newfangled league playoffs were altogether another matter. In the inaugural A.L.C.S. matchup of 1969, Baltimore's Orioles disposed of Billy Martin's men in three straight without breaking a sweat; the following autumn the high-flying Birds of Manager Earl Weaver enjoyed even greater dominance with a second straight three-game sweep. The 1970 A.L.C.S. found Baltimore outscoring Minnesota 27–10 and outhitting the over-matched Twins by nearly 100 points (.330 to .238). But this performance was something of an improvement over the 1969 A.L.C.S., however, when the ice-cold Twins compiled a stunning composite .155 BA from a lineup featuring Killebrew, Carew, Oliva, Rich Reese, and Bob Allison.

The first half of the 1970s brought several altogether lean years to the Minnesota baseball scene. The 1971 team began an ominous pattern by dropping 24 full games off the pennant-winning pace of 1970, eeking out a disappointing fifth-place finish in the division, and posting the worst composite ERA in the west. Bill Rigney lasted only a season and a half after the debacle of the 1970 league playoff series, although at the time of his replacement in mid-season 1972, Rigney had quietly compiled the third highest managerial winning percentage (behind one-year wonder Billy Martin and steady Sam Mele) in the Twins' first quarter-century of franchise history.

The next several seasons saw the revamped Twins under manager Frank Quilici hovering at the .500 mark for three consecutive summers. Identical .500 marks and third-place finishes in 1972 and 1973 were followed by a two-game improvement in 1974 and a fall to fourth place and seven games under .500 in 1975. Things didn't improve much in the second half of the decade; the five years from 1975 through 1979 witnessed one third-place finish and four seasons in fourth. The best finish of this nine-year stretch was a mere eight games over .500 in 1976 under first-year skipper Gene Mauch. Yet Mauch's first club finished only third and his next three would slip back to a consistent fourth-place slot. While the veteran no-nonsense Mauch was brought in by Griffith to restore order to a young ballclub that reportedly lacked discipline under Quilici, a depleted mound corps during this period should have suggested that the problems were perhaps more in the front office than in the clubhouse or dugout. During the Twins' one serious rush at the top in 1976 it was the bullpen which provided the only adequate pitching, as Bill Campbell tied an American League record with 17 wins in relief and Tom Burgmeier sparkled with an 8–1 tally and 2.50 ERA. Finishing only five games behind the pennant-winning Kansas City Royals, this was a team for which the addition of adequate front-line pitching might well have been enough to assure Minnesota a third Western Division title in Mauch's first summer at the helm.

There were a handful of stars and some remarkable performances in the 1970s, however, and the list of memorable moments is headed by the often spectacular batting feats of Rod Carew and Tony Oliva. Oliva's 15-year career was winding down at the beginning of the decade (he hit .300 for the final time in 1972), yet he closed out his playing days by leaving a remarkable legacy. Oliva posted league-leading hit totals in five different seasons, established Twins single-season standards for total bases (374 in 1964) and extra base hits (84 in 1964), and compiled a career franchise mark for doubles (329). Rod Carew, on the other hand, dominated American League hitters for an entire decade like no one since Ty Cobb. There were four straight league batting titles (1972–1975) and six over seven seasons. Another star for Minnesota during the painfully long and often dry decade of the 1970s was Bert Blyleven. The Dutch-born righthander compiled 99 wins in less than seven campaigns before being dealt to the Texas Rangers as part of a dramatic six-player deal in June 1976. The seemingly ageless righthander (who would return to the Twins in 1986) was at the prime of his career in the mid-seventies and set most of the club pitching marks during this decade. The eventual club career leader (for Minnesota) in complete games (134), shutouts (29), and strikeouts (1,890), Blyleven would also set Twins single-season standards that still stand in four different categories during his remarkable 1973 campaign: innings pitched (325), shutouts (9), complete games (25), and strikeouts (258).

Twins' attendance in Metropolitan Stadium dipped steadily during much of the decade, as on-field play had slumped and the colorful sluggers of the 1960s had long since departed. Carew was the toast of baseball throughout the seventies, yet singles hitters rarely sell many grandstand seats. By summer 1971 attendance had slid under the million mark for the first time in Minnesota, and it remained there until 1977; 1979 was the only other season of one million or more fans during this dry spell that would stretch on until the 1984 campaign. While 1977 and 1979 did witness something of an attendance surge in Minneapolis-St. Paul, these would be the last two seasons of genuine fan excitement until hoopla surrounding a new domed stadium facility brought back record numbers of patrons in the middle of the next decade.

While Killebrew had always been surrounded by a fleet of adjunct sluggers and some of the more talented American League pitching of the mid-1960s as well, Carew was aided by few such supporting characters. His four consecutive A.L. batting titles coincided with four Frank Quilici-led ballclubs that never seriously challenged for a division flag; nor did this contingent of castoffs and retreds quicken the pulse rates of many serious Minnesota baseball fans. By decade's end the Griffith family trademark of tightfisted fiscal policy had again reared its ugly head and popular sluggers Larry Hisle (A.L. RBI king in 1977 with 119) and Lyman Bostock (.336 BA in 1977 and .323 in 1976) were lost to rampant free agency before the 1978 season opened. Rod Carew himself was dealt to California the following winter by Griffith, as well, under threat of the seven-time batting champion's own defection to the bulging free agent market. All in all, by the close of the 1979 season, the Minnesota Twins were clearly a baseball franchise in drastic need of a quick infusion of spirit and color, to say nothing of an injection of winning baseball.

Baseball in a Bubble—The Yo-Yo Minnesota Twins of the 1980s

Things turned much worse at Metropolitan Stadium in Minnesota before they got better, and the early 1980s was unarguably the true low-point of the Minnesota baseball franchise. Off-season in 1979 provided reason enough for optimism among diehard Twins supporters; the 1979 ballclub had remained a contender into the final weeks of September and had ultimately finished only six games short of the division title. Jerry Koosman had again emerged as a mound star with his 20 victories, and Mike Marshall had provided the stellar pitching story of the entire Junior Circuit in 1979. Marshall had appeared in a league-record 90 games, fashioned an impressive 2.64 ERA, and paced the circuit with 32 saves. Roy Smalley slammed 24 homers, knocked in 95 runs, batted an impressive .340 before the All-Star break, and also led A.L. shortstops in putouts, assists, and double plays. The Twins had also gotten off to their fastest start ever that season, and Minnesota fans had responded with an outpouring of crowd enthusiasm that produced only the third turnout of the entire decade totalling a million-plus fans.

And the starting lineup of this surprising 1979 ballclub had been held intact as 1980 spring training opened once again in Orlando. The 1980 season itself brought with it only a mediocre ballclub, however, and (in a complete turnaround from the previous summer) one of the lowest attendance figures for the entire first two decades of Minnesota baseball. The fifth and final season under skipper Gene Mauch would prove again, beyond any shadow of a doubt, that Minnesota baseball fans could not be counted upon to support at the gate anything less than a legitimate division contender.

Unlike several previous seasons, the 1980 version of the Twins faded in April rather than waiting around until August to perform their expected annual nose dive. As veteran Minnesota baseball historians Dave Mona and Dave Jarzyna observe in their fine pictorial history of the club's first quarter-century, the 1980 Minnesota Twins were not only inept, they were indeed altogether boring.[4] While other Minnesota clubs finished lower in the standings or compiled worse records, such off-years usually featured some promising if inexperienced young hitters and pitchers, or at least a handful of colorful ballplayers entertaining to watch. This club, which limped home seven games under .500 and 19½ games out, in third place, could boast no such redeeming entertainment value. John Castino paced the hitters with a .302 average and 13 homers; Jerry Koosman was the only moderately effective hurler with an unassuming 16–13 mark and resoundingly unimpressive 4.04 ERA. The slumping bullpen hero of 1979, Mike Marshall, was surprisingly released early in the campaign after proving totally ineffective in the months of April and May (1–3, 6.19 ERA). Even skipper Gene Mauch found this 1980 ballclub altogether painful to watch, and by late August Mauch had apparently seen more than enough; the veteran manager formally stepped down on August 25, after almost five complete seasons at the helm. His replacement, Johnny Goryl, would himself last less than three months on the job.

The baseball season of 1981, in turn, was one of the most forgettable in all big-league history. This was a season torn asunder by an unpopular players' strike which commenced in June and lasted past the normal All-Star break. It was a season also made laughable by a make-shift split-season format instituted by the owners upon the resumption of play. Resulting from this insanity of scheduling was a playoff system which excluded the team with 1981's best composite record—the Cincinnati Reds—yet included a team which finished in sixth place during the second half-season of play—the New York Yankees. What the players set out to ruin with their greed-driven labor action early in the 1981 campaign, the shortsighted owners had finished off altogether after August, with their avaricious and narrow views of a baseball playoff system seemingly driven by the golden egg of television revenues alone.

That unprecedented 1981 campaign also saw one of the most forgettable baseball summers in Minnesota's Twin Cities. Johnny Goryl was fired on May 22 and replaced by ex-Senators and Twins infielder Billy Gardner only 36 games into the soon-to-be interrupted season. Goryl's brief managerial tenure of 72 games was the second shortest ever in club history up to that time, through 21 full seasons of Minnesota big-league baseball. Yet substitutions in the manager's office hardly seemed the prescribed solution. This was a Minnesota team without even a .270 hitter (infielder John Castino paced the club among regulars at .268), or a home run hitter with double figures in roundtrippers (Roy Smalley was tops with seven), or a pitcher with even 10 wins (Pete Redfern came closest at nine wins and eight defeats). If the strike-shortened season was partially to blame for their frail numbers, weak hitting and laughable pitching were even more accountable. Thus these 1981 Twins were not only last in the composite league standings; they also were dead last in team batting (.240) and, not surprisingly, second worst in team ERA (3.98, ahead of only Seattle).

This was also the end of a pioneering baseball era in Minnesota. In late September of a long-lost 1981 season the final home game was routinely played out with little spectacle in Bloomington's Metropolitan Stadium. Thus came a sadly quiet end to exactly two decades of outdoor major league baseball in the Twin Cities of Minneapolis and St. Paul. The demise of "The Met" took place with little of the recognizable fanfare that might be expected to surround such an event. With the strike-shortened season having already put a complete damper on attendance from at least early June on through season's end, less than 500,000 customers had made baseball expeditions to Metropolitan Stadium during its final summer of play. That was an anemic average of only 7,951 fans per game, a startling big-league number more appropriate to, say, Seattle or Atlanta, or perhaps to some AAA franchise located deep off the beaten path in America's rural heartland. Less than 2,000 Twins faithful were in evidence on September 30 when Roy Smalley slapped a weak infield fly that abruptly brought to a close the life of a ballpark which had hosted 1,571 games and in which over 22.3 million composite fans had paid to see the Twins play between 1961 and 1981. And true to their 1981 form, Minnesota proceeded to lose that final game to Kansas City in a 5–2 laugher.

If Metropolitan Stadium disappeared almost without a noticeable whimper, its space-age inflatable-roof replacement was ushered in the following spring with a resounding bang. On April 6, 1982, 52,279 fans gleefully crowded into the downtown Hubert H. Humphrey Metrodome to watch the Twins inaugurate a new era of baseball history. This sudden surge in attendance from the waning days of 1981 could, of course, be attributed largely to media hype and glamour surrounding an historic opening befitting the television age of indoor baseball. The Twins, for their part, launched their new home with an 11–7 loss to the Seattle Mariners, a lackluster performance which provided appropriate foreshadow of the dismal season that was to lie ahead. The American League home opener with Seattle was in actuality the second big-league game to be played in the sterility of the spanking new Metrodome, having been preceded by an April 2 exhibition contest with the Philadelphia Phillies in which baseball's eventual all-time hit leader Pete Rose was to register the first base hit in the inflatable-dome ballpark. If the new downtown Minneapolis dome did not prove quite the same bucolic baseball atmosphere as the venerable "Met" which it replaced, it was (like so many present-day big-league facilities) built, after all, primarily to keep the city's NFL Vikings from abandoning their Twin Cities residence. And once the novelty of the new facility began to wear off by mid-season, the mediocre play of another cellar-dwelling Twins ballclub again kept Minnesota baseball attendance considerably under the cherished one million standard for the third season in a row.

During its inaugural 1982 season the Hubert H. Humphrey Metrodome quickly developed a league-wide reputation as a launching pad for cheap home runs. Perhaps part of this reputation came from the fact that the Minnesota ballclub had itself coincidentally acquired some sorely needed power for the first time in several years. But a more important factor was seemingly the air pressure of the dome itself. With the addition of adequate air conditioning the following summer, the stadium home run output would soon drop measurably, from 191 in 1982 to 147 in 1983. This was still a considerable increase, at any rate, from the limited total of 115 homers poked in spacious Metropolitan Stadium during the strike-shortened season of 1981. While the 148 homers supplied by the young Twins sluggers of 1982 (81 in the Metrodome) pales when compared with the record-setting 225 by Killebrew and company in 1963, it was by a wide margin the most by a Minnesota ballclub since 1970. Such young Minnesota sluggers as Kent Hrbek (23 homers), Gary Gaetti (25), Tom Brunansky (20), and Gary Ward (28) seemed at least in part, then, responsible for the newly proclaimed 1982 reputation of the rechristened Hubert H. Humphrey "Homerdome."

One thing that the new dome did not accomplish was to provide anything resembling an immediate change of fortunes for the inept Twins ballclub on the field of play. The summer of 1982 witnessed the worst year ever for the Twins since setting up camp in Minnesota two decades earlier. For the first time since leaving the nation's capital the ballclub lost over 100 games. And for the second season in a row the Twins were firmly cemented into the American League West cellar by season's end. On the heels of this continued tailspin registered during Billy Gardner's first full season at the helm, the 1983 ballclub showed only moderate improvement, as the Twins gained 10 more victories than the previous summer and in the process tied with California's Angels for fifth, beating out only baseball's weakest club, the Seattle Mariners. Only 130 victories measured against 194 defeats in two full seasons, accompanied by a continued drought in attendance despite a spanking new showcase ballpark, certainly did not bode well for Bill Gardner's future security with the Minnesota ballclub.

If one era of outdoor baseball had come to an end with the 1982 baseball season in Minnesota, an even more significant evolution was about to transpire only two brief years later in June 1984. On the 22nd of that month, accompanied by a lavish public ceremony, Calvin Griffith tearfully turned over control of the Twins franchise to new owner Carl Pohlad before a packed house of Metrodome well-wishers. Thus ended a 60-year personal and professional relationship between Griffith and professional baseball, as well as nearly six-decades of control over the Senators-Twins franchise by the proud Griffith family. When young Calvin Robertson had come to Washington from his Montreal home in 1922 to live with the Clark Griffith family, he had inauspiciously begun his long baseball career as an 11-year-old batboy for the ballclub owned by the famous uncle who would soon become both his adoptive father and life-long mentor. (Calvin's brother, Sheny Robertson, followed a similar route and wound up with a nearly decade-long big-league career as a utility infielder on Senators' rosters of the late forties and early fifties.) Calvin Robertson Griffith had worked his way up through all aspects of the family baseball business— serving as stadium concessionaire, traveling secretary, director of minor league operations, minor league club president (Chattanooga), and major league club vice president. He had also found time in his youth to perform as a reserve catcher and later manager for the Charlotte ballclub of the Tri-State League. There was little about baseball's athletic or business sides that Calvin Griffith did not know intimately. Yet the dawning of free agency had made the game a far different one from the national pastime Griffith had long known and loved, and by the mid-eighties it was time to step aside. Always the craftiest of businessmen, Calvin Griffith did not walk away empty-handed in 1984, selling the baseball franchise that had remained a family jewel for over 70 years for a handsome profit of $32 million.

The first three seasons under new ownership provided little noticeable improvement in the league standings, yet considerable reason for optimism. A host of new and talented hometown stars soon began appearing on the scene. Homegrown Minneapolis product Kent Hrbek hit the longball with regularity after 1982, compiling 150 homers in his first six big-league seasons. Gary Gaetti was soon one of the more talented and more colorful third basemen in the league and an added potent bat in the revamped Twins lineup (with 34 homers in 1986 and 31 in 1987). And above all else, Kirby Puckett flashed onto the scene as a can't-miss prospect, averaging only a hair below 200 hits per year in his first four major league summers.

But all this was not enough to prepare fans for the "dream season" summer that was to unfold storybook style in 1987. Despite charging from sixth place (20 games under .500) in 1986 to the middle of a tight pennant race by late 1987, the first-place Twins remained the butt of jokes all season long from those who doubted the legitimacy of any pennant-pretender from the apparently weak-sister A.L. Western Division. This pennant-winning 1987 Twins edition also seemed to be a ballclub that could only impersonate a true winner while playing within the friendly confines of its own noisy inflatable dome. But the underrated young Twins of second-year skipper Tom Kelly indeed had the last laugh of the topsy-turvey 1987 pennant race, as well as the subsequent A.L.C.S. showdown against Eastern Division leader Detroit. Given little chance against the potent Tigers who had won 98 ball games and ripped Toronto in a final weekend pennant-ending series, Minnesota paid little heed to its universally negative press clippings and routinely flattened the high-flying Tigers in five games. Opening up with an anticipated two-game sweep at the Homerdome, Kelly's overachieving Twins then took two final contests at Tiger Stadium, after losing a nip-and-tuck middle game by but one run. The acknowledged series heroes were outfielder Tom Brunansky with a .412 BA and two homers, as well as relief ace Jeff Reardon, who registered saves in each of the final two A.L.C.S. contests.

The Fall Classic of 1987 brought baseball indoors for the first time in World Series history. And the venue was to prove a major factor in the Series itself, as the Twins continued their much ballyhooed home field superiority which had run through the entire fairytale season. Despite eerie indoor surroundings more befitting the Super Bowl, the 1987 World Series proved as well to be one of the most dramatic of the decade. Opponents were the light-hitting St. Louis Cardinals, themselves surprise winners in the National League pennant chase. Lacking both power and dominant pitching, and relying almost exclusively on their awesome team speed, this Cardinal ballclub was reminiscent of Chicago's 1959 Go-Go White Sox—the hitless wonders of Nellie Fox, Luis Aparacio, Jim Landis, and Minnie Minoso. The St. Louis club had, in fact, earned only about as much respect around the Senior Circuit as had the underrated Twins among A.L. rivals. Whitey

Herzog's Cardinals had ridden the arms of a well-balanced pitching staff (Danny Cox, Greg Matthews, and Bob Forsch) to best New York by three games in the N.L. East and then topple the San Francisco Giants in a dramatic comeback seven-game N.L.C.S. playoff. With slugging star Jack Clark (35 homers, 106 RBIs) sidelined for the World Series, and with no hurler boasting even 15 victories for the campaign (Cox, Matthews, and Forsch all won 11 and John Tudor registered 10 triumphs), the Cardinals boasted neither obvious power nor a dominating pitching punch. Yet sparks flew when these two respect-poor baseball cousins met in a head-to-head contest for the bragging rights of America's heartland.

The 1987 World Series proved to follow form in one respect only—it was truly a Series of homefield advantage from first game to last. The Twins, of course, had thrived all season on games played in the Dome, where they had proved to be practically unbeatable through the "dog days" of the late season. Minnesota played at an incredible .691 clip in "The Bubble" yet had the worst road record in the entire division (also the worst of any club ever to appear in World Series play). By season's end Tom Kelly's ballclub had compiled a 56–25 homefield mark, while playing at only a .358 clip (29–52) on the road—the worst of all-time by any division-winning or pennant-winning big-league club. St. Louis had, by contrast, led the Senior Circuit in both home and road performance. While the Cardinals squeaked out victories in all three well-played mid-Series games in St. Louis, the Twins thoroughly bashed the hitless Cards in Minnesota, outscoring St. Louis in four Dome games by 33 to 12. While the Twins managed to outhit the Cardinals by only 10 points in overall Series batting (.269 to .259), 10–1 and 11–5 drubbings at the Metrodome in Game One and Game Six seemed to set an irreversible tone for the final Minnesota on-slaught. When Jeff Reardon fittingly registered the only save of the Series for the Twins in Game Seven (he had garnered a second-best A.L. total of 31 in regular season play), Minnesota (nee Washington) had captured only its second World Championship—its first since the glorious triumph of Walter Johnson in Griffith Stadium 63 years earlier.

The Twins of 1987 had too much talent to be a mere fluke—a previously uncharted bright supernova which would burst upon the scene and then suddenly flash from view. The hitting trio of Puckett, Hrbek, and Gaetti was as talented as any in the league; Blyleven and Viola were a formidable righty-lefty starting duo, and Jeff Reardon was still the best closer in the league. The Twins might well have repeated quite easily in 1988, in fact, had it not been for a formidable sleeping giant that had been lurking silently throughout 1987 in the divisional wings. The Oakland Athletics had been only a .500 club in

1987, despite the potent home run power of young sluggers Mark McGwire and Jose Canseco and the solid batting of veteran Carney Lansford. Once Oakland came up with sufficient pitching strength, however, they shot past Minnesota and the remaining divisional rivals, waltzing home by 13 full games over the Twins in 1988 and by seven over runner-up Kansas City in 1989.

By the 1989 season Tom Kelly's Cinderella ballclub had slumped to a second-division finish, two games under .500. A few of the stars of 1987 continued to shine brightly, however, and Frank Viola enjoyed a Cy Young season during the summer of 1988, pacing the league with a 24–7 mark and registering a 2.65 ERA (third best in the league). Yet after holding out for a hefty 1989 contract extension, Viola started slowly the following spring and was promptly dealt away to the New York Mets of the National League. Puckett, on the other hand, continued to improve by leaps and bounds, emerging as one of baseball's all-around best by the end of the 1989 campaign. But pitching talent in the Twin Cities was clearly no match for that in Oakland, especially once the Athletics under Tony LaRussa had added (via the trade route and free agency market) such stalwarts as Mike Moore, Storm Davis, and Bob Welch to complement star hurler Dave Stewart. A new power-house had arisen in Oakland, and with the rapid improvement of pitching-rich Kansas City and the revamped California Angeles as well, what had seemed the worst division in baseball was suddenly being touted as the best. The end result was a predictable and painful slide for the overmatched Twins, to a disappointing second place in 1988, and then all the way down to fifth place in 1989.

Despite these two summers of disappointments which followed the giddy world championship year of 1987, Minnesota baseball fans had plenty of reason for optimism as modern-age big-league baseball turned into the final decade of its first full century. By the beginning of the 1990s baseball had again seemed to turn a significant corner in Minneapolis and St. Paul. There could be little argument that the Twin Cities franchise would be entering the decade of the 1990s on a far more optimistic note than it had entered the volatile 1980s. Attendance in Minnesota was up over 2 million paying customers for the first time in both 1987 and 1988. And in November of 1989 local idol Kirby Puckett made significant history as the sport's first three-million-dollar-a-year media star and diamond hero. Puckett was coming off perhaps his finest all-around season ever, sporting a league-leading .339 BA and 215 hits, an effort sufficient to break the four-year stranglehold on league batting honors exercised by Boston's third sacker Wade Boggs. While 1989 represented Puckett's first batting crown, it was the third consecutive season for the speedy and power-ful centerfielder at the top of the Junior Circuit in total hits.

After tumbling all the way to the basement of the west in 1990, Kelly's 1991 edition of the "fighten' Twins" rushed to a division title and ALCS romp over Toronto that set up a history-making World Series meeting of two first-time-ever "last-to-first" ballclubs. And the seven-game Fall Classic showdown with Atlanta's Braves lived up to all the pre-Series hype and then some. Minnesota's thrilling extra-inning triumph in the tiebreaker (both clubs won all contests on their home turf) capped what many pundits and fans alike labelled (perhaps a bit over-enthusiastically, but not by much) as the greatest post-season classic ever played. Individual Series heroes were many in Minnesota: Kirby Puckett's homer in the 11th-inning of Game 6 set up the dramatic finale; Series MVP Jack Morris went the distance in the final game to pick up his second victory. Five games of this extraordinary shootout were decided by but one run, three contests went into extra frames, and the final outcome wasn't decided until pinch-hitter Gene Larkin singled home Dan Gladden to give the Twins a narrow 1–0 victory and their second World Championship in but five short years.

Notes

1. Puckett's statistics indeed compare quite favorably with those of Willie Mays after five-plus seasons of play, except in the single category of home runs. Puckett sports a .320 BA while Mays stood at 311 (with a final career average of only .302). Willie Mays had driven home 509 runs while Puckett accounts for 506; Mays also outdistances Puckett 531–467 in runs scored, yet trails by 1,028–903 in total hits. Willie had cracked 187 homers, however, to Kirby's 96. These totals are arrived at by counting Mays' seasons of 1951–52 and 1954–57, since Mays played only 34 games in his sophomore 1952 season and lost all of 1953 to military service. Certainly the difference between them (in terms of pure numbers alone) is minimal to date.

2. Much of the relevant newspaper literature surrounding the colorful history of Washington's moribund Griffith Stadium has been gathered together for researchers in handouts which accompanied an exceptional research presentation offered by Gordon M. Thomas at the 1987 annual meeting of the Society for American Baseball Research (Washington, DC). Mr. Thomas is indisputably the reigning authority on the Senators' historic ballpark and his SABR presentation has been an important road map for this present chapter.

3. Gerald Vaughn has provided invaluable assistance with information regarding the Washington Senators farm system of the 1940s and 1950s. Vaughn's unpublished article on the topic provides some of the best information on the building of Griffith's minor-league baseball organization during the World War II years.

4. For fans and students of the Minnesota Twins franchise, the handsome booklet by Mona and Jarzyna is must reading, despite its numerous shortcomings and oversights. Sold at the Humphrey Metrodome during the team's 25th anniversary season, this softcover coffee-table book is designed more for the casual fan than for the serious student of baseball history; it was clearly written by casual observers and not serious historians of the Minnesota baseball franchise (see further comments in the bibliography).

References

Boyd, Brendan C., and Fred C. Harris. 1973. *The Great American Baseball Card Flipping, Trading, and Bubble Gum Book.* Boston: Little, Brown and Company.

McCannon, Jimmy. "Deep in Debris Lies Pebble, Buried With Nat Memories." In *The Sporting News* (June 13, 1964): 23.

Meany, Thomas. 1949. "The Boy Wonder: The 1924 Washington Senators." In *Baseball's Greatest Teams,* pp. 209–224. New York: A. S. Barnes.

Mona, Dave, and Dave Jarzyna. 1986. *Twenty-Five Seasons: The First Quarter Century of the Minnesota Twins.* Minneapolis, Minn.: Mona Publications.

Povich, Shirley, 1966. "The Minnesota Twins." In: *The American League,* pp. 83–121. New Revised Edition. Edited by Ed Fitzgerald. New York: Grosset and Dunlap Publishers.

Thorn, John, and Pete Palmer, eds. 1989. *Total Baseball.* New York: Warner Books (Warner Communications).

Vaughn, Gerald F. 1984. "Building the Pre–1961 Washington Senators Farm System." Unpublished manuscript. Washington, D.C.

Wood, Bob. 1988. *Dodgers Dogs to Fenway Franks . . . And All the Wieners in Between—The Ultimate Guide to America's Top Baseball Parks.* New York: McGraw-Hill.

Annotated Bibliography

Bealle, Morris A. *The Washington Senators.* Washington, D.C.: Columbia Publishing Company, 1947.

> A rare collector's item, this treasured volume provides a colorful narrative of the Senators from the earliest days down through the lean World War II years. If located, Bealle's volume is excellent for its portraits of Walter Johnson, Clark Griffith, Bucky Harris, and other lesser Senators stars and journeymen of the decades between the two great wars. Bealle's history is no more useful than Povich's (see below) excellent study, however, which is written in a more lively manner and far more easily located around the country in libraries and used book shops.

Meany, Thomas. "The Boy Wonder: The 1924 Washington Senators." In *Baseball's Greatest Teams,* pp. 209–224. New York: A. S. Barnes, 1949.

> A charming portrait of Clark Griffith's "boy wonder" manager Bucky Harris—who took the reins of the 1924 Senators team at the raw age of 27—and of the underrated team Harris piloted to its first American League crown. Goose Goslin and Walter Johnson were the stars on a surprising team that pulled one of the biggest upsets in American League history. Meany includes here a rare background story of Bucky Harris' brief off-season involvement with professional basketball as well.

Mona, Dave, and Dave Jarzyna. *Twenty-Five Seasons: The First Quarter Century of the Minnesota Twins.* Minneapolis, Minn. Mona Publications, 1986.

> Over-sized concession-stand volume crammed with both color and black and white photographs and featuring a 72-page statistical section. Individual statistical summaries for all Twins players of the first quarter-century provide a potentially useful feature; however, statistics are sometimes incomplete and even inaccurate for some of the lesser players (breakdowns of Minnesota statistics are not provided for players who split seasons with other franchises in cases of in-season trades). This yearbook-format publication is best recommended for its pictorial-style history, but there are also some valuable if condensed summaries of the earliest sea-

sons in Minnesota, as well as good background discussion of the transfer of the franchise from the nation's capital in 1960–1961.

Oliva, Tony, with Bob Fowler. *Tony O!—The Trials and Triumphs of Tony Oliva.* New York: Hawthorn Books, 1973.

A colorful upbeat biography of one of Minnesota's great baseball stars and certainly one of Cuba's finest players ever. While the focus of this inspirational autobiography is unarguably on Oliva's own rags to riches rise from impoverished Cuban farmboy to American League Rookie of the Year, much of the flavor of the Twins' young franchise of the early and mid-sixties is also captured here.

Povich, Shirley. *The Washington Senators.* New York: G. P. Putnam and Sons, 1954.

In-depth coverage of the first half-century of Washington Senators baseball, along with excellent background material on baseball in the nation's capital before the advent of the American League back in 1901. In-depth portraits are featured for such stars as Walter Johnson, Edgar (Sam) Rice, Heinie Manush, Goose Goslin, Bucky Harris, and Clark Calvin Griffith. This is the most thorough and best history of the Washington franchise and is complete right up to the year before Griffith's death in 1955. Lively writing and many little-known facts about the early-day Senators are here compiled by the legendary sportswriter who covered the team for several decades as baseball beat writer for the *Washington Post.*

Povich, Shirley. "The Minnesota Twins." In: *The American League,* pp. 83–121. New Revised Edition. Edited by Ed Fitzgerald. New York: Grosset and Dunlap Publishers, 1966.

Anecdotal team history, from the earliest playing days in Washington during the first decades of the current century, through the Walter Johnson era and inter-war years, and on to the first American League pennant for Minnesota in 1965. The Washington Senators portion of this essay is drawn largely from Povich's 1954 book-length history cited above. This essay is part of a two-volume series of often uneven team histories written with a young adult audience in mind; unfortunately, both volumes are poorly edited and typos, infelicities, and historical inaccuracies abound throughout.

Terzian, James. *The Kid from Cuba—Zoilo Versalles.* Garden City, N.Y.: Doubleday and Company, 1967.

The frustrations and failures of hot Cuban infield prospect, Zoilo Versalles, and the parallel disappointments of the Minnesota Twins' expansion franchise of the early sixties. Versalles is finally able to turn around his ill-starred career by the 1965 season, and the Twins themselves rise to the occasion and capture a first American League flag for the baseball-crazy Twin Cities.

Year-by-Year Standings and Season Summaries
Washington Senators (1901–1960)

Year	Pos.	Record	Pct.	GB	Manager	Player	BA	Player	HR	Player	W-L	ERA
1901	6th	61–73	.455	21.0	Manning	Dungan	.324	Grady	9	Carrick	14–23	3.75
1902	6th	61–75	.449	22.0	Loftus	Delehanty	.376*	Delehanty	10	Orth	19–18	3.97
1903	8th	43–94	.314	7.5	Loftus	Selbach	.252	Ryan	7	Patten	11–22	3.60
1904	8th	38–113	.251	55.5	Donovan	Stahl	.261	Stahl	3	Patten	14–23	3.07
1905	7th	64–87	.421	29.5	Stahl	Anderson	.279	Stahl	5	Patten	14–21	3.14
1906	7th	55–95	.367	37.5	Stahl	Hickman	.284	Hickman	9	Patten	19–16	2.17
1907	8th	49–102	.325	43.5	Cantillon	Anderson	.289	Delehanty	2	Patten	12–16	3.56
1908	7th	67–85	.441	22.5	Cantillon	Unglaub	.286	Pickering	2	Hughes	18–15	2.21
1909	8th	42–110	.276	56.0	Cantillon	Lelivelt	.292	Unglaub	3	Johnson	13–25	2.21
1910	7th	66–85	.437	36.5	McAleer	Milan	.279	several	2	Johnson	25–17	1.35
1911	7th	64–90	.416	38.5	McAleer	Schaefer	.334	Gessler	4	Johnson	25–13	1.89
1912	2nd	91–61	.599	14.0	Griffith	Laporte	.311	Moeller	6	Johnson	32–12	1.39*
1913	2nd	90–64	.584	6.5	Griffith	Gandil	.318	Moeller	5	Johnson	36*–7	1.09*
1914	3rd	81–73	.526	19.0	Griffith	Milan	.295	Shanks	4	Johnson	28*–18	1.72
1915	4th	85–68	.556	17.0	Griffith	Gandil	.291	several	2	Johnson	27*–13	1.55
1916	7th	76–77	.497	14.5	Griffith	Milan	.273	Smith	5	Johnson	25*–20	1.89
1917	5th	74–79	.484	25.5	Griffith	Rice	.302	Judge	2	Johnson	23–16	2.30
1918	3rd	72–56	.563	4.0	Griffith	Milan	.290	several	1	Johnson	23*–13	1.27*
1919	7th	56–84	.400	32.0	Griffith	Rice	.321	Menosky	6	Johnson	20–14	1.49
1920	6th	68–84	.447	29.0	Griffith	Rice	.338	Roth	9	Zachery	15–16	3.77
1921	4th	80–73	.523	18.0	McBride	Rice	.330	Miller	9	Mogridge	18–14	3.00
1922	6th	69–85	.448	25.0	Bush	Goslin	.324	Judge	10	Johnson	15–16	2.99
1923	4th	75–78	.490	23.5	Bush	Rice	.316	Goslin	9	Johnson	17–12	3.53
1924	1st	92–62	.597	+2.0	Harris	Goslin	.344	Goslin	12	Johnson	23*–7	2.72*
1925	1st	96–55	.636	+8.5	Harris	Rice	.350	Goslin	18	Coveleski	20–5	2.84
1926	4th	81–69	.540	8.0	Harris	Goslin	.354	Goslin	17	Coveleski	14–11	3.12
1927	3rd	85–69	.552	25.0	Harris	Goslin	.334	Goslin	13	Lisenbee	18–9	3.57
1928	4th	75–79	.487	26.0	Harris	Goslin	.379*	Goslin	17	Jones	17–7	2.84
1929	5th	71–81	.467	34.0	Johnson	Rice	.323	Goslin	18	Marberry	19–12	3.06

Year	Pos.	Record	Pct.	GB	Manager	Player	BA	Player	HR	Player	W–L	ERA
1930	2nd	94–60	.610	8.0	Johnson	Manush	.350	Cronin	14	Crowder	15–9	3.60
1931	3rd	92–62	.597	16.0	Johnson	West	.333	Cronin	12	Crowder	18–11	3.88
1932	3rd	93–61	.604	14.0	Johnson	Manush	.342	Manush	14	Crowder	26*–13	3.33
1933	1st	99–53	.651	+7.0	Cronin	Manush	.336	Kuhel	11	Crowder	24*–15	3.97
1934	7th	66–86	.434	34.0	Cronin	Manush	.349	Manush	11	Whitehill	14–11	4.52
1935	6th	67–86	.438	27.0	Harris	Myer	.349*	Powell	6	Whitehill	14–13	4.29
1936	4th	82–71	.536	20.0	Harris	Stone	.341	Kuhel	16	Newsom	17–15	4.32
1937	6th	73–80	.477	28.5	Harris	Travis	.344	Lewis	10	Ferrell	11–13	3.94
1938	5th	75–76	.497	23.5	Harris	Wright	.350	Bonura	22	Leonard	12–15	3.43
1939	6th	65–87	.428	41.5	Harris	Lewis	.319	Lewis	10	Leonard	20–8	3.54
1940	7th	64–90	.416	26.0	Harris	Travis	.322	Walker	13	Chase	15–17	3.23
1941	6th	70–84	.455	31.0	Harris	Travis	.359	Early	10	Leonard	18–13	3.45
1942	7th	62–89	.357	39.5	Harris	Spence	.323	Vernon	9	Hudson	10–17	4.36
1943	2nd	84–69	.549	13.5	Bluege	Case	.294	Spence	12	Wynn	18–12	2.91
1944	8th	64–90	.416	25.0	Bluege	Spence	.316	Spence	18	Leonard	14–14	3.06
1945	2nd	87–67	.565	1.5	Bluege	Myatt	.296	Clift	8	Wolff	20–10	2.12
1946	4th	76–78	.494	28.0	Bluege	Vernon	.353*	Spence	16	Haefner	14–11	2.85
1947	7th	64–90	.416	33.0	Bluege	Spence	.279	Spence	16	Wynn	17–15	3.64
1948	7th	56–97	.366	40.0	Kuhel	Stewart	.278	Coan	7	Scarborough	15–8	2.82
1949	8th	50–104	.325	47.0	Kuhel	Robinson	.294	Robinson	18	Hudson	8–17	4.22
1950	5th	67–87	.435	31.0	Harris	Coan	.303	Noren	14	Hudson	14–14	4.09
1951	7th	62–92	.403	36.0	Harris	Coan	.303	Yost	12	Marrero	11–9	3.90
1952	5th	78–76	.506	17.0	Harris	Runnels	.285	Yost	12	Porterfield	13–14	2.72
1953	5th	76–76	.500	23.5	Harris	Vernon	.337*	Vernon	15	Porterfield	22*–10	3.35
1954	6th	66–88	.428	45.0	Harris	Busby	.298	Sievers	24	Stone	12–10	3.22
1955	8th	53–101	.344	43.0	Dressen	Vernon	.301	Sievers	25	McDermott	10–10	3.75
1956	7th	59–95	.383	38.0	Dressen	Runnels	.310	Sievers	29	Stobbs	15–15	3.50
1957	8th	55–95	.357	43.0	Lavagetto	Sievers	.301	Sievers	42*	Ramos	12–10	4.79
1958	8th	61–93	.396	31.0	Lavagetto	Sievers	.295	Sievers	39	Hyde	10–3	1.75
1959	8th	63–91	.409	31.0	Lavagetto	Lemon	.279	Killebrew	42*	Pascual	17–10	2.64
1960	5th	73–81	.474	24.0	Lavagetto	Green	.294	Lemon	38	Pascual	12–8	3.03

Minnesota Twins (1961–1992)

Year	Pos.	Record	Pct.	GB	Manager	Player	BA	Player	HR	Player	W-L	ERA
1961	7th	70–90	.438	38.0	Lavagetto Mele	Battey	.302	Killebrew	46	Pascual	15–16	3.46
1962	2nd	91–71	.562	5.0	Mele	Rollins	.298	Killebrew	48*	Pascual	20–11	3.32
1963	3rd	91–70	.565	13.0	Mele	Rollins	.307	Killebrew	45*	Pascual	21–9	2.46
1964	6th	79–83	.488	20.0	Mele	Oliva	.323*	Killebrew	49*	Kaat	17–11	3.22
1965	1st	102–60	.630	+7.0	Mele	Oliva	.321*	Killebrew	25	Grant	21*–7	3.30
1966	2nd	89–73	.549	9.0	Mele	Oliva	.307	Killebrew	39	Kaat	25*–13	2.75
1967	2nd	91–71	.562	1.0	Mele Ermer	Carew	.292	Killebrew	44*	Chance	20–14	2.73
1968	7th	79–83	.488	24.0	Ermer	Oliva	.289	Allison	22	Chance	16–16	2.53
1969	1st**	97–65	.599	+9.0	Martin	Carew	.332*	Killebrew	49*	J. Perry	20–6	2.82
1970	1st	98–64	.605	+9.0	Rigney	Oliva	.325	Killebrew	41	J. Perry†	24*–12	3.03
1971	5th	74–86	.463	26.5	Rigney	Oliva	.337*	Killebrew	28	Blyleven	16–15	2.82
1972	3rd	77–77	.500	15.5	Rigney Quilici	Carew	.318*	Killebrew	26	Blyleven	17–17	2.73
1973	3rd	81–81	.500	13.0	Quilici	Carew	.350*	Darwin	18	Blyleven	20–17	2.52
1974	3rd	82–80	.506	8.0	Quilici	Carew	.364*	Darwin	25	Blyleven	17–17	2.66
1975	4th	76–83	.478	20.5	Quilici	Carew	.359*	Ford	15	Blyleven	15–10	3.00
1976	3rd	85–77	.525	5.0	Mauch	Carew	.331	Ford	20	Campbell	17–5	3.00
1977	4th	84–77	.522	17.5	Mauch	Carew	.388*	Hisle	28	Goltz	20*–11	3.36
1978	4th	73–89	.451	19.0	Mauch	Carew	.333*	Smalley	19	Goltz	15–10	2.49
1979	4th	82–80	.506	6.0	Mauch	Wilfong	.313	Smalley	24	Koosman	20–13	3.38
1980	3rd	77–84	.478	19.5	Mauch Goryl	Castino	.302	Castino	13	Koosman	16–13	4.04

530

Year	Pos.	Record	Pct.	GB	Manager	Player	BA	Player	HR	Player	W–L	ERA
1981	7th	17–39	.304	18.0	Goryl	Castino	.268	Smalley	7	Redfern	9–8	4.06
					Gardener							
1981***	4th	24–29	.453	6.0								
	7th	41–68	.376	23.0								
1982	7th	60–102	.370	33.0	Gardner	Hrbek	.301	Ward	28	Castillo	13–11	3.66
1983	5th	70–92	.432	29.0	Gardner	Hrbek	.297	Brunansky	28	Schrom	15–8	3.71
1984	2nd	81–81	.500	3.0	Gardner	Hrbek	.311	Brunansky	32	Viola	18–12	3.21
1985	4th	77–85	.475	14.0	Gardner	Puckett	.288	Brunansky	27	Viola	18–14	4.09
					Miller							
1986	6th	71–91	.438	21.0	Miller	Puckett	.328	Gaetti	34	Blyleven	17–14	4.01
					Kelly							
1987	1st	85–77	.525	+2.0	Kelly	Puckett	.332	Hrbek	34	Viola	17–10	2.90
1988	2nd	91–71	.562	13.0	Kelly	Puckett	.356	Gaetti	28	Viola†	24*–7	2.64
1989	5th	80–82	.494	19.0	Kelly	Puckett	.339*	Hrbek	25	Anderson	17–10	3.80
1990	7th	74–88	.457	29.0	Kelly	Harper	.294	Hrbek	22	Tapani	12–8	4.07
1991	1st	95–67	.586	+8.0	Kelly	Puckett	.319	C. Davis	29	Erickson	20–8	3.18
1992	2nd	90–72	.556	6.0	Kelly	Puckett	.329	Puckett	19	Smiley	16–9	3.21

*Led the American League.
**American League West (first season of divisional play).
***Split Season Totals (Players' Union Strike).
†Cy Young Award Winner

**All-Time Washington Senators-Minnesota Twins Career
and Season Records**

Washington Senators Career Batting Leaders (1901–1960)

Games Played	Sam Rice	2,307
At Bats	Sam Rice	8,943
Runs Scored	Sam Rice	1,467
Hits	Sam Rice	2,889
Batting Average (300 or	Heinie Manush	.3234
more games)	Sam Rice	.3230
	Goose Goslin	.3228
Home Runs	Roy Sievers	180
Runs Batted In	Sam Rice	1,045
Stolen Bases	Clyde Milan	495

Minnesota Twins Career Batting Leaders (1961–1992)

Games Played	Harmon Killebrew	1,939
At Bats	Harmon Killebrew	6,593
Runs Scored	Harmon Killebrew	1,047
Hits	Rod Carew	2,085
Batting Average (300 or more games)	Rod Carew	.334
Home Runs	Harmon Killebrew	475
Doubles	Tony Oliva	329
Triples	Rod Carew	90
Runs Batted In	Harmon Killebrew	1,325
Stolen Bases	Rod Carew	271
Grand Slam Home Runs	Harmon Killebrew	10
Total Bases	Harmon Killebrew	3,412

Washington Senators Career Pitching Leaders (1901–1960)

Innings Pitched	Walter Johnson	5,923.2
Earned Run Average (400-plus innings)	Walter Johnson	2.17
Wins	Walter Johnson	416
Losses	Walter Johnson	279
Strikeouts	Walter Johnson	3,508
Walks	Walter Johnson	1,405
Games	Walter Johnson	802
Shutouts	Walter Johnson	110
Saves	Firpo Marberry	96
Complete Games	Walter Johnson	531

Minnesota Twins Career Pitching Leaders (1961–1992)

Innings Pitched	Jim Kaat	2,958
Earned Run Average (400-plus innings)	Al Worthington	2.62
Wins	Jim Kaat	189
Losses	Jim Kaat	152
Winning Percentage (50 decisions)	Camilo Pascual	.607 (88–57)

All-Time Washington Senators-Minnesota Twins Career and Season Records *(continued)*

Strikeouts	Bert Blyleven	1,890	
Walks	Jim Kaat	694	
Games	Jim Kaat	468	
Shutouts	Bert Blyleven	29	
Saves	Ron Davis	108	
Complete Games	Bert Blyleven	134	

Washington Senators Single-Season Batting Records (1901–1960)

Batting Average (350 ABs)	Goose Goslin	.379	1928
Home Runs	Harmon Killebrew	42	1959
	Roy Sievers	42	1957
Home Runs (lefthanded)	Mickey Vernon	20	1954
Runs Batted In	Goose Goslin	129	1924
Runs Scored	Joe Cronin	127	1930
Hits	Sam Rice	227	1925
Singles	Sam Rice	182	1925
Doubles	Mickey Vernon	51	1946
Triples	Goose Goslin	20	1925
	Dan Moeller	20	1914
Slugging Percentage	Goose Goslin	.614	1928
Stolen Bases	Clyde Milan	88	1912
Strikeouts	Jim Lemon	138	1956
Walks	Eddie Yost	151	1956
Hitting Streak	Heinie Manush	33	1933
Hit by Pitch	Bucky Harris	21	1920
Games	Eddie Yost	157	1952

Minnesota Twins Single-Season Batting Records (1961–1992)

Batting Average (350 ABs)	Rod Carew	.388	1977
Home Runs	Harmon Killebrew	49	1964,1969
Home Runs (lefthanded)	Kent Hrbek	34	1987
Runs Batted In	Harmon Killebrew	140	1969
Runs Scored	Rod Carew	128	1977
Hits	Rod Carew	239	1977
Singles	Rod Carew	180	1974
Doubles	Zoilo Versalles	45	1965
Triples	Rod Carew	16	1977
Slugging Percentage	Harmon Killebrew	.606	1961
Extra Base Hits	Tony Oliva	84	1964
Game-Winning RBIs	Tom Brunansky	15	1983
Sacrifice Bunts	Rob Wilfong	25	1979
Stolen Bases	Rod Carew	49	1976
Strikeouts	Danny Darwin	145	1972
Total Bases	Tony Oliva	374	1964
Hitting Streak	Ken Landreaux	31	1980
Grand Slam Home Runs	Bob Allison	3	1961
	Rod Carew	3	1976
	Kent Hrbek	3	1985
Hit by Pitch	Cesar Tovar	17	1968
Games	Cesar Tovar	164*	1967

534   Encyclopedia of Baseball Team Histories: American League

**All-Time Washington Senators-Minnesota Twins Career
and Season Records** (*continued*)

Washington Senators Single-Season Pitching Records (1901–1960)

ERA (150 innings)	Walter Johnson	1.09	1913
Wins	Walter Johnson	36	1913
Losses	John Townsend	26	1904
	Robert Groom	26	1909
Winning Pct. (10 decisions)	Walter Johnson	.837 (36–7)	1913
Strikeouts	Walter Johnson	313	1910
Walks	Bobo Newsom	146	1936
Saves	Firpo Marberry	22	1926
Games	Firpo Marberry	64	1926
Complete Games	Walter Johnson	38	1910
Games Started	Walter Johnson	42	1910
Shutouts	Walter Johnson	12	1913
Innings Pitched	Walter Johnson	374	1910
Consecutive Games Won	Walter Johnson	16	1912
Consecutive Games Lost	Paul Calvert	14	1949
Hit Batsmen	Walter Johnson	20	1923
Wild Pitches	Walter Johnson	21	1910

Minnesota Twins Single-Season Pitching Records (1961–1992)

ERA (150 innings)	Camilo Pascual	2.47	1963
Wins	Jim Kaat	25	1966
Losses	Pedro Ramos	20	1961
Winning Pct. (10 decisions)	Bill Campbell	.773 (17–5)	1976
Strikeouts	Bert Blyleven	258	1973
Walks	Jim Hughes	127	1975
Saves	Jeff Reardon	42	1988
Games	Mike Marshall	90**	1970
Complete Games	Berty Blyleven	25	1973
Games Started	Jim Kaat	42	1965
Shutouts	Bert Blyleven	9	1973
Innings Pitched	Bert Blyleven	325	1973
Home Runs Allowed	Bert Blyleven	50**	1986
Consecutive Games Won	Stan Williams	9	1970
Consecutive Games Lost	Terry Felton	13	1982
Consecutive Scoreless Innings	Jim Kaat	29.2	1966
Hit Batsmen	Jim Kaat	18	1962
Wild Pitches	Dave Goltz	15	1976
	Mike Smithson	15	1986
Balks	Roger Erickson	5	1981
	Les Straker	5	1987

*American League Record.
**Major League Record.

14
Washington Senators-
Texas Rangers
There Are No Dragons in Baseball, Only Shortstops

PETER C. BJARKMAN

There are no dragons in baseball, only shortstops.
A. Bartlett Giamatti, Late Commissioner of Baseball
and Former President of the National League.

Something extraordinary happened along the way to the Hot Stove League winter sessions of December 1988, as in baseball lore and legend almost everything imaginable seems somehow to spring forth sooner or later. The 1988 major league winter meetings in Atlanta, Georgia, proved considerably more interesting for Texas Rangers fans than the entire 1988 or 1989 action-packed baseball seasons combined. In fact, one might well include a dozen more seasons before 1988 and the statement would still stand unchallenged. But then, what transpired during the Hot Stove League baseball winter of 1988 (the signing of superstar free agent pitcher Nolan Ryan and the acquisitions by trade of proven hitting stars Julio Franco from the Indians and Rafael Palmeiro from the Cubs) was actually a far more inspiring story than almost the entire previous history of the Texas Rangers baseball franchise—with a full decade of expansion baseball under the name of the Washington Senators thrown in for good measure. In fact, it is fair to say that the story of Nolan Ryan's remarkable accomplishments in Texas in 1989 and 1990 is almost the single boasting point in the entire two decades of Texas Rangers big league history.

Remember, devoted baseball fans, we are talking here about the perennial cellar-dwelling and almost always disappointing Texas Rangers, that transplanted but hardly refurbished version of the resurrected New Age Washington Senators, an eminently forgettable and usually lackluster baseball team unsurpassed in expansion-era ineptness. Not even the Seattle Mariners come close to the Texas Rangers in monopolizing expansion-era blues; the M's have merchandized baseball disappointment for only slightly more than a decade in the port city of Seattle, a chronological fact which translates into only half as many summers of hopeless second-division baseball. The Mariners have also been privileged to host the league's mid-summer All-Star Classic (in their third season of 1979) to the delight of their sparse and otherwise abused fandom.

The Texas Rangers, by sad contrast, remains the only franchise since the beginning of expansion baseball in the late 1960s never to host either post-season play or a major league All-Star Game. They are also one of only three impoverished ballclubs in the 20-year expansion-era never to win a division title (throw in newcomer Seattle and the octogenarian Cleveland Indians to complete this exclusive club). And the other two franchises involved here have compensating factors to mollify this hurt. The proud Indians can at least offer long-suffering Cleveland fans glorious nostalgic memory trips back into three of the most dramatic World Series appearances ever (those of 1920, 1948, and 1954); Cleveland also boasts a century of genuine diamond stars and a bevy of Hall-of-Famers (Feller, Speaker, Wynn, Lemon, Rosen, Colavito, etc.). And Seattle's lame Mariners have only been around for slightly more than a decade and therefore never seriously expected to rise above their fated second-division moorings.

This Texas ballclub is also the same franchise that under the loose-spending policies of former owner Brad Corbett created the greatest free-agent spending bonanza in baseball history. Corbett's buyout of the Rangers from Robert Short coincided with the ballclub's first successful season—a second-place finish in the A.L. Western Division of 1974 and a club-first .500 season in the Lone Star State—and ushered in the team's most successful six-year span ever. In the half-decade during which he owned the ballclub, Corbett never saw his team dip below third place (despite several sub-.500 ledgers) until his final year at the helm in 1980. But Corbett's reign in Texas purchased only moderate success at the expense of a mortgaged team future and reckless front-office behavior. It was Corbett as much as any other club owner (George Steinbrenner not withstanding) who recklessly ushered in the age of astronomical free agent salaries and fool-hardy long-term contracts. A millionaire many times over in the plastic pipe business, Corbett squandered many of those millions on worn-down veterans and overrated prospects in the desperate attempt to bankroll winning baseball. Among the most noteworthy of these financial boondoggles were an infamous 1977 deal which handed free-swinging outfielder Richie Zisk a 10-year $2.95 million contract to leave the White Sox and sign on in Texas; a $1 million deal that same winter for fading shortstop Bert Campaneris; and a December 1977 22-year package which paid veteran pitcher Bert Blyleven a reported

$2 million. And it was not just Brad Corbett's spendthrift ways that exasperated the local faithful and endangered the game's solvency, but also his penchant for casting aside his investments almost as soon as they were purchased. Zisk awarded his overly generous employer with three mediocre seasons (he stroked over 20 homers but once and never reached the 90 RBI mark) and then was sent packing to Seattle; Campaneris hit only .186 in his first millionaire season and was also immediately unloaded; and Bert Blyleven was quite incredibly shipped off to Pittsburgh in exchange for Al Oliver only days after his unaccountable windfall in Texas.

And it is the Lone Star State American League ballclub, furthermore, whose outrageously pecuniary ownership once created an avoidable event that still overshadows all the best baseball heroics yet played out over the history of Arlington Stadium. This was the infamous food ban of Opening Day 1984, a embarrassing "public happening" which transpired when club officials announced a curious policy preventing fans from bringing further snacks and popular picnic lunches to the home ballpark. While the club had announced the new policy weeks before the scheduled home opener, families nonetheless packed their picnic baskets off to the ballpark on April 3, as they had done in each of the dozen preceding seasons. On the first evening of enforcement thousands of sandwiches and thermos bottles were confiscated at the gate and many irate fans later reported witnessing turnstile workers and ushers dining voraciously on the harvest of harmless snacks in full view of disgruntled customers leaving the stadium at game's end. While public outrage soon put an end to this unpopular anti-snack policy, Rangers fans fittingly had their own form of appropriate revenge only two brief seasons later. When an April 26, 1986, Arlington Stadium crowd of 25,499 was rewarded for its attendance with free baseballs, a seemingly harmless ballpark promotion suddenly turned to further embarrassment and near disaster for the increasingly unpopular Rangers management. Mired in a horrible slump and suffering their second straight shellacking at the hands of the Milwaukee Brewers, helpless Rangers players and startled umpires were pelted with a downpour of souvenir balls from the grandstands when irate fans unloaded their frustration in the midst of a seventh-inning Milwaukee rally. The events of Food Ban 1984 and Ball Night 1986 were among the most embarrassing moments in Texas Rangers history; unfortunately, the near total absence of spectacular baseball happenings has also made them perhaps the two most memorable events of Arlington Stadium history as well.

Brad Corbett and his exhausted checkbook are now long gone from the scene in Arlington. Yet the Rangers' unproductive free-spending ways continue to illustrate some of the worst of expansion-era baseball. Bradford G. Corbett was, after all, only the later alter ego of reckless first Rangers owner Bob Short, the man who launched Texas baseball history. Short had nearly bankrupted the franchise at every turn from the very start in the nation's capital, and long-range tremors of "short-sighted" spending policies in both Washington and Arlington are still being felt by followers of Texas Rangers baseball down to the present hour. It was seemingly only a temporary reprieve, then, when Corbett abandoned ship and sold his holdings to a triumvirate headed by Fort Worth oilman Eddie Chiles in February 1980. In his own nearly 10 years at the helm (the last several of which were preoccupied with desperate and often futile efforts to sell the ballclub), the equally free-spending and baseball-naive Chile roared through 11 managers, countless trades, and often importunate free-agent signings, all of which have brought preciously little baseball stability and a rash of second-division finishes to the ballclub throughout the long and disappointing decade of the 1980s.

When Chiles' own plans for selling his unprofitable ballclub temporarily fell through for the third or fourth time just prior to the 1988 Atlanta major league winter meetings, it seemed that the increasingly unpopular and largely detached owner had suddenly changed his stratagems in midstream. Unleashing the previous muffled skills of his young general manager Tom Grieve, Chiles set in motion a series of transactions during the off-season of 1988 which were destined to give Rangers fans their first serious hopes for ballpark respectability since the near pennant-winning clubs of the late 1970s under the brief managerial reigns of Frank Lucchesi and Billy Hunter. Grieve, in a few short weeks, had put together deals which had made the Rangers the talk of the baseball world, signing free-agent pitching phenomenon Nolan Ryan of the Astros, and acquiring via trade the potent bats of Julio Franco and Rafael Palmeiro while unloading such unproductive if talented dead wood as first sacker Pete O'Brien, utility infielder Curtis Wilkerson, erratic relief fireballer Mitch Williams, and disappointing flychaser Oddibe McDowell. Few teams of recent memory had ever cleaned house so drastically and gotten quite so much return value in the bargain.

The 1989 edition of "Rangers Ball" proved the most interesting club to watch in franchise history, though this is not to claim a great deal in the face of three decades dotted with second-division baseball. Ruben Sierra emerged as a true superstar, nearly winning American League MVP honors, and pacing the Junior Circuit in total bases (344), triples (14), RBIs (119), and slugging percentage (.543). Julio Franco rivaled Sierra for honors as the hitting star throughout much of the season while he posted the fifth highest average in the circuit (.316) and stood fourth in the league as well in multi-hit games with 56. While

Rafael Palmeiro didn't pan out quite as expected (having boasted the second highest National League BA in 1988 with the Cubs), he did add further flair to the Rangers attack with 154 hits (.275 BA) despite fading badly in the second half. And Harold Baines (.309 BA, 16 homers, 72 RBIs) came on board to fill the designated-hitter role in midseason and to give the Rangers the most potent top-to-bottom offense in the American League. However, the very trade which brought a veteran and somewhat damaged Baines to Arlington and shipped away solid second sacker Scott Fletcher and several promising rookies (especially Sammy Sosa) also hung like a dark shadow over the upbeat 1989 campaign. By early 1990 storm clouds were already brewing as the flashy outfield play and solid slugging of Sosa for Chicago's White Sox began suggesting that the Rangers may well have given away cheaply another Ruben Sierra, and some talented young pitching in Wilson Alvarez to boot.

Of course, the single unrivaled story in Texas during the summer of 1989 was one Lynn Nolan Ryan. The seemingly ageless Ryan (now 43) was, in fact, a clear choice as "Baseball Story of the Year" for 1989. In a season dominated by the relentless negative news of Pete Rose's sordid betting scandal and ultimate baseball ban, the untimely tragic death of Commissioner Bart Giamatti, and the earthquake-plagued Giants-Athletics World Series which many already consider the worst in all baseball history, Ryan was perhaps the one inspirational baseball story of the summer. His unprecedented feat of 301 strikeouts at age 42, his relentless march past the unthinkable 5,000 career strikeout barrier, and his near misses on perfection during two occasions in which he flirted with an unparalleled sixth career no-hitter—all held a nation of baseball fans spellbound. As if an encore were needed, Ryan's marvelous first season in Arlington was already proving no fluke as the certain future Hall-of-Famer opened the first month of the 1990 campaign with a perfect 4–0 record and a sterling one-hit performance against the Chicago White Sox which tied Bob Feller's career mark for one-hitters at 12. In that very same April 1990 game Ryan surpassed the single-game Rangers strikeout mark, as well, with 16, bringing his career standard to over 5,100 with a full 1990 season still ahead. All agree today that the remarkable Ryan is an even better pitcher at age 43 than he was in his prime a decade earlier.

Yet for all the pitching feats of Ryan and stellar reliever Jeff Russell, and all the hitting of Sierra and the other potent Rangers bats, in the end this was again not a very good Texas team. By season's end Texas had slumped to fourth place, 16 games behind the runaway Athletics and only three ahead of the fifth-place and decimated Minnesota Twins. While four games over .500 and fifth in the league in hitting, this showing was hardly a joyous fulfillment of overly bright preseason prognostications for the largely revamped Texas ballclub. Texas Rangers pitching was only barely adequate, with a composite seventh-best league ERA, but with only six saves from the entire bullpen staff outside of Russell, and only one winning starter (Kevin Brown at 12–9) outside of Ryan.

This story of baseball ineptness that has been the Texas Rangers stretches back well into baseball's lost decade—the tumultuous 1960s, a period of change, turmoil, lost dreams, and broken promises, both on the major league baseball diamond and in twentieth-century America. The newborn 1960s Washington Senators franchise which inherited a half-century of baseball disillusionment in the nation's capital from their departed namesakes of Clark and Calvin Griffith, were themselves one of baseball's most inglorious expansion sagas—a ballclub which rose above fifth place (fourth in the first summer of division play) but once in 11 seasons of play. The original Senators ballclub which had called Griffith Stadium home for five decades always boasted at least a handful of colorful stars (from Walter Johnson on the eve of the world's first great war to Mickey Vernon and Roy Sievers in the afterglow of its second) if providing few pennant victories. But this new Washington team of the sixties offered nothing in the way of gate attraction which could compare with Walter Johnson, Goose Goslin, Heinie Manush, Roy Sievers, or Harmon Killebrew. Yet it is here—with castoff veterans like Gene Woodling, Dick Donovan, Dale Long and Johnny Klippstein, and with hopeless journeymen like Marty Keough, Billy Klaus, Hector Maestri, Coot Veal, and Pete Daley—that we begin the saga of what has become the greatest test of fan patience in the history of the nation's favorite pastime.

Three Strikes and You Should Be Out—Reincarnations of the Stumblebum Senators

> *But in four years as Short's manager, Ted Williams went from exaltation to depression—and the team from winner to loser, Washington to Texas, bubbling illusion to cold-cement reality.*
>
> Shelby Whitfield, *Kiss It Goodbye.*

The old saying has it that Washington could always be counted on to be "first in war, first in peace, and last in the American League." While this dry witticism proved accurate often enough, it should be also noted that the Washington baseball franchise gave the national pastime some other notable firsts as well. Not least among these was the fact that it was Washington—through its farsighted if often pecuniary owner Calvin Griffith—that brought the expansion age to the American League, a short three years after Walter O'Malley and Horace Stoneham had boldly broken baseball's East Coast stranglehold by moving their Brooklyn and New York National League franchises to the sunny climes of Southern California.

While Calvin Griffith launched one of the great success stories of modern-era baseball with his expansion Minnesota Twins (see the preceding chapter), the fallout of Griffith's dreams for big-league expansion to the untapped regions of the northwest had yet a further and altogether less fortunate ancillary effect. That effect, an equal part of the baseball expansion story of the early 1960s, was the birth of the newly revamped replacement Washington Senators. If baseball fans of the nation's capital—some of the truest and most long-suffering in the land—had agonized for decades with the lowly original Senators, and then been dealt a cruel blow by Griffith with the departure of a promising young team comprised of Killebrew and Allison and Jim Kaat, perhaps the deepest cut was still to come. And that slap to the dignity of American League baseball fans began with the announcement of November 17, 1960, that American League owners—giddy at the thought of new ballclubs in Minnesota and Los Angles—had approved the bid of General Elwood R. (Pete) Quesada for a new Washington franchise, one designed to carry on the Nats treasured name (and certainly their habit for decades of losing baseball) in dilapidated downtown Griffith Stadium.

The new Washington Senators were assembled on paper and in the front office perhaps more quickly than any other team in major league history. Two days after the new franchise was approved, Ed Doherty, president of the American Association, was tabbed as club general manager. On this very same day, longtime Senators favorite Mickey Vernon was introduced, as well, as the new field skipper. Vernon had been American League batting champion twice while playing for the old Senators and was a particular boyhood favorite of new boss Pete Quesada. And on December 10 a club public relations officer was formally announced to the media. Burton Hawkins would soon prove one of the more durable front-office figures of the youthful franchise, surviving three changes of ownership and still holding his position with the transplanted Texas Rangers well into the early 1980s.

The business of assembling a ballclub took its most serious turn only a month later—with the American League expansion draft held between the new Washington and Los Angeles clubs in Boston on December 14, 1960. Choosing ahead of all other teams in the winter minor league draft in November, the Senators had earlier tabbed infielder Danny O'Connell and pitchers John Gabler and Ray Semproch as the first franchise players. When the major league draft got under way, after a one-day delay due to a paralyzing snowstorm in the Hub City of Boston, Washington culled a host of familiar names from existing big-league rosters at the bargain price of $75,000 each;

included were such stalwarts of the 1950s as Gene Woodling, Bobby Shantz, Dick Donovan, Dale Long, and speedy Boston Red Sox outfielder Willie Tasby. The complete roster of Senators draftees provided initial credence to Quesada's pledge to produce "as fine a ball club as money and know-how could put together" (Gilbert, 1988, 28).

Draft List of the 1960 Expansion Washington Senators

Player	Former Team
Pitchers	
Pete Burnside*	Detroit Tigers
Dick Donovan*	Chicago White Sox
Rudy Hernandez*	Washington Senators (Minnesota Twins)
Ed Hobaugh*	San Diego (Pacific Coast League)
Johnny Klippstein*	Cleveland Indians
Hector Maestri*	Washington Senators (Minnesota Twins)
Carl Mathias*	Cleveland Indians
Bobby Shantz	New York Yankees
Dave Sisler*	Detroit Tigers
Tom Sturdivant*	Boston Red Sox
Hal Woodeshick*	Washington Senators (Minnesota Twins)
Infielders	
Chester Boak*	Kansas City Athletics
Bob Johnson*	Kansas City Athletics
Billy Klaus*	Baltimore Orioles
Dale Long*	New York Yankees
Jim Mahoney*	Boston Red Sox
John Schaive*	Washington Senators (Minnesota Twins)
Coot Veal*	Detroit Tigers
Marion Zipfel*	Birmingham (Southern Association)
Outfielders	
Joe Hicks*	Chicago White Sox
Charley Hinton*	Stockton (Pacific Coast League)
Jim King*	Toronto (International League)
Willie Tasby*	Boston Red Sox
Gene Woodling*	Baltimore Orioles
Catchers	
Pete Daley*	Kansas City Athletics
Dutch Dotterer*	Cincinnati Reds
Gene Green*	Baltimore Orioles

*Players on 1961 Senators' Spring Training roster.

    In January 1961 the Senators leased rickety Griffith Stadium for one year, and the first summer of Washington Senators expansion baseball was fully under way. A crowd of 26,725 faithful packed comfortably into the ancient ballpark at the corner of Georgia and Florida Avenues (31,000 was capacity) on April 10 for one of the most unusual "franchise openers" of baseball history. This was the same named and similarly uniformed team, and the same stadium, that Washingtonians had experienced for years. The nation's chief executive (this time John Fitzgerald Kennedy, whose youthful arm hurled a ball over the heads of the entire contingent of waiting players and media) was there to honor timeworn tradition and throw out a ceremonial first pitch.

And yet this was expansion baseball! In fact, this was the very first game featuring the very first expansion team in twentieth-century major league baseball history (the other interloper launched that year, the Angels of Los Angeles, did not begin play until the following day). And if there were any doubts that time-tested incompetence had merely been replaced with expansion-age ineptitude, the play of this new Washington ballclub over the next several months would quickly put them to rest. The shoddy defensive play of the new Senators was all too apparent from the outset on Opening Day. Dick Donovan pitched well against his old teammates but received little support; throwing errors let in both the tying and winning runs for Chicago's visiting White Sox. Washington thus dropped their "historic" opener by a 4–3 count, and it was ironically ex-Senators star Roy Sievers who did the major damage, first with a homer, and then with the game-winning sacrifice fly. New local hero Dale Long, always known for his booming bat and not for his leaden glove, assisted in the historic downfall by messing up a routine ground ball which led to the tying Chicago run in inning number seven.

On April 14 Washington defeated Cleveland's Indians 3–2 for the inaugural victory in franchise history; unfortunately there wouldn't be too many similar highlights over the course of the next several seasons. Despite starting fast and surprising even themselves with 30 victories in their first 60 ball games, the neophyte Senators would ultimately drop an even 100 games and finish 47½ games behind the league leader; the 1962 club in turn managed to lose a full 101 contests and limp home a distant 35½ games off the pace. And overall team statistics clearly reflected the ineptitude of play by Washington those first two seasons. The 1961 team tallied the fewest runs (65 fewer than their closest rival) and registered the lowest team BA (.244) in the Junior Circuit; the 1962 entry outhit both Chicago and Cleveland yet scored fewer runs than any big-league club except Houston.

Actually the 1961 Senators played well for a few heady weeks at the outset of their inaugural season. After two-plus months they were still at .500 and ensconced in fourth place. But then came a devastating weekend series in Boston, when Mickey Vernon's ballclub plunged below the .500 plateau with a resounding thud, dropping the full four-game series and blowing substantial leads in each game along the way. The true turning point of that first season came in the opening game of a Sunday doubleheader that fateful weekend in Beantown, when Boston scored eight times with two out in the bottom of the ninth. Light-hitting catcher Jim Pagliaroni of the Bosox enjoyed a full career wrapped within that one weekend, blasting three homers, including a grand slam in the ninth-inning debacle of game one on Sunday and a game-winner in the 13th inning of the nightcap that same day. After that devastating weekend in the not-so-friendly confines of venerable Fenway Park, the youthful Senators never recovered, winning but 20 of their next 71 outings and falling 31 games below .500 over the next several months. Only veteran ball-hawk Gene Woodling provided steady offensive and defensive play, contributing a club-high .313 BA and driving home 57 runs (third behind Tasby and Green with 63 and 62 respectively) despite a limited 342 official at-bats.

Dick Donovan, however, was the highlight of the first expansion year in Washington. The crafty veteran righthander, who had previously enjoyed several solid if unspectacular seasons for Chicago in the mid-1950s, paced the entire American League in ERA with a sterling 2.40. Yet Donovan still disappointed owner Quesada and manager Vernon in the won-lost column with a 10–10 ledger that trailed club leader Bennie Daniels, who wound up 12–10 despite a soaring 3.44 ERA. Injuries throughout the season had limited Donovan's effectiveness and kept him out of the starting rotation for almost two full months. At season's end Dick Donovan was not surprisingly dispatched from Washington as part of a four-player package (including club home run leader Gene Green, infielder Jim Mahoney, and a player to be named later) which brought flamboyant outfielder Jim Piersall over from Cleveland. Piersall was a popular if erratic flychaser who had gamely battled mental illness and consequently failed to live up to lofty promise for more than a decade in Boston and Cleveland. This was hardly an addition to the lineup (despite the potential gate attraction represented by Piersall's flashy style of outfield play) worth sacrificing the club's one legitimate slugger, and the league's stingiest pitcher in the bargain. Jim Piersall predictably disappointed as well in 1962, batting at .244 (78 points below the previous season with the Indians) in 135 games and supplying but four homers and 31 RBIs. Piersall himself would be gone from Washington only a month into the 1963 season.

A landmark of early Senators history came in September of 1962. On the 12th of that month journeyman righthander Tom Cheney pitched one of the most remarkable games in modern American

League history, striking out 21 astonished Baltimore Orioles in a record-setting 16-inning performance. Cheney had demonstrated great promise with a 2.71 ERA over 21 starts during 1963, but injuries soon limited his effectiveness and a severe elbow injury suffered in July of that season all but ended his ill-fated career. In all, the hard-thrower registered eight shutouts in his 19 big-league victories, yet he would win only one more game in the majors after a disappointing 1963 campaign.

With the expansion Senators, ineptitude was not reserved exclusively for athletes on the field of play. Former Senators' marketing director and current baseball author Bill Gilbert curtly highlights the atmosphere of bungling and confusion surrounding the newly minted Washington Senators baseball operation in a candid essay appearing in the Spring 1988 issue of the journal *Sports Heritage*. Quesada pinched pennies at every quarter and impetuously fired his most competent front-office personnel; he feuded as well with the press and issued scathing charges in late 1962 that an uncooperative press and unsupportive business community were entirely to blame for the Nats' on-field failures. By the end of the 1962 season, Quesada cut back the flow of club funds so severely that daily front-office operations almost came to a complete halt. Wily Bill Veeck is credited with making the most cogent observation on the sad state of baseball affairs in Washington during the late summer of 1962: "Quesada has every reason to be worried about losing a quarter of a million dollars in his first season," exhorted Veeck. "If he were doing his job right he'd have lost five million!" (Gilbert, 1988, 33). Yet while the front office was floundering and the ballclub provided minimal big-league entertainment value, there were still some high points in the first several summers of Washington expansion baseball. The opening of play in 1962 found the Senators occupying a proud new home at District of Columbia Stadium in downtown Washington. With President John F. Kennedy again filling the traditional presidential box in the plush new grandstands, the Senators outscored the Detroit Tigers 4–1 on Opening Day of 1962 to fittingly christen their new showcase ballpark. Less than three weeks later it was Roger Maris—fresh off his controversial 1961 record-breaking 61-homer performance—who smashed the first roundtripper to reach the upper deck of the mammoth and pitcher-friendly D.C. Stadium.

July 10 of 1962 brought the All-Star Game to Washington's new ballpark as well. This was the first of two 1962 All-Star Games (under a procedure that had begun in 1959 and was to last through 1962) and the National League emerged triumphant by the count of 3–1 before a mammoth D.C. crowd of 45,480 fanatics. Former original

Senators star Camilo Pascual ironically took the loss for the American Leaguers, while recently departed expansion hero Dick Donovan of the Indians also appeared briefly in a relief role.

September of 1962 would be witness to an event which seemed to have little enough direct connection with the Senators at the time, yet would prove altogether fateful in the future course of franchise history almost a decade later. On the 18th of that month, league owners convened a special closed-door session in Kansas City to investigate Charles Finley's proposals concerning the merits of big league expansion into the Dallas-Fort Worth area. A Texas delegation headed by Arlington Mayor Tom Vandergriff was soon disappointed by the refusal of A.L. owners to sanction Finley's proposals. In a fitting piece of ironic doubletalk, the owners committee announced that the Dallas-Fort Worth area had plenty to recommend it as a future expansion site, but that baseball would be irrevocably harmed by jumping in and out of an existing big-league city (in this case Kansas City) within the very same decade. Little mention of this pressing concern would be made, of course, when these same owners would again convene nine seasons later in Boston to consider Bob Short's identical petition to move his Washington Senators (also in the nation's capital for less than a full decade) into this identical lucrative Texas baseball market.

The beginning of the 1963 season brought a much welcomed shift in ownership for the faltering Senators, after only two painfully long and deteriorating seasons under the tight-fisted control of cantankerous majority partner General Elwood Quesada. A replacement triumvirate of Washington businessmen which included James H. Johnston, James H. Lemon, and George Bunker was successful in buying out five original shareholders (including the unpopular Quesada) and obtaining a controlling 80 percent of existing club stock. Thus the rest of the league breathed a sigh of collective relief at the departure of the meddlesome and increasingly reckless original Washington owner. In reality, most other American League owners had seen enough and had arranged themselves for transfer (at a handsome enough profit to the departing General) of Quesada's controlling 10 percent of the club ownership. But even new management could not bring any immediate transformation of play on the field, and the 1963 Washington Senators were arguably the worst team in the history of either lackluster Senators franchise. This totally inept ballclub lost 105 games and swooned home 48½ games back of the Yankees and 23 games in arrears of the entire first division. Manager Mickey Vernon predictably did not survive the season, being replaced by another erstwhile star first baseman of the previous decade—former Brooklyn Dodgers hero Gil Hodges. The team's top pitcher, Tom Cheney, sported only an 8–9 record; its top hitter, Chuck Hinton, stroked the ball at a .269 clip;

only journeyman Don Lock showed respectable power numbers with 27 dingers and 82 runs knocked home.

The following four-year period under the continued tutelage of new skipper Gil Hodges saw a slow but steady improvement in the heretofore dreadful Washington Senators. There was a climb up to ninth place in 1964 (the final Washington season at 100 or more losses), followed by two eighth-place campaigns, and then a jump to lofty sixth-place status in 1967. By 1967 the Senators had even edged near the coveted demarcation point of .500 baseball and thus finished the season only 15½ games behind the winners (Boston), a rather remarkable summer indeed by Washington baseball standards.

This same period of the mid-1960s would also witness the emergence of the greatest slugging longball folkhero of Washington-Texas baseball history. Ex-collegiate basketball All-American Frank Howard, only a few seasons off a remarkable Rookie-of-the-Year campaign with the 1960 Los Angeles Dodgers, was acquired in a massive seven-player deal with Los Angeles on December 4, 1964. This uplifting deal was easily the best ever engineered by a franchise which would soon be distinguished around the league by its incompetent trading policies. Howard was a giant of a player, both in physical stature (6'7" and 255 lbs.) and hitting performance. For the next six years he led the Washington club in batting, and for seven consecutive seasons he was the home run leader as well. Howard's best seasons were 1968, 1969, and 1970, during two of which he paced the A.L. in longball production, and for one of which he was RBI king as well.

Several other noteworthy events marked the "Frank Howard Era" of Washington baseball. In September of 1964, 25-year-old lefthander Claude Osteen (15–13, 3.00 ERA) became the first Senators hurler to win more than 12 games in a single summer. Yet three months later it was Osteen who was traded away as part of the landmark Frank Howard deal. By January 1965 the tandem of James H. Johnston and James H. Lemon was able to gain complete control over Senators ownership, buying out the remaining stock still held by partners George Bunker and Floyd Ackers. And in June 1966 the Washington ballclub was fortunate to draft promising high school outfielder Tom Grieve of Pittsfield, Massachusetts, later star player and eventual successful general manager and vice president during the club's second resurrection two decades later in Arlington, Texas.

By 1968 the Senators' seemingly upbeat fortunes took a distinct turn for the worst, however. An all-too-brief productive era ended abruptly when Gil Hodges departed to manage the expansion Mets of New York. Former slugger Jim Lemon of the original Washington franchise became the new Senators field boss and experienced a rude greeting in the form of a talentless ballclub which lost 96 games and slipped back to 10th place on the very heels of his arrival. This slide came despite the first of Frank "Hondo" Howard's three most productive offensive seasons, and also despite the surprising return to prominence of former Senators pitching star Camilo Pascual. Arriving unexpectedly back in D.C. from the late-departed Twins through a December 1966 trade, Pascual capped his brilliant career with 12 Washington victories in 1967 and 13 more in 1968. Howard was first in the A.L. in homers and second in RBIs in 1968 as well; yet Washington still managed collectively to post the second-lowest team BA in the entire Junior Circuit, and the league's worst composite mark for ERA as well.

Perhaps the most truly unusual play in Washington Senators history (including here both the old Senators franchise of half-a-century as well as the new Senators of a mere decade's life-span) occurred on July 30, 1968, against the Cleveland Indians. On that night Ron Hansen became only the eighth player in big-league history to turn a rare unassisted triple play. As if the previous Washington experience of Dick Donovan and Claude Osteen were not enough to have him already glancing warily over his shoulder, three days later a shocked Hansen found he had been traded away to the Chicago White Sox for light-hitting infielder Tim Cullen. This unique moment of unprecedented achievement turned to bitter rejection perhaps best sums up the ineptitude and bizarre overtones which filled almost every dimension of the second abortive attempt to bring major league baseball to the nation's capital.

The single-season slide under short-lived skipper Jim Lemon was indeed temporary, and 1969 proved rather surprisingly to be the best season in the decade-long saga of Washington Senators expansion baseball. With the eye-opening addition of Hall-of-Famer Ted Williams at the controls, the 1969 Washington entry set the baseball world back on its heels with a 21-game improvement and fourth-place finish during the inaugural summer of league divisional play. In large part the credit for such a sudden upswing must be attributed to the impact of the new manager—certainly not a new face to the nation's millions of devoted baseball fans. Ted Williams, perhaps the game's greatest hitter ever and certainly its greatest living legend, enjoyed a remarkable first campaign in his novel role as field boss and was fittingly rewarded for the progress of his team with recognition as A.L. Manager of the Year. Great players are rarely great managers, yet Williams' auspicious debut seemed to defy the maxim. It was a bright summer on other fronts as well, as Washington fans also enjoyed their second All-Star Game in Robert F. Kennedy Memorial Stadium, a seventh-straight N.L. victory on July 23 before a teeming crowd of 45,259 excited stalwarts. And the picturesque oval ballpark in the nation's capital, only recently renamed for a fallen national hero, also enjoyed its largest fan turnouts throughout this most memorable of Senators' baseball summers.

Actually the renaming of D.C. Stadium had itself been immersed in the kind of less-than-ideal circumstances which seemed to constantly plague this new Senators franchise throughout their Washington years. Rechristened almost immediately upon the shocking assassination of the younger Kennedy in springtime of 1968, the besieged ballpark weathered weeks of racial tension which subsequently beset Washington and the remainder of the nation on the heels of a second assassination of Martin Luther King on April 4. The traditional baseball season's opener in the Washington ballpark was itself postponed as a direct result of the King murder, held off until April 10, and then played with a large contingent of National Guardsmen and 82nd Airbourne Division troops patrolling streets throughout the adjacent neighborhood while Vice President Hubert Humphrey attended opening game ceremonies. This uneasy atmosphere in the nation's capital was sufficient for the already financially strapped ballclub to reschedule several ensuing American League games during daylight hours at considerable revenue losses—a necessary if unwelcome means of allaying public fears over attending games in the racially mixed district which housed the city's showcase ballpark.

The final two summers for the beleaguered Senators of Washington were anticlimactic to claim the least. Big Frank Howard continued to hit at a lusty clip, barely missing the triple crown in 1970, with league-leading totals in homers (44) and RBIs (126) and a respectable .286 BA. And a new pitching star emerged in the person of Dick Bosman, a mean-spirited righty who finished the 1970 campaign with a 16–12 ledger and 3.00 ERA. (Bosman reportedly once admonished his teammates "if you don't hustle while I'm pitching I'll kick your ass!"—then ironically proceeded to lose a perfect game while hurling for Cleveland on his own inexcusable fielding error.) But despite the individual heroics, the Senators settled back into the pack with two undistinguished seasons good for fifth place and then sixth place. On both occasions Williams' team was an embarrassing 38 games in arrears of the league pacesetter.

While Washington baseball was disintegrating on the field, it was slipping away even faster in the front office. On October 9, 1970, the Washington brain trust engineered perhaps the worst trade in franchise history, one of the worst in the saga of all famous baseball business deals. Solid veteran pitcher Joe Coleman, along with defensive stalwarts Ed Brinkman and Aurelio Rodriguez, plus reserve pitcher Jim Hannan and cash to boot, were blithely shipped over to Detroit in a barrel for a washed-up two-year-wonderboy Denny

McLain (3–5, with a 4.65 ERA in 1970, after his spectacular Cy Young seasons of 1968 and 1969) and several altogether undistinguished throw-ins. McLain, baseball's original "Bad Boy" and malcontent, was never to contribute a lick in Washington, winning 10 and losing 22 in his single season with the Senators. If the McLain deal were not enough to shatter the few remaining faithful, autumn 1970 also witnessed the beginning of the brief yet absurd events surrounding notorious baseball free agent Curt Flood. Washington management had obtained negotiating rights from the Philadelphia Phillies to the ex-Cardinals outfielder who had waited out the entire 1970 campaign in protest over baseball's reserve clause. To get the much-touted but clearly washed-up Flood, the Senators had dished out a landmark $110,000 contract and parted with several marginal players, but it was all for naught as the aging flychaser hit an anemic .200 in 13 games in Washington pinstripes and then announced his sudden retirement from the game before the end of April 1971.

By December 1968 the now laughingstock franchise had once again changed hands, and once more the front-office shift had seemingly breathed new momentary life into the struggling ballclub. At baseball's winter meetings in San Francisco, Hollywood celebrity and longtime superfan Bob Hope had withdrawn one attractive bid for the Senators, but a second offer was apparently far too lucrative for profit-minded American League club owners to ignore. The new owner this time around would be Democratic National Committee Treasurer Robert E. Short, a fast dealing sports entrepreneur best known for purchasing the Minneapolis Lakers of the National Basketball Association a decade earlier on a shoe string and then spiriting that goldmine franchise off to California, where it was eventually unloaded for huge personal profit (a reported capital gain for Short of over $5 million). The Senators franchise was a dream-come-true corporate tax shelter for Short, a property which could be depreciated at full value over the coming five years. And from the beginnings of his new reign in the nation's capital Mr. Short did little to veil his desires to take the newly purchased ballclub to greener pastures as well. "I'm not committed to keeping the team in Washington if D.C. Stadium is not made safe for the fans," Short exhorted within weeks of assuring A.L. club owners in San Francisco that "I did not buy the Washington team to move it" (Whitfield, 1973, 15). In little less than a month the already unpopular owner was ranting in the press that "if they don't want the Senators here, if there is no radio, no box office support, Dallas or Milwaukee or some other places do" (Whitfield, 19).

The opportunities for Short to seek richer hunting grounds were not long in coming either. On September 20, 1971, after several secret meetings with Arlington Mayor Tom Vandergriff, Robert Short gained the necessary approval of fellow owners (a 10–2 vote emerging from a marathon 13-hour session in Boston) for a coveted franchise relocation. With two weeks of the season still remaining, stunned players and fans had to sit through a painful lame duck episode featuring a ballclub that was abandoning its traditional American League home of three quarters of a century. The final game of Washington baseball proved to be the most bizarre final chapter imaginable to the painful saga of the Washington Senators. With the hometown club leading the Yankees 7–5 and two outs recorded in the ninth inning, hundreds of fans enraged by the latest franchise shift stormed onto the turf at RFK Stadium. When order could not be restored, Umpire-in-Chief Jim Honochick had little choice but to forfeit the disrupted game to the rival Yankees.

By November Bob Short had made his final triumphant appearance in Dallas, new home of the erstwhile Washington ballclub. The franchise move was not to be a cheap one, as the Washington owner had agreed to pay six surviving Texas League franchises $40,000 apiece for territorial invasion, as well as agreeing to an annual exhibition game with a Texas League All-Star team at no expense to the minor league ballclubs. The black side of the ledger for the conniving Short was the offer of an immediate $7.5 million in cash arranged by Vandergriff in exchange for 10 years of radio-TV rights; Short needed the cash to pay off Washington debts, and put his ballclub on solid financial footing at the time of the franchise shift. Ever the flashy promoter, Short was feted as honored guest at a luncheon of 800 prominent area business leaders. At that Dallas banquet the club's new name and logo, sporting the egotistical owner's own initials, were proudly unveiled. But there was already apprehension in the air. *Dallas Morning News* sports editor Sam Blair seemed to tap the mood of public concern when he reported that "I've made a study of Bob Short's method of operations, and I don't think we're getting any bargain" (Whitfield, 249).

Flop of the Century—Expansion Baseball Stumbles Upon Texas

> *The story of the Texas Rangers is the story of some firsts, some lasts and some nevers. It's the story of a team that wants to be the greatest in baseball—and just might pull it off.*
> Bill Shaw, *Texas Rangers* (1982)

"In 1955 there were 77,263,127 male American human beings. And every one of them . . . would have given two arms, a leg and his collection of Davy Crockett iron-ons to be Teddy Ballgame." With these inspired lines humorists Brendan Boyd and Fred Harris (*The Great American Baseball Card Flipping, Trading, and Bubble Gum Book*, 1973, 36) characterize the grip that Ted Williams once held upon the nation of America's youth. But Williams—like all our baseball deities—was also excessively human, and all the frailties of that humanity were to come tumbling out before Teddy Ballgame's painful association with the Texas Rangers (nee Washington Senators) came crashing to its predictable conclusion in the discontented winter of 1972.

From the first disembarking in Dallas there was little question that the long-awaited baseball club which had finally arrived in Texas was a clear extension of the ego and personality of one Robert E. Short, super finagler and ruthless entrepreneur. Short even underscored this fact with the unveiling of the new team uniforms—the red and blue-trimmed letters spelling out "RangerS" had the first and last letters capitalized in honor of the egocentric owner's own initials. But more serious evidence also lurked everywhere that owner Short was far more interested in his own personal perks and portfolio gains than he ever was in the community service of professional baseball. Rumors were afloat from the outset that Short was already looking for the proper opportunity to sell out in two more brief seasons (when IRS rules allowed full depreciation of his investment) and take a huge tax profit in the bargain.

The beginnings of major league baseball play in the Dallas and Fort Worth metroplex were celebrated with anything but an auspicious debut. The franchise opener pencilled in for April 6, 1972, was cancelled by a short-lived players' strike which interrupted the outset of the new season. If that were not foreboding enough, the first exhibition game of the Grapefruit League spring itself had to be broadcast without a radio sponsor, as none had yet been enlisted. And when season's play finally did begin, only 20,105 curious fans (35,694 was capacity) showed up for the inaugural April 21 home game victory, played in a hastily revamped Arlington Stadium (renamed from Turnpike Stadium) against the visiting California Angels. Of this second largest crowd of the Rangers' maiden season, most were still unfortunately trapped in a gigantic traffic gridlock at several toll plazas along the Dallas-Fort Worth Turnpike when Frank Howard provided the season's first highlight at the half-empty ballpark when he clouted a mammoth 400-foot first-inning homer over the distant center-field fence.

Attendance, in fact, was the continuing bane of the new franchise. From the first, the fans and press provided little enough welcome for the new Texas ballclub. Only 660,000 turned out for the first season of play, despite a 20 percent reduction in the league-high ticket prices charged the final season in Washington, and in blissful ignorance of owner Short's continual harangues that 800,000 was the minimal season draw needed to keep the young franchise solvent. And the press was altogether negative as well: "Even if our people were enthused, which they don't seem to be, it's too damned hot to go to a ball park!"

carped the Dallas *Times-Herald* senior sports editor Blackie Sherrod (Whitfield, 1972, 249). Low attendance had some obvious enough explanations, though none of them seemed more plausible than the questionable quality of the team itself and the justifiable suspicions surrounding its wheeling and dealing supercilious owner. The turnpike stadium itself, of course, still under considerable renovation and without benefit of a sheltering upper deck or grandstand roof, was not at all conducive to watching the nation's pastime in comfort or even in safety in a land of sparrow-sized mosquitoes and blazing sunshine.

When 1972 league play finally did begin a week late, franchise firsts were inevitably recorded in the season opening series against the Angels in California. Catcher Hal King achieved the first club base hit in the second inning of game one against Andy Messersmith. Game two brought the first victory, 5–1, with Pete Broberg logging the first pitching triumph credited to a Texas hurler and Elliot Maddox stroking the first franchise extra base hit, a double. Once back in Arlington, the Rangers did manage to win their franchise home opener, a nail-biting 7–6 count over the same Angels, though the game itself yielded enough ominous signs of things to come. Lenny Randle led the hitting with two singles and a double, while Dave Nelson and Frank Howard recorded the first home ballpark roundtrippers. But then an onslaught of errors almost gave the game away as the home side promptly blew an early 6–1 third-inning lead.

The 1972 team fielded by Short and his "baseball people" was one of the worst of recent memory in the American League—"The Worst Darn Team in Baseball"—and the 54–100 won-loss record was unfortunately not the singular marker of team futility. The Rangers managed to finish at or near the bottom of the league in almost every imaginable offensive and defensive category as well. Play on the field certainly did not help boost community support, and the most visible rewards of last-place play were found in the team's radio and television contracts, both of which collapsed after only one year. Hall-of-Fame pitcher Don Drysdale, a member of the initial Rangers broadcast crew, left Texas for greener pastures after only a single season of attempting to chronicle unparalleled baseball ineptitude.

Ted Williams' relationship with Bob Short also had deteriorated precipitously over the course of a final frustrating season in Washington and a first full summer of ineptitude in Arlington, and on September 30, 1972, the Hall-of-Fame slugger announced somewhat bitterly that he was stepping down as Rangers manager. The choice for Williams' 1973 replacement, more surprising even than Ted's expected departure, was a little-known talent plucked out of the New York Mets organization, former Senators and Athletics utility outfielder Dorrel "Whitey" Herzog. Herzog, who less than a decade later would emerge as one of the premier managers (and general managers to boot) of baseball history, had little enough chance to display future brilliance with the short hand dealt him in Texas, and before the first season of his tenure was out Herzog had been dismissed with a less-than-glowing 47–91 record and memories of a badly floundering sixth-place ballclub.

Perhaps the biggest news of the second Rangers season came several months before the first 1973 pitch was thrown in Arlington Stadium. In a most productive January free-agent draft, the Rangers utilized the nation's number one pick to garner PAC-Eight All-Star shortstop Roy Smalley, Jr., fresh from the campus of the University of Southern California, as well as exercising their second pick for future all-star catcher Jim Sundberg out of Galesburg, Illinois. Smalley would have only a brief career in Texas, before contributing elsewhere. Sundberg, however, would jump directly to the parent club after batting .298 in a single season of AA ball, soon becoming one of the most dependable and durable players in team history. Today the recently retired Sundberg still boasts several franchise career hitting records (1,436 games played, 4,537 ABs, 1,151 hits); he has caught the third most games in major league history; averaged 140 games per season behind the plate for over a decade; tied the A.L. record with 155 games caught in his second full season; and remains the only catcher in big-league history to be awarded six gold gloves.

Draft dealings continued as the hot story throughout the 1973 season, as in June the Rangers plucked 18-year-old lefthander David Clyde from the campus of Houston's Westchester High School. Signed to a phenomenal $125,000 bonus by owner Bob Short and rushed directly to the big time against the stern warnings of most Rangers scouts, Clyde enjoyed a short-lived glory that first summer befitting one of baseball's all-time bizarre tales of unfulfilled diamond promise. The flamethrowing lefty's major league debut later that same month was one of the most auspicious in baseball's storied history. Before the first sellout crowd in Arlington Stadium history (35,698), hometown hero Clyde allowed but one hit and struck out eight in five innings of impressive work to gain his first big-league triumph over the baffled Minnesota Twins. But the raw lefty's quick-flaming star was to plunge just as rapidly as it had ascended, and after only 39 starts over his first two seasons, arm troubles would cut short the true-to-life myth that was David Clyde. The young phenom would win only seven games for the Rangers, and his best season would see him post an undistin-guished 8–11 mark (4.28 ERA) during a brief career-ending stay with the Cleveland Indians in 1978. For Short, quick promotion of his promising young homegrown phenom had proved a welcomed one-night box-office bonanza; yet for the struggling expansion franchise and its hungry fans the whole sordid affair had led directly to little more than ruination of a seemingly unlimited pitching talent that might well have been enjoyed for years down the road.

Three separate managers guided the Rangers through a second dismal season in 1973, the last being colorful Billy Martin, signed on six days after his release by the Detroit Tigers in early September. Martin was on board in Arlington for only the tail end of what proved an agonizing 57–105 season, surpassed for ineptitude in club annals only by the horrendous 1963 showing back in the nation's capital. Perhaps the single highlight of this otherwise bungled campaign was a franchise-first no-hit game authored by Jim Bibby on July 30 against the Oakland A's. Bibby also struck out 13 that evening, while Jeff Burroughs aided the hometown cause with a resounding first-inning grandslam homer. (Burroughs produced a highlight reel of his own, in fact, with three prodigious grandslams socked within the 10-day stretch between July 26 and August 4, a team mark which would stand unchallenged until Larry Parrish collected three in one week a decade later.) Bibby's only career masterpiece was indeed unrivaled as the brightest evening of an otherwise painfully long second baseball summer in sunbaked Arlington.

Two other rather noteworthy events surrounded the Texas Rangers ballclub in 1973. On September 19 California Angels outfielder Frank Robinson homered in Arlington Stadium, giving the future Hall-of-Famer a record of 32 major league parks in which he had stroked at least one circuit clout. More on the plus side for the Texas ballclub, an October 26 deal with the Chicago Cubs brought Ferguson Jenkins to Arlington. Over the next several seasons the tall righthander would prove the most successful hurler in club history. Before he was through, Jenkins would own single-season club records for innings pitched (328, 1974), starts (41, 1974), winning percentage (.692, 1978) and victories (25, 1974), as well as career standards for shutouts (17), complete games (90), and victories (93, since surpassed by Charlie Hough).

The 1974 season itself was hardly under way when the long-expected deal transpired which would finally remove Robert Short from ownership of the Texas Rangers. In late May, plastics tycoon Bradford G. Corbett successfully formed a group to purchase the ballclub from the disillusioned and now largely detached original owner. Short had been rumored ready to sell by the end of 1973 season, exactly at the end of a five-year depreciation period for tax purposes which would allow full write-off of the original $9 million purchase price invested in the club. Precisely as many pundits had speculated (and precisely as he had done earlier with the Los Angeles Lakers basketball franchise), the penny-pinching Short walked away from baseball in Texas with a handsome capital gain of close to $14 million. The new owners, in turn, were greeted with the traditional optimism expected of blindly loyal baseball fans, and one of Corbett's first and best moves was to persuade former Yankee infield star Bobby Brown to leave his successful career as a heart specialist and take over as Texas Rangers president. Brown, of course, was eventually to serve as president of the entire American League.

The American League campaign also brought improvement on the ballfield as well as in the front office for the team which now carried the standard of Dallas-Fort Worth into the 1974 baseball wars. On October 2 the Rangers defeated Minnesota, cementing second spot over the Twins and garnering as well their 84th win, a remarkable 27-game turnaround over the previous season. For the first time in Texas and only the second in club history, the franchise boasted a winning record, and this winning standard reflected a solid .500-plus performance from top to bottom of the ledger: the club was 42–38 (.525) both at home and on the road, 63–57 (.525) at night, 21–19 (.525) for day games. Consistency on the upside of the scale had finally arrived in Arlington. The Rangers' remarkable season of 1974 was topped off with still further honors when Billy Martin was selected the league's top skipper, first baseman Mike Hargrove was named A.L. Rookie of the Year, and outfielder Jeff Burroughs became only the third player in major league history to be named a league MVP in his second full season of play. A final highlight of the Rangers' best year to date was the league-leading 25–10 (2.83 ERA) record of mound star Ferguson Jenkins. This was the seventh time in eight seasons (as well as the last time) that the future Canadian Baseball Hall-of-Famer would post in excess of 20 victories; it was also to remain the best all-around season of Jenkins' spectacular 19-year career.

The 1975 season again began with significant developments in the winter amateur draft, as the Rangers exercised the number one overall pick to select diminutive Elliot "Bump" Wills, son of former Los Angeles Dodgers star Maury Wills. In the later June amateur draft the Rangers were again as fortuitous as foresighted in selecting big-stick first baseman Pat Putnam. Putnam was soon to enjoy several quality years in the Rangers organization, beginning with a spectacular second season at Ashville in 1976 which saw him emerge as the first Class A player ever tabbed as *Sporting News* Minor League Player of the Year. Further significant player personnel moves came in June of the same year when Texas engineered a major trade for established righthanded pitcher Gaylord Perry. This headline-grabbing deal saw hurlers Jim Bibby, Jackie Brown, and Rick Waits all depart to the Cleveland Indians, where the trio won a composite total of 12 games (the same as Perry at Texas) over the remainder of the 1975 summer season.

Yet Gaylord Perry aside, the glow of the 1974 "Rangers Resurrection" had already tarnished by mid-summer, as pugnacious skipper Billy Martin rapidly fell out of favor with the new front office in Arlington—much as he was to do elsewhere throughout his unusually explosive managerial career. The flamboyant purveyor of "Billy Ball" was fired on July 21, with the club riding a 44–51 record and already slipping far behind frontrunners Oakland and Minnesota. It is telling, perhaps, that Texas was the only place the combative Martin managed where he was unable to merge on-field success with off-field hi-jinx and controversy. Martin would win league pennants or divisional flags everywhere else he stopped, however, briefly—Minnesota (1969), Detroit (1972), Oakland (1981), and New York (1976, 1977). In Texas, however, "Billy Ball" never really got off the ground or out of the starting gate. Martin may well have been as colorful in Texas as he was everywhere else, but he had also proven to be nowhere near as capable of maintaining the affection of management as he was in inspiring undying loyalty among the ticket-buying fans.

Billy Martin's immediate replacement was third base coach Frank Lucchesi, and over the remainder of the season under the laconic Lucchesi, Texas was a more respectable 35–32 down the stretch. The surprisingly successful new skipper, hired initially on an interim basis, was immediately rewarded with a contract extension through the end of the subsequent season. Nonetheless the beleaguered Rangers still closed out the campaign in the third spot in the imbalanced Western Division, 19 full games off the sizzling pace set by the pennant-winning Oakland A's.

Between the close of the 1975 campaign and the middle of the 1976 season, two significant trades drastically altered the Texas Rangers pitching staff. In November 1975 Fergie Jenkins was peddled to the Red Sox for utility outfielder Juan Beniquez and undistinguished hurlers Steve Barr (a lifetime three-game winner) and Craig Skok (who earned only four major league victories). In June of 1976 the Rangers compensated somewhat for the loss of Jenkins by acquiring Bert Blyleven (who already boasted 99 career wins in but six seasons) from the Minnesota Twins, giving up regular infielders Roy Smalley and Mike Cubbage plus two unheralded pitchers in the process. Another significant trade in the late off-season of 1976 saw 1974 MVP Jeff Burroughs dealt away to Atlanta for five players (the best of whom was pitcher Roger Moret, who would post a 47–27 career mark yet win only three games for Texas) and significant cash. Both the Jenkins and Burroughs trades, a year apart, seemed to be establishing an unfortunate pattern at the spacious Dallas ballpark. Big-named stars were regularly sent packing for truckloads of everyday players who simply didn't pan out once their bags were unpacked in the Arlington clubhouse.

The campaign of 1976 (fourth place and 14 games out) proved an altogether disappointing season, but 1977, by stark contrast, brought one of the more heady performances in club history. Just as Billy Martin had turned things around in this first full season at the helm, Frank Lucchesi seemed prepared for a similar feat in his second full year on the Texas bench. But the unlucky Lucchesi had little enough chance to enjoy the fruits of the ballclub he had been rapidly rebuilding. Unpredictable owner Brad Corbett showed little patience when Lucchesi's young charges were slow to get untracked and fired his manager on June 22, with the team mark standing at an even .500. Eddie Stanky was surprisingly brought in after a 10-year absence from managing, yet Stanky lasted only a single afternoon (a 10–8 win over the Twins) before hastily deciding that the radically altered game of the seventies was no longer to his taste. After a brief six-day tenure by interim skipper Connie Ryan (two wins and four defeats), Billy Hunter was hired on as the fourth field boss of the season. Despite these musical chairs in the manager's office, the club soon soared back into the second spot, winning 31 of the first 40 under Hunter and charging down the stretch with a remarkable 60–33 record. The year's final total of 94 victories remains today the all-time high in the combined Senators-Rangers franchise history. Hunter, an undistinguished infielder with six American League clubs during the 1950s, had the surprising Rangers playing at a remarkable .645 clip over the final two-thirds of the remarkable rebound season.

The 1977 campaign also had its several bizarre sidelights. The afternoon of August 8 (in the second game of a twinbill against the Oakland Athletics) brought that most unpredictable of moments: the first and only triple play in franchise history. Hurler Roger Moret invited the improbable with walks to Mitchell Page and Rich McKinney; Manny Sanguillen than banged out a sharp grounder to Toby Harrah and it was promptly "around the horn" to second sacker Bump Wills and first baseman Mike Hargrove for the rare triple killing. Harrah and Wills then enjoyed a second moment with destiny on August 27, as they banged out even rarer back-to-back inside the park homers off consecutive pitches by New York Yankees righthander Ken Clay. On September 22, Bert Blyleven tossed the second no-hitter in club history, this one against the Angels in Anaheim. It proved to be something of a special year for no-hitters, in fact, as Jim Colborn also became the first pitcher to no-hit the Rangers in a May 14 game at Kansas City.

Summer 1978 welcomed the popular Fergie Jenkins (reacquired from the Red Sox in December 1977) back into a friendly Rangers uniform. In retrospect, December 1977 might well have been the most active trading period in Rangers club history, surpassed only in magnitude by the bold dealing which 11 years later would bring franchise players Nolan Ryan and Julio Franco to Arlington. Ironically, Tom Grieve, major architect of the 1988 Ranger's rebuilding program, was involved in the 1977 winter deals as well. First the Rangers bartered with the Mets, giving up the hard-hitting Grieve, along with first sacker Willie Montanez, for hurler Jon Matlack and first baseman John Milner. On the same day (December 8), ace Bert Blyleven was off to Pittsburgh (in a package deal with the newly acquired and much-traveled Milner) for slugging Al Oliver and shortstop Nelson Norman. Six days later Jenkins was acquired for pitcher John Poloni and cash. The addition of Matlack to the Texas staff was good for 15 additional wins in 1978 alone. Jenkins' own 18–8 mark that first season back in the fold would give him an outstanding 60–38 mark in Texas over a three-season span (1974–1975, 1978).

Despite such apparent improvements to their previously weak-armed mound corps, the Rangers slipped slightly in the won-lost column for 1978, their seventh but hardly charmed campaign in the Texas heartland. An upside was that they remained the same in the standings (second) and actually improved in the margin of games behind the leader (from eight in 1977 to five in 1978). New hero Al Oliver (.324 BA) and one-year-wonder Bobby Bonds (29 homers after coming to Texas in early May) emerged as the hitting stars that summer. At season's close the ballclub had drawn 1.4 million fans and remained competitive, yet field boss Billy Hunter (who managed at a composite .576 clip during his brief season and two thirds at the helm) was nonetheless given his walking papers only hours before the season finale in Arlington. Third base coach Pat Corrales was immediately named as the new skipper for the upcoming 1979 campaign, the ninth bench boss in seven seasons of Texas Rangers baseball. More significant even than the continuation of revolving managers which brought 1978 to a close was the largely unheralded November deal which shipped off minor league hurler Dave Righetti (a future big-league star) in a mammoth 10-player swap with the Yankees, a deal which also brought veteran relief artist Sparky Lyle briefly into the Rangers' fold.

The decade was to be closed out in Arlington with another respectable if uninspired year—a third-place 1979 finish at slightly over .500 (83–79), five games behind the leader for the second consecutive season. Al Oliver continued as the ballclub's most consistent hitter (.323, for the fifth best average in the league), and Jim Kern enjoyed a remarkable year in the Texas bullpen. Kern's numbers were as impressive as any reliever in club history: 13–5 record, a league second-best 29 saves, 1.57 ERA. For his efforts, Kern was named American League Rolaids Relief Man of the Year. Newcomer Buddy Bell at third—acquired in a notable off-season trade with Cleveland for veteran shortstop Toby Harrah—enjoyed a highly productive year at the plate, tying Richie Zisk and first sacker Pat Putnam for the home run lead at 18 apiece. Other standouts for the season were Steve Comer, whose career-high 17 wins were fifth best in the league, and Pat Putnam, whose play at first base would win him A.L. Rookie-of-the-Year honors from *The Sporting News.*

With the close of the 1979 season the Rangers had again topped the 1.5 million attendance standard. Three finishes near the top of the A.L. West seemed to signal a bright enough future for a club which was stocked with such young and experienced hitting stalwarts as Oliver, Bell, Zisk, and Putnam. The midseason acquisition of speedy centerfielder Mickey Rivers from the Yankees had strengthened an already potent Texas attack, as well as cementing the outfield play alongside rookie standout Billy Sample. But a fateful pattern had developed in Arlington throughout the 1970s—promising seasons of considerable expectation intermingled with repeated plunges into the lower echelons of what remained baseball's consensus worst division. And with another drastic ownership upheaval only months down the road, baseball fortunes in Texas were indeed nowhere near as bright as they might have appeared when the 1979 season wound to an upbeat close.

A Very Ugly Baby, Indeed!—Texas Rangers of the 1980s

> *That was some ugly baby. Before the 1987 season Rangers veteran Larry Parrish said that "people expect the labor pains to be over. They expect to see the baby." It was an ugly baby from the first squall.*
>
> Bill James, *The Bill James Baseball Abstract 1988*

February of 1980 brought a landmark transition in the short history of the Texas Rangers baseball franchise. On the 27th of that month Bradford Corbett, one of baseball's most unpopular owners ever, finally sold off his extensive holdings in the Texas Rangers, terminating a chaotic six-year reign as chairman of the board and chief operating officer of the still struggling franchise. Corbett had for years been the chum of greedy player agents and high salaried veterans facing contract renegotiations, and the whipping boy of frustrated fans. The former were often quoted as rating him the "owner they would most like to deal with" (since you always seemed to get precisely what you asked for from Corbett when it came to contract settlements);

a large contingent of the latter regularly sported tee shirts at the ballpark which read "Trade Chuckles the Clown"—in cold derision of the unpopular owner who had unloaded their favorite players so frequently and freely. Eddie Chiles, Fort Worth oilman, was now the new top man in the front office, having joined forces with two other major stockholders, Fort Worth publisher Amon Carter and attorney Dee Kelly, to buy out Corbett's full interest in the club.

The strike-marred season of 1981—one of the least memorable in all baseball history—ironically provided one of the few highlight years in the long-suffering saga of Rangers baseball. A pre-strike surge seemed to maneuver the Texas club into a position to make a serious run at the division title: had they won against Milwaukee on the day before the June 12 players walkout, they would have moved percentage points ahead of Oakland at the top of the Western Division and qualified for the league's makeshift playoffs at season's end. Then a second-half collapse (third place in the division and two games below .500) emphasized that it was still business as usual in Arlington. Yet the season was not without its considerable high points. There was a club-record four consecutive shutouts by a surprising Rangers mound staff during the season's first month, capped by Rick Honeycutt's blanking of Kansas City on April 30; journeyman infielder Bill Stein established an A.L. record with his seventh-straight successful pinch hit on May 25; DH Al Oliver hit .309 for the campaign to cop a second straight *Sporting News* Silver Bat Award; Doc Medich tied for the league lead in shutouts with four.

The summer of 1982 was destined to be Don Zimmer's swan song in Arlington. Having engineered the ballclub safely through the split-personality strike-shortened 1981 campaign with an overall 57–48 mark, second best in the Western Division for the composite season, Zimmer quickly fell on hard times with a 1982 ballclub which started slow and tumbled into the division cellar by midsummer, on the way to a highly embarrassing 64–98 ledger and a sixth-place final roost. The club had come within a scant two defeats of its first 100-loss year since the inaugural two Arlington summers, and as a result Zimmer was predictably out and coach Darrell Johnson in on July 28. And another familiar face was now missing as well, as popular slugger Al Oliver had been shipped off to Montreal during spring training for inconsistent outfielder Dave Hostetler and talented batsman Larry Parrish. The deal proved to have its merits, as Parrish would slam out an all-time Texas club standard 149 homers over the next six seasons, as well as a single-season mark of 32 in 1987. Parrish also began with something of a bang in 1982, blasting three grandslams in a single week in July to tie a major league record set by Jim Northrup of the Tigers during the Bengals championship year of 1968.

The mid-1980s saw the Rangers continue a tradition of rollercoaster seasons—the well-established pattern of one hopeful charge at the top after another, always resulting in the inevitable collapse that lay just around the corner. The debacle of 1982 (50 more losses than the previous season) was followed by slight improvement in 1983 under first-year manager Doug Rader, the ninth regular skipper and 12th overall in Texas club history. Rader's first Rangers club came in third in the Western Division, despite remaining under .500 and over 20 games off the pace, and despite the ex-shortstop's reputation for wacky and outrageous behavior both on the field and off. There were, in fact, considerable signs of marked improvement on the 1983 ballclub, as Rader's charges finished but two games out of second and gave up the fewest runs of any American League team. On the upside for Texas fans, the fact that the Rangers were so far off the pace had in large part to do with the runaway season of the unstoppable Chicago White Sox.

Manager Doug Rader's quick start of 1983, however, was followed by the familiar old story that has haunted this ballclub throughout the course of the past decade. In 1984 the once-promising Rangers reverted to form and lost 92 games; in 1985 the loss column totalled 99 as the club fell 28½ games off the pace and remained buried deep in seventh place. But Doug Rader himself was not around for the finale of the 1985 campaign; one of baseball's most flaky and eccentric figures was gone from the Texas dugout after only 32 disappointing games. By mid-May once-promising Dodger outfielder Bobby Valentine, Texas skipper number 13, was now on board for the duration of a long and dismal losing campaign.

The season of 1984 also witnessed another important front-office move in Texas, equally as important in the long run if somewhat less ballyhooed than the firing of Rader and the hiring of manager Valentine. On September 1, at the tender age of 36, former Rangers first baseman Tom Grieve was appointed vice president and general manager, thus becoming the youngest person at the time ever to hold such a lofty executive role with a big-league club. Grieve grew slowly in his new position, but the off-season of 1988 was to test his true medal with deals which obtained Nolan Ryan, Julio Franco, Rafael Palmeiro, and a handful of other potential contributors for the talent-thin Texas ballclub. It would be Grieve's contribution in the final seasons of the decade which were mostly responsible for earning a franchise citation as *Baseball America's* 1989 Major League Organization of the Year.

The history of trades involving the Rangers has been so poor that even when the Texas ballclub makes an astute personnel move they get little enough credit for it. As SABRmetrician Bill James points out in his 1986 annual review of the Rangers ballclub, everyone loves to kick a losing ballclub when it is down, and the Rangers have long been favorite whipping boys of hardened professional baseball critics. One of the worst Texas deals in the decade of the 1980s involved the loss of promising reliever Tom Henke to the Toronto Blue Jays. The Rangers had made the unproductive move of signing free-agent DH Cliff Johnson, which resulted immediately in losing Henke through the established player compensation pool. Henke, of course, went on to perform brilliantly with Toronto, registering 119 saves over the next five seasons. The backside of the story, however, is that the Rangers' GM Tom Grieve next traded the disappointing Johnson back to the Blue Jays in the waning months of the same 1985 season and acquired, among others, promising fireballer Mitch Williams. Williams' immediate performance in 1986 was almost enough to make the trade an even deal, as the charismatic bullpen stopper led the A.L. in game appearances with 80. However, the Rangers were to gain still further from the complicated Cliff Johnson deal. Three seasons later Williams was a major component in the blockbuster 1988 Cubs trade which brought Rafael Palmeiro to Texas. The verdict is still largely out on the later deal, as Williams himself was a key component in the Cubs' pennant season of 1989. But at worst the whole saga involving Johnson-Henke-Williams-Palmeiro seems to be one of the least disastrous (and least credited) maneuvers the Rangers have made over the past two decades.

Bobby Valentine's first full campaign at the helm in 1986 resulted in rather remarkable improvement and a new soaring of previously dashed hopes at the Arlington ballpark. For starters, there was a 25-game turnaround and an improvement of five full slots in the standings. The 87 victories were the second most in club history, matching the 1978 second-place season and falling short of only the 1977 high-water mark. Two new hitting stars had suddenly emerged in Oklahoma State All-American Pete Incaviglia (30 homers) and journeyman infielder Scott Fletcher (.300 BA with over 500 ABs). Veteran knuckleballer Charlie Hough enjoyed his best season ever on the mound (17–10, 3.79 ERA), after spending much of May on rehabilitation assignment at AAA Oklahoma City. The 1987 and 1988 seasons soon revealed as well, however, that Valentine's fortunes would likely follow the noxious pattern so firmly established by his predecessors Corrales, Zimmer, and Rader. One improved season was quickly followed with several lackluster ones (a dip to sixth place in both 1987 and 1988) in the now time-worn Texas Rangers' tradition. Yet Rangers' front-office management was quick enough this time around to underscore unbending faith in skipper Valentine and to silence inevitable criticism (including substantial rumors of rampant player dissatisfaction), issuing a pointed forceful statement of public support for the beleaguered manager late in the 1988 campaign.

A little-noticed and less trumpeted star for the Texas ballclub throughout the entire decade of the 1980s had been knuckleballing mainstay Charlie Hough. Pitching for perhaps any other club in the league (except perhaps Seattle or the hapless White Sox), Hough might well have been a regular yearly all-star selection. As it was, his numbers were impressive indeed: 174 wins (with 157 losses) spread over 17 big-league summers; 127 victories with the Rangers, including eight consecutive campaigns with 10 or more wins; league-leading totals for games started in both 1984 and 1987; five consecutive seasons as club leader in wins before the arrival of Nolan Ryan in 1988; a team record for consecutive scoreless innings pitched (36 in 1983). Charlie Hough also maintains Texas Rangers career standards in five separate pitching categories: wins (127), losses (111), strikeouts (1,338), walks (846), and game appearances (282). The apparently ageless knuckleballer also hurled one and two-thirds innings of the 1986 All-Star Game at Houston and has thrown one one-hitter, four two-hitters, and 12 three-hitters since putting on a Rangers uniform for the first time in 1980. And all this came on the heels of a successful decade-long career (47–46, 3.50 ERA) as a middle reliever with the Los Angeles Dodgers throughout the 1970s.

The summer of 1989 was arguably the most exciting in the combined history of the Texas Rangers and Washington Senators, if only for the season-long saga of baseball's most remarkable rubber-armed hurler, the incomparable Nolan Ryan. It was also a season which saw the Texas club display far more punch individually than it was to muster collectively. At summer's end the team boasted league leaders in strikeouts (Ryan), runs batted in (Sierra), total bases (Sierra again), and saves (Jeff Russell); collectively they slumped badly in late summer and finished a distant divisional fourth, 16 games off the pace and a mere four games over .500. Yet it was over the .500 mark nonetheless—for the first time in four dryspell seasons. The irrepressible Ryan was the showcase piece, of course, striking out his 5,000th career batter on August 22 (Rickey Henderson of Oakland was the victim), posting a club-best 16–10 mark, twice flirting with that elusive sixth career no-hitter (achieved in 1990), and pacing both leagues with a remarkable 301 strikeouts. It was a record sixth time that the ageless Ryan passed the 300 strikeout barrier, and the first time since he had worn the uniform of the California Angels a dozen full seasons earlier.

If 1989 was largely the passion play of 22-year mound veteran Nolan Ryan and his remarkable geriatric pitching feats, it was also the pageant of youthful stardom for 23-year-old Puerto Rican slugger Ruben Sierra. Considered by many to be the brightest young hitting star of the American League—perhaps even a player in the mold of his Hall-of-Fame countryman, Roberto Clemente—the switch-hitting Sierra largely lived up to advanced billing with a truly remarkable offensive campaign. Leading the league in slugging average (.545), RBIs (119), total bases (344), and triples (14), and finishing in the top 10 in hitting (.307), home runs (29), hits (194), and runs scored (101), Ruben Sierra not surprisingly finished a very close second to Milwaukee Brewers' centerfielder Robin Yount in the A.L. MVP balloting as well. Many veteran observers of the baseball scene were convinced that only the lack of media attention directed toward the Texas franchise (outside of Ryan's pitching feats, of course) kept Sierra from walking away with honors as the Junior Circuit's most valued all-around performer.

Another noteworthy performance in Texas during the Rangers resurgent year of 1989 was that turned in by Jeff Russell, the A.L. leader in saves with 38 (a margin of four over his closest challenger, Bobby Thigpen of Chicago). Russell emerged out of nowhere in 1989 as one of the truly dominant short relievers in the game. Moving from a starter's role (10–9, 3.82 ERA) in his second full big-league campaign of 1988, Russell became a true staff workhorse, appearing in 71 games (fourth in the league) and registering a phenomenal 1.98 ERA, far outdistancing the scant five career saves of his two previous abbreviated bullpen seasons in 1985 and 1986. Acquired from Cincinnati in a controversial 1985 deal which had sent popular Buddy Bell to the National League, Russell was perhaps the biggest surprise in an altogether surprising season for the fast-starting and slow-finishing men of fifth-year mentor Bobby Valentine.

The Rangers have always been a baseball franchise given to a rash inconsistencies and a truly inexplicable lack of front-office commitment. Given this sad state of affairs, it is not at all disarming that the frenzied free-agent activities of winter 1988 were followed with the less-than-stimulating off-season developments of December 1989. Unlike the 1988 bonanza of talent which brought Ryan, Palmeiro, and Franco to Arlington, while at the same time clearing out deadwood veteran players (O'Brien, Wilkerson, Williams, and McDowell), the 1989 post-season saw but one uninspired sortie into the free-agent market. The Rangers inked veteran center fielder Gary Pettis, fresh off what can only be called a busted season for cellar-dwelling Detroit. While Pettis—known largely for his outfield prowess and speed afoot—tied for fourth among American Leaguers in stolen bases and was ninth in walks with a career high 84 (leading the Tigers with a .375 on-base percentage), he batted only .257 with but one homer and 18 RBIs in 119 games during his second summer in Detroit. The switch-hitting Pettis does not come without exciting defensive credentials: he captured Gold Glove Awards for his center-field play in 1985, 1986, and 1988, and he was the only major league outfielder with more than 300 putouts in less than 120 games during 1989. A lifetime .239 average and only 197 RBIs in 832 games, however, hardly suggests the kind of player likely to make an impact on a fourth-place club seeking to move up in what may now be baseball's toughest division. As the 1990 season loomed around the corner, prospects were again not bright for the baseballers of Arlington; and again it appeared that Bill James' proverbial baby that has been the Texas Rangers ballclub of the late 1980s (James 1988, 71) would not soon shed any of its recognizably ugly "baby fat"—nor discard any of its still troublesome predictability.

The Rangers (nee Senators) American League franchise—quite arguably the most disappointing and uninspired in baseball's long history—has been repeatedly characterized from the earliest years by a ceaseless parade of bungling egotistical owners, disastrous trades and inexplicable personnel moves, remarkably inept yearly play, and little support from the baseball faithful in two consistently abused big-league cities. General Pete Quesada, Robert Short, Brad Corbett, and Ed Chiles (the featured front-office players) have collectively maintained a relentless three-decade saga of unpopular team management, featuring callous exploitation of local fans for the shameless purpose of huge corporate profits, and offering preciously little baseball entertainment in return. Baseball is, of course, a high-priced corporate entertainment business; and yet without the expected entertainment, the bottom-line business is distasteful at best. In this sense, Robert E. Short has left his unalterable mark on the franchise he purchased in the swan song days of the Washington Senators and jettisoned for huge personal profit at the end of but two dreadful seasons in the Promised Land of Arlington, Texas. As the struggling Rangers franchise now limps into the new decade of the 1990s under its sixth ownership in less than 30 seasons, it remains the only expansion ball-club outside of the Seattle Mariners (who boast less than half the lifespan) never to appear in league post-season play. Arlington Stadium, as well remains the only current big-league park never to host even a major league All-Star Game, much less an inning of A.L.C.S. play.

The Texas Rangers baseball club enters the nineties much as it entered its first decade of the seventies—as a team with a severe identity crisis. The new ownership of George W. Bush and his wealthy Texas oil-industry associates promises renewed dreams for the stability and long-term baseball planning which has so far consistently eluded this lackluster franchise. The false high hopes and mediocre results enfolding the Rangers' most recent season, however, seem to proffer little firm evidence that much has changed for long-suffering and admirably stoic Texas Rangers baseball fans.

References

Boyd, Brendan C., and Fred C. Harris. 1973. *The Great American Baseball Card Flipping, Trading, and Bubble Gum Book.* Boston: Little, Brown and Company.
Gilbert, Bill. 1988. "First of the Worst—Why Washington No Longer Has a Major League Team." *Sports Heritage* 2:1 (Spring): 28–34.
James, Bill. 1986. *The Bill James Baseball Abstract 1986.* New York: Ballantine Books (Random House Publishers) ("Texas Rangers: An Essay on the Origins and Effects of Mediocrity"—pp. 104–109).
———. 1988. *The Bill James Baseball Abstract 1988.* New York: Ballantine Books (Random House Publishers) ("Texas Rangers"—pp. 71–75).
Shaw, Bill, 1982. *Texas Rangers.* Major League Baseball Team History Series. Mankato, Minn. Creative Education Publishing Company.
Whitfield, Shelby. 1973. *Kiss It Goodbye.* New York: Abelard and Schuman Publishing Company.

Annotated Bibliography

Gilbert, Bill. "First of the Worst—Why Washington No Longer Has a Major League Team." *Sports Heritage* 2:1 (Spring 1988): 28–34.
    A fascinating firsthand portrait of the debacle surrounding first-season play of a newly created Washington Senators franchise, during the historic 1961 American League expansion season. The author (a marketing director for the expansion Senators during their first two seasons) provides enticing arguments that bungling front-office management and unimaginative marketing strategies fostered by incompetent franchise owner Elwood "Pete" Quesada led directly and predictably to the eventual collapse of the final Washington ballclub a decade later. While the laughingstock Senators lost 100 games in each of those first two expansion years with their usual rotten on-field play, they lost even more via inept front-office dealings—support of both loyal fans and the local press.
Keating, Bern. *An Illustrated History of the Texas Rangers.* Chicago: Rand McNally Publishers, 1976. 126 pp.
    Covering the first four seasons of Rangers baseball in Dallas, this standard coffee-table volume is predictably thin and uninspired, offering little insightful text and nothing unusual or memorable in the way of historical baseball photographs. The first Texas Rangers seasons under managers Ted Williams, Whitey Herzog, and Billy Martin provided preciously little excitement (a distant second-place finish in the 1974 A.L. West) and few superstars (Ferguson Jenkins and Jeff Burroughs). A few scattered rare photographs of the earliest manifestations of Turnpike Stadium (Arlington Stadium after the arrival of the Rangers in 1972) stand out as this book's single visual highlight.
Shiffer, Don. "The Washington Senators." In *The American League,* New Revised Edition, edited by Ed Fitzgerald, pp. 326–337. New York: Grosset and Dunlap Publishers, 1966.
    An unfortunately cryptic, unevenly written, and largely uninspired "team history" of the first four seasons of the new expansion Washington Senators franchise. Game accounts of several important early contests are jumbled and in some places even inaccurate; little is said about the front-

office incompetence and team mismanagement prevalent during the first
two expansion seasons under owner Pete Quesada. This essay—the shortest and least satisfying of the volume—is the final entry in the first install-
ment of a much prized two-volume series of team histories produced with
young adult readers in mind and issued in two readily available editions
(Grosset and Dunlap, 1966, and A. S. Barnes, 1952).

Shaw, Bill. *Texas Rangers.* Major League Baseball Team History Series. Mankato, Minn: Creative Education Publishing Company, 1982. 48 pp.

Although written as a juvenile history (part of a series covering all 26 big-
league franchises) and therefore not expected to be overly scholarly or
complete, this small volume deserves special mention as one of the silliest,
most inaccurate, and most misleading baseball histories ever committed
to print. The uninformed author spends nearly three-quarters of the
volume (31 of 48 pages) detailing the glory years of this franchise in the
first half of the century as the Washington Senators under Clark Griffith
and Bucky Harris, quite oblivious to the fact that the first Senators franchise ended up in Minneapolis as the Twins and not in Arlington as the
Texas Rangers. Six brief pages of text devoted to the Rangers falsely
claim as well that during the first decade in Arlington the Rangers were
mostly a winning ballclub (when in fact for six of those seasons the team
finished well under .500).

Whitfield, Shelby. *Kiss It Goodbye.* New York: Abelard and Schuman Publishing
Company, 1973. 271 pp.

The radio "voice of the Washington Senators" in 1969 and 1970, before
being fired by unpredictable owner Bob Short, Whitfield tells the "no-
holds-barred" story of the final dreadful years of Washington major
league baseball, culminating in the surprising move of the Senators to
Dallas-Fort Worth at the beginning of the 1972 season. Whitfield clearly
has an axe to grind, and the portrait he paints of baseball during its final
few seasons in the nation's capital and its first lean years in the Texas
heartland is anything but an inspiring saga. Whitfield's account provides
instead a tale of bungled management decisions, uncontrolled entrepreneurial ego, disillusioned front-office staffers, abused fans, and sorry on-
field big-league play by one of the worst teams in baseball's long history.
And all is dominated by the shortsighted and pecuniary vision of Senators'
mercurial owner Bob Short, a man who left Washington baseball fans
without any team at all and Texas fans with a team they didn't deserve
and certainly didn't turn out in record numbers to watch.

Rogers, Phil. *The Impossible Takes a Little Longer: The Texas Rangers, from
Pretenders to Contenders.* Dallas: Taylor Publishing Company, 1990.

It is indeed a formidable task to make gripping historical narrative out
of the twenty-year saga of the Texas American League ballclub. This
is the challenge accepted and only partially met by Dallas sportswriter
and Rangers' beat writer Phil Rogers. Rogers relates with loving attention the insider's details and perspectives concerning two decades of
futile effort to build a winning baseball tradition in the heart of the
lone-star state. But in the absence of pennants and future hall-of-fame
hotshots the baseball excitement is often as thin in print as it is in the
half-filled bleachers of Arlington Stadium. A brief "Introduction" by
strikeout king Nolan Ryan offers name-recognition for the dust jacket
but little real insight into the history of the franchise whose banner he
now carries almost single-handedly.

Year-by-Year Standings and Season Summaries
Washington Senators (1961–1971)

Year	Pos.	Record	Pct.	GB	Manager	Player	BA	Player	HR	Player	W-L	ERA
1961	10th	61–100	.379	47.5	Vernon	Woodling	.313	Green	18	Donovan	10–10	2.40*
1962	10th	60–101	.373	35.5	Vernon	Hinton	.310	Hinton	17	Stenhouse	11–12	3.65
								Bright	17			
1963	10th	56–106	.346	48.5	Vernon Hodges	Hinton	.269	Lock	27	Cheney	8–9	2.71
1964	9th	62–100	.383	37.0	Hodges	Hinton	.274	Lock	28	Osteen	15–13	3.33
1965	8th	70–92	.432	32.0	Hodges	Howard	.289	Howard	21	Richert	15–12	2.60
1966	8th	71–88	.447	25.5	Hodges	Howard	.278	Howard	18	Richert	14–14	3.37
1967	6th	76–85	.472	15.5	Hodges	Howard	.256	Howard	36	Pascual	12–10	3.28
1968	10th	65–96	.404	37.5	Lemon	Howard	.274	Howard	44*	Pascual	13–12	2.69
1969	4th**	86–76	.531	23.0	Williams	Howard	.296	Howard	48	Bosman	14–5	2.19*
1970	6th	70–92	.432	38.0	Williams	Howard	.283	Howard	44*	Bosman	16–12	3.00
1971	5th	63–96	.396	38.5	Williams	Nelson	.280	Howard	26	Bosman	12–16	3.72

Texas Rangers, 1972–1992

Year	Pos.	Record	Pct.	GB	Manager	Player	BA	Player	HR	Player	W-L	ERA
1972	6th***	54–100	.351	38.5	Williams	Biittner-	.259	Ford	14	Hand	10–14	3.32
						Harrah	.259					
1973	6th	57–105	.352	37.0	Herzog- Wilber Martin	Johnson	.287	Burroughs	30	Bibby	9–10	3.24
1974	2nd	84–76	.525	5.0	Martin	Burroughs	.301	Burroughs	25	Jenkins	25*–10	2.83
1975	3rd	79–83	.483	19.0	Martin- Lucchesi	Hargrove	.303	Burroughs	29	G. Perry	12–8	3.03
1976	4th	76–86	.469	14.0	Lucchesi	Hargrove	.287	Grieve	20	G. Perry	15–14	3.24

Texas Rangers, 1972–1992

Year	Pos.	Record	Pct.	GB	Manager	Player	BA	Player	HR	Player	W-L	ERA
1977	2nd	94–68	.580	8.0	Lucchesi Stanky Ryan Hunter	Hargrove	.305	Harrah	27	Alexander	17–11	3.65
1978	2nd	87–75	.537	5.0	Hunter Corrales	Oliver	.324	Bonds	29	Jenkins	18–8	3.04
1979	3rd	83–79	.512	5.0	Corrales	Oliver	.323	Bell Zisk Putnam	18 18 18	Kern	13–5	1.57
1980	4th	76–85	.472	20.5	Corrales	Rivers	.333	Oliver Zisk	19 19	Darwin	13–4	2.62
1981	2nd	33–22	.600	1.5	Zimmer	Oliver	.309	Bell	10	Medich	10–6	30.8
	3rd	24–26	.480	4.5								
1981†	2nd	57–48	.543	5.0								
1982	6th	64–98	.395	29.0	Zimmer Johnson	Bell	.296	Hostetler	22	Hough	16–13	3.95
1983	3rd	77–85	.475	22.0	Rader	Bell	.277	Parrish	26	Honeycutt	14–8	2.42
1984	7th	69–92	.429	14.5	Rader	Bell	.315	Parrish	22	Hough	16–14	3.76
1985	7th	62–99	.385	28.5	Rader Valentine	Ward	.287	O'Brien	22	Hough	14–16	3.31
1986	2nd	87–75	.537	5.0	Valentine	Fletcher	.300	Incaviglia	30	Hough	17–10	3.79
1987	6th	75–87	.463	10.0	Valentine	Fletcher	.287	Parrish	32	Hough	18–13	3.79
1988	6th	70–91	.435	33.5	Valentine	Fletcher	.276	Sierra	23	Hough	15–16	3.32
1989	4th	83–79	.512	16.0	Valentine	Franco	.316	Sierra	29	Ryan	16–10	3.20
1990	3rd	83–79	.512	20.0	Valentine	Palmeiro	.319	Incaviglia	24	B. Witt	17–10	3.36
1991	3rd	85–77	.525	10.0	Valentine	Franco	.341*	Gonzalez	27	J. Guzman	13–7	3.08
1992	4th	77–85	.475	19.0	Valentine/ Harrah	Palmeiro	.268	Gonzalez	43*	Brown	21*–11	3.32

*Led the American League.
**American League East (first season of divisional play).
***American League West
†Split Season Totals (Players' Union Strike).

All-Time Rangers (Washington Senators) Career and Season Records

Washington Senators Career Batting Leaders (1961–1971)

Games Played	Ed Brinkman	1,142
At Bats	Ed Brinkman	3,845
Runs Scored	Frank Howard	516
Hits	Frank Howard	1,071
Home Runs	Frank Howard	237
Runs Batted In	Frank Howard	670
Extra Base Hits	Frank Howard	403
Total Bases	Frank Howard	1,968

Texas Rangers Career Batting Leaders (1972–1992)

Games Played	Jim Sundberg	1,512
At Bats	Jim Sundberg	4,684
Runs Scored	Toby Harrah	582
Hits	Jim Sundberg	1,180
Batting Average (300 or more games)	Al Oliver	.319
Home Runs	Ruben Sierra	153
Doubles	Buddy Bell	193
Triples	Ruben Sierra	30
Runs Batted In	Ruben Sierra	663
Stolen Bases	Bump Wills	161
Grand Slam Home Runs	Jeff Burroughs	5
Extra Base Hits	Ruben Sierra	417
Total Bases	Ruben Sierra	1,916

Washington Senators Career Pitching Leaders (1961–1971)

Innings Pitched	Joe Coleman	860.2
Wins	Dick Bosman	49
Losses	Bennie Daniels	60
Strikeouts	Joe Coleman	561
Walks	Bennie Daniels	309
Games	Ron Kline	260
Shutouts	Tom Cheney	7
	Joe Coleman	7
Saves	Ron Kline	83
Complete Games	Joe Coleman	36

Texas Rangers Career Pitching Leaders (1972–1992)

Innings Pitched	Charlie Hough	2,307.2	
Earned Run Average (400-plus innings)	Bert Blyleven	2.74	
Wins	Charlie Hough	139	
Losses	Charlie Hough	123	
Winning Pct. (50 decisions)	Nolan Ryan	.575	(46–34)
Strikeouts	Charlie Hough	1,452	
Walks	Charlie Hough	965	
Games	Charlie Hough	314	
Shutouts	Ferguson Jenkins	17	

All-Time Rangers (Washington Senators) Career and Season Records
(continued)

Saves	Jeff Russell	43	
Complete Games	Ferguson Jenkins	90	

Washington Senators Single-Season Batting Records (1961–1971)

Batting Average (350 ABs)	Chuck Hinton	.310	1962
Home Runs	Frank Howard	48	1969
Home Runs (lefthanded)	Mike Epstein	30	1969
Runs Batted In	Frank Howard	126	1970
Runs Scored	Frank Howard	111	1969
Hits	Frank Howard	175	1969
Singles	Ed Brinkman	144	1970
Doubles	Aurelio Rodriguez	31	1970
Triples	Chuck Hinton	12	1963
Slugging Percentage	Frank Howard	.574	1969
Extra Base Hits	Frank Howard	75	1968
Sacrifice Bunts	Danny O'Connell	15	1961
Stolen Bases	Ed Stroud	29	1970
Strikeouts	Frank Howard	155	1967
Total Bases	Frank Howard	340	1969
Hitting Streak	Ken McMullen	19	1967
Hit by Pitch	Mike Epstein	13	1968
Games	Frank Howard	161	1969,1970

Texas Rangers Single-Season Batting Records (1972–1992)

Batting Average (350 ABs)	Julio Franco	.341	1991
Home Runs	Juan Gonzalez	43	1992
Home Runs (lefthanded)	Pete O'Brien	23	1986, 1987
Home Runs (switch-hitter)	Ruben Sierra	30	1987
Runs Batted In	Ruben Sierra	119	1989
Runs Scored	Rafael Palmeiro	115	1991
Hits	Mickey Rivers	210	1980
Singles	Mickey Rivers	165	1980
Doubles	Rafael Palmeiro	49	1991
Triples	Ruben Sierra	14	1989
Slugging Percentage	Ruben Sierra	.545	1989
Extra Base Hits	Ruben Sierra	78	1989
Game-Winning RBIs	Larry Parrish	17	1983
Sacrifice Bunts	Bert Campaneris	40	1977
Stolen Bases	Bump Wills	52	1978
Strikeouts	Pete Incaviglia	185	1986
Total Bases	Ruben Sierra	344	1989
Hitting Streak	Mickey Rivers	24	1980
Grand Slam Home Runs	Jeff Burroughs	3	1973
	Larry Parrish	3	1982
On-Base Percentage	Toby Harrah	.432	1985
Hit by Pitch	Scott Fletcher	12	1988
Hitting for the Cycle	Oddibe McDowell	1	(July 23,1985)
Games	Al Oliver	163	1980

All-Time Rangers (Washington Senators) Career and Season Records

Washington Senators Single-Season Pitching Records (1961–1971)

ERA (150 Innings)	Dick Bosman	2.19	1969
Wins	Dick Bosman	16	1970
Losses	Denny McLain	22	1971
Winning Pct. (10 decisions)	Dick Bosman	.737 (14–5)	1969
Strikeouts	Pete Richert	195	1966
Walks	Joe Coleman	100	1969
Saves	Ron Kline	29	1965
Games	Ron Kline	74	1965
Complete Games	Claude Osteen	13	1964
Games Started	Claude Osteen	36	1964
	Joe Coleman	36	1969
Shutouts	Tom Cheney	4	1963
	Frank Bertaina	4	1967
	Camilo Pascual	4	1968
	Joe Coleman	4	1969
Innings Pitched	Claude Osteen	257	1964
Home Runs Allowed	Pete Richert	36	1969
Consecutive Games Won	Dick Bosman	8	1969
Consecutive Games Lost	Bennie Daniels	10	1962
Wild Pitches	Frank Bertaina	17	1968

Texas Rangers Single-Season Pitching Records (1972–1992)

ERA (150 innings)	Mike Paul	2.17	1972
ERA (100 innings)	Jim Kern	1.57	1979
Wins	Ferguson Jenkins	25	1974
Losses	Jim Bibby	19	1974
Winning Pct. (10 decisions)	Ferguson Jenkins	.692 (18–8)	1978
Strikeouts	Nolan Ryan	301	1989
Walks	Bobby Witt	143	1986
Saves	Jeff Russell	38	1989
Games	Mitch Williams	85	1987
Complete Games	Ferguson Jenkins	29	1974
Games Started	Ferguson Jenkins	41	1974
	Jim Bibby	41	1974
Shutouts	Ferguson Jenkins	6	1974
	Bert Blyleven	6	1976
Innings Pitched	Ferguson Jenkins	328	1974
Home Runs Allowed	Ferguson Jenkins	40	1979
Consecutive Games Won	Danny Darwin	8	1980
Consecutive Games Lost	David Clyde	9	1974
Consecutive Scoreless Innings	Charlie Hough	36	1983
Hit Batsmen	Charlie Hough	19	1987
Wild Pitches	Bobby Witt	22	1986
Balks	Jose Guzman	12	1988

Notes on Contributors

Paul Adomites (Seattle Pilots-Milwaukee Brewers). Publications Director for the Society of American Baseball Research who resides in Pittsburgh and edits *The SABR Review of Books,* an annual discussion of baseball's numerous books and rich literature. Author of *The Bridges of Pittsburgh* and also of articles on topics as diverse as ethnic cooking and the history of technology.

Marty Appel (New York Yankees). Television executive who resides in Larchmont, New York, and has been executive producer of New York Yankees broadcasts over WPIX-TV. Former Public Relations Director of the New York Yankees and collaborator on books with Bowie Kuhn, Tom Seaver, and Thurmon Munson, as well as author of *Yesterday's Heroes* (Morrow, 1989). Public Relations Director for 1996 Atlanta Olympics.

Richard E. Beverage (Los Angeles Angels-California Angels). Author of two books on the history of minor league baseball in the Pacific Coast League and member of the Society of American Baseball Research. A resident of Placentia, California, he has also written for *The SABR Review of Books.*

Peter C. Bjarkman (a.k.a. "Doctor Baseball") (Toronto Blue Jays, Washington Senators-Minnesota Twins, Texas Rangers). Freelance author who has published coffee-table histories of the Dodgers, Reds and Blue Jays, written baseball biographies (Roberto Clemente, Duke Snider, Ernie Banks) for juvenile readers, and is presently completing books on baseball's role in American literature and on Latin American baseball history. Author of *The Baseball Scrapbook* (Dorset, 1991).

Bill Carle (Kansas City Royals). Chair of the Biographical Committee for the Society for American Baseball Research and current member of the SABR Board of Directors. Resident of Grandview, Missouri, and specialist on baseball biographical data.

Morris A. Eckhouse (Cleveland Indians, Detroit Tigers). Freelance author of baseball books and articles and Executive Director of SABR since 1990. Co-author of *This Date in Pittsburgh Pirates History* (Stein and

Day, 1980) and of a forthcoming juvenile biography of Bob Feller, and currently a resident of South Euclid, Ohio.

Bill Felber (St. Louis Browns-Baltimore Orioles). Executive editor of *The Manhattan Mercury* (Manhattan, Kansas) and author of numerous baseball history articles in such journals as *The National Pastime* and *Baseball History*. A member of the Society of American Baseball Research and former associate editor of *The National Pastime,* SABR's annual glossy pictorial journal.

Frederick Ivor-Campbell. (Boston Red Sox). Freelance writer and former university English professor (University of Rhode Island) who currently resides in Warren, Rhode Island. Author of chapters on team histories, post-season play, and the All-Star Game in *Total Baseball* (Warner, 1989).

Richard C. Lindberg (Chicago White Sox). Chicago-based freelance writer who specializes in baseball of the nineteenth century and in Chicago history and has also published three books on the history of the Chicago White Sox. Contributor of several recent articles to *Chicago History* and the official baseball history consultant to the Chicago Historical Society.

Norman L. Macht (Philadelphia Athletics-Kansas City Athletics-Oakland A's). Author of a forthcoming biographical study of Connie Mack and frequent contributor of articles to *Baseball Digest* magazine. A resident of Greenville, Delaware, and chairman of SABR's active Oral History Committee.

James O'Donnell (Seattle Mariners). English instructor at Edmonds Community College in Seattle, Washington, and specialist on baseball fiction and juvenile baseball literature. Organizer of the "Baseball Literature Panel" held at the annual SABR national convention since 1987.